XView Programming Manual

The X Window System Series

The books in the X Window System series from O'Reilly and Associates are based in part on the original MIT X Window System documentation, but are far more comprehensive and easy to use. Over 20 computer vendors recommend or license volumes in the series. In short, these are the definitive guides to the X Window System.

Volume 0, X Protocol Reference Manual
A complete programmer's reference to the X Network Protocol, the language in which computers communicate all the information between the X server and X clients. 414 pages, $30.00

Volume 1, Xlib Programming Manual
A complete guide to programming with the X library (Xlib), the lowest level of programming interface to X. 664 pages, $34.95—or sold as a set with the *Xlib Reference Manual* for $60.00.

Volume 2, Xlib Reference Manual
A complete programmer's reference for Xlib. 725 pages, $34.95—or sold as a set with the *Xlib Programming Manual* for $60.00.

Volume 3, X Window System User's Guide
Describes window system concepts and the most common client applications available for X, Release 3. For experienced users, later chapters explain customizing the X environment and include an alternate *.uwmrc* file. 576 pages, $26.95

Other X manuals soon to be available
Volumes 4 and 5, *X Toolkit Intrinsics Programming Manual* and *X Toolkit Intrinsics Reference Manual*.

For orders or a free catalog of all our books, please contact us. For international orders (outside U.S. or Canada) see our list of distributors in the back of this book.

NUTSHELL
HANDBOOKS

O'Reilly & Associates, Inc.

Creators and publishers of Nutshell Handbooks
632 Petaluma Avenue • Sebastopol CA 95472
email: uunet!ora!nuts • 1-800-338-6887 • in CA 1-800-533-6887 • +1 707-829-0515

Volume Seven

XView Programming
Manual

---

for Version 11 of the
X Window System

by Dan Heller

O'Reilly & Associates, Inc.

Table of Contents

Page

Preface xxiii

Please Read This Section! xxiii
How to Use This Manual xxiv
Assumptions xxvi
Font Conventions Used in This Manual xxvi
Related Documents xxvii
Requests For Comments xxvii
Acknowledgements xxviii

1 XView and the X Window System 3

1.1 The X Window System 3
   1.1.1 The Server and Client 5
1.2 The Software Hierarchy 6
1.3 Extensions to X 9
1.4 The Window Manager 9
1.5 Handling Events 10
1.6 Development of the XView Toolkit 12
1.7 OPEN LOOK Graphical User Interface 13

2 The XView Programmer's Model 17

2.1 Object-oriented Programming 17
   2.1.1 Object Class Hierarchy 18
   2.1.2 Object Handles 19
2.2 Attribute-based Functions 21
   2.2.1 Creating and Manipulating Objects 21
   2.2.2 Changing Object Attributes 22
2.3 Types of Attributes 22
2.4 Types of Objects 23
   2.4.1 Generic Objects 24
   2.4.2 Window Objects 25
   2.4.3 Frames and Subframes 26
   2.4.4 Subwindows 28
   2.4.5 Nonvisual Objects 33
2.5 The Notifier Model 35
   2.5.1 Callback Style of Programming 35
   2.5.2 Why a Notification-based System? 35
   2.5.3 Relationship Among the Notifier, Objects and the Application ... 35

2.5.4 Calling the Notifier Directly 38

3 Creating XView Applications 41

3.1 Interface Overview 41
   3.1.1 Compiling XView Programs 41
   3.1.2 XView Libraries 42
   3.1.3 Header Files 42
   3.1.4 Naming Conventions 42
   3.1.5 Example of XView-style Programming 43
3.2 Initializing XView 45
3.3 Creating and Modifying Objects 46
   3.3.1 Using xv_create() 47
   3.3.2 Using xv_find() 49
   3.3.3 Using xv_destroy() 50
   3.3.4 Using xv_set() and xv_get() 50
3.4 xv_main_loop() and the Notifier 52
3.5 Registering Event Handlers 53
3.6 Error Recovery 54

4 Frames 59

4.1 Types of Frames 60
   4.1.1 The Role of the Window Manager 61
4.2 Base Frames 61
   4.2.1 XView Initialization and Base Frames 62
   4.2.2 Headers and Footers 63
   4.2.3 Closed Base Frames 64
   4.2.4 Quit Confirmation 66
4.3 Command Frames 67
   4.3.1 Manually Displaying Frames 67
   4.3.2 The Pushpin 68
   4.3.3 The FRAME_DONE_PROC Procedure 70
   4.3.4 Showing Resize Corners 71
4.4 Miscellaneous Attributes 72
   4.4.1 Busy Frames 72
   4.4.2 Frame Sizes 72
   4.4.3 Frame Colors 73
   4.4.4 Child Windows 74
4.5 Destroying Frames 75
4.6 Frame Package Summary 76

5 Canvases and Openwin 79

5.1 Canvas Model 80

5.2 Creating a Canvas 82
    5.2.1 Drawing in a Canvas 83
5.3 The Repaint Procedure 85
5.4 Controlling Canvas Sizes 91
    5.4.1 Automatic Canvas Sizing 92
    5.4.2 Explicit Canvas Sizing 92
    5.4.3 Tracking Changes in the Canvas Size 94
5.5 Scrolling Canvases 94
5.6 Splitting Canvas Views 95
    5.6.1 Splitting Views Using Scrollbars 95
    5.6.2 Splitting Views Using xv_set() 96
    5.6.3 Getting View Windows 96
5.7 Handling Input in the Canvas Package 99
    5.7.1 Default Events 99
    5.7.2 Notification of Events 99
5.8 Canvas and Openwin Package Summaries 103

6 Handling Input 107

6.1 Introduction to Events in XView 107
6.2 Classes of Events 108
6.3 Registering Events 109
    6.3.1 Specifying X Event Masks 110
    6.3.2 Specifying XView Events 111
6.4 The Event Handler 115
6.5 The Event Structure 115
6.6 Determining the Event 116
    6.6.1 Keyboard Events 117
6.7 Interpreting Client Messages 120
    6.7.1 Drag and Drop 120
    6.7.2 Sending and Reading Client Messages 124
6.8 Reading Input Directly 125
6.9 Sample Program 126

7 Panels 135

7.1 Creating a Panel 137
7.2 Creating Panel Items 138
7.3 Panel Layout 139
    7.3.1 Explicit Item Positioning 140
    7.3.2 General Positioning of Items 140
    7.3.3 Layout of Panel Items with Values 141
    7.3.4 Sizing Panels 142
7.4 Panel Item Values 143
7.5 Iterating Over a Panel's Items 144
7.6 Panel Item Classes 144

7.7 Button Items 145
   7.7.1 Button Selection 145
   7.7.2 Menu Buttons 146
7.8 Choice Items 147
   7.8.1 Display and Layout of Item Choices 148
   7.8.2 Parallel Lists 149
   7.8.3 Exclusive and Nonexclusive Choices 150
   7.8.4 Checkbox Choices 151
   7.8.5 Abbreviated Choices 151
7.9 Scrolling Lists 153
   7.9.1 Displaying List Items 153
   7.9.2 Adding and Deleting List Entries 156
   7.9.3 List Selection 157
   7.9.4 List Notification 157
7.10 Message Items 157
7.11 Slider Items 159
   7.11.1 Displaying Sliders 159
   7.11.2 Slider Selection 159
   7.11.3 Slider Notification 159
   7.11.4 Slider Value 160
7.12 Text Items and Numeric Text Items 161
   7.12.1 The Current Text Item 162
   7.12.2 Text Selection 162
   7.12.3 Text Notification 162
   7.12.4 Writing Your Own Text Notify Procedure 164
   7.12.5 Text Value 165
7.13 Numeric Text Items 165
7.14 Advanced Panel Usage 165
7.15 Attaching Data to Panel Items 166
7.16 Repainting Panels 169
   7.16.1 Using PANEL_REPAINT_PROC 169
   7.16.2 Painting Panel Items 172
7.17 Panel Event Handling 172
   7.17.1 Using WIN_EVENT_PROC 173
   7.17.2 Using PANEL_BACKGROUND_PROC 174
   7.17.3 Using PANEL_EVENT_PROC 174
   7.17.4 Event Handling Example 175
7.18 Panel Package Summary 176

8 Text Subwindows 181

8.1 Creating Text Subwindows 182
8.2 Setting Text Subwindow Attributes 182
8.3 Text Subwindow Contents 182
8.4 Editing a Text Subwindow 183
   8.4.1 Loading a File 183
   8.4.2 Checking the Status of the Text Subwindow 183

8.4.3 Writing to a Text Subwindow 185
8.4.4 Reading from a Text Subwindow 185
8.4.5 Deleting Text 186
8.4.6 Emulating an Editing Character 187
8.4.7 Replacing Characters 187
8.4.8 The Editing Log 188
8.4.9 Which File is Being Edited? 188
8.5 Saving Edits in a Subwindow 189
8.5.1 Storing Edits 189
8.5.2 Discarding Edits 190
8.6 Setting the Contents of a Text Subwindow 190
8.6.1 TEXTSW_FILE_CONTENTS 190
8.6.2 TEXTSW_CONTENTS 191
8.6.3 TEXTSW_INSERT_FROM_FILE 191
8.7 Positioning the Text Displayed in a Text Subwindow 192
8.7.1 Screen Lines and File Lines 192
8.7.2 Absolute Positioning 192
8.7.3 Relative Positioning 193
8.7.4 Which File Lines are Visible? 193
8.8 Finding and Matching a Pattern 194
8.8.1 Matching a Span of Characters 194
8.8.2 Matching a Specific Pattern 195
8.9 Marking Positions 196
8.9.1 Getting a Text Selection 197
8.9.2 Setting the Primary Selection 198
8.10 Dealing with Multiple Views 198
8.11 Notifications from a Text Subwindow 199
8.12 Text Subwindow Package Summary 202

9 TTY Subwindows 205

9.1 Creating a TTY Subwindow 205
9.2 Driving a TTY Subwindow 207
9.3 Monitoring the Program in the TTY Subwindow 210
9.4 Talking Directly to the TTY Subwindow 211
9.5 Package Summary 213

10 Scrollbars 217

10.1 Creating Scrollbars 218
10.2 Relationship Between Scrollbars and Objects 220
10.3 An Example 221
10.4 Managing Your Own Scrollbar 227
10.5 Scrollbar Package Summary 227

11 Menus 231

11.1 Menu Types 231
    11.1.1 Pop-up Menus 232
    11.1.2 Pulldown Menus 232
    11.1.3 Pullright Menus 232
11.2 Menu Items 234
    11.2.1 Choice Items 234
    11.2.2 Exclusive Items 234
    11.2.3 Nonexclusive Items 235
11.3 Creating Menus 235
11.4 Displaying Menus 236
11.5 A Simple Program 237
11.6 Creating Menu Items 240
    11.6.1 Using MENU_ITEM 240
    11.6.2 Using MENU_ACTION_ITEM 241
    11.6.3 Using MENUITEM 241
    11.6.4 Using MENU_GEN_PROC 242
11.7 Adding Menu Items 242
11.8 Pullright Menus 243
    11.8.1 Menu-generating Procedures 245
11.9 Using Toggle Menus 246
11.10 Menu Layout 247
11.11 Making Pin-up Menus 248
11.12 Notification Procedures 249
11.13 Finding Menu Items 252
11.14 Initial and Default Menu Selections 253
11.15 Destroying Menus 253
    11.15.1 Freeing Allocated Strings 254
    11.15.2 Freeing Pullright Menus 254
    11.15.3 Menu Client Data 255
11.16 Example Program 255
11.17 Menu Package Summary 258

12 Notices 263

12.1 Creating and Displaying Notices 264
    12.1.1 Response Choices and Values 266
    12.1.2 Notice Triggers 267
12.2 Another Example 269
12.3 Notice Package Summary 272

13 Cursors 275

13.1 Creating Cursors 275
    13.1.1 simple_cursor.c 276

13.2 Predefined Cursors 277
13.3 The Hotspot and Cursor Location 278
13.4 Color Cursors 280
13.5 Cursor Package Summary 281

14 Icons 285

14.1 Creating and Destroying Icons 286
14.2 The Icon's Image 286
   14.2.1 The Icon Text 288
14.3 Icon Package Summary 289

15 Nonvisual Objects 293

15.1 The Display 293
15.2 The Screen Object 294
15.3 The SERVER Package 295
   15.3.1 Creating a Server (Establishing a Connection) 295
   15.3.2 Getting the Server 296
15.4 Server Images 297
   15.4.1 Creating Server Images 297
15.5 The FULLSCREEN Package 300
15.6 Nonvisual Package Summary 302

16 Fonts 307

16.1 Creating Fonts 308
   16.1.1 Font Families and Styles 311
   16.1.2 Font Sizes 312
   16.1.3 Scaling Fonts 313
   16.1.4 Fonts by Name 314
16.2 Font Dimensions 315
16.3 Font Package Summary 317

17 Resources 319

17.1 Predefined Defaults 319
17.2 XView Resource Database Functions 322
   17.2.1 Boolean Resources 323
   17.2.2 Integer Resources 323
   17.2.3 Character Resources 324
   17.2.4 String Resources 324
   17.2.5 Enumerated Resources 325

18 The Selection Service 331

18.1 The XView Selection Model 333
18.2 Using the Selection Service 334
18.3 Getting the Current Selection 335
   18.3.1 The Seln_request Structure 337
18.4 Using selection_query() 343
18.5 Selection Package Summary 349

19 The Notifier 353

19.1 Basic Concepts 353
   19.1.1 Mainline Input Handling 353
   19.1.2 Event-driven Input Handling 354
19.2 Functions of the Notifier 354
19.3 How the Notifier Works 354
   19.3.1 Restrictions 355
19.4 What is a Notifier Client? 356
19.5 Signal Handling 357
   19.5.1 Signals to Avoid 357
   19.5.2 A Replacement for signal() 358
   19.5.3 Timers 360
   19.5.4 Handling SIGTERM 364
   19.5.5 Handling SIGCHLD 364
19.6 Client Events 366
   19.6.1 Posting Client Events 367
   19.6.2 Posting with an Argument 368
   19.6.3 Posting Destroy Events 369
   19.6.4 Delivery Time of Destroy Events 369
19.7 Receiving Client Events 370
19.8 Reading and Writing through File Descriptors 370
   19.8.1 Reading Files 371
   19.8.2 Reading and Writing on Pipes 373
19.9 Interposition 378
   19.9.1 Uses of Interposition 378
   19.9.2 Interface to Interposition 379
   19.9.3 An Interposition Example 379
   19.9.4 Interposing on Resize Events 381
   19.9.5 Modifying a Frame's Destruction 381
19.10 Notifier Control 384
   19.10.1 Implicit Dispatching 385
   19.10.2 Explicit Dispatching 387
19.11 Error Codes 388
19.12 Issues 390

20 Color 395

20.1 XView Color Model 396
    20.1.1 Color and Pixel Values 396
20.2 Creating Colormap Segments 397
20.3 Changing Colormap Entries 402
20.4 Foreground and Background Colors 402
20.5 Coloring XView Objects 403
20.6 Coloring Panel Items 408

A Attribute Summary 411

B Summary of Procedures and Macros 445

C Data Types 471

D Event Codes 479

E Command Line Arguments 485

F OPEN LOOK User Interface Compliance 491

Level 1 Features Not Supported in XView 1.0 491
    Keyboard and Mouse Customization 491
    Input Focus Feedback 492
    Menu Default Setting 492
    Default Buttons in Pop Ups 493
    Help 493
    Window Background 493
    Notices 493
    Text Functions 493
    Control Items 494
    Scrolling Lists 494
    Property Windows 495
    Inactive Controls 495
Level 2 Features Supported in XView 1.0 496
Level 2 Features Not Supported in XView 1.0 496

G Example Programs 501

item_move.c 502
xv_termsw.c 508
scroll_cells2.c 510
menu_dir2.c 514
type_font.c 519
fonts.c 521
seln.c 526
seln_line.c 529
x_draw.c 531

Index 535

Figures

Page

1-1 An X application and a traditional text terminal 3
1-2 Selecting a menu item with the pointer 4
1-3 Applications can run on any system across the network 6
1-4 The software architecture of X applications 7
1-5 The Notifier exists between the server and the XView application 10
1-6 A sample OPEN LOOK workspace 13
2-1 XView class hierarchy 18
2-2 Object creation is top down; attribute setting is bottom up 24
2-3 Fully-featured base frame (includes optional elements) 26
2-4 Sample unpinned command frame 27
2-5 Sample help window 27
2-6 Sample notice 27
2-7 A window with multiple views 29
2-8 A control area above a subwindow 30
2-9 A control area to the right of a pane 30
2-10 A control area in a command window 30
2-11 Example of a pop-up menu with a pullright submenu 32
2-12 Vertical scrollbar components 32
2-13 Flow of control in a conventional program 34
2-14 Flow of control in a Notifier-based program 35
2-15 Flow of input events in an XView application 37
3-1 A frame containing a Quit button 44
4-1 Three base frames 59
4-2 Simple base frame created without any FRAME attributes specified 62
4-3 A sample header label display in a frame 63
4-4 Headers and footers on base frame 64
4-5 Default icon and application icon 65
4-6 Command frame with pop-up frame 67
5-1 A canvas subwindow with multiple views 79
5-2 Canvases, views, and paint windows 80
5-3 Window before and after an Expose event 86
5-4 Window with two views before and after an Expose event 87
5-5 A window created with canvas_event.c 103
7-1 Controls in an OPEN LOOK GUI implementation* 135
7-2 Layout of panel items 139
7-3 Layout of panel item with value 141
7-4 Visual feedback for button controls 145
7-5 Sample menu button (unselected and selected) 147
7-6 Sample panel with exclusive choices 150
7-7 Sample panel with nonexclusive choices 150
7-8 Sample panel with checkbox 151
7-9 Sample panel with abbreviated choice (unselected and selected) 152

7-10   Sample panel with scrolling list 153
7-11   Output of program list_glyphs.c 155
7-12   Sample panel with message item 158
7-13   Sample panel with slider item 160
7-14   Sample panel with text item 161
7-15   Panel with gray background 171
7-16   Output of item_move.c in use 175
8-1   A sample text subwindow 181
8-2   A caret marks the insertion point 182
8-3   A text selection 197
9-1   Output of sample_tty.c 206
9-2   Output of textsw_to_ttysw.c 209
10-1   An OPEN LOOK scrollbar 217
10-2   Relationship between a scrollbar and the object it scrolls 218
10-3   Splitting a text subwindow twice 221
10-4   Model for scroll_cells.c 221
11-1   The Window menu 232
11-2   Menu buttons each with a pulldown menu 232
11-3   Pushpins in a menu and a submenu 232
11-4   Exclusive settings on a menu 234
11-5   Nonexclusive settings on a submenu 235
11-6   Output of simple_menu.c when the menu is popped up 239
11-7   Output of xv_menu.c 251
12-1   A sample notice window 263
12-2   Output of simple_notice.c while the notice is up 266
14-1   Three bordered default icons 285
16-1   The Courier font in different styles and sizes 311
18-1   Dragging the pointer to select text 331
18-2   Byte stream after selection_ask() returns the current text selection 338
18-3   How selection_query() is used 344
19-1   Output of animate.c 363
19-2   Flow of control in interposition 378

Examples

Page

3-1 The quit.c program 44
3-2 xv_create() creates XView objects 47
4-1 The simple_frame.c program 61
4-2 Creating a base frame after calling xv_init() 62
4-3 Setting separate values for a frame header 63
4-4 Creating a footer 64
4-5 Creating a subframe 67
4-6 Using several frame attributes 68
4-7 The subframe.c program 70
4-8 Setting colors in a frame 73
5-1 The line.c program 89
5-2 Repainting objects within a damaged region 90
5-3 The canvas_event.c program 100
6-1 The drag_n_drop.c program 121
6-2 The canvas_input.c program 127
7-1 The quit.c program 137
7-2 The btn_menu.c program 146
7-3 The list_glyphs.c program 154
7-4 The stop_frame.c program 158
7-5 The client_data.c program 167
7-6 The panel_repaint.c program 169
8-1 Client notify procedure for a text subwindow 199
9-1 The sample_tty.c program 205
9-2 The textsw_to_ttysw.c program 207
9-3 The ttycurses.c program 211
10-1 The scroll_cells.c program 223
11-1 The simple_menu.c program 237
11-2 The xv_menu.c program 250
11-3 Creating individual menu items 254
11-4 The menu_dir.c program 255
12-1 The simple_notice.c program 264
12-2 The trigger_notice.c program 268
12-3 The notice.c program 270
13-1 The simple_cursor.c program 276
13-2 The hot_spot.c program 278
14-1 The icon_demo.c program 286
14-2 Redefining an icon's size to include its label 289
15-1 Getting a pointer for a particular frame object (screen.c) 294
15-2 The svrimage.c program 299
15-3 The fullscreen.c program 301
16-1 The simple_font.c program 308
17-1 The default_text.c program 321

17-2 The default_size.c program 326
18-1 The simple_seln.c program 336
18-2 The text_seln.c program 339
18-3 The long_seln.c program 345
19-1 The animate.c program 361
19-2 Demonstrating a wait3 handler 365
19-3 The notify_input.c program 372
19-4 The ntfy_pipe.c program 374
19-5 Transferring control through the Notifier 380
19-6 The interpose.c program 383
19-7 The ntfy_do_dis.c program 386
20-1 The x_draw.c program 398
20-2 The color_objs.c program 403
G-1 The item_move.c program 502
G-2 The xv_termsw.c program 508
G-3 The scroll_cells2.c program 510
G-4 The menu_dir2.c program 514
G-5 The type_font.c program 519
G-6 The fonts.c program 521
G-7 The seln.c program 526
G-8 The seln_line.c program 529
G-9 The x_draw.c program 531

Tables

Page

2-1. XView Objects, Owners, Packages, and Data Types 20
2-2. Generic Functions 21
3-1. Reserved Prefixes 43
3-2. Default Ownership of Objects 48
4-1. Frame Attributes 76
5-1. Canvas Attributes, Procedures and Macros 103
5-2. Openwin Attributes, Procedures and Macros 104
7-1. Text Item Notification Level 163
7-2. Return Values for Text Item Notify Procedures 163
7-3. Default Event to Action Mapping 173
7-4. Panel Procedures and Macros 176
7-5. Panel Attributes 177
8-1. Range of Values for Status Variables 184
8-2. Textsw_action Attributes 200
8-3. Text Subwindow Attributes, Procedures and Macros 202
9-1. TTY Subwindow Attributes, Procedures and Macros 213
10-1. Scrollbar Attributes 227
11-1. Menu Attributes 259
12-1. Notice Attributes, Procedures and Macros 272
13-1. Cursor Attributes, Procedures and Macros 281
15-1. Fullscreen Attributes 303
15-2. Screen, Server, and Server Image Attributes 303
17-1. Resources and Default Values Understood by XView 319
18-1. Selecting Text 332
18-2. Selection Procedures 349
18-3. Selection Attributes 349
19-1. Notifier Error Codes 388
D-1. Event Codes 479
E-1. XView Command Line Arguments 485
E-2. Resource Names of Command Line Arguments 487

Preface

Please Read This Section! xxiii
How to Use This Manual xxiv
Assumptions xxvi
Font Conventions Used in This Manual xxvi
Related Documents xxvii
Requests For Comments xxvii
Acknowledgements xxviii

Preface

XView (**X** Window-System-based Visual/Integrated Environment for Workstations) is a user-interface toolkit to support interactive, graphics-based applications running under the X Window System. This toolkit, developed by Sun Microsystems, Inc., is derived from earlier toolkits for the SunView™ windowing system. With over 2000 SunView applications in the workstation market, there are many programmers already familiar with SunView application programmer's interface (API). XView makes it possible for SunView applications to enter the up and coming X marketplace.

XView has many advantages for programmers developing new applications in X, such as a mature and proven API based on the development experience of SunView programmers. It features an object-oriented style interface that is straightforward and simple to learn.

Like any X toolkit, XView provides a set of pre-built, user-interface objects such as canvases, scrollbars, menus, and control panels. The appearance and functionality of these objects follow the OPEN LOOK Graphical User Interface (GUI) specification. Jointly developed by Sun Microsystems and AT&T as the graphical user interface standard for System V Release 4, OPEN LOOK provides users with a simple, consistent and efficient interface for performing tasks within an application.

XView is based upon Xlib, the lowest level of the X Window System available to the programmer. While developing XView user-interfaces does not require Xlib programming experience, there are good reasons for learning more about Xlib, especially if your application renders graphics.

Please Read This Section!

This book provides a basic introduction to developing applications using the XView Toolkit. You do not need any knowledge of SunView, and prior experience with the X Window System is helpful, but also not required. Nonetheless, like any complex system, a programmer needs to know a lot to program effectively in XView.

For each functional area in XView, there are chapters that present the basic concepts and suggest some common ways to implement and use a particular function. Also addressed are some snags to watch out for when implementing certain combinations of functions. Care was taken to keep the content of the chapters brief and to the point. Simple and straightforward functions are not discussed in depth. The appendices provide a reference summary of XView, along with longer sample programs.

If you can't figure out how to accomplish a task because it is not documented here, don't despair—that does not mean it cannot be done. Some features in XView are not addressed in this book—especially the more advanced ones. You are encouraged to experiment with the toolkit and discover new ways of using XView.

At this writing, XView is still under development. There are more features to add, more bugs to fix, and further design changes to improve existing functionality. We have described the XView Toolkit as accurately as possible, but consult the release notes that accompany your distribution for recent changes. Future editions of this book will incorporate these changes.

How to Use This Manual

The chapters in the book are designed to be read sequentially. However, this is not a strong requirement. Reading ahead probably won't affect your understanding of the material, although later chapters might reference earlier material.

The following paragraphs briefly describe contents of this book:

Chapter 1, *XView and the X Window System*, provides a conceptual overview of the X Window System, the role of the XView toolkit and the Open Look graphical user interface. It provides a general introduction to basic X terminology, but it does not go into great detail about X.

Chapter 2, *The XView Programmer's Model*, provides an overview of XView as an object-oriented programming system. The programmer creates and modifies objects that implement the OPEN LOOK interface. This chapter also discusses windows as objects that receive events. It introduces callback functions as the method of registering application-specific event handlers.

Chapter 3, *Creating XView Applications*, begins from the application developer's point of view and explains the basic elements of an XView application. It describes what is involved in initializing XView and creating XView objects such as frames and subwindows.

Chapter 4, *Frames*, explains how to create window frames. There are two basic types of frames: base frames and command frames. Each application has at least one base frame that manages subwindows, panels and other objects. It presents the routines used to create and manage frames.

Chapter 5, *Canvases and Openwin*, presents canvases as the most basic type of subwindow or window pane. It presents the canvas model, which permits a drawing surface larger than what is visible in the canvas subwindow.

Chapter 6, *Handling Input*, explains how events are handled by X, the Notifier and XView objects.

Chapter 7, *Panels*, explains a variety of OPEN LOOK controls that are implemented as items on a control panel. It demonstrates how to create and use contain buttons, check boxes, choices, lists, messages, toggles, text items and sliders. A set of panel attributes controls the behavior in common with all panel items. There are also item-specific attributes.

Chapter 8, *Text Subwindows*, describes how to create a text subwindow and how to use its text editing features.

Chapter 9, *TTY Subwindows*, describes the TTY subwindow that performs terminal emulation functions.

Chapter 10, *Scrollbars*, covers the creation and use of scrollbars. A scollbar is a window attached to another window, such as a canvas or text subwindow or a panel. The scrollbar package only manages the scrollbar; the application must gauge the impact of scrolling on its windows.

Chapter 11, *Menus*, explains how to implement various sorts of pop-up menus.

Chapter 12, *Notices*, explains how pop-up windows serve as notices or dialog boxes.

Chapter 13, *Cursors*, shows various OPEN LOOK pointers and demonstrates their use.

Chapter 14, *Icons*, describes the use of bitmap images as application icons. When an application is closed, or iconified, the application is represented on the screen as an icon.

Chapter 15, *Nonvisual Objects*, describes objects that do not contain windows: Server, Screen and Fullscreen.

Chapter 16, *Fonts*, describes how to load and use fonts from the X server.

Chapter 17, *Resources*, describes the implications of X resources for an XView application. Resources allow individual users to control and customize their computing environment

Chapter 18, *The Selection Service*, discusses how XView applications communicate with other applications, including window managers and applications that are not OPEN LOOK compliant. It shows how XView provides for selection and for other functions, as stated by the *Inter-Client Communication Conventions Manual*.

Chapter 19, *The Notifier*, describes the Notifier and advanced event handling. It describes the relationship of the Notifier and X to the host operating system.

Chapter 20, *Color*, discusses issues concerning color in windows and other XView objects.

Appendix A, *Attribute Summary*, provides alphabetically arranged descriptions of all attributes.

Appendix B, *Summary of Procedures and Macros*, provides alphabetically arranged descriptions of all procedures and macros.

Appendix C, *Data Types*, lists the data types defined by XView.

Appendix D, *Event Codes*, lists the event codes in numerical order by value.

Appendix E, *Command Line Arguments*, lists the values and defaults for command line arguments.

Appendix F, *OPEN LOOK User Interface Compliance*, discusses XView's compliance with the *OPEN LOOK GUI Functional Specification*.

Appendix G, *Example Programs*, presents nine supplementary programs.

Assumptions

Readers should be proficient in the C programming language, although examples are provided for infrequently used features of the language that are necessary or useful when programming with X. In addition, general familiarity with the principles of raster graphics is helpful. Finally, if you do not understand how to use Xlib routines to render graphics, then writing useful programs might be difficult, although you should be able to build OPEN LOOK user interfaces easily.

Font Conventions Used in This Manual

Italics are used for:

- UNIX® pathnames, filenames, program names, user command names, and options for user commands
- New terms where they are introduced

`Typewriter Font` is used for:

- Anything that would be typed verbatim into code, such as examples of source code and text on the screen
- XView packages.*
- The contents of include files, such as structure types, structure members, symbols (defined constants and bit flags), and macros
- XView and Xlib functions
- Names of subroutines of the example programs

`Italic Typewriter Font` is used for:

- Arguments to XView functions, since they could be typed in code as shown but are arbitrary

Helvetica Italics are used for:

- Titles of examples, figures, and tables

Boldface is used for:

- Chapter and section headings

---

*When referring to all members of a particular package, such as `CANVAS`, the notation `CANVAS_*` will be used. This should not be interpreted as a C-language pointer construct.

Related Documents

The C Programming Language by B. W. Kernighan and D. M. Ritchie

The following documents are included on the X11 source tape:

OPEN LOOK Graphical User Interface Functional Specification

OPEN LOOK Graphical User Interface Style Guide

The following books in the X Window System series from O'Reilly and Associates, Inc. are currently available:

Volume One, *Xlib Programming Manual*
> A programmer's guide to the X library. Topics include window attributes, graphics contexts, and events.

Volume Two, *Xlib Reference Manual*
> A programmer's reference to the X library, describing each Xlib function and including many quick-reference aids.

Volume Three, *X Window System User's Guide*
> A guide to the standard clients available in the MIT X distribution.

Volume Four, *X Toolkit Intrinsics Programming Manual*
> A programmer's guide to the X Toolkit, including the Xt functions.

Volume Five, *X Toolkit Intrinsics Reference Manual*
> A programmer's reference to the Xt functions and widget classes.

Requests For Comments

Please write to tell us about any flaws you find in this manual or how you think it could be improved, to help us provide you with the best documentation possible.

Our U.S. mail address, e-mail address, and phone number are as follows:

O'Reilly and Associates, Inc.
632 Petaluma Avenue
Sebastopol, CA 95472
in USA 1-800-338-6887, in CA 1-800-533-6887
international +1 707-829-0515

UUCP: uunet!ora!xview   Internet: xview@ora.UU.NET

Acknowledgements

I always wanted to do this—but for my first *record album!* :−)

This book was influenced by an amalgamation of several sources: *The SunView Programmer's Manual* for design and structure of the chapters, the people on the XView development team at Sun Microsystems for technical detail and the latest up-to-the-minute changes, and my personal experience in programming for narrative content. This book was created using SoftQuad's *sqtroff*™, a Postscript™ laser printer, and a Sun 3/60 color workstation running *xnews*.

Special thanks go to everyone at O'Reilly & Associates for their diligent efforts. Dale Dougherty, the project manager, coordinated the editing and production tasks. His experience in writing books has been priceless in providing direction and guidance. Daniel Gilly, the production editor, stayed up late nights with me fixing all my grammatical and spelling errors. Laurel Katz created superb graphics. Ruth Terry provided speedy help in copy-editing. Many others pitched in for the final push to complete this book.

At Sun Microsystems, I'd like to thank Tom Jacobs, for keeping everything in order and reading *all that e-mail*, Tony Hillman and the rest of the reviewing squad.

Also, Bart Schaefer, for taking care of Mush while I've been too busy. Mike Ilnicki for continuing to play racquetball with me. Penguin's frozen yogurt for nutrition. David Letterman for being on at the perfect time: dinner.

...and most of all, I'd like to thank Tim O'Reilly—the only one who could talk me, a cast-in-stone programmer, into trying my hand at technical writing. Thanks for the confidence in me.

1

XView and the X Window System

In This Chapter:

The X Window System 3
    The Server and Client 5
The Software Hierarchy 6
Extensions to X 9
The Window Manager 9
Handling Events 10
Development of the XView Toolkit 12
OPEN LOOK Graphical User Interface 13

XView and X

1

XView and the X Window System

The XView Toolkit allows a programmer to build the interface to an application without having to learn many of the details of the underlying windowing system. However, it is valuable to have some understanding of X before attempting to build applications under XView. This chapter introduces many of the most important concepts on which the X Window System is based and describes the computing environment for X applications. It also describes the role of the XView Toolkit in the X Window System.

For the most part, this chapter assumes that you are new to programming the X Window System. This chapter describes the basics of the X Window System—further details will be described as necessary later in the manual. However, this book does not repeat the detailed description of Xlib programming found in Volume One, *Xlib Programming Manual*. If you already have some experience programming the X Window System, you might wish to begin at Chapter 2, *The XView Programmer's Model*.

1.1 The X Window System

X controls a bit-mapped display in which every pixel (dot on the screen) is individually controllable. This allows drawing of pictures in addition to text. Until recently, individual control of screen pixels was widely available only on personal computers (PCs) and high-priced technical workstations, while more general-purpose machines were limited to output on text-only terminals. X brings the same world of graphic output to both PCs and more powerful machines. Figure 1-1 shows an X application in comparison with a traditional text terminal.

Like other windowing systems, X divides the screen into multiple input and output areas called windows, each of which can act as an independent *virtual terminal*. Using a terminal emulator, windows can run ordinary text-based applications. However, windows can also run applications designed to take advantage of the graphic power of the bitmapped display.

X takes user input from a *pointer*, which is usually a mouse but could just as well be a trackball or tablet. The pointer allows the user to point at certain graphics on the screen and use the buttons on the mouse to control a program without using the keyboard. This method of using programs is often easier to learn than traditional keyboard control, because it is more intuitive. Figure 1-2 shows a typical pointer being used to select a menu item.

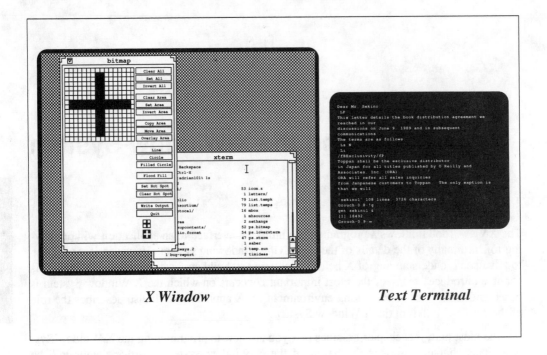

Figure 1-1. An X application and a traditional text terminal

Of course, X also handles keyboard input. The pointer is used to direct the input focus of the keyboard (often called the *keyboard focus*) from window to window with only one application at a time able to receive keyboard input.

In X, as in many other window systems, each application need not (and in fact usually does not) consist of only a single window. Any part of an application can have its own separate window, simplifying the management of input and output within the application code. Such *child* windows are only visible within the confines of their parent window. Each window has its own coordinate system where the origin is the upper-left corner of the window inside its border. In basic X, windows are rectangular and oriented along the same axes as the edges of the display. The application or the user can change the dimensions of windows.

Many of the above characteristics are also true of several other window systems. What has made X a standard is that X is based on a network protocol—a predefined set of requests and replies—instead of system-specific procedure calls. The *X Protocol* can be implemented for different computer architectures and operating systems, making X device-independent. Another advantage of a network-based windowing system is that programs can run on one architecture while displaying on another. Because of this unique design, the X Window System can make a network of different computers cooperate. For example, a computationally-intensive application might run on a supercomputer but take input from and display output on a workstation across a network.

Figure 1-2. Selecting a menu item with the pointer

1.1.1 The Server and Client

To allow programs to be run on one machine and display on another, X was designed as a network protocol between two processes, one of which is an application program called a *client*, and the other, the *server*. The server is a resource server, controlling a user's resources (such as the display hardware, keyboard, and pointer) and making these resources available to user applications. In other words, the X server isolates the device-specific code from the application.

The server performs the following tasks:

*   Allows access to the display by multiple clients. The server can deny access from clients running on certain machines.

*   Interprets network messages from clients and acts on them. These messages are known as requests. Some requests command the server to do two-dimensional drawing or move windows, while others ask the server for information.

*   Passes user input to clients sending network messages known as events, which represent key or button presses, pointer motion and so forth. Events are generated asynchronously, and events from different devices might be intermingled. The server must de-multiplex the event stream and pass the appropriate events to each client.

Maintains complex data structures, including windows and fonts, so that the server can perform its tasks efficiently. Clients refer to these abstractions by ID numbers. Server-maintained abstractions reduce the amount of data that has to be maintained by each client and the amount of data that has to be transferred over the network.

In X, the term *display* is often used as a synonym for server, as is the combined term *display server*. However, the terms *display* and *screen* are not synonymous. A screen is the actual piece of hardware on which the graphics are drawn. Both color and monochrome displays are supported. A server might control more than one screen. For example, one server might control a color screen and a monochrome screen for a user who wants to be able to debug an application on both types of screens without leaving his or her seat.

The communication path between a client and the server is called a *connection*. Several clients may be connected to a single server. Clients may run on the same machine as the server if that machine supports multitasking, or clients may run on other machines in the network. In either case, the X Protocol is used by the client to send requests to draw graphics or to query the server for information; it is used by the server to send user input or replies to requests back to the client. All communication from the client to the server and from the server to the client takes place using the X Protocol.*

It is common for a user to have programs running on several different hosts in the network, all invoked from and displaying their windows on a single screen (see Figure 1-3). Clients running remotely can be started from the remote machine or from the local machine using the network utilities *rlogin* or *rsh*.

This use of the network is known as *distributed processing*. The most important application of this concept is to provide graphic output for powerful systems that cannot have built-in graphics capabilities. However, distributed processing can also help solve the problem of unbalanced system loads. When one host machine is overloaded, the users running clients on that machine can arrange for programs to run on other hosts.

1.2 The Software Hierarchy

There are many different ways to write X applications because X is not restricted to a single language, operating system, or user interface. The only requirement of an X application is that it generate and receive X Protocol messages.

Figure 1-4 shows the layering of software in an X application. Xlib is the lowest-level C language interface to X. The main task of Xlib is to translate C data structures and procedures into X Protocol events; it then sends them off and receives protocol packets in return that are unpacked into C data structures. Xlib provides full access to the capabilities of the X protocol but does little to make programming easier. It handles the interface between an application and the network and includes some optimizations that encourage efficient network

---

*The X Protocol is independent of the networking hardware and runs on top of any network that provides point-to-point packet communication. TCP/IP and DECnet are the only networks currently supported. For more information about the X Protocol, see Volume Zero, *The X Protocol Reference Manual*.

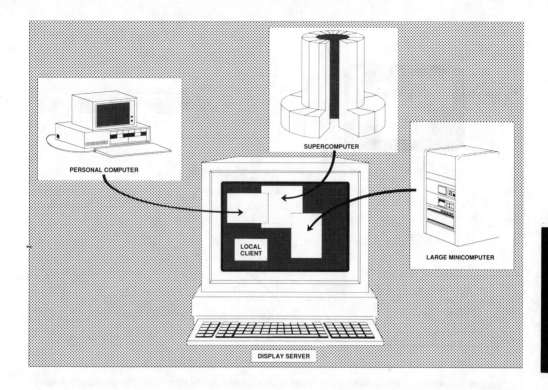

Figure 1-3. Applications can run on any system across the network

usage. The list of functions that Xlib performs is so extensive that if the programmer were responsible for handling all these pieces directly, application programs would be too large and prone to performance degradation and potential bugginess. For this reason, *toolkits* are used to modularize the more common functions that handle the user interface portion of an application.

XView is one of a half-dozen or so toolkits available for the X Window System. If you are familiar with other toolkits, you will recognize that the XView Toolkit is equivalent to the Xt Intrinsics and a widget set. Like the Intrinsics, XView is built upon Xlib. It is an object-oriented toolkit that provides reusable, configurable user-interface components, equivalent to widgets.*

Toolkits handle many things for the programmer. They provide a framework for combining prebuilt user-interface components with application-specific code. For example, if the application needs to prompt the user for a filename, a toolkit should provide a component (a *command frame*) that is functionally capable of displaying the query to the user and providing the user's response to the application.

---

*Widget sets are sometimes loosely referred to as toolkits. However, a toolkit comprises the functions of the Xt Intrinsics layer and one widget set (e.g., the Athena widget set). There are several different widget sets from various vendors that are designed to work with Xt. For more information on Xt Intrinsics-based toolkits, see Volume Four, *X Toolkit Intrinsics Programming Manual*.

Figure 1-4. The software architecture of X applications

Any user interface component also needs to manage the interpretation of events delivered from the window system. When events are generated, the toolkit decides whether or not to propagate the event to the application or to use it for its own internal purposes. To continue the example, when the user types a filename in the command frame, events are generated in which the interface must decide whether that object should interpret the input or whether it should be sent to the application. A toolkit thus comprises a mechanism to dispatch events and a set of prebuilt interface objects that define the look and feel of an application.

Note that using a toolkit does not preclude calling Xlib directly to accomplish certain tasks such as drawing. In XView, graphics rendering is done most efficiently by using Xlib drawing routines, for instance.

1.3 Extensions to X

Another thing to know about X is that it is *extensible*. The code includes a defined mechanism for incorporating extensions, so that vendors are not forced to modify the existing system in incompatible ways when adding features. An extension requires an additional piece of software on the server side and an additional library at the same level as Xlib on the client side. After an initial query to see whether the server portion of the extension software is installed, these extensions are used just like Xlib routines and perform at the same level.

Among the extensions currently being developed are support for 2-D spline curves, for 3-D graphics, and for Display PostScript™. These extensions can be used in Toolkit applications just like Xlib can.

1.4 The Window Manager

Because multiple applications can be running simultaneously, rules must exist for arbitrating conflicting demands for input. For example, does keyboard input automatically go to whichever window the pointer is in or must the user explicitly select a window for keyboard input?

Unlike most window systems, X itself makes no rules about this kind of thing. Instead, there is a special client called the *window manager* that manages the positions and sizes of the main windows of applications on a server's display. The window manager is just another client, but by convention, it is given special responsibility to mediate competing demands for the physical resources of a display including screen space, color resources, and the keyboard. The window manager allows the user to move windows around on the screen, resize them, and usually start new applications. The window manager also defines much of the visible behavior of the window system, such as whether windows are allowed to overlap or are tiled (side by side), and whether the keyboard focus simply follows the pointer from window to window or whether the user must click a pointer button in a window to change the keyboard focus (click-to-type).

Applications are required to give the window manager certain information that helps the window manager mediate competing demands for screen space or other resources. For example, an application specifies its preferred size and size increments. These are known as *window manager hints* because the window manager is not required to honor them. The XView Toolkit provides an easy way for applications to set the window manager hints.

The conventions for interaction with the window manager and with other clients have been standardized by the X Consortium as of July 1989 in a manual called the *Inter-Client Communications Conventions Manual* (ICCCM, for short). The ICCCM provides basic policy intentionally omitted from X itself, such as the rules for transferring data between applications (selections), transfer of keyboard focus, layout schemes, colormap installation, and so on. As long as applications and window managers follow the conventions set out in the ICCCM, applications created with different toolkits will be able to coexist and work together on the same server. Toolkit applications should be immune to the effects of the change from earlier conventions.

1.5 Handling Events

The window that X provides is the connection between the XView application and the X server. The reason X windows are important to XView is that these windows are the input targets for the user's focus. They are the actual objects that get events from the user and pass the events through to the XView world.

An X *event* is a data structure sent by the server that describes something that just happened that is of interest to the application. The sources of events are the user's input, the window system, the operating system, and the application programs. For example, the user's pressing a key on the keyboard or clicking a mouse button generates an event, and a window's being moved on the screen also generates events if it changes the visible portions of other applications. It is the server's job to distribute events to the various windows on the screen.

In XView, between the server and the application, there is an event dispatch mechanism called the Notifier, as shown in Figure 1-5.

After the set-up phase of the application, where you create XView objects such as buttons or scrollbars and determine how they will interact with your application code, you have several choices for input distribution. The simplest method is to hand off control of your application to XView. From then on, the XView Notifier automatically distributes events to the objects created by the application. These objects process many events internally so that your application does not need to get involved.

The key point is that your application is only told about events for which it specifically requested to be notified. By responding to these events, the application can perform its tasks. For example, if the user types the letter *A* in a window, X will pass the event to XView, which in turn can pass it to the application. An application's event handler can interpret this event and display the letter typed in the window. Finally, control returns to the top level so the next event can be read. This is a typical cycle of events that happens for each event generated by the user.

If the application created a scrollbar, then it would track certain events, such as when the scroll button is pressed. XView actually sends a request to the X server to create the X window that will become part of the scrollbar object. In the application's request, it can ask to be notified about or to ignore certain user events in the X window created.

The window system dictates which window gets an event. If the window currently has the keyboard focus and that window does not want to process the event, it has the option of throwing away the event or dropping it to the window below it. This is usually the parent of the window. For instance, if a panel item gets a keyboard press (the user typed an *A*) and if the panel item does not want to deal with the event, then the panel item might be configured so that the event is passed to the item's parent: the panel itself.

The Notifier does not just do input distribution; it also allows selection of different input sources. In addition to handling window system events, your application can also handle a number of interrupts that might be generated by the operating system. Your application can respond to signals, input on a file descriptor, and interval timers. You could also pass events between clients in the same process, interpose on a Notifier client to change its behavior, and receive notification on the death of a child process which you have spawned. The use of

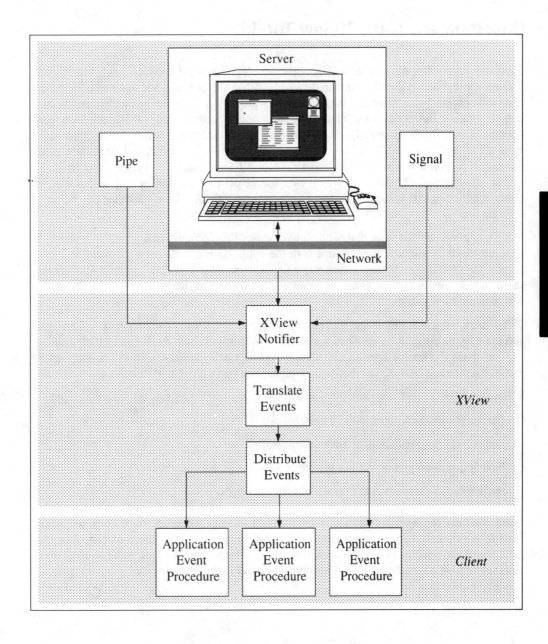

Figure 1-5. The Notifier exists between the server and the XView application

some of these input sources requires you to call the Notifier directly. The Notifier is covered again in the next two chapters as well as in Chapter 19, *The Notifier*.

1.6 Development of the XView Toolkit

Over the years, Sun Microsystems, Inc. has developed several toolkits, each more well-defined, more functional and aesthetically superior than the last. SunView 1 was perhaps the first well-accepted user interface toolkit Sun provided. It had all the basic elements necessary to make a functional user interface—including a well-defined API (application programmer's interface). It introduced the attribute-value interface, which we'll examine in more detail in Chapter 2, *The XView Programmer's Model*. It has very few procedure calls. For instance, you use a single function to create all user interface objects. You have the option of using default values, in which case the object is created with only a few lines of code, or of setting the values of specific attributes as required. These attributes can be set at the time the object is created, or later on, by using a different function.

The SunView 1 toolkit was based on SunWindows™, a kernel-based window system. It required that a single computer control both the application and the user's display and keyboard. The X Window System represents a new generation of window systems. It is server-based, which means that the client application can run on a different system than the server that controls the display.

Today there are several thousand SunView applications, and one of the aims of XView is to make it easy to bring those applications to the X Window System marketplace. In addition, Sun has made the source code to the XView Toolkit freely available. It will be shipped as part of the standard MIT X distribution as well as with UNIX System V Release 4.

XView provides a set of windows that include:

- *Canvases* on which programs can draw.

- *Text subwindows* with built-in editing capabilities.

- *Panels* containing items such as buttons, choice items, and sliders.

- *tty subwindows* that emulate character-based terminals.

These windows are arranged as *subwindows* within *frames*, which are themselves windows. Frames can be transitory or permanent. Transient interactions with the user can also take place in *menus* which can pop up anywhere on the screen. We will look more at all XView objects when we cover the XView programming model in the next chapter.

1.7 OPEN LOOK Graphical User Interface

An important feature of the XView Toolkit is that it implements the OPEN LOOK Graphical
User Interface (GUI). The OPEN LOOK GUI aims to provide users with a simple, consistent
and efficient interface. An example of an OPEN LOOK workspace is shown in Figure 1-6.
OPEN LOOK is supported by Sun and AT&T as the graphical user interface standard for System V Release 4. Users and developers benefit from a standard because it ensures consistent
behavior across a number of diverse applications. Programmers can concentrate on the
design of the application without having to "invent" a user interface.

Figure 1-6. A sample OPEN LOOK workspace

A well-defined user interface should be generalized enough so that it can be implemented on
any operating system, windowing system or graphics display. Because OPEN LOOK is not
bound by any of these constraints, XView was built entirely based on specifications that
could be mapped easily into the X Window System.

The visual design of OPEN LOOK is restrained. The design of each component in the user
interface is simple and uncomplicated. The interface is based on a few simple concepts that
result in a system that is easy to learn initially. And an XView application is relatively

simple and easy to implement because many of the default values of interface components are adequate for most applications.

We will attempt to summarize the OPEN LOOK interface where appropriate in this document. However, the definitive document on OPEN LOOK for application programmers is the *OPEN LOOK Graphical User Interface Style Guide*. This book provides guidelines for developers on using the elements of the OPEN LOOK GUI in applications. Where appropriate, we will show examples, such as Figure 1-6, which are taken from the *OPEN LOOK GUI Specification Guide*.

2

The XView Programmer's Model

In This Chapter:

Object-oriented Programming 17
    Object Class Hierarchy 18
    Object Handles 19
Attribute-based Functions 21
    Creating and Manipulating Objects 21
    Changing Object Attributes 22
Types of Attributes 22
Types of Objects 23
    Generic Objects 24
    Window Objects 25
    Frames and Subframes 26
    Subwindows 28
    Nonvisual Objects 33
The Notifier Model 35
    Callback Style of Programming 35
    Why a Notification-based System? 35
    Relationship Among the Notifier, Objects and the Application ... 35
    Calling the Notifier Directly 38

2

The XView Programmer's Model

XView is intended to simplify application development under the X Window System by providing the programmer with a set of predefined user interface components. These components implement the "look and feel" of the OPEN LOOK Graphical User Interface, developed by Sun Microsystems, Inc. and AT&T.

This chapter presents a model of XView for the programmer. It is important to understand this model before you begin writing XView applications. However, you might wish to skim the concepts presented in this chapter and proceed to Chapter 3, *Creating XView Applications*, to examine sample programs.

2.1 Object-oriented Programming

To the programmer, XView is an *object-oriented* toolkit. XView objects can be considered building blocks from which the user interface of the application is assembled. Each piece can be considered an *object* from a particular *package*. Each package provides a list of properties from which you can choose to configure the object. By selecting objects from the available packages, you can build the user interface for an application.

XView is based on several of the fundamental principles of object-oriented programming:

- Objects are represented in a class hierarchy.

- Objects are opaque data types.

- Objects have attributes which can be set via message passing functions.

- Objects may have callback procedures that are trigged by events. We will look at how these concepts are implemented in XView in the sections that follow.

2.1.1 Object Class Hierarchy

XView defines classes of objects in a tree hierarchy. For example, *frame* is a subclass of the more general class *window*, which in turn is a subclass of *drawable*. Drawable, like user interface object classes, is a subclass of the *Generic Object* class. Figure 2-1 shows the XView class hierarchy and the relationships between the classes. Each class has identifying features that make it unique from other classes or packages. In XView, a class is often called a *package*, meaning a set of related functional elements. However, there are XView packages that are not members of the object class hierarchy, such as the Notifier package.

Some objects are visual and others are not. Visual objects include windows, scrollbars, frames, panels and panel items, among others. Nonvisual objects are objects which have no appearance, per se, but they have information which aids in the display of visual objects. Examples of nonvisual objects include the server, screen, and font objects. The screen, for example, provides information such as the type of color it can display or the default foreground and background colors that objects might inherit. The display can provide information about what fonts are available for objects that display text.

All objects, both visual and nonvisual, are a part of this object classing system. The system is extensible, so you can create new classes that might or might not be based on existing classes.

XView uses static subclassing and chained inheritance as part of its object-oriented model. All objects of a particular class inherit the properties of the parent class (also known as a superclass). The Generic Object XV_OBJECT contains certain basic properties that all objects share. For example, the same object can appear in many places on the screen to optimize storage. To keep a record of this, the Generic Object maintains a reference count of its instances. Since all objects have an owner, the parent of the object is stored in a field of the generic part of the object. As the needs of an object get more specific to a particular look or functionality, lower-level classes define properties to implement it.

Each class contains properties that are shared among all instances of that object. For example, *panels* are a part of the PANEL package, which has properties that describe, among other things, its layout (horizontal or vertical) or the spacing between items (buttons) in the panel. All panels share these properties, even though the state of the properties might differ for each instance of the object.

As mentioned earlier, XView uses subclassing so that each package can inherit the properties of its superclass. The PANEL package is subclassed from the WINDOW package, which has properties specific to all windows, such as window dimensions, location on the screen, border thickness, depth, visual and colormap information. The WINDOW package is subclassed from the root object XV_OBJECT, as are all objects, and the panel can access generic information such as the size and position of itself.

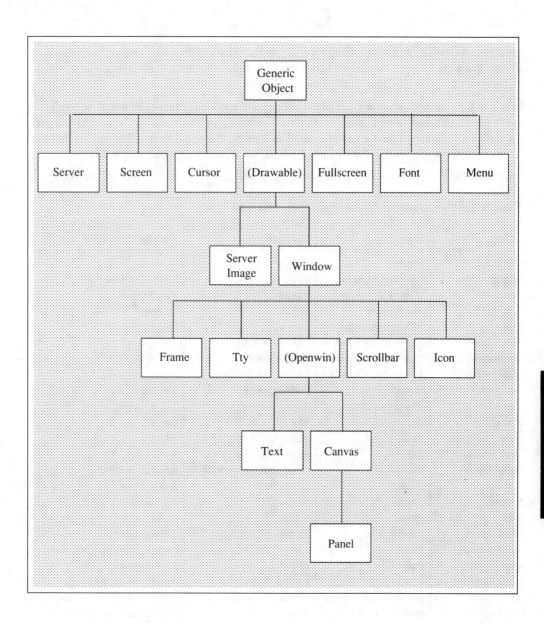

Figure 2-1. XView class hierarchy

2.1.2 Object Handles

When you create an object, the XView function returns a *handle* for the object. Later, when you wish to manipulate the object or inquire about its state, you pass its handle to the appropriate function. This reliance on object handles is a way of *information-hiding*. The handles are *opaque* in the sense that you cannot see through them to the actual data structure which represents the object.

Each object type has a corresponding type of handle. Since C does not have an opaque type, all the opaque data types mentioned above are typedef'd to the XView type Xv_opaque or Xv_object.

In addition to the opaque data types, there are several typedefs that refer not to pointers but to structures: Event, Rect, and Rectlist. Generally pointers to these structures are passed to XView functions, so they are declared as Event *, Rect *, etc. The reason that the asterisk (*) is not included in the typedef is that the structures are publicly available.

Table 2-1 lists each XView object, its owner, the package that defines it, and its data type:

Table 2-1. XView Objects, Owners, Packages, and Data Types

Object	Owner	Package	Handle Data Type
canvas	frame	CANVAS	Canvas
canvas view	window or screen	CANVAS_VIEW	Canvas_view
cursor	window or screen	CURSOR	Xv_Cursor
font	root window	FONT	Xv_Font
frame	frame or root window	FRAME	Frame
base frame	frame or root window	FRAME_BASE	
command frame	frame or root window	FRAME_CMD	
property frame	frame or root window	FRAME_PROPS	
fullscreen	root window	FULLSCREEN	Fullscreen
icon	window or screen	ICON	Icon
menu	null	MENU	Menu
command menu	null	MENU_COMMAND_MENU	Menu
choice menu	null	MENU_CHOICE_MENU	Menu
toggle menu	null	MENU_TOGGLE_ITEM	Menu
menu item	menu	MENUITEM	Menu_item
openwin	frame	OPENWIN	Openwin
panel	frame	PANEL	Panel
panel button	panel	PANEL_BUTTON	Panel_button_item
panel choice	panel	PANEL_CHOICE	Panel_choice_item
panel item	panel	PANEL_ITEM	Panel_item
panel list	panel	PANEL_LIST	Panel_list_item
panel message	panel	PANEL_MESSAGE	Panel_message_item
panel numeric text	panel	PANEL_NUMERIC_TEXT	Panel_numeric_text_item
panel slider	panel	PANEL_SLIDER	Panel_slider_item
panel text	panel	PANEL_TEXT	Panel_text_item
screen	null	SCREEN	Screen
scrollbar	panel or canvas	SCROLLBAR	Scrollbar
server	null	SERVER	Server
server image	screen	SERVER_IMAGE	Server_image
text subwindow	frame	TEXTSW	Textsw
tty	frame	TTY	Tty
window	frame	WINDOW	Xv_Window

2.2 Attribute-based Functions

A model such as that used by XView, which is based on complex and flexible objects, presents the problem of how the client is to manipulate the objects. The basic idea behind the XView interface is to provide a small number of functions, which take as arguments a large set of *attributes*. For a given call to create or modify an object, only a subset of the set of all applicable attributes will be of interest.

2.2.1 Creating and Manipulating Objects

There is a common set of functions that allows the programmer to manipulate any object by referencing the object handle. The functions are listed in Table 2-2:

Table 2-2. Generic Functions

Function	Role
xv_init()	Establishes the connection to the server, initializes the Notifier and the Defaults/Resource-Manager database, loads the Server Resource-Manager database, and reads the ~/.*Xdefaults* database and any passed attributes.
xv_create()	Creates an object.
xv_destroy()	Destroys an object.
xv_find()	Finds an object that meets certain criteria; or if the object doesn't exist, creates it.
xv_get()	Gets the value of an attribute.
xv_set()	Sets the value of an attribute.

Using these six routines, objects can be created and manipulated from all packages available in XView. When the programmer wants to create an instance of an object from a certain package, the routine xv_create() is used. For example:

```
Panel panel;
panel = xv_create(panel_parent, PANEL, NULL);
```

Here, an instance of a panel has been created from the PANEL package. All its attributes are set to the panel's *default* properties because no object-specific attributes have been specified. A handle to the new panel object is returned and stored in the variable panel. This handle is not a pointer and does not contain any useful information about the object itself.

The next section goes into detail about the use of xv_set() and xv_get(). Chapter 3, *Creating XView Applications*, discusses the use of xv_init(), xv_destroy() and xv_find().

XView Model

2.2.2 Changing Object Attributes

The programmer uses the handle returned from the `xv_create()` function as a parameter to the functions `xv_get()` and `xv_set()` to get and set attributes of the object.

```
panel = xv_create(...)
xv_set(panel, PANEL_LAYOUT, PANEL_HORIZONTAL, NULL);
```

Here, the handle to the panel (`panel`) is used to change a `PANEL` package attribute, `PANEL_LAYOUT`, whose value is set to `PANEL_HORIZONTAL`. The attribute and value form an *attribute-value pair*. The functions `xv_create()`, `xv_destroy()`, `xv_find()`, `xv_set()` and, to some extent, `xv_get()` use attribute-value pairs. The functions can have any number of pairs associated with the function call. These *variable argument lists* are always terminated by a `NULL` pointer as the last argument in the list. Note that `NULL`, not the constant 0 (zero), should be used as the terminating argument.

The effect of this function call is to change the layout of the panel from the previous value, whatever it might be, to horizontal.

2.3 Types of Attributes

Attributes can be divided into three categories. Those that apply to all XView objects are termed *generic* attributes. Attributes that are supported by many, but not all objects, are termed *common* attributes. Attributes that are associated with a particular package or class of objects are called *specific* attributes.

XView uses naming conventions to simplify the identification of the task of an attribute. Those attributes that apply to a specific package have their name prefixed by the package name. The attributes have prefixes that indicate the type of object they apply to, i.e. `CAN-VAS_*`, `CURSOR_*`, `FRAME_*`, `ICON_*`, `MENU_*`, `PANEL_*`, `SCROLLBAR_*`, `TEXTSW_*`, `TTY_*`, etc.

Common and generic attributes apply to several different object types and are prefixed by `XV_`. For example, the generic attribute `XV_HEIGHT` applies to all objects since all objects must have a height. In contrast, attributes that apply only to windows are prefixed by `WIN_`. Attributes such as `WIN_HEIGHT` and `WIN_WIDTH` apply to all windows regardless of whether they happen to be panels or canvases.

The value part of an attribute-value pair can differ from attribute to attribute. The reason for this is that the attribute may describe a wide range of values. If the attribute describes the height or width of an object, the value associated with the attribute will be an integer. However, sometimes the attribute requires a variable-length list of values—this too must be `NULL`-terminated.

Look at the following code fragment that specifies an attribute-value list at the creation of a panel item:

```
Panel_item panel_item;
panel_item = xv_create(panel, PANEL_CYCLE,
     XV_WIDTH,               50,
     XV_HEIGHT,              25,
     WIN_RIGHT_OF,           other_panel_item,
     PANEL_LABEL_X,          100,
     PANEL_LABEL_Y,          100,
     PANEL_LABEL_STRING,     "Open File"
     PANEL_CHOICE_STRINGS,   "Append to file",
                             "Overwrite contents",
                             NULL,

     NULL);
```

All the attributes except PANEL_CHOICE_STRINGS take a single value. The PANEL_CHOICE_STRINGS attribute takes a list of strings, and that list is NULL-terminated. The last NULL terminates the list of attribute-value pairs passed to the xv_create() function.

Don't worry for now what each of these attributes does. Simply notice the mixture of generic attributes (XV_WIDTH and XV_HEIGHT) with common attributes (WIN_RIGHT_OF) and class-specific attributes (all the PANEL_* attributes). Because all packages are subclasses of the XV_OBJECT package, the XV_* attributes can be used with all xv_create() calls. The WIN_ attributes can be used because the PANEL package is a subclass of the WINDOW package.

2.4 Types of Objects

The following section describes on a conceptual level the different types of objects that XView offers. In many cases, figures taken from the *OPEN LOOK GUI Specification Guide* are used to show the appearance of the object. Details about the objects themselves, how to create them, their properties, their default values and so forth are discussed in later chapters that are specific to those object packages. A list of the objects that can be created include:

- Generic Objects

- Windows

- Frames

- Openwins

- Canvases

- Text Windows

- Menus

- Scrollbars

2.4.1 Generic Objects

The Generic Object is the root object of the class hierarchy. One never creates an instance of a Generic Object because, by itself, it has no function. Figure 2-2 shows the path taken when an object is created.

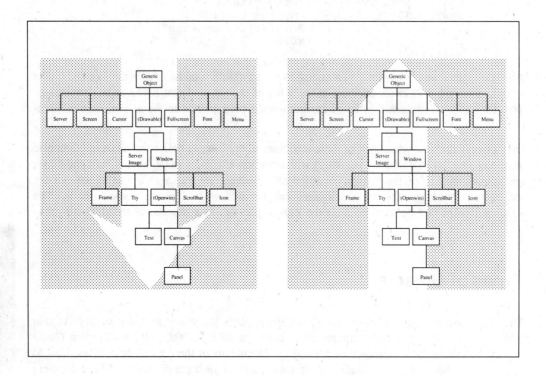

Figure 2-2. Object creation is top down; attribute setting is bottom up

First, the Generic Object is created; then the subclass of that object is created all the way down until the object class of the type of object desired is created. At that point, a complete instance of the object has been created with all the default properties of the classes set. If there were any attribute-value pairs specified in the `xv_create()` call, those attributes are set in reverse order—the attributes specific to the class of the instance of the object are set first, followed by its parent's class attributes and so on, until the generic attributes are set.

Consider the code below, which creates a panel:

```
extern xv_font font;
Panel panel;

panel = xv_create(frame, PANEL,
                  XV_Y,         5,
                  WIN_HEIGHT,   50,
                  PANEL_FONT,   font,
                  NULL);
```

When the panel is created, the first thing created is a generic object. Next a window instance is created, followed by a canvas and finally a panel object. Each is created with the default properties of the object specific to each class.

Now the reverse traversal takes place, and the attributes specified in the xv_create() call for each class are set to override the default properties inherited from the class. First, the panel package attributes are set. The panel's default font is controlled by the attribute PANEL_FONT; its assigned value, *font*, must be previously initialized. Then the window package attributes are set. The panel's window width is controlled by the attribute CAN-VAS_WIDTH which is not explicitly set, so its assigned value defaults to WIN_EXTEND_TO_EDGE. This value indicates that the width of the window should always be the width of its parent. The height of the window, however, is specified. So the window package sets the height to be 50 pixels. Finally, the generic attributes are set. The panel's *x* and *y* location, indicating where it should be placed within its parent, is controlled by setting the XV_X and XV_Y attributes. The example sets the *y* position only; the *x* position is not set because the window package is told to extend the width of the panel to the edges of its parent. The parent in this case is the object frame (which is presumed to be from the FRAME package).

2.4.2 Window Objects

Many XView objects contain X windows in order to display themselves and receive events. Examples include frames, tty windows, scrollbars and icons.

The XView window class, like the Generic Object class, is a hidden class: a *window* object is never explicitly created. Rather, an object that is a subclass of the window class is created. This includes most visual objects with the exception of panel items.

Nonvisual objects are so named because they do not contain, or are not a subclass of, windows. Fonts, for example, are displayed in windows, or in a memory image, or somewhere that contains a bitmap, but fonts do not contain or require windows to be used.

Some attributes of windows include depth (XV_DEPTH), the border width around its perimeter (WIN_BORDER_WIDTH) as well as foreground and background colors.

2.4.3 Frames and Subframes

There are two kinds of frames:

- *Base Frames*

- *Pop-up Frames*

With one exception, all frames are free-floating windows that contain subwindows that are bound by the frame and tiled (they do not overlap one another). Base frames reside on the root window and are not constrained by any other window, though all frames can overlap one another. The base frame is also known as the application's frame. (More than one base frame may be associated with an application.) Subframes are frames whose owner is a frame; they are controlled by the base frames of the application. For example, extraneous dialog boxes (subframes) will go away if the main application's base frame is *iconified* (closed). Figure 2-3 shows an example of a fully featured base frame from the *OPEN LOOK GUI Specification Guide*.

Figure 2-3. Fully-featured base frame (includes optional elements)

Chapter 4, *Frames*, goes into more detail about the elements of a frame and how to set attributes and override default values. It should be noted that many features of the frame are attributes of the window manager. Figure 2-3 assumes an OPEN LOOK-compliant window manager; if another window manager is used, base frames might not look the same. XView defines attributes that give hints to the window manager to provide such features such as title bar information, resize corners, and so on. If a non-OPEN LOOK window manager is used, there is no guarantee that these attributes will have any effect.

Pop-up frames are typically used to perform one or more transient functions. They are not intended to stay up after the set of functions has been completed, although they might remain up if the user or the application chooses so. This functionality can be handled by a pushpin at the upper-left corner of the frame. There are different kinds of pop-up frames:

Command Frames   give operands and set parameters needed for a command. This is implemented as a subframe that contains a default panel.

Help Frames   display help text for the object under the pointer. This is implemented as a text subwindow within a subframe.

Notices   are special pop-up windows that are used to confirm requests, to display messages and conditions that must be brought to the user's attention and handled immediately. These require immediate attention and suspend the application from running by disallowing the focus from leaving the Notice.

Figure 2-4 shows a sample unpinned command frame from the *OPEN LOOK GUI Specification Guide*.

Figure 2-4. Sample unpinned command frame

The user may select the option, and the frame will be *dismissed* (be undisplayed). The pushpin at the upper-left corner is out of its hole. If the pushpin were in, the command frame would remain visible even after the user selects an action to take. Figure 2-5 shows a sample pinned help frame from the *OPEN LOOK GUI Specification Guide*.

Figure 2-6 shows a sample notice from the *OPEN LOOK GUI Specification Guide*.

The user can do nothing but choose either Save or Cancel. Choosing either one will cause the notice to be dismissed immediately.

Figure 2-5. Sample help window

Figure 2-6. Sample notice

2.4.4 Subwindows

Subwindows differ from frames in several basic ways. They never exist independently; they are always owned and maintained by a frame or another window, and they may not themselves own frames. While frames can be moved freely around the screen, subwindows are constrained to fit within the borders of the frame to which they belong. Also, in contrast to frames, subwindows are *tiled*—they may not overlap each other within their frame. Within these constraints (which are enforced by a run-time *boundary manager*), subwindows may be moved and resized by either a program or a user.

XView Programming Manual

Canvas subwindows and text subwindows are subclassed from the OPENWIN package, a hidden class which implements the notion of *splittable views* described by OPEN LOOK. Figure 2-7 shows an example of one canvas object providing separate views into one graphic image. Each view into the object has scrollbars attached. The scrollbars provide the ability to scroll independently from all the other views attached to the subwindow and to split the views again.

Figure 2-7. A window with multiple views

All the views, however, are still a part of the same OPENWIN object. Using the scrollbars, the user can split or join different views.

Canvas Subwindows

The canvas is the most basic type of subwindow. It provides a drawing surface—a place in which the result of Xlib graphics calls can be displayed. A canvas object can be configured to permit the application to draw on an area larger than the size of the visible window. The entire region representing the drawing surface is a window called the *paint window*. The visible portion of the paint window is the *view window*. It is the view window that appears in the canvas subwindow. In the previous figure, the paint window contains a picture of an astronaut. Multiple view windows each show a particular region of the paint canvas. The view windows are independent of each other. See Chapter 5, *Canvases and Openwin*, for a full discussion and illustration of the Canvas model.

Text Subwindows

Another basic window type is a text subwindow. It provides basic text editing capabilities using the OPEN LOOK text editing model.

Panels

Panels (or *control areas*) are an unbordered region of a window where controls such as buttons and settings are displayed. The panel also controls the arrangement of its controls in a horizontal or vertical fashion. The panel shown in Figure 2-8 presents the typical positioning of the control area—the top of a base frame with a canvas subwindow under it.

Figure 2-8. A control area above a subwindow

The panel shown in Figure 2-9 presents a control area that is to the right of a canvas subwindow.

Control areas within panes usually contain varied combinations of the following controls:

- Buttons
- Exclusive and nonexclusive choice lists
- Check boxes
- Sliders
- Text and numeric fields

A command frame (subframe) contains only a panel and no other subwindows. Figure 2-10 shows a control area in a command frame. It contains text fields, choice lists, and buttons. See Chapter 7, *Panels*, for a discussion of panel items and the PANEL package.

Figure 2-9. A control area to the right of a pane

Figure 2-10. A control area in a command window

Menus

Menus are subclassed from the Generic Object. A menu by itself is a windowless object. Only when the menu is activated by the user is it bound to a window. This implementation avoids creating multiple X11 windows (one for each menu) since not all the menus will be displayed at once. XView has three types of menus:

1. Pop-up menus that are displayed when the user presses the menu button in a window.

2. Pullright menus that are displayed as a menu to the right of a menu.

3. Pulldown menus that are displayed below a menu button on a panel.

Figure 2-11 shows an example of a pop-up menu on the left; on the right, a pullright submenu is displayed.

Pushpins can be used in some menus, allowing them to be *pinned* so that the menu remains on the screen for repeated use.

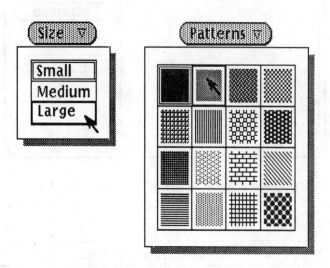

Figure 2-11. Example of a pop-up menu with a pullright submenu

Scrollbars

Scrollbars implement the OPEN LOOK metaphor of an elevator on a cable. These components are shown in Figure 2-12.

A scrollbar is an object that can exist independently or it can attach itself to various types of subwindows. The scrollbar is subclassed from the WINDOW class since it is a visual object. However, because its functionality is very tightly bound to other objects, the scrollbar is sometimes considered to be a property of those objects. OPENWIN subclasses (canvas and text-based packages) require scrollbars to provide splittable views, and scrollbars can be created automatically by such objects. Typically, it is your responsibility to pass a hint to the object that it should create the scrollbar using the appropriate attribute-value pair. Nevertheless, scrollbars can be manually attached or detached to OPENWIN objects or can be created independently of these objects for other purposes entirely.

The SCROLLBAR package manages only the scrollbar window. It does not control the window to which it is attached. When a scrolling action results from the user clicking on a portion of the scrollbar, the window to which the scrollbar is attached must modify its data (a view in most cases). It is not the scrollbar's responsibility to notify the window it is attached to. The scrollbar informs the object interested in its scrolling by use of callback routines that the owner of the scrollbar must install.

Figure 2-12. Vertical scrollbar components

Scrollbars can be oriented vertically or horizontally, but some packages might not allow a particular scrollbar orientation. Text subwindows, for example, contain vertical scrollbars by default but do not permit horizontal scrollbars.

Icons

An icon is a small image representing the application when the application's frame is in a closed, or iconified, state. The ICON package is very small. It is subclassed from the WINDOW package because it is a window that displays graphics and accepts input. The only attributes that you can set in the ICON package specify the image to display in the window and the geometry of the image. Other important attributes that an icon can have (such as width, height, label and font) are attributes of the generic class.

2.4.5 Nonvisual Objects

There are several nonvisual objects that cannot be represented on the screen but are subclassed from the Generic Object:

SERVER   This package interacts with the X server. The window-server is the program that does the drawing to the screen and receives the user's input. The server also maintains font information and user-configurable resources, which can be set for specific applications.

SCREEN   This object describes the visual and other characteristics of the physical screen. This object is separate from Xlib SCREEN object.

FONT   The font package allows the programmer to request fonts of varying attributes such as font *family* and *style*. Fonts can be accessed by name, size or scaling.

CURSOR   The cursor, or pointer, is a visual object indicating the mouse location on the screen.

These objects are closely tied with the X Window System and they are manipulated by making requests to set or get attributes from X. While there are Xlib calls that can be used to acquire the same information, these packages simplify the work required to do so.

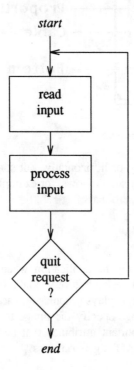

Figure 2-13. Flow of control in a conventional program

2.5 The Notifier Model

XView is a *notification-based* system. The Notifier acts as the controlling entity within a user process, reading input from the operating system, and formatting it into higher-level *events*, which it distributes to the different XView objects.*

2.5.1 Callback Style of Programming

In the conventional style of interactive programming, the main control loop resides in the application. An editor, for example, will read a character, take some action based on the character, then read the next character, and so on. When a character is received that represents the user's request to quit, the program exits. Figure 2-13 illustrates this approach.

Notification-based systems invert this straight line control structure. The main control loop resides in the Notifier, not the application. The Notifier reads events and *notifies*, or *calls out* to, various procedures which the application has previously registered with the Notifier. These procedures are called *notify procs* or *callback procs*. This control structure is shown in Figure 2-14.

2.5.2 Why a Notification-based System?

If you are not used to it, this callback style of programming takes some getting used to. Its big advantage is that it takes over the burden of managing a complex, event-driven environment. In XView, an application typically has many objects. In the absence of a centralized Notifier, each application must be responsible for detecting and dispatching events to all the objects in the process. With a centralized Notifier, each component of an application receives only the events the user has directed towards it.

2.5.3 Relationship Among the Notifier, Objects and the Application

It is not necessary for you to interact with the Notifier directly in your application. XView has a two-tiered scheme in which the packages that support the various objects—panels, canvases, scrollbars, etc.—interact with the Notifier directly, registering their own callback procedures. The application, in turn, registers its own callback procedures with the object.

Typically, when writing a XView application, you first create the various windows and other objects you need for your interface and register your callback procedures with the objects. Then you pass control to the Notifier. The work is done in the various callback procedures.

---

*XView events are in a form which you can easily use: an ASCII key has been pressed, a mouse button has been pressed or released, the mouse has moved, the mouse has entered or exited a window, etc. Events are described in detail in Chapter 6, *Handling Input*.

Application Code | Notifier

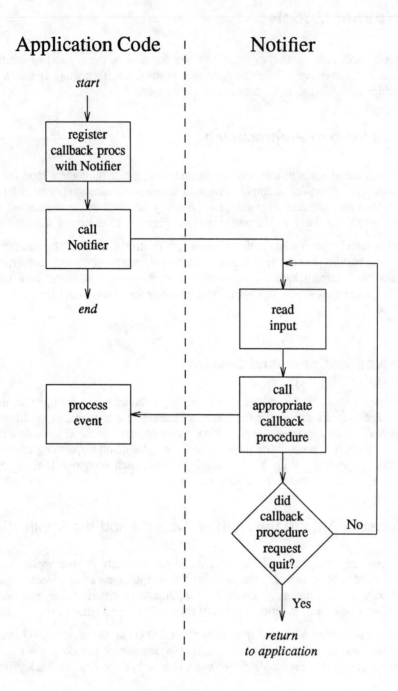

Figure 2-14. Flow of control in a Notifier-based program

Let's illustrate the relationship of the Notifier, the XView objects and the application by taking a sample application. Figure 2-15 illustrates how the Notifier receives X events from the

X server, as well as operating system "events" such as signals or input on file descriptors. Event procedures are supplied by XView packages as well as the application itself.

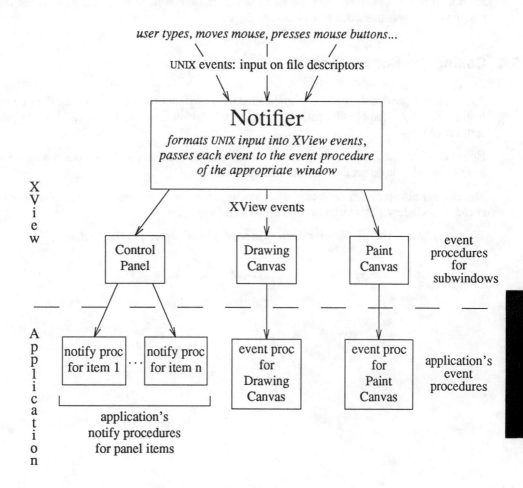

Figure 2-15. Flow of input events in an XView application

The main point of Figure 2-15 is to clarify the double-tiered callback scheme. How you register the callback procedures will be explained in Chapter 5, *Canvases and Openwin*, and Chapter 7, *Panels*.

One point worth mentioning is the distinction between the *event procedures* for the canvases and the *notify procedures* for the panel items. They are all callback procedures, but they have different purposes. The canvas's event procedure does not do much work—basically, it calls out to the application's event procedure each time an event is received. The application sees every event and is free to interpret the events however it likes.

The event procedure for panels, on the other hand, does quite a bit of processing. It determines which item should receive the event and places its own interpretation on events—the middle mouse button is ignored, and the left mouse button down over an item is interpreted as a tentative activation of the item, etc. It does not call back to the notify procedure for the item until it receives a left mouse button up over the item. So panel item notify procedures are not so much concerned with the event which caused them to be called as with the fact that the button was pushed, a new choice made, etc.

2.5.4 Calling the Notifier Directly

As mentioned previously, for many applications, you will not need to call or be called by the Notifier directly—the Notifier calls back to the subwindows, which in turn call back to your application.

However, if you need to use signals or be notified of the death of a child process which you have spawned, you do need to call the Notifier directly.

The Notifier also provides calls that allow you to insert your own routine in the event stream ahead of a window. This technique is known as *interposition*.

When and how to call the Notifier directly is covered in Chapter 19, *The Notifier*.

3

Creating XView Applications

In This Chapter:

Interface Overview 41
    Compiling XView Programs 41
    XView Libraries 42
    Header Files 42
    Naming Conventions 42
    Example of XView-style Programming 43
Initializing XView 45
Creating and Modifying Objects 46
    Using xv_create( ) 47
    Using xv_find( ) 49
    Using xv_destroy() 50
    Using xv_set( ) and xv_get( ) 50
xv_main_loop( ) and the Notifier 52
Registering Event Handlers 53
Error Recovery 54

Creating
Applications

3
Creating XView Applications

This chapter covers the XView programming interface. It describes the basic XView distribution and how you use it to compile and link XView applications. It also presents the proper structure for XView applications. The structure can be summarized as:

- Initialize XView using xv_init().

- Create a top-level window (FRAME) to manage subwindows.

- Add subwindows as children of the FRAME.

- Add objects to subwindows.

- Specify notification callbacks and select input events.

- Call xv_main_loop() to start the dispatching of events.

This chapter also discusses error recovery procedures.

3.1 Interface Overview

This section gives an overview of the XView programming interface. It covers reserved words and naming conventions in XView. It also includes a complete sample program, which we will look at more closely when describing the calling sequence for a program.

3.1.1 Compiling XView Programs

To compile an XView program, you must link with several XView libraries. Because they are built one on top of another, their order is important. For example, to compile a typical XView application whose source is *myprog.c*, you type in the command:

```
% cc myprog.c -lxview -lX11 -o myprog
```

The X11 library is not included in the XView library, so it must be specified in addition to *-lxview*.

3.1.2 XView Libraries

XView functions are found mostly in the library *libxvol.a*. These libraries include the code to create and manipulate high-level objects such as frames, panels, scrollbars and icons. These packages in turn call routines in *libxvin.a* to create and manipulate windows and interact with the Notifier. These libraries are both included in the library *libxview.a*. The XView libraries call routines in the Xlib library (*libX11.a*) that do the drawing on the screen.

3.1.3 Header Files

The basic definitions needed by an XView application (windows, frames, menus, icons and cursors) are obtained by including the header file *<xview/xview.h>*. All XView applications should have the line:

```
#include <xview/xview.h>
```

This header file includes many other header files that set up standard types. It also declares external functions and includes some system-specific header files that are required by all the XView header files. Once *<xview/xview.h>* has been included, other include files specific to the packages are included. Each object package has its own header file to declare object types, to provide definitions for frequently used macros, and to make external definitions for routines that are specific to that object's package. Frequently these files include other files, which in turn may include other packages or system header files.

For instance, if your code uses the FRAME, PANEL and FONT packages, then these include files must be specified:

```
#include <xview/xview.h>
#include <xview/frame.h>
#include <xview/panel.h>
#include <xview/font.h>
```

However, investigation shows that some header files include other header files by default. For example, *<xview/xview.h>* includes *<xview/frame.h>*. Since there are "wrappers" inside the XView header files which prevent them from being included more than once, if the file has already been included and is inadvertently included again, the second and subsequent attempts to include it are discarded. Because of this, it is safe to include header files more than once.

3.1.4 Naming Conventions

All the examples throughout this book follow a consistent method in the naming of data types, package names, and even variable names. Because of the large number of packages and data types, you could easily confuse what a lexical string represents. Therefore, you are advised to follow certain criteria when naming variables and declaring data types that are not specific to XView. Whatever naming convention you choose, you should always try to be consistent.

Reserved Names

XView reserves names beginning with the object types, as well as certain other prefixes, for its own use. The prefixes in Table 3-1 should not be used by applications in lower, upper or mixed case.

Table 3-1. Reserved Prefixes

attr_	icon_	seln_
canvas_	menu_	server_
cursor_	notify_	server_image_
defaults_	panel_	termsw_
ei_	pixrect_	text_
es_	pr_	textsw_
ev_	pw_	tty_
event_	rect_	ttysw_
font_	rl_	win_
frame_	screen_	window_
fullscreen_	scroll_	wmgr_
generic_	scrollbar_	xv_

To help you choose what *not* to use for data types and other lexical tokens in your application, review Table 2-1, "XView Objects, Owners, Packages, and Data Types."

3.1.5 Example of XView-style Programming

The flavor of the XView programming interface is illustrated by the code in Example 3-1. This program, *quit.c*, creates a frame containing a panel with one item: a button labeled Quit.

There are a few things to notice in the program. First, note the NULL that terminates the attribute lists in the xv_create() and xv_set() calls. The most common mistake in using attribute lists is to forget the final NULL. This will not be flagged by the compiler as an error. The results are actually unpredictable, but the most common result is that XView will generate a run-time error message and the program will exit.

Second, the object returned by the xv_create() for the PANEL_BUTTON is not stored into a variable. This is primarily because it is not needed by any other portion of the code. One of the most common programming inefficiencies is the use of global variables when they are not needed. If you are not going to reference an object created via xv_create(), you should not retain its handle. If you need its handle, but only temporarily, then it should be a local variable, not a global or static one. For example, the panel variable (type Panel) is used as a local variable.

Creating
Applications

Example 3-1. The quit.c program

```
/*
 * quit.c -- simple program to display a panel button that says "Quit".
 * Selecting the panel button exits the program.
 */
#include <xview/xview.h>
#include <xview/frame.h>
#include <xview/panel.h>

Frame frame;

main (argc, argv)
int argc;
char *argv[];
{
    Panel panel;
    void quit();

    xv_init (XV_INIT_ARGC_PTR_ARGV, &argc, argv, NULL);

    frame = (Frame)xv_create (NULL, FRAME,
        FRAME_LABEL,      argv[0],
        XV_WIDTH,         200,
        XV_HEIGHT,        100,
        NULL);

    panel = (Panel)xv_create (frame, PANEL, NULL);

    (void) xv_create (panel, PANEL_BUTTON,
            PANEL_LABEL_STRING,        "Quit",
            PANEL_NOTIFY_PROC,         quit,
            NULL);

    xv_main_loop (frame);
    exit(0);
}

void
quit()
{
    xv_destroy_safe(frame);
}
```

Figure 3-1 shows the output resulting from *quit.c*. In the sections that follow, we are going to look at how this program demonstrates the structure of XView programs.

Figure 3-1. A frame containing a Quit button

3.2 Initializing XView

Initializing the XView system should be done as soon as possible in the application. The `xv_init()` function performs many tasks, including:

* Opening the connection to the server.
* Initializing the Notifier.
* Initializing the Resource Manager database.*

The form of `xv_init()` is:

```
void
xv_init(attrs)
    <attribute-value list> attrs;
```

Initialization should be done before the application attempts to parse its own command line options. Since many programs tend to have command line parameters, a program tends to report unknown parameters as illegal arguments. Because XView parameters can also be specified on the command line to the application, the program must be able to distinguish between the application's parameters and XView's parameters.

`xv_init()` accepts the attributes `XV_INIT_ARGS` and `XV_INIT_ARGC_PTR_ARGV` for purposes of parsing command line arguments. These attributes both take two parameters as values: `argc` and `argv`. These are typically the same ones passed into `main()`. Using the `XV_INIT_ARGC_PTR_ARGV` attribute, the `xv_init()` function can be told to modify `argc` and `argv` by removing parameters that are XView-specific, like so:

```
(void) xv_init(XV_INIT_ARGC_PTR_ARGV, &argc, argv, NULL);
```

When `xv_init` returns, `argv` contains only those parameters that are not specific to XView, and the application can now assume that all remaining arguments are specific to the application. So a hypothetical command line might look like this:

---

*See Chapter 17, *Resources*, for more information about the resource database.

```
% program -display maui:0
```

The command line is first parsed by xv_init(), and in this case, all arguments are stripped from the argv variable, leaving just argv[0], whose value is program. argc is modified to have the value 1 (it was originally 3). The example command line parameters change the default server to be the X server running on the machine named *maui*.

The macro XV_INIT_ARGS is similar:

```
(void) xv_init(XV_INIT_ARGS, argc, argv, NULL);
```

Here, argc and argv are not modified at all and are returned unchanged by xv_init(). Therefore, the *value*, not the address, of argc is used. This method is less advantageous for initializing XView because it leaves the application with the responsibility of parsing XView command line parameters later.

NOTE

Once XView has been initialized, subsequent calls to xv_init() are ignored, as are all parameters consisting of XV_INIT_ARGS or XV_INIT_ ARGC_PTR_ARGV.

A common error that users make is to enter bad command line arguments. These arguments can be specific to XView or specific to the application, so XView handles the XView-specific argument and then expects the programmer to handle application-specific arguments.

Upon receiving a bad argument, XView prints an error message, indicating what XView-specific values are legal, and then calls exit(1). The function that provides this message is specified by the attribute XV_USAGE_PROC. In most cases, you want to leave this alone because it is *not* the way you handle application-specific arguments.

The attribute XV_ERROR_PROC is used to install an error recovery routine. See Section 3.6, "Error Recovery," later in this chapter.

3.3 Creating and Modifying Objects

After the system has been initialized, objects can be created and modified using xv_create(), xv_find(), xv_get(), and xv_set(). A closer look at xv_create() and xv_find() shows how these functions can be used to create new objects or find existing objects with particular attributes from various packages.

3.3.1 Using xv_create()

xv_create() is typically used as in Example 3-2:

Example 3-2. xv_create() creates XView objects

```
#include <xview/xview.h>

main(argc, argv)
char *argv[];
{
    Frame frame;

    xv_init(XV_INIT_ARGC_PTR_ARGV, &argc, argv, NULL);
    frame = (Frame)xv_create(NULL, FRAME, NULL);
    xv_main_loop(frame);
}
```

In Example 3-2, a frame is created from the FRAME package and no additional attribute-value pairs are specified. Therefore, all the default properties from the frame class are set into the instance of this new frame when it is created.

The form of xv_create() is:

```
Xv_object
xv_create(owner, package, attrs)
    Xv_object          owner;
    Xv_pkg             package;
    <attribute-value list> attrs
```

In most cases, owner is another XView object. As shown in the example, when the frame is created, it has no owner, per se. This means that the owner should default to a pre-specified owner that XView has in mind. Defaulting is not always possible, but for this base frame, the default owner is the root window of the current server. As a child of the root window, the frame is under the constraints that the window manager might impose upon it (the colormap, for example).

Objects must have an owner for several reasons. One reason is that the X server may not be running on the same machine as the application (client) program. Therefore, because XView is running on the client side, objects that are created by the application have to contact the server. There could be more than one server to contact if the application supports multiple displays or runs on several machines simultaneously. To do this, XView needs to know what server or screen a particular object is associated with.

Another reason is that certain attributes are inherited from the owner, such as color and event masks. It is up to the individual package to determine what it inherits from its owner.

When owner is NULL, the owner of the object being created is either defaulted to a predetermined owner, or the object is said to have *delayed binding*. That is, the object is not associated with any other object until it is displayed on the screen. A scrollbar that is created with a NULL owner will not be displayed until it is attached to an object, and this object becomes its owner. Most objects are required to have owners at the time of their creation. Frames, windows and fonts must have a valid (default) owner because they need to access the screen's default colors, available fonts, and so on.

Table 3-2 shows the default owner if `owner` is NULL in the call to `xv_create`.

Table 3-2. Default Ownership of Objects

Object's Package	Owner	If Owner is NULL
FRAME	Another frame or the root window	The window manager of `xv_default_screen`
CANVAS, TEXT, PANEL	Another window	The window manager of `xv_default_screen`
Panel Items	Panel	NULL owner not allowed
MENU	Ignores its owner	Always use NULL
Menu Items	Menu	Allows delayed binding
CURSOR	Window, screen or anything that returns XV_ROOT	The window manager of `xv_default_screen`
ICON	Same as cursor	Same as cursor
SCROLLBAR	An openwin object	Allows delayed binding
SCREEN, FULLSCREEN	Server	`xv_default_server`
SERVER	Doesn't matter	Always use NULL
SERVER_IMAGE	Screen	`xv_default_screen`

The object that is returned from `xv_create()` is an opaque data type called `Xv_object`. The return value should be coerced into the type of the object being created.

Each time `xv_create()` is used, it creates a new and entirely different object. The type of object that is returned depends on the *package* specified.

```
Panel panel;
panel = (Panel)xv_create(frame, PANEL, NULL);
```

Here, a panel is created as a child of a frame. As in the previous example, there are no attribute-value pairs specified, so the panel is created with all the default values intrinsic to a generic panel object from the PANEL package. The panel is then installed inside the frame accordingly. Panel items can be installed inside the panel as:

```
Panel_item button;
button = (Panel_item)xv_create(panel, PANEL_BUTTON,
    PANEL_LABEL_STRING,   "Quit",
    PANEL_NOTIFY_PROC,    quit,
    NULL);
```

Here, `xv_create()` is used to create a panel item of type PANEL_BUTTON. This is a special type of object that is created inside of panels only. That is why the owner of the item is the panel created in the previous example. In the attribute-value list provided in this example, the label is set by specifying the PANEL_LABEL_STRING attribute and a string as the value portion of the pair. Similarly, the callback routine specified is the routine called `quit()`. Because the intent of panel buttons is to select them with the pointer, the callback routine is the function to call if the user presses the mouse button in the panel button item.

3.3.2 Using xv_find()

In all the examples so far, the routine `xv_create()` has been used to create new objects of different types or classes. However, it might not always be possible to know whether or not a particular object has been created. The best way to handle such cases is to use `xv_find()`. If the object has been created, `xv_find()` returns the handle to the pre-existing object; if not, `xv_find()` creates it. The definition of the routine follows:

```
Xv_opaque
xv_find (owner, package, attrs)
    Xv_object          owner;
    Xv_pkg             package;
    <attribute-value list>   attrs;
```

As you can see, the form of `xv_find()` is the same as `xv_create()`. Fonts are objects that usually only need to be created once and are then used throughout the application wherever necessary. For example, say the application needs to use the font named *fixed* (because it is usually available on any X server and is almost guaranteed to be found). Several places in the application need to use the font, but only one instance of the font needs to be created. To avoid multiple instances of the object, the following function call is made:

```
Xv_Font my_font;
my_font = xv_find(frame, FONT,
    FONT_NAME, "fixed",
    NULL);
```

This code segment demonstrates how `xv_find()` tries to find an existing font named *fixed* that has already been created by the application. If the application has not yet created this font, then `xv_find()` acts just like `xv_create()`, and a new font is created. This function is not intended to replace `xv_create()` at all. It is intended to be used in the case where only one instance of an object is desired and that one instance is shared throughout the application. While you could use `xv_find()` rather than `xv_create()` in the other examples shown so far, the problem arises if you need two copies of a particular instance of an object. For example, if you were going to create another PANEL using all the default values of the PANEL package, then `xv_find()` would return the previously created panel. Any new objects attached to that panel would also be attached to the other panel because they are, in fact, one and the same.

As shown, fonts* are frequent users of the `xv_find()` function.

_____
*Chapter 16, *Fonts*, describes how to create fonts using `xv_find()`.

3.3.3 Using xv_destroy()

The correct way for an XView application to exit is to destroy all objects created and then exit properly. The function `xv_destroy()` destroys an instance of an XView object. The function `xv_destroy_safe()` does the same thing but ensures that it is *safe* to do so.* In general, it is better to be safe than sorry. The definition of these routines are as follows:

```
int
xv_destroy_safe(object)
    Xv_opaque object;

int
xv_destroy(object)
    Xv_opaque object;
```

The return value from the routines is either XV_OK or XV_ERROR. Example 3-1 shows a base frame containing a panel subwindow with one panel button created inside it. The callback routine for the panel item, `quit()`, is intended to exit the application. Rather than actually calling `exit()`, a more elegant way to exit would be to destroy all the objects that have been created. If a text subwindow had its text modified since the last update, this would give the package an opportunity to prompt the user for an update. Or you might install a routine that interposes any request for destruction on a particular object (such as a frame).†

The `quit()` routine looks something like this:

```
void
quit()
{
    if (xv_destroy_safe(frame) == XV_OK)
        exit(0);
}
```

Rather than calling `xv_destroy_safe()` on all objects, it is only called for the base frame. Because the base frame is the owner of all the other objects, `xv_destroy()` and `xv_destroy_safe()` descend into the objects' children and destroys all of them with the same call.

3.3.4 Using xv_set() and xv_get()

As discussed in the previous chapter, attributes about objects can be set, reset, and retrieved using the calls `xv_set()` and `xv_get()`. The definition of these routines are:

```
Xv_opaque
xv_set(object, attrs)
    Xv_object          object;
    <attribute-value list>  attrs;
```

---

*Chapter 19, *The Notifier*, discusses the difference between a safe and an *immediate* destruction of an object.
†Chapter 19, *The Notifier*, describes how to install destroy interpose functions.

```
    Xv_opaque
    xv_get(object, attrs)
        Xv_object          object;
        <attribute-value list>   attrs;
```

xv_set() is just like xv_create() with respect to the attribute-value parameters. Use xv_set() to set or change the value of one or more attributes of an object that has already been created. The following code segment uses a single xv_set() call to change three attributes of a frame:

```
#include <xview/xview.h>

main()
{
    Frame frame;
    frame = xv_create(NULL, FRAME, NULL);
    ...
    xv_set(frame,
        FRAME_LABEL,        "XView Demo",
        FRAME_SHOW_LABEL,   TRUE,
        FRAME_NO_CONFIRM,   TRUE,
        NULL);
    ...
    xv_main_loop(frame);
}
```

xv_get() is different from xv_set() in that the value parameter is not passed to the function—instead, the value is returned from xv_get():

```
Xv_Window root_win;
Frame frame;
Rect *rect;

/* create the base frame for the application */
frame = xv_create(NULL, FRAME, NULL);

/* get the root window of the base frame of the application */
root_win = (Xv_Window *) xv_get(frame, XV_ROOT);

/* get the dimensions (rectangle) of the root window */
rect = (Rect *) xv_get(root_win, XV_RECT);
```

Because xv_get() returns the value of the attribute specified, only one attribute of the object can be retrieved by an xv_get() call. The return value for the function is going to be an opaque data type, so it must be *typecast* into the type expected. However, note that the value XV_ERROR might be returned in the event that the object passed is not a valid object or if an attribute does not apply. In this case, the return value should be checked to see if it is XV_ERROR. One potential problem is that the value of XV_ERROR might happen to be the same as the expected return value. Fortunately, an error returned from xv_get() is unlikely in a properly debugged application.

In many packages, certain properties may be retrieved but not set. That is, you may use xv_get() for the property FRAME_FOREGROUND_COLOR to get the foreground color of a frame, but you may not use xv_set() to set the foreground color. In this case, xv_set

Creating
Applications

returns XV_ERROR.* In the more likely event that the call was successful in setting attributes using xv_set(), then the value XV_OK will be returned.

3.4 xv_main_loop() and the Notifier

Once all the objects have been created, you are ready to have all the windows displayed and have event processing begin. At this point, the program calls xv_main_loop(). The job of xv_main_loop() is to start the Notifier. Once the Notifier has started, the program will begin to receive and process events such as Expose, MapNotify, ConfigureNotify, KeyPress, and so on. The X server generates these events and sends them to the client. While it is up to the client to handle all events that the X server sends to it, the Notifier layer of XView handles much of this work automatically.

The Notifier's main job is to process these events and dispatch them to the client if it has registered a callback routine for that event type with the Notifier. Otherwise, the Notifier might ignore the event. Of course, XView attempts to provide reasonable default actions for all events that the application typically does not want to deal with. For example, a simple application that contains nothing but a command frame (which has nothing but a panel/control area) might not care to handle resize events if the user resizes the window. XView must handle this so it can resize the panel and/or reposition the panel items within it.

Those events that the application would be most interested in are things like KeyPress and ButtonPress events of various types. For events like these, the application should install callback routines for the Notifier to call if one of those events has taken place.

In the examples shown, the only callback routine installed is the one in the panel item, quit(). When selected, the Notifier notifies the application by calling the callback routine associated with the object in which the event took place. In this case, the Notifier calls the routine quit() and the application has control of the program again. As one might expect, the Notifier has relinquished control of the program while the application's callback routine is being called. The Notifier does no more event processing at all until the callback routine has returned. However, the programmer can query events from within the callback routine if necessary.

If the code within the callback routine creates new objects or destroys existing objects, nothing will happen on the display until the callback routine is finished and returns control back to the Notifier.

Just because the Notifier handles the delivery of events to the application, that does not mean that the application will be notified of all events that might occur. The application is only notified of the events that it has registered with the Notifier. Events that the client can register with the Notifier include CreateWindow, MapWindow, ConfigureWindow, Query-Font, GetInputFocus, and so on. These are general X events, not XView-specific events. However, XView has a corresponding event definition for the purpose of registering events with the Notifier. Event registration is covered in detail in Chapter 19, *The Notifier*. Event

---

*The foreground color for a frame can be set only in xv_create(). Once the frame is created, the color cannot be changed. Section 3.6, "Error Recovery," discusses some methods for error recovery.

types and specifications are discussed in Chapter 5, *Canvases and Openwin*, and Chapter 6, *Handling Input*.

When a frame is displayed on the screen, a MapNotify event is generated by the X server (since the frame is *mapped*, or displayed, to the screen). However, there has been no callback routine specified to handle the map event, so the Notifier passes it back to XView, which handles it internally. This default action, in fact, does nothing special; it simply allows the frame to be displayed. Further events are generated: expose events, visibility events (for the frames that are covered up by the new frame), enter and leave events when the user moves the mouse in and out of the frame, motion events, and so on. If none of these events have an application-defined callback routine associated with them, the Notifier handles them.

Note that when objects such as frames or canvases are created, only the objects themselves and the associated attributes of those objects are created. What is *not* created are the objects' windows. These are not created until after xv_main_loop() is called. This is due to the fact that one of the events that is generated is the *realize* event—this indicates that an object has been realized to the screen and a window has been (or needs to be) generated. The objects' packages internally handle the creation of windows at the appropriate time. Since that does not occur until after the call to xv_main_loop(), there should be no attempts to render graphics into objects' windows before then.

3.5 Registering Event Handlers

XView provides a method for specifying which events an object might be interested in. In some cases, the object registers which events it wants to know about by specifying one of various event *masks* in calls to either xv_create() or xv_set(). The following example shows how an object expresses interest in receiving all button and keyboard events:

```
Frame   frame;
Canvas canvas;
void    my_notify_proc();
 . . .
canvas = (Canvas)xv_create(frame, CANVAS,
    WIN_CONSUME_KBD_EVENTS,      TRUE,
    WIN_CONSUME_PICK_EVENTS,     TRUE,
    WIN_NOTIFY_EVENT_PROC,       my_notify_proc,
    NULL);
```

If a KeyPress or ButtonPress event occurs in the canvas window, the routine my_notify_proc() is called from XView, passing it the window in which the event occurred and a pointer to an XEvent.

XView uses #define macros for specifying all possible events that X provides. Many of these defines, as the example above indicates, encompass more than one event type. Chapter 6, *Handling Input*, goes into detail about event structures for X as well as XView. The XView Event type has the corresponding XEvent object embedded in it.

Upon receiving an event, XView calls the procedure that the application has set up to handle that event. For instance, if an application informs XView that a particular object should respond to a ButtonPress event, it must specify what routine to call upon receiving the event. The callback routine is simply an application function that is called when a specified event or set of events occur. The routine performs its task and returns control back to the window system to track the next event.

Your program does not call notify procedures directly; the Notifier calls them when X delivers the repaint event to the application.

3.6 Error Recovery

As you will soon find out, it is quite easy to generate an XView run-time error. Errors can be caused by specifying invalid or unknown attributes, invalid or NULL XView objects, failing to terminate a *list* of values or attribute-value pairs, and so on. Whatever the reason, in the event of an error, XView calls xv_error(). This routine calls another routine that prints the nature of the error to stderr and then either returns or exits.

The form of the function is:

```
Xv_error_action
error_proc(object, severity, avlist)
    Xv_object            object;
    Xv_error_severity  severity;
    Attr_avlist          avlist[ATTR_STANDARD_SIZE];
```

You install the error handler in the call to xv_create().

```
xv_init(XV_INIT_ARGC_PTR_ARGV, &argc, argv,
    XV_ERROR_PROC,   my_error_proc,
    NULL);
```

Because xv_init() can only be called once, the routine cannot be changed or uninstalled. my_error_proc() is called when there is an internal error in XView—not if there is an X protocol error or errors of any other nature. For example, the following call to xv_create() results in a call to the error routine installed as XV_ERROR_PROC.

```
xv_create(NULL, FRAME, FRAME_LABEL, argv[0]);
```

The reason that this example fails is that the attribute-value list given to xv_create() is not NULL-terminated. Even if the value for FRAME_LABEL were NULL, it is still the value of the attribute—XView will still scan for the next attribute in the attribute-value list. The next attribute found is actually undefined; the next item on the stack might be any arbitrary value (commonly referred to as garbage). XView does not know that, though, so if the next attribute has a garbage value, then XView will complain that it is an unknown attribute and call the error routine.

There are two types of errors: recoverable and unrecoverable. Clearly, if the error is unrecoverable, your application should terminate. Otherwise, it may continue on as usual. If you install your own error routine, the choice is yours. Under the current implementation, the most useful feature for this would be to call abort() which forces the program to dump core. This allows you to use debuggers such as adb or dbx and trace exactly where the problem lies.

All the information about the error is provided in the parameters to the error function:

object   This XView object is the object in which the `xv_*` call failed to operate on. If this object is NULL, then chances are, this is the cause of the error. Otherwise, you can get the type of the object by calling `xv_get(object, XV_TYPE)`.

severity   This parameter is of type `Xv_error_severity`, which is an enumerated type whose values consist of `XV_ERROR_RECOVERABLE` and `XV_ERROR_NON_RECOVERABLE`.

attrs   The attribute-value pairs given here describe the nature of the error. Unfortunately, some of the functions necessary to interpret the attribute-value pairs are not publically available.

The header file *<xview/xv_error.h>* contains the definitions of the types and functions used. The following code fragment demonstrate how this works.

```
Xv_error_action
error_proc(object, severity, avlist)
Xv_object          object;
Xv_error_severity  severity;
Attr_avlist        avlist[ATTR_STANDARD_SIZE];
{
    char buf[32];

    if (severity != XV_ERROR_NON_RECOVERABLE) {
        printf("Dump core? "), fflush(stdout);
        gets(buf);
        if (buf[0] == 'y' || buf[0] == 'Y' || buf[0] == NULL)
            return XV_ERROR_CONTINUE;
    }
    abort();
}
```

Clearly, not much is done in this routine to identify the nature of the error. Instead, a core image is made so you can determine the point in the program at which the `xv_*` routine is called incorrectly. If the error is recoverable, the program prints to stdout a prompt asking to dump core. If you answer with a RETURN or anything that starts with a y, then `abort()` is called and the program terminates and a core image is left. If the error is nonrecoverable, the same thing happens except that you are not prompted for the action.

If the error is recoverable and you indicate that you do not want to dump core, then the program continues and no other error message concerning this error is printed. If you do not want to continue and you do not want to dump core, you should *interrupt* the program using CTRL-C (interrupt character).

Creating
Applications

4

Frames

In This Chapter:

Types of Frames 60
    The Role of the Window Manager 61
Base Frames 61
    XView Initialization and Base Frames 62
    Headers and Footers 63
    Closed Base Frames 64
    Quit Confirmation 66
Command Frames 67
    Manually Displaying Frames 67
    The Pushpin 68
    The FRAME_DONE_PROC Procedure 70
    Showing Resize Corners 71
Miscellaneous Attributes 72
    Busy Frames 72
    Frame Sizes 72
    Frame Colors 73
    Child Windows 74
Destroying Frames 75
Frame Package Summary 76

4
Frames

A frame is a container for other windows. It manages the geometry and placement of *subwindows* that do not overlap and are fixed within the boundary of the frame. The OPEN LOOK specification refers to subwindows, or *panes*, as *tiled* windows because they do not overlap one another. Subwindow types include canvases, text subwindows, panels and scrollbars. These subwindows cannot exist without a parent frame to manage them.

Figure 4-1 shows an example of a screen that displays three frames, each one containing at least one subwindow. Note that frames do overlap. The File Manager frame has the keyboard focus, as indicated by the title bar having its foreground and background colors reversed. The setting of the keyboard focus is handled by the window manager, not the FRAME package. In this case, an OPEN LOOK window manager is using click-to-type to set the keyboard focus. This is demonstrated by the cursor's location within an unselected frame (the *Edit: File* frame).

The FRAME package provides the following capabilities:

- A communication path between the application and the window manager.

- A mechanism to receive input for the application.

- A visual container for user interface objects.

- A method to group windows with related functionality.

A frame depends upon the window manager for its *decorations* and many basic operations. The FRAME package does *not* manage headers (title bars), footers, resize corners, or the colors of those objects. These are all strictly functions of the window manager. The application gives hints to the window manager about some of these attributes through the FRAME package (including not to display decorations at all if so desired), but results vary depending on which window manager the user is running. The examples in this book assume the user is running an OPEN LOOK window manager.

Frames

Figure 4-1. Three base frames

4.1 Types of Frames

Basically, two types of frames are available in XView: base frames and command frames. The main frame of the application is called the *base frame*. The base frame resides on the root window; its handle is passed to xv_main_loop() to begin application processing.

A special kind of frame, called a *command frame*, is created with a panel subwindow by default. Command frames are useful as help frames, property frames, and such defined by OPEN LOOK. Programmatically, a command frame is no different from a frame with one subwindow that is a panel.

A base frame's *parent* is the root window, whereas a subframe's parent is another frame (either a base frame or a subframe). When a frame goes away (quit or close), all of its child windows, including subframes, also go away. For example, assume you create a command subframe to display application-specific help. When this command subframe is activated, it might display explanatory text along with an OK button to dismiss the help. If you close the base frame, the help subframe also closes.

XView allows for multiple frames that are not children of the base frame. For instance, you could create a help frame that is independent of the application's base frame. The parent of this frame is the root window of the display and not the base frame. The help frame will remain visible even if the base frame goes away. The term subframe defines a relationship among frames at creation time and a slight difference in functionality.

4.1.1 The Role of the Window Manager

It is important to understand what effect the window manager has in determining the appearance and behavior of an XView frame. As mentioned earlier, many attributes defined in the FRAME package are really hints to the window manager. The window manager is responsible for frame and window decoration, as well as the size and placement of windows on the screen (screen geometry). That is, it is the window manager's job to provide such decorations as title bars and to set attributes such as the color of decorations. It also handles resizing windows, moving windows, closing windows (iconifying), and so on. The application can ask the window manager to do things in a certain way, but the window manager is not obligated to act on these requests.

For your application and the window manager to communicate properly, the window manager must comply with the specifications outlined by the *Inter-Client Communication Conventions Manual* (ICCCM). Since the window manager is a client of the X server just as the application is a client, the two clients must follow specified conventions for communication with one another. The FRAME package assumes it is communicating with an OPEN LOOK-compliant window manager. If not, some of the frame attributes might not work as described here.

For example, using an OPEN LOOK window manager, a command subframe is a pop-up window that has a pushpin in the upper-left corner. The state of the pushpin (unpinned or pinned) determines whether or not the window remains on the screen after the command has been executed. The pin objects are provided by the OPEN LOOK window manager. If XView applications are run with another window manager, they might not necessarily be pinnable.

4.2 Base Frames

Let's first create a base frame using the default attribute settings. To create a frame, use xv_create, specifying the owner of the frame and identifying the FRAME package. The program in Example 4-1 shows how to create a simple base frame:

Example 4-1. The simple_frame.c program

```
#include <xview/xview.h>

main()
{
    Frame frame;
    frame = (Frame)xv_create(NULL, FRAME, `NULL);
    xv_main_loop(frame);
}
```

Frames

Specifying NULL as the owner argument tells the FRAME package to use the default value, which specifies the root window on the current screen. The macro FRAME is defined to be FRAME_BASE, which is the base FRAME package in XView.

Note that the header file associated with the FRAME package, *<xview/frame.h>*, is included indirectly by *<xview/xview.h>*. (A separate inclusion has no harmful effect, however.)

The frame displayed by this program is shown in Figure 4-2.

Figure 4-2. Simple base frame created without any FRAME attributes specified

4.2.1 XView Initialization and Base Frames

The first XView object to be created by an application is typically the base frame. However, xv_init() is always called first to get any command line parameters, initialize the connection to the X server, set resources, and so on. The code segment in Example 4-2 shows how argc and argv can be used in conjunction with xv_init():

Example 4-2. Creating a base frame after calling xv_init()

```
main(argc, argv)
int argc;
char *argv[];
{
    Frame frame;
    ...
    xv_init(XV_INIT_ARGC_PTR_ARGV, &argc, argv, NULL);
    frame = (Frame)xv_create(NULL, FRAME, NULL);
    ...
    xv_main_loop(frame);
    exit(0);
}
```

In this sample code segment, the program expects no parameters that are specific to the program. Any parameters that the user supplies are expected to be specific to XView or X. When `xv_init()` is called with attribute `XV_INIT_ARGC_PTR_ARGV`, `&argc` and `argv` are passed as values; upon return, `argv` is stripped of the parameters that are X or XView-specific. The `argc` variable is also modified to reflect the number of parameters that remain after processing. If the user specified no other parameters, then `argc` should be 1 and `argv` should contain one element in its array of strings: the name of the program (since that is what `argv[0]` is). If there are any more parameters, then the application has the opportunity to look for application-specific parameters or to report unknown parameters as errors.

When the attribute `XV_INIT_ARGS` is used, the value of `argc` (not the address of `argc`) is passed, and neither variable is modified.

4.2.2 Headers and Footers

The OPEN LOOK window manager provides frames with headers and footers that display text. The header typically displays information such as the application name. The text is centered and its font is not alterable by the application. The header also has a Close button at the upper-left corner; selecting the button causes the frame to iconify—that is, the frame turns into a graphical image, or *icon*, and is displayed (probably) elsewhere on the screen. The application's *state* is now closed. This usually indicates that the program is idle.

The footer of a base frame shows text such as error messages, a page number, the date, or other miscellaneous information. The footer is split in two parts: the left footer where text is left justified, and the right footer where the text is right justified.

Unless otherwise specified by giving the appropriate attribute-value pairs, the header of a base frame is displayed, but the footer is not. The header does contain the abbreviated menu button, but there is no default header label. Thus, to create a header with a label, the attribute `FRAME_LABEL` must have a string value. This may be a constant string or a variable pointing to a string. When the frame is displayed, the string will be centered in the header. The header label can be turned off by setting the `FRAME_SHOW_HEADER` attribute to `FALSE`. In this case, even if the header label is set, the header (including the close button) will not be displayed at all. If `FRAME_SHOW_HEADER` is later set to `TRUE`, then the label will be displayed again (see Figure 4-3).

The code segment in Example 4-3 sets `FRAME_SHOW_HEADER` to `FALSE` at creation but sets it to `TRUE` in a separate call. The header displays the name of the program.

Example 4-3. Setting separate values for a frame header

```
...
Frame frame;
frame = (Frame)xv_create(NULL, FRAME,
    FRAME_LABEL, argv[0],
    FRAME_SHOW_HEADER, FALSE, NULL);
...
xv_set(frame, FRAME_SHOW_HEADER, TRUE, NULL);
...
```

Frames

Figure 4-3. A sample header label display in a frame

Footers in base frames are not displayed by default, so setting either the left or right footer messages also requires the boolean FRAME_SHOW_FOOTER to be set to TRUE. Note that setting the footer on and off resizes the total size of the base frame, and while it does not cause any subwindows to be resized, it is rather distracting to change the frame frequently (or at all). Therefore, you should decide ahead of time whether you are going to use footers and set them to be on or off once at the time the frame is created. If the footer is no longer needed, set the left or the right footer string to the null string—*not* the constant NULL. That is, use " ". Figure 4-4 shows what is displayed when the code in Example 4-4 is run:

Example 4-4. Creating a footer

```
...
Frame frame;
frame = (Frame)xv_create(NULL, FRAME,
    FRAME_LABEL,        "hdrs_n_footers",
    FRAME_SHOW_FOOTER,  TRUE,
    FRAME_LEFT_FOOTER,  "left side",
    FRAME_RIGHT_FOOTER, "right side",
    NULL);
...
```

4.2.3 Closed Base Frames

Base frames are unique from other types of frames because they can be closed, or *iconified*. When the frame is closed, an icon replaces the entire base frame, including all subwindows and control areas. If any subframes are associated with the base frame, then they are taken down for as long as the application is closed.* Using the appropriate attribute-value pairs, it

---

*Only base frames have icons associated with them.

Figure 4-4. Headers and footers on base frame

is possible to set the image and size of the icon. By default, no icon is associated with a base frame and the size of the area occupied by an icon is 64x64. See Chapter 14, *Icons*, for more information on creating icons used by frames. The bounding box (or Rect) of the icon is independent of the size of the icon, so the bounding box should be set explicitly if its value is anything other than the default.

Setting the frame's icon and size when the frame is closed is special because they cannot be set until *after* the base frame has been created. Therefore, attempting to set FRAME_CLOSED_RECT or FRAME_ICON on a base frame in the call to xv_create() results in a run-time error. The frame's icon and closed rect should be set using xv_set() once the frame has been created. Figure 4-5 shows what any application or base frame looks like when it is closed, providing that the application uses the base frame with default values. The figure also shows a graphical icon used by an application.

Figure 4-5. Default icon and application icon

To set the icon for the base frame, the icon must already have been created. However, assuming one is available, the icon can be set in the base frame using the FRAME_ICON attribute-value pair. Because the icon might not be the default size (64x64), it is usually a good idea to set the size of the frame when it is in the closed state. To do this, set the attribute FRAME_CLOSED_RECT to be a pointer to a variable of type Rect * (pointer to a Rect). (Rect is an XView data type defined in *<xview/rect.h>*.)

The best way to handle it is to use `xv_set()` after the call to `xv_create()`:

```
    ...
    extern Icon icon;
    Frame       frame;
    Rect        rect;
    ...
    rect.r_width = (int)xv_get(icon, XV_WIDTH);
    rect.r_height = (int)xv_get(icon, XV_HEIGHT);
    frame = (Frame)xv_create(NULL, FRAME, NULL);
    xv_set(frame,
        FRAME_ICON,          icon,
        FRAME_CLOSED_RECT,   &rect,
        NULL);
```

This code segment sets the size of the icon area to be whatever size the icon is. Since `FRAME_CLOSED_RECT` takes a pointer to a variable of type `Rect`, the address of the variable is given as the `value` parameter to the call to `xv_set()`. Also note that the other fields of the `rect` variable, (`r_top`, `r_left`) are not used because `FRAME_CLOSED_RECT` only uses the width and height dimensions from the variable.

The following call can be made to determine whether the frame is currently closed from within the application:

```
    is_closed = (Boolean) xv_get(frame, FRAME_CLOSED);
```

This call is useful for applications that are graphics-intensive. If a complex piece of code is about to be executed, the application could check to see if the frame is open to display the graphics.

4.2.4 Quit Confirmation

OPEN LOOK specifies that a notice is generally not needed to confirm a `quit` action unless data will be lost. The base frame, which usually handles this type of action through the window manager, can be set to ask for confirmation. The attribute `FRAME_NO_CONFIRM`, which defaults to `TRUE`, can be set to `FALSE` to force confirmation:

```
    frame = (Frame)xv_create(NULL, FRAME,
        FRAME_NO_CONFIRM, FALSE,
        NULL);
```

When the attribute `FRAME_NO_CONFIRM` is set to `FALSE` and the user initiates a *quit* action, a notice dialog box will appear to request confirmation.

4.3 Command Frames

Command frames are normally subframes in that they are most often created as children of
base frames. Most of the time, they are pop-up frames that serve one function and then go
away. Instead of having a Close button at in the frame's header, the command frame might
have a pushpin. The pushpin governs whether the frame remains up after the user performs
the functions that the pop-up frame provides. When a command frame is created, a default
panel is also created automatically. The panel on a command frame can be used to hold the
panel items, such as buttons or sliders, that the user interacts with. When command frames
are created, a panel is also created. `xv_get()` can be used on command frames to get the
default panel and to avoid creating a new one.

Example 4-5 shows a simple program that creates a pop-up frame as a child of the base
frame. Figure 4-6 displays the output of this program.

Example 4-5. Creating a subframe

```
/*
 * subframe.c -- display a subframe from a base frame.
 */
#include <xview/xview.h>
main()
{
    Frame frame, subframe;

    xv_init(XV_INIT_ARGC_PTR_ARGV, &argc, argv, NULL);

    frame = (Frame)xv_create(NULL, FRAME,
        XV_WIDTH,       100,
        XV_HEIGHT,      100,
        FRAME_LABEL,    "Base Frame",
        NULL);

    subframe = (Frame)xv_create(frame, FRAME_CMD,
        XV_WIDTH,       100,
        XV_HEIGHT,      100,
        FRAME_LABEL,    "Popup",
        NULL);

    xv_set(subframe, XV_SHOW, TRUE, NULL);

    xv_main_loop(frame);
}
```

4.3.1 Manually Displaying Frames

The attribute XV_SHOW sets whether a window (or frame, in this case) will be displayed. If it
is set to FALSE, the frame will not be seen. Base frames are always displayed because
xv_main_loop sets the XV_SHOW attribute to TRUE. Pop-up frames are not displayed unless
the XV_SHOW attribute is set by the application. An application might create many pop-up
dialog boxes initially and then determine the appropriate time to actually display them. A

Figure 4-6. Command frame with pop-up frame

callback routine invoked by some action (e.g., panel button selection) from the base frame
might be used to display the pop-up frame.

4.3.2 The Pushpin

On a command frame, the pushpin at the upper-right corner is unpinned by default. It can be
pinned by setting the attribute FRAME_CMD_PUSHPIN_IN to TRUE. This attribute can also be
queried using xv_get(), which will return TRUE if the pushpin is in and FALSE if it is not.

A simple example can demonstrate how some of the frame attributes interact. The program
in Example 4-6 builds a base frame with a panel button that says, "Hello." If selected, a command frame pops up. The new frame has a panel button that says, "Push Me," and if pushed,
"Hello World" is printed to *stdout*. If the command frame's pushpin is out, once the Push Me
button is selected, the frame is taken down. To get the frame up again, the user must select
Hello again. However, if the pin is in, then the frame remains up for repeated use. Selecting
Hello while the frame is already up causes the command frame to be raised to the top of the
window tree. This is useful in case the command frame gets obscured by other windows.

Example 4-6. Using several frame attributes
```
/*
 * popup2.c -- popup a frame and allo the user to interact with
 * the new popup frame.
 */
#include <xview/xview.h>
#include <xview/panel.h>

Frame frame;      /* top level application base-frame */
Frame subframe;   /* subframe (FRAME_CMD) is a child of frame */

main(argc, argv)
int argc;
```

Example 4-6. Using several frame attributes (continued)

```
char *argv[];
{
    Panel panel;
    int show_cmd_frame(), pushed();

    xv_init(XV_INIT_ARGC_PTR_ARGV, &argc, argv, NULL);

    /* Create base frame */
    frame = (Frame)xv_create(NULL, FRAME,
        FRAME_LABEL, argv[0],
        NULL);

    /* Install a panel and a panel button */
    panel = (Panel)xv_create(frame, PANEL, NULL);
    (void) xv_create(panel, PANEL_BUTTON,
        PANEL_LABEL_STRING, "Hello",
        PANEL_NOTIFY_PROC,  show_cmd_frame,
        NULL);

    /* Create the command frame -- not displayed until XV_SHOW is set */
    subframe = (Frame)xv_create(frame, FRAME_CMD,
        FRAME_LABEL,        "Popup",
        NULL);

    /* Command frames have panels already created by default -- get it */
    panel = (Panel)xv_get(subframe, FRAME_CMD_PANEL);
    (void) xv_create(panel, PANEL_BUTTON,
        PANEL_LABEL_STRING, "Push Me",
        PANEL_NOTIFY_PROC,  pushed,
        NULL);

    xv_main_loop(frame);
}
/* Called when base frame's button is pushed -- show/raise subframe */
show_cmd_frame(subframe,event)
Frame subframe;
Event *event;
{
    xv_set(subframe, XV_SHOW, TRUE, NULL);
}

/* Called when command frame's button is pushed */
pushed(item,event)
Panel_item  item;
Event  *event;
{
    printf("Hello world.\n");

    /* Check to see if the pushpin is in -- if not, close frame */
    if ((int)xv_get(subframe, FRAME_CMD_PUSHPIN_IN) == FALSE)
        xv_set(subframe, XV_SHOW, FALSE, NULL);
}
```

Several things are noteworthy in this sample program. First, there is only one Panel variable (called panel). It is used to store the handle to the panel created by the base frame. It does not matter that this variable is also used to store the return value of the call to:

```
xv_create(frame, PANEL, NULL)
```

because its use is temporary. This demonstrates that the programmer need not maintain handles to objects that are never referenced. A common programming efficiency error is to declare many variables that reference objects created via xv_create() and then never to use them. The panel is needed, but only long enough to use it as the *owner* of the panel button that is created. Once ownership is established, the handle to that panel is no longer needed. Therefore, the variable is reused in the call that gets the *already created panel* from the subframe. This call is as follows:

```
panel = (Panel)xv_get(subframe, FRAME_CMD_PANEL)
```

The handles to the buttons are never needed, so the return values of those creation calls are ignored. On the other hand, it is always prudent to check for return values in case of error—had the panel creation returned a NULL handle, then the buttons should not be created. The sample programs do not demonstrate this type of error checking in order to keep the examples simple and readable.

4.3.3 The FRAME_DONE_PROC Procedure

If the pushpin is pushed in by the user, the application has no knowledge of this action. However, if the user pulls the pin out, then the application calls the command frame's FRAME_DONE_PROC routine. By default, the routine takes down the subframe. The programmer can override this by setting FRAME_DONE_PROC to another routine. This is only needed if you want to check that the frame can be dismissed. Suppose that the purpose of the subframe is to query for a filename. If the filename was not given, you might want to display a notice indicating the fact and allow the user to type in a filename. In this case, the FRAME_DONE_PROC is responsible for doing the necessary checking and deciding on whether to display a notice or to take the frame down.

When you install your own FRAME_DONE_PROC routine, XView will *not* take down the frame regardless of what your code does. If you want the frame to go down, set it down.

The parameter passed to your routine is a handle to the subframe itself (see Example 4-7:)

Example 4-7. The subframe.c program

```
/*
 * subframe.c -- create a base frame that has an associated subframe.
 * Pull the pin out of the subframe and its FRAME_DONE_PROC procedure
 * gets called.
 */
main()
{
    Frame frame, subframe;
    int done_proc();

    xv_init(XV_INIT_ARGC_PTR_ARGV, &argc, argv, NULL);

    frame = (Frame)xv_create(NULL, FRAME, NULL);

    subframe = (Frame)xv_create(frame, FRAME_CMD,
        FRAME_DONE_PROC, done_proc,
        XV_SHOW,          TRUE,
        NULL);
```

Example 4-7. The subframe.c program (continued)

```
    xv_main_loop(frame);
}
/*
 * when the pushpin is pulled out, this routine is called
 */
done_proc(subframe)
Frame subframe;
{
    /* we have the choice of vetoing or granting the user's
     * request to dismiss the frame -- if we choose to dismiss
     * the frame, we must do it manually.  Like so:
     */
    xv_set(subframe, XV_SHOW, FALSE, NULL);
    /* otherwise, we should push the pin back in */
}
```

The call to xv_set(XV_SHOW, FALSE) is safe because no action is taken at all if this was not the result of the pin being pulled out. The frame will not go down (i.e., the xv_set() is a no-op) if the pin is in or is already out. This gives the programmer the flexibility of using the same function (something like done_proc()) in other places throughout the application. For example, it could be used in a callback routine for a panel button.

If the subframe must be taken down regardless of whether the pin is in or out, the application should forcefully remove the pin using:

```
    xv_set(subframe, FRAME_CMD_PUSHPIN_IN, FALSE, NULL);
```

Forcefully removing the pin in this fashion does not result in the frame's done procedure getting called. This routine is only called when the pin has been removed as a result of an action that the user has taken and when the application has no knowledge of this action.

4.3.4 Showing Resize Corners

It should also be noted that the command frame has no resize corners as the base frame does. This is the default behavior for command frames, but the attribute FRAME_ SHOW_RESIZE_CORNER can be set to TRUE to force the resize corners to be shown. This allows the user to resize command frames the same as base frames. Base frames always have resize corners and they cannot be turned off. Attempting to do so results in a run-time error.

Frames

4.4 Miscellaneous Attributes

The attributes discussed in this section are attributes that are also used by the FRAME package to communicate with the window manager. You will get unpredictable results if the window manager does not understand these attributes, the user is not running an OPEN LOOK window manager, or there is no window manager running at all.

4.4.1 Busy Frames

When running the Push Me application, you might notice a delay between the time that the Hello button is pressed and the time that the subframe is displayed. If a delay might confuse the user about what might be happening, you can provide visual feedback that the application is at work. You can set the FRAME_BUSY attribute for the frame that issues the request that might cause the delay. In Example 4-7, we set the XV_SHOW attribute in the base frame. Thus, show_cmd_frame() might have looked like the following code fragment:

```
show_cmd_frame(subframe,event)
Frame subframe;
Event *event;
{
    xv_set(baseframe, FRAME_BUSY, TRUE, NULL);
    xv_set(subframe, XV_SHOW, TRUE, NULL);
    xv_set(baseframe, FRAME_BUSY, FALSE, NULL);
}
```

The effect of this action is that the base frame's header will be grayed out and the cursor will change to a timeout cursor. When the subframe has been displayed, the base frame's appearance is resumed and the cursor restored. If excessively long delays are expected, then this method might not be adequate—all other buttons and events are suspended until the callback routine has returned control to the Notifier. There are better ways to handle these situations, and they are described in Chapter 19, *The Notifier*.

4.4.2 Frame Sizes

The size of any type of frame can be set or queried using either of two convenience functions available from the FRAME package. They are frame_get_rect() and frame_set_rect(). Both use a Rect data type. The origin of the frame as well as its width and height can be set using frame_set_rect(). Of course, the frame must already be created in order to use this function. In the following code, the frame is set at 10,10 on the screen and the dimensions are set to 200 by 300:

```
        Frame frame;
        Rect rect;

        rect.r_top = rect.r_left = 10;
        rect.r_width = 200;
        rect.r_height = 300;
        . . .
        frame = (Frame)xv_create(NULL, FRAME, NULL);

        frame_set_rect(frame, &rect);
```

Conversely, the dimensions as well as the position of the frame can be gotten:

```
        extern Frame frame;
        extern Rect rect;
        . . .
        frame_get_rect(frame, &rect);
        printf("frame is at %d, %d and is %d by %d\n",
            rect.r_left, rect.r_top, rect.r_width, rect.r_height);
```

4.4.3 Frame Colors

In frames, you can set several attributes pertaining to color. FRAME_FOREGROUND_COLOR
and FRAME_BACKGROUND_COLOR can be set to colors that correspond to the frame's foreground and background colors, respectively. These colors do not affect the frame's header
and footer, but they do affect the window in the frame. Setting these attributes can have little
effect unless the attribute FRAME_INHERIT_COLORS is also set. This attribute tells the
FRAME package to propagate the colors to the subwindows and subframes that the frame
owns. Therefore, if a panel is installed in a frame, the panel will inherit the colors specified
in the frame.

Example 4-8 shows a program that displays a frame with the appropriate foreground and
background colors set in the variables, fg and bg. The panel will inherit those colors from
the frame, so the panel will be brown and the panel button will be yellow.*

Example 4-8. Setting colors in a frame
```
#include <xview/xview.h>

main()
{
    Frame               frame;
    Panel               panel;
    Xv_singlecolor      fg, bg;

    fg.red = 250, fg.green = 230, fg.blue = 20;
    bg.red = 180, bg.green = 100, bg.blue = 20;

    frame = (Frame)xv_create(NULL, FRAME,
        FRAME_BACKGROUND_COLOR, &bg,
        FRAME_FOREGROUND_COLOR, &fg,
        FRAME_INHERIT_COLORS,   TRUE,
```

---

*This depends on your colormap setting and the type of display you have.

Example 4-8. Setting colors in a frame (continued)

```
        NULL);

    panel = (Panel)xv_create(frame, PANEL, NULL);
    (void) xv_create(panel, PANEL_BUTTON,
        PANEL_BUTTON_STRING,    "Push Me",
        NULL);

    xv_main_loop(frame);
}
```

One caveat to setting the colors in frames is that they can be set once and only once in the call to `xv_create()`. Once the colors are set, they cannot be reset. One reason for this is that the colors cannot be propagated to the child objects in the object tree.

Note that only the frame and subordinate objects have the colors specified. The window manager controls the colors of the title bar and other decorations.

4.4.4 Child Windows

The very purpose of frames is to manage subwindows such as panels and canvases. Basically, parenting responsibilities are handled transparently by XView and do not require intervention by the programmer. When creating a new object (such as a panel), you simply specify the frame as the panel's parent or owner.

There are several attributes that can obtain subwindows and subframes from the frame. `FRAME_NTH_SUBWINDOW` and `FRAME_NTH_SUBFRAME` are attributes that can be used with `xv_get()`. Assuming the application has created a subframe, the following code fragment will return the first subframe created:

```
    Frame subframe;

    subframe = xv_get(frame, FRAME_NTH_SUBFRAME, 1);
```

Similarly, if a frame creates a panel and then a canvas, you can get the canvas (because it was the second one created) by using the call:

```
    Canvas canvas;

    canvas = xv_get(frame, FRAME_NTH_SUBWINDOW, 2);
```

If you attempt to get a subwindow or subframe index but it does not exist, `xv_get()` will return `NULL`.

Laying out subwindows in frames is somewhat automatic, but more explicit layouts can be accomplished by using the macro defined in *<xview/frame.h>* called `frame_fit_all()`. This macro loops on `xv_get()` to get each `FRAME_NTH_SUBWINDOW` and call `window_fit()` to make sure that all the subwindows fit in the frame (if possible). See Chapter 5, *Canvases and Openwin*, for more information on `window_fit()`.

4.5 Destroying Frames

When the application wants to exit, the user typically initiates the action via the frame menu. A call to xv_destroy() destroys the object as well as all objects descended from it. Therefore, all the objects created by an application can be destroyed simply by destroying the base frame, assuming that the base frame is the owner of all those objects. Subframes of the base frame are included as are icons and panels and so forth. There are exceptions to this (such as server images or fonts), but those exceptions are covered later in chapters specific to those objects.

The following code segment demonstrates how to destroy a base frame. When the routine quit() is called, which calls xv_destroy_safe() on the base frame, it destroys all the objects in the frame's tree, including panels and panel items.

```
{
    ...
    xv_main_loop(frame);
    puts("The program is now done.");
    exit(0);
}

quit()
{
    xv_destroy_safe(frame);
}
```

What is significant about this segment is that there is code following the call to xv_main_loop() so that the routine will return when no more frames are left to display. The FRAME package keeps track of all the frames in the application. Each time a frame is created or destroyed, the FRAME package updates its internal count of the number of existing frames. This includes frames that are not displayed or frames that are iconified. When the last frame is destroyed, the Notifier stops and xv_main_loop() returns. (Note that the FRAME package has its own destruction procedures.) Most applications simply exit as shown in the code fragment above. However, if desired, more frames can be created and the Notifier can be restarted. For example, the following code shows how the same base frame may be created five times, assuming that the program does not exit in some manner.

```
Frame    frame;
int      i;

for (i = 0; i < 5; i++) {
    frame = (Frame)xv_create(NULL, FRAME, NULL);
    ...
    xv_main_loop(frame);
}
```

For this to work, there must be a call to xv_destroy() for each frame in the application. Granted, this example is rather silly, but consider an application driven by timer interrupts or network traffic listening for a particular request. Here, there may be no frames displayed until the timer goes off or until the network protocol is initiated. Once this happens, the application that requires user input will create the base frames and enter xv_main_loop(). When the user is done and has destroyed all the frames, xv_main_loop() returns and the application can continue waiting for alarm timeouts or listening for network traffic.

Frames

4.6 Frame Package Summary

Table 4-1 lists the attributes in the FRAME package; the procedures and macros are listed below. This information is described fully in Appendices A and B.

```
frame_get_rect()
frame_set_rect()
```

Table 4-1. Frame Attributes

Frame	Base Frame	Command Frame
FRAME_BACKGROUND_COLOR	FRAME_CLOSED	FRAME_CMD_PANEL
FRAME_BUSY	FRAME_CLOSED_RECT	FRAME_CMD_PUSHPIN_IN
FRAME_FOREGROUND_COLOR	FRAME_ICON	FRAME_DEFAULT_DONE_PROC
FRAME_INHERIT_COLORS	FRAME_NO_CONFIRM	FRAME_DONE_PROC
FRAME_LEFT_FOOTER		
FRAME_NTH_SUBFRAME		
FRAME_NTH_SUBWINDOW		
FRAME_RIGHT_FOOTER		
FRAME_SHOW_FOOTER		
FRAME_SHOW_HEADER		
FRAME_SHOW_LABEL		
FRAME_SHOW_RESIZE_CORNER		
XV_LABEL		

5

Canvases and Openwin

In This Chapter:

Canvas Model 80
Creating a Canvas 82
    Drawing in a Canvas 83
The Repaint Procedure 85
Controlling Canvas Sizes 91
    Automatic Canvas Sizing 92
    Explicit Canvas Sizing 92
    Tracking Changes in the Canvas Size 94
Scrolling Canvases 94
Splitting Canvas Views 95
    Splitting Views Using Scrollbars 95
    Splitting Views Using xv_set() 96
    Getting View Windows 96
Handling Input in the Canvas Package 99
    Default Events 99
    Notification of Events 99
Canvas and Openwin Package Summaries 103

5
Canvases and Openwin

Perhaps the most important object in the XView toolkit is a *canvas*—the area in which an application displays graphics and handles input. The canvas object is similar to that of a painter's canvas. The artist's painting is drawn onto the canvas and the canvas is mounted in a frame. The canvas may be larger than the frame, but the person looking at the canvas only sees what is within the boundaries of the frame. If the canvas is larger than what is viewable, the painting can be moved around making different portions of the canvas visible.

An XView canvas object allows the user to view a graphic image that is too large for the window or even the display screen. The viewable portion of the graphic image is part of the *viewport* or *view window* of the image. Many different views of the image can use the same canvas object. While each view maintains its own idea of what it is displaying, the canvas object manages all the view windows as well as the graphic image that all views share. The ability for the canvas to maintain different views of the graphic image is a property that is inherited from the canvas's superclass, the OPENWIN package. These properties provide for *splitting* and *scrolling* views. You cannot create a canvas object with multiple views; views are split and joined generally by the user via the attached scrollbars. It is possible to programmatically split and scroll views, but OPEN LOOK's interface specification indicates that scrollbars provide the ability to split views. When a view is split, each new view may be further split into two more views, and so on. All the views are still a part of the same canvas object.

The OPENWIN package is an example of a *hidden* class. You cannot instantiate an openwin object independently from canvas or text subwindows. Chapter 8, *Text Subwindows*, contains information about text subwindows. The canvas object is different from the text object in that it maintains an image that can be manipulated by the user. The openwin object, and thus the canvas object, are broken down into three parts: the *main subwindow*, the *view window*, and the *paint window*.

Each view displays a portion of a corresponding paint window. The paint window need not be the size of the corresponding view or the canvas subwindow. Figure 5-1 shows an example of one canvas object providing separate views into one graphic image. What each view displays is independent of what the other views display. A view may even display a portion of an image that is currently displayed in another view.

Figure 5-1. A canvas subwindow with multiple views

5.1 Canvas Model

The components of a canvas subwindow and their relationships can be seen in Figure 5-2.

To summarize, three types of windows are involved with the canvas object:

Canvas Subwindow   Owned by a frame and manages one or more views. The canvas is subclassed from the OPENWIN package so all openwin attributes must be set to the instance of the canvas object.

View Window   Represents the visible portion of the paint window—whenever the paint window associated with a view window changes, it is reflected in the view window. If there is more than one view window, the views are tiled. Vertical and/or horizontal scrollbars can be attached to the view subwindow to allow the user to modify which portion of the paint window is displayed for that particular view. The size of the view window can vary among all the views. Only views can be split. No graphics or user events take place in this window.

Paint Window   Graphics and events (mouse/keyboard) take place in the paint window. There is one paint window per view window. All paint windows in the canvas are the same size regardless of the size of the canvas or of the corresponding view windows. When a view is split, the old view reduces in size and a new view is created. With the new

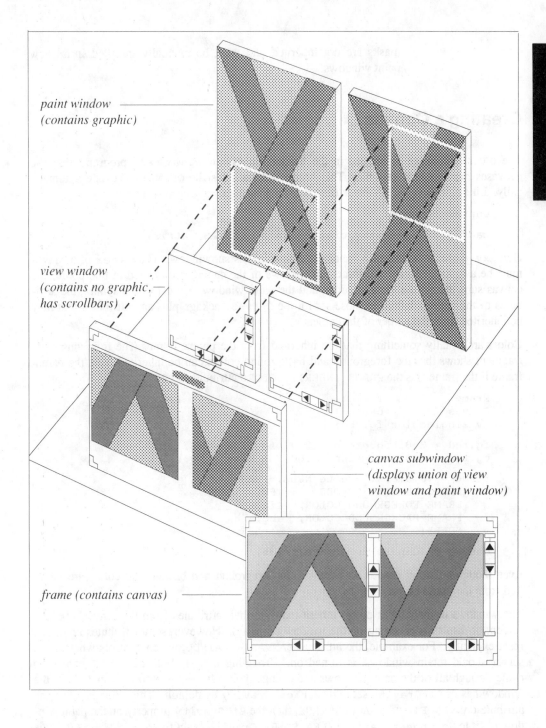

*paint window
(contains graphic)*

*view window
(contains no graphic,
has scrollbars)*

*canvas subwindow
(displays union of view
window and paint window)*

frame (contains canvas)

Figure 5-2. Canvases, views, and paint windows

view, a new paint window is created that is identical to the paint window from the old view. This includes the same visual, width, height, depth, and graphic image. However, callback functions and event masks are not inherited and must be manually installed in all new paint windows.

5.2 Creating a Canvas

The CANVAS package is defined in the header file *<xview/canvas.h>* so programs that use canvases must include this file. This header file includes the OPENWIN package automatically. Like all objects in XView, a canvas is created with xv_create():

```
Canvas canvas;

canvas = (Canvas)xv_create(owner, CANVAS, attrs);
```

Here, xv_create() returns a handle to a new canvas subwindow. The owner of a canvas must be a FRAME object. All three subwindows of the canvas are created at this point: the canvas subwindow, the view window, and the paint window. By using this syntax, the attributes of the canvas default to those set for the CANVAS package plus any attributes that may be inherited from the owner of the canvas.

Colors are usually something that are inherited from the parent frame. The following code fragment shows that the foreground and background colors can be inherited from the parent frame if the frame sets the FRAME_INHERIT_COLORS attribute to TRUE:

```
Frame           frame;
Canvas          canvas;
Xv_singlecolor fg, bg;

fg.red = 250, fg.green = 230, fg.blue = 20;
bg.red = 180, bg.green = 100, bg.blue = 20;

frame = (Frame)xv_create(NULL, FRAME,
    FRAME_INHERIT_COLORS,      TRUE,
    FRAME_FOREGROUND_COLOR,    &fg,
    FRAME_BACKGROUND_COLOR,    &bg,
    NULL);

canvas = (Canvas)xv_create(frame, CANVAS, NULL);
```

Even though a default canvas was created, its foreground and background colors are inherited from the frame object.

The windows in the canvas object inherit many of their attributes from the canvas's parent, screen, or display (depending on the window property). However, some attributes are set or reset explicitly. For example, the attribute CANVAS_RETAINED, which controls whether the server should retain windows, is turned on.* Toggling this attribute causes the canvas to cycle through all of the paint windows and change their WIN_RETAINED attribute. Also, the window has its BitGravity set to NorthWestGravity by default. This value is set by the attribute CANVAS_FIXED_IMAGE. If TRUE, then the BitGravity property on the paint window is set to NorthWestGravity. If FALSE, BitGravity is set to ForgetGravity. This is discussed in more detail in Section 5.3, "The Repaint Procedure."

---

*CANVAS_RETAINED does not affect the view windows, which are not retained.

The width and height of the paint window and the view window default to the size of the canvas when it is realized. Unless otherwise specified, those sizes are governed by the object that is the owner of the canvas.

5.2.1 Drawing in a Canvas

The use of canvases implies that your application wants to display a graphic image that the user can either manipulate or generate. In conventional (not server-client based) windowing systems, when you request to create a window, you usually get a window back that you can draw into. This is not exactly true for X. Although you get a window back from the request, you are not guaranteed to be able to draw into it until it has been successfully mapped (displayed) on the screen. In the general case for XView, this does not happen until `xv_main_loop()` is called. Therefore, you should *not* do the following:

```
canvas = (Canvas)xv_create(frame, CANVAS, NULL);
win = (Window)xv_get(canvas_paint_window(canvas), XV_XID);

XDrawString(dpy, win, gc, x, y, "Hello World.", 11);
```

Instead, you should design your program such that your repaint routine knows exactly what the contents of the canvas should be so that it can reproduce the image. Here are two helpful hints for typical applications:

- *Use your repaint proc.*
  Never call any graphics routines before `xv_main_loop()` is called. Routines that draw anything into windows should be called directly or indirectly from your canvas repaint procedure or event handler.

- *Use internal data.*
  The repaint routine should be able to repaint a canvas window based on some sort of internal data. To maintain system performance, the data should be in core; it should *not* be on disk (in a file), from a network connection, or from interaction with the user. If the data is received from those media, the data should already have been updated by the time the repaint routine is called.

To give you an idea of the issues involved here, we'll look at several common applications that typically use canvases.

Draw Programs

Draw programs are usually applications which maintain a *display list* of geometric shapes such as lines, circles, rectangles, and so on. The user generates these shapes using the mouse or keyboard. The canvas's `WIN_EVENT_PROC` procedure handles mouse and keyboard input from the user, and the user interface generally describes the shape that is currently being drawn.

When the user initiates mouse clicks, drags, or keyboard actions, the event handler picks up these events and is fully expected to modify the canvas window accordingly (e.g., by "rubber banding" the object). Upon receipt of the appropriate event (button release, perhaps), the event handler adds the new geometric item to the display list.

In order to reconstruct what the canvas should be displaying, the repaint routine references the updated display list. Obviously, the display list should contain enough information in it to be able to tell the repaint routine what colors to use, line thickness, and so on.

Paint Programs

Paint programs are *pixel based*, meaning that the image that the user manipulates is typically a bitmap (monochrome) or a color pixmap. In this case, the pixmap is used as the internal data. If the user uses a *brush* to modify the image, the modification to the canvas window is handled in the event procedure as above, but the image that the user is editing is also updated so that when the repaint routine is called, it can use a function such as XCopyArea() to copy the portion of the image onto the canvas window. This is also a case where the event handler may draw directly onto the window.

If the program starts up and already has an image to work with (e.g., the user requests to load a previously saved image that was stored into the file), *do not render the image onto the paint window before* xv_main_loop() *is called.* Eventually, the repaint procedure will be called and the image should be rendered at that time.

Text-based Programs

If you want to display text, as in desktop publishing packages, or if you just want a simple program that displays a window with text, then the same thing applies as with the previous examples: render the text in the repaint routine based on internal data (e.g., a text string or set of strings). Again, the data must contain enough information to allow your repaint routine to repaint the text as it was intended (e.g., font type, style, size, color).

Event-handling routines that accept keyboard input may render the new text directly to the canvas window, but the text entered should also be saved internally for the benefit of the repaint routine.

Visualization Programs

It is common to have an application that displays the time, network traffic, CPU usage, file system integrity, or the current Dow Jones Industrial Averages. Such applications get their data from a variety of sources such as the system clock, UNIX sockets, the file system, or the output of another application that has been forked. In the past, such applications might have been written where the repaint routine accesses the information. This model does not apply in a networked windowing system because of its asynchronous nature; the window system and the application may not be in sync. A program should have a separate method for retrieving data apart from the repaint procedure. See the program *animate.c* in Chapter 19, *The Notifier*, for an example.

In many of these cases (with the possible exception of the *meters*), if the application is well designed, the repaint routines and the event handlers may be calling the same internal routines which render graphics. Therefore, when writing functions that draw into a canvas, you should consider the generic case where the function could be called from a repaint routine, event handler or anywhere else. The program *canvas_event.c* (shown in Example 5-3) calls the repaint routine directly from the event handler.

Rendering Graphics

The preferred form of rendering graphics from an XView application is to use Xlib graphics calls. Volume One, *Xlib Programming Manual*, has a complete discussion of Xlib graphics programming. Throughout this book, you will find examples of drawing into canvases using Xlib graphics routines. Appendix G, *Example Programs*, has several longer programs that demonstrate Xlib graphics. The XView graphics model, which is available, is almost identical to the *SunView* model for graphics and is provided for backwards compatibility with SunView. Because XView graphics calls are wrappers to the underlying Xlib calls, these functions are not recommended for graphics-intensive applications or for use by programmers who are not already familiar with SunView.

5.3 The Repaint Procedure

It is always the responsibility of the application to repaint its canvas at any time. Even though there may be a retained canvas that the X server maintains, there is no guarantee that there will be enough memory for the server to maintain it. For this reason, all canvases should install a routine to handle repainting.

To install a repaint procedure, use the attribute CANVAS_REPAINT_PROC and specify a callback function as its value:

```
extern void my_repaint_proc();
...
canvas = (Canvas)xv_create(frame, CANVAS,
    ...
    CANVAS_REPAINT_PROC,    my_repaint_proc(),
    ...
    NULL);
```

The repaint routine installed is called anytime all or a portion of the canvas needs to be re-displayed. This always happens when the canvas is mapped on the screen for the first time (causing an Expose event). If the canvas is *not* retained, the repaint procedure is called when:

• The canvas is resized.

• The canvas has been moved in front of obscuring windows.

• The user uses the scrollbar to render a different part of the paint window visible.

If the canvas *is* retained and has not changed size, the server refreshes the window without calling the repaint callback. This includes all exposures except for those that are the result of a resize of the window or the initial mapping of the canvas onto the screen. However, if the canvas is not retained, the repaint routine is called in all of these cases.

The repaint callback routine will be called once for each view the canvas is maintaining. If the canvas has been split several times, then the repaint routine will get called for each view that needs repainting. One of the parameters to the callback routine is a variable that describes the region that has been exposed or needs repainting. When a window is initially displayed on the screen, the exposed region is the entire canvas. However, this area may not be a contiguous area of the window. For example, as shown in Figure 5-3, if a window that is partially obscured by two windows is brought forward, two separate areas are exposed.

Before
Window partially obscured

After
Exposed in one view

Figure 5-3. Window before and after an Expose event

The attribute WIN_COLLAPSE_EXPOSURES governs how many times the repaint routine is called. By default, XView collapses Expose (and GraphicsExpose) X events destined for the same window; that is, XView waits for the exposure count member to reach zero. After all exposure X events have arrived (when count == 0), XView generates a WIN_REPAINT event and calls the repaint procedure. This WIN_REPAINT represents all the areas in the window that have been damaged (it can be a disjoint set of rectangles). The X event associated with the WIN_REPAINT event (accessed through the event_xevent() macro) represents a bounding rectangle of all the damaged areas in the window (basically the union of all the damaged areas in the window).

However, sometimes the application wants to monitor the incoming Expose (and GraphicsExpose) X events, monitoring piece by piece the count member in the Expose X event itself. This can be done by setting WIN_COLLAPSE_EXPOSURES to FALSE. As exposures come into a window with this attribute set to FALSE, they will be immediately sent to the client's repaint procedure. The client will thus receive several WIN_REPAINT events, all for the same window. The area of exposure is set to each region as it is exposed.

By default, the repaint routine is called once per window exposed. However, there may be situations where there are more windows exposed in the same canvas object. For example, in Figure 5-4, two view windows have been exposed as a result of bringing the window to the top of the window stack. In this case, the repaint routine will be called twice—once for the paint window of each view exposed. Only one area of each view window is exposed, so the value of the WIN_COLLAPSE_EXPOSURES attribute does not apply.

Before
Window partially obscured

After
Exposed in two views

Figure 5-4. Window with two views before and after an Expose event

Before the repaint routine is called, the window can be cleared in one of two ways. If CANVAS_AUTO_CLEAR is set to TRUE, then the paint window being repainted is automatically cleared. CANVAS_AUTO_CLEAR is really defined as OPENWIN_AUTO_CLEAR since this is a property of the OPENWIN package. Automatically clearing the window happens anytime the window needs repainting. This means that the exposed area represents the entire window. If this attribute is set to FALSE (the default), the repaint routine should prepare to clear all, or portions of, the window that needs to be repainted. The contents of the window in the exposed areas is undefined. If you are going to repaint those areas opaquely (that is, leave no transparent portions), then you do not need to clear the area. However, if any transparent portion of the area will be repainted (e.g., if your gc.function is set to GXxor), you should clear the window first by using XClearArea() or XClearWindow().

Alternatively, the window may be cleared automatically by the Xlib internals if the window has actually changed size. The BitGravity attribute for the window controls whether the data in the window is cleared or just moved around to different locations of the window according to its new size. If BitGravity is set to ForgetGravity, then the data in the window is discarded, resulting in the window getting cleared. As mentioned before, this value can be set by setting the attribute CANVAS_FIXED_IMAGE to FALSE. But to have more direct control over the BitGravity of the window, the window attribute WIN_BIT_GRAVITY may be set to any of the legal values provided by Xlib (ForgetGravity, North-Gravity, NorthWestGravity, and so on). Section 4.3.3, "Bit Gravity," in Volume One, *Xlib Programming Manual*, discusses this in full detail.

The parameters to the repaint routine provide information about which window and which areas within the window need to be repainted.

The repaint procedure takes one of two different forms:

```
void
repaint_proc(canvas, paint_window, repaint_area)
    Canvas        canvas;
    Xv_Window     paint_window
    Rectlist      *repaint_area;
```

or:

```
void
repaint_proc(canvas, paint_window, dpy, xwin, area)
    Canvas        canvas;
    Xv_Window     paint_window
    Display       *dpy;
    Window        xwin;
    Xv_xrectlist  *area;
```

The routine takes the first or second form depending on the value of the attribute CANVAS_X_PAINT_WINDOW. If FALSE, the first, simpler form of the repaint procedure is called. If TRUE, the repaint routine gets passed the parameters shown in the second form. The second method is more useful since it saves you from writing code for extracting the Display and the XID of the paint window.

In both forms, the first two parameters are rather obvious—the paint_window is the paint window associated with the canvas that needs repainting (not the view window). The paint_window contains an X window whose XID can be gotten by using xv_get():

```
Window xwin = (Window)xv_get(paint_window, XV_XID);
```

xwin is set to the actual X window referenced by the paint window. Obtaining the XID from the paint window like this is used because the first form of the repaint procedure (when CANVAS_X_PAINT_WINDOW is FALSE) does not provide a handle for you.

In the first form of the repaint procedure, the only other parameter is the repaint_area. This is a linked list of rectangular areas in the paint window that have been exposed and need to be repainted. The Rectlist type is a linked list of Rect's as shown in *<xview/rect.h>*. The declaration for the Rect type is:

```
typedef struct rectnode {
    coord r_left, r_top;
    short r_width, r_height;
} Rect;
```

The type coord is #define'd as type short. The Rectlist is declared in *<xview/rectlist.h>* as:

```
typedef struct  rectnode {
    struct rectnode *rn_next;  /* Pointer to next rectnode */
```

```
        struct rect        rn_rect;
    } Rectnode;

    typedef struct rectlist {
        coord              rl_x, rl_y; /* Offset to apply to each rect
                                        * in list including bound */
        struct rectnode *rl_head;      /* Pointer to first rectnode */
        struct rectnode *rl_tail;      /* Pointer to last rectnode */
        struct rect       rl_bound;    /* Describes bounding rect of
                                        * all rects in list */
    } Rectlist;
```

The repaint_area parameter is of type Rectlist, so the application has several ways it can approach repainting the window. It could just ignore the parameter and repaint the entire window, or it could repaint the entire area described by the rl_bound field of the rectlist structure, or it could loop through all the Rectnode's and repaint those areas individually. Deciding which method to choose should be based on how complicated the redrawing is.

When CANVAS_X_PAINT_WINDOW is set to FALSE, the internal clipping for the paint window is set to be the same region or regions described by the repaint parameter of the repaint routine. In most cases, this means that OPENWIN_AUTO_CLEAR will only clear those areas—not the entire window.* The default behavior may be overridden by setting WIN_NO_CLIP-PING to TRUE for the *canvas*. Setting this attribute cycles through all the paint windows in the canvas and sets the window property WIN_NO_CLIPPING. Having the clipping on the window turned off means that OPENWIN_AUTO_CLEAR will cause the entire window to be cleared.†

By setting the attribute CANVAS_X_PAINT_WINDOW to TRUE, the repaint routine gets passed the extra X-specific parameters as shown in the second form of the repaint procedure. These extra parameters include handles to the Display and the X window of the paint_window.

Example 5-1 shows how a repaint procedure might be used.

Example 5-1. The line.c program

```
/*
 * line.c -- demonstrates installing a repaint routine in a canvas.
 * The routine is called whenever the canvas needs to be repainted.
 * This usually occurs when the canvas is exposed or resized.
 */
#include <X11/Xlib.h>
#include <xview/xview.h>
#include <xview/canvas.h>
#include <xview/xv_xrect.h>

main(argc, argv)
int argc;
char *argv[];
{
    Frame frame;
    void  canvas_repaint_proc();
```

---

*For those using the SunView-compatible drawing routines such as pw_vector(), rendering is clipped to the area or areas described by repaint_area.

†This also affects the SunView-compatible routines—pw_vector() will not be clipped.

Example 5-1. The line.c program (continued)

```
    xv_init(XV_INIT_ARGC_PTR_ARGV, &argc, argv, NULL);

    frame = (Frame)xv_create(NULL, FRAME, NULL);

    (void) xv_create(frame, CANVAS,
        CANVAS_REPAINT_PROC,      canvas_repaint_proc,
        CANVAS_X_PAINT_WINDOW,   TRUE,
        NULL);

    xv_main_loop(frame);
}
/*
 * repaint routine draws a line from the top left to the bottom right
 * corners of the window
 */
void
canvas_repaint_proc(canvas, paint_window, dpy, xwin, xrects)
Canvas          canvas;         /* unused */
Xv_Window       paint_window;   /* unused */
Display         *dpy;
Window          xwin;
Xv_xrectlist *xrects;           /* unused */
{
    GC gc;
    int width, height;

    gc = DefaultGC(dpy, DefaultScreen(dpy));
    width = (int)xv_get(paint_window, XV_WIDTH);
    height = (int)xv_get(paint_window, XV_HEIGHT);

    XDrawLine(dpy, xwin, gc, 0, 0, width, height);
}
```

Because the program uses Xlib calls (and thus, the repaint routine is being passed different parameters), the header files *<X11/Xlib.h>* and *<xview/xv_xrect.h>* must be added at the top of the program. The parameters display and xwin are handles to the X Display and the X Window, respectively. The GC (graphics context) is taken from the default GC of the screen.

The xrects parameter represents the exposed, or "damaged," region of the paint window. When the canvas is first displayed, this region will be the entire paint window (or the portion that is viewable by the view window). But in cases where another window that has partially obscured it moves away, perhaps only a portion of the paint window will need repainting. Therefore, the xrects variable can aid in setting the clip rectangles in the GC, as shown in Example 5-2.

Example 5-2. Repainting objects within a damaged region

```
/* canvas_repaint_proc()
 *
 * Draws onto the canvas using Xlib drawing functions.
 *
 * Uses the current clipping rectangle to:
 *  1. Restrict graphics output by setting the
 *      clip_mask in the graphics context.
```

Example 5-2. Repainting objects within a damaged region (continued)

```
 *  2. Do "smart repainting" by only painting the objects
 *     that lie within the damaged region (not being done
 *     in this example).
 */
void
repaint_proc(canvas, paint_window, display, xid, xrects)
    Canvas canvas;
    Xv_Window paint_window;
    Display *display;
    Window xwin;
    Xv_xrectlist *xrects;
{
    extern GC gc;
    int width, height;

    width = (int)xv_get(paint_window, XV_WIDTH);
    height = (int)xv_get(paint_window, XV_HEIGHT);

    /*
     * Set clip rects, if any
     */
    if (xrects)
        XSetClipRectangles(display, gc, 0, 0, xrects->rect_array,
            xrects->count, Unsorted);
    else {
        XGCValues gc_val;

        gc_val.clip_mask = None;
        XChangeGC(display, gc, GCClipMask, &gc_val);
    }

    XDrawLine(display, xwin, gc, 0, 0, width, height);
}
```

Because this routine sets the clip mask of the GC, we want to be sure that we *do not use the default GC of the screen* as we did in or it will interfere with other programs (such as the window manager). The GC shown here is declared as `extern`, assuming that the application has created it somewhere else using `XCreateGC()`.

5.4 Controlling Canvas Sizes

The size of the canvas subwindow is usually determined by the frame window. Thus, the canvas changes as the user resizes the frame. Applications largely concern themselves with the size of the paint window.* The paint window does not affect the size of the viewable canvas, but the viewable portion of the paint window is important.

Although the width and height of the canvas subwindow can be set explicitly, unless done so, the default size of the subwindow and the paint window is determined by the parent frame. If the frame resizes, the canvas object resizes proportionally according to how the frame

---

*There may be more than one paint window to a canvas, but all paint windows in a canvas are the same size, so it's a moot point.

chooses to resize the canvas. If several other windows (canvases, panels, whatever) are in the frame, the frame might choose to lay out and size those subwindows differently (according to available and required space from other windows). The canvas window itself, as well as all window objects, can be sized using XV_WIDTH and XV_HEIGHT. Managing the size of the paint windows under the canvas is dealt with later in this chapter.

5.4.1 Automatic Canvas Sizing

The paint window's size may fluctuate with that of the canvas subwindow's size. The attributes CANVAS_AUTO_EXPAND and CANVAS_AUTO_SHRINK maintain the relation of the canvas subwindow and paint window in the event of any kind of window resizing. Both of these attributes default to TRUE, allowing the paint window to always correspond to the size of the canvas subwindow. If the canvas subwindow becomes larger, the paint window size changes to that size. If the frame changes size, the canvas subwindow changes size and so does the paint window. This happens regardless of how many view windows there are. The size of view windows does not affect the size of the paint window.

Specifically, if CANVAS_AUTO_EXPAND is TRUE, then the width and height of the paint window cannot be less than that of the canvas subwindow. Setting CANVAS_AUTO_EXPAND allows the paint window to grow bigger as the user stretches the window. If a resize of the subwindow occurs such that the size of the paint window is less than the size of the canvas subwindow, the paint window is expanded to be at least that size. Conversely, if the canvas subwindow's size shrinks, then the paint canvas size does not change because its size is already greater than or equal to the size of the canvas subwindow—no expansion is necessary.

If CANVAS_AUTO_SHRINK is TRUE, the canvas object checks that width and height of the paint window are not greater than that of the canvas subwindow. Setting CANVAS_AUTO_SHRINK forces the paint window to grow smaller as the size of the canvas subwindow gets smaller. If the user resizes the frame such that the canvas subwindow is smaller than the size of the paint window, then the paint window is reduced to the size of the new subwindow.

You can also set a minimum width and height for the canvas using the attributes CANVAS_MIN_PAINT_WIDTH and CANVAS_MIN_PAINT_HEIGHT.

5.4.2 Explicit Canvas Sizing

The attributes CANVAS_WIDTH and CANVAS_HEIGHT can be set to establish the size of the *paint window*. Automatic sizing should be turned off. Otherwise, as soon as the canvas window is realized, the paint window may be automatically resized to the new dimensions. This all depends on whether either or both of the auto-expand or auto-shrink attributes are set. The following code fragment shows that one can be set and the other unset for specific needs:

```
Canvas canvas;

canvas = (Canvas)xv_create(frame, CANVAS,
    CANVAS_AUTO_SHRINK,  FALSE,
```

```
        CANVAS_AUTO_EXPAND,    TRUE,
        CANVAS_WIDTH,          100,
        CANVAS_HEIGHT,         200,
        NULL);
```

With these settings, the paint window will initially be set to 100 by 200. If the subwindow is realized at a larger size, the canvas will be expanded to the new dimensions. That is, if the frame in which the canvas resides is larger, it may affect the initial size of the paint window. However, if the canvas is realized or resized at smaller dimensions, the canvas will retain its original size. In short, these settings will force the paint window to grow to the maximum size that the window will ever be—it will never shrink. In typical usage, you would set the auto-expand and auto-shrink attributes to FALSE and explicitly set CANVAS_WIDTH and CANVAS_HEIGHT. Alternatively, you would not initialize the width and height and set both CANVAS_AUTO_EXPAND and CANVAS_AUTO_SHRINK to TRUE. A draw program might allow the paint window to be sized automatically, since the display list of geometric objects is the underlying feature of the program. However, a paint program would set explicit width and height attributes of the graphic, disallowing any resizing of that graphic.

The following code fragment creates a canvas with a fixed-size paint window that is not affected by resizing:

```
Canvas canvas;

canvas = (Canvas)xv_create(frame, CANVAS,
        CANVAS_AUTO_SHRINK,    FALSE,
        CANVAS_AUTO_EXPAND,    FALSE,
        CANVAS_WIDTH,          1000,
        CANVAS_HEIGHT,         1000,
        NULL);
```

This call sets the initial size of the paint window to 1000 by 1000 pixels. The origin of the paint window's coordinate system is the upper-left corner (0,0) and the lower-right corner (CANVAS_WIDTH-1, CANVAS_HEIGHT-1). Note that we did not set the size of the canvas subwindow. Instead, we allowed it to be determined by the frame size. The size of the paint window remains constant regardless of how the frame and canvas subwindow is resized. If the frame or the canvas subwindow resizes, the subwindow merely changes its view of the underlying paint window, which remains constant.

In the following code fragment, we set the size of the canvas subwindow, using generic attributes:

```
Canvas canvas;

canvas = (Canvas)xv_create(frame, CANVAS,
        CANVAS_AUTO_SHRINK,    FALSE,
        CANVAS_AUTO_EXPAND,    FALSE,
        CANVAS_WIDTH,          1000,
        CANVAS_HEIGHT,         1000,
        XV_WIDTH,              200,
        XV_HEIGHT,             100,
        NULL);
```

Here, a canvas subwindow is created that is 200 pixels wide and 100 pixels high. All other attributes about this canvas object are the same as the previous example: the paint window is going to be 1000x1000 in width and height. The problem with this canvas is that the user has no way to view different parts of the paint window. To handle that, scrollbars should be attached to the canvas to provide scrolling. See Section 5.5, "Scrolling Canvases."

5.4.3 Tracking Changes in the Canvas Size

In the event that the canvas has been resized, the program has the opportunity to track this event by installing a callback routine. This routine is installed, using CANVAS_ RESIZE_PROC. The client's resize procedure is called whenever the width or height of the canvas changes. Its form is:

```
void
sample_resize_proc(canvas, width, height)
    Canvas canvas;
    int    width;
    int    height;
```

The parameters to the resize procedure are the canvas and the new width and height of the canvas. Unlike the repaint routine, the resize procedure is not called for each view in the canvas. It is just called for the canvas window itself. The resize procedure should never repaint any of the canvas's paint windows. If any new area is to be painted, the repaint procedure will be called separately for each view. The width and height of the new views are available within the repaint routine.

5.5 Scrolling Canvases

Many applications need to view and manipulate a large object through a smaller viewing window. To facilitate this, packages that are subclassed from the openwin class may have *scrollbars* attached to their subwindows.

The following code fragment creates a canvas that can be scrolled in both directions:

```
Canvas      canvas;
Scrollbar   h_scrollbar, v_scrollbar;

canvas = (Canvas)xv_create(frame, CANVAS,
    CANVAS_AUTO_EXPAND,   FALSE,
    CANVAS_AUTO_SHRINK,   FALSE,
    CANVAS_WIDTH,         1000,
    CANVAS_HEIGHT,        1000,
    NULL);

h_scrollbar = (Scrollbar)xv_create(canvas, SCROLLBAR,
    SCROLLBAR_DIRECTION, SCROLLBAR_HORIZONTAL,
    NULL);

v_scrollbar = (Scrollbar)xv_create(canvas, SCROLLBAR,
    SCROLLBAR_DIRECTION, SCROLLBAR_VERTICAL,
    NULL);
```

Because the SCROLLBAR package is being used here, the header file *<xview/scrollbar.h>* must be included. Chapter 10, *Scrollbars*, discusses scrollbars more complete as well as gives furthers examples of how to scroll canvases.

The owner of the scrollbars is the canvas so that the scrollbars are automatically attached to the canvas's view. If the user scrolls the canvas, your canvas's repaint procedure will be called provided that the canvas's WIN_RETAINED attribute is set to FALSE. This is important because setting WIN_RETAINED to TRUE assumes that you are not interested in handling repainting for scrolling. In other words, as long as the user does not do anything that changes the contents of the image, you do not need to be informed when the user scrolls the image. If you want to be informed of scrolling, set WIN_RETAINED to FALSE and your repaint routine will be called with the *exposed area* parameter* describing the new area that just scrolled into view. If there are many views in the canvas, the paint window associated with the view that scrolled is in the second parameter to the repaint function: the paint_window.

5.6 Splitting Canvas Views

There are two methods by which the application may split the views of a canvas (or any openwin-classed object). The first method is for the user to use the scrollbars to split views. This method is more common and complies with the OPEN LOOK specification. The alternate method is for the application to make calls to xv_set() with attribute-value pairs that tell where and how a view should be split.

Whenever views are split, the following attributes are propagated from the split paint window to the new paint window:

- WIN_BACKGROUND_COLOR
- WIN_FOREGROUND_COLOR
- WIN_CMS_DATA
- WIN_CMS_NAME
- WIN_COLUMN_GAP
- WIN_COLUMN_WIDTH
- WIN_CURSOR
- WIN_EVENT_PROC
- WIN_ROW_GAP
- WIN_ROW_HEIGHT
- WIN_X_EVENT_MASK

5.6.1 Splitting Views Using Scrollbars

To set up the canvas so that the user can split it using scrollbars, the canvas should have scrollbars attached as shown in the previous example with the additional attribute SCROLLBAR_SPLITTABLE set to TRUE:

```
h_scrollbar = (Scrollbar)xv_create(canvas, SCROLLBAR,
    SCROLLBAR_DIRECTION,    SCROLLBAR_HORIZONTAL,
```

---

*The exposed area passed to the repaint procedure is of type Xv_xrectlist if CANVAS_X_PAINT_WINDOW is set to TRUE or Rectlist if CANVAS_X_PAINT_WINDOW is set to FALSE.

```
        SCROLLBAR_SPLITTABLE,    TRUE,
        NULL);

    v_scrollbar = (Scrollbar)xv_create(canvas, SCROLLBAR,
        SCROLLBAR_DIRECTION,     SCROLLBAR_VERTICAL,
        SCROLLBAR_SPLITTABLE,    TRUE,
        NULL);
```

With this attribute set, the scrollbars have the ability to split view windows in two. The user splits the view by selecting the *cable anchors* at the endpoints of the scrollbars and dragging them towards the center of the scrollbar. A pop-up menu provided with the scrollbars also provides this functionality. The entire view will be split at the point the mouse button is released, provided there is enough room for a new view at that point. Each view can scroll its own underlying paint window independently of other views.

5.6.2 Splitting Views Using xv_set()

Splitting a view by setting attribute-value pairs in the view is a less common method since the scrollbar already provides this functionality. However, there is a programmatic interface for splitting views whether or not those views that have scrollbars attached to them.

The attribute OPENWIN_SPLIT is followed by a list of attribute-value pairs that indicate specifically how a view is to be split. Only attributes that are prefixed with OPENWIN_SPLIT may be used in this NULL-terminated list. Other attributes are ignored. The following demonstrates how an arbitrary view window can be split into two parts:

```
    Xv_Window view;
    view = (Xv_Window)xv_get(canvas, CANVAS_NTH_VIEW, 0);

    xv_set(canvas,
        OPENWIN_SPLIT,
            OPENWIN_SPLIT_VIEW,        view,
            OPENWIN_SPLIT_DIRECTION,   OPENWIN_SPLIT_HORIZONTAL,
            NULL,
        NULL);
```

This very simple example shows that the first *view window* in the canvas will be split horizontally. The place in which the split takes place is, by default, the position of the scrollbar in the view. Assuming the code fragment above, the window is split so that the new view is the same width as the original view but the height is split at the position of the scrollbar. The original view is the remaining height and is on top of the new view.

5.6.3 Getting View Windows

If a canvas has been split several times resulting in multiple view and paint windows, it is possible to get a handle to a particular view or paint window. This can be done either at the time the view was split or by using xv_get().

Getting the Newest View

If you want to be notified when the user splits or joins views, you can specify the attributes OPENWIN_SPLIT_INIT_PROC for when the user *splits* a view, and OPENWIN_SPLIT_ DESTROY_PROC when the user *joins* a view. These attributes are set in the canvas (or any openwin object). Set these functions by using xv_create() or xv_set() in the following manner:

```
extern void init_split(), join_view();

xv_create(frame, CANVAS,
    ...
    OPENWIN_SPLIT,
        OPENWIN_SPLIT_INIT_PROC,     init_proc,
        OPENWIN_SPLIT_DESTROY_PROC, join_view,
    NULL,
    ...
NULL);
```

Write the split and join functions, which take the following parameters:

```
void
init_split(origview, newview, pos)
    Xv_Window origview, newview;
    int pos;

void
join_view(view)
    Xv_Window view;
```

The origview and the newview parameters in the first function represent the view that was originally split and the new resulting view, respectively. These are *not* the paint windows; these are the views themselves. To get a handle to the associated paint window from these views, you can use:

```
Xv_Window paint_window;

paint_window = (Xv_Window)xv_get(view, CANVAS_VIEW_PAINT_WINDOW);
```

The example in Chapter 6, *Handling Input*, gives an example of handling input in different views.

Getting Arbitrary Views

For each view in an OPENWIN object, you can get either the view window or the paint window for the view by choosing either the CANVAS_NTH_PAINT_WINDOW or the OPENWIN_NTH_VIEW attribute and an integer value for the view window. The first window is 0 and the last window is *n-1*, where *n* is the number of view windows.

```
xv_get(canvas, CANVAS_NTH_PAINT_WINDOW, 1, NULL);
```

The line above shows how to get the second paint window in the canvas. You can get the number of available views by calling:

```
int nviews = (int)xv_get(canvas, OPENWIN_NVIEWS);
```

Remember that the number of views corresponds directly with the number of paint windows.

Each paint window can be accessed in order, using a simple loop like the following:

```
Xv_Window window;
Canvas     canvas;
int        i = 0;

while (window = (Xv_Window)xv_get(canvas, CANVAS_NTH_PAINT_WINDOW, i)) {
    draw_into_window(window);
    i++;
}
```

The call to xv_get() returns NULL if you try to get a window number that does not exist (XView does the error checking). Thus, the loop terminates when xv_get() returns NULL. The value of i represents the number of views in the canvas subwindow.

XView provides a pair of macros that facilitate looping through a set of views in a canvas: CANVAS_EACH_PAINT_WINDOW and CANVAS_END_EACH. The previous loop could be written as:

```
Xv_Window window;
Canvas     canvas;

CANVAS_EACH_PAINT_WINDOW(canvas, window)
    draw_into_window(window);
CANVAS_END_EACH
```

Because the paint windows are different from the view windows, a different method is used for getting view windows. The other method is similar to the paint window method:

```
Xv_Window view;
Canvas     canvas;
int        i = 0;

while (window = (Xv_Window)xv_get(canvas, OPENWIN_NTH_VIEW, i)) {
    /* process window */
    i++;
}
```

There is also a macro that loops through all the views in the canvas:

```
Xv_Window view;
Canvas     canvas;

OPENWIN_EACH_VIEW(canvas, view)
    ...
OPENWIN_END_EACH
```

You can get the paint window associated with a view by using the attribute CANVAS_VIEW_PAINT_WINDOW:

```
Xv_Window view;
Xv_Window paint_window;

paint_window = (Xv_Window)xv_get(view, CANVAS_VIEW_PAINT_WINDOW);
```

This is useful in situations where you are given the view window and need to get the paint window associated with it. For example, the routines called when views are *split* or *joined* are passed handles to view windows. When a view is split, you will need to get the paint window associated with the new view to install event or repaint callbacks.

5.7 Handling Input in the Canvas Package

This section discusses, to a limited degree, the method for handling and specifying events in a canvas. For a detailed discussion on the types of events used and the proper method for handling them, see Chapter 6, *Handling Input*.

5.7.1 Default Events

By default, the CANVAS package enables the following events for its window and paint windows: LOC_WINENTER, LOC_WINEXIT, LOC_MOVE, and the three mouse buttons MS_LEFT, MS_MIDDLE and MS_RIGHT. Other events may be added to the window event mask by using xv_set() and passing the appropriate parameters. This following shows how to add keyboard ASCII events:

```
xv_set(canvas_paint_window(canvas),
    WIN_CONSUME_EVENT, WIN_ASCII_EVENTS,
    NULL);
```

An application needing to track mouse motion while the mouse button is down would enable LOC_DRAG by calling:

```
xv_set(canvas_paint_window(canvas),
    WIN_CONSUME_EVENT, LOC_DRAG,
    NULL);
```

5.7.2 Notification of Events

In addition to specifying which events the application needs to know about, the program should also install an event callback routine that is called when one of the specified events takes place. The callback routine for event handling is installed using WIN_EVENT_PROC. Included are samples that demonstrate how to handle events appropriately using a combination of repaint and event callback routines. However, for a complete discussion of events, you should consult Chapter 6, *Handling Input*, and Chapter 19, *The Notifier*.

In the sample program *canvas_event.c* (see Example 5-3), after a base frame is created, a canvas is created with the attribute CANVAS_X_PAINT_WINDOW set to TRUE because its repaint procedure (repaint_proc) uses Xlib routines to clear the window and draw text strings in the canvas.

Next we specify the events that the application should handle when they occur on the paint_window. We are going to listen for keyboard events, pointer motion events, and pointer button events. We have not assigned any responses to these events yet; we have just registered them for this window with XView so that the application will be called back if they occur.

We then set the paint window's event handling procedure to be event_proc. This is the routine that will decide what to do when the events occur. XView is then started up by calling xv_main_loop(), in which event processing starts.

The event_proc is called by the Notifier whenever a registered event takes place in any view that has an event handling procedure set. The event_proc looks at the type of event it has received and determine the appropriate message to display in the paint window. There is a different message for each type of the events that we have registered. There are three message buffers, one each for: keyboard events, pointer motion events and pointer button events. After the message buffers are updated, then the repaint procedure is called to display them. Note that we are reusing the repaint_proc, instead of writing more code just to display the messages. See Section 5.2.1, "Drawing in a Canvas."

If the event we have received is of no interest to us, then we return. It is important to do this because the events WIN_REPAINT and WIN_RESIZE are delivered regardless of the events we have registered with the Notifier. These two events will eventually result in the Notifier calling the repaint procedure anyway, so it is not necessary to call it redundantly from here. See Chapter 6, *Handling Input*, for details about this.

In *canvas_event.c*, the repaint_proc simply clears the paint window and then displays the three messages in it, at a fixed position and using the default font. In the case of a pure repaint callback (from the Notifier, not the event_proc), the messages will just repeat the last event's messages.

Example 5-3. The canvas_event.c program

```
/*
 *   canvas_event.c
 *   Demonstrates how to get keyboard and mouse events in an canvas
 *   window.  Looks for keyboards, pointer movement and button
 *   events and displays the info in the canvas.
 */
#include <X11/Xlib.h>
#include <xview/xview.h>
#include <xview/canvas.h>
#include <xview/xv_xrect.h>

void      event_proc(), repaint_proc();
char      kbd_msg[128], ptr_msg[128], but_msg[128];

/*
 * main()
 *      Create a canvas specifying a repaint procedure.
 *      Get the paint window for the canvas and set the input
 *      mask and the event procedure.
 */
main(argc, argv)
int argc;
char *argv[];
{
    Frame         frame;
    Canvas        canvas;

    /* Initialize XView */
    xv_init(XV_INIT_ARGC_PTR_ARGV, &argc, argv, NULL);

    /* Create windows -- base frame and canvas. */
    frame = (Frame)xv_create(NULL, FRAME, NULL);

    canvas = (Canvas)xv_create(frame, CANVAS,
        XV_WIDTH,                300,
```

Example 5-3. The canvas_event.c program (continued)

```
        XV_HEIGHT,              110,
        CANVAS_X_PAINT_WINDOW,  TRUE,
        CANVAS_REPAINT_PROC,    repaint_proc,
        NULL);
    window_fit(frame);

    /* Set input mask */
    xv_set(canvas_paint_window(canvas),
        WIN_EVENT_PROC,         event_proc,
        WIN_CONSUME_EVENTS,
            KBD_DONE, KBD_USE, LOC_DRAG, LOC_MOVE, LOC_WINENTER,
            LOC_WINEXIT, WIN_ASCII_EVENTS, WIN_MOUSE_BUTTONS,
            NULL,
        NULL);

    /* Initial messages */
    strcpy(kbd_msg, "Keyboard: key press events");
    strcpy(ptr_msg, "Pointer: pointer movement events");
    strcpy(but_msg, "Button: button press events");

    /* Start event loop */
    xv_main_loop(frame);
}

/*
 * event_proc()
 *      Called when an event is received in the canvas window.
 *      Updates the keyboard, pointer and button message strings
 *      and then calls repaint_proc() to paint them to the window.
 */
void
event_proc(window, event)
Xv_Window window;
Event     *event;
{
    if (event_is_ascii(event))
        sprintf(kbd_msg, "Keyboard: key '%c' %d pressed at %d,%d",
                event_action(event), event_action(event),
                event_x(event), event_y(event));
    else
        switch (event_action(event)) {
            case KBD_USE:
                sprintf(kbd_msg, "Keyboard: got keyboard focus");
                break;
            case KBD_DONE:
                sprintf(kbd_msg, "Keyboard: lost keyboard focus");
                break;
            case LOC_MOVE:
                sprintf(ptr_msg, "Pointer: moved to %d,%d",
                    event_x(event), event_y(event));
                break;
            case LOC_DRAG:
                sprintf(ptr_msg, "Pointer: dragged to %d,%d",
                    event_x(event), event_y(event));
                break;
            case LOC_WINENTER:
                sprintf(ptr_msg, "Pointer: entered window at %d,%d",
```

Example 5-3. The canvas_event.c program (continued)

```
                        event_x(event), event_y(event));
                break;
            case LOC_WINEXIT:
                sprintf(ptr_msg, "Pointer: exited window at %d,%d",
                    event_x(event), event_y(event));
                break;
            case ACTION_SELECT:
            case MS_LEFT:
                sprintf(but_msg, "Button: Select (Left) at %d,%d",
                    event_x(event), event_y(event));
                break;
            case ACTION_ADJUST:
            case MS_MIDDLE:
                sprintf(but_msg, "Button: Adjust (Middle) at %d,%d",
                    event_x(event), event_y(event));
                break;
            case ACTION_MENU:
            case MS_RIGHT:
                sprintf(but_msg, "Button: Menu (Right) at %d,%d",
                    event_x(event), event_y(event));
                break;
            default:
                return;
        }

    /* call repaint proc directly to update messages */
    repaint_proc((Canvas)NULL, window,
        (Display *)xv_get(window, XV_DISPLAY),
        xv_get(window, XV_XID), (Xv_xrectlist *) NULL);
}

/*
 * repaint_proc()
 *      Called to repaint the canvas in response to damage events
 *      and the initial painting of the canvas window.
 *      Displays the keyboard, pointer and button message strings
 *      after erasing the previous messages.
 */
void
repaint_proc(canvas, paint_window, dpy, xwin, xrects)
Canvas          canvas;             /* Ignored */
Xv_Window       paint_window;       /* Ignored */
Display         *dpy;
Window          xwin;
Xv_xrectlist *xrects;               /* Ignored */
{
    GC gc = DefaultGC(dpy, DefaultScreen(dpy));

    XClearWindow(dpy, xwin);
    XDrawString(dpy, xwin, gc, 25, 25, kbd_msg, strlen(kbd_msg));
    XDrawString(dpy, xwin, gc, 25, 50, ptr_msg, strlen(ptr_msg));
    XDrawString(dpy, xwin, gc, 25, 75, but_msg, strlen(but_msg));
}
```

The result produced by Example 5-3 is shown in Figure 5-5.

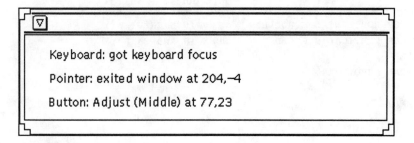

Figure 5-5. A window created with canvas_event.c

5.8 Canvas and Openwin Package Summaries

This section lists the attributes, procedures and macros for the CANVAS and OPENWIN packages. This information is described fully in Appendices A and B.

Table 5-1. Canvas Attributes, Procedures and Macros

Attributes	Procedures and Macros
CANVAS_AUTO_EXPAND	canvas_paint_window()
CANVAS_AUTO_SHRINK	canvas_repaint_proc()
CANVAS_FIXED_IMAGE	canvas_resize_proc()
CANVAS_HEIGHT	CANVAS_EACH_PAINT_WINDOW
CANVAS_MIN_PAINT_HEIGHT	CANVAS_END_EACH
CANVAS_MIN_PAINT_WIDTH	
CANVAS_NO_CLIPPING	
CANVAS_NTH_PAINT_WINDOW	
CANVAS_PAINT_CANVAS_WINDOW	
CANVAS_PAINTWINDOW_ATTRS	
CANVAS_REPAINT_PROC	
CANVAS_RESIZE_PROC	
CANVAS_RETAINED	
CANVAS_VIEW_CANVAS_WINDOW	
CANVAS_VIEW_PAINT_WINDOW	
CANVAS_VIEWABLE_RECT	
CANVAS_WIDTH	
CANVAS_X_PAINT_WINDOW	

Table 5-2. Openwin Attributes, Procedures and Macros

Attributes	Procedures and Macros
OPENWIN_ADJUST_FOR_HORIZONTAL_SCROLLBAR	OPENWIN_EACH_VIEW()
OPENWIN_ADJUST_FOR_VERTICAL_SCROLLBAR	OPENWIN_END_EACH()
OPENWIN_AUTO_CLEAR	
OPENWIN_HORIZONTAL_SCROLLBAR	
OPENWIN_NO_MARGIN	
OPENWIN_NTH_VIEW	
OPENWIN_NVIEWS	
OPENWIN_SELECTED_VIEW	
OPENWIN_SHOW_BORDERS	
OPENWIN_SPLIT	
OPENWIN_SPLIT_DESTROY_PROC	
OPENWIN_SPLIT_DIRECTION	
OPENWIN_SPLIT_INIT_PROC	
OPENWIN_SPLIT_POSITION	
OPENWIN_SPLIT_VIEW	
OPENWIN_SPLIT_VIEW_START	
OPENWIN_VERTICAL_SCROLLBAR	
OPENWIN_VIEW_ATTRS	
OPENWIN_VIEW_CLASS	

6

Handling Input

In This Chapter:

Introduction to Events in XView 107
Classes of Events 108
Registering Events 109
   Specifying X Event Masks 110
   Specifying XView Events 111
The Event Handler 115
The Event Structure 115
Determining the Event 116
   Keyboard Events 117
Interpreting Client Messages 120
   Drag and Drop 120
   Sending and Reading Client Messages 124
Reading Input Directly 125
Sample Program 126

6
Handling Input

In discussing canvases in the previous chapter, we showed how to do some basic event handling in the canvas's paint window. This chapter goes into detail about the content of such events, the breakdown of the Event data structure that describes the event, the different types of input events that can be handled, and the specifics about what gets passed to the program's event handling callback routine. Chapter 19, *The Notifier*, should be reviewed for an in-depth discussion of how to handle events on a somewhat more advanced level. Chapter 19 addresses the event types themselves, how to register which events you want to be notified of, and how to interpret the events you receive.

This chapter discusses the following:

- The design of event handling.
- The breakdown of the Event data structure.
- Registering an event handler and the events you are interested in.
- Interpreting the events your event handler received.
- Sending messages to other windows or clients.
- Explicit reading of events from the server.

6.1 Introduction to Events in XView

Events are generated from several sources, including standard devices such as the keyboard and mouse, special input devices such as graphics tablets, and the window system itself. XView does not directly receive events from the hardware devices; the X server is responsible for managing these events and communicating them to the XView application. The Notifier receives all X events on behalf of the client application and dispatches them to the appropriate callback procedures registered by XView objects.

Because the Notifier multiplexes the input stream between windows, each individual window operates under the illusion that it has the user's full attention. That is, it sees precisely those input events that the user has directed to it. Each window indicates which events it is prepared to handle using *input masks*. An event callback procedure processes the events when they occur. Many windows have default event handlers that are installed internally by certain XView packages. Panels, for example, have a default event notification procedure that is used to identify which panel item received the input. Text subwindows capture events to allow typing and monitor text selection generated by using the mouse. However, some events may result in separate callback procedures being notified as well—repaint and resize events, for example, may have separate callback routines installed.

Applications can send messages to separate windows within the same application or to other applications running under separate processes. The X function XSendEvent() sends client-specified X events to other windows. XClientMessageEvent is one such event that can be sent. XView provides the function xv_send_message() as an interface for sending client messages in this manner.

The X Window System has a full set of events that can be sent to client applications by the server. It is highly recommended that you review Chapter 8, *Events*, in Volume One, *Xlib Programming Manual*, for specifics on the nature of these events.

6.2 Classes of Events

Events are grouped into the following classes:

- Semantic Events

- ASCII Events

- Locator Button Events

- Locator Motion Events

- Function Key Events

- Repaint and Resize Events

- Client Messages

Each of these event types are discussed in Section 6.3, "Registering Events," and Section 6.7, "Interpreting Client Messages." There are separate issues to consider in both cases. However, *semantic* event codes are common to both. We will first address event IDs and semantic events and then move directly on to event registration. After we discuss how to register the events you are interested in, we will discuss how your event handling routine can interpret the events it receives.

Event IDs

Event IDs are integer values that have been assigned somewhat, but not completely, arbitrarily to events that may be generated in X.* Some event IDs represent keyboard events, function key events, window resize and repaint events, and so on. Although both X and XView understand the same events, there is no correlation between the event ID and Xlib's event codes. Thus, keyboard event IDs are *not* key symbols as defined by X's `KeySym` or `XKey-Event.keycode` fields.

Event IDs are helpful when debugging applications; you can stop in event-handling routines and print the value of a particular event ID to identify the specific event type. One helpful hint is that the ASCII event IDs correspond to the ASCII codes generated. That is, if the user presses the *x* key, then the event ID is *x*.

Semantic Events

Also called *action* events, semantic events are used to describe the *meaning* of an event using semantic phrases, so to speak, rather than using the literal event code represented by an event *ID*. That is, the definition of the *macro* describes the value of the event as well as its meaning. When someone presses a key marked HELP on the keyboard, the event ID may represent a large, cryptic numeral such as 65034. However, the semantic code associated with the key event would be `ACTION_HELP`.

There are also cases where the keyboard has been remapped by some applications for other purposes. For example, in OPEN LOOK, the SELECT button defaults to the leftmost physical mouse button, also known as button **one**. Normally this button is activated using the index finger for a right-handed person. A left-handed person who places the mouse on the left may remap the semantics of the leftmost and rightmost buttons (assuming a multibutton mouse). This allows the left-handed user to also use his index finger to activate the SELECT button.

We recommend that you use semantic actions when referring to events for consistency with other applications as well as consistency with different computers.

6.3 Registering Events

Typically, when you specify which events a particular window is interested in, you also specify an event handler for that window. You register an event handler with an XView *window*, not the object with which the window is associated. Specifically, to register an event handler for canvases and panels, you use the *paint window* as in:

---

*This concept is carried over from SunView and is foreign to X.

```
Xv_Window window;
Canvas    canvas;
int       win;

window = (Xv_Window)xv_get(canvas, CANVAS_NTH_PAINT_WINDOW, win);
```

For text subwindows, you use the *view window*:

```
Xv_Window window;
Textsw    textsw;
int       win_no;

window = (Xv_Window)xv_get(textsw, OPENWIN_NTH_VIEW, win_no);
```

Once you have obtained the window, you can install the event handler using the WIN_EVENT_PROC attribute:

```
xv_set(window,
    WIN_EVENT_PROC,      sample_event_proc,
    WIN_CONSUME_EVENTS, WIN_ASCII_EVENTS, WIN_MOUSE_BUTTONS, NULL,
    NULL);
```

The window is of type Xv_Window. The event handler is a function that is called whenever any of the registered events occur in the specified windows. Details about this routine and how to interpret the events delivered to it are discussed later in this chapter, starting with Section 6.4, "The Event Handler."

This section discusses specifically how to register and unregister the events in which you are interested for a particular window. There are several ways to describe events you wish to register. You can specify action (semantic) events, literal events, or event *classes* defined by XView (as shown in the example), or you can use X event masks (familiar to Xlib programmers). Which method you choose for registering events does not affect the function of the event handler; it maintains its function of receiving and understanding events.

6.3.1 Specifying X Event Masks

The simplest and most direct method for people familiar with Xlib programming is to use X event masks.* To register or unregister events using X masks, you can use:

```
WIN_CONSUME_X_EVENT_MASK
WIN_IGNORE_X_EVENT_MASK
```

The value for these attributes is a mask made up of any of the event masks defined in *<X11/X.h>*. Do not confuse event masks with actual event types.

WIN_CONSUME_X_EVENTS appends the specified event mask to the existing event mask for the object. However, to set the event mask explicitly to the specified mask, use WIN_EVENT_MASK. To clear the event mask completely, use:

```
xv_set(window, WIN_X_EVENT_MASK, NoEventMask, NULL);
```

---

*See Volume One, *Xlib Programming Manual*, for a complete discussion on event masks and their implications.

The following code segment demonstrates how a canvas would register interest in the keyboard and mouse buttons:

```
xv_set(window,
    WIN_CONSUME_X_EVENT_MASK, ButtonPressMask | KeyPressMask,
    NULL);
```

Notice that we did not specify `ButtonReleaseMask` or `KeyReleaseMask`. Thus, the event handler is going to receive the down events only.

When you specify event masks with the attribute `WIN_IGNORE_X_EVENT_MASK`, then those events are not delivered to your event handler. You cannot use this attribute to unregister all events and expect that to unregister your event handler. You must set the `WIN_EVENT_PROC` to `NULL` to do that. It is perfectly legal to have no events registered with a window.

6.3.2 Specifying XView Events

XView events (or event *types*) are simply alternate ways to specify events when you register them or interpret them. When using these event types to register events, you are not adding any more functionality than using the Xlib event registration scheme in the previous section. However, XView event types may make it easier to identify more precisely which events you are interested in being notified of.

The header files *<xview/win_input.h>* and *<xview/win_event.h>* have several data types, and most XView event definitions allowing you to register events with windows or the Notifier. There are two methods available to do this: using the `Inputmask` data structure or specifying XView event codes directly.

Although the `Inputmask` method tends to be less elegant than using XView event types, they are necessary in order to use `xv_input_readevent()` and other advanced-usage functions. See Section 6.8, "Reading Input Directly," for details about how the `Inputmask` structure is used.

The attribute `WIN_CONSUME_EVENTS` is used to register events via XView event types. The value for this attribute is a `NULL`-terminated list of the XView events defined in the header files mentioned above. Let's re-examine the example used in the previous section:

```
xv_set(window,
    WIN_EVENT_PROC,      sample_event_proc,
    WIN_CONSUME_EVENTS, WIN_ASCII_EVENTS, WIN_MOUSE_BUTTONS, NULL,
    NULL);
```

The values `WIN_ASCII_EVENTS` and `WIN_MOUSE_BUTTONS` encompass all the ASCII codes from 0 to 127, inclusive, and the mouse button events. The events specified are added to the existing input mask for the window. This does not override what the window had previously; the event mask specified is *appended* to the input mask for that window. To set an explicit event mask, the value `WIN_NO_EVENTS` should be specified first in the list.

```
xv_set(window,
    WIN_EVENT_PROC,        sample_event_proc,
    WIN_CONSUME_EVENTS,
        WIN_NO_EVENTS, WIN_ASCII_EVENTS, WIN_MOUSE_BUTTONS, NULL,
    NULL);
```

All events are cleared at the point in which WIN_NO_EVENTS is given in the list. If it is given in the middle of the list, then the events specified previous to that point are forgotten. If it is the only attribute in the list, then the event mask for the window is cleared. Note that this does not mean that your event handler will receive no events. There are certain events that are sent to your window, and thus to your event handler, whether you want them or not. This is addressed later in this chapter.

You can specify which events to ignore in the same way:

```
xv_set(window,
    WIN_IGNORE_EVENTS,
        WIN_UP_ASCII_EVENTS, LOC_WINENTER, LOC_WINEXIT,
        NULL,
    NULL);
```

Here we are telling the window to ignore the events caused by *releasing* the ASCII keys on the keyboard as well as window-enter and window-exit events. As with WIN_X_ EVENT_MASK, you cannot use WIN_IGNORE_EVENTS to unregister all the events and expect the event handler to be unregistered. It is perfectly legal to have a window that has no events registered with it.

While these attributes take a NULL-terminated list, you can use WIN_CONSUME_EVENT or WIN_IGNORE_EVENT to consume or ignore *one* event. Using these attributes, it is not necessary to specify a list of events.

Mouse Events

The mouse (or *locator*) resides at an (*x,y*) coordinate position in pixels; this position is transformed by XView to the coordinate space of the window receiving an event. You can request mouse motion events by specifying LOC_MOVE or LOC_DRAG. A LOC_MOVE event is reported when the mouse moves, regardless of the state of the locator buttons. If you only want to know about locator motion when a button is down, then enable LOC_DRAG instead of LOC_MOVE. This will greatly reduce the number of motion events that your application has to process. If you have both specified, you will only receive one event or the other; you will never receive one followed by the other.

Even if you do not request move or drag events, you may still monitor when the mouse moves in and out of windows by specifying LOC_WINENTER and LOC_WINEXIT. In the case of LOC_WINENTER, the window installs its colormap into the server, and for LOC_WINEXIT, the window's colormap is uninstalled. If you have registered the colormap notify event (WIN_COLORMAP_NOTIFY), then you will receive the appropriate events when you enter and leave a window.

Each button that is associated with the mouse is assigned an event code; the *i-th* button is assigned the code BUT(i). Thus, the event codes MS_LEFT, MS_MIDDLE, and MS_RIGHT correspond to BUT(1), BUT(2), and BUT(3). These are actual key codes, not semantic codes. You can specify setting the buttons explicitly (as shown here) or as a group (`WIN_MOUSE_BUTTONS`) or as semantic events using `ACTION_SELECT`, `ACTION_ADJUST` and `ACTION_MENU`.

Keyboard Events

In order to be notified of keyboard events, you must specify any one of several XView event types depending on which event you want. Unlike the X event mask `KeyPressMask`, which generates events for all keys on the keyboard, including function keys, XView allows you to be more specific about which keyboard events you are interested in while not having to specify explicit keys.

The following list contains input event descriptors that may be used:

`WIN_ASCII_EVENTS`	Enable ASCII keycodes—these are events that fall between 0 and 127 in the ASCII character set. Using this attribute specifies up events as well as down events.
`WIN_UP_ASCII_EVENTS`	This is used mostly by `WIN_IGNORE_EVENTS` to turn off receiving the release event that usually follows a key press.
`WIN_TOP_KEYS`	This enables notification when any of the function keys on the *top* of the keyboard are specified. This is highly keyboard dependent. XView provides for up to 15 keys in this location. Keys that are labeled differently might produce different key codes.
`WIN_LEFT_KEYS`	This enables notification when any of the function keys on the *left* side of the keyboard are specified. There are also action events associated with each key on the left side of the keyboard. Again, XView provides for 15 keys and your mileage may vary.
`WIN_RIGHT_KEYS`	This enables notification when any of the function keys on the *right* of the keyboard are used. Typically, these include the arrow keys for cursor movement in some applications (like text editors).
`WIN_META_EVENTS`	This enables notification when the *meta* key(s) goes down.
`WIN_UP_META_EVENTS`	To be used with `WIN_IGNORE_EVENT` to ignore key releases.
`WIN_UP_EVENTS`	This is a general facility for ignoring all release events from mouse buttons and keyboard keys.

The XView event types `KBD_USE` and `KBD_DONE` can be specified to notify you when your window obtains the keyboard focus. OPEN LOOK specifies the click-to-type method for keyboard focus, so the you may not get keyboard focus just because the mouse entered a window. The user can specify how keyboard focus should work without letting the application know about it. When a window gets keyboard focus and the window's event mask has `KBD_USE` set, then the window's event procedure is called.

Resize and Repaint Events

When the size of a window is changed (either by the user or programmatically), a WIN_RESIZE event is generated to give the client a chance to adjust any relevant internal state to the new window size. You should *not* repaint the window when receiving a resize event. You will receive a separate WIN_REPAINT event when a portion of the window needs to be repainted.

If you are using a canvas subwindow, you will not need to track resize and repaint events directly. The CANVAS package receives these events, computes the new window dimensions or the precise area requiring repainting, and calls your resize or repaint procedures directly. See Chapter 5, *Canvases and Openwin*, for more details.

NOTE

You will get WIN_REPAINT and WIN_RESIZE events sent to your event handler routine no matter what. These events cannot be prevented from being delivered to your event handler. However, we recommend that you install repaint and resize handling routines using CANVAS_REPAINT_PROC and CANVAS_RESIZE_PROC rather than acting on these events from the event handler

As pointed out in Chapter 5, *Canvases and Openwin*, there may be a WIN_REPAINT event generated for each region of a window that gets exposed. However, you can set whether or not all those exposure events are collapsed into one expose event specifying a region that covers the entire exposed area. The attribute WIN_COLLAPSE_EXPOSURES can be set to TRUE (the default) or FALSE to prevent multiple expose events.

You get graphics exposure events whenever you draw into a window using a GC whose graphics_exposures field set to True. This is another event that you cannot ignore. How you choose to deal with it is specific to your application. If you do not wish to receive this event, you should be sure to set the value to False.

Client Messages

Client messages are events that cannot be ignored by your event handler. Typically, these are messages that are used to implement a predefined protocol between your application and other applications that are familiar with the protocol. Because client messages cannot be ignored, we do not address the issue of client messages in this section. Read Section 6.7, "Interpreting Client Messages," for more information on how to interpret these events.

6.4 The Event Handler

When one of the events in which you have expressed interest occurs, your event handler is called. The form of this routine is:

```
    void
    sample_event_proc(window, event, arg)
        Xv_Window    window;
        Event        *event;
        Notfiy_arg   arg;
```

The arguments to the routine are the window the event occurred in, a pointer to a data structure describing information about the event itself and an optional argument supplied by the XView package responsible for the function being called.*

6.5 The Event Structure

Events that are generated are passed to event handling procedures by the Notifier as `Event` pointers (type `Event *`). This structure is declared in <xview/win_input.h>:

```
typedef struct   inputevent {
    short            ie_code;            /* input code */
    short            ie_flags;
    short            ie_shiftmask;       /* input code shift state */
    short            ie_locx, ie_locy;   /* mouse position */
    struct timeval   ie_time;            /* time of event */
    short            action;             /* keymapped ie_code */
    Xv_object        ie_win;             /* window receiving event */
    char             *ie_string;         /* keycode binding string */
    XEvent           *ie_xevent;         /* actual XEvent struct */
} Event;
```

The `Event` data structure contains all the information about the event. The fields are broken down as follows:

ie_code	Actual XView event ID, as defined in <xview/win_event.h> and <xview/win_input.h>† Event codes can take on any value in the range 0 through 65535. The values are useful when debugging.
ie_flags	Indicates whether the event was an up- or down-event, if applicable. A down-event occurs when a mouse button or keyboard key goes down. There must be a corresponding up-event, although the client may choose to ignore up events.
ie_shiftmask	If a Shift key, control key and/or mouse button was down when the event occurred, this mask will have the appropriate bits set.

---

*This parameter is currently unused by XView packages but is available for new or extensions to XView packages or with advanced Notifier usage. See Section 19.6.2, "Posting with an Argument."

†<xview/panel.h> also has a couple of event definitions, but they are not widely used. See Chapter 7, *Panels*, for details.

`ie_locx, ie_locy`	*x,y* coordinates of the position of the locator (mouse) relative to the window in which the event occurred.
`ie_time`	The time of the event.
`action`	Semantic code representing predefined actions specific to the window manager or OPEN LOOK.
`ie_win`	Window in which the event took place.
`ie_string`	String in which a keycode (found in `ie_code`) is bound to using `XRebindKeysym()`.
`ie_xevent`	The actual event structure generated by X. This event structure arrives untouched by XView for events generated by the server.

6.6 Determining the Event

In the `Event` structure, there is a pointer to the `XEvent` structure that was delivered by the X server as a direct result of the event that it describes. This section discusses how to interpret the event based on information in the `Event` structure only; it does not address the `XEvent` structure.

The header files *<xview/win_input.h>* and *<xview/win_event.h>* contain many macros that should be used rather than referencing fields in the `Event` data structure. If the structure is modified in the future, then the macros will be modified to support the changes and your code will not have to change. For example, to get the window in which the event took place, you should not use (assume *event* is of type `Event *`):

```
window = event->ie_win;
```

Instead you should use:

```
window = event_window(event);
```

To determine the actual event ID, you could use:

```
event_id(event)
```

This macro returns the actual event ID that took place, such as `MS_LEFT` to indicate the left mouse button. However, as discussed earlier, we recommend that you use the semantic action events provided by the macro:

```
event_action(event)
```

In the case where the user selected the left mouse button, `event_action` would return `ACTION_SELECT`. The two values do not map to the same thing; consider the case where left-handed users have remapped the mouse settings. On the other hand, if there is no action associated with an event, `event_action()` is set to `event_id()`. For example, consider when the letter *a* is pressed or when the `Expose` event is generated.

Event States

When a mouse button or keyboard event occurs, the event may be the result of a button or key being released or pressed. The way to determine this state from a particular event is to use one of these two macros:

```
event_is_up(event)
event_is_down(event)
```

Modifier Keys

Modifier keys include the left and right Shift keys, the Control key, and the Meta key. The locations of these keys on the user's keyboard are dependent on the make and model of your keyboard. The functions of modifier keys are to modify particular keyboard or mouse states. For example, the Shift key, when modifying the *a* key, results in the *A* key.

Unless you have explicitly requested to be notified of *modifier* key events, you will not be informed when their state changes (e.g., when a user pressed or releases one of the keys). You probably do not need to know this anyway. Instead, you only need to know the state of the key at the time you are evaluating another event. In this case, you can use any of the following macros:

```
event_shift_is_down(event)
event_ctrl_is_down(event)
event_meta_is_down(event)
```

6.6.1 Keyboard Events

When XView translates keyboard events into `Event` codes, it does translation of the key depending on the state of the modifier keys. For example, when the user types Shift-A, intending to type a capital-A, then the event ID (that is, `event->ie_code`) is *A*. You do not need to use `event_shift_is_down` to translate the key to the upper case.*

In XView, you can use the following macro to determine if an event is an ASCII key:

```
event_is_ascii(event)
```

This result does not tell you if you have a *printable* character. Depending on the font you are using, you may not be able to print anything with this event code. However, you can use any of the macros in *<ctype.h>* to determine whether the character is printable, a control character, a digit, a punctuation mark, and so on. Remember, this works because you are using the *already-translated* version of the event code.

The macro, `event_string()` can be used to determine the string value associated with the event ID. This value the result of a call to `XLookupString()`. For normal ASCII event codes, `event_string()` will return a string value of the same key. However, the key (ASCII or not) could be rebound to a string using `XRebindKeysym()`:

---

*This is in contrast to the value of `XKeyEvent.keycode` used by Xlib.

```
Display *dpy = (Display *)xv_get(frame, XV_DISPLAY);
char *newstring = "Nine";

XRebindKeysym(dpy, XK_9, 0, 0, newstring, strlen(newstring));
```

Here, the 9 key is rebound to generate the string "Nine" whenever it is pressed. The following macro determines whether or not a string is associated with the event:

```
event_is_string(event)
```

In the event callback, the following code could be used:

```
    . . .
    if (event_is_string(event))
        printf("string = %s\n", event_string(event));
    . . .
```

Function keys differ from keyboard to keyboard, and the default key mappings for your server are configurable (at the time you build your server). However, XView has provisions for keyboards that are sectioned off into four sets of fifteen function keys: left, top, right and bottom keys. To determine which set of keys a particular event is associated with, you can use the following macros:

```
event_is_key_left(event)
event_is_key_right(event)
event_is_key_top(event)
event_is_key_bottom(event)
```

To determine which function set a particular function key belongs to, use:

```
KEY_TOP(key)
KEY_LEFT(key)
KEY_RIGHT(key)
KEY_BOTTOM(key)
```

Here, you do not pass the event, you pass the event *ID*. Thus, to test to see if a particular event were the fifth function key in the top row of keys, you would use:

```
    if (event_is_key_top(event) && event_id(event) == KEY_TOP(5))
        /* process the fifth top-function key. */
```

Notice that we are using event_id() rather than event_action(). The reason for this is that some function keys are mapped to particular semantic actions and we wanted to be sure that we knew the user hit the *fifth* function key on the top row. Had we used event_action() instead, the equality test may have failed.

Mouse Events

XView supports a locator device (a mouse) with up to ten buttons on it. This device may generate various different types of events, such as:

Motion events   These events are generated whenever the mouse moves.

Drag events   These events result in mouse movement when any of the mouse buttons are down.

Button events   These events are generated whenever the state of a mouse button changes
                 (e.g., when a button goes up or down).

The following macros determine the state of particular buttons for a three-button mouse (the
most common type).

```
event_is_button(event)
event_left_is_down(event)
event_middle_is_down(event)
event_right_is_down(event)
event_button_is_down(event)
```

Note that this does not indicate an exclusive button state; that is, if event_right_is_down
returns TRUE, this does not exclude the left button being down, too.

You can determine the actual mouse button similar to how you determine a function key
position. You pass the *ID* of the event to:

```
BUT(i)
```

To determine whether the second mouse button was down, you could use:

```
if (event_is_down(event) && event_id(event) == BUT(2))
    /* process button-2 event handling */
```

Again, we recommend that rather than determining the state of a particular mouse button,
you use the semantic codes:

```
if (event_is_down(event) && event_action(event) == ACTION_ADJUST)
    /* process "adjust" event handling */
```

Keyboard Focus

One way for the application to automatically direct keyboard focus to a particular window is
to use win_set_kbd_focus(). The calling parameters are the window and the XID of the
window to get the focus. For example, if a window gets an event LOC_WINENTER, you can
grab the keyboard focus automatically:

```
my_event_proc(window, event)
Xv_Window   window;
Event       *event;
{
    switch (event_id(event)) {
        . . .
        case LOC_WINENTER :
            win_set_kbd_focus(window, xv_get(window, XV_XID));
            break;
        . . .
    }
}
```

win_set_kbd_focus() generates a KBD_USE event for the window that is getting the
focus and a WIN_KBD_DONE event for the window that lost its focus. The window that lost
its focus must have WIN_KBD_DONE specified in its event mask to be notified.

Another way to grab keyboard focus for a window is to grab *all* the input for that window. This can be accomplished in various ways including the use of the FULLSCREEN package described in Chapter 15, *Nonvisual Objects*. However, perhaps a much more convenient method is to use the WIN_GRAB_ALL_INPUT attribute. Setting this attribute to TRUE causes a grab, which forces all input to be directed to that window. Setting to FALSE releases the grab.

This is useful when you want to display a dialog box with panel items and confirmation or cancel buttons indicating that the user must respond to a particular request before interacting with any other portion of the application. In this case, you should set the grab on the paint window of a panel. Be sure to reset this attribute once its no longer needed. Also, be careful that you code the segment of the program that uses the grab carefully or you might generate a grab you cannot get out of.

6.7 Interpreting Client Messages

Client messages may be delivered to your event handler for two reasons.

First, OPEN LOOK has a mechanism known as *drag-and-drop*, which allows the user to move or copy text selections to other windows. In this scenario, the user selects text in a text subwindow and then uses the SELECT button to *drag* it to another location and *drop* it into a new window. Similarly, for cut-and-paste operations, a client message is sent to the recipient window informing it that data is waiting in the *shelf* selection.

For these cases, the Notifier interposes your event handler and replaces the client message event with an action event (described later). From the event handler's point of view, the action describes the type of drop-and-drag action taken or cut-and-paste operations.

Second, your event handler may receive client messages if the event was sent by another source using XSendEvent() or xv_send_message(). This implies that the sender of the message has loaded some arbitrary information into client-message format and has sent it to you directly. In this case, the sender assumes you know how to interpret the information in the message.

Let's consider the OPEN LOOK use of client messages first.

6.7.1 Drag and Drop

A drag-and-drop operation occurs when the user grabs the text selection using the SELECT mouse button, drags it somewhere (perhaps another window or application), and then drops it onto that window. The window onto which the selection has been dropped receives an event (XClientMessage) informing it that data intended for that window is available in the primary selection. The destination window can use the contents of the selection as input data and the selection should be deleted from the original window. Thus, the selection appears to have *moved*.

In this scenario, the receiving window's event handler is called with the `event_action(event)` set to `ACTION_ DRAG_MOVE`. Your event handler is responsible for getting the primary selection and telling the selection holder to delete the selected text from its window (as if the user had moved it to the new location).

Rather than moving the text selection, the user may wish to *copy* it to another window. In this case, the same scenario applies as described above, except that the user has the Control key down at the time the selection was grabbed. After dragging, and when the button is released, the event handler is called with `event_action(event)` set to `ACTION_DRAG_COPY`. The event handler does the same thing except it does not tell the holder of the selection to delete the selected text from its window.

Drag and Load

OPEN LOOK's *file manager* application displays a graphical layout of files and directories on the file system. The user can select and drag an icon (representing a file or directory) and drop it onto a window of another application in the same manner as described for drag and drop. However, when using the file manager, the intent is to have the application act on that file as input. A mail program, for example, might be able to load a file as a mail folder, or a graphics application might interpret that file as if it had page description commands such as PostScript. Thus, the application *loads* the file.

In this case, *file manager*, or any other application that might want to provide similar functionality, would send the action event `ACTION_DRAG_LOAD`. When your event handler receives this action event, it gets the filename from the primary selection and attempts to open that file and process it. It should be sure to do proper error checking on parsing the given file as the user is not restricted as to which file he drops on your window.

CAUTION

The filename specified may not be accessible because the *file manager* application may be running on a different machine than the application that received the event. Thus, this interface may change in the future to actually contain the entire file in the selection.

Example 6-1 shows how drag-and-drop should be handled in an event handler. The program builds a base frame, a canvas and a text subwindow. When running the program, make a selection in the text subwindow and drag it over into the canvas using the methods mentioned earlier. The canvas simply displays the action received and the contents of the selection.

Example 6-1. The drag_n_drop.c program

```
/*
 * drag_n_drop.c -- demonstrate how to handle drag and drop usage in
 * OPEN LOOK. Create a base frame, canvas and text subwindow.  Install
 * an event handler for the canvas to interpret drag-and-drop actions.
 * The text subwindow is there for convenience, but you can drag and
 * drop from anywhere on the screen.  The "file manager" application
 * can be used to generate the ACTION_DRAG_LOAD event/action.  The user
 * can select text and then "drag" the selection on top of the canvas
```

Example 6-1. The drag_n_drop.c program (continued)

```
 * window.  When this happens, the canvas's callback routine is called
 * and the event_action(event) will be set accordingly.
 */
#include <X11/Xlib.h>
#include <xview/xview.h>
#include <xview/canvas.h>
#include <xview/textsw.h>
#include <xview/seln.h>

main(argc, argv)
int      argc;
char     *argv[];
{
    Frame        frame;
    Canvas       canvas;
    void         event_handler();

    xv_init(XV_INIT_ARGS, argc, argv, NULL);

    frame = (Frame)xv_create(NULL, FRAME, NULL);
    canvas = (Canvas)xv_create(frame, CANVAS,
        XV_WIDTH,   300,
        XV_HEIGHT,  300,
        NULL);
    xv_set(canvas_paint_window(canvas),
        WIN_EVENT_PROC, event_handler,
        NULL);
    (void) xv_create(frame, TEXTSW,
        TEXTSW_CONTENTS,
            "This is a test of the emergency broadcasting system.",
        XV_HEIGHT, 300,
        XV_WIDTH,  300,
        NULL);
    window_fit(frame);

    xv_main_loop(frame);
}
/*
 * handle the drag and drop actions.  Also handle the ACTION_PASTE
 * event since it is very similar.  The action specifies how the
 * event was generated.  In all drag-and-drop cases, the contents
 * of the selection is held in the primary selection.  Use the
 * selection service routines to extract the information.
 */
void
event_handler(window, event, arg)
Xv_Window       window;
Event           *event;
Notify_arg      arg;
{
    Display *dpy = (Display *)xv_get(window, XV_DISPLAY);
    char       msg[128];

    /* not interested in action-up events */
    if (event_is_up(event))
        return;
    switch (event_action(event)) {
```

Example 6-1. The drag_n_drop.c program (continued)

```
        case ACTION_PASTE:
        case ACTION_DRAG_LOAD:
        case ACTION_DRAG_COPY:
        case ACTION_DRAG_MOVE: {
            Seln_holder     holder;
            Seln_request    *result;
            Seln_rank       selection;
            char            *data;
            int             read_only;

            /*
             * ACTION_PASTE is generated by hitting L8, or the "paste"
             * key on the left side of the keyboard.  This assumes you
             * have cut (L10) or copied (L6) a selection first.
             */

            if (event_action(event) == ACTION_PASTE) {
                strcpy(msg, "paste from shelf: ");
                selection = SELN_SHELF;
            } else {
                sprintf(msg, "drag and drop (%s): ",
                    event_action(event) == ACTION_DRAG_MOVE ? "move" :
                    event_action(event) == ACTION_DRAG_LOAD ? "load" : "copy");
                selection = SELN_PRIMARY;
            }
            holder = seln_inquire(selection);
            result = seln_ask(&holder,
                SELN_REQ_IS_READONLY,     NULL,
                SELN_REQ_CONTENTS_ASCII, NULL,
                NULL);
            data = result->data;
            data += sizeof(Seln_attribute);

            /* testing read-only is only important if the selection
             * came from a textsw.  If so, then we need to know if
             * it is read-only to head off a drag-move since we won't
             * be able to delete the selection from that window.
             * Note, there is no way to determine the type of the xview
             * object that is holding the selection! :-(
             */

            if ((read_only = *(int *) data) == TRUE &&
                event_action(event) == ACTION_DRAG_MOVE)
                /* can't "move" text from a read-only window. use copy */
                return;
            data += sizeof(int) + sizeof(SELN_REQ_CONTENTS_ASCII);
            strcat(msg, data);
            if (event_action(event) == ACTION_DRAG_MOVE)
                /* ask holder to delete its selection for drag moves */
                seln_ask(&holder, SELN_REQ_DELETE, NULL, NULL);
            break;
        }
        default :
            /* we could go on and on with the above cases ... */
            return;
    }
    XClearWindow(dpy, xv_get(window, XV_XID));
```

Example 6-1. The drag_n_drop.c program (continued)

```
    XDrawString(dpy, xv_get(window, XV_XID),
        DefaultGC(dpy, DefaultScreen(dpy)), 20, 20, msg, strlen(msg));
}
```

6.7.2 Sending and Reading Client Messages

xv_send_message() is used to send client messages to other windows. This is the way that the file manager and the text subwindow implement their drag-and-drop features. When the user performs the correct sequence of events, the applications load the primary selection with the appropriate text and then call xv_send_message() to deliver the event. As described in the previous section, the Notifier handles this case automatically. However, for other uses (specific to the application's needs), regular client messages can still be exchanged using the same function, xv_send_message().

The form for this function is:

```
    Xv_private int
    xv_send_message(window, addressee, msg_type, format, data, len)
        Xv_object       window;
        Xv_opaque       addressee;
        char            *msg_type;
        int             format;
        Xv_opaque       *data;
        int             len;
```

The function sends the message encoded in data to the addressee window. If the addressee parameter is an X window, then the message is sent to that window. Otherwise, the addressee may be either PointerWindow or InputFocus to correspond to the window under wherever the pointer happens to be lying or the window which happens to have the current focus. This is rather dependent on whether the user has click-to-type or focus-follows-mouse mode in the window manager.

The window parameter is an XView window/object from which the event is being sent. This is only used to extract the Display *. The format may be 8, 16, or 32. The value 8 is typically used to represent string values. len is the strlen() of the data.

The actual XEvent that is generated is XClientMessageEvent. When the Notifier detects the event, before passing it onto your event handler, it checks to see if the message content represents a drag-and-drop operation. If so, then the event action is set to the appropriate action. The XEvent structure's ie_xevent field remains unchanged.

If the client message is not a drag-and-drop operation, then you are responsible for deciphering the message. Clearly, this is something you have to be expecting, or there is no way to tell what to do with the information. Thus, you can create your own protocol between clients. You can determine the content of the message using xv_get() and the attributes:

```
    WIN_CLIENT_MESSAGE_DATA
    WIN_CLIENT_MESSAGE_TYPE
    WIN_CLIENT_MESSAGE_FORMAT
```

These attributes map directly to the XClientMessageEvent data structure in <X11/Xlib.h>.

Therefore, you could reference the appropriate fields in the `ie_xevent` pointer from the `Event` structure passed to the callback function. Using the type, format and data of the client message, you can read the message content. See Volume One, *Xlib Programming Manual*, for more information about unwrapping a client message.

6.8 Reading Input Directly

You can read input *immediately* using `xv_input_readevent()`. The function, which returns the window associated with the event read, takes the form:

```
Xv_object
xv_input_readevent(window, event, block, type, im)
    Xv_object      window;
    Event          *event;
    int            block, type;
    Inputmask      *im;
```

The `window` parameter identifies the window you want to read the events from. If `NULL`, `XNextEvent()` is called and the function returns the window that received the next event. In this case, you should probably have a server grab for the window from which you are reading the event. Otherwise, you will have to propagate the received event to the appropriate window later.

The `event` parameter is a pointer to an `Event` type that is filled in when the function returns. The `block` parameter indicates whether or not the function should wait if there are no events pending to be read. If `block` is `FALSE` and there are no events, the function returns immediately without having read an event.

The `type` parameter tells whether to use the input mask already set in the window or whether to use the input mask specified by the `im` parameter. The `Inputmask` is declared in *<xview/win_input.h>*:

```
typedef  struct inputmask {
    short      im_flags;
    char       im_keycode[IM_MASKSIZE];
} Inputmask;
```

The structure consists of a input code array and flags that indicate those user actions to be placed in the input queue. The following macro should be used to initialize the mask:

```
event_init(im)
```

The following macros are used to manipulate XView event codes in an `Inputmask`:

```
win_setinputcodebit(im, code)
win_unsetinputcodebit(im, code)
```

Here, `code` is an XView code as described earlier. The `flags` field may be set to any of the following bits:

IM_NEGEVENT   Send input negative events (release, or "up," events), too. This includes all keyboard keys and mouse buttons.

IM_ASCII   Enable ASCII codes 0 through 127—equivalent to `WIN_ASCII_EVENTS`.

IM_META   Enable META codes 128 through 255—equivalent to WIN_META_EVENTS.

IM_NEGASCII   Enable release, or "up," ASCII codes 0 through 127—this is more specific than IM_NEGEVENT above. This is also primarily used to unset the code bits once ASCII bits have been set.

IM_NEGMETA   Enable release, or "up," META codes 128 through 255—used to unset these code bits.

IM_TOP   Enable TOP function keys.

IM_NEGTOP   Enable release events for TOP function keys.

With these macros, we set the Inputmask that is passed to xv_read_inputevent(). As it turns out, this method can also be used to set the input mask for regular windows. This is not the recommended method for providing the input mask, but it can be done by specifying the attribute WIN_INPUT_MASK:

```
Inputmask im;

win_setinputcodebit(im, WIN_MOUSE_BUTTONS);
win_setinputcodebit(im, WIN_ASCII_EVENTS);
im.im_flags &~ IN_NEGEVENTS;

xv_set(window, WIN_INPUT_MASK, &im, NULL);
```

Similarly, you can get the input mask in the same way:

```
Inputmask *im;

im = (Inputmask *)xv_get(window, WIN_INPUT_MASK);
```

6.9 Sample Program

This section provides a sample program that demonstrates most of what has been discussed in this chapter. In Example 6-2, the canvas window where the events occur may be split into several views. Each new view handles its own events and therefore handles its own graphic rendering into its paint window.

The intent is for the user to split the views several times and move the mouse between the views. Each view prints the events it receives in its own window at the the upper-right corner. New views created from a split view may not be positioned correctly to see the text describing the events. It is not possible to programmatically scroll individual views to arbitrary locations, so the user is required to do this manually.

Pay careful attention to which window receives events so as to get a feeling for how the keyboard focus is handled. In some cases, the keyboard focus does not follow the mouse—a particular view may continue to receive keyboard focus even though the mouse is no longer in that subwindow. Usually, selecting the SELECT mouse button forces the focus to be directed to that view window.

Example 6-2. The canvas_input.c program

```c
/*
 * canvas_input.c --
 * Display a canvas whose views may be split repeatedly.  The event
 * handler is installed for each view, so events are displayed in
 * each paint window.
 */
#include <xview/xview.h>
#include <xview/canvas.h>
#include <xview/scrollbar.h>
#include <xview/xv_xrect.h>

Canvas   canvas;
Frame    frame;
char     msg[128];
void     init_split(), my_event_proc(), my_repaint_proc();

main(argc,argv)
int      argc;
char     *argv[];
{
    /*
     * Initialize, create base frame (with footers) and create canvas.
     */
    xv_init(XV_INIT_ARGS, argc, argv, NULL);
    frame = (Frame)xv_create(NULL,FRAME,
        FRAME_LABEL,             "Split View Windows.",
        FRAME_SHOW_FOOTER,       TRUE,
        NULL);
    canvas = (Canvas)xv_create(frame,CANVAS,
        CANVAS_X_PAINT_WINDOW,   TRUE,
        OPENWIN_SPLIT,
            OPENWIN_SPLIT_INIT_PROC,    init_split,
            NULL,
        CANVAS_REPAINT_PROC,     my_repaint_proc,
        NULL);

    (void) xv_create(canvas, SCROLLBAR,
        SCROLLBAR_SPLITTABLE,    TRUE,
        SCROLLBAR_DIRECTION,     SCROLLBAR_VERTICAL,
        NULL);
    (void) xv_create(canvas, SCROLLBAR,
        SCROLLBAR_SPLITTABLE,    TRUE,
        SCROLLBAR_DIRECTION,     SCROLLBAR_HORIZONTAL,
        NULL);

    /*
     * Set input mask
     */
    xv_set(canvas_paint_window(canvas),
        WIN_CONSUME_EVENTS,
            WIN_NO_EVENTS, WIN_ASCII_EVENTS, KBD_USE, KBD_DONE,
            LOC_DRAG, LOC_WINENTER, LOC_WINEXIT, WIN_MOUSE_BUTTONS,
            NULL,
        WIN_EVENT_PROC, my_event_proc,
        NULL);

    xv_main_loop(frame);
}
```

Example 6-2. The canvas_input.c program (continued)

```
/*
 * when a viewport is split, this routine is called.
 */
void
init_split(splitview, newview, pos)
Xv_Window splitview, newview;
int pos;
{
    Xv_Window    view;
    int          i = 0;

    /*
     * Determine view # from the new view and set its scrollbar to 0,0
     */
    OPENWIN_EACH_VIEW(canvas, view)
        if (view == splitview) {
            /* identify the view # of the view the user just split. */
            sprintf(msg, "Split view #%d", i+1);
            xv_set(frame, FRAME_LEFT_FOOTER, msg, NULL);
        } else if (view == newview) {
            xv_set(xv_get(canvas, OPENWIN_VERTICAL_SCROLLBAR, view),
                SCROLLBAR_VIEW_START, 0,
                NULL);
            xv_set(xv_get(canvas, OPENWIN_HORIZONTAL_SCROLLBAR, view),
                SCROLLBAR_VIEW_START, 0,
                NULL);
        }
        i++;
    OPENWIN_END_EACH
    sprintf(msg, "Total views: %d", i);
    xv_set(frame, FRAME_RIGHT_FOOTER, msg, NULL);
}

/*
 * Called when an event is received in an arbitrary paint window.
 */
void
my_event_proc(window, event, arg)
Xv_Window       window;
Event           *event;
Notify_arg      arg;
{
    register char *p = msg;

    *p = 0;

    /* test to see if a function key has been hit */
    if (event_is_key_left(event))
        sprintf(p, "(L%d) ", event_id(event) - KEY_LEFTFIRST + 1);
    else if (event_is_key_top(event))
        sprintf(p, "(T%d) ", event_id(event) - KEY_TOPFIRST + 1);
    else if (event_is_key_right(event))
        sprintf(p, "(R%d) ", event_id(event) - KEY_RIGHTFIRST + 1);
    else if (event_id(event) == KEY_BOTTOMLEFT)
        strcpy(p, "bottom left ");
    else if (event_id(event) == KEY_BOTTOMRIGHT)
        strcpy(p, "bottom left ");
```

Example 6-2. The canvas_input.c program (continued)

```
    p += strlen(p);

    if (event_is_ascii(event)) {
        /*
         * note that shift modifier is reflected in the event code by
         * virtue of the char printed is upper/lower case.
         */
        sprintf(p, "Keyboard: key '%c' (%d) %s at %d,%d",
            event_action(event), event_action(event),
            event_is_down(event)? "pressed" : "released",
            event_x(event), event_y(event));
    } else switch (event_action(event)) {
        case ACTION_CLOSE :
            xv_set(frame, FRAME_CLOSED, TRUE, NULL);
            break;
        case ACTION_OPEN :
            strcpy(p, "frame opened up");
            break;
        case ACTION_HELP :
            strcpy(p, "Help (action ignored)");
            break;
        case ACTION_SELECT :
            sprintf(p, "Button: Select (Left) %s at %d,%d",
                event_is_down(event)? "pressed" : "released",
                event_x(event), event_y(event));
            break;
        case ACTION_ADJUST :
            sprintf(p, "Button: Adjust (Middle) %s at %d,%d",
                event_is_down(event)? "pressed" : "released",
                event_x(event), event_y(event));
            break;
        case ACTION_MENU :
            sprintf(p, "Button: Menu (Right) %s at %d,%d",
                event_is_down(event)? "pressed" : "released",
                event_x(event), event_y(event));
            break;
        case SHIFT_RIGHT :
            sprintf(p, "Keyboard: right shift %s",
                event_is_down(event)? "pressed" : "released");
            break;
        case SHIFT_LEFT :
            sprintf(p, "Keyboard: left shift %s",
                event_is_down(event)? "pressed" : "released");
            break;
        case SHIFT_LEFTCTRL : case SHIFT_RIGHTCTRL :
            sprintf(p, "Keyboard: control key %s",
                event_is_down(event)? "pressed" : "released");
            break;
        case SHIFT_META :
            sprintf(p, "Keyboard: meta key %s",
                event_is_down(event)? "pressed" : "released");
            break;
        case SHIFT_ALT :
            sprintf(p, "Keyboard: alt key %s",
                event_is_down(event)? "pressed" : "released");
            break;
```

Handling
Input

Example 6-2. The canvas_input.c program (continued)

```
        case KBD_USE:
            sprintf(p, "Keyboard: got keyboard focus");
            break;
        case KBD_DONE:
            sprintf(p, "Keyboard: lost keyboard focus");
            break;
        case LOC_MOVE:
            sprintf(p, "Pointer: moved to %d,%d",
                    event_x(event),event_y(event));
            break;
        case LOC_DRAG:
            sprintf(p, "Pointer: dragged to %d,%d",
                    event_x(event), event_y(event));
            break;
        case LOC_WINENTER:
            win_set_kbd_focus(window, xv_get(window, XV_XID));
            sprintf(p, "Pointer: entered window at %d,%d",
                    event_x(event), event_y(event));
            break;
        case LOC_WINEXIT:
            sprintf(p, "Pointer: exited window at %d,%d",
                    event_x(event), event_y(event));
            break;
        case WIN_RESIZE :
        case WIN_REPAINT :
            return;
        default : ;
            /* There are too many ACTION events to trap -- ignore the
             * ones we're not interested in.
             */
    }

    my_repaint_proc(canvas, window,
        xv_get(canvas, XV_DISPLAY), xv_get(window, XV_XID), NULL);
}

/*
 * my_repaint_proc()
 *      Called to repaint the canvas in response to damage events
 *      and the initial painting of the canvas window.
 *      Displays the keyboard, pointer and button message strings
 *      after erasing the previous messages.
 */
void
my_repaint_proc(canvas, pw, dpy, xwin, xrects)
Canvas          canvas;
Xv_Window       pw;
Display         *dpy;
Window          xwin;
Xv_xrectlist    *xrects;
{
    char        win_num[16];
    Xv_Window   w;
    int         i = 0;
    GC          gc = DefaultGC(dpy, DefaultScreen(dpy));

    /*
```

Example 6-2. The canvas_input.c program (continued)

```
    * Determine which paint window we're writing in.
    */
CANVAS_EACH_PAINT_WINDOW(canvas, w)
    if (w == pw)
        break;
    i++;
CANVAS_END_EACH
sprintf(win_num, "(Window #%d) ", i+1);

XClearWindow(dpy, xwin);
XDrawString(dpy, xwin, gc, 25, 25, win_num, strlen(win_num));
XDrawString(dpy, xwin, gc, 25, 45, msg, strlen(msg));
}
```

This sample program initializes XView and creates a frame. It then creates a canvas with two scrollbars attached to it. Chapter 5, *Canvases and Openwin*, addresses how to attach scrollbars to a canvas. The canvas installs a callback routine that will be called when its views are split. This routine installs the existing event masks and callback routine in the new view's paint window. Remember, this is necessary because new windows need to be initialized by the application.

The callback routine my_event_proc() handles all events for all the windows in the program. It determines which event has taken place and constructs a descriptive message identifying the event. It then calls the repaint routine to display the message in the window in which the event occurred. Note that the repaint callback routine may be called by the application—it is not a function reserved for the window system to call exclusively. In this case, the graphics is limited to calling XDrawString() to display text.

7

Panels

In This Chapter:

Creating a Panel 137
Creating Panel Items 138
Panel Layout 139
    Explicit Item Positioning 140
    General Positioning of Items 140
    Layout of Panel Items with Values 141
    Sizing Panels 142
Panel Item Values 143
Iterating Over a Panel's Items 144
Panel Item Classes 144
Button Items 145
    Button Selection 145
    Menu Buttons 146
Choice Items 147
    Display and Layout of Item Choices 148
    Parallel Lists 149
    Exclusive and Nonexclusive Choices 150
    Checkbox Choices 151
    Abbreviated Choices 151
Scrolling Lists 153
    Displaying List Items 153
    Adding and Deleting List Entries 156
    List Selection 157
    List Notification 157
Message Items 157
Slider Items 159
    Displaying Sliders 159
    Slider Selection 159
    Slider Notification 159
    Slider Value 160
Text Items and Numeric Text Items 161
    The Current Text Item 162
    Text Selection 162

    Text Notification 162
    Writing Your Own Text Notify Procedure 164
    Text Value 165
Numeric Text Items 165
Advanced Panel Usage 165
Attaching Data to Panel Items 166
Repainting Panels 169
    Using PANEL_REPAINT_PROC 169
    Painting Panel Items 172
Panel Event Handling 172
    Using WIN_EVENT_PROC 173
    Using PANEL_BACKGROUND_PROC 174
    Using PANEL_EVENT_PROC 174
    Event Handling Example 175
Panel Package Summary 176

7
Panels

The PANEL package implements the OPEN LOOK *control area*. Panels are used in many different contexts—property sheets, notices, and menus all use panels in their implementation. The main function of a panel is to manage a variety of *panel items*. Figure 7-1 shows examples of panel items from the *OPEN LOOK GUI*. Because some panel items may not contain windows which handle their own events, the PANEL package is responsible for propagating events to the appropriate panel item. This chapter addresses issues specific to panels, the management of panel items, and the distribution of events to those items. We look at basic issues common to all panel items before introducing each of the eight different panel item packages. Finally, we look at several advanced topics regarding panel usage.

The PANEL package is subclassed from the CANVAS package and, hence, the OPENWIN package. In typical usage, you create a panel and set certain panel-specific attributes. None of the openwin- or canvas-specific attributes need to be set or reset to create a panel in an OPEN LOOK-compliant control area. However, these attributes are available.

Since panels are subclassed from canvases, a panel can be used anywhere that a canvas can. The principle difference between canvases and panels is the management of events and the existence of panel items. In canvases, callback routines are installed for events, repaint and resize routines. An input mask is set for notification of certain events that the application is interested in. For panels, the application does not set event masks or install an event callback routine unless the application needs to track events above and beyond what the PANEL package does by default (typical applications will not need to do this).

The PANEL package handles all the repainting and resizing events automatically. Panels are not used to display graphics, so there is no need to capture repaint events. Rather than deal with other events specifically, callback routines are not installed on panels but, rather, set for each panel item. Because of the varying types of panel items, each item's callback function may be invoked by a different action from the user. While clicking on a panel button is all that is necessary to activate the button's callback routine, a text panel item might be configured to call its notification callback routine upon the user pressing the RETURN key.

Since panel items express interest in different events, it is the responsibility of the PANEL package to track all events within the panel's window and dispatch events to the proper panel item depending on its type. In some cases, if an event happens over a certain panel item and that item is not interested in that event, the event may be sent to another panel item. For example, what happens if a key is pressed over a panel button? Because the panel button has

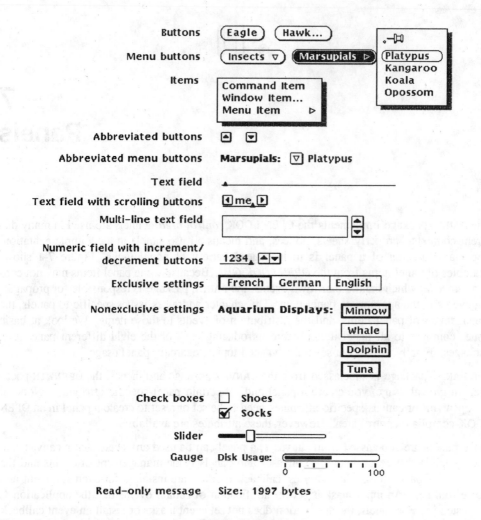

Buttons	(Eagle) (Hawk...)
Menu buttons	(Insects ▽) (Marsupials ▷) (Platypus) Kangaroo Koala Opossom
Items	Command Item Window Item... Menu Item ▷
Abbreviated buttons	⬆ ⬇
Abbreviated menu buttons	**Marsupials:** ▽ Platypus
Text field	▲_____
Text field with scrolling buttons	◀ me ▶
Multi-line text field	
Numeric field with increment/ decrement buttons	1234 ▲▼
Exclusive settings	French | German | English
Nonexclusive settings	**Aquarium Displays:** Minnow Whale Dolphin Tuna
Check boxes	☐ Shoes ☑ Socks
Slider	▬■▭
Gauge	Disk Usage: ▭▬▭ 0 100
Read-only message	Size: 1997 bytes

Figure 7-1. Controls in an OPEN LOOK GUI implementation*

no interest in the event, the panel will send the event to a text panel item, if one exists elsewhere in the panel.

Section 7.14, "Advanced Panel Usage," describes panel event handling and repainting.

---

*XView does not support multiline text items. Also, the scrolling list item is supported but not shown here.

7.1 Creating a Panel

Creating a panel is achieved by calling xv_create() and specifying the PANEL package and a NULL-terminated list of attribute-value pairs. Panels must be created as a child of the frame. All programs that use panels or panel items must include *<xview/panel.h>*. Because panels are uninteresting without panel items, Example 7-1 shows how to create a simple frame, a panel and a panel button. Selecting the panel button causes the program to exit. This is the same *quit.c* program as shown in Chapter 3, *Creating XView Applications*.

Example 7-1. The quit.c program

```
/*
 * quit.c -- simple program to display a panel button that says "Quit".
 * Selecting the panel button exits the program.
 */
#include <xview/xview.h>
#include <xview/frame.h>
#include <xview/panel.h>

Frame frame;

main (argc, argv)
int argc;
char *argv[];
{
    Panel panel;
    void quit();

    xv_init (XV_INIT_ARGC_PTR_ARGV, &argc, argv, NULL);

    frame = (Frame)xv_create (NULL, FRAME,
        FRAME_LABEL,      argv[0],
        XV_WIDTH,         200,
        XV_HEIGHT,        100,
        NULL);

    panel = (Panel)xv_create (frame, PANEL, NULL);

    (void) xv_create (panel, PANEL_BUTTON,
            PANEL_LABEL_STRING,        "Quit",
            PANEL_NOTIFY_PROC,         quit,
            NULL);

    xv_main_loop (frame);
    exit(0);
}

void
quit()
{
    xv_destroy_safe(frame);
}
```

Panels

7.2 Creating Panel Items

Panel items are created using `xv_create()` as usual:

```
Panel_item
xv_create(panel, item_type, attrs)
    Panel panel;
    <item type>              item_type;
    <attribute-value list> attrs;
```

The values for `item_type` must be a panel item from one of the panel item packages:

- `PANEL_BUTTON`
- `PANEL_CHOICE`
- `PANEL_LIST`
- `PANEL_MESSAGE`
- `PANEL_NUMERIC_TEXT`
- `PANEL_SLIDER`
- `PANEL_TEXT`

The items in this list represent the items found in Figure 7-1. Each item's type can be retrieved by calling:

```
Panel_item_type type;
type = (Panel_item_type)xv_get(panel_item, PANEL_ITEM_CLASS);
```

`Panel_item_type` is an enumerated type found in *<xview/panel.h>* and contains the following types:

- `PANEL_BUTTON_ITEM`
- `PANEL_CHOICE_ITEM`
- `PANEL_LIST_ITEM`
- `PANEL_MESSAGE_ITEM`
- `PANEL_NUMERIC_TEXT_ITEM`
- `PANEL_SLIDER_ITEM`
- `PANEL_TEXT_ITEM`
- `PANEL_TOGGLE_ITEM`

Some of these panel items have values that are displayed separately. For example, the choice item displays its choices either vertically or horizontally next to the choice's label.

As panel items are created, they are added to a stack of panel items. The first panel item in a panel is considered at the bottom of the stack. When more items are added, they are added on top of the stack. The first item on the panel is said to be at the bottom, while the last item added is at the top. The order in which items lie on the panel has no effect on the display of the items. If items overlap, the last item to repaint itself will appear to be at the top of the stack despite it's order in on the panel. This behavior is described by the term *Z-order*, because in addition to the (x, y) coordinates of the panel items, there is a virtual z coordinate associated with panel items but has no effect on the graphical representation of the object.

Most panel items are drawn using Xlib calls directly onto the panel window. Thus, these panel items have no windows associated with them. Because there are no windows associated with panel items, panel items should be careful not to overlap one another, because one item will not *clip* the one under it. For event processing, when a button event occurs in a panel, the panel loops through the items in its stack (according to its Z-order) and if the event occurs in the panel item, then that item is notified of the event, even though it is entirely possible that another panel item may share the same space. For this reason, it is important that panel items are *tiled* and do not intersect partially or completely.

Note that this is *not* the case for Xt Intrinsics-based toolkits, whose items may be window based. It is not unusual to do this sort of thing in some toolkits, but you should avoid doing it in XView. If you need to place more than one item at the same location, you should probably have one item's XV_SHOW attribute set to FALSE while the other's is TRUE. Toggle the attribute's values in each of the panel items.

7.3 Panel Layout

A panel lays out panel items in rows and columns. The width and height of the rows and columns may be set by panel and window attributes and/or by the sizes of the panel items themselves.

Whenever panel items are created, they are added to the panel adjacent to one another in either a row-first or a column-first order. As each new item is added, it is placed at the next position depending on the value of the panel's PANEL_LAYOUT attribute. The default value, PANEL_HORIZONTAL, lays out panel items horizontally until the items have reached the edge of the panel. A new row is then started and the next item is placed at the left edge of the panel. Setting the value of PANEL_LAYOUT to PANEL_VERTICAL causes items to be laid out by column first; when the height of the panel is reached, the next column is started.

Use the attributes PANEL_NEXT_ROW and PANEL_NEXT_COL to explicitly specify the row or column gap for the next item only. The value –1 uses the value of WIN_ROW_GAP and WIN_COL_GAP (see Section 7.3.2, "General Positioning of Items").

Since different panel items have different sizes, the grid is not rigidly adhered to and the positions of items may fluctuate within a row. However, it is possible to force items to line up to specific rows and columns as shown later.

The gap between items as they are laid out vertically and horizontally, can be set by the attributes PANEL_ITEM_X_GAP and PANEL_ITEM_Y_GAP. The default gap is 10 pixels in the horizontal direction and 5 pixels in the vertical direction.

Figure 7-2 shows how panels items are laid out as they are created.

Figure 7-2. Layout of panel items

7.3.1 Explicit Item Positioning

To position panel items explicitly, the attributes XV_X and XV_Y are used. These specify absolute positioning relative to the panel. The attributes PANEL_ITEM_X and PANEL_ITEM_Y are specific to panels. These values reflect the coordinates of the last item created. Therefore, they are both get-only attributes. The following code fragment shows how both are used:

```
panel = (Panel)xv_create(frame, PANEL, NULL);

xv_create(panel, PANEL_BUTTON,
    XV_X,               50,
    XV_Y,               75,
    PANEL_LABEL_STRING, "Quit",
    NULL);

printf("The last item in the panel was at %d %d.\n",
    xv_get(panel, PANEL_ITEM_X), xv_get(panel, PANEL_ITEM_Y));
```

This code segment would print:

```
The last item in the panel was at 50 75.
```

When positioning panel items, if the position of the new panel item extends beyond the edges of the panel in the positive direction, the size of the panel increases to include the item. This happens regardless of whether the panel's size was set explicitly at the time it was created.*

7.3.2 General Positioning of Items

Two functions that are available for general positioning of panel items within windows are xv_row() and xv_col(). These functions use the values of WIN_ROW_GAP and WIN_COLUMN_GAP of the panel. While these attributes control the spacing between panel items, the distance between items and the edge of the panel are set by the attributes PANEL_ITEM_X_START and PANEL_ITEM_Y_START. These attributes default to 4 pixels.

---

*Setting an item to negative coordinates does not increase the size of the panel—only if the item is wide enough or high enough to stretch into the panel window will any of it be visible.

For example, `xv_col(panel, 0)` places an item at a distance of `PANEL_ITEM_X_START` from the left edge of the panel, and `xv_col(panel, 1)` places an item at a distance of:

```
PANEL_ITEM_X_START + WIN_COLUMN_GAP
```

from the left edge of the panel.

Consider the following code fragment that positions items within regimented rows and columns:

```
int          rows, cols;
extern char *names[3][5];

frame = (Frame)xv_create(NULL, FRAME, NULL);
panel = (Panel)xv_create(frame, PANEL,
    WIN_ROW_GAP,          70,
    WIN_COLUMN_GAP,       20,
    PANEL_ITEM_START_X,   10,
    PANEL_ITEM_START_Y,   10,
    NULL);

for (rows = 0; rows < 3; rows++)
    for (cols = 0; cols < 5; cols++)
        (void) xv_create(panel, PANEL_BUTTON,
            XV_X,                 xv_col(panel, cols),
            XV_Y,                 xv_row(panel, rows),
            PANEL_LABEL_STRING,   names[rows][cols],
            PANEL_NOTIFY_PROC,    (rows+cols==0)? quit : selected,
            PANEL_CLIENT_DATA,    frame,
            NULL);
```

This code displays a panel with a 10-pixel distance between the panel edges and the panel items and a 70-pixel distance between the upper-left corners of the panel items. This contrasts with `PANEL_ITEM_X_GAP` and `PANEL_ITEM_Y_GAP`, which specify the gap between the right and left sides of adjacent panel items.

The `xv_col()` and `xv_row()` method of explicit panel item placement does not take into account the sizes of the panel items. If not enough space is given between the rows and columns (`WIN_COLUMN_GAP`, `WIN_ROW_GAP`), then items will lie on top of one another.

7.3.3 Layout of Panel Items with Values

For panel items with values, special attributes should be used instead of the `XV_X` and `XV_Y` attributes mentioned above. These panel items display their values by printing a separate piece of the item apart from the panel item's label, as shown in Figure 7-3. Text items, for example, display their values as text strings adjacent to the text item's label.

Text Item Label: Value_____

Figure 7-3. Layout of panel item with value

It is possible to position the text item's label and text string (value) independently of one another. This is accomplished by using the following four attributes:

- PANEL_LABEL_X
- PANEL_LABEL_Y
- PANEL_VALUE_X
- PANEL_VALUE_Y

Setting PANEL_ITEM_X and PANEL_ITEM_Y position the *label* portion of the panel item to the coordinates specified. Similarly, setting PANEL_VALUE_X and PANEL_VALUE_Y position the value portion of the panel item. Each X/Y attribute pair should be used together; otherwise, if one is set, the other's value is changed to a default value. If PANEL_VALUE_X is set to 100 and PANEL_LABEL_X is not specified, the label's position and, thus, *the whole panel item* is moved so that the value portion is aligned with its *x* coordinate at 100.

It is important *not* to use XV_X and XV_Y when using the label and value positioning attributes.

7.3.4 Sizing Panels

The size of a panel, by default, extends to the bottom and right edges of the frame in which it is placed (assuming there are no other subwindows in the frame). Alternatively, the panel's dimensions can be set explicitly using XV_WIDTH and XV_HEIGHT. If it is important to maintain the layout of the panel items in a panel, then the dimensions should be set explicitly and scrollbars may be attached to the panel (since it is subclassed from the OPENWIN package). Note, however, that to attach scrollbars, the attribute OPENWIN_SHOW_BORDERS needs to be set to TRUE in the xv_create() call.*

More often than not, you want the panel to be just the minimum height and width required to encompass all of its items. You can set the minimum height and width using the macros window_fit_height() or window_fit_width(), respectively. You can set both in a single call to window_fit(). These macros are called after all the items have been created.

The attributes PANEL_EXTRA_PAINT_WIDTH and PANEL_EXTRA_PAINT_HEIGHT specify the increment by which a panel will grow in the *x* and *y* directions, respectively.

---

*Panels with scrollbars violate OPEN LOOK's policy on control areas. Attaching scrollbars to panels is handled exactly the same way for panels as it is for canvases. See Chapter 5, *Canvases and Openwin*, for details on how to attach scrollbars.

7.4 Panel Item Values

Many panel items are associated with a specific value. A text item has a *string* value, a text-number item has an integer value, a list item has a list-choice value, a choice item has a current-choice value, and so on.* To set a value, use:

```
xv_set(item, PANEL_VALUE, value, NULL)
```

Of course, the type of `value` is dependent on the type of panel item whose value is being set. Consider the following examples:

```
/* Set the text field in the text item to print "Hello World" */
xv_set(text_item, PANEL_VALUE, "Hello world.", NULL);

/* Set the numeric value of the number-text item to be 10 */
xv_set(text_num_item, PANEL_VALUE, 10, NULL);

/* Set the current choice in choice_item to be the fifth choice */
xv_set(choice_item, PANEL_VALUE, 5, NULL);
```

NOTE

The values for string-valued attributes are dynamically allocated when they are created or set. The value you specify is *copied* into the newly allocated space. If a previous value was present, the panel item frees its old data first.†

Panel item values are retrieved in a similar way:

```
xv_get(item, PANEL_VALUE);
```

Since the `xv_get()` routines are used to retrieve attributes of all types, you should coerce the value returned into the type appropriate to the attribute being retrieved.

```
int val;
val = (int)xv_get(num_text_item, PANEL_VALUE);
printf("The int-value in the num_text_item is: '%d'\n", val);
```

To get the image for a choice item's current choice (assuming the choice item is a choice of `Server_image`'s):

```
Server_image image;
image = (Server_image)xv_get(item, PANEL_CHOICE_IMAGE,
                             xv_get(item, PANEL_VALUE));
```

---

*For details about the value type of a panel item, see the corresponding sections on specific panel items (Sections 7.7 through 7.13).

†This contrasts with menu items. See Chapter 11, *Menus*.

NOTE

`xv_get()` does not dynamically allocate storage for the values it returns. If the value returned is a pointer, it points directly into the panel's private data. It should be considered *read-only*—do not change the contents of the pointer; it is your responsibility to copy the information pointed to.

7.5 Iterating Over a Panel's Items

You can iterate over each item in a panel with the two attributes `PANEL_FIRST_ITEM` and `PANEL_NEXT_ITEM`. A pair of macros, `PANEL_EACH_ITEM()` and `PANEL_END_EACH` are also provided for this purpose. For example, to destroy each item in a panel:

```
Panel_item item;

PANEL_EACH_ITEM(browser, item)
    xv_destroy(item);
PANEL_END_EACH
```

A semicolon is not required after `PANEL_END_EACH`.

7.6 Panel Item Classes

Eight types of panel items are presented here:

- Panel Buttons
- Checkboxes
- Exclusive and Nonexclusive Choices
- Abbreviated Choices
- Scrolling Lists
- Message Items
- Sliders
- Text and Numbered Text Items

Items are made up of one or more displayable components. One component shared by all item types is the *label*. An item label is either a string or a graphic image.

The user interacts with items through various different methods ranging from mouse button selection to keyboard input. This interaction typically results in a *callback* function being called for the panel item. The callback functions also vary on a per-item basis. Each item type is described in the following sections of this chapter.

7.7 Button Items

A button item allows the user to invoke a command or bring up a menu. Examples of various buttons are listed in Figure 7-4. The button's label identifies the name of the command or menu. A button label that ends in three dots (...) indicates that a pop-up menu will be displayed when the button is selected.

Figure 7-4. Visual feedback for button controls

A button requires a label specified by the attribute PANEL_LABEL_STRING or PANEL_LABEL_IMAGE. OPEN LOOK describes which font is used for the button label—it cannot be changed or emboldened.

7.7.1 Button Selection

The user invokes a panel button by clicking the SELECT mouse button on it. When this happens, the button's notify procedure, installed via the attribute PANEL_NOTIFY_PROC, is called. The notify procedure is installed by specifying PANEL_NOTIFY_PROC as in the following example:

```
xv_create(panel, PANEL_BUTTON,
    PANEL_NOTIFY_PROC,   quit_proc,
    PANEL_LABEL_STRING,  "Quit",
    NULL);
```

When the button is selected, the notify procedure is called. The form of the notify procedure for a button is:

```
int
button_notify_proc(item, event)
    Panel_item   item;
    Event        *event
```

The return value from the notify procedure should be XV_OK.

7.7.2 Menu Buttons

It is often useful to associate a menu with a button. The menu may provide alternate values or functions that the button may invoke. Associated with each menu is a notify procedure for either the menu itself or the menu item. Also associated with each menu is a default menu item. If the button is selected without bringing up the menu, the default menu item's notify procedure or the notify procedure for the menu itself is called *after* the notify procedure for the panel button. If the menu *is* used, then the menu item's notify procedure is called and the panel button's notify procedure is *not* called.*

Menu buttons contain a triangle or mark pointing in the direction in which the menu will be displayed.

The *btn_menu.c* program demonstrates how a menu can be attached to a panel button. This program is shown in Example 7-2:

Example 7-2. The btn_menu.c program

```
/*
 * btn_menu.c -- display a panel that has an OPEN LOOK menu button.
 * The choices displayed are Yes, No and Quit.  If Quit is selected
 * in the menu, the program exits.
 */
#include <xview/xview.h>
#include <xview/panel.h>
#include <xview/openmenu.h>

main(argc, argv)
int argc;
char *argv[];
{
    Frame        frame;
    Panel        panel;
    Menu         menu;
    int          selected();
    void         menu_proc();
```

---

*Chapter 11, *Menus*, should be read for details about menus and menu items.

Example 7-2. The btn_menu.c program (continued)

```
    xv_init(XV_INIT_ARGC_PTR_ARGV, &argc, argv, NULL);

    frame = (Frame)xv_create(NULL, FRAME, NULL);
    panel = (Panel)xv_create(frame, PANEL, NULL);

    /* Create the menu _before_ the panel button */
    menu = (Menu)xv_create(NULL, MENU,
        MENU_NOTIFY_PROC,       menu_proc,
        MENU_STRINGS,           "Yes", "No", "Quit", NULL,
        NULL);
    (void) xv_create(panel, PANEL_BUTTON,
        PANEL_LABEL_STRING,     "Y/N/Q",
        PANEL_NOTIFY_PROC,      selected,
        PANEL_ITEM_MENU,        menu, /* attach menu to button */
        NULL);
    window_fit(panel);
    window_fit(frame);
    xv_main_loop(frame);
}
int
selected(item, event)
Panel_item item;
Event *event;
{
    printf("%s selected...\n", xv_get(item, PANEL_LABEL_STRING));
    return XV_OK;
}

void
menu_proc(menu, menu_item)
Menu menu;
Menu_item menu_item;
{
    printf("Menu Item: %s\n", xv_get(menu_item, MENU_STRING));
    if (!strcmp((char *)xv_get(menu_item, MENU_STRING), "Quit"))
        exit(0);
}
```

The output produced by this program is shown in Figure 7-5.

7.8 Choice Items

Choice items provide a list of different choices to the user in which one or more choices may be selected. There are variations of choice items which implement different OPEN LOOK objects such as:

- Exclusive and Nonexclusive Choices (or Settings)

- Abbreviated Choice Items (or Menu Buttons)

- Checkboxes

Figure 7-5. Sample menu button (unselected and selected)

Behind the flexibility of presentation lies a uniform structure consisting of a label, a list of choices, and an indication of which choice or set of choices is currently selected. The choices can be displayed as either text strings (PANEL_CHOICE_STRINGS) or server images (PANEL_CHOICE_IMAGES). For a choice item to be displayed, at the very least, either a choice or a label must be set in the item.

7.8.1 Display and Layout of Item Choices

The attribute PANEL_DISPLAY_LEVEL determines which of an item's choices are actually displayed. The display level may be set to:

PANEL_ALL   The default. All choices are shown.

PANEL_CURRENT   Only the current choice is shown. This setting is used to imple-
                     ment the *Abbreviated Choice Item.*

PANEL_NONE   No choices are shown. This is virtually useless—if you do not
                     want to display any of the choices but would rather display a label
                     and have the choices be chosen by a pop-up menu, do not use
                     choice items; use panel buttons with a menu attached.

The choices are laid out either horizontally or vertically next to the label depending on the value of the item's value for PANEL_LAYOUT. By default, this value is inherited from the parent panel. If you want an explicit layout pattern for the choice item only, you should specify it explicitly by setting the PANEL_LAYOUT attribute for the *panel item*, not the panel.

7.8.2 Parallel Lists

Parallel lists are lists of values for particular attributes that correspond to each choice in the panel item. An example of a parallel list is PANEL_CHOICE_XS and PANEL_CHOICE_YS. These two attributes take as values a NULL-terminated list of coordinates to specify explicit placement of the choices when they are displayed (assuming PANEL_ALL is the display format). These attributes are used to display choices in adjacent rows and columns. Look at the following example:

```
xv_create(panel, PANEL_CHOICE,
    PANEL_CHOICE_STRINGS,       "One", "Two", "Three",
                                "Four", "Five", "Six", NULL,
    PANEL_CHOICE_XS,            10, 70, 130, NULL,
    PANEL_CHOICE_YS,            90, 120, NULL,
    PANEL_VALUE,                2,
    PANEL_NOTIFY_PROC,          notify_proc,
    NULL);
```

The item has three choices: the strings "One", "Two" and "Three." We have specified explicit positioning of the choice items using the PANEL_CHOICE_XS and PANEL_CHOICE_YS attributes. These attributes take precedence over PANEL_LAYOUT, so that layout is ignored if specified. Note that the list PANEL_CHOICE_YS has only one element. When any of the parallel lists are abbreviated in this way, the last element given will be used for the remainder of the choices. So, in the example above:

```
90, NULL
```

serves as shorthand for:

```
90, 90, 90, NULL
```

All the choices will appear at y coordinate 90, while the x coordinates for the choices will be 10, 70, and 130, respectively.

You cannot specify that a choice appear at $x = 0$ or $y = 0$ by using the attributes PANEL_CHOICE_XS or PANEL_CHOICE_YS. Since these attributes take NULL-terminated lists as values, the zero would be interpreted as the terminator for the list. You may achieve the desired effect by setting the positions individually. The attributes PANEL_CHOICE_X or PANEL_CHOICE_Y take as values the number of the choice followed by the desired position. The following example demonstrates setting the position of choice items:

```
Panel_item   choice;
int          i;
extern char *strings[];

choice = (Panel_item)xv_create(panel, PANEL_CHOICE,
    PANEL_CHOOSE_ONE,           FALSE,
    NULL);
for (i = 0; i < sizeof(strings) / sizeof(char *); i++)
    xv_set(choice,
        PANEL_CHOICE_STRING, i, strings[i],
        PANEL_CHOICE_X,      i, i*20,
        PANEL_CHOICE_Y,      i, i*20,
        NULL);
```

After the choice item is created, the *x* and *y* positions of the choices are set individually in a loop.

7.8.3 Exclusive and Nonexclusive Choices

When a default choice item is created, its type is an exclusive choice item allowing the user to select only one choice from the list. The value of the panel item is the currently selected item. In the following example, we create several choice items as exclusive settings:

```
xv_create(panel, PANEL_CHOICE,
     PANEL_LABEL_STRING,      "Choices",
     PANEL_CHOICE_STRINGS,    "One", "Two", "Three", "Four", NULL,
     PANEL_NOTIFY_PROC,       selected,
     PANEL_VALUE,             3,
     NULL);
```

This code fragment produces the panel item shown in Figure 7-6.

Figure 7-6. Sample panel with exclusive choices

Figure 7-6 represents a panel item that has four choices, the third of which is *set*. If the user makes another choice, the value of the item, and therefore the value of PANEL_VALUE, changes to the ordinal number of the choice.

The choice item can be made nonexclusive (allowing more than one of the choices to be selected) when the attribute PANEL_TOGGLE is set to FALSE. This attribute affects the panel item in two ways. More than one choice may be set in the visual feedback, and the value of the item is set as a mask indicating those choices that are selected. In the following, the choice items in the previous example are shown as nonexclusive settings:

```
xv_create(panel, PANEL_CHOICE,
     PANEL_TOGGLE,            FALSE,
     PANEL_LABEL_STRING,      "Choices",
     PANEL_CHOICE_STRINGS,    "One", "Two", "Three", "Four", NULL,
     PANEL_NOTIFY_PROC,       selected,
     PANEL_VALUE,             5,
     NULL);
```

This code fragment would produce the panel item shown in Figure 7-7.

Figure 7-7 represents a panel item that has two choices set, the first and the third. The reason for this is that the panel's value is set to 5, which is a mask that represents the first and third bits. For example, 5 in binary is ... 00101.* In the binary representation, the first and third bits from the right are 1's. This means that the first and third choices are selected. This is

---

*The value for nonexclusive choice items is stored as an unsigned int.

Choices [One] [Two] [Three] [Four]

Figure 7-7. Sample panel with nonexclusive choices

how the value is interpreted on calls to xv_set() or xv_create(), and this is what is returned for calls to xv_get().

7.8.4 Checkbox Choices

Checkboxes can be displayed rather than the default display for choices by using PANEL_CHECK_BOX. The following example demonstrates checkboxes:

```
xv_create(panel, PANEL_CHECK_BOX,
     PANEL_LAYOUT,          PANEL_VERTICAL,
     PANEL_CHOOSE_ONE,      FALSE,
     PANEL_LABEL_STRING,    "Choices",
     PANEL_CHOICE_STRINGS,  "One", "Two", "Three", "Four", NULL,
     PANEL_NOTIFY_PROC,     selected,
     PANEL_VALUE,           5,
     NULL);
```

The only difference from previous examples is that the panel item is marked using checkboxes for selected choices and empty boxes for nonselected choices. The panel items created by this code are shown in Figure 7-8.

Choices ☑ One   ☐ Two   ☑ Three   ☐ Four

Figure 7-8. Sample panel with checkbox

All of the items can be selected in the same way and the values of the items can be set identically.

7.8.5 Abbreviated Choices

Abbreviated choices are similar to choice items. However, only the current value is displayed. A menu is used to display all the choices. To implement abbreviated choice items, specify the macro PANEL_CHOICE_STACK. The following example demonstrates creating abbreviated choice items:

```
xv_create(panel, PANEL_CHOICE_STACK,
    PANEL_LAYOUT,               PANEL_VERTICAL,
    PANEL_LABEL_STRING,         "Choices",
    PANEL_CHOICE_STRINGS,       "One", "Two", "Three", "Four", NULL,
    PANEL_NOTIFY_PROC,          selected,
    PANEL_VALUE,                5,
    NULL);
```

The panel item created by this code is shown in Figure 7-9.

Figure 7-9. Sample panel with abbreviated choice (unselected and selected)

Here, since only the current selection is visible, the only way to make other choices in the item is to bring up a menu. The value of the panel item is similar.

Choice Selection and Notification

The user can make a selection from a choice item by selecting the desired choice directly with the SELECT mouse button.

The procedure specified via the attribute PANEL_NOTIFY_PROC will be called when any of its choices are selected. If a choice item's current selection or value changes as a result of a call to xv_set() from somewhere else, then the notify procedure is not called. The choice notify procedure is passed the item, the current value of the item, and the event that caused notification:

```
choice_notify_proc(item, value, event)
    Panel_item  item;
    int         value;
    Event       *event;
```

For exclusive choices, the value passed to the notify procedure is the ordinal number corresponding to the current choice (the choice that the user has just selected). The first choice has ordinal number zero. For nonexclusive choices, the value is a mask of the currently selected choices in the list (see the previous section).

The event is the event that caused the notify procedure to be called. For these types of choices, the event action will probably be ACTION_SELECT.

7.9 Scrolling Lists

OPEN LOOK's specification for *scrolling lists* is implemented by the PANEL_LIST panel item. List items allow the user to make selections from a scrolling list of choices larger than can be displayed on the panel at one time. The selections can be exclusive or nonexclusive similar to the choice items outlined in the previous section. The list is made up of strings or images and a scrollbar that functions like any scrollbar in XView, except that it cannot be split.* List items are laid out in rows only—one list entry per row. Below is a code fragment for creating a simple list:

```
xv_create(panel, PANEL_LIST,
    PANEL_LIST_STRINGS,      "One", "Two", "Three", NULL,
    NULL);
```

The list items produced by this code are shown in Figure 7-10.

Figure 7-10. Sample panel with scrolling list

7.9.1 Displaying List Items

You can use either text strings or server images to display the choice to the user; you can even intermix them. You specify the choices either one at a time or in a group. To set only one choice, use PANEL_LIST_STRING or PANEL_LIST_GLYPH. Use PANEL_LIST_STRINGS or PANEL_LIST_GLYPHS to set the choices all in a group.

The width of the list item can be set to explicit pixel values using PANEL_LIST_WIDTH. Alternatively, the number of rows that are displayed in the list item can be controlled through

---

*See Chapter 10, *Scrollbars*, for a further description of how scrollbars work.

the value of the PANEL_LIST_DISPLAY_ROWS attribute. This value governs the height of the list item.

The height of each row in the list may be set using PANEL_LIST_ROW_HEIGHT. If the items in the list are glyphs, then the height of each row must be specified by at least the height of the tallest glyph in the list. This should be determined before the list of glyphs is set in the list item. Since entries in the list can be either glyphs or strings, if an entry contains both a string and a glyph, then both are displayed—the glyph on the left and the string on the right. Consider the program in Example 7-3.

Example 7-3. The list_glyphs.c program

```
/*
 * list.c -- show a scrolling list with three items in it.
 * Each item is an icon (a pattern) and a string.
 */
#include <xview/xview.h>
#include <xview/panel.h>
#include <xview/svrimage.h>

#define gray1_width 16
#define gray1_height 16
static char gray1_bits[] = {
    0x55, 0x55, 0xaa, 0xaa, 0x55, 0x55, 0xaa, 0xaa, 0x55, 0x55,
    0xaa, 0xaa, 0x55, 0x55, 0xaa, 0xaa, 0x55, 0x55, 0xaa, 0xaa,
    0x55, 0x55, 0xaa, 0xaa, 0x55, 0x55, 0xaa, 0xaa, 0x55, 0x55,
    0xaa, 0xaa
};

#define gray2_width 16
#define gray2_height 16
static char gray2_bits[] = {
    0x11, 0x11, 0x00, 0x00, 0x44, 0x44, 0x00, 0x00, 0x11, 0x11,
    0x00, 0x00, 0x44, 0x44, 0x00, 0x00, 0x11, 0x11, 0x00, 0x00,
    0x44, 0x44, 0x00, 0x00, 0x11, 0x11, 0x00, 0x00, 0x44, 0x44,
    0x00, 0x00
};

#define gray3_width 16
#define gray3_height 16
static char gray3_bits[] = {
    0x22, 0x22, 0xee, 0xee, 0x33, 0x33, 0xee, 0xee, 0x22, 0x22,
    0xee, 0xee, 0x33, 0x33, 0xee, 0xee, 0x22, 0x22, 0xee, 0xee,
    0x33, 0x33, 0xee, 0xee, 0x22, 0x22, 0xee, 0xee, 0x33, 0x33,
    0xee, 0xee
};

main(argc, argv)
int     argc;
char    *argv[];
{
    Frame          frame;
    Panel          panel;
    Server_image gray1, gray2, gray3;
    extern void exit();

    xv_init(XV_INIT_ARGS, argc, argv, NULL);

    gray1 = (Server_image)xv_create(NULL, SERVER_IMAGE,
```

Example 7-3. The list_glyphs.c program (continued)

```
        XV_WIDTH,                gray1_width,
        XV_HEIGHT,               gray1_height,
        SERVER_IMAGE_BITS,       gray1_bits,
        NULL);
    gray2 = (Server_image)xv_create(NULL, SERVER_IMAGE,
        XV_WIDTH,                gray2_width,
        XV_HEIGHT,               gray2_height,
        SERVER_IMAGE_BITS,       gray2_bits,
        NULL);
    gray3 = (Server_image)xv_create(NULL, SERVER_IMAGE,
        XV_WIDTH,                gray3_width,
        XV_HEIGHT,               gray3_height,
        SERVER_IMAGE_BITS,       gray3_bits,
        NULL);
    frame = (Frame)xv_create(NULL, FRAME, NULL);
    panel = (Panel)xv_create(frame, PANEL, NULL);

    (void) xv_create(panel, PANEL_BUTTON,
        PANEL_LABEL_STRING,      "quit",
        PANEL_NOTIFY_PROC,       exit,
        NULL);

    (void) xv_create(panel, PANEL_LIST,
        PANEL_LIST_ROW_HEIGHT,   16,
        PANEL_LIST_GLYPHS,       gray1, gray2, gray3, NULL,
        PANEL_LIST_STRINGS,      "Pattern1", "Pattern2", "Pattern3", NULL,
        NULL);

    window_fit(panel);
    window_fit(frame);

    xv_main_loop(frame);
}
```

The output produced by *list_glyphs.c* is shown in Figure 7-11.

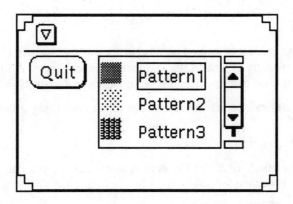

Figure 7-11. Output of program list_glyphs.c

The height of each row in the list is determined by the height of the font used by the string. If glyphs are used, this calculation is not done automatically, so the programmer is responsible for setting row height. In the example, all the glyphs in the list are the same height (16 pixels), so the calculation is easy: PANEL_LIST_ROW_HEIGHT is set to 16. If a glyph is assigned to a row whose height is not as high as the glyph, then a warning is printed and the glyph is ignored.

Note that in Figure 7-11 each string in a scrolling list is *converted* internally into a message item; you do not specify a message item when adding an item to the list. A handle to the newly created message item is given as the item parameter to the list_notify_proc(). See Section 7.9.4, "List Notification," for a discussion of the notify procedure.

7.9.2 Adding and Deleting List Entries

List entries are denoted by row number. The first entry is row 0. They are added and deleted from the list at run-time. The attribute PANEL_LIST_DELETE value specifies the list item to delete. The string and/or image resources are deallocated and the list is updated appropriately.

To add a list item, PANEL_LIST_INSERT is used in the same way. When adding a new list item in this manner, all the succeeding items are incremented and the list size grows by one. Space for a new item is created, and a new string or glyph may be added. These are all done at the time the attribute is evaluated, so they may be combined into one xv_set() call. You can move an item by deleting it from its old location and reassigning it to a new location. Look at the following code:

```
char *buf[128];

strcpy(buf, xv_get(list_item, PANEL_LIST_STRING, 4));

xv_set(list_item,
    PANEL_LIST_DELETE,      4,
    PANEL_LIST_INSERT,      8,
    PANEL_LIST_STRING,      8, buf,
    NULL);
```

The value for the string *must* be copied because as soon as the list item is deleted, the data is freed. When the new entry is created, the old entry number 8 is moved to 9, as are all succeeding items; the new list entry number 8 is set to the string described by buf.

The selected choice(s) can be set at list creation or later by using PANEL_LIST_SELECT. For example:

```
PANEL_LIST_SELECT, 3, TRUE,
```

will set choice 3 as selected. If the list item is nonexclusive, you can set more than one choice at one time. For example:

```
PANEL_LIST_SELECT, 3,  TRUE,
PANEL_LIST_SELECT, 13, TRUE,
PANEL_LIST_SELECT, 14, TRUE,
```

sets the 3rd, 13th, and 14th entries as selected.

To determine if a list entry is selected, use this:

```
xv_get(list_item, PANEL_LIST_SELECTED, i);
```

`xv_get()` returns TRUE if list entry *i* is selected.

7.9.3 List Selection

Items in the list are selected by using the SELECT mouse button while pointing at an item or by dragging the the pointer over the list items. If the list attribute PANEL_CHOOSE_ONE has a value of TRUE, then only one list entry may be selected. Otherwise, more entries may be selected.

7.9.4 List Notification

The procedure specified via the attribute PANEL_NOTIFY_PROC will be called when the item is selected. List notify procedures are passed the item, the current value of the item, and the event which caused notification:

```
list_notify_proc(item, op, event)
    Panel_item          item;
    Panel_list_op       op;
    Event               *event;
```

`item` is the message item corresponding to the string selection made in the scrolling list. To get the string or image associated with the selected entry, use `xv_get()` and the attribute PANEL_LABEL_STRING or PANEL_LABEL_IMAGE, respectively. If the selected list entry contains both a string and an image, then the string item is passed as the parameter.

`op` is either SELECT or DESELECT.

7.10 Message Items

Message items display a text or image message within a panel. The only visible component of a message item is the label itself. Message items are useful for annotations of all kinds, including titles, comments, descriptions, pictures, and dynamic status messages. The message is often used to identify elements on the panel. A message has no value.

You may set or change the label for a message item via PANEL_LABEL_STRING or PANEL_LABEL_IMAGE. Message items, like buttons, are selectable and can have notify procedures. Panel message items are the only panel items whose font can be set to boldface. This is done using the attribute PANEL_LABEL_BOLD.

Since message buttons cannot be selected, their primary use is for display purposes only. In Example 7-4, two message items are used together to give a warning message. The other two panel button items are used for actual functionality.

Example 7-4. The stop_frame.c program

```c
/*
 * stop_frame.c -- Use a server image as a panel message item.
 */
#include <xview/xview.h>
#include <xview/svrimage.h>
#include <xview/panel.h>

static short stop_bits[] = {
    0x3E00, 0x7F00, 0xFF80, 0xFF80, 0xFF80, 0xFF80, 0xFF80, 0x7F00,
    0x3E00, 0x0800, 0x0800, 0x0800, 0x0800, 0x0800, 0x7F00, 0x0000
};

main(argc, argv)
char *argv[];
{
    Frame frame;
    Panel panel;
    Server_image stopsign;

    xv_init();

    frame = (Frame)xv_create(NULL, FRAME,
        FRAME_SHOW_HEADER,  FALSE,
        NULL);
    panel = (Panel)xv_create(frame, PANEL, NULL);

    stopsign = (Server_image)xv_create(NULL, SERVER_IMAGE,
        XV_WIDTH,           16,
        XV_HEIGHT,          16,
        SERVER_IMAGE_DEPTH, 1,
        SERVER_IMAGE_BITS,  stop_bits,
        NULL);

    (void) xv_create(panel, PANEL_MESSAGE,
        PANEL_LABEL_IMAGE,  stopsign,
        NULL);
    (void) xv_create(panel, PANEL_MESSAGE,
        PANEL_LABEL_STRING,
            "This action will cause unsaved edits to be lost.",
        NULL);
    (void)xv_create(panel, PANEL_BUTTON,
        PANEL_NEXT_ROW,     -1,
        XV_X,               110,
        PANEL_LABEL_STRING, "Ok",
        NULL);
    (void)xv_create(panel, PANEL_BUTTON,
        PANEL_LABEL_STRING, "Cancel",
        NULL);

    window_fit(panel);
    window_fit(frame);
    xv_main_loop(frame);
}
```

The output from this program is shown in Figure 7-12.

Figure 7-12. Sample panel with message item

7.11 Slider Items

Slider items allow the graphical representation and selection of a value within a range. Sliders are appropriate for situations where it is desired to make fine adjustments over a continuous range of values. They can be horizontal or vertical. You can also type in the current value for the slider in an optional numeric text field.

7.11.1 Displaying Sliders

A slider has four displayable components: the label, the current value, the slider bar, and the minimum and maximum allowable integral values (the range). When PANEL_SHOW_VALUE is TRUE, the current value is shown after the label in an editable numeric text field. The minimum and maximum allowable values are set with PANEL_MIN_VALUE and PANEL_MAX_VALUE. The width of the slider bar corresponding to the current value is filled with black and can be adjusted using the PANEL_SLIDER_WIDTH attribute. The slider bar is always displayed unless the item is hidden (i.e., XV_SHOW is FALSE). When PANEL_SHOW_RANGE is TRUE, the minimum value of the slider PANEL_MIN_VALUE is shown to the left of the slider bar and the maximum value PANEL_MAX_VALUE is shown to the right of the slider bar.

7.11.2 Slider Selection

Only the slider bar of a slider may be selected. When the SELECT button is pressed within the slider bar, the black area of the bar will advance or retreat with the position of the cursor. The slider value may also be changed via the numeric text field.

7.11.3 Slider Notification

Slider notify procedures are passed the item, the item's value at time of notification, and the event which caused notification:

```
        void
        slider_notify_proc(item, value, event)
            Panel_item  item;
            int         value;
            Event       *event;
```

The notification behavior of a slider is controlled by the value of PANEL_NOTIFY_LEVEL. It can be set to one of two values:

PANEL_DONE   The default. The notify procedure is called only when the select button is released within the panel or when the user types in a new value for the slider's numeric text field.

PANEL_ALL   The notify procedure is called whenever the value of the slider is changed moved; this includes when the user selects, drags, or releases the SELECT button in a slider. For each movement of the mouse while the SELECT button is down, the slider's notify procedure is called.

7.11.4 Slider Value

The value of a slider is an integer in the range PANEL_MIN_VALUE to PANEL_MAX_VALUE. You can retrieve or set a slider's value with the attribute PANEL_VALUE and the functions xv_set() or xv_get().

The following code fragment produces a slider with a label:

```
xv_create(panel, PANEL_SLIDER,
    PANEL_LABEL_STRING,     "Brightness: ",
    PANEL_VALUE,            75,
    PANEL_MIN_VALUE,        0,
    PANEL_MAX_VALUE,        100,
    PANEL_SLIDER_WIDTH,     300,
    PANEL_NOTIFY_PROC,      brightness_proc,
    NULL);
```

The output from this program is displayed in Figure 7-13.

Brightness: 0 ▬▬▬▬▬▬▬▬▬▬▬▬▬▬▬□▭▭▭ 100

Figure 7-13. Sample panel with slider item

7.12 Text Items and Numeric Text Items

A text panel item contains as its value a NULL-terminated string. Typically, it contains only printable ASCII characters with no newlines. When a panel receives keyboard input (regardless of where the pointer is as long as it is in the boundaries of the panel), the keyboard event is passed to the item with the keyboard focus. A caret is used to indicate the insertion point where new text is added. You can type in more text than fits on the text field. If this happens, a right arrow pointing to the left will appear on the left on the field, indicating that some text to the left of the displayed text is no longer visible. Similarly, if text is inserted causing text on the right to move out of the visible portion of the text item, then an arrow pointing to the right will appear to the right of the text.

Numeric text items are a special type of text item. They can include buttons used to increment or decrement the value displayed in the field.

Text items use the attribute PANEL_LABEL_STRING as do most other panel items, to label the text item accordingly. The value of a text item is also a string, as shown by the following code:

```
xv_create(panel, PANEL_TEXT,
    PANEL_LABEL_STRING,   "Name:",
    PANEL_VALUE,          "Edward G. Robinson",
    NULL);
```

The output from this code fragment is shown in Figure 7-14.

Name: Edward G. Robinson

Figure 7-14. Sample panel with text item

If PANEL_LAYOUT is set to PANEL_VERTICAL, the value is placed below the label. The default is PANEL_HORIZONTAL.

The number of characters of the text item's value that are displayed is set via PANEL_VALUE_DISPLAY_LENGTH. The maximum number of characters which can be typed into a text item (independently of how many are displayable) is set via the attribute PANEL_VALUE_STORED_LENGTH. When characters are entered beyond this length, and when PANEL_VALUE_STORED_LENGTH is greater than the display length, the value string is scrolled one character to the left so that the most recently entered character is always visible. As the string scrolls to the left, the leftmost characters move out of the visible display area. The presence of these temporarily hidden characters is indicated by a small left-pointing triangle.

It is sometimes desirable to have a protected field where the user can enter confidential information. The attribute PANEL_MASK_CHAR is provided for this purpose. When the user enters a character, the character you have specified as the value of PANEL_MASK_CHAR will be displayed in place of the character the user has typed. So setting PANEL_MASK_CHAR to an asterisk (*) would produce a string of asterisks instead of the characters typed. The value of the text is still the string the user types.

If you want to disable character echo entirely so that the caret does not advance and it is impossible to tell how many characters have been entered, use the space character as the mask. You can remove the mask and display the actual value string at any time by setting the mask to NULL.

7.12.1 The Current Text Item

A panel may have several text items, exactly one of which may be *current* at any given time. The current text item is the one to which keyboard input is directed and is indicated by a caret at the item's value. Selection of a text item (i.e., pressing and releasing the SELECT mouse button anywhere within the item's bounding box) causes that item to become the current text item.

You can find out which text item has the caret or give the caret to a specified text item, by means of the panel attribute PANEL_CARET_ITEM.

```
current_item = (Panel_item)xv_get(panel, PANEL_CARET_ITEM);
xv_set(panel, PANEL_CARET_ITEM, another_item, NULL);
```

You can set the current item to the next or previous text item in the panel by using the following two routines:

```
Panel_item
panel_advance_caret(panel)
    Panel panel;

Panel_item
panel_backup_caret(panel)
    Panel panel;
```

They return the text panel items that now have the caret. Advancing past the last text item places the caret at the first text item while backing up past the first text item places the caret at the last text item.

7.12.2 Text Selection

You can use the *selection service* to select text within a text panel item. Chapter 18, *The Selection Service*, goes into detail about how to get the current selection from a text item. You can use the examples in that chapter to get the current selection from the selection's owner and set the text item's value to the text from the selection.

7.12.3 Text Notification

The notification behavior of text items is rather more complex than that of the other item types. You can control whether your notify procedure is called on each input character or only on selected characters.

When your notify procedure will be called is determined by the value of `PANEL_NOTIFY_LEVEL`. Possible values are given in Table 7-1:

Table 7-1. Text Item Notification Level

Notification Level	Level Causes Notify Procedure to be Called ...
`PANEL_NONE`	Never
`PANEL_NON_PRINTABLE`	On each non-printable input character
`PANEL_SPECIFIED`	If the input char is found in the string given for the attribute `PANEL_NOTIFY_STRING`
`PANEL_ALL`	On each input character

The default for `PANEL_NOTIFY_LEVEL` is `PANEL_SPECIFIED`, and the default for `PANEL_NOTIFY_STRING` is \n\r\t (i.e., notification on line-feed, carriage-return and tab).

The user's editing characters are treated specially. If you have asked for the character by including it in `PANEL_NOTIFY_STRING`, the `PANEL` package will call your notify procedure. After the notify procedure returns, the appropriate editing operation will be applied to the value string. (Note that the editing characters are never appended to the value string, regardless of the return value of the notify procedure.)

Characters other than the special characters described above are treated as follows. If the character typed by the user does *not* result in your notify procedure getting called, then the character, if printable, is appended to the value string. If it is not printable, it is ignored. If your notify procedure *is* called, what happens to the value string and whether the caret moves to another text item is determined by the notify procedure's return value. Table 7-2 shows the possible return values.

Table 7-2. Return Values for Text Item Notify Procedures

Value Returned	Action Caused
`PANEL_INSERT`	Character is appended to item's value
`PANEL_NEXT`	Caret moves to next text item
`PANEL_PREVIOUS`	Caret moves to previous text item
`PANEL_NONE`	Ignore the input character

If you do not specify your own notify procedure, the default procedure, `panel_text_notify()`, is called at the appropriate time as determined by the setting of `PANEL_NOTIFY_LEVEL`.

7.12.4 Writing Your Own Text Notify Procedure

By writing your own notify procedure, you can tailor the notification behavior of a given text item to support whatever the needs are for the application. On one extreme, you may want to process each character as the user types it in. For a different application, you may not care about the characters as they are typed in and may only want to look at the value of the string in response to some other button. A typical example is getting the value of a filename field when the user presses a **Load File** panel button.

The form of the text notification procedure is:

```
Panel_setting
panel_text_notify(item, event)
    Panel_item  item;
    Event       *event;
```

This procedure returns a panel setting enumeration which has the following side effects:

PANEL_NONE   Do not advance the caret to the next text item. The current text item and insertion point remain unchanged.

PANEL_NEXT   The caret moves to the *next* text item (defined by the text item that was created *after* the current text item). If there is no next text item, the first text item in the panel is used.

PANEL_PREVIOUS   The caret moves to the *previous* text item in the panel (defined by the text item that was created *before* the current text item). If there is no previous text item, the last text item in the panel is used.

PANEL_INSERT   The character which caused the notification procedure to be called is inserted into the text item's value at the location of the caret (insertion point).

The input character is referenced by event_action(event). The code fragment below calls the notify procedure name_proc when the ESCAPE key, the RETURN key or the TAB key is typed by the user. If any of these three keys are typed, the caret moves to the next panel item. However, output is only generated when the ESCAPE key or the RETURN key is used; the TAB key simply advances the caret without taking an action.

```
    ...
    name_item = (Panel_item)xv_create(panel, PANEL_TEXT,
        PANEL_LABEL_STRING,    "Enter Name Here:",
        PANEL_NOTIFY_LEVEL,    PANEL_SPECIFIED,
        PANEL_NOTIFY_STRING,   "\n\r\t\033",
        PANEL_NOTIFY_PROC,     name_proc,
        NULL);
    ...

    Panel_setting
    name_proc(item, event)
    Panel_item  item;
    Event       *event;
    {
        switch (event_action(event)) {
            case '\n':
            case '\r' :
```

```
        case '\033': /* [Esc] */
            printf("Entered value: '%s'\n",
                xv_get(item, PANEL_VALUE));
            /* FALL THRU */

        case '\t': /* [tab] just advance caret -- don't print */
            return (PANEL_NEXT);

        default:
            return (panel_text_notify(item, event));
    }
}
```

7.12.5 Text Value

You can set or get the value of a text item at any time via PANEL_VALUE. The following call
retrieves the value of name_item into name:

```
Panel_item name_item;
char name[NAME_ITEM_MAX_LENGTH];
    ...
strcpy(name, (char *)xv_get(name_item, PANEL_VALUE));
```

Note that name_item should have been created with a PANEL_VALUE_STORED_LENGTH not
greater than NAME_ITEM_MAX_LENGTH so the buffer name will not overflow.

7.13 Numeric Text Items

Numeric text items are virtually the same as panel text items except that the value displayed
is of type int. Also, convenience features (such as increment and decrement buttons) ease
the manipulation of the text string's numeric value, but there is little programmatic difference between the text item and the numeric text item. You can create a numeric text item
using the PANEL_NUMERIC_TEXT attribute. You can also set the minimum and maximum
range for the numeric text field by using PANEL_MIN_VALUE and PANEL_MAX_VALUE,
respectively.

7.14 Advanced Panel Usage

The sections that follow address some advanced topics dealing with panels. They cover
attaching data to panel items, repainting panels (installing a repaint procedure), and handling
events in panels and in panel items. Handling panel repainting and panel events are features
which are available but are not generally used by most applications. Attaching data to panel
items should be a practice closely followed for more efficient programs.

7.15 Attaching Data to Panel Items

Callback routines are called separately and independently from the application's main routine. If the callback routine needs data, there are two ways to make it available. One way is to store the data in global variables or data structures so the callback routine can reference the data or the data can be attached directly to panel items (which the notification procedure already has a handle to).

In the spirit of good programming practice, it is wise to avoid creating global variables if possible and feasible. So, the preferred method for making data available to callback routines is to *attach* the data to the panel items. A handle to the panel item is already made available to the callback function as the first parameter to the function. Two attributes can be used to attach data to panel items: XV_KEY_DATA or PANEL_CLIENT_DATA.*

Using XV_KEY_DATA requires a *key*, which must be some arbitrary, but unique, integer. An example of usage would be:

```
#define PANEL_ITEM_KEY     123
...
xv_create(panel, PANEL_BUTTON,
    PANEL_BUTTON_LABEL,      "Push Me",
    XV_KEY_DATA,             PANEL_ITEM_KEY,     "text",
    PANEL_NOTIFY_PROC,       my_notify_proc,
    ...
    NULL);
```

If this method is used, my_notify_proc() retrieves the data using xv_get():

```
char *data = (char *)xv_get(item, XV_KEY_DATA, PANEL_ITEM_KEY);
```

The common element in this case is the use of the constant PANEL_ITEM_KEY. A constant need not be used, but it is better than creating a global int variable to store the key. If that were the case, you might as well make the *data* portion that you wanted to attach the the panel item a global variable.

One advantage to using XV_KEY_DATA is that you can specify any number of keys and attach as many pieces of data to objects as you like.

An alternate method for attaching data to panel items is to use PANEL_CLIENT_DATA. This attribute is similar to XV_KEY_DATA in that the data is attached to the item, but in this case, you can only attach one piece of data to the panel item. You can, however, use *both* XV_KEY_DATA and PANEL_CLIENT_DATA on the same panel item. The advantage to using PANEL_CLIENT_DATA is that you do not have to keep track of a key. Since you can only attach one piece of data to a panel item, xv_get() returns only that data.

For a real example of this situation, let's modify the *quit.c* program (from the beginning of this chapter), which displays a frame, panel and a panel item labeled Quit. The modified program, *client_data.c*, is shown in Example 7-5. Selecting the panel button exits the program gracefully. The call to xv_destroy_safe(frame) causes the frame to be destroyed and thus, xv_main_loop() returns and the program exits.

---

*These attributes may be used with any XView object.

Example 7-5. The client_data.c program

```
/*
 * client_data.c -- demonstrate the use of PANEL_CLIENT_DATA attached
 * to panel items.  Attach the base frame to the "Quit" panel item so
 * that the notify procedure can call xv_destroy_safe() on the frame.
 */
#include <xview/xview.h>
#include <xview/panel.h>

main(argc, argv)
int argc;
char *argv[];
{
    Frame   frame;
    Panel   panel;
    int     quit();

    xv_init(XV_INIT_ARGC_PTR_ARGV, &argc, argv, NULL);

    frame = (Frame)xv_create(XV_NULL, FRAME, NULL);
    panel = (Panel)xv_create(frame, PANEL, NULL);
    (void) xv_create(panel, PANEL_BUTTON,
        PANEL_LABEL_STRING,     "Quit",
        PANEL_NOTIFY_PROC,      quit,
        PANEL_CLIENT_DATA,      frame,
        NULL);

    xv_main_loop(frame);
    puts("The program is now done.");
    exit(0);
}

quit(item)
Panel_item item;
{
    Frame frame = (Frame)xv_get(item, PANEL_CLIENT_DATA);
    xv_destroy_safe(frame);
}
```

In this program, the `frame` object is not a global variable; it es a local, or *automatic*, variable. Since there is a close association between the panel button and the frame (meaning that the panel button is going to access the handle to the frame in the callback routine), we attach the frame to the panel button as *client data*. `PANEL_CLIENT_DATA` takes a generic address of type `caddr_t`. In the callback routine for the panel button, the first parameter to the callback function is the panel item that called the notification. From that handle, the frame is retrieved via `xv_get()`.

This worked because the frame was created via `xv_create()`. That is, the object was *allocated*. You cannot attach data that has not been allocated. Thus, the following code segment is not advised:

```
dummy_functon()          /* Wrong way */
{
    char *home = (char *)getenv("HOME");
    xv_set(panel_item, XV_KEY_DATA, HOME_KEY, home);
}
```

The reason for this is that getenv() returns a pointer to static data that is *overwritten on each call*. The next call that the application makes to getenv() will change the value for the panel item XV_KEY_DATA. Likewise, the following should also not be used:

```
dummy_function()        /* Also wrong */
{
    char home[MAXPATHLEN], *ptr;
    if ((ptr = (char *)getenv("HOME")) != NULL) {
        (void) strcpy(home, ptr);
        xv_set(panel_item, XV_KEY_DATA, HOME_KEY, home);
    }
}
```

This does not work because as soon as dummy_function() returns, the value of home is lost because it is an automatic variable. The correct way to handle this is to make home either a static variable or a pointer whose storage is allocated via malloc().

The problem with home being static is that if dummy_function() is called more than once, the value of home will be overwritten on each call. So, the *best* way to handle this case is to allocate the data:

```
dummy_function()        /* Best way */
{
    extern char *malloc(), *getenv();
    char *home, *ptr;
    if ((ptr = getenv("HOME")) != NULL &&
        (home = malloc(strlen(ptr)+1))) {
        (void) strcpy(home, ptr);
        xv_set(panel_item, XV_KEY_DATA, HOME_KEY, home);
    }
}
```

Having allocated data for XV_KEY_DATA, we now assume the responsibility of freeing that data when the object is destroyed. Otherwise, the data is left free with no references to it. This is also known as creating a *core leak*. Because you don't always know when an object is being destroyed (destroying a panel may or may not cause a panel item to be destroyed), you can specify a function that explicitly frees the data pointed to by XV_KEY_DATA. To do this, use the attribute XV_KEY_DATA_REMOVE_PROC:

```
dummy_function()
{
    extern void free_data();
    extern char *malloc(), *getenv();
    char *home, *ptr;
    if ((ptr = getenv("HOME")) != NULL &&
        (home = malloc(strlen(ptr)+1))) {
        (void) strcpy(home, ptr);
        xv_set(panel_item,
            XV_KEY_DATA,                    HOME_KEY, home,
            XV_KEY_DATA_REMOVE_PROC, free_data,
            NULL);
    }
}
```

```
        void
        free_data(object, key, data)
        Xv_object object;
        int       key;
        caddr_t   data;
        {
            free(data);
        }
```

Whenever an object is freed, all the "key data" objects are scanned and if "remove procedures" are associated with them, they are called with the key data as the parameter. In this case, free_data() is called—it merely frees the data associated with that paricular key.

If you need to assign a new key to the *same* key data of an object, the old key data is automatically freed by XView by calling the remove procedure (if it exists). If you wish to delete a key without having to assign a new key, then you can call:

```
        xv_set(object, XV_KEY_DATA_REMOVE, key, NULL);
```

7.16 Repainting Panels

Due to the differences between panels and canvases, repainting and resizing of panels should be treated much differently than with canvases. OPEN LOOK describes control areas as being an unbordered region of a window where application controls (panel items) are displayed. Typically, these areas are painted with a solid background color and the panel items are displayed using either or both the foreground and background colors. These colors are inherited from the parent frame if the parent has FRAME_INHERIT_COLORS set to TRUE. But this appearance is not *required* by OPEN LOOK—you may, if you so choose, write a repaint routine that will paint the panel's window however you want: render another color, a pattern, or an image of some sort.

7.16.1 Using PANEL_REPAINT_PROC

There are already facilities in the CANVAS package to handle repaint events. However, because the panel must repaint the panel items within it, the canvas repaint method does not work; it will paint over the panel items. Therefore, the PANEL package provides an alternative property for installing a repaint routine. This repaint routine is called before the panel items have been rendered again but otherwise conforms to all other qualities of the canvas repaint routine.

The following code fragment demonstrates how a repaint routine can be installed on a panel. This repaint routine draws a gray background on the panel behind any existing panel items.

Example 7-6. The panel_repaint.c program

```
/*
 * panel_repaint.c -- repaint a panel background without disturbing
 * the repainting of panel items.
 */
```

Example 7-6. The panel_repaint.c program (continued)

```c
#include <xview/xview.h>
#include <xview/panel.h>
#include <xview/svrimage.h>
#include <X11/Xlib.h>
#include <X11/X.h>
#include <X11/bitmaps/gray1>

#define PANEL_GC_KEY     101  /* any arbitrary number */

main(argc, argv)
int argc;
char *argv[];
{
    Display      *display;
    Frame        frame;
    Panel        panel;
    int          quit();
    void         panel_repaint();
    XGCValues    gcvalues;
    Server_image grey;

    Mask         gcmask = 0L;
    GC           gc;

    xv_init(XV_INIT_ARGC_PTR_ARGV, &argc, argv, NULL);

    frame = (Frame)xv_create(XV_NULL, FRAME, NULL);
    panel = (Panel)xv_create(frame, PANEL,
        PANEL_REPAINT_PROC,      panel_repaint,
        NULL);

    (void) xv_create(panel, PANEL_BUTTON,
        PANEL_LABEL_STRING,      "Quit",
        PANEL_NOTIFY_PROC,       quit,
        PANEL_CLIENT_DATA,       frame,
        NULL);

    window_fit(frame);

    grey = (Server_image)xv_create(NULL, SERVER_IMAGE,
        XV_WIDTH,                gray1_width,
        XV_HEIGHT,               gray1_height,
        SERVER_IMAGE_DEPTH,      1, /* clarify for completeness*/
        SERVER_IMAGE_BITS,       gray1_bits,
        NULL);

    display = (Display *)xv_get(panel, XV_DISPLAY);
    gcvalues.stipple = (Pixmap) xv_get(grey, XV_XID);
    gcvalues.fill_style = FillOpaqueStippled;
    gcvalues.plane_mask = 1L;
    gcvalues.graphics_exposures = False;
    gcvalues.foreground = BlackPixel(display, DefaultScreen(display));
    gcvalues.background = WhitePixel(display, DefaultScreen(display));
    gcmask = GCStipple | GCFillStyle | GCPlaneMask |
        GCGraphicsExposures | GCForeground | GCBackground;
    gc = XCreateGC(display, xv_get(panel, XV_XID), gcmask, &gcvalues);

    /* attach the GC to the panel for use by the repaint proc above */
    xv_set(panel, XV_KEY_DATA, PANEL_GC_KEY, gc, NULL);
```

Example 7-6. The panel_repaint.c program (continued)

```
    xv_main_loop(frame);
    exit(0);
}

/*
 * repaint procedure for the panel paints a gray pattern over the
 * entire panel.  Use the GC attached to the panel via XV_KEY_DATA.
 */
void
panel_repaint(panel, pw)
Panel panel;
Xv_Window pw;
{
    /* get the GC attached to the panel in main() */
    GC gc = (GC)xv_get(panel, XV_KEY_DATA, PANEL_GC_KEY);

    /* call XFillRectangle on the entire size of the panel window */
    XFillRectangle(xv_get(panel, XV_DISPLAY), xv_get(pw, XV_XID), gc,
        0, 0, xv_get(pw, XV_WIDTH), xv_get(pw, XV_HEIGHT));
}

quit(item)
Panel_item item;
{
    Frame frame = (Frame)xv_get(item, PANEL_CLIENT_DATA);
    xv_destroy_safe(frame);
}
```

The output produced by this program is shown in Figure 7-15.

Figure 7-15. Panel with gray background

The PANEL package does not retain its paint windows by default, so the repaint routine may be called more frequently than one might expect. Therefore, when the panel is created, the attribute WIN_RETAINED may be set to TRUE; otherwise, the routine should try to be as computationally cheap as possible so as to maintain good performance. It is not recommended that you retain the canvas unless you have provided your own repaint routine which perhaps make expensive use of graphics. Typically, you will set the background to a solid color, render a pattern, or display an image.

If a panel item is added, deleted or moved, then the repaint routine is called regardless of whether or not the panel's window is retained.

7.16.2 Painting Panel Items

To repaint either an individual item or an entire panel, use:

```
panel_paint(panel_object, paint_behavior)
    Panel_item     panel_object;
    Panel_setting paint_behavior;
```

The panel_object may be a panel item or a panel itself. If it is a panel, the items within the panel are repainted one by one. The argument paint_behavior is either PANEL_CLEAR, which causes the rectangle occupied by the panel or item to be cleared prior to repainting, or PANEL_NO_CLEAR, which causes repainting to be done without any prior clearing. This setting will override the default paint behavior set in the panel item's PANEL_PAINT attribute.

7.17 Panel Event Handling

This section describes how the PANEL package handles events. If you require a behavior not provided by default, you can write your own event handling procedure for either an individual item or the panel as a whole.

The default event handling mechanism for panels processes events for all the panel items in a uniform way. A single routine reads the events, updates an internal state machine, and maps the event to an *action* to be taken by the item. Actions fall into two categories: *previewing* and *accepting*. The previewing action gives the user visual feedback indicating what will happen when the mouse button is released. The accepting action causes the item's value to be changed and/or its notify procedure to be called, with the event passed as the last argument.

The default event-to-action mapping is given in Table 7-3:

Table 7-3. Default Event to Action Mapping

Event	Action
Left button down or drag in w/left button down	Begin previewing
Drag with left button down	Update previewing
Drag out of item rectangle with left button down	Cancel preview
Left button up	Accept
Right button down	Display menu & accept user's selection
Keystroke	Accept keystroke if text item

What actually happens when an item is told to perform one of the above actions depends on the type of the item. For example, when asked to begin previewing, a button item inverts its label, a message item does nothing, a slider item redraws the shaded area of its slider bar, etc.

ASCII events and some `action` events (described in Chapter 6, *Handling Input*) are automatically redirected towards the item with keyboard focus. Since only one text item may receive keyboard events, if there is more than one text item in the panel, the one that is receiving events has a solid caret.* You may use `PANEL_CARET_ITEM` with `xv_set()` or `xv_get()` to set or get the text item that currently has the active caret. Panel list items have their own windows, so events that occur in them are not propagated (even to text items).

Handling events by the application in panels is a task best avoided since the panel does this automatically. But there are certainly situations where the application might like to supervise or handle events itself. In such situations, there are several methods available for event handling in panels. You can use:

- The usual `WIN_EVENT_PROC` method (described in Chapter 6, *Handling Input*, and Chapter 5, *Canvases and Openwin*)

- `PANEL_BACKGROUND_PROC`

- `PANEL_EVENT_PROC`

Depending on the needs of the application, one of these is usually sufficient.

7.17.1 Using WIN_EVENT_PROC

To use `WIN_EVENT_PROC`, the event routine should be installed on the panel's paint window(s) exactly as it is done for canvases.

```
extern void my_event_proc();

panel = (Panel)xv_create(frame, PANEL, NULL);
xv_set(canvas_paint_window(panel),
    WIN_EVENT_PROC,    my_event_proc,
    NULL);
```

---

*Noncurrent text panel items have a gray caret to show the insertion point.

The panel has already set up the correct event masks, so setting event masks explicitly is not recommended. The example above sets up `my_event_proc()` to receive events in the panel's window. This does not interfere with the normal event processing handled by the panel. Selecting panel items still takes place, but now `my_event_proc()` will also know about the occurrence of such events.

7.17.2 Using PANEL_BACKGROUND_PROC

The `PANEL_BACKGROUND_PROC` is similar to the `WIN_EVENT_PROC` except that the notification routine is only notified of events that do not happen in, or are redirected to, panel items. It is probably the case that the application would want to know about events that are not sent to panel items.

```
extern void my_event_proc();

panel = (Panel)xv_create(frame, PANEL,
    PANEL_BACKGROUND_PROC,   my_event_proc,
    NULL);
```

Another difference between using `PANEL_BACKGROUND_PROC` and `WIN_EVENT_PROC` is that `PANEL_BACKGROUND_PROC` is installed in the *panel*, not the panel's subwindow as is the case for the `WIN_EVENT_PROC` method. Also, the calling parameters to the routine are different. The parameters to the routine for `PANEL_BACKGROUND_PROC` are:

```
my_event_proc(panel, event)
    Panel   panel;
    Event *event;
```

The `panel` here is not the window of the panel but the panel object itself.

The `PANEL_BACKGROUND_PROC` does not, by default, get keyboard events passed to it. Therefore, rather than trying to set this mask explicitly in the panel's window, the attribute `PANEL_ACCEPT_KEYSTROKE` can be set to `TRUE`. With this attribute set, ASCII events and function key events are passed to the routine.

7.17.3 Using PANEL_EVENT_PROC

Just as `PANEL_BACKGROUND_PROC` specifies a routine to handle events that happen outside of panel items, you can also get events that happen only *within* panel items using `PANEL_EVENT_PROC`. When this routine is installed in the panel, the default event procedure for all successively created items calls the installed event handler. If the `PANEL_EVENT_PROC` is later set to `NULL`, then the panel item's default event procedure is called.

```
xv_set(panel, PANEL_EVENT_PROC, my_event_proc, NULL);
```

Using this routine causes the default event handling for that item to be ignored in favor of the new event procedure. In other words, this routine *does* interfere with the normal event processing for panel items and the panel item's callback routine is no longer automatically called by the `PANEL` package.

If the `PANEL_EVENT_PROC` routine for the panel item is not interested in the event, or if that routine intends for the panel item to process the event normally, it may call `panel_default_handle_event()`. The public routine takes the form:

```
Xv_public void
panel_default_handle_event(item, event)
    Panel_item    item;
    Event         *event;
```

There are two special event codes especially for panel events: `PANEL_EVENT_CANCEL` and `PANEL_EVENT_DRAG_IN`. These two events are special because they track situations which are not always easily traced. Consider what happens when a panel button is selected. It is inverted, and as long as the pointer remains in the button, it should remain *highlighted* (inverted). But if the user drags the pointer out while the button is still down, the application needs to restore the button (turn highlighting off). In this case, the event `PANEL_EVENT_CANCEL` is sent to the routine installed as the `PANEL_EVENT_PROC`. Similarly, if the pointer is dragged into the window (with the button down), then the routine will receive the `PANEL_EVENT_DRAG_IN` event.

7.17.4 Event Handling Example

The program *item_move.c* (a longer program listed in Appendix G, *Example Programs*) demonstrates how events can be handled in panels. The program allows you to create, destroy and move around three different types of panel items. Two panels are displayed (see Figure 7-16). The control panel contains three panel items: a quit button (to exit the program), a text item to type in panel item names, and a choice item providing the different item types that may be created. The other panel is where newly created panel items are placed. After items are created, you may move them around the panel using the ADJUST mouse button. Moving the item off the panel deletes the item.

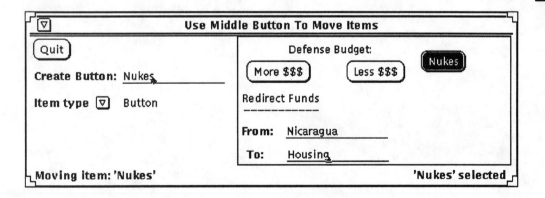

Figure 7-16. Output of item_move.c in use

item_move.c focuses on the use of `WIN_EVENT_PROC` to handle events within a panel. This does not interfere with the normal event processing for the panel; events continue to be dispatched to the panel items. Since the program is only interested in ADJUST button events that occur on panel items, it would seem appropriate to use PANEL_EVENT_PROC since it is designed to notify the routine only when panel items receive events. However, we chose not to use this method because when the mouse button is *dragged* around the frame to move the item, the dragging events may move outside of the button and the event callback would not be called.

Because panel items have no sense of Z-order (see Section 7.2, "Creating Panel Items"), care is taken to disallow panel items from being moved on top of one another.

7.18 Panel Package Summary

Table 7-4 lists the procedures and macros for the PANEL package; Table 7-5 lists the attributes. This information is described fully in Appendices A and B.

Table 7-4. Panel Procedures and Macros

Panel Procedures and Macros	
panel_advance_caret()	PANEL_EACH_ITEM()
panel_backup_caret()	PANEL_END_EACH()
panel_default_handle_event()	panel_paint()
PANEL_CHECK_BOX	panel_text_notify()
PANEL_CHOICE_STACK	PANEL_TOGGLE

Table 7-5. Panel Attributes

Panel Area	Panel Item	Panel List Item
PANEL_ACCEPT_KEYSTROKE	PANEL_ACCEPT_KEYSTROKE	PANEL_LIST_CHOOSE_NONE
PANEL_BACKGROUND_PROC	PANEL_EVENT_PROC	PANEL_LIST_CHOOSE_ONE
PANEL_CARET_ITEM	PANEL_INACTIVE	PANEL_LIST_CLIENT_DATA
PANEL_DEFAULT_ITEM	PANEL_ITEM_CLASS	PANEL_LIST_CLIENT_DATAS
PANEL_EVENT_PROC	PANEL_ITEM_COLOR	PANEL_LIST_DELETE
PANEL_EXTRA_PAINT_HEIGHT	PANEL_ITEM_RECT	PANEL_LIST_DISPLAY_ROWS
PANEL_EXTRA_PAINT_WIDTH	PANEL_LABEL_IMAGE	PANEL_LIST_FONT
PANEL_FIRST_ITEM	PANEL_LABEL_STRING	PANEL_LIST_FONTS
PANEL_ITEM_X	PANEL_LABEL_WIDTH	PANEL_LIST_GLYPH
PANEL_ITEM_X_GAP	PANEL_LABEL_X	PANEL_LIST_GLYPHS
PANEL_ITEM_Y	PANEL_LABEL_Y	PANEL_LIST_HEIGHT
PANEL_ITEM_Y_GAP	PANEL_LAYOUT	PANEL_LIST_INSERT
PANEL_LAYOUT	PANEL_NEXT_COL	PANEL_LIST_NROWS
PANEL_REPAINT_PROC	PANEL_NEXT_ITEM	PANEL_LIST_ROW_HEIGHT
	PANEL_NEXT_ROW	PANEL_LIST_SELECT
	PANEL_NOTIFY_PROC	PANEL_LIST_SELECTED
	PANEL_PAINT	PANEL_LIST_STRING
	PANEL_PARENT_PANEL	PANEL_LIST_STRINGS
	PANEL_READ_ONLY	PANEL_LIST_WIDTH
	PANEL_REPAINT_PROC	
	PANEL_VALUE_X	
	PANEL_VALUE_Y	
	XV_SHOW	

Panel Choice Item	Panel Slider Item	Panel Text Item
PANEL_CHOICE_FONT	PANEL_MAX_VALUE	PANEL_LABEL_WIDTH
PANEL_CHOICE_IMAGE	PANEL_MIN_VALUE	PANEL_MASK_CHAR
PANEL_CHOICE_IMAGES	PANEL_NOTIFY_LEVEL	PANEL_NOTIFY_LEVEL
PANEL_CHOICE_STRING	PANEL_SHOW_RANGE	PANEL_NOTIFY_STRING
PANEL_CHOICE_STRINGS	PANEL_SHOW_VALUE	PANEL_READ_ONLY
PANEL_CHOOSE_ONE	PANEL_SLIDER_WIDTH	PANEL_VALUE
PANEL_DEFAULT_VALUE	PANEL_VALUE	PANEL_VALUE_DISPLAY_LENGTH
PANEL_DISPLAY_LEVEL		PANEL_VALUE_STORED_LENGTH
PANEL_FEEDBACK		PANEL_VALUE_UNDERLINED
PANEL_TOGGLE_VALUE		
PANEL_VALUE		

Panel Button Item	Panel Message Item
PANEL_ITEM_MENU	PANEL_LABEL_BOLD

8

Text Subwindows

In This Chapter:

Creating Text Subwindows 182
Setting Text Subwindow Attributes 182
Text Subwindow Contents 182
Editing a Text Subwindow 183
   Loading a File 183
   Checking the Status of the Text Subwindow 183
   Writing to a Text Subwindow 185
   Reading from a Text Subwindow 185
   Deleting Text 186
   Emulating an Editing Character 187
   Replacing Characters 187
   The Editing Log 188
   Which File is Being Edited? 188
Saving Edits in a Subwindow 189
   Storing Edits 189
   Discarding Edits 190
Setting the Contents of a Text Subwindow 190
   TEXTSW_FILE_CONTENTS 190
   TEXTSW_CONTENTS 191
   TEXTSW_INSERT_FROM_FILE 191
Positioning the Text Displayed in a Text Subwindow 192
   Screen Lines and File Lines 192
   Absolute Positioning 192
   Relative Positioning 193
   Which File Lines are Visible? 193
Finding and Matching a Pattern 194
   Matching a Span of Characters 194
   Matching a Specific Pattern 195
Marking Positions 196
   Getting a Text Selection 197
   Setting the Primary Selection 198
Dealing with Multiple Views 198
Notifications from a Text Subwindow 199

Text Subwindow Package Summary 202

8
Text Subwindows

This chapter describes the TEXTSW package, which allows a user or client to display and edit a sequence of ASCII characters. Figure 8-1 shows an example of a text subwindow. The text contains a vertical scrollbar but may not contain a horizontal scrollbar. The vertical scrollbar can be used to split views into several views (see Chapter 5, *Canvases and Openwin* for this openwin functionality). The font used by the text can be specified using the XV_FONT generic attribute, but only one font per text subwindow can be used, regardless of how many views there may be. See the program *textsw.font.c* in Appendix G, *Example Programs*, for an example about changing fonts in text subwindows.

The contents of a text subwindow are stored in a file or in memory on the client side, not on the X server. Whether the *source* of the text is stored on disk or in memory is transparent to the user. When the user types characters in the text subwindow, the source might be changed immediately or synchronized later depending on how the text subwindow is configured. The TEXTSW package provides basic text editing features such as inserting arbitrary text into a file. It also provides complex operations such as searching for and replacing a string of text.

Figure 8-1. A sample text subwindow

8.1 Creating Text Subwindows

Applications need to include the file *<xview/textsw.h>* to use text subwindows. You create a text subwindow the same way that you create any XView object, by calling `xv_create()` with the appropriate type parameters:

```
Textsw textsw;
textsw = (Textsw)xv_create(base_frame, TEXTSW, NULL);
```

8.2 Setting Text Subwindow Attributes

As for all XView objects, you can set attribute-value pairs to configure the text subwindow accordingly. Like the CANVAS package, the text subwindow object is subclassed from the OPENWIN package and can therefore be split into separate views. The package handles all of its own events and redisplaying of text, so none of these things is handled by the application.

Most text subwindow attributes are orthogonal; that is, attribute order does not effect the object. In a few cases, however, the attributes in a list might interact, so you must specify them in a particular order. Such cases are noted in the sections that follow. For example, you must pass TEXTSW_STATUS first in any call to `xv_create()` or `xv_set()` *only* if you want to find the status after setting some other attribute in the same call.

8.3 Text Subwindow Contents

The contents of a text subwindow are a sequence of characters. Each character can be uniquely identified by its position in the sequence (type `Textsw_index`). Editing operations, such as inserting and deleting text, can cause the index of successive characters to change. The valid indices are 0 through *length* −1 inclusive, where *length* is the number of characters currently in the text subwindow, returned by the TEXTSW_LENGTH attribute.

The text subwindow has a notion of the current index after which the next character will be inserted. This is called the *insertion point* and is indicated by a caret, as shown in Figure 8-2.

```
The contents of a text subwindow are a sequence of characters.
Each character can be uniquely identified by its position
```

Figure 8-2. A caret marks the insertion point

8.4 Editing a Text Subwindow

A text subwindow can be edited by the user or by a client program. When you create a text subwindow, the user is normally allowed to edit it. By using the special attributes discussed in this section, the client program can edit the subwindow. These edits are then stored in */tmp/textProcess-id.Counter*.

The next five sections explain the functions and attributes that you will use to load, read, write, edit, and finally save a text file.

8.4.1 Loading a File

You can load a file into a text subwindow by using TEXTSW_FILE, as in:

```
xv_set(textsw, TEXTSW_FILE, file_name, NULL);
```

Keep in mind that if the existing text has been edited, then these edits will be lost. To avoid such loss, first check whether there are any outstanding edits by calling:

```
int modified = (int)xv_get(textsw, TEXTSW_MODIFIED)
```

If there have been updates, you may choose to synchronize with the *source* if necessary. That is, if the existing text is part of a file, you can overwrite the existing changes before loading in a new file.

The above call to xv_set(), which loads the new file, positions the new text so that the first character displayed has the same index as the first character that was displayed in the previous file. This is probably not what you want. The code segment below shows how to load the file at a set position:

```
xv_set(textsw,
    TEXTSW_FILE,  file_name,
    TEXTSW_FIRST, position,
    NULL);
```

The first character displayed has its index set by position. The order of these attributes matters. Because attributes are evaluated in the order given, reversing the order would first reposition the existing file, then load the new file. This would cause an unnecessary repaint. It would also mis-position the old file if it was shorter than position.

8.4.2 Checking the Status of the Text Subwindow

Both of the calls in the previous example blindly trust that the load of the new file was successful. This is, in general, a bad idea. The following code segment shows how to find out whether the load succeeded, and if not, why it failed:

```
Textsw_status status;

xv_set(textsw,
    TEXTSW_STATUS,      &status,
    TEXTSW_FILE,        file_name,
    TEXTSW_FIRST,       position,
    NULL);
```

NOTE

The TEXTSW_STATUS attribute and handle must appear in the attribute list
before the operation whose status you want to determine.

The range of values for such a variable are enumerated in Table 8-1. Note that in the first
column, each value begins with the prefix TEXTSW_STATUS_, which has been omitted from
the table to improve readability.

Table 8-1. Range of Values for Status Variables

Value (TEXTSW_STATUS_ ...)	Description
OKAY	The operation encountered no problems.
BAD_ATTR	The attribute list contained an illegal or unrecognized attribute.
BAD_ATTR_VALUE	The attribute list contained an illegal value for an attribute, usually an out-of-range value for an enumeration.
CANNOT_ALLOCATE	A call to calloc(2) or malloc(2) failed.
CANNOT_OPEN_INPUT	The specified input file does not exist or cannot be accessed.
CANNOT_INSERT_FROM_FILE	The operation encountered a problem when trying to insert from file.
OUT_OF_MEMORY	The operation ran out of memory while editing in memory.
OTHER_ERROR	The operation encountered a problem not covered by any of the other error indications.

8.4.3 Writing to a Text Subwindow

To insert text into a text subwindow at the current insertion point, call:

```
Textsw_index
textsw_insert(textsw, buf, buf_len)
    Textsw  textsw;
    char    *buf;
    int     buf_len;
```

The return value is the number of characters actually inserted into the text subwindow. This number will equal `buf_len` unless either the text subwindow has had a memory allocation failure or the portion of text containing the insertion point is read only. The insertion point is moved forward by the number of characters inserted.

This routine does not do terminal-style interpretation of the input characters. Thus, editing characters (such as CTRL-H or DEL for character erase) are simply inserted into the text subwindow rather than performing edits to the existing contents of the text subwindow. To emulate a terminal, scan the characters to be inserted and invoke `textsw_edit()` where appropriate, as described in the next section.

Setting the Insertion Point

The attribute `TEXTSW_INSERTION_POINT` is used to interrogate and set the insertion point. For instance, the following call determines where the insertion point is:

```
Textsw_index point;

point = (Textsw_index)xv_get(textsw, TEXTSW_INSERTION_POINT);
```

Whereas the following call sets the insertion point to be just before the third character of the text:

```
xv_set(textsw, TEXTSW_INSERTION_POINT, 2, NULL);
```

To set the insertion point at the end of the text, set `TEXTSW_INSERTION_POINT` to the special index `TEXTSW_INFINITY`. This call does not ensure that the new insertion point will be visible in the text subwindow, even if `TEXTSW_INSERT_MAKES_VISIBLE` is TRUE. To guarantee that the caret will be visible afterwards, call `textsw_possibly_normalize()`, a procedure that is described later in this chapter.

8.4.4 Reading from a Text Subwindow

Many applications that incorporate text subwindows never need to read the contents of the text directly from the text subwindow. For instance, the text subwindow might display text for the user to view but not to edit.

Even when the user is allowed to edit text, some applications simply wait for the user to perform some action that indicates that all of the edits have been made. The application can then use either `textsw_save()` or `textsw_store_file()` to place the text in the file.

The text can then be read via the usual file input utilities, or the file itself can be passed off to another routine or program.

It is, however, useful to be able to directly examine the text in the text subwindow. You can do this using the TEXTSW_CONTENTS attribute. The code fragment below illustrates how to use TEXTSW_CONTENTS to get a span of characters from the text subwindow. It gets 1000 characters beginning at position 500 out of the text subwindow and places them into a NULL-terminated string.

```
#define TO_READ 1000

char          buf[TO_READ+1];
Textsw_index next_pos;

next_pos = (Textsw_index) xv_get(textsw, TEXTSW_CONTENTS, 500,
                                 buf, TO_READ);

if (next_pos != 500+TO_READ) {
    /* handle error case */
} else
    buf[TO_READ] = '\0';
```

8.4.5 Deleting Text

You can delete a contiguous span of characters from a text subwindow by calling:

```
Textsw_index
textsw_delete(textsw, first, last_plus_one)
    Textsw          textsw;
    Textsw_index  first, last_plus_one;
```

first specifies the first character of the span that will be deleted; last_plus_one specifies the first character *after* the span that will *not* be deleted. first should be less than or equal to last_plus_one. To delete to the end of the text, pass the special value TEXTSW_INFINITY for last_plus_one.

The return value is the number of characters deleted or:

```
last_plus_one - first
```

unless all or part of the specified span is read-only. In this case, only those characters that are not read-only will be deleted, and the return value will indicate how many such characters there were. If the insertion point is in the span being deleted, it will be left at first.

A side effect of calling textsw_delete() is that the deleted characters become the contents of the global Clipboard. To remove the characters from the text subwindow without affecting the Clipboard, call:

```
Textsw_index
textsw_erase(textsw, first, last_plus_one)
    Textsw          textsw;
    Textsw_index  first, last_plus_one;
```

Again, the return value is the number of characters removed, and last_plus_one can be TEXTSW_INFINITY.

Both of these procedures will return 0 if the operation fails.

8.4.6 Emulating an Editing Character

You can emulate the behavior of an editing character, such as CTRL-H, with textsw_edit():

```
Textsw_index
textsw_edit(textsw, unit, count, direction)
     Textsw    textsw;
     unsigned   unit, count, direction;
```

Depending on the value of unit, this routine will erase either a character, a word or a line. Set unit to:

- TEXTSW_UNIT_IS_CHAR to erase individual characters.

- TEXTSW_UNIT_IS_WORD to erase the span of characters that make up a word (including any intervening white space or other nonword characters).

- TEXTSW_UNIT_IS_LINE to erase all characters in the line on one side of the insertion point.

If the direction parameter is 0, the operation will affect characters after the insertion point; otherwise, it will affect characters before the insertion point.

The count parameter determines the number of times the operation will be applied. Set it to 1 to do the edit once or to a value greater than 1 to do multiple edits in a single call. textsw_edit() returns the number of characters actually removed.

For example, suppose you want to interpret the function key F7 as meaning *delete word forward*. On receiving the event code for the F7 key, you would make the call:

```
textsw_edit(textsw, TEXTSW_UNIT_IS_WORD, 1, NULL);
```

8.4.7 Replacing Characters

While a span of characters can be replaced by calling textsw_erase() followed by textsw_insert(), character replacement is done most efficiently by calling:

```
Textsw_index
textsw_replace_bytes(textsw, first, last_plus_one, buf, buf_len)
     Textsw          textsw;
     Textsw_index    first, last_plus_one;
     char            *buf;
     int             buf_len;
```

The span of characters to be replaced is specified by first and last_plus_one, just as in the call to textsw_erase(). The new characters are specified by buf and buf_len, just as in the call to textsw_insert(). Once again, if last_plus_one is TEXTSW_INFINITY, the replace operation affects all characters from first to the end of the text. If the insertion point is in the span being replaced, it will be left at:

```
first + buf_len
```

The return value is the net number of bytes inserted. The number is negative if the original string is longer than the one that replaces it. If a problem occurs when an attempt is made to replace a span, it will return an error code of 0.

`textsw_replace_bytes()`, like `textsw_erase()`, does *not* put the characters it removes on the global Clipboard.

8.4.8 The Editing Log

All text subwindows allow the user to undo editing actions. The `TEXTSW` package keeps a running log of all the edits. If a file is associated with the text subwindow, this log is kept in a file in the */tmp* directory. This file can grow until the file system in which this directory resides runs out of space. To limit the size of the edit log and to avoid filling up all of */tmp*, the user can set the text wrap-around size with `TEXTSW_WRAPAROUND_SIZE`. If there is no associated file, the edit log is kept in memory, and the maximum size of the log is controlled by the attribute `TEXTSW_MEMORY_MAXIMUM`, which defaults to 20,000 bytes.

Unfortunately, once a memory-resident edit log has reached its maximum size, no more characters can be inserted into or removed from the text subwindow. In particular, since deletions as well as insertions are logged, space cannot be recovered by deleting characters.

It is important to understand how the edit log works, since you might want to use a text subwindow with no associated file to implement a temporary scratch area or error message log. If such a text subwindow is used for a long time, the default limit of 20,000 bytes might well be reached, and either the user or your code will be unable to insert any more characters, even though only a few characters might be visible in the text subwindow. Therefore, it is recommended to set `TEXTSW_MEMORY_MAXIMUM` to a much higher value, say 200,000.

8.4.9 Which File is Being Edited?

To find out the name of the file in the text subwindow, call:

```
int
textsw_append_file_name(textsw, name)
    Textsw   textsw;
    char    *name;
```

If the text subwindow is editing memory, then this routine will return a nonzero value. Otherwise, it will return 0 and append the name of the file to the end of `name`. The following code gets the name of the current file:

```
char name[BUFSIZ];

name[0] = '\0';
if (textsw_append_file_name(textsw, name) == 0)
    printf("File name is: %s\n", name);
```

Interactions with the File System

Suppose the current file is called *myfile*. If the user chooses 'Save Current File' from the subwindow's menu (or if the client code invokes `textsw_save()`), the following sequence of file operations occurs:

- *myfile* is copied to *myfile%*.

- The contents of *myfile%* are combined with information from the edit log file (*/tmp/TextProcess-id.Counter*) and written over *myfile*, thereby preserving all its permissions, etc.

- The edit log file is removed from */tmp*.

If *myfile* is a symbolic link to *../some_dir/otherfile*, then the backup file is created as *../some_dir/otherfile%*.

Keep in mind that the user can change the current directory by selecting 'Load File' or 'Set Directory' from the text subwindow menu. If *myfile* is a relative path name, then both the copy to *myfile%* and the save take place in the current directory.

8.5 Saving Edits in a Subwindow

To save any edits made to a file currently loaded into a text subwindow call:

```
unsigned
textsw_save(textsw, locx, locy)
    Textsw  textsw;
    int     locx, locy;
```

`locx` and `locy` are relative to the upper-left corner of the text subwindow and are used to position the upper-left corner of the alert should the save fail for some reason—usually they should be 0. The return value is 0 if and only if the save succeeded.

8.5.1 Storing Edits

The text subwindow might not contain a file, or the client might wish to place the edited version of the text (whether or not the original text came from a file) in some specific file. To store the contents of a text subwindow to a file call:

```
unsigned
textsw_store_file(textsw, filename, locx, locy)
    Textsw  textsw;
    char    *filename;
    int     locx, locy;
```

Again, `locx` and `locy` are used to position the upper-left corner of the message box. The return value is 0 if and only if the store succeeded.

By default, this call changes the file that the text subwindow is editing, so that subsequent saves will save the edits to the new file. To override this policy, set the attribute TEXTSW_STORE_CHANGES_FILE to FALSE.

8.5.2 Discarding Edits

To discard the edits performed on the contents of a text subwindow, call:

```
void
textsw_reset(textsw, locx, locy)
    Textsw    textsw;
    int       locx, locy;
```

locx and locy are as above. Note that if the text subwindow contains a file that has not been edited, the effect of textsw_reset is to unload the file and replace it by memory provided by the TEXTSW package; thus, the user will see an absolutely empty text subwindow. Alternatively, if the text subwindow was already editing memory, then another, untouched, piece of primary memory will be provided and the edited piece will be deallocated.

8.6 Setting the Contents of a Text Subwindow

The rest of this chapter describes the other functions that are available for text subwindows. These features include setting the contents of a subwindow, setting the primary selection, and dealing with multiple or split views.

You might want to set the initial contents of a text subwindow that your application uses. To set the initial contents of a text subwindow, use one of three attributes: TEXTSW_INSERT_FROM_FILE, TEXTSW_FILE_CONTENTS and TEXTSW_CONTENTS. Each attribute is illustrated in code fragments given below.

8.6.1 TEXTSW_FILE_CONTENTS

The attribute TEXTSW_FILE_CONTENTS allows a client to initialize the text subwindow contents from a file yet still edit the contents in memory. The user can return a text subwindow to its initial state after an editing session by choosing 'Undo All Edits' in the text menu.

The code fragment below shows how you would use this attribute:

```
extern char *filename;

xv_set(textsw,
    TEXTSW_FILE_CONTENTS, filename,
    TEXTSW_FIRST,          0,
    NULL);
```

When the client calls the undo routine and filename is not a null string, the memory used by the text subwindow is reinitialized with the contents of the file specified by filename.

When the client calls the undo routine and the `filename` is a null string, the memory used by the text subwindow is reinitialized with the previous contents of the text subwindow.

8.6.2 TEXTSW_CONTENTS

`TEXTSW_CONTENTS` lets you insert a text string from memory, instead of a file, into the text subwindow. The default for this attribute is `NULL`.

Using `xv_create()` with this attribute specifies the initial contents for a nonfile text subwindow.

Using `xv_set()` with this attribute sets the contents of a window, as in:

```
xv_set(textsw, TEXTSW_CONTENTS, "text", NULL);
```

If you use `xv_get()` with this attribute, you will need to provide additional parameters, as in:

```
xv_get(textsw, TEXTSW_CONTENTS, pos, buf, buf_len);
```

The return value is the next position to be read. The buffer array:

```
buf[0 ... buf_len-1]
```

is filled with the characters from `textsw` beginning at the index `pos` and is `NULL`-terminated only if there were too few characters to fill the buffer.

8.6.3 TEXTSW_INSERT_FROM_FILE

`TEXTSW_INSERT_FROM_FILE` allows a client to insert the contents of a file into a text subwindow at the current insertion point. It is the programming equivalent of a user choosing 'Include File' from the text menu.

The code below demonstrates this attribute:

```
Textsw            textsw;
Textsw_status     status;

xv_set(textsw,
    TEXTSW_STATUS,             &status,
    TEXTSW_INSERT_FROM_FILE,   filename,
    NULL);
```

Three status values can be returned for this attribute when the argument `TEXTSW_STATUS` is passed in the same call to `xv_create()` or `xv_set()`:

```
TEXTSW_STATUS_OKAY
TEXTSW_STATUS_CANNOT_INSERT_FROM_FILE
TEXTSW_STATUS_OUT_OF_MEMORY
```

8.7 Positioning the Text Displayed in a Text Subwindow

Usually, more text is managed by the text subwindow than can be displayed all at once. As a result, it is often necessary to determine the indices of the characters that are being displayed and to control exactly which portion of the text is visible.

8.7.1 Screen Lines and File Lines

When there are long lines in the text, it is necessary to distinguish between two definitions of "line of text."

A *screen line* reflects what is actually displayed on the screen. A line begins with the left-most character in the subwindow and continues across until either a newline character or the right edge of the subwindow is encountered. A *file line*, on the other hand, can only be terminated by the newline character. It is defined as the span of characters starting after a newline character (or the beginning of the file) running through the next newline character (or the end of the file).

Whenever the right edge of the subwindow is encountered before the newline, if the following attribute-value pair were specified:

```
TEXTSW_LINE_BREAK_ACTION, TEXTSW_WRAP_AT_CHAR
```

then the next character and its successors would be displayed on the next lower screen line. In this case, there would be two screen lines, but only one file line. From the perspective of the display there are two lines; from the perspective of the file, only one. On the other hand, if the following attribute-value pair were specified:

```
TEXTSW_LINE_BREAK_ACTION, TEXTSW_WRAP_AT_WORD
```

then the entire word would be displayed on the next line.

Unless otherwise specified, all text subwindow attributes and procedures use the *file line* definition. Line indices have a zero-origin, like the character indices; that is, the first line has index 0, not 1.

8.7.2 Absolute Positioning

Two attributes are provided to allow you to specify which portion of the text is displayed in the text subwindow.

Setting the attribute TEXTSW_FIRST to a given index causes the first character of the line containing the index to become the first character displayed in the text subwindow. Thus, the following call causes the text to be positioned so that the first displayed character is the first character of the line that contains index 1000:

```
xv_set(textsw, TEXTSW_FIRST, 1000, NULL);
```

Since the text subwindow is subclassed from the OPENWIN package and can be split into several views, the previous code fragment would only cause the positioning of one view. To position all of the views in a text subwindow, use the attribute `TEXTSW_FOR_ALL_VIEWS`, as in the following call:

```
xv_set(textsw,
    TEXTSW_FOR_ALL_VIEWS,  TRUE,
    TEXTSW_FIRST,          1000,
    NULL);
```

Conversely, the following call retrieves the index of the first displayed character:

```
index = (Textsw_index)xv_get(textsw, TEXTSW_FIRST);
```

A related attribute, useful in similar situations, is `TEXTSW_FIRST_LINE`. When used in a call on `xv_set()` or `xv_get()`, the value is a file line index within the text.

You can determine the character index that corresponds to a given line index (both zero-origin) within the text by calling:

```
Textsw_index
textsw_index_for_file_line(textsw, line)
    Textsw   textsw;
    int      line;
```

The return value is the character index for the first character in the line, so character index 0 always corresponds to line index 0.

8.7.3 Relative Positioning

To move the text in a text subwindow up or down by a small number of lines, call the routine:

```
void
textsw_scroll_lines(textsw, count)
Textsw   textsw;
int      count;
```

A positive value for `count` causes the text to scroll up, while a negative value causes the text to scroll down.

When calling `textsw_scroll_lines()`, you might want to know how many screen lines are in the text subwindow. You can find this out by calling:

```
int
textsw_screen_line_count(textsw)
    Textsw   textsw;
```

8.7.4 Which File Lines are Visible?

Exactly which file lines are visible on the screen is determined by calling:

```
void
textsw_file_lines_visible(textsw, top, bottom)
    Textsw   textsw;
    int      *top, *bottom;
```

This routine fills in the addressed integers with the file line indices of the first and last file lines being displayed in the specified text subwindow.

Guaranteeing What is Visible

To ensure that a particular line or character is visible, call:

```
void
textsw_possibly_normalize(textsw, position)
    Textsw        textsw;
    Textsw_index position;
```

The text subwindow must be displayed on the screen before this function will work.

If the character at the specified `position` is already visible, then this routine does nothing. If it is not visible, then it repositions the text so that it is visible and at the top of the subwindow.

If a particular character should always be at the top of the subwindow, then calling the following routine is more appropriate:

```
void
textsw_normalize_view(textsw, position)
    Textsw        textsw;
    Textsw_index position;
```

Ensuring that the Insertion Point is Visible

Most of the programmatic editing actions do not update the text subwindow to display the caret, even if `TEXTSW_INSERT_MAKES_VISIBLE` is set. If you want to ensure that the insertion point is visible, use:

```
textsw_possibly_normalize(textsw,
    (Textsw_index) xv_get(textsw, TEXTSW_INSERTION_POINT));
```

8.8 Finding and Matching a Pattern

A common operation performed on text is to find a span of characters that match some specification. The text subwindow provides several rudimentary pattern matching facilities. This section describes two functions that you can call in order to perform similar operations.

8.8.1 Matching a Span of Characters

To find the nearest span of characters that match a pattern, call:

```
int
textsw_find_bytes(textsw, first, last_plus_one, buf,
                  buf_len, flags)
```

```
Textsw          textsw;
Textsw_index *first, *last_plus_one;
char            *buf;
unsigned        buf_len;
unsigned        flags;
```

The pattern to match is specified by `buf` and `buf_len`. The matching operation looks for an exact and literal match—it is sensitive to case and does not recognize any kind of meta-character in the pattern. `first` specifies the position at which to start the search. If `flags` is 0, the search proceeds forward through the text; if `flags` is 1, the search proceeds backwards. The return value is –1 if the pattern cannot be found; otherwise it is some non-negative value, in which case the indices addressed by `first` and `last_plus_one` will have been updated to indicate the span of characters that match the pattern.

8.8.2 Matching a Specific Pattern

Another useful operation is to find delimited text. For example, you might want to find the starting and ending brace in a piece of code. To find a matching pattern, call:

```
int
textsw_match_bytes(textsw, first, last_plus_one,
                   start_sym, start_sym_len,
                   end_sym, end_sym_len, field_flag)
Textsw          textsw;
Textsw_index *first, *last_plus_one;
char            *start_sym, *end_sym;
int             start_sym_len, end_sym_len;
unsigned        field_flag;
```

`first` stores the starting position of the pattern that you want to search for. `last_plus_one` stores the cursor position of the end pattern. Its value is one position past the text. `start_sym` and `end_sym` store the beginning position and ending position of the pattern, respectively. `start_sym_len` and `end_sym_len` store the starting and ending pattern's length, respectively.

Use one of the following three field flag values to search for matches:

TEXTSW_DELIMITER_FORWARD	Begins from `first` and searches forward until it finds `start_sym` and matches it forward with `end_sym`.
TEXTSW_DELIMITER_BACKWARD	Begins from `first` and searches backward for `end_sym` and matches it backward with `start_sym`.
TEXTSW_DELIMITER_ENCLOSE	Begins from `first` and expands both directions to match `start_sym` and `end_sym` of the next level.

If no match is found, then `textsw_match_bytes()` will return a value of –1. If a match is found, then it will return the index of the first match.

The code fragment below can be used to find delimited text. Notice that the `field_flag` value is `TEXTSW_DELIMITER_FORWARD`.

```
Textsw_index      first, last_plus_one, pos;

first = (Textsw_index) xv_get(textsw, TEXTSW_INSERTION_POINT);
pos = textsw_match_bytes(textsw, &first, &last_plus_one,
                    "/*", 2,
                    "*/", 2, TEXTSW_DELIMITER_FORWARD);
if (pos > 0) {
    textsw_set_selection(textsw, first, last_plus_one, 1);
    xv_set(textsw, TEXTSW_INSERTION_POINT, last_plus_one, NULL);
} else
    (void) window_bell(textsw);
```

This code searches forward from first until it finds the starting /* and matches it forward
with the next */. If no match is found, a bell will ring in the text subwindow.

8.9 Marking Positions

Often a client wants to keep track of a particular character or group of characters that are in
the text subwindow. Given that arbitrary editing can occur in a text subwindow and that it is
very tedious to intercept and track all of the editing operations applied to a text subwindow, it
is often easier to simply place one or more marks at various positions in the text subwindow.
These marks are automatically updated by the text subwindow to account for user and client
edits. There is no limit to the number of marks you can add.

A new mark is created by calling:

```
Textsw_mark
textsw_add_mark(textsw, position, flags)
    Textsw          textsw;
    Textsw_index    position;
    unsigned        flags;
```

The flags argument is either TEXTSW_MARK_DEFAULTS or TEXTSW_MARK_
MOVE_AT_INSERT. The latter causes an insertion at the marked position to move the mark to
the end of the inserted text, whereas the former causes the mark to not move when text is
inserted at the mark's current position. As an example, suppose that the text managed by the
text subwindow consists of the two lines:

```
this is the first line
not this, which is the second
```

Assume a mark is set at position 5 (just before the *i* in *is* on the first line) with flags of
TEXTSW_MARK_MOVE_AT_INSERT.

If the user makes a selection just before the *is* (thereby placing the insertion point before the
i, at position 5) and types an *h*, making the text read:

```
this his the first line
not this, which is the second
```

the mark moves with the insertion point and they both end up at position 6.

However, if the `flags` had been `TEXTSW_MARK_DEFAULTS`, then the mark would remain at position 5 after the user typed the *h*, although the insertion point moved on to position 6.

Now, suppose instead that the user made a selection before the *this* on the first line, and typed *Kep*, making the text read:

```
Kepthis is the first line
not this, which is the second
```

In this case, no matter what `flags` the mark had been created with, it would end up at position 8, still just before the *i* in *is*.

If a mark is in the middle of a span of characters that is subsequently deleted, the mark moves to the beginning of the span. Going back to the original scenario, with the original text and the mark set at position 5, assume that the user deletes from the *h* in *this* through the *e* in *the* on the first line, resulting in the text:

```
te first line
not this, which is the second
```

When the user is done, the mark will be at position 1, just before the *e* in *te*.

The current position of a mark is determined by calling:

```
Textsw_index
textsw_find_mark(textsw, mark)
    Textsw        textsw;
    Textsw_mark   mark;
```

An existing mark is removed by calling:

```
void
textsw_remove_mark(textsw, mark)
    Textsw        textsw;
    Textsw_mark   mark;
```

Note that marks are dynamically allocated, and it is the client's responsibility to keep track of them and to remove them when they are no longer needed.

8.9.1 Getting a Text Selection

A user selects a portion of the contents of the text subwindow using a pointer. A text selection is indicated on the screen with reverse-video highlighting. An application needs to know which window has the current selection and what the contents of a text selection are. The TEXTSW package does not provide procedures to get this information. Instead, these functions are carried out by the Selection Service. For an example of how this is done, see Chapter 18, *The Selection Service*. Figure 8-3 shows a text selection:

The contents of a text subwindow are a sequence of characters.
Each character can be uniquely identified by its position
in the sequence (type \f(CWTextsw_index)\fR.
Editing operations, such as inserting and deleting text, may cause the
index of successive characters to change.

Figure 8-3. A text selection

8.9.2 Setting the Primary Selection

Primary and secondary selections are maintained. The primary selection can be set by calling:

```
void
textsw_set_selection(textsw, first, last_plus_one, type)
    Textsw          textsw;
    Textsw_index    first, last_plus_one;
    unsigned        type;
```

A value of 1 for type means *primary selection*, while a value of 2 means *secondary selection*, and a value of 17 is *pending delete*. Note that there is no requirement that all or part of the selection be visible; use textsw_possibly_normalize() to guarantee visibility (see Section 8.7.4, "Which File Lines are Visible?").

8.10 Dealing with Multiple Views

By splitting a text view, the user can create multiple views of the text being managed by the text subwindow. Although these additional views are usually transparent to the client code controlling the text subwindow, it might occasionally be necessary for a client to deal directly with all of the views. This is accomplished by using the following routines, with the knowledge that split views are simply extra text subwindows that happen to share the text of the original text subwindow.

```
Textsw
textsw_first(textsw)
    Textsw textsw;
```

Given an arbitrary view out of a set of multiple views, textsw_first() returns the first view (currently, this is the original text subwindow that the client created). To move through the other views of the set, call:

```
Textsw
textsw_next(textsw)
    Textsw textsw;
```

Given any view of the set, textsw_next() returns some other member of the set or NULL if there are none left to enumerate. The loop coded below is guaranteed to process all of the views in the set:

```
    for (textsw = textsw_first(any_split); textsw;
                    textsw = textsw_next(textsw)) {
        /* processing involving textsw */
    }
```

When you create a text subwindow, take into account that the user might split the window. If you try to do something like enlarge the window, you might run into problems.

8.11 Notifications from a Text Subwindow

The text subwindow notifies its client about interesting changes in the subwindow's or text's state by calling a notification procedure. It also calls this procedure in response to user actions. If the client does not provide an explicit notification procedure by using the attribute TEXTSW_NOTIFY_PROC, then the text subwindow provides a default procedure. The declaration for this procedure looks like:

```
void
notify_proc(textsw, avlist)
    Textsw          textsw;
    Attr_avlist     avlist;
```

avlist contains attributes that are the members of the Textsw_action enumeration.

Your notification procedure must be careful either to process all of the possible attributes or to pass through the attributes that it does not process to the standard notification procedure. This is important because among the attributes that can be in the *avlist* are those that cause the standard notification procedure to implement the possible *Front*, *Back*, *Open*, *Close* and *Quit* accelerators of the user interface.

Example 8-1 presents a client notify procedure for a text subwindow:

Example 8-1. Client notify procedure for a text subwindow
```
int (*default_textsw_notify)();

void
client_notify_proc(textsw, attributes)
Textsw          textsw;
Attr_avlist     attributes;
{
    int   pass_on   = FALSE;
    Attr_avlist     attrs;

    for (attrs = attributes; *attrs; attrs = attr_next(attrs)) {
        switch ((Textsw_action)(*attrs)) {
            case TEXTSW_ACTION_CAPS_LOCK:
                /* Swallow this attribute */
                ATTR_CONSUME(*attrs);
                break;
            case TEXTSW_ACTION_CHANGED_DIRECTORY:
                /* Monitor the attribute, don't swallow it */
                strcpy(current_directory, (char *)attrs[1]);
                pass_on = TRUE;
                break;
```

Example 8-1. Client notify procedure for a text subwindow (continued)

```
            default:
                pass_on = TRUE;
                break;
        }
    }
    if (pass_on)
        (void) default_textsw_notify(textsw, attributes);
}
default_textsw_notify =
    (void (*) ())xv_get(textsw, TEXTSW_NOTIFY_PROC);
xv_set(textsw, TEXTSW_NOTIFY_PROC, client_notify_proc, NULL);
```

The `Textsw_action` attributes that can be passed to your notify procedure are listed in
Table 8-2. Note that in the first column, each attribute begins with the prefix
`TEXTSW_ACTION_`, which has been omitted from the table to improve readability. Remember that the attributes constitute a special class that are passed to your text subwindow notification procedure. They are not attributes of the text subwindow in the usual sense and cannot be retrieved or modified using `xv_get()` or `xv_set()`.

Table 8-2. Textsw_action Attributes

Attribute (TEXTSW_ACTION_ ...)	Type	Description
CAPS_LOCK	Boolean	The user pressed the Caps Lock key to change the setting of the Caps Lock (it is initially 0, meaning off).
CHANGED_DIRECTORY	char *	The current working directory for the process has been changed to the directory named by the provided string value.
EDITED_FILE	char *	The file named by the provided string value has been edited. Appears once per session of edits (see below).
EDITED_MEMORY	none	Monitors whether an empty text subwindow has been edited.
FILE_IS_READONLY	char *	The file named by the provided string value does not have write permission.
LOADED_FILE	char *	The text subwindow is being used to view the file named by the provided string value.
TOOL_CLOSE	(no value)	The frame containing the text subwindow should become iconic.
TOOL_DESTROY	Event *	The tool containing the text subwindow should exit, without checking for a veto from other subwindows. The value is the user action that caused the destroy.

Table 8-2. Textsw_action Attributes (continued)

Attribute (TEXTSW_ACTION_ ...)	Type	Description
TOOL_QUIT	Event *	The tool containing the text subwindow should exit normally. The value is the user action that caused the exit.
TOOL_MGR	Event *	The tool containing the text subwindow should do the window manager operation associated with the provided event value.
USING_MEMORY	(no value)	The text subwindow is being used to edit a string stored in primary memory, not a file.

The attribute TEXTSW_ACTION_EDITED_FILE is a slight misnomer, as it is given to the notify procedure *after* the first edit to *any* text, whether or not it came from a file. This notification only happens once per session of edits, where notification of TEXTSW_ACTION_LOADED_FILE is considered to terminate the old session and start a new one.

NOTE

The attribute TEXTSW_ACTION_LOADED_FILE must be treated very carefully because the notify procedure gets called with this attribute in several situations: after a file is initially loaded, after any successful 'Save Current File' menu operation, after an 'Undo All Edits' menu operation, and during successful calls to textsw_reset(), textsw_save() and textsw_store().

The appropriate response by the procedure is to interpret these notifications as being equivalent to:

The text subwindow is displaying the file named by the provided string value; no edits have been performed on the file yet. In addition, any previously displayed or edited file has been either reset, saved, or stored under another name.

Text
Subwindows

8.12 Text Subwindow Package Summary

Table 8-3 lists the attributes, procedures and macros for the TEXTSW package. This information is described fully in Appendices A and B.

Table 8-3. Text Subwindow Attributes, Procedures and Macros

Attributes	Procedures and Macros
TEXTSW_AGAIN_RECORDING	textsw_add_mark()
TEXTSW_AUTO_INDENT	textsw_append_file_name()
TEXTSW_AUTO_SCROLL_BY	textsw_delete()
TEXTSW_BLINK_CARET	textsw_edit()
TEXTSW_BROWSING	textsw_erase()
TEXTSW_CHECKPOINT_FREQUENCY	textsw_file_lines_visible()
TEXTSW_CLIENT_DATA	textsw_find_bytes()
TEXTSW_CONFIRM_OVERWRITE	textsw_find_mark()
TEXTSW_CONTENTS	textsw_first()
TEXTSW_CONTROL_CHARS_USE_FONT	textsw_index_for_file_line()
TEXTSW_DISABLE_CD	textsw_insert()
TEXTSW_DISABLE_LOAD	textsw_match_bytes()
TEXTSW_EDIT_COUNT	textsw_next()
TEXTSW_FILE	textsw_normalize_view()
TEXTSW_FILE_CONTENTS	textsw_possibly_normalize()
TEXTSW_FIRST	textsw_remove_mark()
TEXTSW_FIRST_LINE	textsw_replace_bytes()
TEXTSW_HISTORY_LIMIT	textsw_reset()
TEXTSW_IGNORE_LIMIT	textsw_save()
TEXTSW_INSERT_FROM_FILE	textsw_screen_line_count()
TEXTSW_INSERT_MAKES_VISIBLE	textsw_scroll_lines()
TEXTSW_INSERTION_POINT	textsw_set_selection()
TEXTSW_LENGTH	textsw_store_file()
TEXTSW_LINE_BREAK_ACTION	
TEXTSW_LOWER_CONTEXT	
TEXTSW_MEMORY_MAXIMUM	
TEXTSW_MODIFIED	
TEXTSW_MULTI_CLICK_SPACE	
TEXTSW_MULTI_CLICK_TIMEOUT	
TEXTSW_NOTIFY_PROC	
TEXTSW_READ_ONLY	
TEXTSW_STATUS	
TEXTSW_STORE_CHANGES_FILE	
TEXTSW_SUBMENU_EDIT	
TEXTSW_SUBMENU_FILE	
TEXTSW_SUBMENU_FIND	
TEXTSW_SUBMENU_VIEW	
TEXTSW_UPPER_CONTEXT	

9

TTY Subwindows

In This Chapter:

Creating a TTY Subwindow 205
Driving a TTY Subwindow 207
Monitoring the Program in the TTY Subwindow 210
Talking Directly to the TTY Subwindow 211
Package Summary 213

9
TTY Subwindows

The TTY (or *terminal emulator*) subwindow emulates a standard terminal, the principal difference being that the row and column dimensions of a tty subwindow can vary from that of a standard terminal. In a tty subwindow, you can run arbitrary programs, including a complete interactive shell. Or you can emulate terminal interface applications that use the *curses*(3X) terminal screen optimization package without actually running a separate process. The TTY subwindow accepts the standard ANSI escape sequences for doing ASCII screen manipulation, so you can use *termcap* or *termio* screen-handling routines. This chapter discusses the TTYSW package.

9.1 Creating a TTY Subwindow

Programs using tty subwindows must include the file *<xview/tty.h>*. Like all XView windows, you create a tty subwindow by calling xv_create() with the appropriate type parameter, as in:

```
Tty tty;
tty = xv_create(frame, TTY, NULL);
```

The default tty subwindow will fork a shell process and the user can use it interactively to enter commands. This program does not interact with the processing of the application in which the TTY subwindow resides; it is an entirely separate process. For example, if you want to start the tty subwindow with another program, say *man*, you can do so by specifying the name of the program to run via the TTY_ARGV attribute, as shown in Example 9-1:

Example 9-1. The sample_tty.c program

```
/*
 * sample_tty.c -- create a base frame with a tty subwindow.
 * This subwindow runs a UNIX command specified in an argument
 * vector as shown below.  The example does a "man cat".
 */
#include <xview/xview.h>
#include <xview/tty.h>

char *my_argv[] = { "man", "cat",  NULL };
```

Example 9-1. The sample_tty.c program (continued)

```
main(argc, argv)
char *argv[];
{
    Tty tty;
    Frame frame;

    xv_init();
    frame = (Frame)xv_create(NULL, FRAME, NULL);
    tty = (Tty)xv_create(frame, TTY,
        WIN_ROWS,       24,
        WIN_COLUMNS,    80,
        TTY_ARGV,       my_argv,
        NULL);

    window_fit(frame);
    xv_main_loop(frame);
}
```

The output of Example 9-1 is shown in Figure 9-1.

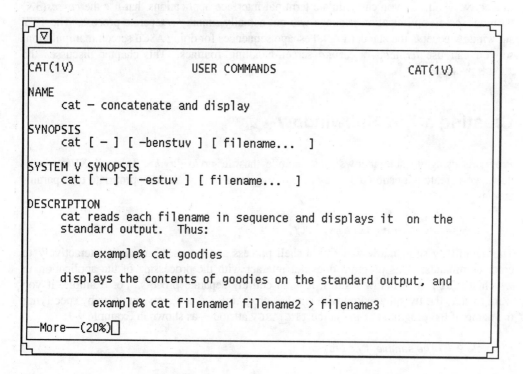

Figure 9-1. Output of sample_tty.c

Note that you can have only one tty subwindow per process.

9.2 Driving a TTY Subwindow

You can drive the terminal emulator programmatically. There are procedures both to send input to the terminal emulator (as if the user had typed it in the tty subwindow) and to send output (as if a program running in the tty subwindow had output it). You can send input to a tty subwindow programmatically with the function:

```
int
ttysw_input(tty, buf, len)
    Tty    tty;
    char *buf;
    int    len;
```

`ttysw_input()` appends the character sequence in `buf` that is `len` characters long onto `tty`'s input queue. It returns the number of characters accepted. The characters are treated as if they were typed from the keyboard in the tty subwindow. `ttysw_input()` provides a simple way for a window program to send input to a program running in its tty subwindow. You can send output to a tty subwindow programmatically with the function:

```
int
ttysw_output(tty, buf, len)
    Tty    tty;
    char *buf;
    int    len;
```

`ttysw_output()` runs the character sequence in `buf` that is `len` characters long through the terminal emulator of `tty`. It returns the number of characters accepted. The effect is similar to executing this:

```
echo character_sequence > /dev/ttyN
```

where `ttyN` is the pseudo-tty associated with the tty subwindow. `ttysw_output()` can be used to send ANSI escape sequences to the tty subwindow.

Note the differences between the input and output TTY routines. If an application is running in the tty subwindow, then the characters sent to the tty subwindow using `ttysw_input()` are sent to that program as its `stdin`. Characters sent to the tty subwindow using `ttysw_ouput()` are sent to the tty subwindow itself and have nothing to do with the application that might be running in the window.

The program in Example 9-2 creates a text subwindow in which the user can type input. There is a panel button called "Text to Tty" which, if selected, reads the data in the text subwindow and sends it to the tty subwindow using `ttysw_input()`.

Example 9-2. The textsw_to_ttysw.c program

```
/*
 * textsw_to_ttysw.c -- send text from a text subwindow to a
 * tty subwindow using ttysw_output()
 */
#include <stdio.h>
#include <xview/panel.h>
#include <xview/xview.h>
#include <xview/textsw.h>
#include <xview/tty.h>
```

Example 9-2. The textsw_to_ttysw.c program (continued)

```
Textsw    textsw;
Tty       ttysw;

main(argc,argv)
int       argc;
char      *argv[];
{
    Frame          frame;
    Panel          panel;
    void           text_to_tty(), exit();

    xv_init(XV_INIT_ARGC_PTR_ARGV, &argc, argv, NULL);

    frame = (Frame)xv_create(XV_NULL, FRAME,
        FRAME_LABEL, argv[0],
        NULL);
    panel = (Panel)xv_create(frame, PANEL,
        PANEL_LAYOUT, PANEL_VERTICAL,
        NULL);
    (void) xv_create(panel, PANEL_BUTTON,
        PANEL_LABEL_STRING,     "Quit",
        PANEL_NOTIFY_PROC,      exit,
        NULL);
    (void) xv_create(panel, PANEL_BUTTON,
        PANEL_LABEL_STRING,     "Text To Tty",
        PANEL_NOTIFY_PROC,      text_to_tty,
        NULL);
    window_fit(panel);

    textsw = (Textsw)xv_create(frame, TEXTSW,
        WIN_ROWS,       10,
        WIN_COLUMNS,    80,
        NULL);
    ttysw = (Ttysw)xv_create(frame, TTY,
        WIN_BELOW,      textsw,
        WIN_X,          0,
        TTY_ARGV,       TTY_ARGV_DO_NOT_FORK,
        NULL);

    window_fit(frame);
    xv_main_loop(frame);
}

/*
 * callback routine for the panel button -- read text from textsw
 * and send it to the ttysw using ttysw_output()
 */
void
text_to_tty(item, event)
Panel_item item;
Event *event;
{
    char buf[BUFSIZ];

    (void) xv_get(textsw, TEXTSW_CONTENTS, 0, buf, sizeof buf);
    ttysw_output(ttysw, buf, strlen(buf));
}
```

Figure 9-2 shows the output of the previous example.

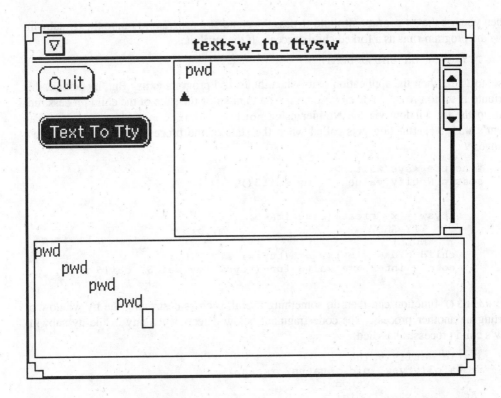

Figure 9-2. Output of textsw_to_ttysw.c

Using `ttysw_output()` shows that the text is simply output to the dummy terminal emulator described by `ttysw`. `ttysw_input()` is useful for sending data as input to a program running in the tty subwindow. For example, a window-based front end for a text editor could be written where all the common functions such as Save and Next Page can be programmed into panel buttons. Selecting one of those panel buttons would cause a constant string to be sent to the application to be processed as input. The *write filename* function in *vi* could have a button that uses `ttysw_input()` to send the string "w!\n" to the tty subwindow containing the program.

9.3 Monitoring the Program in the TTY Subwindow

When you use the TTY_ARGV attribute to pass the name of a program to run to the tty subwindow, the program runs as a forked child process. If the attribute

```
TTY_QUIT_ON_CHILD_DEATH
```

is set to TRUE, then the application exits when the forked program exits. But, by default, this attribute is set to FALSE. You can use TTY_PID to monitor the state of the child process running in the tty window via the Notifier using notify_interpose_wait3_func(). The client's wait3() function gets called when the state of the process in the tty subwindow changes*:

```
#include <sys/wait.h>
static Notify_value     my_wait3();

    ...
    ttysw = xv_create(base_frame, TTY,
        TTY_ARGV,                      my_argv,
        NULL);
    child_pid = (int)xv_get(ttysw, TTY_PID);
    notify_interpose_wait3_func(ttysw, my_wait3, child_pid);
    ...
```

The wait3() function can then do something useful, such as destroying the tty window or starting up another process. The code fragment below detects when any of the tty subwindow's child processes has died.

```
static Notify_value
my_wait3(ttysw, pid, status, rusage)
Tty             ttysw;
int             pid;
union wait      *status;
struct rusage   *rusage;
{
    int     child_pid;

    notify_next_wait3_func(ttysw, pid, status, rusage);
    if (!(WIFSTOPPED(*status))) {
    /* rerun the program */
        xv_set(ttysw, TTY_ARGV, my_argv, NULL);
        child_pid = (int)xv_get(ttysw, TTY_PID);
        notify_interpose_wait3_func(ttysw, my_wait3, child_pid);
    }
    return NOTIFY_DONE;
}
```

You can set TTY_PID as well as get it, but if you set it, you are responsible for setting

```
notify_interpose_wait3_func()
```

to catch the child's death. You are also responsible for directing the standard input and standard output of the child to the pseudo-tty.

---

*This includes when the program *stops* in addition to when it exits.

9.4 Talking Directly to the TTY Subwindow

Setting `TTY_ARGV` to `TTY_ARGV_DO_NOT_FORK` tells the system not to fork a child in the tty subwindow. In combination with `TTY_TTY_FD`, this allows the tool to use standard I/O routines to read and write to the tty subwindow by getting the file descriptor of the pseudo-tty associated with the tty subwindow. You can then use this to read and write to the pseudo-tty using standard UNIX I/O routines.

Example 9-3 uses a tty subwindow to create a pseudo *terminal* in which *curses* routines can be used. Five panel items are displayed. Along with the usual Quit button to exit the program, a Print button displays the text in the text panel item at the coordinates input in the X and Y numeric text items.

Example 9-3. The ttycurses.c program

```
/*
 * ttycurses.c -- An application that uses a tty subwindow that
 * emulates a tty so well, you can use curses(3X) routines in it.
 * This program does not handle resizes -- resizing the base frame
 * produces unpredictable results.  To handle resizing properly,
 * the application should install a resize event handler and
 * call endwin() followed by initscr() to reinitialize curses
 * to reflect the size of the window.
 *
 * cc ttycurses.c -lxview -lcurses -ltermlib
 */

#include <curses.h>
#undef WINDOW /* defined by curses.h -- needs to be undefined */
#include <xview/xview.h>
#include <xview/panel.h>
#include <xview/textsw.h>
#include <xview/tty.h>

/* panel items contain the x,y info for outputting text to the ttysw */
Panel_item  x, y, text;

main(argc,argv)
int      argc;
char     *argv[];
{
    Frame        frame;
    Panel        panel;
    Tty          ttysw;
    char         buf[16];
    void         output(), exit();

    xv_init(XV_INIT_ARGC_PTR_ARGV, &argc, argv, NULL);

    frame = xv_create(XV_NULL, FRAME,
        FRAME_LABEL,             argv[0],
        FRAME_SHOW_FOOTER,       TRUE,
        NULL);

    panel = (Frame)xv_create(frame, PANEL, NULL);
    (void) xv_create(panel, PANEL_BUTTON,
        PANEL_LABEL_STRING,              "Quit",
```

Example 9-3. The ttycurses.c program (continued)

```
            PANEL_NOTIFY_PROC,                exit,
            NULL);
    (void) xv_create(panel, PANEL_BUTTON,
            PANEL_LABEL_STRING,              "Print",
            PANEL_NOTIFY_PROC,               output,
            NULL);
    x = (Panel_item)xv_create(panel, PANEL_NUMERIC_TEXT,
            PANEL_LABEL_STRING,              "X:",
            PANEL_VALUE_DISPLAY_LENGTH,      3,
            NULL);
    y = (Panel_item)xv_create(panel, PANEL_NUMERIC_TEXT,
            PANEL_LABEL_STRING,              "Y:",
            PANEL_VALUE_DISPLAY_LENGTH,      3,
            NULL);
    text = (Panel_item)xv_create(panel, PANEL_TEXT,
            PANEL_LABEL_STRING,              "Text:",
            PANEL_VALUE_DISPLAY_LENGTH,      10,
            PANEL_VALUE,                     "X",
            NULL);
    window_fit(panel);

    ttysw = (Tty)xv_create(frame, TTY,
            WIN_BELOW,          panel,
            WIN_X,              0,
            TTY_ARGV,           TTY_ARGV_DO_NOT_FORK,
            NULL);
    window_fit(frame);

    dup2((int)xv_get(ttysw, TTY_TTY_FD), 0); /* dup2 closes 0 first */
    dup2((int)xv_get(ttysw, TTY_TTY_FD), 1); /* dup2 closes 1 first */

    /* initscr() initializes the curses package and determines
     * characteristics about the window as if it were a terminal.
     * The curses specific variables, LINES and COLS are now set
     * to the row and column sizes of the window.
     */

    initscr();

    xv_set(x, PANEL_MAX_VALUE, COLS-1, NULL);
    xv_set(y, PANEL_MAX_VALUE, LINES-1, NULL);
    sprintf(buf, "LINES: %d", LINES-1);
    xv_set(frame, FRAME_LEFT_FOOTER, buf, NULL);
    sprintf(buf, "COLS: %d", COLS-1);
    xv_set(frame, FRAME_RIGHT_FOOTER, buf, NULL);

    xv_main_loop(frame);
}
/*
 * callback routine for the <print> panel button.  Get the coordinates
 * and the text to print on the tty subwindow and use curses library
 * routines to render the text.
 */

void
output()
{
    int X = (int)xv_get(x, PANEL_VALUE);
    int Y = (int)xv_get(y, PANEL_VALUE);
```

Example 9-3. The ttycurses.c program (continued)

```
    char *Text = (char *)xv_get(text, PANEL_VALUE);
    mvaddstr(Y, X, Text);
    refresh();
}
```

9.5 Package Summary

Table 9-1 lists the attributes, procedures and macros for the TTYSW package are listed below. This information is described fully in Appendices A and B.

Table 9-1. TTY Subwindow Attributes, Procedures and Macros

Attributes	Procedures and Macros
TTY_ARGV	ttysw_input()
TTY_ARGV_DO_NOT_FORK	ttysw_output()
TTY_CONSOLE	
TTY_PAGE_MODE	
TTY_PID	
TTY_QUIT_ON_CHILD_DEATH	
TTY_TTY_FD	

10

Scrollbars

In This Chapter:

Creating Scrollbars 218
Relationship Between Scrollbars and Objects 220
An Example 221
Managing Your Own Scrollbar 227
Scrollbar Package Summary 227

10
Scrollbars

Scrollbars are used to change what you view in a subwindow. For instance, in a text subwindow, scrollbars are used to scroll through a document. In a canvas subwindow, scrollbars can be used to see another portion of the paint window (which can be larger than the canvas subwindow). This chapter addresses specific functions of scrollbars themselves. These functions are applicable to any XView package that has scrollbars attached. If you are interested in how to utilize scrollbars for a particular package, you should consult the chapter that discusses that package.

OPEN LOOK describes scrollbars using the visual metaphor of an elevator riding on a cable, which is attached at both ends to anchors. Figure 10-1 shows a scrollbar from the *OPEN LOOK GUI Specification Guide*.

Figure 10-1. An OPEN LOOK scrollbar

The elevator contains directional arrows and a drag box. A subwindow can have vertical or horizontal scrollbars. Horizontal scrollbars are placed to the right of the subwindow while vertical scrollbars are placed at the bottom. OPEN LOOK defines precisely how scrollbars look and behave—the programmer or user cannot change it. All the programmer can control is the scrollbar's color, length, and various other common and generic attributes.

One of the functions of the scrollbar is the ability to *split a view*. The OPENWIN package provides objects such as text subwindows and canvases that may be split into several views; the scrollbar provides the functional interface. Certain XView packages, such as text subwindows, automatically create their own scrollbars. Canvases, on the other hand, require the programmer to create scrollbars and attach scrollbars.

The scrollbar's look and feel is related to the size of the object it scrolls. Attributes are associated with each of the following terms:

Orientation   The orientation of a scrollbar indicates whether it is horizontal or vertical.

Object Length   The length of the object is registered with the scrollbar. The *proportional indicator* (the darkened part of the elevator cable) uses this value. For example, the object length for a text subwindow is the number of lines in the editing buffer.

Page Length   When the object length is larger than what the view window can contain, the overall area is broken up into *pages*. When the user selects the elevator cable, the scrollbar scrolls in page segments in the direction of the cursor (e.g., left, right, up or down) relative to the elevator.

Unit Length   When the user clicks on the elevator arrows, the scrollbar scrolls one *unit*. Units are measured in pixels, so arbitrary or abstract objects that are to be scrolled should be measured in terms of pixels so that scrolling seems consistent with the object. For example, a text subwindow sets its scrollbar's unit length to the size of the characters in the font. Unit scrolling results in the window moving line by line up or down.

View Length   The view length is the same size as the height or width of the subwindow the scrollbar is associated with depending on the scrollbar's orientation.

Figure 10-2 illustrates the terminology used above.

10.1 Creating Scrollbars

The definitions necessary to use scrollbars are found in the header file *<xview/scrollbar.h>*. The basic scrollbar is created using the following code fragment:

```
Scrollbar scrollbar;

scrollbar = (Scrollbar)xv_create(owner, SCROLLBAR, NULL);
```

The owner may be NULL, which indicates that the scrollbar will have delayed binding—it should be attached to an object later. However, if the scrollbar has a valid owner when it is created, then the scrollbar inherits certain attributes while other attributes are initialized automatically. For example, if the owner of the scrollbar is a canvas, the scrollbar's color is inherited from the canvas, while the scrollbar's object length is set by the canvas explicitly;

(values measured in units)

object being scrolled

SCROLLBAR_VIEW_START (2)

SCROLLBAR_VIEW_LENGTH (5)

SCROLLBAR_OBJECT_LENGTH (8)

SCROLLBAR_VIEW_START

SCROLLBAR_VIEW_LENGTH

unit size

Figure 10-2. Relationship between a scrollbar and the object it scrolls

that is, you are not required to set this. This is usually desirable when creating objects that are used together.

10.2 Relationship Between Scrollbars and Objects

Most scrollbar attributes describe the relationship between the scrollbar and the object such as a canvas or text subwindow that is affected by scrolling. The foremost is SCROLLBAR_PIXELS_PER_UNIT, which describes the number of pixels in a scrolling *unit*. For text subwindows, the unit is the text width and height. For canvases, it is one pixel (by default). If you were to build a canvas subwindow intended to browse a set of 64x64 bitmaps, then you would set this to 64. Scrolling actions occur in scrollbar units, so this would mean that the clicking on one of the elevator arrows causes a scrolling movement of 64 pixels at a time. Most scrollbar attribute values are based on the *unit* value.

The size of the object itself (a graphic image, text stream, or whatever) is stored as the SCROLLBAR_OBJECT_LENGTH while the size of the viewable window is represented as the scrollbar's SCROLLBAR_VIEW_LENGTH. After having been scrolled, the scrollbar's current offset into the object is reflected in SCROLLBAR_VIEW_START. When *paging* is done (selecting the *cable* portion of the elevator), the amount scrolled is set by SCROLLBAR_PAGE_LENGTH. These values are in object units, so to get their values in pixels, multiply by the value of SCROLLBAR_PIXELS_PER_UNIT.

The scrollbar manages its own events, resizes and repaints automatically. It is not necessary to interpose event handlers for the scrollbar. By default, the event handling mechanism determines the type of scrolling that has been done and changes the appropriate attributes. All OPENWIN objects that support scrollbars also redisplay the window to show the results of scrolling.

Even though you do not need to know when the scrollbar is scrolled to manage the scrolling, you might be interested in knowing when the scrolling action occurs. XView objects such as text subwindows that manage their own data (text, in this case) handle this automatically. See Chapter 5, *Canvases and Openwin*, for discussion on scrolling canvases.

If a window that has a scrollbar is resized, the scrollbar is resized accordingly. If the window is sized too small for all of the parts of the scrollbar to be visible or usable, then those parts cannot be available. At the very least, the scrolling *arrows* must be visible. Figure 10-3 shows a text subwindow that has been split twice. Notice the scrollbars to the right of the text subwindows. The uppermost window can not be split again because the minimum size of the scrollbar has been reached.

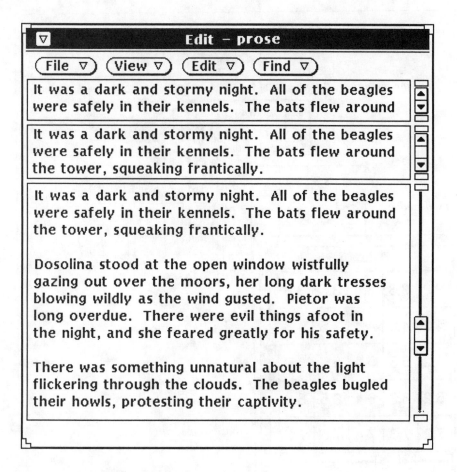

Figure 10-3. Splitting a text subwindow twice

10.3 An Example

Let's suppose that you want to display a list of icons that have dimensions of 64x64. You wish to display the icons in rows and columns in a canvas. Because there may be more icons than the canvas can display at once, you attach scrollbars to the canvas. When the user uses the scrollbars to view the icons, each scrolling action should scroll an entire icon or set of icons into view. *Paging* should scroll the next *page* of icons into view.

For demonstration purposes, rather than display actual icons, we present a grid where each *cell* in the grid represents an icon (see Figure 10-4).

Each cell is considered a *unit* to the scrollbars, so the number of pixels per scrollbar-unit must be set to the size of the cell. Thus, the attribute SCROLLBAR_PIXELS_PER_UNIT is set to 64 for each scrollbar (the width and height are the same). With this attribute set, when the user selects an arrow on the scrollbar, an entire cell is scrolled into view (depending on which arrow is selected).

Figure 10-4. Model for scroll_cells.c

We set SCROLLBAR_PAGE_LENGTH to be the same as SCROLLBAR_VIEW_LENGTH to specify the paging size. When the user selects any part of the scrollbar cable, the view is paged and a new set of icons is scrolled into view (depending on which side of the elevator is selected). The page length could be set to one unit less than the view length, so that paging causes the last cell in the old block to be the first cell in the new block. Remember, the "lengths" mentioned here are given in *units*.

The setting of the scrollbar unit size also assures that the upper-left corner of a cell maps to the upper-left corner of the window so as not to display a portion of the cell. This guarantee cannot be made for the lower and right-hand edges of the window because we cannot control the resizing of the frame by the user.

In the program in Example 10-1, the variable `cell_map` is a `Pixmap` of depth 1. But, the depth is arbitrary—we use 1 because we know that the icons we are displaying are of depth 1. The canvas, on the other hand, may be any depth at all; color canvases have a depth greater than 1. Copying drawables of different depths onto one another is an X protocol error, so we use `XCopyPlane()` to guarantee that the pixmap is rendered into the canvas correctly.

Example 10-1. The scroll_cells.c program

```
/*
 * scroll_cells.c -- scroll a bitmap of cells around in a canvas.
 * The cells are rectangular areas labeled with numbers which may
 * represent arbitrary data such as icon images.  The cell sizes are
 * defined to be 64 by 64 aligned in rows and columns.  This example
 * is used to demonstrate how to configure scrollbars to accommodate
 * arbitrary data within a window.
 */
#include <stdio.h>
#include <X11/X.h>
#include <X11/Xlib.h>    /* Using Xlib graphics */
#include <xview/xview.h>
#include <xview/canvas.h>
#include <xview/scrollbar.h>
#include <xview/font.h>
#include <xview/xv_xrect.h>

#define CELL_WIDTH             64
#define CELL_HEIGHT            64
#define CELLS_PER_HOR_PAGE     5 /* when paging w/scrollbar */
#define CELLS_PER_VER_PAGE     5 /* when paging w/scrollbar */
#define CELLS_PER_ROW          8
#define CELLS_PER_COL          16

Pixmap          cell_map;           /* pixmap copied onto canvas window */
Scrollbar       horiz_scrollbar;
Scrollbar       vert_scrollbar;
GC              gc;                  /* General usage GC */

main(argc, argv)
int argc;
char *argv[];
{
    Frame       frame;
    Canvas      canvas;
    void        repaint_proc();

    /* Initialize, create frame and canvas... */
    xv_init(XV_INIT_ARGC_PTR_ARGV, &argc, argv, NULL);

    frame = (Frame)xv_create(XV_NULL, FRAME,
        FRAME_LABEL,            argv[0],
        FRAME_SHOW_FOOTER,      TRUE,
        NULL);

    canvas = (Canvas)xv_create(frame, CANVAS,
        /* make subwindow the size of a "page" */
        XV_WIDTH,               CELL_WIDTH * CELLS_PER_HOR_PAGE,
        XV_HEIGHT,              CELL_HEIGHT * CELLS_PER_VER_PAGE,
        /* canvas is much larger than the window */
```

Example 10-1. The scroll_cells.c program (continued)

```
        CANVAS_WIDTH,               CELL_WIDTH * CELLS_PER_ROW + 1,
        CANVAS_HEIGHT,              CELL_HEIGHT * CELLS_PER_COL + 1,
        CANVAS_AUTO_EXPAND,         FALSE,
        CANVAS_AUTO_SHRINK,         FALSE,
        /* don't retain window -- we'll need
         * to repaint it all the time */
        CANVAS_RETAINED,            FALSE,
        /* we're using Xlib graphics calls in repaint_proc() */
        CANVAS_X_PAINT_WINDOW,      TRUE,
        CANVAS_REPAINT_PROC,        repaint_proc,
        /* we'll be repainting over exposed areas,
         * so don't bother clearing */
        OPENWIN_AUTO_CLEAR,         FALSE,
        NULL);

    /*
     * Create scrollbars attached to the canvas.  When user clicks
     * on cable, page by the page size (PAGE_LENGTH).  Scrolling
     * should move cell by cell, not by one pixel (PIXELS_PER_UNIT).
     */
    vert_scrollbar = xv_create(canvas, SCROLLBAR,
        SCROLLBAR_DIRECTION,             SCROLLBAR_VERTICAL,
        SCROLLBAR_PIXELS_PER_UNIT,       CELL_HEIGHT,
        SCROLLBAR_OBJECT_LENGTH,         CELLS_PER_COL,
        SCROLLBAR_PAGE_LENGTH,           CELLS_PER_VER_PAGE,
        SCROLLBAR_VIEW_LENGTH,           CELLS_PER_VER_PAGE,
        NULL);
    horiz_scrollbar = xv_create(canvas, SCROLLBAR,
        SCROLLBAR_DIRECTION,             SCROLLBAR_HORIZONTAL,
        SCROLLBAR_PIXELS_PER_UNIT,       CELL_WIDTH,
        SCROLLBAR_OBJECT_LENGTH,         CELLS_PER_ROW,
        SCROLLBAR_PAGE_LENGTH,           CELLS_PER_HOR_PAGE,
        SCROLLBAR_VIEW_LENGTH,           CELLS_PER_HOR_PAGE,
        NULL);

    /*
     * create pixmap and draw cells into it ... this is the abstraction.
     * The cell_map is copied into the window via XCopyPlane in the
     * repaint procedure.
     */
    {
        short           x, y, pt = 0;
        Xv_Font         font;
        XPoint          points[256]; /* keep Xlib calls to a minimum */
        XGCValues       gcvalues;
        Display *dpy = (Display *)xv_get(canvas, XV_DISPLAY);

        font = (Xv_Font)xv_find(frame, FONT,
            FONT_NAME,          "icon",
            XV_AUTO_CREATE,     FALSE,
            NULL);
        cell_map = XCreatePixmap(dpy, DefaultRootWindow(dpy),
            CELLS_PER_ROW * CELL_WIDTH + 1,
            CELLS_PER_COL * CELL_HEIGHT + 1,
            1); /* We only need a 1-bit deep pixmap */

        /* Create the gc for the cell_map -- since it is 1-bit deep,
```

Example 10-1. The scroll_cells.c program (continued)

```
       * use 0 and 1 for fg/bg values.  Also, limit number of
       * events generated by setting graphics exposures to False.
       */
      gcvalues.graphics_exposures = False;
      gcvalues.background = 0;
      gcvalues.foreground = 1;
      if (font)
          gcvalues.font = (Font)xv_get(font, XV_XID);
      gc = XCreateGC(dpy, cell_map,
          GCForeground|GCBackground|GCGraphicsExposures, &gcvalues);

      if (!font) {
          /* dot every other pixel */
          for (x = 0; x <= CELL_WIDTH * CELLS_PER_ROW; x += 2)
              for (y = 0; y <= CELL_HEIGHT * CELLS_PER_COL; y += 2) {
                  if (x % CELL_WIDTH != 0 && y % CELL_HEIGHT != 0)
                      continue;
                  points[pt].x = x, points[pt].y = y;
                  if (++pt == sizeof points / sizeof points[0]) {
                      XDrawPoints(dpy, cell_map, gc, points, pt,
                          CoordModeOrigin);
                      pt = 0;
                  }
              }
          if (pt != sizeof points) /* flush remaining points */
              XDrawPoints(dpy, cell_map, gc,
                          points, pt, CoordModeOrigin);
      }
      /* Icon font not available.  Instead, label each cell
       * with a string describing the cell's coordinates.
       */
      for (x = 0; x < CELLS_PER_ROW; x++)
          for (y = 0; y < CELLS_PER_COL; y++) {
              char buf[8];
              if (!font) {
                  sprintf(buf, "%d,%d", x+1, y+1);
                  XDrawString(dpy, cell_map, gc,
                      x * CELL_WIDTH + 5, y * CELL_HEIGHT + 25,
                      buf, strlen(buf));
              } else {
                  buf[0] = x + y * CELLS_PER_COL;
                  XDrawString(dpy, cell_map, gc,
                      x * CELL_WIDTH, y * CELL_HEIGHT, buf, 1);
              }
          }
      /* we're now done with the cell_map, so free gc and create
       * a new one based on the window that will use it.  Otherwise,
       * the GC may not work because of different depths.
       */
      if (font)
          xv_destroy(gc);
      XFreeGC(dpy, gc);
      gcvalues.background = WhitePixel(dpy, DefaultScreen(dpy));
      gcvalues.foreground = BlackPixel(dpy, DefaultScreen(dpy));
      gcvalues.plane_mask = 1L;
      gc = XCreateGC(dpy, DefaultRootWindow(dpy),
```

Example 10-1. The scroll_cells.c program (continued)

```
                    GCForeground|GCBackground|GCGraphicsExposures, &gcvalues);
    }

    /* shrink frame to minimal size and start notifier */
    window_fit(frame);
    xv_main_loop(frame);
}

/*
 * The repaint procedure is called whenever repainting is needed in
 * a paint window.  Since the canvas is not retained, this routine
 * is going to be called anytime the user scrolls the canvas.  The
 * canvas will handle repainting the portion of the canvas that
 * was in view and has scrolled onto another viewable portion of
 * the window.  The xrects parameter will cover the new areas that
 * were not in view before and have just scrolled into view.  If
 * the window resizes or if the window is exposed by other windows
 * disappearing or cycling through the window tree, then the number
 * of xrects will be more than one and we'll have to copy the new
 * areas one by one.  Clipping isn't necessary since the areas to
 * be rendered are set by the xrects value.
 */
void
repaint_proc(canvas, paint_window, dpy, win, xrects)
Canvas          canvas;
Xv_Window       paint_window;
Display         *dpy;
Window          win;
Xv_xrectlist    *xrects;
{
    int x, y;

    x = (int)xv_get(horiz_scrollbar, SCROLLBAR_VIEW_START);
    y = (int)xv_get(vert_scrollbar, SCROLLBAR_VIEW_START);

    for (xrects->count--; xrects->count >= 0; xrects->count--) {
        printf("top-left cell = %d, %d -- %d,%d %d,%d\n", x+1, y+1,
            xrects->rect_array[xrects->count].x,
            xrects->rect_array[xrects->count].y,
            xrects->rect_array[xrects->count].width,
            xrects->rect_array[xrects->count].height);

        XCopyPlane(dpy, cell_map, win, gc,
            xrects->rect_array[xrects->count].x,
            xrects->rect_array[xrects->count].y,
            xrects->rect_array[xrects->count].width,
            xrects->rect_array[xrects->count].height,
            xrects->rect_array[xrects->count].x,
            xrects->rect_array[xrects->count].y, 1L);
    }
}
```

10.4 Managing Your Own Scrollbar

A scrollbar may have *delayed binding*—that is, it may be created without an owner and attached to objects that were created separately.

In most cases, you would probably never need to create a scrollbar that was not part of a text subwindow or a canvas. These two packages handle all of the dirty work involved in managing and maintaining the types of attributes mentioned above. If you are using the CANVAS or TEXTSW packages, you do not need to worry about any of this. If you do try to create your own scrollbars and have them manage your own windows, you will probably find that you will have reinvented the wheel in the form of the CANVAS package.

Such advanced scrollbar usage is beyond the scope of this book. However, if you are going to attempt it anyway, you will need to follow these guidelines:

- Maintain the relationship between the object to be scrolled and the scrollbar itself. This includes using all the scrollbar attributes mentioned in Section 10.1, "Creating Scrollbars."

- Manage geometry (size, position and orientation) of the scrollbar. You must place the scrollbars in the appropriate places around the object you intend to scroll. Typically, the scrollbars should match the width and height of the object being scrolled.

- Install appropriate SCROLLBAR_NORMALIZE_PROC and SCROLLBAR_COMPUTE_ SCROLL_PROC procedures to change the display of the scrolling object.

10.5 Scrollbar Package Summary

The procedures and macros in the SCROLLBAR package are listed below:

```
scrollbar_default_compute_scroll_proc()
scrollbar_paint()
```

Table 10-1 lists the attributes in the SCROLLBAR package. This information is described fully in Appendices A and B.

Table 10-1. Scrollbar Attributes

Scrollbar Attributes

SCROLLBAR_COMPUTE_SCROLL_PROC	SCROLLBAR_OBJECT_LENGTH
SCROLLBAR_DIRECTION	SCROLLBAR_PAGE_LENGTH
SCROLLBAR_LAST_VIEW_START	SCROLLBAR_PIXELS_PER_UNIT
SCROLLBAR_MENU	SCROLLBAR_SPLITTABLE
SCROLLBAR_NORMALIZE_PROC	SCROLLBAR_VIEW_LENGTH
SCROLLBAR_NOTIFY_CLIENT	SCROLLBAR_VIEW_START

11
Menus

In This Chapter:

Menu Types 231
    Pop-up Menus 232
    Pulldown Menus 232
    Pullright Menus 232
Menu Items 234
    Choice Items 234
    Exclusive Items 234
    Nonexclusive Items 235
Creating Menus 235
Displaying Menus 236
A Simple Program 237
Creating Menu Items 240
    Using MENU_ITEM 240
    Using MENU_ACTION_ITEM 241
    Using MENUITEM 241
    Using MENU_GEN_PROC 242
Adding Menu Items 242
Pullright Menus 243
    Menu-generating Procedures 245
Using Toggle Menus 246
Menu Layout 247
Making Pin-up Menus 248
Notification Procedures 249
Finding Menu Items 252
Initial and Default Menu Selections 253
Destroying Menus 253
    Freeing Allocated Strings 254
    Freeing Pullright Menus 254
    Menu Client Data 255
Example Program 255
Menu Package Summary 258

11
Menus

Menus play an important role in an application's user interface. An OPEN LOOK menu may display text or graphics. Menus may be attached to most XView objects such as *menu buttons*, *scrollbars* or *text subwindows*, or they may exist independently from objects and be displayed on demand.

The user may cause a menu to be pinned up by selecting an optional *pushpin* in the pop-up menu. When this happens, the menu is taken down and a corresponding command frame is put up at the same location. Panel items in the pinup window correspond to the menu items in the menu. Once a menu has been pinned up, the user continues to interact with it just as if the menu were popped up each time. Menus that are used frequently are good candidates for having pushpins so the user does not have to repeat the sequence of redisplaying the menu to make selections.

OPEN LOOK requires that menus have titles. Menus or submenus that originate from *menu buttons* or *pullright* items do not need to have titles, since the name of the menu button or menu item acts as the title.

Fonts may not be specified in either menu items or menu titles; menu items follow the same constraints outlined for *panel buttons*. However, if text is not used, then menu items may contain graphic images, in which case, the font is of no concern. That is, you could specify a `Server_image` that has a string rendered in a particular font.

11.1 Menu Types

There are three different types of menus: *pop-up*, *pulldown* and *pullright* menus. The general term *pop-up menu* may describes all three types in certain contexts since menus are *popped up*. However, pulldown and pullright menus have distinct characteristics that make them unique.

11.1.1 Pop-up Menus

Pop-up menus are displayed when the user selects the MENU mouse button over XView objects such as *scrollbars* or *text subwindows*. An OPEN LOOK window manager also utilizes pop-up menus in the root window and from base frame title bars. XView objects handle the display of menus automatically. Applications may wish to track ACTION_MENU events in objects such as canvases and display their own pop-up menus. Figure 11-1, from the *OPEN LOOK GUI Specification Guide*, shows a *Window* menu-generated from the title bar of an OPEN LOOK base frame.

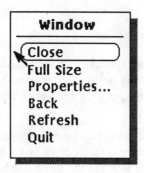

Figure 11-1. The Window menu

11.1.2 Pulldown Menus

Pulldown menus are attached to *menu buttons*. Menu buttons have a set of choices associated with them that the user can access only via the pulldown menu. When the user presses the MENU mouse button over a menu button, the choices are displayed in the form of a pulldown menu. If the menu button is selected using the SELECT button, the default menu item is selected. See Chapter 7, *Panels*, for details on creating menu buttons. Figure 11-2, from the *OPEN LOOK GUI Specification Guide*, shows sample pulldown menus activated from a menu button.

11.1.3 Pullright Menus

OPEN LOOK provides for items in the menu to have *pullright menus* associated with them. Also called *cascading menus*, these menus are activated from the user dragging the MENU mouse button to the right of a menu item that has an arrow pointing to the right. The cascading menu that results is a pop-up menu that can also have menu items with pullrights attached. Figure 11-3, from the *OPEN LOOK GUI Specification Guide*, shows a pullright menu originating from a menu item in a pulldown menu.

Figure 11-2. Menu buttons each with a pulldown menu

Figure 11-3. Pushpins in a menu and a submenu

11.2 Menu Items

In addition to the menu types, there are different types of menu items: *choice, exclusive* and *nonexclusive*. The different menu item types may be associated with each type of menu.

Each menu has a *default selection* associated with it. This item is displayed uniquely from other menu items and designates a default action to take if the user wants to select the menu without displaying it (see *pulldown menus* below). Typically, the first item in the menu is the default, but that may be changed either by the application or by the user.

11.2.1 Choice Items

The *choice* item is the default menu item type used when a menu is created. The default selection in a menu has a ring around it. When a pop-up menu is displayed, it is positioned so that the mouse is pointing at the default item. Choice menu items may have pullright menus associated with them, in which case there is a pullright arrow at the right side of the item. If the selection of a menu item brings up a dialog box (command frame), then the label for the menu item typically ends in ellipses (...).

11.2.2 Exclusive Items

When a choice item is selected, an action is taken and the menu forgets about it. Exclusive menu items retain the fact that they are selected even after the menu has popped down. If the user selects a new item, the new item is remembered. Because this is an exclusive menu, only one choice may be selected at a time. The *default* item is indicated by a double-lined box around the item. Figure 11-4 is from the *OPEN LOOK GUI Specification Guide*.

Figure 11-4. Exclusive settings on a menu

When exclusive settings are used on menus, the current choice has a bold border when the pointer is not on a menu choice. When the user drags the pointer onto other settings, the bold border follows the pointer. Exclusive choice menus may not have items with pullright menus.

11.2.3 Nonexclusive Items

Also called *toggle items*, menus that have toggle items support multiple choices from the menu to be selected at the same time. That is, the user may *toggle* whether a particular choice is selected. This action has no affect on the other menu items. Figure 11-5 shows an example of a menu that has items and a submenu that has nonexclusive settings.

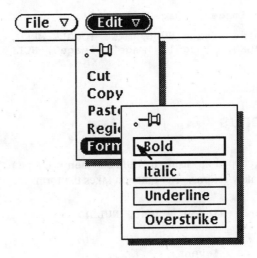

Figure 11-5. Nonexclusive settings on a submenu

In this figure, the chosen settings on the submenu are Bold and Italic. The choices not selected are Underline and Overstrike.

11.3 Creating Menus

The header file for the MENU package is *<xview/openmenu.h>*, but the file is already included by *<xview/xview.h>*. The basic menu is created using xv_create():

```
Menu menu;

menu = (Menu)xv_create(NULL, MENU, NULL);
```

The owner of a menu is ignored when creating both menus and menu items (which are discussed later). Menus (and sometimes menu items) are discrete objects that may have *delayed binding*. That is, they may be created independently from any XView object and attached later using attributes specific to that object (like the way PANEL_ITEM_MENU may be used to attach an existing menu to a *menu button*). In any case, menus are never owned by other objects.*

Exclusive menus are created using the MENU_CHOICE_MENU package, as in the following example:

```
Menu menu;

menu = (Menu)xv_create(NULL, MENU_CHOICE_MENU,
    MENU_STRINGS,  "choice1", "choice2", "choice3", NULL,
    NULL);
```

Nonexclusive menus are created using the MENU_TOGGLE_MENU package, as in the following example:

```
Menu menu;
Server_image image1, image2, image3;

menu = (Menu)xv_create(NULL, MENU_TOGGLE_MENU,
    MENU_IMAGES,  image1, image2, image3, NULL,
    NULL);
```

11.4 Displaying Menus

Menus are displayed (popped up) using the function menu_show().† It displays the specified menu and immediately returns. The function takes the form:

```
void
menu_show(menu, window, event, NULL);
    Menu            menu;
    Xv_Window       window;
    Event           *event;
```

The menu is a menu created from xv_create() or a menu extracted from an existing XView object (such as a button menu). The X window associated with the menu calls XGrabPointer() to grab the server's mouse events. The pointer grab stays in effect until the user releases the MENU mouse button (e.g., the ACTION_MENU action with event_is_up() being TRUE). This is independent of the event that caused the menu to be displayed. Releasing the MENU button results in the user having either made a selection, *not* made a selection, or pinned up the menu (provided that the menu has a pushpin).

The window attribute defines the window where the menu appears. The event parameter contains the event that caused the decision to display the menu. The most common use for it is to extract the *x,y* coordinate pair so as to remember the location of the pointer at the time the menu was displayed. This event structure can be retrieved later by calling:

```
Event *event = (Event *)xv_get(menu, MENU_FIRST_EVENT);
```

---

*Except when they are *pinned* up, in which case they are owned by another frame (typically the base frame).
†This function is called internally by other XView objects such as scrollbars, menu buttons and text subwindows to display menus associated with them.

Similarly, when the user releases the MENU button, this event can be retrieved using the MENU_LAST_EVENT attribute.

The last parameter to menu_show() must be NULL. It actually represents a list of attribute-value pairs but is used internally by other XView packages that utilize menus.

Menus can also be created at run time by procedures that are called whenever a menu is needed. This is covered in Section 11.8.1, "Menu-generating Procedures."

11.5 A Simple Program

Given the information provided so far, we can demonstrate how to pop up a menu. Example 11-1 shows how the canvas object tracks for pointer events and calls menu_show() when the ACTION_MENU event occurs.

Example 11-1. The simple_menu.c program

```
/*
 * simple_menu.c -
 * Demonstrate the use of an XView menu in a canvas subwindow.
 * A Menu is brought up with the MENU mouse button.  The choices
 * in the menu toggle the display of the scrollbar next to the canvas.
 */
#include <xview/xview.h>
#include <xview/canvas.h>
#include <xview/scrollbar.h>

#define SCROLLBAR_KEY    100
#define MENU_KEY         200

main(argc,argv)
int      argc;
char     *argv[];
{
    Frame          frame;
    Canvas         canvas;
    Scrollbar      scrollbar;
    Menu           menu;
    void           menu_notify_proc(), pw_event_proc();

    xv_init(XV_INIT_ARGC_PTR_ARGV, &argc, argv, NULL);

    /*
     * Create a frame, canvas and menu.
     * A canvas receives input in its canvas_paint_window().
     */
    frame = (Frame)xv_create(NULL, FRAME,
        FRAME_LABEL,      argv[0],
        NULL);
    canvas = (Canvas)xv_create(frame, CANVAS,
        XV_WIDTH,         300,
        XV_HEIGHT,        200,
        NULL);
    scrollbar = (Scrollbar)xv_create(canvas, SCROLLBAR,
        SCROLLBAR_DIRECTION,      SCROLLBAR_VERTICAL,
```

Example 11-1. The simple_menu.c program (continued)

```
        NULL);

    menu = (Menu)xv_create(canvas, MENU,
        MENU_TITLE_ITEM,          "Scrollbar",
        MENU_STRINGS,             "On", "Off", NULL,
        MENU_NOTIFY_PROC,         menu_notify_proc,
        XV_KEY_DATA,              SCROLLBAR_KEY, scrollbar,
        NULL);

    xv_set(canvas_paint_window(canvas),
        WIN_EVENT_PROC,           pw_event_proc,
        XV_KEY_DATA,              MENU_KEY, menu,
        NULL);

    window_fit(frame);
    window_main_loop(frame);
}
/*
 * menu_notify_proc - toggle the display of the scrollbar
 * based on which menu item was chosen.
 */
void
menu_notify_proc(menu, menu_item)
Menu menu;
Menu_item menu_item;
{
    char *menu_choice = (char *)xv_get(menu_item, MENU_STRING);
    int show_it = !strcmp(menu_choice, "On");

    xv_set(xv_get(menu, XV_KEY_DATA, SCROLLBAR_KEY),
        XV_SHOW,          show_it,
        NULL);
}

/*
 * Call menu_show() to display menu.
 */
void
pw_event_proc(canvas_pw, event)
Xv_Window          canvas_pw;
Event *event;
{
    if (event_action(event) == ACTION_MENU && event_is_down(event)) {
        Menu menu = (Menu)xv_get(canvas_pw, XV_KEY_DATA, MENU_KEY);
        menu_show(menu, canvas_pw, event, NULL);
    }
}
```

In Example 11-1 above, *simple_menu.c* shows the simplest and most common method for creating and using pop-up menus. The menu, menu items, and the callback routine are all created at the same time using the call:

```
menu = (Menu)xv_create(canvas, MENU,
    MENU_TITLE_ITEM,        "Scrollbar",
    MENU_STRINGS,           "On", "Off", NULL,
    MENU_NOTIFY_PROC,       menu_notify_proc,
    NULL);
```

Figure 11-6 shows the result of running *simple_menu.c* and selecting the menu.

Figure 11-6. Output of simple_menu.c when the menu is popped up

Since this menu is not attached to a menu button panel item and is not a pullright menu of
another menu item, a title bar is added using MENU_TITLE_ITEM. The attribute
MENU_STRINGS takes a list of strings and creates a menu item for each string.

NOTE

The MENU package, in contrast to the PANEL package, does not save strings
which you pass in as the menu item's label (string). You should either pass a
constant string, as in the example above, or static storage that you have dynamically allocated (e.g., malloc()).

menu_notify_proc() is a routine that is called whenever any of the menu items are
selected. The routine is passed a handle to the menu and the menu item selected. The canvas
serves no other purpose than to capture events—the event callback routine for the canvas
determines if the user generated the ACTION_MENU event and, if so, calls menu_show().

The use of XV_KEY_DATA is used to associate one object with another. In this case, we associate the scrollbar with the menu so when the menu callback routine is called, the scrollbar
can be retrieved easily. The menu, on the other hand, is associated with the canvas's paint
window since that window is going to get the event that pops up the menu.

The use of XV_KEY_DATA removes the need for the menu and the scrollbar to be global variables. It also clarifies the association between the objects that would otherwise not be as clear. Other examples of XV_KEY_DATA, including a complete discussion on usage, can be found in Chapter 7, *Panels*, and Chapter 3, *Creating XView Applications*.

11.6 Creating Menu Items

As noted, the use of MENU_STRINGS results in the creation of menu items *in line*; that is, they are created automatically by the MENU package during the creation of the menu object. Other methods for creating menu items in-line include using the attributes, MENU_ITEM and MENU_ACTION_ITEM.*

MENU_ACTION_ITEM is used as a shortcut for separately specifying a label and a callback routine:

```
menu = (Menu)xv_create(NULL, MENU,
    MENU_ACTION_ITEM,  "item1",  callback1,
    MENU_ACTION_ITEM,  "item2",  callback2,
    ...
    NULL);
```

Two other methods for creating menu items are to:

- Use a separate call to xv_create() with the MENUITEM package.

- Provide a menu-generation routine.

The following subsections discuss the use of MENU_ITEM to create menu items *in-line*, MENUITEM to create separate menu items, and MENU_GEN_PROC to specify a routine that creates menus.

11.6.1 Using MENU_ITEM

Using the attribute MENU_ITEM indicates that a new menu item is to be created and appended to the existing menu. Use of this attribute means that the menu item is created *in-line* so a separate call to xv_create() is not necessary. The form of the value portion of the attribute is a NULL-terminated list of menu-item, attribute-value pairs:

---

*The attributes MENU_IMAGES and MENU_ACTION_IMAGE are just like MENU_STRINGS and MENU_ACTION_ITEM except that Server_images are used as labels rather than text.

```
extern void on_notify_proc(), off_notify_proc();

menu = (Menu)xv_create(NULL, MENU,
    MENU_TITLE_ITEM,        "Toggle",
    MENU_ITEM,
        MENU_STRING,        "On",
        MENU_NOTIFY_PROC, on_notify_proc,
        NULL,
    MENU_ITEM,
        MENU_STRING,        "Off",
        MENU_NOTIFY_PROC, off_notify_proc,
        NULL,
    NULL);
```

The code fragment shown above creates a menu with the same two menu items as shown in the previous example, except that the menu items are created more directly by the use of MENU_ITEM. Here we can specify item-specific attributes rather than accept all the defaults for the menu. In this case, we set a different notification routine for each menu item.*

If you have a Server_image to display rather than a string, you can replace MENU_STRING above with MENU_IMAGE and specify a Server_image rather than a string.

11.6.2 Using MENU_ACTION_ITEM

Rather than specifying menu item creation using a separate attribute-value list, the attribute MENU_ACTION_ITEM can be used as a shortcut, as shown in the example below:

```
menu = (Menu)xv_create(NULL, MENU,
    MENU_TITLE_ITEM,        "Toggle",
    MENU_ACTION_ITEM,       "On",    on_notify_proc,
    MENU_ACTION_ITEM,       "Off",   off_notify_proc,
    NULL);
```

The attribute MENU_ACTION_IMAGE, with a Server_image as its value, may be used interchangeably with MENU_ACTION_STRING and its string value.

11.6.3 Using MENUITEM

The MENUITEM package allows you to create separate menu items using separate calls to xv_create(). The attributes used are menu item-specific attributes—the same as those that are used in the MENU_ITEM attribute above.

_____
*Notification (callback) routines are discussed in Section 11.12, "Notification Procedures."

```
Menu_item    on, off;

on = (Menu_item)xv_create(NULL, MENUITEM,
    MENU_STRING,          "On",
    MENU_NOTIFY_PROC,     on_notify_proc,
    NULL);

off = (Menu_item)xv_create(NULL, MENUITEM,
    MENU_STRING,          "Off",
    MENU_NOTIFY_PROC,     off_notify_proc,
    NULL);

xv_set(menu,
    MENU_APPEND_ITEM,     on,
    MENU_APPEND_ITEM,     off,
    NULL);
```

These menu items are not created *in-line*; they are created independently using separate calls to xv_create(). They must therefore be added to the menu independently. In this case, they are added using MENU_APPEND_ITEM (see Section 11.7, "Adding Menu Items").

11.6.4 Using MENU_GEN_PROC

This attribute takes as its value a procedure that creates a menu item. If you do not know what the item will show as text or as an image at the time the menu is created or if there is other information that is not known, you can defer the creation of the menu item until the item is actually needed by specifying the item creation routine. Creating menu items using this method is identical for creating menus. See Section 11.8.1, "Menu-generating Procedures," for more information.

11.7 Adding Menu Items

There are several methods for adding separately created menu items to menus. For a list of menu item attributes, see the package summary at the end of this chapter. These attributes can be used when you are using xv_set() on a menu.

The code fragment below demonstrates the use of MENU_APPEND_ITEM. The menu items are created independently of the menu itself. They are added to the menu as they are created by using the attribute MENU_APPEND_ITEM:

```
char         *names[] = { "One", "Two", "Three", "Four", "Five" };
Menu          menu;
Menu_item     mi;
int           i;
void          my_notify_proc();

menu = (Menu)xv_create(NULL, MENU, NULL);

for (i = 0; i < 5; i++) {
    mi = (Menu_item)xv_create(NULL, MENUITEM,
        MENU_STRING,          names[i],
        MENU_NOTIFY_PROC,     my_notify_proc,
```

```
        MENU_RELEASE,
        NULL);
    xv_set(menu, MENU_APPEND_ITEM, mi, NULL);
}
```

This use of MENU_RELEASE is to indicate that the menu item is intended to be freed when when the item's parent menu is destroyed. This attribute takes *no value*; specifying it is equivalent to specifying a TRUE value. Not specifying it implies FALSE. *In-line* menu items have this attribute set by default, but menu items that are not created in-line must set this attribute explicitly if you want them to be freed automatically. You do not want to set this attribute if you intend to use this menu item in more than one menu or if you want to reuse it later. See Section 11.15, "Destroying Menus," later in this chapter.

11.8 Pullright Menus

A pullright menu is simply another menu that is attached to a menu item. Note that for a menu item to contain a pullright menu, the menu must already have been created. This means that any menu group should be created from the bottom up. The attributes MENU_PULLRIGHT, MENU_PULLRIGHT_ITEM, and MENU_PULLRIGHT_IMAGE all allow a pullright menu to be attached to a menu item.

In the first case, MENU_PULLRIGHT can be assigned to a menu item to attach an existing menu to it, as shown below:

```
extern Server_image image1, image2, image3;
Menu image_menu, menu;
void image_notify_proc();

image_menu = (Menu)xv_create(NULL, MENU,
    MENU_IMAGES,        image1, image2, image3, NULL,
    MENU_NOTIFY_PROC,   image_notify_proc,
    NULL);

menu = (Menu)xv_create(NULL, MENU,
    MENU_ITEM,
        MENU_STRING,      "images",
        MENU_PULLRIGHT,   image_menu,
        NULL,
    NULL);
```

In the previous example, a menu of server images is created and is initialized to contain three images. Another menu is created that is initialized for one menu item, but that menu item has a pullright menu that is set to the menu_images menu.

The menu item created may also be initialized using the MENU_PULLRIGHT_ITEM attribute. This attribute takes two parameters as its *value*: a string and a menu. Therefore, the above code fragment could have been written:

```
menu = (Menu)xv_create(NULL, MENU,
    MENU_PULLRIGHT_ITEM, "images", image_menu,
    NULL);
```

Had the label for the pullright menu item been a *Server_image* rather than a string, the call would look like:

```
extern Server_image label_image;

menu = (Menu)xv_create(NULL, MENU,
    MENU_PULLRIGHT_IMAGE, label_image, image_menu,
    NULL);
```

In the code fragment below, we use another piece of code to demonstrate the same principle. This example demonstrates how a menu that represents font sizes may be set as the pullright menu for a list of fonts:

```
Menu        font_menu, size_menu;
Menu_item   mi;
int         i;
void        notify_font();
char        buf[4], *p;
...
size_menu = (Menu)xv_create(NULL, MENU,
    MENU_NOTIFY_PROC,   notify_size,
    NULL);

for (i = 8; i <= 20; i += 2) {
    sprintf(buf, "%d", i);
    p = strcpy(malloc(strlen(buf)+1), buf);
    mi = (Menu_item)xv_create(NULL, MENUITEM,
        MENU_STRING,        p,
        MENU_RELEASE,
        MENU_RELEASE_IMAGE,
        MENU_NOTIFY_PROC, notify_font,
        NULL);
    xv_set(size_menu, MENU_APPEND_ITEM, mi, NULL);
}

font_menu = (Menu)xv_create(NULL, MENU,
    MENU_TITLE_ITEM,        "Fonts",
    MENU_PULLRIGHT_ITEM, "courier",          size_menu,
    MENU_PULLRIGHT_ITEM, "boston",           size_menu,
    MENU_PULLRIGHT_ITEM, "times-roman",      size_menu,
    MENU_PULLRIGHT_ITEM, "lucidasans",       size_menu,
    MENU_PULLRIGHT_ITEM, "palatino-roman", size_menu,
    NULL);
```

Each item in the main menu (font_menu) has a pullright menu (size_menu) associated with it. In the for loop where the string for the menu item is assigned, the data is allocated using malloc() and buf is copied into the allocated data using strcpy(). We cannot use buf directly, because unlike panel items, the menu item string is not copied by the MENU package—we must pass in allocated data. Because of this, we also specify the attribute MENU_RELEASE_IMAGE so that when the item is destroyed, the allocated data will be freed. Also note that because we used xv_create() to create the menu item, we specify MENU_RELEASE to indicate that the menu item should be freed when the parent menu is destroyed.

11.8.1 Menu-generating Procedures

In certain situations, the menu items for a particular menu cannot be known ahead of time. For example, a mail application allows users to write mail messages to files in a designated *folder directory*. If a menu is going to display the current folders in that directory, then the menu items should be updated any time a folder is created or deleted from that directory. But rather than updating the folder at the time the directory contents change, it would be better to scan the directory and use each filename in the directory as a menu item.

For such situations, it is necessary to defer the creation of the folder menu until it needs to be displayed. Therefore, you still create the pullright menu item so the user can select the item. But rather than specifying a pullright menu associated with the item, specify a routine that will generate the menu. When the menu needs to be displayed, the routine is called which returns a menu.

To do this, you specify the attribute MENU_GEN_PULLRIGHT when creating the menu item, as shown below:

```
Menu menu, gen_folder_menu();
void change_to_folder();

menu = (Menu)xv_create(NULL, MENU,
    MENU_TITLE_ITEM,        "Mail Folders",
    MENU_NOTIFY_PROC,       change_to_folder,
    MENU_STRINGS,           "/usr/spool/mail", "~/mbox", NULL,
    MENU_ITEM,
        MENU_STRING,        "~/Mail"
        MENU_GEN_PULLRIGHT, gen_folder_menu,
        NULL,
    NULL);
```

There is a shortcut attribute that allows you to specify both the menu item's string and the MENU_GEN_PULLRIGHT procedure in the same call. The attribute is MENU_GEN_PULLRIGHT_ITEM. It is used as follows:

```
MENU_GEN_PULLRIGHT_ITEM, "~/Mail", gen_folder_menu,
```

The menu-generating routine may do whatever is necessary to build a new menu, but you should be careful that the routine does not take too much processing time, since the user is waiting with the MENU button pressed for the menu to be displayed. Also remember that a pointer grab is going on, so the routine should avoid any interaction with the user (such as error dialog boxes).

The form of the menu-generating procedure is:

```
Menu
menu_gen_proc(menu_item, op)
    Menu_item menu_item;
    Menu_generate op;
```

This routine may be called *each time* the menu is needed. If the menu need only be created once, you can to return the same menu all the time.

The op parameter is one of the following enumerated types:

```
typedef enum {
    MENU_DISPLAY,
    MENU_DISPLAY_DONE,
    MENU_NOTIFY,
    MENU_NOTIFY_DONE
} Menu_generate;
```

op indicates the condition in which your routine has been called. The MENU_DISPLAY value indicates that the menu is going to be displayed while MENU_DISPLAY_DONE indicates that the menu has been displayed and dismissed. If your menu is truly dynamic (e.g., it may change upon each invocation), then you should destroy the menu when op equals MENU_DISPLAY_DONE.

The MENU_NOTIFY value indicates that the user has chosen a menu item and the MENU_NOTIFY_PROC associated with the menu item selected or the menu's notify procedure is about to be called. After the generating procedure has been called, the notify routine is called. After the notify routine for the menu or menu item is called, the menu-generating procedure is called again with op set to MENU_NOTIFY_DONE. At this point, you should destroy the menu if you do not intend to reuse it. A debugging hint: if your menu-generating routine generates a run-time error, be careful when trying to debug the program under a debugger. The problem is that when you run the program in a debugger and the program generates a run-time error, the debugger will stop execution and wait for input. In the meantime, the server has a pointer grab so keyboard focus is directed to the menu's window which is not able to receive input.

At this point, there is no way to interact with any program on the console—you will have to go to another server, computer or terminal connected to your workstation and kill the debugger (this will terminate the program and release the pointer grab). You may think of more clever ways to handle this situation depending on your workstation configuration, but the point is that you should be aware of the extremely inconvenient side effects whenever you play with server grabs.

The sample program *menu_dir2.c* in Appendix G, *Example Programs*, demonstrates how a menu-generating routine is used.

11.9 Using Toggle Menus

Toggle menus are menus with nonexclusive settings. The user can toggle menu items, turning them *on* or *off*. More than one menu item may be selected at a time. The only difference for creating these menu items is that MENU_TOGGLE_MENU is used as the *package* parameter to xv_create() and that menu items may not have pullright menus associated with them. Therefore, these are typically simple menus.

In the code below, we build a toggle menu that has three items in it. If the menu has been displayed and the user makes a selection, on or off, the notification routine is called no differently from any other menu notification procedure:

```
       void toggle_bold(), toggle_size(), toggle_italic();
       Menu menu;

       menu = (Menu)xv_create(NULL, MENU_TOGGLE_MENU,
           MENU_TITLE_ITEM,      "Text Rendering",
           MENU_ACTION_ITEM,     "Bold Style",       toggle_bold,
           MENU_ACTION_ITEM,     "Large Font",       toggle_size,
           MENU_ACTION_ITEM,     "Italics",          toggle_italic,
           NULL);
```

In this case, we are specifying three different notify procedures for each menu item. Since each performs a completely separate function, the menu items need not call the same routine.

To determine exactly which menu items are selected, you must loop through all the items in the menu:

```
       toggle_notify(menu, item)
       Menu menu
       Menu_item item;
       {
           int i;

           for (i = (int)xv_get(font_menu, MENU_NITEMS); i > 0; i--)
               if (xv_get(xv_get(font_menu, MENU_NTH_ITEM, i),
                   MENU_SELECTED)) {
                   printf("item %d selected\n", i);
                   /* do whatever other processing may need to be done */
               }
       }
```

This loop starts at the last item and works towards the first. The first item starts at 1, not 0; the *0th* item is the menu's title item, and it cannot be retrieved.

11.10 Menu Layout

By default, pop-up menus place their items vertically. If there are too many items, a new column may be started in order to display the entire menu on the screen. You can specify the number of rows and columns for the menu by using the attributes MENU_NROWS and MENU_NCOLS.

Although specifying menu item layout is certainly legal and acceptable to OPEN LOOK, explicit menu item layout should be avoided for anything other than static menus. Dynamic menus will have problems maintaining menu item order, and if you use a pin-up menu, the command frame will almost certainly not match the appearance of the menu. To guarantee that your pin-up menu looks the same as the menu, specify your own pin-up procedure. (See the following section for more information.)

11.11 Making Pin-up Menus

As the programmer, you may give the user the option of pinning up a menu by providing the pushpin in the pop-up menu. For the simple case where menus are static and there are not going to be any modifications to the menu or the menu items, XView provides the attribute MENU_GEN_PIN_WINDOW. If specified, XView generates the pin window frame automatically by creating a command frame, a panel and a series of panel items that correspond to the menu items.

This attribute takes two values as parameters. One is a base frame; the other is a string that acts as a title for the frame, as shown below:

```
Frame     frame;
Menu      menu;
void      func1(), func2();
...
/* Create base frame for the application */
frame = (Frame)xv_create(NULL, FRAME, NULL);
...
menu = (Menu)xv_create(NULL, MENU,
    /* the pinup menu subframe is a child of the base frame */
    MENU_GEN_PIN_WINDOW,    frame,  "title",
    MENU_ITEM,
        MENU_STRING,        "item1",
        MENU_NOTIFY_PROC,   func1,
        NULL,
    MENU_ITEM,
        MENU_STRING,        "item2",
        MENU_NOTIFY_PROC,   func2,
        NULL,
    NULL);
...
```

The new command frame is created as a subframe of the frame value. The title label for the menu and the frame is the *title* value. Note that you should not use MENU_TITLE_ITEM if you are using MENU_GEN_PIN_WINDOW.

When using MENU_GEN_PIN_PROC, there must be a callback routine specified with each menu item given. The notify procedure assigned to the menu itself is ignored, so it should not be specified.

When the menu is displayed as a result of a call to menu_show(), a pushpin in the upper-left corner of the menu is displayed allowing the user to pin up the menu, that causes the menu to go away and the subframe to be displayed. You can get a handle to this subframe if you need it by calling:

```
Frame subframe = (Frame)xv_get(menu, MENU_PIN_WINDOW);
```

You can get a handle the panel associated with that frame by calling:

```
Panel panel = (Panel)xv_get(frame, FRAME_CMD_PANEL);
```

MENU_GEN_PIN_WINDOW should be used only for *static* menus. You should *not* use this attribute on menus which have items that may change or be removed, added, or modified in any way. The command frame, panel and panel items built by MENU_GEN_PIN_PROC are not updated or maintained by XView. If you have a menu that changes in any way, you must manage the pin window yourself or create your own.

If you choose to write your own pin window, there are several attributes that you might find helpful in implementing your routines:

MENU_PIN   This Boolean attribute indicates that the menu has a pushpin.

MENU_PIN_WINDOW   This attribute assigns the command frame you created to the menu's pin window. Once the pushpin is pushed in, the MENU package automatically sets the command frame's XV_SHOW attribute to TRUE, allowing the frame to be displayed.

MENU_PIN_PROC   This attribute provides the menu with a procedure that is called when the user pushes the pin in. You may override the default procedure that shows the pin_window of the menu by providing your own routine using this attribute. This routine overrides the default behavior of setting XV_SHOW on the command frame, so this responsibility lies in this routine.

MENU_DONE_PROC   This routine is called whenever a pop-up menu has been taken down after a menu item has been selected, pinned up, or simply dismissed without a selection being made. Again, this overrides the default action of setting XV_SHOW to FALSE, so this responsibility lies with the MENU_DONE_PROC routine.

11.12 Notification Procedures

When a menu item is selected, a notification procedure is called to notify the host application that the user has made a selection. If the menu item does not have a notify procedure, the parent menu's notification procedure is called instead. If the menu does not have a notification procedure, no action is taken. Be sure that each menu item or its parent menu has a MENU_NOTIFY_PROC routine associated with it. Otherwise, choosing a menu item has no effect. If you wish to make a menu item *inactive*, you should set the attribute MENU_INAC-TIVE to TRUE.

The primary difference between the MENU package and the PANEL package with respect to the notification mechanism is that if a menu item has no notification procedure associated with it, the notify procedure of the parent menu is used. The PANEL package has no such feature. To differentiate between the notify procedure of a *menu* and the notify procedure of a *menu item*, the term *action procedure* is sometimes used to refer to the menu item's notify procedure. Thus, you may come across the term *action procedure* or the attribute MENU_ACTION_PROC outside of this book.

However, because there is functionally no difference between the MENU_ACTION_PROC and the MENU_NOTIFY_PROC and since all other XView objects use *notify* procedures to register their callbacks, we are going to attempt to maintain consistency and avoid potential confusion with the terms by referring to both notify procedures commonly using MENU_NOTIFY_PROC.

The form of the callback routine is:

```
void
menu_notify_proc(menu, menu_item)
    Menu menu;
    Menu_item menu_item;
```

The program in Example 11-2 demonstrates several of the concepts introduced in the chapter so far. *xv_menu.c* creates a simple frame, a canvas and a pop-up menu. The menu is a *static* menu because all the menu items are created in-line with the menu-generating procedure. The menu itself has a notify procedure which is called if any of the menu items specified by MENU_STRINGS are selected. The result is to display the text of the selected item in the header of the frame. An additional menu item is specified that has a pullright menu that can be pinned up.

Example 11-2. The xv_menu.c program

```
/*
 * xv_menu.c -
 *      Demonstrate the use of an XView menu in a canvas subwindow.
 *      Menu is brought up with right mouse button and the selected
 *      choice is displayed in the canvas.  Allows menu to be pinned.
 */
#include <xview/xview.h>
#include <xview/canvas.h>

Frame     frame;

main(argc,argv)
int       argc;
char      *argv[];
{
    Canvas         canvas;
    Menu           menu;
    void           my_notify_proc(), my_event_proc();
    extern void exit();

    xv_init(XV_INIT_ARGC_PTR_ARGV, &argc, argv, NULL);

    frame = (Frame)xv_create(NULL, FRAME,
        FRAME_LABEL,      argv[0],
        NULL);
    canvas = (Canvas)xv_create(frame, CANVAS,
        XV_WIDTH,          300,
        XV_HEIGHT,         200,
        NULL);
    menu = (Menu)xv_create(NULL, MENU,
        MENU_TITLE_ITEM,           "Junk",
        MENU_STRINGS,              "Yes", "No", "Maybe", NULL,
        MENU_NOTIFY_PROC,          my_notify_proc,
        MENU_ITEM,
            MENU_STRING,           "Save",
            MENU_NOTIFY_PROC,      my_notify_proc,
            MENU_PULLRIGHT,
                xv_create(canvas, MENU,
                    MENU_GEN_PIN_WINDOW,          frame, "Save",
                    MENU_ITEM,
                        MENU_STRING,              "Update Changes",
                        MENU_NOTIFY_PROC,         my_notify_proc,
```

Example 11-2. The xv_menu.c program (continued)

```
                        NULL,
                NULL),
        NULL,
    MENU_ITEM,
            MENU_STRING,          "Quit",
            MENU_NOTIFY_PROC,     exit,
            NULL,
        NULL);

    xv_set(canvas_paint_window(canvas),
        WIN_CONSUME_EVENTS,      WIN_MOUSE_BUTTONS, NULL,
        WIN_EVENT_PROC,          my_event_proc,
        /* associate the menu to the canvas win for easy retrieval */
        WIN_CLIENT_DATA,         menu,
        NULL);

    window_fit(frame);
    window_main_loop(frame);
}

/*
 * my_notify_proc - Display menu selection in frame header.
 */
void
my_notify_proc(menu, menu_item)
Menu menu;
Menu_item menu_item;
{
    xv_set(frame,
        FRAME_LABEL,      xv_get(menu_item, MENU_STRING),
        NULL);
}

/*
 * Call menu_show() to display menu on right mouse button push.
 */
void
my_event_proc(window, event)
Xv_Window window;
Event *event;
{
    if (event_action(event) == ACTION_MENU && event_is_down(event)) {
        Menu menu = (Menu)xv_get(window, WIN_CLIENT_DATA);
        menu_show(menu, window, event, NULL);
    }
}
```

The output of Example 11-2 is shown in Figure 11-7.

Figure 11-7. Output of xv_menu.c

11.13 Finding Menu Items

You can use xv_find() to locate menu items that match certain attribute-value pairs. The form of using xv_find() for menus is:

```
Menu_item item;

item = (Menu_item) xv_find(menu, MENU,
    <attribute-value list>,
    NULL);
```

xv_find() returns menu items, not menus. By default, when you search for items, each item in a menu is searched before descending into a menu item's pullright menu, should it exist. However, you can override this default behavior by specifying the attribute MENU_DESCEND_FIRST. During a menu search, if an item with a pullright is found, then this attribute indicates whether the search should continue through the pullright or to the next item in the current menu.

If a menu item or a menu item's pullright is a *generate* procedure, the generate procedure is called despite the fact that the menu or menu item will not be displayed. No matter how many attributes are given, xv_find() will return the first item found that matches all given attributes even though the item may have more attributes associated with it.

When specifying attribute-value pairs, you specify attributes in the same way as when you use xv_create(). For example, if you want to find a menu item with the string value of "fonts" and the callback routine of my_notify_proc, you would use:

```
menu_item = (Menu_item) xv_find(menu, MENUITEM,
    MENU_STRING,       "fonts,"
    MENU_NOTIFY_PROC,  my_notify_proc,
    NULL);
```

Unless the attribute XV_AUTO_CREATE is set to FALSE, if xv_find() does not find the menu item that you are looking for, a new menu item will be created.

11.14 Initial and Default Menu Selections

Two special menu items are the *default item* (MENU_DEFAULT_ITEM) and the *selected item* (MENU_SELECTED_ITEM). The default item defaults to the *first* item in the menu, and the *selected item* is the selected item (or items for MENU_TOGGLE_MENU menus).

Although the default menu item may be set by using xv_set(), the user may interactively change the default menu item by holding down the CONTROL key while also selecting a menu item with the MENU button. Therefore, if the user selects a menu item that has a pullright menu, *but the pullright menu is not activated*,* when your notify procedure is called, you may choose to descend into the pullright menu and find the default menu item and call that item's callback routine.

11.15 Destroying Menus

Destruction of menus is an important task because menus are frequently used and, if their resources are not freed adequately, you could find the size of your application growing rapidly until your system runs out of available memory. Therefore, proper cleanup of menu destruction is imperative. Menus are destroyed using xv_destroy(). In the case of *static menus*, nothing more is required than calling xv_destroy(). This is because the internals of XView automatically set attributes discussed in this section.

Be aware of several situations, such as when you:

- Allocate your own strings or server images as menu item labels.

- Create your own menu items using xv_create(NULL, MENUITEM, ...).

- Generate your own pullright menus.

The destruction phase walks down each menu item in the menu and tests each menu item to see if it has the MENU_RELEASE attribute set. This is not a Boolean attribute—it has no value associated with it at all. If you specify the attribute, the attribute is set. If you do not specify it, then the attribute is not set. As noted, menu items that have been created in-line have MENU_RELEASE set already.

Menu items that you create yourself do not have MENU_RELEASE set by default. You also may or may not *want* it set. If you plan to reuse menu items—a need that is common—then you do not want to set this attribute. However, you must maintain a handle to the menu item or it is lost. If the attribute is set, then the menu item is freed, but no other data associated with the menu item is destroyed. Only the item itself is. If you have any allocated data

---

*This might happen if the user did not drag the mouse far enough to the right.

associated with the menu item, then you either need to free it yourself or give a hint to XView to free it for you.

The following subsections discuss other data allocated for menu items. Remember that freeing menus and menu items is not done automatically; this only happens as a result of your calling xv_destroy(). So, if you decide to free menus or menu items, you should be sure to free pullright menus and/or client data yourself beforehand.

11.15.1 Freeing Allocated Strings

If you create a menu item with allocated data, you should *not* use them in a MENU_STRINGS list. Instead, you should create the menu items individually, as shown in Example 11-3.

Example 11-3. Creating individual menu items

```
char *str1;
if (str1 = malloc(strlen(buf)+1))
    strcpy(str1, buf);
menu = xv_create(NULL, MENU,
    MENU_ITEM,
        MENU_STRING,     str1,
        MENU_RELEASE_IMAGE,
        NULL,
    NULL);
```

The code in Example 11-3 shows a menu item that is created *in-line* because it is created using the MENU_ITEM attribute. However, because the string used as the menu item's label is allocated, we need to provide XView with a hint to release this data.

Similarly, if we used xv_create() to create a Server_image as the menu item's label, the MENU_RELEASE_IMAGE attribute suffices to free that data as well.

11.15.2 Freeing Pullright Menus

Even though a menu item has MENU_RELEASE set, if a pullright menu is associated with it, the menu will not be freed. In many cases, this is acceptable because many menu items may share the same pullright menu. If you are sure you do not need the menu anymore, then you should free it. Note that freeing the menu will attempt to free the menu items within it.

This is most commonly done in menu-generating routines installed as the MENU_GEN_ PULLRIGHT attribute.

11.15.3 Menu Client Data

If a menu item is freed, you should be sure to free any client data you may be associated with it. Client data may have been attached to the menu item using XV_KEY_DATA or MENU_CLIENT_DATA.

If you created menus for panel buttons, and you destroy the MENU button (or the panel associated with that button), then you are responsible for destroying the menu you created. The panel does not handle this for you. Destroying the menu attached to menu buttons is done the same way as it is for menus.

11.16 Example Program

The following brief descriptions are introductory notes about the programs *menu_dir.c* (listed here) and *menu_dir2.c* (listed in Appendix G, *Example Programs*). The comments in the programs as well as the code itself should be read for full details.

menu_dir.c demonstrates many of the features of the MENU package presented in this chapter. It displays a menu that contains all the files from the current directory. If a pathname is given on the command line, that directory is used. The entire menu hierarchy is built initially at start-up time, so directories that do not have extremely long paths should be specified.*

For each directory found, a new menu is created and the directory is descended building items for the new menu. *menu_dir2.c* also builds cascading menus for directories, but instead of descending into the directory tree, a menu-generating routine is called only if the user tries to go into a pullright.

Example 11-4. The menu_dir.c program

```
/*
 * menu_dir.c -
 * Demonstrate the use of an XView menu in a canvas subwindow.
 * A menu is brought up with the MENU mouse button and displays
 * menu choices representing the files in the directory.  If a
 * directory entry is found, a new pullright item is created with
 * that subdir as the pullright menu's contents.  This implementation
 * creates the entire directory tree initially.  Do not attempt to
 * build a tree from /.  You will most likely run out of resources.
 *
 * argv[1] indicates which directory to start from.
 */
#include <xview/xview.h>
#include <xview/canvas.h>
#include <sys/stat.h>
#include <sys/dir.h>
#include <X11/Xos.h>
#ifndef MAXPATHLEN
#include <sys/param.h> /* probably sun/BSD specific */
```

---

*Don't even think of specifying /.

Example 11-4. The menu_dir.c program (continued)

```
#endif /* MAXPATHLEN */

Frame    frame;

/*
 * main -
 *      Create a frame, canvas and menu.
 *      A canvas receives input in its canvas_paint_window().
 *      Its callback procedure calls menu_show().
 */
main(argc,argv)
int      argc;
char     *argv[];
{
    Canvas          canvas;
    extern void exit();
    void            my_event_proc();
    Menu            menu;
    Menu_item    mi, add_path_to_menu();

    xv_init(XV_INIT_ARGC_PTR_ARGV, &argc, argv, NULL);

    frame = (Frame)xv_create(NULL, FRAME,
        FRAME_LABEL,             argv[1]? argv[1] : "cwd",
        FRAME_SHOW_FOOTER,       TRUE,
        NULL);
    canvas = (Canvas)xv_create(frame, CANVAS,
        FRAME_LABEL,     argv[0],
        XV_WIDTH,        400,
        XV_HEIGHT,       100,
        NULL);

    mi = add_path_to_menu(argc > 1? argv[1] : ".");
    menu = (Menu)xv_get(mi, MENU_PULLRIGHT);

    /* associate the menu to the canvas win for easy retrieval */
    xv_set(canvas_paint_window(canvas),
        WIN_CONSUME_EVENTS,     WIN_MOUSE_BUTTONS, NULL,
        WIN_EVENT_PROC,         my_event_proc,
        WIN_CLIENT_DATA,        menu,
        NULL);

    window_fit(frame);
    window_main_loop(frame);
}

/*
 * my_action_proc - display the selected item in the frame footer.
 */
void
my_action_proc(menu, menu_item)
Menu     menu;
Menu_item        menu_item;
{
    xv_set(frame,
        FRAME_LEFT_FOOTER,      xv_get(menu_item, MENU_STRING),
        NULL);
}

/*
```

Example 11-4. The menu_dir.c program (continued)

```
 * Call menu_show() to display menu on right mouse button push.
 */
void
my_event_proc(canvas, event)
Canvas   canvas;
Event *event;
{
    if ((event_id(event) == MS_RIGHT) && event_is_down(event)) {
        Menu menu = (Menu)xv_get(canvas, WIN_CLIENT_DATA);
        menu_show(menu, canvas, event, NULL);
    }
}

/*
 * return an allocated char * that points to the last item in a path.
 */
char *
getfilename(path)
char *path;
{
    char *p;

    if (p = rindex(path, '/'))
        p++;
    else
        p = path;
    return strcpy(malloc(strlen(p)+1), p);
}

/*
 * The path passed in is scanned via readdir().  For each file in the
 * path, a menu item is created and inserted into a new menu.  That
 * new menu is made the PULLRIGHT_MENU of a newly created panel item
 * for the path item originally passed it.  Since this routine is
 * recursive, a new menu is created for each subdirectory under the
 * original path.
 */
Menu_item
add_path_to_menu(path)
char *path;
{
    DIR                 *dirp;
    struct direct       *dp;
    struct stat         s_buf;
    Menu_item           mi;
    Menu                next_menu;
    char                buf[MAXPATHLEN];

    /* don't add a folder to the list if user can't read it */
    if (stat(path, &s_buf) == -1 || !(s_buf.st_mode & S_IREAD))
        return NULL;
    if (s_buf.st_mode & S_IFDIR) {
        int cnt = 0;
        if (!(dirp = opendir(path)))
            /* don't bother adding to list if we can't scan it */
            return NULL;
        next_menu = (Menu)xv_create(XV_NULL, MENU, NULL);
```

Example 11-4. The menu_dir.c program (continued)

```
        while (dp = readdir(dirp))
            if (strcmp(dp->d_name, ".") && strcmp(dp->d_name, "..")) {
                (void) sprintf(buf, "%s/%s", path, dp->d_name);
                if (!(mi = add_path_to_menu(buf)))
                    /* unreadable file or dir - deactivate item */
                    mi = xv_create(XV_NULL, MENUITEM,
                        MENU_STRING,            getfilename(dp->d_name),
                        MENU_RELEASE,
                        MENU_RELEASE_IMAGE,
                        MENU_INACTIVE,          TRUE,
                        NULL);
                xv_set(next_menu, MENU_APPEND_ITEM, mi, NULL);
                cnt++;
            }
        closedir(dirp);
        mi = xv_create(XV_NULL, MENUITEM,
            MENU_STRING,            getfilename(path),
            MENU_RELEASE,
            MENU_RELEASE_IMAGE,
            MENU_NOTIFY_PROC,       my_action_proc,
            NULL);
        if (!cnt) {
            xv_destroy(next_menu);
            /* An empty or unsearchable directory - deactivate item */
            xv_set(mi, MENU_INACTIVE, TRUE, NULL);
        } else {
            xv_set(next_menu, MENU_TITLE_ITEM, getfilename(path), NULL);
            xv_set(mi, MENU_PULLRIGHT, next_menu, NULL);
        }
        return mi;
    }
    return (Menu_item)xv_create(NULL, MENUITEM,
        MENU_STRING,            getfilename(path),
        MENU_RELEASE,
        MENU_RELEASE_IMAGE,
        MENU_NOTIFY_PROC,       my_action_proc,
        NULL);
}
```

11.17 Menu Package Summary

Table 11-1 lists the attributes in the MENU package; the procedures and macros are listed below. This information is described fully in Appendices A and B.

```
menu_action_proc()
menu_return_item()
menu_return_value()
menu_show()
```

Table 11-1. Menu Attributes

Menu	Menu Item
MENU_ACTION_IMAGE	MENU_ACTION_IMAGE
MENU_ACTION_ITEM	MENU_ACTION_ITEM
MENU_APPEND_ITEM	MENU_ACTION_PROC
MENU_CLASS	MENU_FEEDBACK
MENU_COL_MAJOR	MENU_GEN_PROC
MENU_DEFAULT	MENU_GEN_PROC_IMAGE
MENU_DEFAULT_ITEM	MENU_GEN_PROC_ITEM
MENU_DESCEND_FIRST	MENU_GEN_PULLRIGHT
MENU_DONE_PROC	MENU_GEN_PULLRIGHT_IMAGE
MENU_FIRST_EVENT	MENU_GEN_PULLRIGHT_ITEM
MENU_GEN_PIN_WINDOW	MENU_IMAGE
MENU_GEN_PROC	MENU_IMAGE_ITEM
MENU_GEN_PULLRIGHT_IMAGE	MENU_INACTIVE
MENU_GEN_PULLRIGHT_ITEM	MENU_INVERT
MENU_IMAGE_ITEM	MENU_PULLRIGHT
MENU_IMAGES	MENU_PULLRIGHT_IMAGE
MENU_INSERT	MENU_PULLRIGHT_ITEM
MENU_INSERT_ITEM	MENU_RELEASE
MENU_ITEM	MENU_RELEASE_IMAGE
MENU_LAST_EVENT	MENU_SELECTED
MENU_NCOLS	MENU_STRING
MENU_NITEMS	MENU_STRING_ITEM
MENU_NOTIFY_PROC	MENU_TITLE
MENU_NROWS	MENU_TYPE
MENU_NTH_ITEM	MENU_VALUE
MENU_PIN	
MENU_PIN_PROC	
MENU_PIN_WINDOW	
MENU_PULLRIGHT_IMAGE	
MENU_PULLRIGHT_ITEM	
MENU_REMOVE	
MENU_REMOVE_ITEM	
MENU_REPLACE	
MENU_REPLACE_ITEM	
MENU_STRINGS	
MENU_TITLE_IMAGE	
MENU_TITLE_ITEM	
MENU_TYPE	
MENU_VALID_RESULT	

12

Notices

In This Chapter:

Creating and Displaying Notices 264
    Response Choices and Values 266
    Notice Triggers 267
Another Example 269
Notice Package Summary 272

Notices

12
Notices

A notice is a pop-up window that notifies the user of a problem or asks a question that requires an immediate response. The notice grabs the entire screen so no other windows or applications can receive input until the user responds to the notice. Figure 12-1 shows an example of a notice window from the *OPEN LOOK GUI Specification*.

Figure 12-1. A sample notice window

Notices are implemented using the FULLSCREEN package to grab the keyboard and pointer events from the server. (The FULLSCREEN package is described in Chapter 15, *Nonvisual Objects*.) The notice window, which owns the fullscreen object, is a nonrectangular transient X window with the X-window attribute override_redirect* set. When the notice is

_____
*override_redirect tells the window manager not to provide window decorations.

created, the notice window is immediately displayed. When the user responds to one of the available choices, the notice-session ends.

12.1 Creating and Displaying Notices

To use the NOTICE package in applications, the header file *<xview/notice.h>* must be included. Notices are special XView objects because they are not created via xv_create(). Also, they cannot be modified using xv_set(). Notices are created using the special procedure notice_prompt():

```
int
notice_prompt(owner, event, attrs)
    Xv_Window    owner;
    Event        *event;
    attributes ...
```

When creating a notice, the owner must be a valid XView object that has a window associated with it. This can be a panel or a frame, but it is typically the window that causes the notice to be created. If the user tries to type in a read-only text subwindow, a notice might appear from that window informing the user of the error. The event might be NULL if you are not using NOTICE_TRIGGER (see Section 12.1.2, "Notice Triggers").

Because the notice window is not a part of any other XView package and it does not allow window-specific attributes, you cannot use any generic, common or window attributes to configure the notice window; you can only use NOTICE_* attributes.

Notice windows are explicitly specified by OPEN LOOK and cannot be modified. If you wish to create a notice-type interface that is not OPEN LOOK compliant, which is not recommended, you need to learn more about the fullscreen object described in Chapter 15, *Nonvisual Objects*.

Your application has control over the messages that are displayed in the notice window as well as the choices available to the user as responses. notice_prompt() creates a window, grabs the server, waits for the user to make a selection on one of the available button choices, then destroys the window. You never have a handle to the notice *object* itself—only the resulting choice made by the user. The result is the return value of the notice_prompt() function.

A very simple case of a notice prompt is demonstrated in Example 12-1:

Example 12-1. The simple_notice.c program

```
/*
 * simple_notice.c -- Demonstrate the use of notices.
 */
#include <xview/xview.h>
#include <xview/panel.h>
#include <xview/notice.h>

main(argc,argv)
int     argc;
char    *argv[];
```

Example 12-1. The simple_notice.c program (continued)

```
{
    Frame        frame;
    Panel        panel;
    Xv_opaque    my_notify_proc();

    /*
     * Initialize XView, create a frame, a panel and one panel button.
     */
    xv_init(XV_INIT_ARGS, argc, argv, NULL);

    frame = (Frame)xv_create(XV_NULL, FRAME, NULL);
    panel = (Panel)xv_create(frame, PANEL, NULL);
    xv_create(panel, PANEL_BUTTON,
        PANEL_LABEL_STRING,       "Quit",
        PANEL_NOTIFY_PROC,        my_notify_proc,
        NULL);

    /* make sure everything looks good */
    window_fit(panel);
    window_fit(frame);

    /* start window event processing */
    xv_main_loop(frame);
}

/*
 * my_notify_proc() -- called when the user selects the Quit button.
 *      The notice appears as a result of notice_prompt().  Here
 *      the user must chooses YES or NO to confirm or deny quitting.
 */
Xv_opaque
my_notify_proc(item, event)
Panel_item    item;
Event         *event;
{
    int          result;
    Panel        panel = (Panel)xv_get(item, PANEL_PARENT_PANEL);
    Window       win;
    Window       root = (Window)xv_get(xv_get(panel, XV_ROOT), XV_XID);
    int          x, y;

    XTranslateCoordinates(xv_get(panel, XV_DISPLAY),
        xv_get(panel, XV_XID), root, event_x(event), event_y(event),
        &x, &y, &win);

    result = notice_prompt(panel, NULL,
        NOTICE_MESSAGE_STRINGS, "Do you really want to quit?", NULL,
        NOTICE_FOCUS_XY,        x, y,
        NOTICE_BUTTON_YES,      "Yes",
        NOTICE_BUTTON_NO,       "No",
        NULL);

    if (result == NOTICE_YES)
        exit(0);
}
```

The program *simple_notice.c* contains a panel with a Quit button. When the user selects the Quit button, a notice pops up to prompt the user for confirmation. What the user sees is shown in Figure 12-2. If the user presses Yes, the program exits.

Figure 12-2. Output of simple_notice.c while the notice is up

The position from which the notice shadow emanates is described by the attribute
NOTICE_FOCUS_XY. This value defaults to the current mouse position when the application
calls notice_prompt(). As shown in *simple_notice.c*, the point from which the notice
shadow emanates appears to be the same position as the location where the panel button was
selected. Due to possible delays with the X server, by the time the notice_prompt() routine gets called, the location of the mouse may have moved from the place where the panel
button was selected. To be sure that the notice prompt appears to emanate from the original
mouse-down location, we convert the coordinates of the mouse button from the panel-
relative coordinates (given in the Event parameter) to root-window coordinates using
XTranslateCoordinates(). Once translated, we now have the values for
NOTICE_FOCUS_XY.

12.1.1 Response Choices and Values

Two responses are normally present whenever a notice appears: Yes and No. These are
defined for convenience in *<xview/notice.h>*:

```
#define NOTICE_YES   1
#define NOTICE_NO    0
```

These are the return values that notice_prompt() might return that correspond directly to
the attributes NOTICE_BUTTON_YES and NOTICE_BUTTON_NO. As shown in
simple_notice.c, these are the only two choices made available to the user.

These two choices are special in another way: they respond to *accelerator* keys. That is, the RETURN key can be used instead of selecting the NOTICE_BUTTON_YES button with the pointer, and the STOP key can be used instead of selecting NOTICE_BUTTON_NO.

Also, when these choices are used, the cursor is immediately warped to the button associated with NOTICE_BUTTON_YES because this is the *default* response to the notice. As a hint to the programmer, it is always desirable to word all questions such that the default answer is Yes.

It is quite common for the application to have more than one appropriate response to some kind of notice prompt. Suppose that your application is an editor of some kind. If the user selects the Quit button and there have been changes to the file that have not been accounted for, you might wish to inform the user and allow more than one response: quit, updating changes; quit, ignoring changes; or cancel the quit all together. To implement these new choices, use the NOTICE_BUTTON attribute to define the choices available:

```
result = notice_prompt(panel, NULL,
    NOTICE_MESSAGE_STRINGS,
        "There have been modifications since your last update",
        "Would you like to quit or continue editing?",
        NULL,
    NOTICE_BUTTON,      "Quit, Update changes",     101,
    NOTICE_BUTTON,      "Quit, Ignore changes",     102,
    NOTICE_BUTTON,      "Continue Editing",         103,
    NULL);
```

The NOTICE_BUTTON attribute takes two parameters: the button label* and the return value if that button is selected. In this case, the possible return values for the call to notice_prompt are 101, 102, and 103 (in addition to possible error return values). The application should make its decision on how to proceed based on the return value.

Because the NOTICE_BUTTON attribute is used, there is no default choice and no accelerators associated with the notice; the user must use the pointer to select one of the available choices.

12.1.2 Notice Triggers

If you want to assign accelerators to notice buttons, or if you find it necessary to give the user the choice of using mouse buttons or keyboard events to respond to a notice, you can identify *triggers* that cause the notice to return. The value returned in this case is NOTICE_TRIGGERED, and the event that caused the trigger will be in the Event * passed in the call to notice_prompt(). When triggers are not used, the Event * can be NULL.

Example 12-2 shows how one might use the NOTICE_TRIGGER to get a particular event:

---

*The button can display text only; no graphic images can be displayed.

Example 12-2. The trigger_notice.c program

```
/*
 * trigger_notice.c -- Demonstrate the use of triggers in notices.
 */
#include <xview/xview.h>
#include <xview/panel.h>
#include <xview/notice.h>

main(argc,argv)
int      argc;
char     *argv[];
{
    Frame          frame;
    Panel          panel;
    Xv_opaque      my_notify_proc();
    extern void exit();

    /*
     * Initialize XView, create a frame, a panel and one panel button.
     */
    xv_init(XV_INIT_ARGS, argc, argv, NULL);
    frame = (Frame)xv_create(XV_NULL, FRAME, NULL);
    panel = (Panel)xv_create(frame, PANEL, NULL);
    (void) xv_create(panel, PANEL_BUTTON,
        PANEL_LABEL_STRING,       "Quit",
        PANEL_NOTIFY_PROC,        exit,
        NULL);
    (void) xv_create(panel, PANEL_BUTTON,
        PANEL_LABEL_STRING,       "Move",
        PANEL_NOTIFY_PROC,        my_notify_proc,
        NULL);

    /* make sure everything looks good */
    window_fit(panel);
    window_fit(frame);

    /* start window event processing */
    xv_main_loop(frame);
}

/*
 * my_notify_proc() -- called when the user selects the "Move"
 * panel button.  Put up a notice_prompt to get new coordinates
 * to move the main window.
 */
Xv_opaque
my_notify_proc(item, event)
Panel_item  item;
Event       *event;
{
    int            result, x, y;
    Panel          panel = (Panel)xv_get(item, PANEL_PARENT_PANEL);
    Frame          frame = (Frame)xv_get(panel, XV_OWNER);

    x = event_x(event), y = event_y(event);
    printf("original click relative to panel: %d, %d\n", x, y);
    result = notice_prompt(panel, event,
        NOTICE_MESSAGE_STRINGS,
            "You may move the window to a new location specified by",
            "clicking the Left Mouse Button somewhere on the screen.",
```

Example 12-2. The trigger_notice.c program (continued)

```
        NULL,
    NOTICE_TRIGGER,            MS_LEFT,
    NOTICE_NO_BEEPING,         TRUE,
    NULL);

if (result == NOTICE_TRIGGERED) {
    x += event_x(event) + (int)xv_get(frame, XV_X);
    y += event_y(event) + (int)xv_get(frame, XV_Y);
    printf("screen x,y: %d, %d\n", x, y);
    xv_set(frame, XV_X, x, XV_Y, y, NULL);
}
}
```

When this program is run and the user selects the Move panel button, a notice is displayed instructing the user to select a new position for the application window. When the user selects a new location, the window frame moves to that position. Note that the window manager adds a title bar and other decorations around the frame, so do not expect the upper-left corner of the frame to move to the new position. The real frame's origin is moved to the new position, and the frame's decorations are moved as well but not aligned to the same values (it will be somewhat higher).

When notice_prompt() returns, the Event structure that was passed to it contains the event that triggered the notice to return. The x and y coordinates in the Event structure are relative to the origin of the notice shadow. Thus, if you clicked at the point in which the shadow emanates from the screen, the Event structure's x and y coordinates will be 0,0.

To translate these coordinates to screen-specific coordinates, we save the original event location and add to that the (x, y) coordinates returned when notice_prompt() returns as well as the current coordinates of the frame (main application).

Before leaving trigger_notice.c, we should mention the attribute NOTICE_NO_BEEPING that is used to prevent the notice from beeping when it is displayed. Beeping the screen is usually done when there is an error condition of some sort you wish to alert the user about. In this example, there is no error condition—it is a simple dialog with the user.

12.2 Another Example

In the previous example, we used many of the attributes covered in this section in addition to using some generic and common attributes for the panel items. Example 12-3 goes a little further to demonstrate how the NOTICE package works in conjunction with the rest of XView. It creates a frame, a panel with two panel buttons, and a message item. Initially, only the Quit button and the Commit button are displayed. When the user selects either button, a notice pops up asking the user to confirm or cancel the proposed action. If the user confirms quitting the program, the program quits. Otherwise, the result, either Confirmed or Canceled, is displayed as the text of the message item.

Example 12-3. The notice.c program

```c
/*
 * notice.c --
 * This application creates a frame, a panel, and 3 panel buttons.
 * A message button, a Quit button (to exit the program) and a
 * dummy "commit" button.  Extra data is attached to the panel
 * items by the use of XV_KEY_DATA.  The callback routine for the
 * quit and Commit buttons is generalized enough that it can apply
 * to either button (or any arbitrary button) because it extracts
 * the expected "data" (via XV_KEY_DATA) from whatever panel
 * button might have called it.
 */
#include <xview/xview.h>
#include <xview/panel.h>
#include <xview/notice.h>

/*
 * assign "data" to panel items using XV_KEY_DATA ... attach the
 * message panel item, a prompt string specific for the panel
 * item's notice_prompt, and a callback function if the user
 * chooses "yes".
 */
#define MSG_ITEM        10 /* any arbitrary integer */
#define NOTICE_PROMPT   11
#define CALLBACK_FUNC   12

main(argc,argv)
int     argc;
char    *argv[];
{
    Frame       frame;
    Panel       panel;
    Panel_item  msg_item;
    Xv_opaque   my_notify_proc();
    extern int  exit();

    /*
     * Initialize XView, and create frame, panel and buttons.
     */
    xv_init(XV_INIT_ARGS, argc, argv, NULL);
    frame = (Frame)xv_create(XV_NULL, FRAME,
        FRAME_LABEL,            argv[0],
        NULL);
    panel = (Panel)xv_create(frame, PANEL,
        PANEL_LAYOUT,           PANEL_VERTICAL,
        NULL);
    msg_item = (Panel_item)xv_create(panel, PANEL_MESSAGE, NULL);
    (void) xv_create(panel, PANEL_BUTTON,
        PANEL_LABEL_STRING,     "Quit",
        PANEL_NOTIFY_PROC,      my_notify_proc,
        XV_KEY_DATA,            MSG_ITEM,       msg_item,
        /*
         * attach a prompt specific for this button used by
         * notice_prompt()
         */
        XV_KEY_DATA,            NOTICE_PROMPT,  "Really Quit?",
        /*
         * a callback function to call if the user answers "yes"
```

Example 12-3. The notice.c program (continued)

```
                * to prompt
                */
              XV_KEY_DATA,               CALLBACK_FUNC,   exit,
              NULL);
      /*
       * now that the Quit button is under the message item,
       * layout horizontally
       */
      xv_set(panel, PANEL_LAYOUT, PANEL_HORIZONTAL, NULL);
      (void) xv_create(panel, PANEL_BUTTON,
          PANEL_LABEL_STRING,        "Commit...",
          PANEL_NOTIFY_PROC,         my_notify_proc,
          XV_KEY_DATA,               MSG_ITEM,        msg_item,
          /*
           * attach a prompt specific for this button used by
           * notice_prompt()
           */
          XV_KEY_DATA,               NOTICE_PROMPT,   "Update all changes?",
          /*
           * Note there is no callback func here, but one could be
           * written
           */
          NULL);

      window_fit(panel);
      window_fit(frame);
      xv_main_loop(frame);
}
/*
 * my_notify_proc()
 * The notice appears as a result of notice_prompt().
 * The "key data" associated with the panel item is extracted via
 * xv_get().  The resulting choice is displayed in the panel
 * message item.
 */
Xv_opaque
my_notify_proc(item, event)
Panel_item  item;
Event       *event;
{
    int          result;
    int          (*func)();
    char         *prompt;
    Panel_item   msg_item;
    Panel        panel;

    func = (int(*)())xv_get(item, XV_KEY_DATA, CALLBACK_FUNC);
    prompt = (char *)xv_get(item, XV_KEY_DATA, NOTICE_PROMPT);
    msg_item = (Panel_item)xv_get(item, XV_KEY_DATA, MSG_ITEM);
    panel = (Panel)xv_get(item, PANEL_PARENT_PANEL);
    /*
     * Create the notice and get a response.
     */
    result = notice_prompt(panel, NULL,
        NOTICE_MESSAGE_STRINGS,
                prompt,
```

Example 12-3. The notice.c program (continued)

```
                    "Press YES to confirm",
                    "Press NO to cancel",
                    NULL,
        NOTICE_BUTTON_YES,        "YES",
        NOTICE_BUTTON_NO,         "NO",
        NULL);

    switch(result) {
        case NOTICE_YES:
            xv_set(msg_item, PANEL_LABEL_STRING, "Confirmed", NULL);
            if (func)
                (*func)();
            break;
        case NOTICE_NO:
            xv_set(msg_item, PANEL_LABEL_STRING, "Cancelled", NULL);
            break;
        case NOTICE_FAILED:
            xv_set(msg_item, PANEL_LABEL_STRING, "unable to pop-up",
                NULL);
            break;
        default:
            xv_set(msg_item, PANEL_LABEL_STRING, "unknown choice",
                NULL);
    }
}
```

12.3 Notice Package Summary

Table 12-1 lists the attributes, procedures and macros for the NOTICE package. This information is described fully in Appendices A and B.

Table 12-1. Notice Attributes, Procedures and Macros

Attributes	Procedures and Macros
NOTICE_BUTTON	notice_prompt()
NOTICE_BUTTON_NO	
NOTICE_BUTTON_YES	
NOTICE_FOCUS_XY	
NOTICE_FONT	
NOTICE_MESSAGE_STRINGS	
NOTICE_MESSAGE_STRINGS_ARRAY_PTR	
NOTICE_NO_BEEPING	
NOTICE_TRIGGER	

13

Cursors

In This Chapter:

Creating Cursors 275
   simple_cursor.c 276
Predefined Cursors 277
The Hotspot and Cursor Location 278
Color Cursors 280
Cursor Package Summary 281

13
Cursors

A *cursor* is an image that tracks the mouse on the display. Each window has its own cursor which you can change. There are some cursors defined by OPEN LOOK that correspond to specific window manager operations such as resizing or dragging windows. For these cases, you cannot redefine a cursor. However, for windows in your application, you can assign any cursor image you like.

13.1 Creating Cursors

To use the CURSOR package, include the header file *<xview/cursor.h>*. It provides the necessary types and definitions for using the package. The cursor object's type is Xv_Cursor. In general, to create a cursor, create an image and a cursor using that image as the CURSOR_IMAGE data:

```
Server_image  svr_image;
Xv_Cursor     cursor;

cursor = (Xv_Cursor)xv_create(owner, CURSOR,
    CURSOR_IMAGE,  svr_image,
    NULL);
```

The owner of the cursor may be any XView object. The root window associated with the XView object is used internally by the CURSOR package. If NULL, then the root window of the default screen is used.

The cursor is then assigned to a window associated with an XView object such as a frame, canvas, or panel:

```
xv_set(window, WIN_CURSOR, cursor, NULL);
```

It is illegal to assign a cursor to a window if the screens do not match. This is normally not a problem unless you are using multiple displays in your application. In this case, you should be sure to use an XView object that has a common display as the owner for the cursor. In the code line above, *window* should be the visible window to the application. For canvases and panels, this should be the *paint window*, not the canvas or panel object itself.* If you assign

---

*See Chapter 5, *Canvases and Openwin*, for more information about the paint window.

your own cursor to an openwin object (such as a canvas or panel) and the object has been split (either by the user *splitting views* or by the application), then the application is responsible for assigning the cursor to each new paint window.

13.1.1 simple_cursor.c

To introduce how to use the CURSOR package, we'll start with a short program that shows how to set the cursor for a canvas.

Example 13-1. The simple_cursor.c program

```
/*
 * simple_cursor.c -- create a cursor (looks like an hourglass) and
 * assign it to a canvas window.
 */
#include <xview/xview.h>
#include <xview/panel.h>
#include <xview/cursor.h>
#include <xview/svrimage.h>

/* data that describes the cursor's image -- see SERVER_IMAGE below */
short cursor_bits[] = {
/* Width=16, Height=16, Depth=1, */
    0x7FFE,0x4002,0x200C,0x1A38,0x0FF0,0x07E0,0x03C0,0x0180,
    0x0180,0x0240,0x0520,0x0810,0x1108,0x23C4,0x47E2,0x7FFE
};

main(argc, argv)
int argc;
char *argv[];
{
    Frame        frame;
    Canvas       canvas;
    Xv_Cursor    cursor;
    Server_image svr_image;

    xv_init(XV_INIT_ARGC_PTR_ARGV, &argc, argv, NULL);

    /*
     * create a server image to use as the cursor's image.
     */
    svr_image = (Server_image)xv_create(XV_NULL, SERVER_IMAGE,
        XV_WIDTH,           16,
        XV_HEIGHT,          16,
        SERVER_IMAGE_BITS,  cursor_bits,
        NULL);
    /*
     * create a cursor based on the image just created
     */
    cursor = (Xv_Cursor)xv_create(XV_NULL, CURSOR,
        CURSOR_IMAGE,           svr_image,
        NULL);

    /*
     * Create a base frame and a canvas
     */
    frame = (Frame)xv_create(XV_NULL, FRAME, NULL);
```

Example 13-1. The simple_cursor.c program (continued)

```
canvas = (Canvas)xv_create(frame, CANVAS,
    XV_WIDTH,                    100,
    XV_HEIGHT,                   100,
    NULL);
/*
 * set the cursor to the paint window for the canvas
 * Do not set it for the canvas itself.
 */
xv_set(xv_get(canvas, CANVAS_NTH_PAINT_WINDOW, 0),
    WIN_CURSOR,                  cursor,
    NULL);

window_fit(frame);
window_main_loop(frame);
}
```

Beware that if a canvas (or any openwin object) is split, the new view (which has a corresponding paint window) does not inherit the cursor from the old view window.* Note that the server images used in cursors must be 1-bit deep. Cursors can have two colors associated with them by specifying foreground and background colors; you cannot specify server images whose depths are greater than 1. See Section 13.4, "Color Cursors."

13.2 Predefined Cursors

A number of predefined cursors are available in the CURSOR package for use as OPEN LOOK cursors. To use these cursors, you may specify the CURSOR_SRC_CHAR and CURSOR_MASK_CHAR attributes with certain predefined constants as values for these attributes. In <xview/cursor.h>, there are some OPEN LOOK cursor defines prefixed by OLC_. When using these attributes, you should not use the CURSOR_IMAGE attribute since you cannot use both simultaneously. Using the previous example, we can remove the SERVER_IMAGE references and modify the call to create the cursor:

```
cursor = xv_create(NULL, CURSOR,
    CURSOR_SRC_CHAR,    OLC_BUSY_PTR,
    NULL);
```

Predefined cursors are really images from a prebuilt font. The *value* in the attribute-value pair is the character to use from that font—or rather, it is the index into the array of glyphs that the font contains. The glyph from the font is extracted and used as the image. You can use the attribute CURSOR_MASK_CHAR similarly. This image is used as the mask for the source image. If no mask is given, the same image used as the source is used as the mask.†

---

*Chapter 5, *Canvases and Openwin*, discusses splitting views.
†See XCreateGlyphCursor and XCreatePixmapCursor from Volume Two, *Xlib Reference Manual.*

Cursors

13.3 The Hotspot and Cursor Location

The *hotspot* on a cursor is the location in which the cursor is located if the user generates an event like pressing a mouse button or typing at the keyboard, or if you were to query its position. For example, if a cursor is shaped like an arrow, the hotspot should be at the tip of the arrow. If the hotspot for a cursor were set to (0, 0) then the hotspot would be the upper-left corner of the image used. A cursor shaped like a bull's eye (16x16) might have its hotspot at (7, 7) to indicate that the focus for the cursor is in the middle.* You can find out what the current position of the cursor is by using the attribute WIN_MOUSE_XY, as in:

```
r = (Rect *)xv_get(window, WIN_MOUSE_XY);
```

The return value from xv_get() is a pointer to a Rect structure. The r_width and r_height fields of this structure are unused (0, 0), but the r_top and r_left indicate the position of the hotspot for the cursor with respect to the window, window. The program in Example 13-2 demonstrates how this is used, and it shows how to create your own pixmap for a cursor image.

Example 13-2. The hot_spot.c program

```
/*
 * hot_spot.c -- create a cursor and query it's position on the
 * screen and in the panel's window.
 * Our own function, create_cursor(), attaches a new cursor to the
 * window parameter passed into the function.
 */
#include <X11/X.h>
#include <X11/Xlib.h>                    /* for the xlib graphics */
#include <xview/xview.h>
#include <xview/panel.h>
#include <xview/cursor.h>
#include <xview/svrimage.h>

main(argc, argv)
int argc;
char *argv[];
{
    Frame          frame;
    Panel          panel;
    void           do_it();

    xv_init(XV_INIT_ARGC_PTR_ARGV, &argc, argv, NULL);

    /*
     * Create a base frame, a panel, and a panel button.
     */
    frame = (Frame)xv_create(XV_NULL, FRAME, NULL);
    panel = (Panel)xv_create(frame, PANEL, NULL);
    create_cursor(xv_get(panel, CANVAS_NTH_PAINT_WINDOW, 0));
    (void) xv_create(panel, PANEL_BUTTON,
        PANEL_LABEL_STRING,     "Push Me",
        PANEL_NOTIFY_PROC,      do_it,
        NULL);
```

---

*The value 7, 7 is used because the origin is at 0, 0—not 1, 1.

Example 13-2. The hot_spot.c program (continued)

```
        window_fit(panel);
        window_fit(frame);
        window_main_loop(frame);
}
/*
 * when user selects the panel button, the current mouse location is
 * printed relative to the panel's window and to the screen.
 * This location is governed by the hot spot on the cursor.
 */
void
do_it(item, event)
{
    Rect *r;
    Panel panel = (Panel)xv_get(item, PANEL_PARENT_PANEL);

    r = (Rect *)xv_get(xv_get(panel, XV_ROOT), WIN_MOUSE_XY);
    printf("Root window: %d %d\n", r->r_left, r->r_top);
    r = (Rect *)xv_get(xv_get(panel, CANVAS_NTH_PAINT_WINDOW, 0), WIN_MOUSE_XY);
    printf("Panel window: %d %d\n", r->r_left, r->r_top);
}

/*
 * create_cursor() creates a bull's eye cursor and assigns it
 * to the window (parameter).
 */
create_cursor(window)
Xv_Window window;
{
    Xv_Cursor       cursor;
    Server_image    image;
    Pixmap          pixmap;
    Display         *dpy = (Display *)xv_get(window, XV_DISPLAY);
    GC              gc;
    XGCValues       gcvalues;

    image = (Server_image)xv_create(XV_NULL, SERVER_IMAGE,
        XV_WIDTH,       16,
        XV_HEIGHT,      16,
        NULL);
    pixmap = (Pixmap)xv_get(image, XV_XID);
    /* Create GC with reversed foreground and background colors to
     * clear pixmap first.  Use 1 and 0 because pixmap is 1-bit deep.
     */
    gcvalues.foreground = 0;
    gcvalues.background = 1;
    gc = XCreateGC(dpy, pixmap, GCForeground|GCBackground, &gcvalues);
    XFillRectangle(dpy, pixmap, gc, 0, 0, 16, 16);
    /*
     * Reset foreground and background values for XDrawArc() routines.
     */
    gcvalues.foreground = 1;
    gcvalues.background = 0;
    XChangeGC(dpy, gc, GCForeground | GCBackground, &gcvalues);
    XDrawArc(dpy, pixmap, gc, 2, 2, 12, 12, 0, 360 * 64);
    XDrawArc(dpy, pixmap, gc, 6, 6, 4, 4, 0, 360 * 64);
```

Example 13-2. The hot_spot.c program (continued)

```
    /* Create cursor and assign it to the window (parameter) */
    cursor = xv_create(XV_NULL, CURSOR,
        CURSOR_IMAGE,   image,
        CURSOR_XHOT,    7,
        CURSOR_YHOT,    7,
        NULL);
    xv_set(window, WIN_CURSOR, cursor, NULL);

    /* free the GC -- the cursor and the image must not be freed. */
    XFreeGC(dpy, gc);
}
```

When running the program, each time the panel button is pushed, the program prints the cursor's position relative to the panel's window and relative to the root window (absolute screen coordinates). You can move the base frame around on the screen to see how the root window coordinates change.

The routine create_cursor() creates a bull's eye cursor for the window passed as the parameter to the routine. The cursor image must be a Server_image, so we first create a server image, then get the Pixmap associated with it using the XV_XID, and use Xlib graphics to draw two circles in the pixmap.

We need a GC, so we create one based on the pixmap obtained from the server image. The pixmap is one bit deep, so the foreground and background colors are set to 0, 1 (to clear the pixmap first), then to 1, 0 so as to draw the two circles. We then create the cursor using the server image and setting the hotspots accordingly. We free the gc, but the Server_image (which contains the pixmap) and the cursor must not be freed so the cursor can be maintained by the window.

If you would rather set the cursor for a window using raw Xlib calls such as XCreate-PixmapCursor, XCreateGlyphCursor or XCreateFontCursor, use the X Window associated with the Xv_Window parameter. To get it, use:

```
    xv_get(window, XV_XID)
```

and assign an X Cursor object to that window.*

13.4 Color Cursors

You can define the foreground and background colors of a cursor independently of the window the cursor is assigned to. You may not have more than two colors per cursor because X does not support color images as cursor glyphs. Thus, to create or modify an existing cursor to have color, you need to specify foreground and background colors. Because of the use of color, the header file <xview/cms.h> must be included. The colors are of type Xv_singlecolor and should be initialized before use:

---

*See Volume One, *Xlib Programming Manual*.

```
#include <xview/cms.h>
...
Xv_singlecolor    fg, bg;

bg.red = 250, bg.green = 230, bg.blue = 30;
fg.red = 180, fg.green = 100, fg.blue = 20;

cursor = xv_create(NULL, CURSOR,
    CURSOR_IMAGE,                image,
    CURSOR_FOREGROUND_COLOR,    &fg,
    CURSOR_BACKGROUND_COLOR,    &bg,
    NULL);
```

13.5 Cursor Package Summary

Table 13-1 lists the attributes, procedures and macros for the CURSOR package. This information is described fully in Appendices A and B.

Table 13-1. Cursor Attributes, Procedures and Macros

Attributes	Procedures and Macros
CURSOR_BACKGROUND_COLOR	cursor_copy()
CURSOR_FOREGROUND_COLOR	
CURSOR_IMAGE	
CURSOR_SHOW_IMAGE	
CURSOR_X_HOT	
CURSOR_Y_HOT	

14

Icons

In This Chapter:

Creating and Destroying Icons 286
The Icon's Image 286
   The Icon Text 288
Icon Package Summary 289

14
Icons

A user may *close* an application to save space on the display. The program is still running and it may even be active, but it is not receiving input from the user. In order to represent the application in its closed state, an *icon* is used. An icon is a small picture that represents the application as shown in Figure 14-1 from the *OPEN LOOK GUI Specification Guide*.

Figure 14-1. Three bordered default icons

The graphic image that icons use may be used for other purposes and, therefore, may be shared among other objects in the application. But the icon image should be designed to easily identify the application while in a closed state. Icons may also have text associated with them. Space is limited, so the text is usually the name of the application.

Icons

14.1 Creating and Destroying Icons

To use the ICON package, include the header file *<xview/icon.h>*. The form for creating an icon is:

```
Icon icon;

icon = (Icon)xv_create(owner, ICON, attributes, NULL);
```

The owner of an icon is a base frame, but it may be created with a NULL owner. Once an icon is assigned to a frame, the owner of the icon is changed to that frame. This is another example of *delayed binding*.

When destroying an icon, the server image associated with the icon is not destroyed—it is your responsibility to free the server image and the pixmap associated with the icon if needed.

14.2 The Icon's Image

The most important thing about the icon is its graphic representation, so you will also need to be familiar with the SERVER_IMAGE package described in Chapter 15, *Nonvisual Objects*. Once an image is created, you can create an icon and assign it to a frame.

The program in Example 14-1 creates two server images—it uses *open.icon* as the image for the panel button and *closed.icon* for the application's icon.* Pressing the panel button causes the application to *close* to its iconic state. You must use a window manager function to open the application back up again.

Example 14-1. The icon_demo.c program

```
/*
 * icon_demo.c -- demonstrate how an icon is used.  Create a server
 * image and create an icon object with the image as the ICON_IMAGE.
 * Use the icon as the frame's icon.
 */
#include <xview/xview.h>
#include <xview/panel.h>
#include <xview/svrimage.h>
#include <xview/icon.h>

short open_bits[] =  {
#include "open.icon"
};

short closed_bits[] =  {
#include "closed.icon"
};

main(argc, argv)
```

---

*The files *open.icon* and *closed.icon* are not included in this book due to their length and complexity. They are bit-map files represented in ASCII *hex* notation. The files may be included with your XView distribution.

Example 14-1. The icon_demo.c program (continued)

```
int      argc;
char     *argv[];
{
    Frame                frame;
    Panel                panel;
    Server_image         open_image, closed_image;
    Icon                 icon;
    void                 close_frame();

    xv_init(XV_INIT_ARGC_PTR_ARGV, &argc, argv, NULL);

    frame = (Frame)xv_create(XV_NULL, FRAME, NULL);
    panel = (Panel)xv_create(frame, PANEL, NULL);

    open_image = (Server_image)xv_create(NULL, SERVER_IMAGE,
        XV_WIDTH,                64,
        XV_HEIGHT,               64,
        SERVER_IMAGE_BITS,       open_bits,
        NULL);

    closed_image = (Server_image)xv_create(NULL, SERVER_IMAGE,
        XV_WIDTH,                64,
        XV_HEIGHT,               64,
        SERVER_IMAGE_BITS,       closed_bits,
        NULL);

    (void) xv_create(panel, PANEL_BUTTON,
        PANEL_LABEL_IMAGE,       open_image,
        PANEL_NOTIFY_PROC,       close_frame,
        NULL);

    icon = (Icon)xv_create(frame, ICON,
        ICON_IMAGE,              closed_image,
        XV_X,                    100,
        XV_Y,                    100,
        NULL);
    xv_set(frame, FRAME_ICON, icon, NULL);

    window_fit(panel);
    window_fit(frame);
    xv_main_loop(frame);
}

void
close_frame(item, event)
Panel_item item;
Event *event;
{
    Frame frame = (Frame)xv_get(xv_get(item,
        PANEL_PARENT_PANEL), XV_OWNER);
    xv_set(frame, FRAME_CLOSED, TRUE, NULL);
}
```

The callback routine for the panel button, close_frame(), makes a call to an XView routine which sends window manager requests from the client to the window manager. In this case, we set the frame's FRAME_CLOSED attribute to TRUE to request that the window manager iconify the application associated with the frame parameter.*

---

*Window manager functions are discussed in Chapter 4, *Frames*.

The position of the image with respect to the icon is set using the attribute ICON_IMAGE_RECT, which takes as its value a pointer to a Rect structure. The r_top and r_left fields of the structure indicate the offset from the upper-left corner of the icon where the image is placed. The r_width and r_height fields describe the size of the image. If the icon is going to be a different size from the size of the icon's image, or if there is going to be text used with this icon, then the ICON_IMAGE_RECT attribute should be used. Section 14.2.1, "The Icon Text," has an example.

Color Icons

Color icons are accomplished in several ways. You can create a color server image and use that as the ICON_IMAGE. You can set the foreground and background colors for a mono-chrome image (single bit deep image) and change the colormap of the icon. For example:

```
Icon             icon;
unsigned long    foregound_index, background_index;
Server_image     image; /* assume 1-bit deep monochrome image */

icon = (Icon)xv_create(frame, ICON,
    ICON_IMAGE,        image,
    WIN_CMS_NAME,      "colormap1",
    WIN_FOREGROUND,    foreground_index,
    WIN_BACKGROUND,    background_index,
    NULL);
```

The icon created assumes that the colormap named *colormap1* has been created. The foreground and background colors are indexes into the colormap. The image is rendered with the "on" bits in the foreground color and the "off" bits in the background color. See the program *xv_color.c* in Appendix G, *Example Programs*.

14.2.1 The Icon Text

Each icon may have text associated with it. This text is not part of the icon's image; it is rendered on top of the image after the image is rendered. To specify the text displayed in the icon, use the generic attribute XV_LABEL. By default, the text is displayed at the bottom of the icon area. This may overlap the icon's image. You can change the position in which the text is rendered by using the attribute ICON_LABEL_RECT. The value of the attribute describes a rectangular region in which the text will overwrite anything underneath it. If the text does not fit, it is clipped by this region. To keep the entire image on the icon and display the text without writing over the image, define your icon to be large enough to include both the image and the extents of the text without these regions overlapping. This might make your icon a nonstandard size, however. (The size of an icon is typically 64x64 pixels.)

The code fragment in Example 14-2 implements the added sizes to compensate for text while preserving enough area to display the entire icon:

Example 14-2. Redefining an icon's size to include its label

```
. . .
Rect            image_rect, label_rect;
Server_image image;
Icon            icon;
. . .
rect_construct(&image_rect, 0, 20, 64, 64);
rect_construct(&label_rect, 0, 0, 64, 20);
icon = xv_create(frame, ICON,
    XV_WIDTH,               64,
    XV_HEIGHT,              64 + 20,
    XV_LABEL,               "Sample",
    ICON_LABEL_RECT,        &label_rect,
    ICON_IMAGE,             closed_image,
    ICON_IMAGE_RECT,        &image_rect,
    NULL);
xv_set(frame, FRAME_ICON, icon, NULL);
```

The first thing we do is construct the image and label Rects by using the rect_ con-
truct() macro found in *<xview/rect.h>*. The image is positioned at 0, 20 and is a size of
64x64. The text is positioned at the upper-left corner (0, 0) and extends to the width of the
icon and is 20 pixels high. The size of the icon is 64, and the height of the text is 20, so when
we create the icon, we set the height of the icon object using XV_HEIGHT to be 64+20.

14.3 Icon Package Summary

There are no procedures or macros in the ICON package. The attributes for the ICON package
are listed below. This information is described fully in Appendix A, *Attribute Summary*.

```
ICON_IMAGE
ICON_IMAGE_RECT
ICON_LABEL_RECT
XV_LABEL
```

Icons

15

Nonvisual Objects

In This Chapter:

The Display 293
The Screen Object 294
The SERVER Package 295
   Creating a Server (Establishing a Connection) 295
   Getting the Server 296
Server Images 297
   Creating Server Images 297
The FULLSCREEN Package 300
Nonvisual Package Summary 302

15
Nonvisual Objects

This chapter addresses nonvisual objects—objects that are not elements of the user interface. Nonvisual objects include the screen, the display, the X11 server, and server images. The FULLSCREEN package is used to grab the X server, and an instance of it is considered a nonvisual object. Nonvisual objects are not viewed on the screen, but they have a place in the XView object hierarchy. Like all XView objects, they share many of the generic and common properties and can be manipulated using xv_create(), xv_set(), xv_get() or xv_find().

Nonvisual objects are typically used internally by XView and are seldom used directly in an application. Therefore, this chapter contains advanced material that may not be essential to all programmers.

15.1 The Display

There is no XView *Display* object. If you need the Display data structure as defined by X, you can get the value of the attribute XV_DISPLAY. This can be used on virtually any visible XView object except for panel items. For example, to get the display associated with the frame object, use this:

```
Display *dpy;
dpy = (Display *)xv_get(frame, XV_DISPLAY);
```

The object does not have to be displayed or visible—just created. To do this, the header file *<X11/Xlib.h>* must be included for the declaration of the Display data structure. This structure contains a great deal of information that describes attributes of the workstation, the server being used, and more. See Volume One, *Xlib Programming Manual*, and Volume Two, *Xlib Reference Manual*, for more information.

15.2 The Screen Object

An `Xv_Screen` is associated with virtually all XView objects (similar to the `Display` pointer described in the previous section). To use the `Xv_Screen` object, you must include the file *<xview/screen.h>*. To get a handle on the current screen, use `xv_get()` on an object:

```
Xv_Screen xv_screen;

xv_screen = (Xv_Screen)xv_get(frame, XV_SCREEN);
```

The `Xv_Screen` object carries useful information such as the screen number of the root window, all the visuals, the colormap, the server, and so on, that are all associated with that screen.

The XView Screen object (`Xv_Screen`) differs from the `Screen` data structure defined by Xlib and, in fact, has nothing to do with the X11 `Screen` data type (defined in *<X11/Xlib.h>*). That is, you cannot use:

```
xv_get(xv_screen, XV_XID)   /* Doesn't work */
```

to get a corresponding `Screen` pointer.

Because the X `Screen` type provides information not available from the `Xv_Screen` object, it may be useful to get the X `Screen`. Once the XView screen is obtained, the X `Screen` type can be gotten by using the `SCREEN_NUMBER` of the screen and the `Display` pointer associated with an arbitrary visual object. Example 15-1 demonstrates how to do this for a frame:

Example 15-1. Getting a pointer for a particular frame object (screen.c)

```
/*
 * screen.c -- get some simple info about the current screen:
 * width, height, depth.
 */
#include <X11/Xlib.h>
#include <xview/xview.h>
#include <xview/screen.h>

main(argc, argv)
int      argc;
char     *argv[];
{
    Frame               frame;
    Xv_Screen           screen;
    Display             *dpy;
    int                 screen_no;

    xv_init(XV_INIT_ARGC_PTR_ARGV, &argc, argv, NULL);

    frame = (Frame)xv_create(XV_NULL, FRAME, NULL);

    dpy = (Display *)xv_get(frame, XV_DISPLAY);
    printf("Server display = '%s'\n", dpy->vendor);
    screen = (Screen)xv_get(frame, XV_SCREEN);

    screen_no = (int)xv_get(screen, SCREEN_NUMBER);
    printf("Screen #%d:\n\twidth: %d\n\theight: %d\n\tdepth: %d\n",
        screen_no,
```

Example 15-1. Getting a pointer for a particular frame object (screen.c) (continued)

```
            DisplayWidth(dpy, screen_no),
            DisplayHeight(dpy, screen_no),
            DefaultDepth(dpy, screen_no));
}
```

As shown in Example 15-1 above, you can use any of the macros defined in *<X11/Xlib.h>* to get information about the default screen such as the width, height, depth and so on. From this information, you can get information about the physical framebuffer. These are Xlib-related issues not covered in this book.

15.3 The SERVER Package

The SERVER package may be used to initialize the connection with the X server running on an arbitrary workstation on the network. Once the connection has been made, the package allows you to query information about the server. This package is automatically called by xv_init() and should not be called by most client applications except in advanced applications not covered at this time.

15.3.1 Creating a Server (Establishing a Connection)

When making any reference to Server objects, applications should include *<xview/server.h>*. You can open a connection to an arbitrary server by using xv_create():

```
Server server;
extern char *server_name;

server = (Server)xv_create(NULL, SERVER,
                           XV_NAME, server_name, NULL);
```

Because there is no owner for a server, the owner parameter is ignored and may be set to NULL. The server described by server_name is assumed to have been initialized already. It should be set to the standard format:

hostname : *display.screen*

For example:

```
maui:0.1
```

connects the second screen on the first display on the host named *maui*. If the connection fails, NULL is returned.

There is no real advantage to creating a server in this way because the *user* should be able to control which server is used—not the application itself. The user may control this by using the *-display* option, which is parsed by the call to:

```
xv_init(XV_INIT_ARGC_PTR_ARGV, &argc, argv, NULL);
```

If the application is intended to run on a named host, then the display information should be identified on the command line by the user:

```
% program_name -display maui:0
```

The Default Server

If `xv_init()` has not been called by the time the first call to `xv_create()` is called, the call to `xv_create()` calls `xv_init()` internally. This means that when the program gets around to calling `xv_init()`, it is a no-op. Likewise, `xv_init()` creates a server instance, so you cannot establish the initial server after calling `xv_init()`.

Thus, the *only* way to establish a connection to a constant, unalterable server is to coerce the `argv` parameter to `xv_init()` to always specify a `-display` argument.

Creating the server is typically done by XView internals and not by most XView applications. However, getting information from the server may be of some use.

15.3.2 Getting the Server

The server to which the application is connected can be gotten only from the `Xv_Screen` object described in the previous section.

```
server = (Server)xv_get(xv_get(frame, XV_SCREEN), SCREEN_SERVER);
```

With the server object, you can tell the server to synchronize with your application by calling:

```
Server server;
...
xv_set(server, SERVER_SYNC, TRUE, NULL);
```

If set to TRUE, the server will remain synchronized with your application until it is turned off by setting the attribute to FALSE.

To synchronize once, but not have the server maintain its synchronous behavior, call:

```
Server server;

xv_set(server, SERVER_SYNC_AND_PROCESS_EVENTS, NULL);
```

Note that this attribute takes no value—you specify it and no other attributes. This attribute makes sense only in `xv_set()`.

15.4 Server Images

A server image is a graphic image stored on the X server. Images on the client side can be stored as XImages or as memory *pixrects*.* The XView Server_image object is not equivalent to X Pixmaps, although pixmaps are part of the Server_image object. Even though pixmaps are stored on the server, the XView object is a client-side object. Because it is an XView object, you can query the dimensions of a Server_image by using XV_WIDTH or XV_HEIGHT—this is something you cannot do with X11 Pixmaps.

15.4.1 Creating Server Images

Applications that wish to use the SERVER_IMAGE package should include <*xview/svrimage.h*>. Server_image objects can be created using xv_create():

```
#include <xview/svrimage.h>
...
Server_image image;

image = (Server_image)xv_create(owner, SERVER_IMAGE,
    attrs,
    NULL);
```

The owner in the call to xv_create() is an Xv_Screen object. The server that owns this screen owns the newly created image. If the owner is NULL, then the default screen is used. The dimensions of Server_image objects are 16 by 16 by 1 unless the attributes XV_WIDTH, XV_HEIGHT, or SERVER_IMAGE_DEPTH are specified. The bitmap data for the server image may be set using either SERVER_IMAGE_BITS or SERVER_IMAGE_X_BITS depending on the format of the data. The data format choices are arrays of short or char types. X11 bitmap data is represented as array of chars, while Sun's pixrect library represents the data as an array of shorts.† The following code segment uses SERVER_IMAGE_BITS to produce a 1-bit-deep image that looks like a trash can:

```
short image_bits[] = {
#include <images/trash.icon>
};

Server_image = (Server_image)xv_create(NULL, SERVER_IMAGE,
    XV_WIDTH,           32,
    XV_HEIGHT,          30,
    SERVER_IMAGE_BITS,  image_bits,
    NULL);
```

Here, the trash can icon was created with its bits store in an array of shorts. To load an image stored as an array of chars (the format used by X11), use SERVER_IMAGE_X11_BITS:

---

*The term *pixrect* is a data type brought over from SunView.

† Many of Sun's existing applications should use SERVER_IMAGE_BITS when porting to XView. This attribute must be used in order to load bitmap data created by *iconedit*.

```
#include <X11/bitmaps/xlogo32>
```

```
xlogo_image = (Server_image)xv_create(NULL, SERVER_IMAGE,
    XV_HEIGHT,              xlogo32_width,
    XV_WIDTH,               xlogo32_height,
    SERVER_IMAGE_X_BITS,    xlogo32_bits,
    NULL);
```

In both of these cases, the file specified on the #include line must be accessible at the time the program is *compiled*. Once compiled, the data for the image is stored in the program and the file is no longer needed (e.g., the file may be deleted and the program still displays the image).

Rather than including the file containing the image's bitmap data, you could specify the actual file:

```
char *file = "/usr/include/X11/bitmaps/xlogo32";
```

```
server_image = (Server_image)xv_create(NULL, SERVER_IMAGE,
    SERVER_IMAGE_BITMAP_FILE,   file,
    NULL);
```

Be aware that this file must exist and be accessible by any person who runs this program at *run time*. If the file is not accessible for some reason, then an error is generated. And because the program may be run from any directory, a full pathname should be specified. As shown, the file points to a static string, but file could have a value that is changed by selecting from a list of bitmap filenames. In this case, the code fragment could use xv_set() to set the file name and thus, the Server_image's data. Whenever xv_set() is used to change the data of the image like this, the values of XV_WIDTH and XV_HEIGHT are automatically updated.

Many XView objects require Server_images as values (such as MENU_IMAGE_STRINGS in the MENU package). If you have already created a pixmap and wish to attach it to a server image, you can use:

```
image = (Server_image)xv_set(NULL, SERVER_IMAGE,
    SERVER_IMAGE_PIXMAP,   pixmap,
    NULL);
```

The attribute SERVER_IMAGE_PIXMAP may also be used in xv_get() to return the XID of the pixmap associated with the Server_image.

Normally, a Server_image destroys its pixmap when a new pixmap is created using SERVER_IMAGE_BITS, SERVER_IMAGE_X_BITS or SERVER_IMAGE_PIXMAP. This default behavior can be turned off by setting the SERVER_IMAGE_SAVE_PIXMAP attribute to TRUE. Be sure to maintain a handle to the pixmap if you specify this attribute and destroy the Server_image.

If the depth of an image is unspecified, it defaults to 1. To create a color image, use SERVER_IMAGE_DEPTH to specify an alternate depth that can support color. You can also specify a colormap to use with this image by specifying SERVER_IMAGE_COLORMAP. This is used for multiplane color images and must be specified before the image bits are set. The colormap specified is assumed to have been created already including the WIN_CMS_DATA associated with the colormap name.

Example 15-2 demonstrates how to use a server image by creating a frame with a panel. On the panel is a button that uses a server image as the PANEL_LABEL_IMAGE. The bits used are the same as the *trash.icon* used above.

Example 15-2. The svrimage.c program

```
/*
 * svrimage.c -- demonstrate how a server image can be created and
 * used.  The "bits" used to create the image are taken arbitrarily
 * from <images/trash.icon>
 */
#include <xview/xview.h>
#include <xview/panel.h>
#include <xview/svrimage.h>
#include <X11/Xlib.h>

short image_bits[] =  {
    0x0000,0x0000, 0x0000,0x0000, 0x0000,0x0000, 0x0000,0x0000,
    0x0007,0xE000, 0x0004,0x2000, 0x03FF,0xFFC0, 0x0200,0x0040,
    0x02FF,0xFF40, 0x0080,0x0100, 0x00AA,0xAB00, 0x00AA,0xAB00,
    0x00AA,0xAB00, 0x00AA,0xAB00, 0x00AA,0xAB00, 0x00AA,0xAB00,
    0x00AA,0xAB00, 0x00AA,0xAB00, 0x00AA,0xAB00, 0x00AA,0xAB00,
    0x00AA,0xAB00, 0x00AA,0xAB00, 0x00AA,0xAB00, 0x00AA,0xAB00,
    0x00AA,0xAB00, 0x00AA,0xAB00, 0x00AA,0xAB00, 0x0091,0x1300,
    0x00C0,0x0200, 0x003F,0xFC00
};

main(argc, argv)
int     argc;
char    *argv[];
{
    Frame              frame;
    Server_image       image;
    Panel              panel;
    void               exit();

    xv_init(XV_INIT_ARGC_PTR_ARGV, &argc, argv, NULL);

    image = (Server_image)xv_create(NULL, SERVER_IMAGE,
        XV_WIDTH,             32,
        XV_HEIGHT,            30,
        SERVER_IMAGE_BITS,    image_bits,
        NULL);

    frame = (Frame)xv_create(NULL, FRAME, NULL);
    panel = (Panel)xv_create(frame, PANEL, NULL);
    (void) xv_create(panel, PANEL_BUTTON,
        PANEL_LABEL_IMAGE,    image,
        PANEL_NOTIFY_PROC,    exit,
        NULL);

    window_fit(panel);
    window_fit(frame);
    xv_main_loop(frame);
}
```

15.5 The FULLSCREEN Package

The FULLSCREEN package allows XView clients to grab the server for keyboard and/or pointer use either exclusively or nonexclusively with other applications. This package is used primarily to prompt the user for immediate feedback on a question or to notify the user of an error that needs attention. Typically, the user responds with a button press or a keyboard event. The NOTICE package uses the FULLSCREEN package extensively to implement its functionality. In most cases, you need nothing more than the NOTICE package and should rarely need to use the FULLSCREEN package. The need for this package arises if you choose to implement your own notice or perhaps a user-interface item that is not OPEN LOOK-compliant. In either case, this is advanced usage and is beyond the scope of this book. Using the FULLSCREEN package can be very dangerous because it uses the X server's grabbing functions in Xlib. It is possible to get into a state in which you cannot get out, except by killing the server remotely or rebooting your workstation. Be extremely careful when using a debugger that you do not set breakpoints within code where the server is in the middle of a grab of some kind. Whatever you do, *do not step through code that creates a* FULLSCREEN *instance*. If this is unavoidable, you should prepare for this by making sure you have remote access to your workstation or attach a terminal to it so you can kill the debugger to free the server.

The flow of control for client code using the FULLSCREEN package is to create a fullscreen instance (grabbing the server), scan for a particular event, and destroy the fullscreen instance (freeing the server).

Creating a fullscreen object (grabbing the server) involves xv_create() as usual:

```
Fullscreen fs;

fs = xv_create(owner, FULLSCREEN, NULL);
```

The owner in this case may be a visible XView object that has a window associated with it* and is currently displayed on the screen (e.g., XV_SHOW is TRUE). If owner is NULL, then the root window of the default screen is used as the owner.

Example 15-3 uses the FULLSCREEN package. A simple panel with two panel buttons is created. The Quit button quits the program, and the Fullscreen button calls the grab() routine that grabs the server using the FULLSCREEN package and waits for a button to be pressed. Once this happens, the routine frees the fullscreen object, thus releasing the server. In the default case, there is no event mask that the FULLSCREEN package has been instructed to allow to pass through to the client, so event types should be specified in the creation call. Similarly, since the call to xv_input_readevent() is used, a similar input mask should be set up.†

---

*This does not include panel items.
†See Chapter 6, *Handling Input*, for more information about xv_input_readevent().

Example 15-3. The fullscreen.c program

```
/*
 * fullscreen.c
 * Demonstrate the fullscreen package.  Create a panel button that
 * creates a fullscreen instance, thus grabbing the X server.  User
 * presses a mouse button to release the server.
 */
#include <xview/xview.h>
#include <xview/panel.h>
#include <xview/fullscreen.h>

main(argc, argv)
char *argv[];
{
    Frame           frame;
    Panel           panel;
    void            exit(), grab();

    xv_init(XV_INIT_ARGC_PTR_ARGV, &argc, argv, NULL);

    frame = (Frame)xv_create(XV_NULL, FRAME, NULL);
    panel = (Panel)xv_create(frame, PANEL, NULL);
    (void) xv_create(panel, PANEL_BUTTON,
        PANEL_LABEL_STRING,     "Quit",
        PANEL_NOTIFY_PROC,      exit,
        NULL);
    (void) xv_create(panel, PANEL_BUTTON,
        PANEL_LABEL_STRING,     "Fullscreen",
        PANEL_NOTIFY_PROC,      grab,
        NULL);

    window_fit(panel);
    window_fit(frame);
    xv_main_loop(frame);
}
/*
 * Notify procedure for when the "Fullscreen" button is pushed.
 * Create a fullscreen instance, scan for a button event, then
 * destroy it.
 */
void
grab(item, event)
Panel_item item;
Event *event;
{
    Panel           panel = (Panel)xv_get(item, PANEL_PARENT_PANEL);
    Fullscreen      fs;
    Inputmask       im;

    /* set up an input mask for the call to xv_input_readevent(). */
    win_setinputcodebit(&im, MS_LEFT);
    win_setinputcodebit(&im, MS_MIDDLE);
    win_setinputcodebit(&im, MS_RIGHT);
    win_setinputcodebit(&im, LOC_MOVE);

    /*
     * Create a fullscreen object (initialize X server grab).
     * Specify which events should be allowed to pass through.
     * These events should match the input mask coded above.
```

Example 15-3. The fullscreen.c program (continued)

```
    */
    fs = xv_create(panel, FULLSCREEN,
        WIN_CONSUME_EVENTS,
            WIN_MOUSE_BUTTONS, LOC_MOVE, NULL,
        NULL);

    /* Loop till user generates a button event */
    while (xv_input_readevent(panel, event, TRUE, TRUE, &im) != -1)
        if (event_is_button(event))
            break;

    /* Destroy the fullscreen (release the X server grab) */
    xv_destroy(fs);

    /* Report which button was pushed. */
    printf("event was button %d\n", event_id(event) - BUT_FIRST + 1);
}
```

When this program is run and the user selects the Fullscreen panel item, the X server is grabbed and the user must select one of the mouse buttons to release it. To users, it may appear as though they can select another panel button. Although the panel window is the owner of the fullscreen object, events that occur while the server is grabbed by the fullscreen object are *not* propagated to XView objects under the pointer. In Example 15-3, if the user presses the button on top of a panel button while in fullscreen, the button-*down* event will trigger the call to xv_input_readevent() and break the loop. The corresponding button-up event is not read yet and will get read by normal event processing after the call to grab() returns. If the button-up event happened over a panel button, then the panel button's notify routine will be called.

The event masks set by the FULLSCREEN package and by the Inputmask do not interfere with the event masks in any XView window.

15.6 Nonvisual Package Summary

There are no nonvisual procedures or macros. Table 15-1 lists the attributes in the FULLSCREEN package. Table 15-2 lists the attributes in the SCREEN, SERVER and SERVER-IMAGE packages. This information is described fully in Appendix A, *Attribute Summary*.

Table 15-1. Fullscreen Attributes

Fullscreen Attributes

FULLSCREEN_ALLOW_EVENTS	FULLSCREEN_KEYBOARD_GRAB_PTR_MODE
FULLSCREEN_ALLOW_SYNC_EVENT	FULLSCREEN_INPUT_WINDOW
FULLSCREEN_COLORMAP_WINDOW	FULLSCREEN_OWNER_EVENTS
FULLSCREEN_CURSOR_WINDOW	FULLSCREEN_PAINT_WINDOW
FULLSCREEN_GRAB_KEYBOARD	FULLSCREEN_POINTER_GRAB_KBD_MODE
FULLSCREEN_GRAB_POINTER	FULLSCREEN_POINTER_GRAB_PTR_MODE
FULLSCREEN_GRAB_SERVER	FULLSCREEN_RECT
FULLSCREEN_KEYBOARD_GRAB_KBD_MODE	FULLSCREEN_SYNC

Table 15-2. Screen, Server, and Server Image Attributes

Screen Attributes	Server Attributes	Server Image Attributes
SCREEN_NUMBER	SERVER_NTH_SCREEN	SERVER_IMAGE_BITS
SCREEN_SERVER	SERVER_SYNC	SERVER_IMAGE_COLORMAP
	SERVER_SYNC_AND_PROCESS_EVENTS	SERVER_IMAGE_DEPTH
	XV_NAME	XV_HEIGHT
		XV_WIDTH

16

Fonts

In This Chapter:

Creating Fonts 308
   Font Families and Styles 311
   Font Sizes 312
   Scaling Fonts 313
   Fonts by Name 314
Font Dimensions 315
Font Package Summary 317

Fonts

16
Fonts

In X, a large number of fonts are provided on the server. Deciding on which font to use and then trying to specify fonts by name can be difficult since there are many different styles and sizes of fonts. Most fonts are used to render text strings, so the images, or *glyphs*, represent a character set defined mostly by the English language. However, a font may be built to support glyphs for other languages or to provide a set of glyphs that have nothing to do with a language. Fonts are stored on the server and are associated with the display of your workstation. The *font ID* is stored in the graphics context (GC), which is used by Xlib functions like `XDrawString()`. Using fonts to render text is perhaps the most common application. For example, the `Courier` font family displays the classic typewriter or constant-width character set. This text is set in Times-Roman, a proportionally spaced font. Often within a font family, there are different styles, such as **bold** or *italic*, and different point sizes.* For example, *Helvetica bold 14* refers to the Helvetica font family; bold is the style and 14 is the point size.

Not all server fonts have a variety of styles and sizes. These special-purpose fonts are generally specified by name only—there are no corresponding styles or families for these fonts.

When accessing fonts, you typically want to specify a font either by *name* or by the *family*, *style*, and *size* or *scale* of the font. In addition, XView provides an interface for determining the dimensions (in pixels) of characters and strings rendered in a specified font.

OPEN LOOK uses predefined fonts for certain items such as panel buttons and other user interface elements. These items may not be changed, but you may assign fonts to panel choices, text subwindows and other types of windows. We will address these issues later in this chapter.

---

*Note that point sizes on workstations are based on pixels, whereas point sizes for typesetters and printers are based on inches.

16.1 Creating Fonts

Applications that use the FONT package must include the header file, *<xview/font.h>*. In XView, when a font object is created, it loads the font from the X server. When we say, "create a font," we really mean, "load a font from the server and create an XView font object associated with that font."

While fonts can be created using xv_create(), it may not be necessary to create a new instance of a font. Fonts are typically cached on the server, and XView may already have a handle to a particular font. Therefore, you would rather obtain a handle to the font, if it already exists, rather than opening another instance of the same font. xv_find() can be used to return the handle of an existing font. If the handle does not exist, xv_find() can create a new instance of the font. In general, if the attribute is set to false, xv_find() does *not* create a new object.

Both xv_find() and xv_create() will return an object of the type Xv_Font when using the FONT package. The form of the call is:

```
Xv_Font font;
font = (Xv_Font) xv_create(parent, FONT, attrs, NULL);
```

Or:

```
Xv_Font font;
font = (Xv_Font) xv_find(parent, FONT, attrs, NULL);
```

The *parent* of the font is usually the window in which the font is going to be used. Fonts may be used on any window or in memory pixmaps or Server_image, but these objects must have the same display associated with them as the font or you will get an X Protocol error. If the parent is NULL, the default server is used. Otherwise, the server as determined from the parent object is used. This is only an issue if your XView application is running on several servers at the same time.

Once a font object is created, it can be used to render text by assigning the font's XV_XID to the font field of a graphics context (GC) and then using any of the Xlib routines that use fonts such as XDrawString(). Example 16-1 lists *simple_font.c*, a program that builds a simple frame and canvas. The repaint routine for the canvas displays the string "Hello World" at the upper-left corner of the window.

Example 16-1. The simple_font.c program

```
/*
 * simple_font.c -- very simple program showing how to render text
 * using a font gotten from xv_find().  Hello World is printed in
 * the upper-left corner of a canvas window.
 */
#include <stdio.h>
#include <X11/X.h>
#include <X11/Xlib.h>    /* X.h and Xlib.h used for Xlib graphics */
#include <xview/xview.h>
#include <xview/canvas.h>
#include <xview/font.h>
#include <xview/xv_xrect.h>
```

Example 16-1. The simple_font.c program (continued)

```
#define GC_KEY  10 /* any arbitrary number -- used for XV_KEY_DATA */

main(argc, argv)
int     argc;
char    *argv[];
{
    Frame           frame;
    Canvas          canvas;
    XGCValues       gcvalues;
    Xv_Font         font;
    void            my_repaint_proc();
    Display         *dpy;
    GC              gc;

    xv_init(XV_INIT_ARGC_PTR_ARGV, &argc, argv, NULL);

    frame = (Frame)xv_create(XV_NULL, FRAME, NULL);

    canvas = (Canvas)xv_create(frame, CANVAS,
        XV_WIDTH,               400,
        XV_HEIGHT,              200,
        CANVAS_X_PAINT_WINDOW,  TRUE,
        CANVAS_REPAINT_PROC,    my_repaint_proc,
        NULL);
    window_fit(frame);

    dpy = (Display *)xv_get(frame, XV_DISPLAY);
    font = (Xv_Font)xv_find(frame, FONT, FONT_NAME, "courier", NULL);
    if (!font) {
        fprintf(stderr, "%s: cannot use font: courier.\n", argv[0]);
        font = (Xv_Font)xv_get(frame, XV_FONT);
    }
    /* Create a GC to use with Xlib graphics -- set the fg/bg colors
     * and set the Font, which is the XV_XID of the XView font object.
     */
    gcvalues.font = (Font)xv_get(font, XV_XID);
    gcvalues.foreground = BlackPixel(dpy, DefaultScreen(dpy));
    gcvalues.background = WhitePixel(dpy, DefaultScreen(dpy));
    gcvalues.graphics_exposures = False;
    gc = XCreateGC(dpy, RootWindow(dpy, DefaultScreen(dpy)),
        GCForeground | GCBackground | GCFont | GCGraphicsExposures,
        &gcvalues);

    /* Assign the gc to the canvas object so we can use the same
     * gc each time we draw into the canvas.  Also avoids a global
     * variable to store the GC.
     */
    xv_set(canvas, XV_KEY_DATA, GC_KEY, gc, NULL);
    xv_main_loop(frame);
}
/*
 * Called every time the window needs repainting.
 */
void
my_repaint_proc(canvas, pw, dpy, xwin, xrects)
Canvas          canvas;
Xv_Window       pw;
```

Example 16-1. The simple_font.c program (continued)

```
Display          *dpy;
Window           xwin;
Xv_xrectlist     *xrects;
{
    GC gc = (GC)xv_get(canvas, XV_KEY_DATA, GC_KEY);

    XDrawString(dpy, xwin, gc, 10, 20,
        "Hello World", 11); /* 11 = strlen("Hello World") */
}
```

The program attempts to create the font named "courier."* If the font is not found, the frame's font is used as a backup. This font must exist, so there is no need to check for a failed return value.

Since the text is rendered using Xlib graphics, we need to use a GC that has the right attributes set: the foreground and background colors and a font. Because this GC is specifically used for the canvas window, we are going to *attach* the GC to the canvas by use of the generic attribute XV_KEY_DATA. Using a unique key, GC_KEY (which can be any integer since no other keys have been assigned to the object yet), the GC is attached with the call:

```
    xv_set(canvas, XV_KEY_DATA, GC_KEY, gc, NULL);
```

Later, in my_repaint_proc(), the GC is retrieved:

```
    GC gc = (GC)xv_get(canvas, XV_KEY_DATA, GC_KEY);
```

This method of storing the GC by using XV_KEY_DATA avoids the need for a global variable.

When creating some fonts, it may take quite some time for the font to be found and completely loaded—especially large fonts, since they may be created at run time. Loading the font may result in the user having to wait longer than expected. So it is recommended that the application provide visual feedback if the user must wait for some time. Do this by setting the FRAME_BUSY attribute to TRUE for the parent frame:

```
    xv_set(frame, FRAME_BUSY, TRUE, NULL);
    font = (Xv_Font) xv_find(frame, FONT,
        FONT_NAME,  "Courier-22",
        NULL);
    xv_set(frame, FRAME_BUSY, FALSE, NULL);
```

This code fragment attempts to create a 22-point size font. Note that not all servers can do this either because of memory limitations or because the server cannot arbitrarily scale fonts. In this case, the font returned may be NULL.

---

*Font names are case-sensitive—courier and Courier are two different fonts.

16.1.1 Font Families and Styles

One way to create fonts is to specify a font family, style and size. The family of a font describes its basic characteristics. Figure 16-1 shows the Courier family in different styles and a range of point sizes.

Courier plain

10 12 14 16 18

Courier bold

10 **12 14 16 18**

Courier italic

10 12 14 16 18

Figure 16-1. The Courier font in different styles and sizes

Some font families and styles known to XView are predefined in <*xview/font.h*>. To use a font other than the ones listed, you may specify any font family and style known by your X server. You may also specify fonts by *name* (see Section 16.1.4, "Fonts by Name"). The list of XView font families include:

- FONT_FAMILY_DEFAULT
- FONT_FAMILY_DEFAULT_FIXEDWIDTH
- FONT_FAMILY_LUCIDA
- FONT_FAMILY_LUCIDA_FIXEDWIDTH
- FONT_FAMILY_ROMAN
- FONT_FAMILY_SERIF
- FONT_FAMILY_COUR
- FONT_FAMILY_OLGLYPH*
- FONT_FAMILY_OLCURSOR*

The FONT_FAMILY_DEFAULT font is the default font for the server. This may be redefined depending on how the X server has been configured. The FONT_FAMILY_DEFAULT_ FIXEDWIDTH font is guaranteed to be a fixed-width font, regardless of the kind of font used as the default font. All the characters in fixed-width fonts occupy the same amount of space. Other fonts are proportionally spaced; that is, each character was a different amount of space.

---

*The families FONT_FAMILY_OLGLYPH and FONT_FAMILY_OLCURSOR are used by the SCROLLBAR and CURSOR packages, respectively. They are not for general/public use.

The available styles are:

- FONT_STYLE_DEFAULT
- FONT_STYLE_NORMAL
- FONT_STYLE_BOLD
- FONT_STYLE_ITALIC
- FONT_STYLE_BOLD_ITALIC

The default style indicates the default for that particular font family—this style may be any of the other styles (normal, bold, italic, or bold-italic).

The call to xv_find() in *simple_font.c* could have been written to specify the family and style of the font rather than the name of the font:

```
font = (Xv_Font)xv_find(frame, FONT,
    FONT_FAMILY,     FONT_FAMILY_COUR,
    FONT_STYLE,      FONT_STYLE_NORMAL,
    NULL);
```

Since normal is the default style of the font, this example renders the same font as in the earlier example. However, we could specify a different style:

```
font = (Xv_Font)xv_find(frame, FONT,
    FONT_FAMILY,     FONT_FAMILY_COUR,
    FONT_STYLE,      FONT_STYLE_BOLD,
    NULL);
```

This call returns a bold style of the Courier font. For most font families, you can specify a font family with any style, although some families may not support an italic or bold style of the font. Therefore, you should be prepared to handle a NULL return from the call to xv_create() or xv_find():

```
if (!(font = (Xv_Font)xv_find(canvas, FONT,
    FONT_FAMILY,     FONT_FAMILY_FIXED,
    FONT_STYLE,      FONT_STYLE_ITALIC,
    NULL))) {
    /* Handle the case where the font fails. */
    font = (Xv_Font)xv_get(canvas, XV_FONT);
}
```

16.1.2 Font Sizes

Fonts can be specified in any size from one point on up, as long as there is enough memory in the server to support the font in that size. The server must also support scaleable fonts. When a size is specified, provided the font is not already loaded, a new font is created at run time according to the family and style in the size specified, as below:

```
Xv_Font font;

font = (Xv_Font)xv_find(canvas, FONT,
    FONT_FAMILY,     FONT_FAMILY_ROMAN,
    FONT_STYLE,      FONT_STYLE_BOLD,
    FONT_SIZE,       36,
    NULL);
```

This code fragment attempts to find or create a font from the Times-Roman font family, in bold and in 36 point. The font may already exist in the server, or the font's family may exist but not the size. In the latter case, the server must attempt to scale the font to the specified size. If the the font cannot be created because of memory limitations, the call to xv_find() will return NULL. Because a 36-point font takes a lot of memory, it might take a while to load this font.

16.1.3 Scaling Fonts

Bitmapped fonts are not scaleable but are provided in several different sizes giving the appearance that some fonts may be scaled to arbitrary sizes. On the other hand, some fonts are scaleable because the font is not stored as a static bitmap. While some fonts are scaleable, the server must support the ability to scale arbitrary fonts. Sun's *xnews* server is an example of such a server.

When fonts are created, four additional sizes of the font in the specified family and style are attempted to be created as well. This is limited by the constraints outlined above. You can request a relative scale of the font with respect to other fonts within the same family. The relative scales are *small*, *medium*, *large* and *extra large*. These scales are represented by the attributes WIN_SCALE_SMALL, WIN_SCALE_MEDIUM, WIN_SCALE_LARGE and WIN_SCALE_EXTRALARGE. These attributes are members of the enumerated type Window_rescale_state.

These are WINDOW attributes because of the fact that windows may be scaled accordingly. For example, if your application is resized to a larger or smaller size, you may wish to reset the fonts for some windows according to different scaling sizes. By default, the sizes of the fonts corresponding to the scale is as follows:

Attribute	Font Size
WIN_SCALE_SMALL	10
WIN_SCALE_MEDIUM	12
WIN_SCALE_LARGE	14
WIN_SCALE_EXTRALARGE	19

If FONT_SIZE is not specified, then when a font is requested, the size will correspond to the *medium* scale size. Specifying the font size overrides the request for the scaling factor. The code fragment below requests a font from the Lucida family with an italic style in large scale:

```
Xv_Font    font;

font = (Xv_Font)xv_find(canvas, FONT,
    FONT_FAMILY,     FONT_FAMILY_LUCIDA,
```

```
FONT_STYLE,      FONT_STYLE_ITALIC,
FONT_SCALE,      WIN_SCALE_LARGE,
NULL);
```

If you have already created a font and wish to get the same font in a different scale, the attribute FONT_RESCALE_OF is specified with two values: a font and a Window_rescale_state.

```
Xv_Font   font, small_font;

font = (Xv_Font)xv_find(canvas, FONT,
    FONT_FAMILY,      FONT_FAMILY_LUCIDA,
    FONT_STYLE,       FONT_STYLE_BOLD,
    NULL);

    . . .

small_font = (Xv_Font)xv_find(canvas, FONT,
    FONT_RESCALE_OF,      font, WIN_SCALE_SMALL,
    NULL);
```

When a font is created for the first time, it has at least four sizes corresponding to the scaling factors mentioned above. Thus, when requesting a scaled version of an existing font, it is very important to use xv_find() rather than xv_create(); the chances are that the font exists for that scaling factor. Using xv_create() may unnecessarily create a new version of the font.

You can reset the sizes of fonts' scale factors by using the attribute FONT_SIZES_FOR_SCALE. This attribute takes four *values* that correspond to each scaling factor:

```
font = (Xv_Font)xv_find(canvas, FONT,
    FONT_FAMILY,           FONT_LUCIDA,
    FONT_STYLE,            FONT_STYLE_NORMAL,
    FONT_SIZES_FOR_SCALE,  12, 14, 16, 22,
    NULL);
```

In this example, the lucida font is created such that the small, medium, large and extra-large scaling sizes are 12, 14, 16 and 22, respectively. The font size returned is 14-point.

16.1.4 Fonts by Name

When specifying a font by name, the entire name of the font is given as it appears in the output of a program such as *xlsfonts* or by the Xlib call XListFonts().* These programs provide a complete list of all the fonts available by the server.

In Example 16-1 above, the program *simple_font.c* demonstrated how to load a font using a given name:

```
font = (Xv_Font) xv_find(canvas, FONT, FONT_NAME, "Courier", NULL);
```

When specifying fonts by name, you cannot specify a family, style, scale or size; these attributes are ignored in favor of the font name. However, in some cases, you can specify style and size attributes as part of the name of the font. For example, to create a Courier font, you

---

*See Volume Two, *Xlib Reference Manual*, for a description of XListFonts().

can specify the font named "Courier":

```
font = (Xv_Font)  xv_find(canvas, FONT,
    FONT_NAME,      "Courier",
    NULL);
```

We can also specify a style along with the font family:

```
font = (Xv_Font)  xv_find(canvas, FONT,
    FONT_NAME,      "Courier-boldoblique",
    NULL);
```

This creates a bold-italic, 16-point font from the Courier family. Of course, if you have chosen to use the family/style method of specifying fonts, then you can use xv_get() with the attribute FONT_NAME to get the name of the returned font. For example, if you created a font in the following manner:

```
Xv_Font      font;
font = (Xv_Font)  xv_create(frame, FONT,
    FONT_FAMILY,      FONT_FAMILY_COUR,
    FONT_STYLE,       FONT_STYLE_BOLD_ITALIC,
    NULL);
```

You could retrieve the name of the font just created by calling:

```
char *name = (char *)xv_get(font, FONT_NAME);
```

This call would return the string "Courier-boldoblique".

16.2 Font Dimensions

Once the font is created, it can be used in applications using Xlib routines, as demonstrated in *simple_font.c* earlier in the chapter. In the program, text is rendered using the Xlib routine XDrawString(). This routine uses the font ID from the GC parameter. This ID is extracted from the font using xv_get() and XV_XID. You can also get a pointer to the font's XFontStruct structure, by specifying the attribute FONT_INFO to xv_get(). This data structure is what describes the characteristics about the font such as the width and height for each character in the font and so on. See Volume One, *Xlib Programming Manual*, for more information.

You can get information about the sizes of individual characters or the dimensions of entire strings of characters in a particular font using several methods. You can use the information in the XFontStruct data structure obtained from the font, or you can use Xlib routines such as XTextWidth() or XTextExtents(), or you can use xv_get() along with XView attributes such as FONT_CHAR_WIDTH, FONT_CHAR_HEIGHT, FONT_DEFAULT_CHAR_HEIGHT, FONT_DEFAULT_CHAR_WIDTH, and FONT_STRING_DIMS.

The usage is as follows:

```
Xv_Font   font;
int       width, height;
```

The following code shows how to get the dimensions of a particular character in a font:

```
width  = (int)xv_get(font, FONT_CHAR_WIDTH, 'm');
```

```
height = (int)xv_get(font, FONT_CHAR_HEIGHT, 'm');
```

The calls to xv_get() return the width and height of the characters in pixels for that particular font. If you are using a fixed-width font, then each character will be the same width—thus, you may specify the default character width and height of the font. The following code shows how to get the dimensions of characters for a fixed-width font:

```
Xv_Font font;
int width, height;

width  = (int)xv_get(font, FONT_DEFAULT_CHAR_WIDTH);
height = (int)xv_get(font, FONT_DEFAULT_CHAR_HEIGHT);
```

If you use FONT_DEFAULT_CHAR_WIDTH (or height) on a variable-width font, you will get the *average* width of a character in that font.

To get the width and height dimensions of a complete string of text in a given font, use the FONT_STRING_DIMS attribute:

```
extern Xv_Font      font;
Font_string_dims    dims;

(void) xv_get(font, FONT_STRING_DIMS, "Hello World", &dims);
```

In this case, the call to xv_get() returns a pointer to the dims structure passed as the last argument. The return value may be ignored since the dims parameter will have the value filled in upon return of xv_get(). The Font_string_dims data structure is as follows:

```
typedef struct {
    int   width;
    int   height;
} Font_string_dims;
```

Thus, the xv_get() returns the extents of the string for the font specified. This would be equivalent to calling XTextExtents() in the manner below:

```
Font_string_dims dims;
extern char     *str;
int              len = strlen(str);
extern Xv_Font font;
XFontStruct     *font_info = (XFontStruct *)xv_get(font, FONT_INFO);
int              direction, ascent, descent;
XCharStruct      overall_return;

(void) XTextExtents(font_info, str, len,
          &direction, &ascent, &descent, &overall_return);

dims.width = overall_return.width;
dims.height = ascent + descent;
```

16.3 Font Package Summary

There are no procedures or macros in the FONT package. The attributes in the FONT package are listed below. They are described fully in Appendix A, *Attribute Summary*.

```
FONT_CHAR_HEIGHT
FONT_CHAR_WIDTH
FONT_DEFAULT_CHAR_HEIGHT
FONT_DEFAULT_CHAR_WIDTH
FONT_FAMILY
FONT_RESCALE_OF
FONT_SCALE
FONT_SIZE
FONT_SIZES_FOR_SCALE
FONT_STRING_DIMS
FONT_STYLE
```

17

Resources

In This Chapter:

Predefined Defaults 321
XView Resource Database Functions 324
    Boolean Resources 325
    Integer Resources 325
    Character Resources 326
    String Resources 326
    Enumerated Resources 327

Resources

17
Resources

In the X Window System, the user may configure the interface according to options available in specific applications. The user accomplishes this through a *resource database* that resides in the X server. The X Protocol provides many ways to access the resource database, as well as many functions to aid in this task. You should consult Chapter 11, *Managing User Preferences*, in Volume One, *Xlib Programming Manual*, for a complete, in-depth discussion of X resource specification and management. Related programs include *xrdb*, and related functions can be found in Volume Two, *Xlib Reference Manual*.

XView provides many functions that allow the programmer to interact with the server to get or set resources specified by the user. Robust applications should account for user-definable defaults. That is, your programs should always consider the user's wishes for changing attribute values for things like fonts, colors, and maybe even window sizes, as long as the values do not interfere with the normal running of the program. You should also provide the user with a list of resources that can be set and should test for them in your application.

17.1 Predefined Defaults

All of the packages in XView look for predefined defaults that the user can set in his resource environment. Table 17-1 outlines these defaults.

Table 17-1. Resources and Default Values Understood by XView

Type	Name	Default	Legal Values
string	**window.scale**	Medium	Small, Medium, Large, Extra_Large
string	**font.name**	NULL	*fontname-size*
boolean	**window.mono.disableRetained**	False	True, False
string	**server.name**	getenv(DISPLAY)	*hostnamedisplay*
boolean	**alarm.audible**	True	True, False
boolean	**alarm.visible**	True	True, False
string	**window.header**	NULL	*header string*
integer	**window.columns**	80	—

Type	Name	Default	Legal Values
integer	window.rows	34	—
integer	window.width	80 columns	Greater than 0
integer	window.height	34 rows	Greater than 0
integer	window.x	0	—
integer	window.y	0	—
boolean	window.iconic	False	True, False
integer	window.inheritcolor	1	
string	window.color.foreground	"0 0 0"	3 RGB values, 0-255
string	window.color.background	"255 255 255"	3 RGB values, 0-255
string	icon.font.name	NULL	*fontname-size*
string	icon.pixmap	NULL	*pixmap filename*
string	icon.footer	NULL	*footer string*
integer	icon.x	0	—
integer	icon.y	0	—
integer	openWindows.dragRightDistance	5	—
boolean	notice.jumpCursor	True	True, False
integer	notice.beepCount	1	—
integer	OpenWindows.MultiClickTimeout	4	1 through 10 (in sec/10)
integer	scrollbar.repeatDelay	500	0, 999 (msec delay interval)
integer	scrollbar.pageInterval	100	0, 999 (msec delay interval)
integer	scrollbar.lineInterval	1	0, 999 (msec delay interval)
integer	cmdtool.checkpointFrequency	0	0, 0x77777777
integer	cmdtool.maxLogFileSize	0x77777777	0, 0x77777777
integer	text.checkpointFrequency	0	0, 0x77777777
boolean	text.enableScrollbar	True	True, False
integer	text.againLimit	1	0, 500
boolean	text.autoIndent	False	True, False
integer	text.autoScrollBy	1	0, 100
boolean	text.blinkcaret	True	True, False
boolean	text.confirmOverwrite	True	True, False
boolean	text.displayControlChars	False	True, False
integer	text.undoLimit	50	0, 500
string	text.insertMakesCaretVisible	If_auto_scroll	If_auto_scroll, Always
string	text.lineBreak	Wrap_word	Clip, Wrap_char, Wrap_word
integer	text.margin.bottom	0	–1, 50
integer	mouse.multiclick.space		
boolean	text.storeChangesFile	True	True, False
integer	text.margin.top	2	–1, 50
integer	text.margin.left	8	0, 2000
integer	text.margin.right	0	0, 2000
integer	text.tabWidth	8	0, 50
string	text.extrasMenuFilename	*.text_extra_menu* (in */usr/lib*)	*filename*
integer	text.maxDocumentSize	20000	0, 0x80000000

Type	Name	Default	Legal Values
boolean	text.retained	False	True, False
string	keyboard.arrowKeys	Yes	Yes, No
string	keyboard.leftHanded	No	Yes, No
boolean	term.enableEdit	True	True, False
string	term.boldStyle	Invert	None, OFFSET_X, OFFSET_Y, OFFSET_X_AND_Y, OFFSET_X_AND_XY, OFFSET_Y_AND_XY, OFFSET_X_AND_Y_AND_XY, OFFSET_XY, INVERT
string	term.inverseStyle	Enable	ENABLED, DISABLED, SAME_AS_BOLD
string	term.underlineStyle	Enable	ENABLED, DISABLED, SAME_AS_BOLD

XView provides many functions to get resource values from the database. Basically, values come in several types: `int`, `character` (strings), `boolean` (which can be specified using a number of string values; see below), and `enumerated` values.

Example 17-1 lists a simple application that introduces the use of one of the functions provided by the `defaults` package. The program *default_text.c* creates a frame with a text subwindow whose font is specified by the user's resource `textsw.font`.

Example 17-1. The default_text.c program

```
/*
 * default_text.c -- use the defaults package to get a font name from
 * the resource database to set the textsw's font.
 */
#include <xview/xview.h>
#include <xview/font.h>
#include <xview/defaults.h>
#include <xview/textsw.h>

main(argc, argv)
char *argv[];
{
    Frame       frame;
    Xv_Font     font;
    char        *name;

    xv_init(XV_INIT_ARGC_PTR_ARGV, &argc, argv, NULL);

    frame = (Frame)xv_create(NULL, FRAME, NULL);

    name = defaults_get_string("textsw.font","Textsw.Font", "fixed"),
    font = xv_find(frame, FONT,
        FONT_NAME,      name,
        NULL);

    xv_create(frame, TEXTSW,
        XV_FONT,        font,
```

Example 17-1. The default_text.c program (continued)

```
        WIN_COLUMNS,     80,
        WIN_ROWS,        10,
        NULL);

    window_fit(frame);
    xv_main_loop(frame);
}
```

default_text.c shows how an XView program queries the resource database for a string value
associated with a name-class pair. `defaults_get_string()` gets the string value associated with `Textsw.Font`. If the resource database has this attribute, then the value is
returned. If not, the default (`fixed`) is returned.

17.2 XView Resource Database Functions

The functions that XView provides are defined in *<xview/defaults.h>*. The following functions are provided by XView for setting and getting resource values to and from the database.
Note that when setting resources *to* the database, the database on the *server* is updated—not
the user's *defaults* database. Resources not updated to the user's defaults database are not
retained for the next time the X server is started.

```
    void
    defaults_init_db()
```

This function is called automatically by `xv_init()`, so it need not be called by your application. `defaults_init_db()` calls `XrmInitialize()`.

```
    void
    defaults_load_db(filename)
        char *filename;
```

`defaults_load_db()` loads the database residing in the specified filename or the server
database if filename is `NULL`. The database found in `filename` is loaded via `XrmGetFile-`
`Database()` and is merged into the existing resource database via `XrmMerge-`
`Databases()`.

```
    void
    defaults_store_db(filename)
        char *filename;
```

This function writes the database to the specified file via `XrmPutFileDatabase()`. This
must be done in order to ensure that the database is accessible the next time the server is
started.*

```
    Bool
    defaults_exists(name, class)
        char *name;
        char *class;
```

This function returns `TRUE` if the resource exists in the database via `XrmGetResource()`.

---

*The file *Xdefaults* in the user's home directory is a good candidate for *filename*.

17.2.1 Boolean Resources

```
Bool
defaults_get_boolean(name, class, default_value)
    char *name, *class;
    int   default_value;

void
defaults_set_boolean(resource, value)
    char *resource;
    Bool  value;
```

defaults_get_boolean() looks up the name-class pair in the resource database and returns TRUE if the value is one of:

- True
- Yes
- On
- Enabled
- Set
- Activated
- 1

It returns FALSE if the value is one of:

- False
- No
- Off
- Disabled
- Reset
- Cleared
- Deactivated
- 0

If the value is none of the above, a warning message will be displayed and the default value will be returned. If the resource is not found, no error message is printed but the default value is still returned.

defaults_set_boolean() sets the resource to the value specified.

17.2.2 Integer Resources

```
int
defaults_get_integer(name, class, default_value)
    char *name;
    char *class;
    int   default_value;
```

```
int
defaults_get_integer_check(name, class, default_value,
                           minimum, maximum)
    char *name;
    char *class;
    int   default_value;
    int   minimum;
    int   maximum;
void
defaults_set_integer(resource, value)
    char *resource;
    int   value;
```

defaults_get_integer() looks up the name-class pair in the resource database and returns the resulting integer value. If the database does not contain the resource, the default value is returned.

defaults_get_integer_check() looks up the name-class pair in the resource database and returns the resulting integer value. If the value in the database is not between the values minimum and maximum (inclusive), an error message is printed and the default value is returned. If the resource is not found, no error message is printed but the default value is returned.

defaults_set_integer() sets the resource to the value specified.

17.2.3 Character Resources

```
char
defaults_get_character(name, class, default_char)
    char *name;
    char *class;
    char  default_char;
void
defaults_set_character(resource, character)
    char *resource;
    char  character;
```

defaults_get_character() looks up the name-class pair in the resource database and returns the resulting character value. If the resource is not found, then the default char is returned.

defaults_set_character() sets the resource to the character value.

17.2.4 String Resources

```
char *
defaults_get_string(name, class, default_str)
    char *name;
    char *class;
    char *default_str;
```

```
void
defaults_set_string(resource, string)
    char *resource;
    char *string;
```

`defaults_get_string()` returns the string value associated with the specified name-class pair in the resource database. If the resource is not found, the default string value is returned.

`defaults_set_character()` sets the resource to the specified string.

17.2.5 Enumerated Resources

Enumerated resources are those whose values are string values, but the legal values for the resource are restricted to a predefined list. For example, say you want to allow the user to specify the font scale for the font `lucidasans`. The legal `scale` values are: small, medium, large, and extra large. You could use `defaults_get_string()` and determine, using `strcmp()`, whether the value returned is one of the legal scale values. Or you could use `defaults_get_enum()` and pass in a table describing the legal values. The *table* is an array of elements of the type:

```
typedef struct _default_pairs {
    char    *name;  /* Name of pair */
    int     value; /* Value of pair */
} Defaults_pairs;
```

The *name* is a string, and the *value* is the returned value associated with the name. This value may be your own value and need not be sequential, but it must be an `int`.

```
int
defaults_get_enum(name, class, pairs)
    char            *name;
    char            *class;
    Defaults_pairs *pairs;
```

`defaults_get_enum()` looks up the value associated with name and class and scans the Pairs table and return the associated value. If no match is found, an error is generated and the value associated with last entry is returned. `defaults_get_enum()` calls `defaults_get_string()` and determines the value returned by calling `defaults_lookup()` (below) passing the returned string as the name parameter.

```
int
defaults_lookup(name, pairs)
    char            *name;
    Defaults_pairs *pairs;
```

`defaults_lookup()` linearly scans the `pairs` array looking for `name`. The value associated with `name` is returned. The `pairs` array *must* contain a last element with a NULL name and a legal `value` associated with it. This value is the default returned if the name in `name` is not found in the `name` field of any of the elements in `pairs`.

Example 17-2 shows a program that implements the idea discussed earlier for allowing the user to specify a scale for a font to use.

Example 17-2. The default_size.c program

```
/*
 * default_scale.c -- demonstrate the use of defaults_get_enum().
 * Specify a table of font scales and query the resource database
 * for legal values.  For example, you may have the following in
 * your .Xdefaults (which must be loaded into the resource database):
 *      font.scale: large
 */
#include <xview/xview.h>
#include <xview/font.h>
#include <xview/defaults.h>
#include <xview/textsw.h>

Defaults_pairs size_pairs[] = {
    "small",            WIN_SCALE_SMALL,
    "medium",           WIN_SCALE_MEDIUM,
    "large",            WIN_SCALE_LARGE,
    "extralarge",       WIN_SCALE_EXTRALARGE,
    /* the NULL entry is the default if Resource not found */
    NULL,               WIN_SCALE_MEDIUM,
};

main(argc, argv)
char *argv[];
{
    Frame       frame;
    Xv_Font     font;
    int         scale;

    xv_init(XV_INIT_ARGC_PTR_ARGV, &argc, argv, NULL);

    frame = (Frame)xv_create(NULL, FRAME, NULL);

    scale = defaults_get_enum("font.scale", "Font.Scale", size_pairs);
    /* get the default font for the frame, scaled to resource */
    font = xv_find(frame, FONT,
        FONT_RESCALE_OF,        xv_find(frame, FONT, NULL), scale,
        NULL);

    xv_create(frame, TEXTSW,
        XV_FONT,                font,
        WIN_COLUMNS,            80,
        WIN_ROWS,               10,
        NULL);

    window_fit(frame);
    xv_main_loop(frame);
}
```

In *default_size.c*, the Defaults_pairs table describes an association between string constants and scaling factors. The resource database may specify the resource font.scale that describes a scaling factor. If the value in the resource is not one of the legal values included in the table, an error message is printed to inform the user that he has misspecified the resource. In this case, or in the case where the resource is not specified, the *default* resource (associated with the NULL entry) is returned. In this case, it is WIN_SCALE_MEDIUM.

NOTE

The `value` field in the `Defaults_pair` data structure is an `int`, so do not attempt to assign pointers, functions, or attributes to this field. You can assign enumerated types since they are interpreted as `int`.

18

The Selection Service

In This Chapter:

The XView Selection Model 331
Using the Selection Service 332
Getting the Current Selection 333
   The Seln_request Structure 335
Using selection_query() 341
Selection Package Summary 347

18
The Selection Service

The X Window System provides several methods for separate applications to exchange information with one another. One of these methods is the use of the selection service. A *selection* transfers arbitrary information between two clients. An in-depth discussion of the selection mechanism that X provides is discussed in Volume One, *Xlib Programming Manual*. This chapter addresses XView's programmatic interface to the selection service provided by the X server.

While XView provides all the functions for applications to set and get selections of various sorts, OPEN LOOK applications must follow the conventions outlined in the *OPEN LOOK GUI Specification Guide*. All XView packages that have interactive text entry support the ability to make selections and to get selections from the server. Figure 18-1, from the *OPEN LOOK GUI Specification Guide*, shows one way to select text.

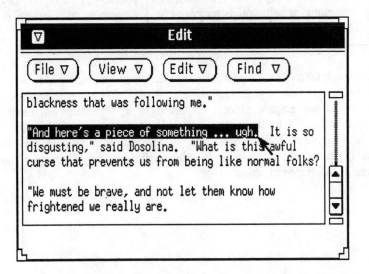

Figure 18-1. Dragging the pointer to select text

In OPEN LOOK, you select objects in basically the same way that you select windows or icons—using the SELECT and ADJUST mouse buttons. OPEN LOOK describes three functions that operate on selected objects: CUT, COPY and PASTE. These are *core functions* that are accessed from the keyboard.* CUT, COPY and PASTE operations use the *clipboard* to keep track of selected objects. The clipboard temporarily stores items selected via the selection service; it does not store selected windows or icons since these are not considered selectable objects by the *selection service*. Table 18-1 summarizes text selection for the OPEN LOOK GUI.

Table 18-1. Selecting Text

Action	Off Selection	On Selection
Click SELECT	Insert point is set at the pointer location.	When SELECT is released, insert point is set at pointer location and selection is cleared.
Drag SELECT	Text is highlighted as pointer is dragged (wipe-through selection).	Text move pointer is displayed. When you release SELECT, text is moved to pointer location if that location is outside the highlighted area.
Click ADJUST	Extends the highlighting to the pointer location extending either the beginning or the end of the current selection.	Moves the end of the highlighting to the pointer location. Beginning of selection is preserved.
Drag ADJUST	Adjusts an existing selection as the pointer is dragged (wipe-through). Beginning of selection is anchored at insert point.	Adjusts an existing selection as pointer is dragged (wipe-through). Beginning of selection is anchored at insert point.

Note that although OPEN LOOK specifies the selection of graphic objects, no XView objects currently support selection of graphical objects. A possible implementation is to have a canvas object, which has graphic objects displayed in it, set selections based on the event sequences outlined in Table 18-1. The reason for this is that what constitutes a complete graphic object is application-dependent. A *draw* application might consider a drawn geometric shape as a graphic object, whereas a *paint* application might consider the pixels in an arbitrary area as the graphical object.

---

*The function keys that are bound to these functions vary from keyboard to keyboard depending on the make and model of the computer.

18.1 The XView Selection Model

The XView selection model is based upon the requestor/owner model of peer-to-peer communications. The *owner* has the data representing the value of its selection, and the *requestor* receives it.

In the X environment, *all* data transferred between an owner and a requestor must transfer via the server. An X client cannot assume that another client can open the same files or even communicate directly. Such assumptions might result in an application that does not work in all network configurations or across heterogeneous computer architectures.

X makes provisions for selections and therefore generates certain events such as `Property-Notify` when a selection is acquired. For XView to implement its selection service, XView tracks all events that might be generated from selections. Because of this, you may not use any of the selection mechanisms provided by Xlib. If you do, you will generate events that you will not be able to receive and that XView will be confused about.

The XView selection library deals with four discrete *ranks* under the general term *selection*. Those ranks are: Primary, Secondary, Shelf and Caret. Most familiar is the *Primary* selection, which is normally indicated on the screen by inverting (*highlighting*) its contents. Selections made while a function key is held down (usually indicated with an underscore under the selection) are considered secondary selections.* These selections are used when the primary selection must be left undisturbed. The *Shelf* (or *Clipboard*) selection is used by the CUT and COPY operations to load the selection, while the PASTE operation retrieves the selection. Finally, the *Caret* (the insertion point for interactive text objects) is also treated as a selection even though it has no contents.

When a user interface element, such as a text subwindow, wants to allow the user make a selection, it must have a selection *client*. Through this client, the text subwindow can acquire a selection rank (primary, secondary, etc) and provide it with data (text). An application can have many such clients, but there is typically one client per XView object. Each selection rank is associated with each client—a separate client need not be created just to utilize other selection ranks. However, only one client can be the holder of a particular selection rank at any one time. If a client wishes to acquire the selection, the current selection *holder* must *yield* the selection to the new requestor. The client becomes the new holder of the selection and might provide any data it chooses.

Selection Service

---

*Which function key depends on your particular computer. By default the L6 function key should work for Sun Workstations or the F6 key for other computers.

18.2 Using the Selection Service

It is not necessary to create a selection service client just to query the holder of a selection or to get its contents. Since this is the most common usage, most of this chapter is dedicated to explaining this level of functionality. Creating a selection is typically used internally by packages in the XView library or by applications that wish to create their own objects that need to communicate via the selection service. This is generally very intricate and complicated and is beyond the scope of this book. Although no programs demonstrate how to create an object with data to provide to the selection service, later sections of this chapter (beginning with *Creating a Selection*) address the conceptual issues involved.

Nevertheless, to understand how to create a selection service client, it is best to learn how to request information from an existing client. Once you understand what to expect from a selection, you can understand how to create a client that provides information from other requests. Therefore, the bulk of the chapter addresses the process of querying for selections already provided by XView packages or other X-based applications.

OPEN LOOK assigns to function keys the special functions COPY, CUT, and PASTE. The function keys generate and correspond to the XView events ACTION_CUT, ACTION_COPY, and ACTION_PASTE. An OPEN LOOK application checks the state of these keys and modifies the selection rank accordingly. Note that it is the responsibility of the XView application (more specifically, each XView package) to set the state of the server's selection rank according to the state of some function keys. Unless you are writing your own XView package (a topic that this book does not address), you need not concern yourself about it.

Even though XView packages might query for the state of function keys, this does not interfere with normal event processing. All events that your application has registered to receive are not affected by the selection service. Note, however, that while the selection service might react to the state of these function keys, any action you take as a result of these keys might result in a *dual action* and might confuse the user. For example, if your application is coded to change the font of a text subwindow in the event of an L8-up event, you will not only get that event, but the selection service also gets it and will PASTE the contents of the *Shelf* selection.

Whenever using the selection service either as a client or to query the selection from another client, application code must include the header file *<xview/seln.h>*. This file includes the files *<xview/sel_svc.h>* and *<xview/sel_attrs.h>*, which provide external declarations of available functions and data types.

18.3 Getting the Current Selection

Determining the current selection involves two steps: determining the *holder* of the current selection and getting the actual selection *data* from the holder. To determine who is holding the selection of a specified *rank*:

```
Seln_holder
selection_inquire(server, rank)
    Xv_Server server;
    Seln_rank rank;
```

The returned `holder` is used in other selection routines that allow you to access selection data for that *rank*. For example, the call `selection_ask()` asks for the data held by the holder of the selection. The form of the call is:

```
Seln_request *
selection_ask(server, holder, attrs)
    Xv_Server        server;
    Seln_holder     *holder;
    <attribute-value list>  attrs
```

The `holder` in this case is the address of the holder returned from the call to `selection_inquire()`.

The *server* is important to all the selection service routines because it identifies the X server in which the selection is associated. Because X applications can communicate with more than one server, specifying different servers can result in getting different selections.

The `Seln_rank` specifies which selection type you want. Its value corresponds with the four selection ranks outlined in the beginning of the chapter. However, there are six legal values in this enumerated data type:

SELN_UNKNOWN   This is an error value, not a value you would use as a parameter or a legal or known *rank*.

SELN_CARET   The caret selection is used with text subwindows and text panel items. It is usually used to describe where the insertion point is within the corresponding text stream of the object so there is no *data* associated with the caret selection. This selection type is not very widely used.

SELN_PRIMARY   The primary selection is the most widely used and is usually the default type used in most user interfaces and applications.

SELN_SECONDARY   As noted earlier, the secondary selection is only used if the primary selection must not be removed or lost—or if it must remain clearly visible (visually selected) on the screen.

SELN_SHELF   The selection buffers are stored in files. Clients of the selection service do no access these files; the selection service just uses them as temporary storage for data. As noted, this is not a good place to hold selections.

Selection
Service

When this rank is used, either the primary or the secondary
                       selection is used depending on the state of the appropriate function
                       keys. This is usually passed as the `rank` parameter to
                       `selection_inquire()`.

`selection_ask()` returns a pointer to a `Seln_request` data structure. The function goes
out and asks the server for the selection associated with the rank described in the *holder*
parameter. All the information about the selection is held in this data structure. The
attribute-value list following the `holder` parameter describes what attributes about the
selection you are interested in.

Before we go on, let's show an example program that illustrates what we have covered so far.
The simple program in Example 18-1 has a panel button that prints the current primary
selection to the standard output. The selection can be held by any client on the server.

Example 18-1. The simple_seln.c program

```
/*
 * seln.c -- print the primary selection by pressing the panel
 * button.  The selection may have originated from any window or
 * application on the server.
 */
#include <stdio.h>
#include <xview/xview.h>
#include <xview/panel.h>
#include <xview/server.h>
#include <xview/seln.h>

Xv_Server server;

main(argc, argv)
char *argv[];
{
    Frame       frame;
    Panel       panel;
    void        exit();
    int         print_seln();

    xv_init(XV_INIT_ARGC_PTR_ARGV, &argc, argv, NULL);

    frame = (Frame) xv_create(NULL, FRAME,
        FRAME_LABEL,            argv[0],
        NULL);
    panel = (Panel)xv_create(frame, PANEL,
        WIN_WIDTH,              WIN_EXTEND_TO_EDGE,
        NULL);
    (void) xv_create(panel, PANEL_BUTTON,
        PANEL_LABEL_STRING,     "Quit",
        PANEL_NOTIFY_PROC,      exit,
        NULL);
    (void) xv_create(panel, PANEL_BUTTON,
        PANEL_LABEL_STRING,     "Print Selection",
        PANEL_NOTIFY_PROC,      print_seln,
        NULL);
    window_fit(panel);
    window_fit(frame);

    server = (Xv_Server)xv_get(xv_get(frame, XV_SCREEN), SCREEN_SERVER);
```

Example 18-1. The simple_seln.c program (continued)

```
    xv_main_loop(frame);
}

/*
 * Get the selection using selection_ask().  Note that if the
 * selection is bigger than about 2K, the whole selection will
 * not be gotten with one call, thus this method of getting
 * the selection may not be sufficient for all situations.
 */
int
print_seln(item, event)
Panel_item item;
Event *event;
{
    Seln_holder         holder;
    Seln_request        *response;
    char                text[BUFSIZ];

    /* get the holder of the primary selection */
    holder = selection_inquire(server, SELN_PRIMARY);
    response = selection_ask(server, &holder,
        SELN_REQ_CONTENTS_ASCII, NULL,
        NULL);

    strcpy(text, response->data + sizeof (SELN_REQ_CONTENTS_ASCII));
    printf("---selection---\n%s\n---end seln---\n", text);

    return XV_OK;
}
```

selection_ask() does not return until it has contacted the server and gotten a response
back from it. This implies that if the server does not respond, the application *blocks* until
either a time-out occurs or the selection is received. The attribute-value pair that is passed
(SELN_REQ_CONTENTS_ASCII, NULL) indicates that we are interested in the ASCII contents of the selection. Whether the selection is successful or not, a pointer to a
Seln_request structure is returned. If there was an error, the status field of the structure
will indicate so. If it succeeded, then the selection contents will be in the data field of the
structure. All this is clarified in the next section.

18.3.1 The Seln_request Structure

The Seln_request data structure returned from selection_ask() contains information
about the selection requested. The pointer returned points to static data that is overwritten on
each call. Thus, if you need to save any of this data, it should be copied. The
Seln_request structure is defined as follows:

```
typedef struct {
    Seln_replier_data      *replier;
    Seln_requester          requester;
    char                   *addressee;
    Seln_rank               rank;
    Seln_result             status;
    unsigned                buf_size;
    char                    data[SELN_BUFSIZE];
} Seln_request;
```

If there is no selection or if the selection fails in any way, the status field in the data structure is set to one of the values in the enumerated type Seln_result. If status is set to SELN_FAILED, then the data field should not be examined as it will not contain any reliable values.

On the other hand, if selection_ask() returns successfully, the same attributes that were passed into the function are copied into the data byte array along with the new values (see Figure 18-2).

```
Seln_request  *request;

...

request = selection_ask(server, &holder,
    SELN_REQ_FIRST,           NULL,
    SELN_REQ_LAST,            NULL,
    SELN_REQ_CONTENTS_ASCII,  NULL,
    NULL);
```

Figure 18-2 above shows what is returned assuming that the selection contained the string "Now is the time for all..." The data field contains all the attributes passed in to selection_ask(), but the attributes and the values are all aligned to 4-byte boundaries. This includes the *string* returned from the selection. If the selection string is not a multiple of 4, then it is NULL-padded. The NULL-terminating byte of the string is required—if the last character of the string aligns to a 4-byte boundary, the NULL-terminator pushes it into the next 4-byte block and three more NULLs are required to align to the next boundary.

The value of buf_size is the number of bytes in the data array that is used by attribute-value pairs including the text selection and alignment padding. The attributes SELN_REQ_FIRST and SELN_REQ_LAST return the first and last indexes into the object in which the selection resides.*

To further demonstrate the use of the selection service, we will examine another program (see Example 18-2) that is a little more intricate but that still follows the same principles outlined in the first program. The new program, *text_seln.c*, also helps explain some of the new concepts introduced in this section.

text_seln.c contains a text subwindow in which selections can be made. Also, a panel button that prints the current primary selection is provided. If the selection is made in the provided

---

*Currently, the text subwindow is the only XView object that responds to these requests—panel text items do not.

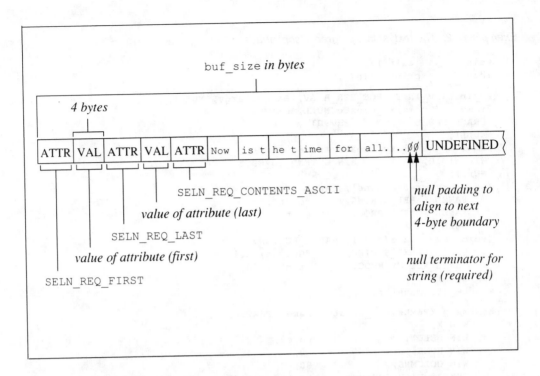

Figure 18-2. Byte stream after selection_ask() returns the current text selection

text subwindow, information is printed about the relationship between the selected text and the rest of the subwindow. The program makes more extensive use of the selection_ask() function.

Example 18-2. The text_seln.c program

```
/*
 * seln.c -- print the primary selection from the server.  If the
 * selection is in a text subwindow, also print information about
 * the line number(s) the selection spans and the indexes of
 * the bytes within the textsw's buffer.
 */
#include <stdio.h>
#include <xview/xview.h>
#include <xview/textsw.h>
#include <xview/panel.h>
#include <xview/server.h>
#include <xview/seln.h>

Xv_Server       server;
Textsw          textsw;

char *get_selection();

main(argc, argv)
char *argv[];
{
    Frame       frame;
    Panel       panel;
```

The Selection Service

339

Example 18-2. The text_seln.c program (continued)

```
    void        exit();
    int         print_seln();

    xv_init(XV_INIT_ARGC_PTR_ARGV, &argc, argv, NULL);
    frame = (Frame)xv_create(NULL, FRAME,
     FRAME_LABEL,           argv[0],
     NULL);
    panel = (Panel)xv_create(frame, PANEL,
     WIN_WIDTH,             WIN_EXTEND_TO_EDGE,
     NULL);
    (void) xv_create(panel, PANEL_BUTTON,
        PANEL_LABEL_STRING,     "Quit",
        PANEL_NOTIFY_PROC,      exit,
        NULL);
    (void) xv_create(panel, PANEL_BUTTON,
        PANEL_LABEL_STRING,     "Get Selection",
        PANEL_NOTIFY_PROC,      print_seln,
        NULL);
    window_fit(panel);

    textsw = (Textsw)xv_create(frame, TEXTSW,
        WIN_X,                  0,
        WIN_BELOW,              panel,
        WIN_ROWS,               10,
        WIN_COLUMNS,            80,
        TEXTSW_FILE_CONTENTS,   "/etc/passwd",
        NULL);
    window_fit(frame);

    server = (Xv_Server)xv_get(xv_get(frame, XV_SCREEN), SCREEN_SERVER);

    xv_main_loop(frame);
}

int
print_seln()
{
    char *text = get_selection();

    if (text)
        printf("---selection---\n%s\n---end seln---\n", text);

    return XV_OK;
}

/*
 * Get the selection using selection_ask().  Note that if the
 * selection is bigger than about 2K, the whole selection will
 * not be gotten with one call, thus this method of getting the
 * selection may not be sufficient.
 */
char *
get_selection()
{
    long            sel_lin_num, lines_selected;
    Textsw_index    first, last;
    Seln_holder     holder;
    Seln_result     result;
    int             len;
```

Example 18-2. The text_seln.c program (continued)

```
Seln_request           *response;
static char            selection_buf[BUFSIZ];
register char          *ptr;

/* get the holder of the primary selection */
holder = selection_inquire(server, SELN_PRIMARY);

/* If the selection occurs in the text subwindow, print lots of
 * info about the selection.
 */
if (seln_holder_same_client(&holder, textsw)) {
    /* ask for information from the selection service */
    response = selection_ask(server, &holder,
        /* get index of the first and last chars in the textsw */
        SELN_REQ_FIRST,             NULL,
        SELN_REQ_LAST,              NULL,
        /* get the actual selection bytes */
        SELN_REQ_CONTENTS_ASCII,    NULL,
        /* Now fool the textsw to think entire lines are selected */
        SELN_REQ_FAKE_LEVEL,        SELN_LEVEL_LINE,
        /* Get the line numbers of beginning and ending of the
         * selection */
        SELN_REQ_FIRST_UNIT,        NULL,
        SELN_REQ_LAST_UNIT,         NULL,
        NULL);
    /* set the ptr to beginning of data -- SELN_REQ_FIRST */
    ptr = response->data;
    /* "first" is data succeeding SELN_REQ_FIRST -- skip attr */
    first = *(Textsw_index *)(ptr += sizeof(SELN_REQ_FIRST));
    ptr += sizeof(Textsw_index); /* skip over value of "first" */
    /* "last" is data succeeding SELN_REQ_LAST -- skip attr */
    last  = *(Textsw_index *)(ptr += sizeof(SELN_REQ_LAST));
    ptr += sizeof(Textsw_index); /* skip over value of "last" */

    /* advance pointer past SELN_REQ_CONTENTS_ASCII */
    ptr += sizeof(SELN_REQ_CONTENTS_ASCII);
    len = strlen(ptr); /* length of string in response */
    (void) strcpy(selection_buf, ptr);
    /*
     * advance pointer past length of string.  If the string length
   * isn't aligned to a 4-byte boundary, add the difference in
   * bytes -- then advance pointer passed "value".
     */
    if (len % 4)
        len = len + (4 - (len % 4));
    ptr += len + sizeof(Seln_attribute); /* skip over "value" */

    /* advance pointer past SELN_REQ_FAKE_LEVEL, SELN_LEVEL_LINE */
    ptr += sizeof(SELN_REQ_FAKE_LEVEL) + sizeof(SELN_LEVEL_LINE);

    sel_lin_num = *(long *)(ptr += sizeof(SELN_REQ_FIRST_UNIT));
    ptr += sizeof(long);
    lines_selected = *(long *)(ptr += sizeof(SELN_REQ_LAST_UNIT));
    ptr += sizeof(long);

    /* hack to workaround bug with SELN_REQ_LAST_UNIT always
   * returning -1.  Count the lines explicitly in the selection.
     */
```

Selection
Service

Example 18-2. The text_seln.c program (continued)

```
        if (lines_selected < 0) {
            register char *p;
            lines_selected++;
            for (p = selection_buf; *p; p++)
                if (*p == '\n')
                    lines_selected++;
        }
        printf("index in textsw: %d-%d, line number(s) = %d-%d\n",
            first+1, last+1, sel_lin_num+1,
          sel_lin_num + lines_selected + 1);
    } else {
        /* the selection does not lie in our text subwindow */
        response = selection_ask(server, &holder,
            SELN_REQ_CONTENTS_ASCII, NULL,
            NULL);
        if (response->status != SELN_SUCCESS) {
            printf("selection_ask() returns %d\n", response->status);
            return NULL;
        }
        (void) strcpy(selection_buf,
            response->data + sizeof(SELN_REQ_CONTENTS_ASCII));
    }
    return selection_buf;
}
```

There are several points of interest here. In the function `get_selection()`, once the holder of the client has been obtained, it is tested to see if the holder is the text subwindow using `seln_holder_same_client()`. If so, `selection_ask()` is called requesting information specific to the text subwindow. If the text subwindow is not the holder of the selection, then `selection_ask()` is called requesting only the ASCII contents. If there is no selection, then the `status` field of the structure is set to `SELN_FAILED`.

In the case where the holder is the text subwindow, we ask it for the first and last indices of the selection relative to the beginning of the text stream. Note that we might not be able to request this information from any object. For example, if the selection were inside an *xterm*, then this information is not available and the *xterm*'s selection client will not respond to such requests.

The next attribute (`SELN_REQ_CONTENTS_ASCII`) requests the ASCII contents of the selection actually made. Following that, the attribute-value pair:

```
SELN_REQ_FAKE_LEVEL, SELN_LEVEL_LINE
```

fools the text subwindow into thinking that the user selected an entire line of text (in OPEN LOOK, this would have meant a triple-click with the SELECT mouse button). Had this attribute-value pair been listed *before* the request for ASCII contents, the text returned by the request would have contained the entire line of text on which the selection occurred *regardless of whether the selection began at the beginning of the line*.

The reason we *fake* the text window into thinking the entire line has been selected is this: the attributes `SELN_REQ_FIRST_UNIT` and `SELN_REQ_LAST_UNIT` request the line numbers that the selection spans. As the names of the attributes imply, the request is for the first and last *units* selected. Setting the `SELN_REQ_FAKE_LEVEL` attribute to `SELN_LEVEL_LINE` indicates that the unit type should be `line`. Note that we fake the fact that the selection unit is set to `line` just to get the start and end line numbers of the selection. If we wanted to actually set the level, we would have used `SELN_REQ_SET_LEVEL`.

After `selection_ask()` returns a pointer to a `Seln_request` structure, the values of the requested attributes are found in `data`, the byte stream. As demonstrated in Example 18-2 above, the way to retrieve these values is by moving a pointer along the array.

```
Seln_request  *response;
char          *ptr;
long           value;
. . .
response = selection_ask(server, &holder,
    ATTR1,       NULL,
    ATTR2,       NULL,
    . . .
    NULL);
. . .
/* set the ptr to beginning of data response -- first attribute */
ptr = response->data;
/* value is data succeeding first attribute -- skip over attr */
value = *(long *)(ptr += sizeof(Seln_attribute));
ptr += sizeof(long); /* skip over the size of the type of value */
```

There is no need to test the attributes as you scan `data`; they are the same attributes that you used in `selection_ask()` and they remain in the same order. The values you get back are almost always `long`.* The exception to this is the text string returned when `SELN_REQ_CONTENTS_ASCII` is specified. However, the text string is padded to a 4-byte boundary to make sure that the alignment is correct. *text_seln.c* demonstrates how this is done.

18.4 Using selection_query()

One problem with using `selection_ask()` is handling large selections. In this context, *large* means a text string that is long enough so that it, along with all its attributes and values, does not fit in the `data` byte-stream. Of course, the fewer attributes that are requested, the more text is returned from the selection.

In this case, the problem is that there is an upper limit to the number of bytes that can be retrieved from the selection. There is no guarantee that the user is not going to select a large number of bytes from some arbitrary application on the screen. However, there is another way to get the selection, regardless of how large it is, and that is by using `selection_query()`:

---

*Architectures whose `int` type does not equal its `long` type must be sure to compensate for this.

The Selection Service

Selection Service

```
Seln_result
selection_query(server, holder, reader, context, attrs)
    Xv_Server        server;
    Seln_holder      *holder;
    Seln_result      (*reader)();
    char             *context;
    <attribute-value list> attrs
```

The primary feature of this routine is that you provide it with a pointer to a function that does the scanning of the `data` array in the `Seln_request` structure as demonstrated earlier. Your `reader` function is called by `selection_query()`, and it gets the `Seln_request` structure as the sole parameter to your function. Your function takes the form of:

```
Seln_result
reader(request)
    Seln_request *request;
```

Your function should return `SELN_SUCCESS` provided that you encountered no problems with scanning `request->data`. `selection_query()` returns the same `Seln_result` that your `reader` function returns. Your `reader` function is called by `selection_query()` for each *chunk* of data in the selection.* The flowchart in Figure 18-3 shows the sequence of operations.

The program in Example 18-3 demonstrates the use of `selection_query()`. It is similar to *text_seln.c*, but this new program also provides for selections from one of three selection ranks. The user chooses the selection rank from the panel choice item. When the Get Selection button is pressed, the current selection from that selection rank is displayed.

The point of the program is to demonstrate the flow of control between `selection_query()` and the client-installed `reader` procedure. The text subwindow in the application loads the file */etc/termcap*. When a selection is made, `selection_query()` is called, which in turn calls the reader procedure. You can make an arbitrarily large selection to show how `read_proc` is called many times. Start by intializing the selection and then *scrolling* the window and *extending* the selection by using the ADJUST mouse button on later text. Select the Get Selection panel button and the output is directed to `stdout`. Because the selection size can be large, the output text is truncated to the first 20 characters of the selection.

---

*A *chunk* is the largest text string that will fit in the `data` field of the `Seln_request` structure.

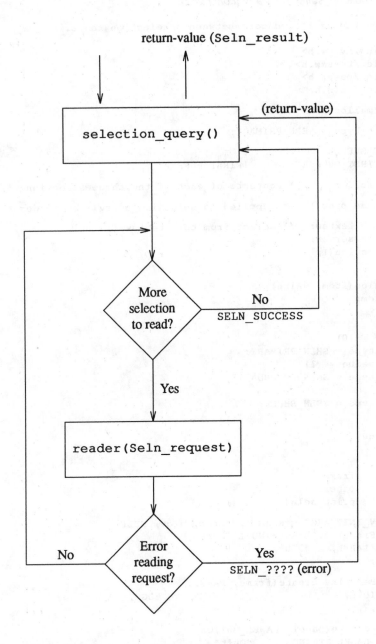

return-value (Seln_result)

selection_query()

(return-value)

More
selection
to read?

No
SELN_SUCCESS

Yes

reader(Seln_request)

No

Error
reading
request?

Yes
SELN_???? (error)

Figure 18-3. How selection_query() is used

Example 18-3. The long_seln.c program

```
/*
 * long_seln.c shows how to get an arbitrarily large selection by
 * providing a reading procedure to selection_query().  The panel
```

Example 18-3. The long_seln.c program (continued)

```
 * items allow the user to choose between 3 selection ranks.
 */
#include <xview/xview.h>
#include <xview/textsw.h>
#include <xview/panel.h>
#include <xview/seln.h>

extern char *malloc();

Seln_rank seln_type = SELN_PRIMARY;

#define FIRST_BUFFER              0
#define NOT_FIRST_BUFFER          !FIRST_BUFFER

char *seln_bufs[3];      /* contents of each of the three selections */

Seln_result read_proc(); /* supplied to selection_query() as reader */

Textsw            textsw;  /* select from this textsw */
Xv_Server         server;
char *get_selection();

void
change_selection(item, value)
Panel_item item;
int value;
{
    if (value == 0)
        seln_type = SELN_PRIMARY;
    else if (value == 1)
        seln_type = SELN_SECONDARY;
    else
        seln_type = SELN_SHELF;
}

main(argc, argv)
char *argv[];
{
    Frame         frame;
    Panel         panel;
    void          print_seln(), exit();

    xv_init(XV_INIT_ARGC_PTR_ARGV, &argc, argv, NULL);
    frame = (Frame) xv_create(NULL, FRAME,
        FRAME_LABEL, argv[0],
        NULL);

    panel = (Panel)xv_create(frame, PANEL,
        WIN_WIDTH,                WIN_EXTEND_TO_EDGE,
        NULL);

    (void) xv_create(panel, PANEL_BUTTON,
        PANEL_LABEL_STRING,       "Quit",
        PANEL_NOTIFY_PROC,        exit,
        NULL);
    (void) xv_create(panel, PANEL_BUTTON,
        PANEL_LABEL_STRING,       "Get Selection",
        PANEL_NOTIFY_PROC,        print_seln,
        NULL);
    (void) xv_create(panel, PANEL_CHOICE,
```

Example 18-3. The long_seln.c program (continued)

```
        PANEL_LABEL_STRING,        "Selection Type",
        PANEL_CHOICE_STRINGS,      "Primary", "Secondary", "Shelf", NULL,
        PANEL_NOTIFY_PROC,         change_selection,
        NULL);
    window_fit(panel);

    textsw = (Textsw)xv_create(frame, TEXTSW,
        WIN_X,                     0,
        WIN_BELOW,                 panel,
        WIN_ROWS,                  10,
        WIN_COLUMNS,               80,
        TEXTSW_FILE_CONTENTS,      "/etc/termcap",
        NULL);
    window_fit(frame);
    server = (Xv_Server)xv_get(xv_get(frame, XV_SCREEN), SCREEN_SERVER);
    xv_main_loop(frame);
}

void
print_seln()
{
    char *text = get_selection();

    if (text)
        printf("---seln---\n%.*s [...]0-end seln---0, 20, text);
}

/*
 * return the text selected in the current selection rank.  Use
 * selection_query() to guarantee that the entire selection is
 * retrieved.  selection_query() calls our installed routine,
 * read_proc() (see below).
 */
char *
get_selection()
{
    Seln_holder    holder;
    Seln_result    result;
    Seln_request   *response;
    char           context = FIRST_BUFFER;

    holder = selection_inquire(server, seln_type);
    printf("selection type = %s\n",
        seln_type == SELN_PRIMARY? "primary" :
        seln_type == SELN_SECONDARY? "secondary" : "shelf");

    /* result is based on the return value of read_proc() */
    result = selection_query(server, &holder, read_proc, &context,
        SELN_REQ_BYTESIZE,                 NULL,
        SELN_REQ_CONTENTS_ASCII,           NULL,
        NULL);
    if (result == SELN_FAILED) {
        puts("couldn't get selection");
        return NULL;
    }

    return seln_bufs[seln_type];
}
```

Example 18-3. The long_seln.c program (continued)

```
/*
 * Called by selection_query for every buffer of information received.
 * Short messages (under about 2000 bytes) will fit into one buffer.
 * For larger messages, read_proc is called for each buffer in the
 * selection.  The context pointer passed to selection_query is
 * modified by read_proc so that we know if this is the first buffer
 * or not.
 */
Seln_result
read_proc(response)
Seln_request *response;
{
    char *reply;  /* pointer to the data in the response received */
    long seln_len; /* total number of bytes in the selection */
    static long seln_have_bytes;
        /* number of bytes of the selection
         * which have been read; cumulative over all calls for
         * the same selection (it is reset when the first
         * response of a selection is read)
         */

    printf("read_proc status: %s (%d)\n",
        response->status == SELN_FAILED? "failed" :
        response->status == SELN_SUCCESS? "succeeded" :
        response->status == SELN_CONTINUED? "continued" : "???",
        response->status);
    if (*response->requester.context == FIRST_BUFFER) {
        reply = response->data;

        /* read in the length of the selection -- first attribute.
         * advance "reply" passed attribute to point to actual data.
         */
        reply += sizeof(SELN_REQ_BYTESIZE);
        /* set seln_len to actual data now. (bytes selected) */
        seln_len = *(int *)reply;
        printf("selection size is %ld bytes\n", seln_len);
        /* advance "reply" to next attribute in list */
        reply += sizeof(long);

        /* create a buffer large enough to store entire selection */
        if (seln_bufs[seln_type] != NULL)
            free(seln_bufs[seln_type]);
        if (!(seln_bufs[seln_type] = malloc(seln_len + 1))) {
            puts("out of memory");
            return(SELN_FAILED);
        }
        seln_have_bytes = 0;

        /* move "reply" passed attribute so it points to contents */
        reply += sizeof(SELN_REQ_CONTENTS_ASCII);
        *response->requester.context = NOT_FIRST_BUFFER;
    } else {
        /* this is not the first buffer, so the contents of the
         * response is just more of the selection
         */
        reply = response->data;
    }
```

Example 18-3. The long_seln.c program (continued)

```
    /* copy data from received to the seln buffer allocated above */
    (void) strcpy(&seln_bufs[seln_type][seln_have_bytes], reply);
    seln_have_bytes += strlen(reply);

    return SELN_SUCCESS;
}
```

18.5 Selection Package Summary

Table 18-2 lists the procedures and macros in the SELECTION package; Table 18-3 lists the attributes in the SELECTION package. This information is described fully in Appendices A and B.

Table 18-2. Selection Procedures

Selection Procedures

selection_acquire()	selection_inform()
selection_ask()	selection_init_request()
selection_clear_functions()	selection_inquire()
selection_create()	selection_inquire_all()
selection_destroy()	selection_query()
selection_done()	selection_report_event()
selection_figure_response()	selection_request()
selection_hold_file()	selection_yield_all()

Table 18-3. Selection Attributes

Selection Attributes	Advanced Selection Attributes
SELN_REQ_BYTESIZE	SELN_REQ_COMMIT_PENDING_DELETE
SELN_REQ_CONTENTS_ASCII	SELN_REQ_CONTENTS_PIECES
SELN_REQ_DELETE	SELN_REQ_FAKE_LEVEL
SELN_REQ_END_REQUEST	SELN_REQ_FIRST
SELN_REQ_FILE_NAME	SELN_REQ_FIRST_UNIT
SELN_REQ_YIELD	SELN_REQ_LAST
	SELN_REQ_LAST_UNIT
	SELN_REQ_LEVEL
	SELN_REQ_RESTORE
	SELN_REQ_SET_LEVEL

Selection
Service

19

The Notifier

In This Chapter:

Basic Concepts 353
    Mainline Input Handling 353
    Event-driven Input Handling 354
Functions of the Notifier 354
How the Notifier Works 354
    Restrictions 355
What is a Notifier Client? 356
Signal Handling 357
    Signals to Avoid 357
    A Replacement for signal() 358
    Timers 360
    Handling SIGTERM 364
    Handling SIGCHLD 364
Client Events 366
    Posting Client Events 366
    Posting with an Argument 367
    Posting Destroy Events 368
    Delivery Time of Destroy Events 369
Receiving Client Events 369
Reading and Writing through File Descriptors 370
    Reading Files 371
    Reading and Writing on Pipes 373
Interposition 377
    Uses of Interposition 378
    Interface to Interposition 378
    An Interposition Example 379
    Interposing on Resize Events 380
    Modifying a Frame's Destruction 381
Notifier Control 384
    Implicit Dispatching 385
    Explicit Dispatching 387
Error Codes 388
Issues 389

Notifier

19
The Notifier

In this chapter, we look at the Notifier in fuller detail, discussing its role in processing events for an XView application.

19.1 Basic Concepts

The Notifier maintains the flow of control in an application. To understand the basic concepts of the Notifier, we must distinguish between two different styles of input handling, *mainline* input and *event-driven* input, and consider how they affect where the flow of control resides within a program.

19.1.1 Mainline Input Handling

The traditional type of input handling of most text-based applications is mainline-based and input-driven. The flow of control resides in the main routine and the program *blocks* when it expects input. That is to say, no other portion of the program may be executed while the program is waiting for input. For example, in a mainline-driven application, a C programmer will use fgets() or getchar() to wait for characters that the user types. Based on the user's input, the program chooses an action to take. Sometimes, that action requires more input, so the application calls getchar() again. The program does not return to the main routine until the processing for the current input is done.

The tight control represented by this form of input handling is the easiest to program since you have control at all times of what to expect from the user and you can control the direction the application goes. There is only one source of input—the keyboard—and the user can only respond to one interface element at a time. A user's responses are predictable in the sense that you know that the user is going to type *something*, even if you do not know what it is.

Notifier

19.1.2 Event-driven Input Handling

Windowing systems are designed such that many sources of input are available to the user at any given time. In addition to the keyboard, there are the mouse and perhaps other input devices. Each keystroke and mouse movement causes an *event* that the application might consider. Further, there are other sources of events such as the window system itself and other processes. Another aspect of event-driven input handling is that you are not guaranteed to have any predictable sequence of events from the user. That is, a user can position the mouse on an object that receives text as input. Before the user is done typing, the user can move the mouse to another window and select on a panel button of some sort. The application cannot (and should not) expect the user to type in window *A* first, then move to window *B* and select the button. A well-written program should expect input from any window to happen at any time.

19.2 Functions of the Notifier

The Notifier is used to do any of the following:

- Handle *software interrupts*—specifically, UNIX signals such as SIGINT or SIGCONT.

- Notice state changes in processes that your process has spawned (e.g., a child process that has died).

- Read and write through file descriptors (e.g., files, pipes and sockets).

- Receive notification of the expiration of timers so that you can regularly flash a caret or display animation.

- Extend, modify or monitor XView Notifier clients (e.g., noticing when a frame is opened, closed or about to be destroyed.)

- Use a non-notification-based control structure while running under XView (e.g., porting programs to XView).

The Notifier also has provisions, to a limited degree, to allow programs to run in the Notifier environment without inverting their control structure.

19.3 How the Notifier Works

Up until now, we have been saying that you should register an event handler for objects when they want to be notified of certain events such as mouse motion or selection or keyboard input. What you may not have been aware of is that you are indirectly registering these event handlers with the *Notifier*. When you specify *callbacks* or *notify procedures*, the XView object specified is said to be the *client* of the Notifier. Look at the following code:

```
    extern void my_event_handler();

xv_set(canvas,
    CANVAS_PAINTWINDOW_ATTRS,
        WIN_CONSUME_X_EVENT_MASK,   ButtonPressMask | KeyPressMask,
        WIN_EVENT_PROC,             my_event_handler,
        NULL,
    NULL);
```

In the above code, each paint window of the canvas becomes a client of the Notifier.*

Generally stated, the Notifier detects events in which its clients have expressed an interest and dispatches these events to the proper clients in a predictable order. In the X Window System, events are delivered to the application by the X server. In XView, it is the Notifier that receives the events from the server and dispatches them to its clients. After the client's notify procedure processes the event, control is returned back to the Notifier.

19.3.1 Restrictions

The Notifier imposes some restrictions on its clients. Designers should be aware of these restrictions when developing software to work in the Notifier environment. These restrictions exist so that the application and the Notifier do not interfere with each other. More precisely, since the Notifier is multiplexing access to user process resources, the application needs to respect this effort so as not to violate the sharing mechanism.

For example, a client should not call signal(3). The Notifier is catching signals on behalf of its clients. If a client sets up its own signal handler, then the Notifier will never notice the signal. The program should call notify_set_signal_func() instead of signal(3). (See Section 19.5, "Signal Handling.")

System Calls to Avoid

Assuming an environment with multiple clients and an unknown notifier usage pattern, you should not use any of the following system calls or C library routines:

signal(3)   The Notifier is catching signals on the behalf of its clients. If you set up your own signal handler over the one that the Notifier has set up, then the Notifier will never notice the signal.

sigvec(2)   The same applies for sigvec(2) as does for signal(3) above.

setitimer(2)   The Notifier is managing two of the process's interval timers on the behalf of its many clients. If you access an interval timer directly, the Notifier could miss a timeout. Use notify_set_itimer_func() instead of setitimer(2).

---

*CANVAS_PAINTWINDOW_ATTRS tells the CANVAS package to register the input mask and callback routine for each of its paint windows.

alarm(3)	Because alarm(3) sets the process's interval timer directly, the same applies here as setitimer(2), above.
getitimer(2)	When using a Notifier-managed interval timer, you should call notify_itimer_value() to get its current status. Otherwise, you can get inaccurate results.
wait3(2)	The Notifier notices child process state changes on behalf of its clients. If you do your own wait3(2), then the Notifier may never notice the change in a child process or you may get a change of state for a child process in which you have no interest. Use notify_set_wait3_func() instead of wait3(2).
wait(2)	The same applies for wait(2) as does for wait3(2), above.
ioctl(2) (..., FIONBIO, ...)	This call sets the blocking status of a file descriptor. The Notifier needs to know the blocking status of a file descriptor in order to determine if there is activity on it. fcntl(2) has an analogous request that should be used instead of ioctl(2).
ioctl(2) (..., FIOASYNC, ...)	This call controls a file descriptor's asynchronous IO (input/output) mode setting. The Notifier needs to know this mode in order to determine if there is activity on it. fcntl(2) has an analogous request that should be used instead of ioctl(2).
system(3)	In the SunOS, this function calls signal(3) and wait(2). Hence, you should avoid using this for the reasons mentioned above.

19.4 What is a Notifier Client?

A *client* of the Notifier is anything that has registered a callback routine with it. In XView, a client is an object such as a canvas or panel that you have created using xv_create(). Typically, most of the event registration happens at the time such clients are created. However, to the Notifier, a client is nothing more than an ID that distinguishes it from all other Notifier clients. Thus, you could identify a client using a number such as "43" or the address of an object as in &foo. XView objects are commonly used as Notifier clients because xv_create() returns a unique handle to an object that has been allocated dynamically.

The client ID which is of type Notify_client as declared in <xview/notify.h>.

```
Notify_func      func();
Frame            frame;

frame = (Frame)xv_create(NULL, FRAME, NULL);

notify_interpose_destroy_func(frame, func);
```

Up until the call to notify_interpose_destroy_func(), the frame object may not have been registered as a client to the Notifier. Internally, the Notifier package looks up in its table of clients whether there is any other client that is using that identifier (the frame handle is the identifier). If so, the Notifier operation specified affects that client. Otherwise, a new client is allocated and the frame handle is also used as a handle to the new Notifier client.

The client can unregister the interposition by specifying NOTIFY_FUNC_NULL as the func parameter to the function. The same method is used to unregister all clients with the Notifier, not just interposers. If there are no more registrations involved with the client, the client is removed from the Notifier's list of clients.

Notifier clients are *not* XView objects for you to create or manipulate using xv_create() or xv_set(). In fact, the Notifier is completely independent of XView and can be used in applications that do not even use XView objects.

19.5 Signal Handling

Signals are UNIX software interrupts. The Notifier multiplexes access to the UNIX signal mechanism. A Notifier client may ask to be notified that a UNIX signal occurred either when it is received (asynchronously) and/or later during normal processing (synchronously).

Clients may define and register a signal event handler to respond to any UNIX signal desired. However, some of the signals that you might catch in a traditional UNIX program should instead be caught by the Notifier.

CAUTION

Clients of the Notifier should not directly catch any UNIX signals using signal(3) or sigvec(2). There are critical stages of event reading and dispatching that, if interrupted, the program could jump to another location and interrupt the communication protocol between the X server and the application.

Exceptions to this are noted later in this section.

19.5.1 Signals to Avoid

Clients should not have to catch any of the following signals (even via notify_set_signal_func() described below). If you are, you are probably utilizing the Notifier inappropriately. The Notifier catches these signals itself under a variety of circumstances and handles them appropriately.

SIGALRM   Caught by the Notifier's interval timer manager. Use notify_set_itimer_func() instead.

SIGVTALRM   The same applies for SIGVTALRM as does for SIGALRM above.

SIGTERM   Caught by the Notifier so that it can tell its clients that the process is going away. Use notify_set_destroy_func() if that is why you are catching SIGTERM.

Notifier

SIGCHLD	Caught by the Notifier so that it can do child process management. Use `notify_set_wait3_func()` instead.
SIGIO	Caught by the Notifier so that it can manage its file descriptors that are running in asynchronous IO mode. Use `notify_set_input_func()` or `notify_set_output_func()` if you want to know when there is activity on your file descriptor.
SIGURG	Caught by the Notifier so that it can dispatch exception activity on a file descriptor to its clients. Use `notify_set_exception_func()` if you are looking for out-of-band communications when using a socket.

The last two signals in the list are considered advanced topics and are not covered in this book.

19.5.2 A Replacement for signal()

Instead of using `signal()` to catch signals delivered by UNIX, you should register a signal event handler by calling `notify_set_signal_func()`. This function allows you to have a function called when a specified signal is generated. The function takes the form:

```
Notify_func
notify_set_signal_func(client, signal_func, signal, when)
    Notify_client      client;
    Notify_func        signal_func;
    int                signal;
    Notify_signal_mode when;
```

The `signal_func` is the function to call when the signal described by `sig` occurs.*

The `when` parameter is either `NOTIFY_SYNC` or `NOTIFY_ASYNC`. `NOTIFY_SYNC` causes notification during normal processing; that is, the delivering of the signal is delayed so as to avoid interrupting Xlib protocol communication between the X server and the application. When it is safe to do so, your `signal_func` function is called at which time you can display a notice, exit, or jump to another place in the program without risking a break in the Xlib protocol between the server and your application. Typically, there is a very short time between the signal delivery and the notification of the signal to your callback routine; signal delivery is virtually as instantaneous as it is when using `signal()`.

`NOTIFY_ASYNC` causes notification immediately as the signal is received—this mode mimics the UNIX `signal`(3) semantics.

---

*See *<signal.h>* for a list of signals and definitions.

CAUTION

When using asynchronous signals, your routine might set a variable, a condition, or a flag indicating that the signal was received, or change any internal state to your program. Do *not* make any XView, Xlib or Notifier calls or any function that might manipulate any XView data structures. Also, do not call `longjmp()` or `setjmp()` as these calls may set the program state inconsistently with what the protocol might be expecting.

`notify_set_signal_func()` returns a pointer to the function that was installed before you set the new function. You should use this to reset the function if you want to unregister your installed function.

When the specified signal occurs, your `signal_func` is called:

```
Notify_value
signal_func(client, sig, when)
    Notify_client      client;
    int                sig;
    Notify_signal_mode when;
```

The parameters to the signal handler are not the same parameters that are given to a signal handler specified using the call to `signal`(3). However, it is not advised to use either one except in unusual circumstances. As a general rule, you should use `notify_set_signal_func()` to do all signal handling. If you want the signal *code* or *context* from the signal that was generated (two parameters that are passed to a normal UNIX signal handler), you can use:

```
int
notify_get_signal_code()

struct sigcontext *
notify_get_signal_context()
```

These two functions take no parameters—they return the signal code and context (respectively) of the last signal generated. If you wish to save these values, they should be copied.

Using the Notifier, you can catch any signal with the exception of SIGKILL and SIGSTOP, since these signals cannot be caught by a UNIX application. Attempting to do so generates an error. An example of how common signal handling is done is shown below:

```
#include <xview/notify.h>

...
extern Notify_value sigint_func();

notify_set_signal_func(frame, sigint_func, SIGINT, NOTIFY_SYNC);
...
```

Notifier

```
Notify_value
sigint_func(client, sig, when)
Notify_client client;
int sig;
{
    puts("received interrupt -- exiting");
    xv_destroy_safe(frame);
    return NOTIFY_DONE;
}
```

The return value of your signal handler tells whether you handled the signal or ignored it.*

19.5.3 Timers

One specific type of signal is a *timer*. Timers can be set up to call a routine after the passage of a specified amount of time.† This routine may cause a caret to flash on regular intervals or allow a clock application to change the time display. The timer is handled differently from other signals so that multiple timers can be installed for various clients (say a flashing caret and a clock in the same application).

Because the Notifier handles timers, you should not make calls to such routines as sleep() or setitimer(). As pointed out already, you should not attempt to use signal() to catch SIGALRM or SIGVTALRM to trap timer-signals. To set timers and be notified when they expire, use notify_set_itimer_func(). The form of the call is:

```
Notify_func
notify_set_itimer_func(client, timer_func, which, value, ovalue)
    Notify_client   client;
    Notify_func     timer_func;
    int             which;
    struct itimerval *value, *ovalue;
```

The parameter which indicates which type of timer you want to use. Its value is either ITIMER_REAL or ITIMER_VIRTUAL.

The value parameter is a pointer to an itimerval that indicates the initial timeout and an interval timeout. The interval timeout is what is used after the initial timeout times out. If the initial timeout is 0, then the timer is not called regardless of the value of the interval timer. The granularity of the timer is dependent on your hardware architecture and operating system. It is perhaps unwise to assume that you will be notified as frequently as 30 milliseconds or less. Some cases may have higher minimum limits—your mileage may vary.

The ovalue is also a pointer to an itimerval structure. If there was a previous timeout that has yet to expire, this structure will have that time filled in. You may pass a NULL as ovalue if you are not interested in this value.

The timer_func parameter is the function to call when the timer expires. notify_set_itimer_func() returns the function that was previously set for this client (see notify_set_signal_func above). The form of the timer_func is:

---

*Currently, the return value is ignored.

†Event processing still takes place during this time segment.

```
        void
        timer_func(client, which)
            Notify_client client;
            int            which;
```

Example 19-1 demonstrates one possible use of notify_set_itimer_func(). The program displays an animation of several icons that are stored in the *icon* font. When animating, the next icon in a sequence is displayed using XDrawString() (since the icon is part of the font). The slider controls the rate at which the next icon is drawn. If the slider is set to 0, the animation stops. The slider is a panel item whose callback routine makes calls to notify_set_itimer_func() to set the timer to the new value or to turn it off by setting the function to NOTIFY_FUNC_NULL.

Example 19-1. The animate.c program

```
/*
 * animate.c -- use glyphs from the "icon" font distributed with XView
 * to do frame-by-frame animation.
 */
#include <stdio.h>
#include <ctype.h>
#include <X11/X.h>
#include <X11/Xlib.h>
#include <X11/Xos.h>                    /* for <sys/time.h> */
#include <xview/xview.h>
#include <xview/panel.h>
#include <xview/font.h>
#include <xview/notify.h>

Frame           frame;
Display         *dpy;
GC              gc;
Window          canvas_win;
Notify_value    animate();
struct itimerval timer;

#define ArraySize(x)   (sizeof(x)/sizeof(x[0]))
char *horses[] = { "N", "O", "P", "Q", "R" };
char *boys[] = { " 07", " 05", " 07", " 10" };
char *men[] = { "\\", "]", "Y", "Z", "[" };
char *eyes[] = {
    "2", "5", "4", "3", "4", "5",
    "2", "1", "0", "/", "0", "1"
};

int max_images = ArraySize(horses);
char **images = horses;
int cnt;

main(argc, argv)
int     argc;
char    *argv[];
{
    Panel           panel;
    Canvas          canvas;
    XGCValues       gcvalues;
    Xv_Font         _font;
    XFontStruct     *font;
```

Example 19-1. The animate.c program (continued)

```
    void            adjust_speed(), change_glyph();
    extern void exit();

    xv_init(XV_INIT_ARGC_PTR_ARGV, &argc, argv, NULL);

    frame = (Frame)xv_create(XV_NULL, FRAME,
        FRAME_LABEL,             argv[0],
        FRAME_SHOW_FOOTER,       TRUE,
        NULL);

    panel = (Panel)xv_create(frame, PANEL,
        PANEL_LAYOUT,            PANEL_VERTICAL,
        NULL);
    xv_create(panel, PANEL_BUTTON,
        PANEL_LABEL_STRING,      "Quit",
        PANEL_NOTIFY_PROC,       exit,
        NULL);
    xv_create(panel, PANEL_SLIDER,
        PANEL_LABEL_STRING,      "Millisecs Between Frames",
        PANEL_VALUE,             0,
        PANEL_MAX_VALUE,         120,
        PANEL_NOTIFY_PROC,       adjust_speed,
        NULL);
    xv_create(panel, PANEL_CHOICE,
        PANEL_LABEL_STRING,      "Glyphs",
        PANEL_LAYOUT,            PANEL_HORIZONTAL,
        PANEL_DISPLAY_LEVEL,     PANEL_ALL,
        PANEL_CHOICE_STRINGS,    "Horse", "Man", "Boy", "Eye", NULL,
        PANEL_NOTIFY_PROC,       change_glyph,
        NULL);
    window_fit(panel);

    canvas = (Canvas)xv_create(frame, CANVAS,
        XV_WIDTH,                64,
        XV_HEIGHT,               64,
        CANVAS_X_PAINT_WINDOW,   TRUE,
        NULL);
    canvas_win = (Window)xv_get(canvas_paint_window(canvas), XV_XID);

    window_fit(frame);

    dpy = (Display *)xv_get(frame, XV_DISPLAY);
    _font = (Xv_Font)xv_find(frame, FONT,
        FONT_NAME,       "icon",
        NULL);
    font = (XFontStruct *)xv_get(_font, FONT_INFO);

    gcvalues.font = font->fid;
    gcvalues.foreground = BlackPixel(dpy, DefaultScreen(dpy));
    gcvalues.background = WhitePixel(dpy, DefaultScreen(dpy));
    gcvalues.graphics_exposures = False;
    gc = XCreateGC(dpy, RootWindow(dpy, DefaultScreen(dpy)),
        GCForeground | GCBackground | GCFont | GCGraphicsExposures,
        &gcvalues);

    xv_main_loop(frame);
}

void
change_glyph(item, value)
```

Example 19-1. The animate.c program (continued)

```
Panel_item item;
int value;
{
    cnt = 0;
    if (value == 0) {
        max_images = ArraySize(horses);
        images = horses;
    } else if (value == 1) {
        max_images = ArraySize(men);
        images = men;
    } else if (value == 2) {
        max_images = ArraySize(boys);
        images = boys;
    } else if (value == 3) {
        max_images = ArraySize(eyes);
        images = eyes;
    }
    XClearWindow(dpy, canvas_win);
}

/*ARGSUSED*/
Notify_value
animate()
{
    XDrawImageString(dpy, canvas_win, gc, 5, 40, images[cnt], 1);
    cnt = (cnt + 1) % max_images;

    return NOTIFY_DONE;
}

void
adjust_speed(item, value)
Panel_item item;
int value;
{
    if (value > 0) {
        timer.it_value.tv_usec = (value + 20) * 1000;
        timer.it_interval.tv_usec = (value + 20) * 1000;
        notify_set_itimer_func(frame, animate,
            ITIMER_REAL, &timer, NULL);
    } else
        /* turn it off */
        notify_set_itimer_func(frame, NOTIFY_FUNC_NULL,
            ITIMER_REAL, NULL, NULL);
}
```

Figure 19-1 shows one frame of an animated horse sequence, produced by *animate.c*.

Notifier

Figure 19-1. Output of animate.c

19.5.4 Handling SIGTERM

The SIGTERM signal is a software *terminate* signal. If you receive a SIGTERM signal, another process is telling your application to terminate. Rather than handling this signal using notify_set_signal_func(), you could use notify_set_destroy_func(). It takes the form:

```
Notify_func
notify_set_destroy_func(client, destroy_func)
    Notify_client   client;
    Notify_func     destroy_func;
```

Like the other Notifier functions, this one also returns the previously set function that was handling this signal. Note that this function only interprets SIGTERM—it does not get called if the application chooses to kill itself by calling either exit() or xv_destroy() on the base frame or if the user selects the *quit* option from the title bar (provided by the OPEN LOOK window manager).

19.5.5 Handling SIGCHLD

Let's say that you want to fork a process to run another program. UNIX requires that you perform some housekeeping of that process. The minimum housekeeping required is to notice when that process dies and reap it. Normally, the system call wait() is used to do this. By default, wait() will block until a spawned process has terminated—when wait() returns, it has information about the process that died. Rather than have the application sit and *wait* for a spawned (child) process to die, it should continue processing events and be notified automatically when the process dies.

To handle this, you can register a `wait3` event handler* that the Notifier will call whenever a child process changes state (dies) by calling the following:

```
Notify_func
notify_set_wait3_func(client, wait3_func, pid)
    static Notify_client client;
    Notify_func            wait3_func;
    int                    pid;
```

In the above call, the `pid` identifies the particular child process that the client wants to wait for. The `wait3_func` is the function to call when that child has died. Another reason that an application should use `notify_set_wait3_func()` is due to the semantics of the `wait3(2)` system call. `wait3(2)` will return with status about *any* process that has changed state. Thus, if two clients are managing different child processes, they should hear only about their own process. The Notifier keeps straight which client is managing which process.

Reaping Dead Processes

Many clients using child process control simply need to perform the required reaping after a child process dies. These clients can use the predefined `notify_default_wait3()` as their `wait3` event handler. This default handler does nothing but return—the fact that it handled the event is good enough for UNIX. The Notifier automatically removes a dead process's `wait3` event handler.

The code segment in Example 19-2 demonstrates how a *wait3* handler might be set up.

Example 19-2. Demonstrating a wait3 handler

```
#include <xview/notify.h>
#include <sys/wait.h>
#include <sys/time.h>
#include <sys/resource.h>

/* canvas created in another part of the program */
extern Canvas canvas;

/* declare our own wait3 handler */
Notify_value my_wait3_handler();

fork_it(argv)
char *argv[];
{
    int pid;

    /* here's the fork -- two processes are going to execute code
     * from this point down.
     */
    switch (pid = fork()) {
        case -1:
            perror("fork");
            return;
```

---

*The name *wait3 event* originates from the `wait3(2)` system call. There are other forms of *wait* including `wait()`, `wait2()` and `wait4()`. Since `wait4()` is not generally available, `wait3()` is the most efficient form of the *wait* functionality.

Example 19-2. Demonstrating a wait3 handler (continued)

```
        case 0: /* this is the child of the fork -- the new process */
            /* execute the specified command */
            execvp(*argv, argv); /* execvp doesn't return unless failed */
            perror("execvp");
            _exit(0); /* don't call exit() -- man exec() for info */
        default: /* this is the parent -- the original process */
            /* Register a wait3 event handler */
            (void) notify_set_wait3_func(canvas, my_wait3_handler, pid);
    }
    /* parent returns -- child is happily processing away */
}

static Notify_value
my_wait3_handler(me, pid, status, rusage)
    Notify_client   me;
    int             pid;
    union wait      *status;
    struct rusage *rusage;
{

    if (WIFEXITED(*status)) {
        /* Child process exited with return code */
        printf("child exited with status %d\n", status->w_retcode);
        /* Tell the Notifier that you handled this event */
        return (NOTIFY_DONE);
    }
    /* Tell the Notifier that you ignored this event */
    return (NOTIFY_IGNORED);
}
```

Example 19-2 is a simple example for demonstration only. There are other things to consider for a complete and *proper* method for forking new processes. See Section 19.8, "Reading and Writing through File Descriptors," for a full example program that uses `notify_set_wait3_func()`.

19.6 Client Events

Client events are used by the application to communicate with clients of the Notifier. Using this mechanism, you can have any portion of your application send an event to itself that the Notifier will dispatch to any of its clients that have expressed interest in that particular client event. Thus, these events may be considered as *broadcast messages* for the entire application.

The process for the delivery of client events is similar to that of signals described above. However, because the entire process happens in the application, more control can be maintained by the Notifier. For example, optional parameters (extra information) may be passed to client message event handlers.

The need and use of client events is far reaching and is utilized frequently by the internals to XView. Use is also available by the application—say the application wants to notify all interested Notifier clients that input has been received from a pipe (see Section 19.8,

"Reading and Writing through File Descriptors"); once data has been read, the application can *post* the data to the Notifier.

From the Notifier's point of view, *client events* are defined and generated by the application. Client events are not interpreted by the Notifier in any way; the Notifier does not *detect* client events, it just detects X events. However, when client events are *posted* to the Notifier, it dispatches these events to the receiving client's *event handler*.

19.6.1 Posting Client Events

A client event may be posted with the Notifier at any time. The poster of a client event may suggest to the Notifier when to deliver the event, but this is only a hint. The Notifier will see to it that it is delivered at an appropriate time (more on this below). The call to post a client event is:

```
typedef char * Notify_event;

Notify_error
notify_post_event(client, event, when_hint)
    Notify_client      client;
    Notify_event       event;
    Notify_event_type  when_hint;
```

The `client` handle from `notify_set_event_func()` is passed to `notify_post_event()`. `event` is defined and interpreted solely by the `client`. A return code of `NOTIFY_OK` indicates that the notification has been posted. Other values indicate an error condition. `NOTIFY_UNKNOWN_CLIENT` indicates that `client` is unknown to the Notifier. `NOTIFY_NO_CONDITION` indicates that `client` has no client event handler registered with the Notifier.

Usually it is during the call to `notify_post_event()` that the client event handler is called. Sometimes, however, the notification is queued up for later delivery. The Notifier chooses between these two possibilities by noting which kinds of client event handlers `client` has registered, whether it is safe, and what the value of `when_hint` is. Here are the cases broken down by the kind of client event handlers `client` has registered:

Immediate only   If `when_hint` is `NOTIFY_SAFE` or `NOTIFY_IMMEDIATE`, the event is delivered immediately.

Safe only   If `when_hint` is `NOTIFY_SAFE` or `NOTIFY_IMMEDIATE`, the event is delivered when it is safe.

Both safe and immediate
    A client may have both an immediate client event handler as well as a safe client event handler. If `when_hint` is `NOTIFY_SAFE`, then the notification is delivered to the safe client event handler when it is safe. If `when_hint` is `NOTIFY_IMMEDIATE`, then the notification is delivered to the immediate client event handler right away. If the immediate client event handler returns `NOTIFY_IGNORED`, then the same notification will be delivered to the safe client event handler when it is safe.

Notifier

19.6.2 Posting with an Argument

XView posts a fixed field structure with each event. Sometimes additional data must be passed with an event. For instance, when the scrollbar posts an event to its owner to do a scroll, the scrollbar's handle is passed as an argument along with the event. `notify_post_event_and_arg()` provides this argument passing mechanism (see below).

When posting a client event, there is the possibility of delivery being delayed. In the case of XView, the event being posted is a pointer to a structure. The Notifier avoids an invalid (dangling) pointer reference by copying the event if delivery is delayed. It calls routines the client supplies to copy the event information and later to free up the storage the copy uses. `notify_post_event_and_arg()` provides this storage management mechanism.

```
Notify_error
notify_post_event_and_arg(client, event, when_hint, arg,
                          copy_func, release_func)
    Notify_client        client;
    Notify_event         event;
    Notify_event_type    when_hint;
    Notify_arg           arg;
    Notify_copy          copy_func;
    Notify_release       release_func;

typedef caddr_t Notify_arg;

typedef Notify_arg (*Notify_copy)();
#define NOTIFY_COPY_NULL    ((Notify_copy)0)

typedef void (*Notify_release)();
#define NOTIFY_RELEASE_NULL  ((Notify_release)0)
```

`copy_func()` is called to copy `arg` (and, optionally, `event`) when `event` and `arg` needed to be queued for later delivery. `release_func()` is called to release the storage allocated during the copy call when `event` and `arg` were no longer needed by the Notifier.

Any of `arg`, `copy_func()`, or `release_func()` may be NULL. If `copy_func` is not NOTIFY_COPY_NULL and `arg` is NULL, then `copy_func()` is called anyway. This allows `event` the opportunity to be copied because `copy_func()` takes a pointer to `event`. The pointed to event may be replaced as a side affect of the copy call. The same applies to a NOTIFY_RELEASE_NULL release function with a NULL `arg` argument.

The `copy()` and `release()` routines are client-dependent so you must write them yourself. Their calling sequences follow:

```
Notify_arg
copy_func(client, arg, event_ptr)
    Notify_client  client;
    Notify_arg     arg;
    Notify_event   *event_ptr;

void
release_func(client, arg, event)
    Notify_client  client;
    Notify_arg     arg;
    Notify_event   event;
```

19.6.3 Posting Destroy Events

When a destroy notification is set, the Notifier also sets up a synchronous signal condition for SIGTERM that will generate a DESTROY_PROCESS_DEATH destroy notification. Otherwise, a destroy function will not be called automatically by the Notifier. One or two (depending on whether the client can veto your notification) explicit calls to notify_post_destroy() need be made.

```
Notify_error
notify_post_destroy(client, status, when)
    Notify_client        client;
    Destroy_status       status;
    Notify_event_type    when;
```

NOTIFY_INVAL is returned if status or when is not defined. After notifying a client to destroy itself, all references to client are purged from the Notifier.

19.6.4 Delivery Time of Destroy Events

Unlike a client-event notification, the Notifier does not try to detect when it is safe to post a destroy notification. Thus, a destroy notification can come at any time. It is up to the good judgement of a caller of notify_post_destroy() or notify_die() (described in the Section "Notifier Control") to make the call at a time that a client is not likely to be in the middle of accessing its data structures.

If status is DESTROY_CHECKING and when is NOTIFY_IMMEDIATE then notify_post_destroy() may return NOTIFY_DESTROY_VETOED if the client does not want to go away. See Section 19.9.5, "Modifying a Frame's Destruction," for details on these values.

Often you want to tell a client to go away at a safe time. This implies that delivery of the destroy event will be delayed, in which case the return value of notify_post_destroy() ca not be NOTIFY_DESTROY_VETOED because the client has not been asked yet. To get around this problem, the Notifier will flush the destroy event of a checking/destroy pair of events if the checking phase is vetoed. Thus, a common idiom is:

```
(void) notify_post_destroy(client, DESTROY_CHECKING, NOTIFY_SAFE);
(void) notify_post_destroy(client, DESTROY_CLEANUP, NOTIFY_SAFE);
```

19.7 Receiving Client Events

To register a client event handler call, use:

```
Notify_func
notify_set_event_func(client, event_func, when)
    Notify_client       client;
    Notify_func         event_func;
    Notify_event_type   when;

typedef enum notify_event_type {
    NOTIFY_SAFE       = 0,
    NOTIFY_IMMEDIATE  = 1,
} Notify_event_type;
```

The when parameter indicates whether the event handler will accept notifications only when it is safe NOTIFY_SAFE) (or at less restrictive times NOTIFY_IMMEDIATE).

The calling sequence of a client event handler is:

```
Notify_value
event_func(client, event, arg, when)
    Notify_client       client;
    Notify_event        event;
    Notify_arg          arg;
    Notify_event_type   when;
```

The client is the client that called notify_set_event_func(). The event is passed through from notify_post_event(). The arg and event parameters are completely defined by the client. The types Notify_arg and Notify_event are of type caddr_t—a generic pointer type. The when parameter is the actual situation in which event is being delivered. It may have the value NOTIFY_SAFE or NOTIFY_IMMEDIATE and may be different from when_hint of notify_post_event().

The return value is one of NOTIFY_DONE or NOTIFY_IGNORED.

19.8 Reading and Writing through File Descriptors

The Notifier is set up for testing if there is input pending on file descriptors as well as testing whether file descriptors are available to accept data for writing. The file descriptors can represent files, pipes and sockets. System calls such as read() or write() may be used on any of these file descriptors.

In an event-driven system, the application cannot wait for data to be read—instead it is better for the system to notify the application when data can be read. System calls such as read() will *block* if there is no input to be read. That is, read() waits until there is something to read before it returns. If your application is blocking on a read, then it cannot process events that the user may be generating such as selecting a panel button. Rather than blocking on a call to read(), the Notifier can inform you when there is input ready on that file descriptor so that when you finally call read(), it immediately returns.

To handle this, the Notifier provides functions such as `notify_set_input_func()` and `notify_set_output_func()` to test whether a file descriptor has data to be read or is ready for writing. These functions inform you of the status of file descriptors whether they are files, pipes, or sockets.*

```
Notify_func
notify_set_input_func(client, input_func, fd)
    Notify_client    client;
    Notify_func      input_func;
    int              fd;
Notify_func
notify_set_output_func(client, output_func, fd)
    Notify_client    client;
    Notify_func      output_func;
    int              fd;
```

The `input_func()` is your function that is called whenever the file descriptor (`fd`) has data to be read.† The `output_func()` is a function that is called whenever the file descriptor (`fd`) is ready to receive data.

Generally, file descriptors open for writing are always ready to receive data, so this function may not be as widely used as the input function case. However, it is important if you are writing to a pipe where another process is probably on the other side of the pipe. Pipes have buffers which, when full, will not accept any more data on them until the process on the other side of the pipe reads the data written so far (thus, emptying the buffer). If the process on the other side of the pipe is slow in reading the data you have written to it, then you may need to use `notify_set_output_func()` so you can be notified when the pipe is ready to have more data written to it.

The `input_func()` and `output_func()` take the following form:

```
Notify_value
func(client, fd)
    Notify_client    client;
    int              fd;
```

19.8.1 Reading Files

Our first example demonstrates how `notify_set_input_func()` can be used to read data from a file. The program is quite simple; it does not bother using any XView objects such as frames or canvases. Because of this, the program makes use of `notify_start()`, which is covered in Section 19.10, "Notifier Control."

---

*`notify_set_exception_func()` is also available for determining if out-of-band data is available on a socket, but it is not covered in this book.
†Exceptions to this are discussed in Section 19.8.1, "Reading Files."

Notifier

Example 19-3. The notify_input.c program

```
/*
 * notify_input.c -- use notify_set_input_func to monitor the state of
 * a file.  The notifier is running and checking the file descriptors
 * of the opened files associated with the command line args.  The
 * routine installed by notify_set_input_func() is called whenever
 * there is data to be read.  When there is no more data to be read
 * for that file, the input function is unregistered.  When all files
 * have been read, notify_start() returns and the program exits.
 */
#include <stdio.h>
#include <sys/ioctl.h>
#include <xview/notify.h>

main(argc, argv)
char *argv[];
{
    Notify_value    read_it();
    Notify_client   client = (Notify_client)10101; /* arbitrary */
    FILE            *fp;

    while (*++argv)
        if (!(fp = fopen(*argv, "r")))
            perror(*argv);
        else {
            (void) notify_set_input_func(client, read_it, fileno(fp));
            client++; /* next client is new/unique */
        }

    /* loops continuously */
    notify_start();
}

/*
 * read_it() is called whenever there is input to be read.  Actually,
 * it's called continuously, so check to see if there is input to be
 * read first.
 */
Notify_value
read_it(client, fd)
Notify_client   client;
int fd;
{
    char buf[BUFSIZ];
    int bytes, i;

    if (ioctl(fd, FIONREAD, &bytes) == -1 || bytes == 0)
        (void) notify_set_input_func(client, NOTIFY_FUNC_NULL, fd);
    else
        do
            if ((i = read(fd, buf, sizeof buf)) > 0)
                (void) write(1, buf, i);
        while (i > 0 && bytes -= i > 0);
    return NOTIFY_DONE;
}
```

The comments in this sample program describe what is going on up front. However, behind the scenes, there are interesting things happening.

The first thing you might notice is that the *clients* used in the Notifier start at 10101 and, for each file on the command line, the client is incremented by one. Remember, the client is an arbitrary identifier and can be any unique value. Since there are no other clients of the Notifier, we know that 10101 is going to be unique.

The function read_it() is installed to read data from the files given on the command line. The first thing that read_it() does is check to see if there is data to be read. The ioctl() call returns the number of bytes to read in the bytes variable. If there is data to be read, then read() is used to read buffers (of size BUFSIZ) until it has read all the bytes pending. This continues until the program has read the entire file. Once this happens, the ioctl() call will return that there are no bytes to read. Normally, it would return -1 indicating that the end of file has been reached. However, the Notifier has modified the state of the file descriptor for internal purposes (to set nonblocking mode). When we have reached the end of the file, we unregister the client by calling notify_set_input_func() with a notify_func of NOTIFY_FUNC_NULL.

notify_input.c is not terribly interesting because you do not need to be notified of data to be read on a *file*; you can just open the file, read it till EOF and then close it. But if you know that the file is going to have data continuously added to it, you might want to be informed when there is new data to be read and then print it out.

This can be accomplished by not unregistering the input function with the Notifier when there is no data to be read. Unfortunately, your function is going to be called continuously whether there is new data to be read or not. This is true *only for file descriptors that represent files* and is not the case for pipes.

19.8.2 Reading and Writing on Pipes

A far more interesting and likely situation is for an application to execute another program while being able to send data to the program and read the output from it. The best way to handle this problem is to follow these steps:

- Setup a pipe for each stream (such as stdin and stdout). This is done using the pipe() system call.

- fork() a new process. The child will execute the program (using execvp()) and have its input and output redirected to the appropriate ends of the pipes (using dup2()).

- The parent registers *input* and *output* functions to read and write from the "other" ends of the pipes (using notify_set_input_func()). Also, the parent calls notify_set_wait3_func() (discussed earlier).

The example program used to demonstrate this capability is a little longer, but it is still rather simple. It follows the steps outlined above and is the minimum work needed to accomplish the task of spawning a new process. Again, no XView objects are created to keep the code short and simple; the existence of XView objects would not affect the program in any way.

Notifier

The way to run this program is to specify a command on the command line of the program. For example:

```
% ntfy_pipe cat
```

Remember, there are *two* processes involved here: the parent process (ntfy_pipe) and the child process (cat). Both programs read from their respective stdin and write to their own stdout. However, because the child process (cat) was spawned off from the parent, we need to handle the IO (input/output) of the new process. After the call to fork(), its stdin and stdout must be redirected to the pipe that was set up before the fork. The parent, however, retains its IO—its stdin and stdout remain directed towards the window in which you typed the command.

Example 19-4. The ntfy_pipe.c program

```c
/*
 * notify_pipe.c -- fork and set up a pipe to read the IO from the
 * forked process.  The program to run is specified on the command
 * line.  The functions notify_set_input_func() and
 * notify_set_output_func() are used to install functions which read
 * and write to the process' stdin and stdout.
 * The program does not use any xview code -- just the notifier.
 */
#include <stdio.h>
#include <errno.h>
#include <sys/time.h>
#include <sys/types.h>
#include <sys/wait.h>
#include <sys/resource.h>
#include <sys/ioctl.h>
#include <xview/notify.h>

Notify_client client1 = (Notify_client)10;
Notify_client client2 = (Notify_client)11;

int pipe_io[2][2]; /* see diagram */
/*
 *                     [0]                              [1]
 *      child reads:  |========== pipe_io[0] ========| <- parent writes
 *    pipe_io[0][0]                                       pipe_io[0][1]
 *
 *      parent reads: |========== pipe_io[1] ========| <- child writes
 *    pipe_io[1][0]                                       pipe_io[1][1]
 *
 * The parent process reads the output of the child process by reading
 * pipe_io[1][0] because the child is writing to pipe_io[1][1].
 * The child process gets its input from pipe_io[0][0] because the
 * parent writes to pipe_io[0][1].  Thus, one process is reading from
 * one end of the pipe while the other is writing at the other end.
 */
main(argc, argv)
char *argv[];
{
    Notify_value        read_it(), write_it(), sigchldcatcher();
    int                 pid;
    FILE                *fp;

    if (!*++argv)
```

Example 19-4. The ntfy_pipe.c program (continued)

```
            puts("specify a program [w/args]"), exit(1);
    pipe(pipe_io[0]); /* set up input pipe */
    pipe(pipe_io[1]); /* set up output pipe */
    switch (pid = fork()) {
        case -1:
            close(pipe_io[0][0]);
            close(pipe_io[0][1]);
            close(pipe_io[1][0]);
            close(pipe_io[1][1]);
            perror("fork failed");
            exit(1);
        case  0: /* child */
         /* redirect child's stdin (0), stdout (1) and stderr(2) */
            dup2(pipe_io[0][0], 0);
            dup2(pipe_io[1][1], 1);
            dup2(pipe_io[1][1], 2);
            for (i = getdtablesize(); i > 2; i--)
                (void) close(i);
            for (i = 0; i < NSIG; i++)
                (void) signal(i, SIG_DFL);
            execvp(*argv, argv);
            if (errno == ENOENT)
                print("%s: command not found.\n", *argv);
            else
                perror(*argv);
            perror("execvp");
            _exit(-1);
        default: /* parent */
            close(pipe_io[0][0]); /* close unused portions of pipes */
            close(pipe_io[1][1]);
        }

    /* when the process outputs data, read it */
    notify_set_input_func(client1, read_it, pipe_io[1][0]);
    notify_set_wait3_func(client1, sigchldcatcher, pid);

    /* wait for user input -- then write data to pipe */
    notify_set_input_func(client2, write_it, 0);
    notify_set_wait3_func(client2, sigchldcatcher, pid);

    notify_start();
}
/*
 * callback routine for when there is data on the parent's stdin to
 * read.  Read it and then write the data to the child process via
 * the pipe.
 */
Notify_value
write_it(client, fd)
Notify_client    client;
int fd;
{
    char buf[BUFSIZ];
    int bytes, i;

    /* only write to pipe (child's stdin) if user typed anything */
```

Notifier

Example 19-4. The ntfy_pipe.c program (continued)

```
        if (ioctl(fd, FIONREAD, &bytes) == -1 || bytes == 0) {
            notify_set_input_func(client, NOTIFY_FUNC_NULL, pipe_io[0][1]);
            close(pipe_io[0][1]);
        } else
            while (bytes > 0) {
                if ((i = read(fd, buf, sizeof buf)) > 0) {
                    printf("[Sending %d bytes to pipe (fd=%d)]\n",
                        i, pipe_io[0][1]);
                    write(pipe_io[0][1], buf, i);
                } else if (i == -1)
                    break;
                bytes -= i;
            }
    return NOTIFY_DONE;
}

/*
 * callback routine for when there is data on the child's stdout to
 * read.  Read, then write the data to stdout (owned by the parent).
 */
Notify_value
read_it(client, fd)
Notify_client   client;
register int fd;
{
    char buf[BUFSIZ];
    int bytes, i;

    if (ioctl(fd, FIONREAD, &bytes) == 0)
        while (bytes > 0) {
            if ((i = read(fd, buf, sizeof buf)) > 0) {
                printf("[Reading %d bytes from pipe (fd=%d)]\n",
                    i, fd);
                (void) write(1, buf, i);
                bytes -= i;
            }
        }
    return NOTIFY_DONE;
}

/*
 * handle the death of the child.  If the process dies, the child
 * dies and generates a SIGCHLD signal.  Capture it and disable the
 * functions that talk to the pipes.
 */
Notify_value
sigchldcatcher(client, pid, status, rusage)
Notify_client client; /* the client noted in main() */
int pid; /* the pid that died */
union wait *status; /* the status of the process (unused here) */
struct rusage *rusage; /* resources used by this process (unused) */
{
    if (WIFEXITED(*status)) {
        printf("Process termined with status %d\n", status->w_retcode);
        /* unregister input func with appropriate file descriptor */
        notify_set_input_func(client, NOTIFY_FUNC_NULL,
            (client == client1)? pipe_io[1][0] : 0);
```

Example 19-4. The ntfy_pipe.c program (continued)

```
        return NOTIFY_DONE;
    }
    puts("SIGCHLD not handled");
    return NOTIFY_IGNORED;
}
```

Assuming that the program was run with cat(1) as described earlier, input to the child process comes from the function write_it(). That is, write_it() is the function which *writes* to the other side of the pipe that the child is reading from. This function was set up as the *input_func* for the *parent's* stdin. The function gets its input from whatever you type in the window in which you ran the program. It could have gotten its input from a text panel item or a selection using the selection service. It reads whatever data is sent through the pipe and ends up as the stdin for the child process.

Similarly, when the child process writes anything to its stdout, the data is redirected through the pipe. The parent reads from the other end of the pipe in read_it(). Whatever the parent reads is written to the parent's stdout, which is the user's tty window. It does this by calling write(1, buf, i). This line of the program can easily be replaced by:

```
    textsw_insert(textsw, buf, i);
```

This demonstrates how you can redirect the output (including stderr output) from a child process to a text subwindow.

The last thing to mention about the program is the treatment of extraneous file descriptors and signals handled by the child process after forking. When using fork(), the child process inherits all the file descriptors* and signal handling set up by the parent. This could seriously affect your program if the child process gets certain signals. The best thing to do, in this case, is for the child to loop through all the signals that are dealt with by the parent and reset them to SIG_DFL using signal(3) and close all file descriptors except for the child's stdin (0), stdout (1) and stderr (2) descriptors.

We use the signal() system call here because it is assumed the child is not going to execute any of the XView code in the parent's program. Therefore, the child does not need to use the notify_set_signal_func() routine to unregister the signals. Releasing these signals using this method completely disassociates the program from the parent.

This very general program is used as an example, but it is quite useful to use in all your applications that need to run external processes. The only modifications necessary would be to provide alternate sources for the input and output of the parent. main() could be replaced by a general function which simply gets an argv parameter that contains the program (with arguments) to execute.

The program could be modified to be used as a replacement for the system(3) call. Even if you do not expect to read the child's stdout or send data to its stdin, the child process still needs to be handled differently from system(3) because that function calls wait() and attempts to do its own signal handling.

---

*Unless the file descriptors were set to *close on exec* using: ioctl(fd, FIOCLEX, 0).

Notifier

19.9 Interposition

The Notifier provides a mechanism called *interposition,* with which you can intercept control of the internal communications within XView. Interposition is a powerful way to both monitor and modify window behavior in ways that extend the functionality of a window object.

Interposition allows a client to intercept an event before it reaches the *base event handler.* The base event handler is the one set originally by a client. The client can call the base event handler before or after its own handling of the event or not at all.

There may be more than one interposer per Notifier client. As each interposer is added, it is inserted ahead of the last interposer installed. When an event arrives, the Notifier calls the function at the top of the interposer list for that client. An interposed routine may (indirectly) call the next function in the interposition sequence and receive its results.

Figure 19-2 illustrates the flow of control with interposition. Note that the interposer could have stopped the flow of control to the base event handler.

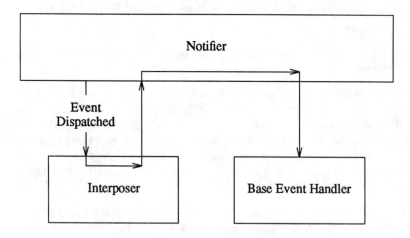

Figure 19-2. Flow of control in interposition

19.9.1 Uses of Interposition

Typically, it is application-level code that uses interposition. But, in general, any client's creator may want to use interposition. There are many reasons why an application might want to interpose a function in the call path to a client's event handler.

- An application may want to use the fact that a client has received a particular event as a trigger for some application specific processing.

- An application may want to filter the events to a client, thus modifying the client's behavior.

- An application may want to extend the functionality of a client by handling events that the client is not programmed to handle.

XView window objects utilize the Notifier for much of their communication and cooperation. Thus, if an application wanted to monitor the user actions directed to a particular window, then the application would use interposition to get into the flow of control.

19.9.2 Interface to Interposition

The Notifier supports interposition by keeping track of how interposition functions are ordered for each type of event for each client. Here is a typical example of interposition:

- An application creates a client. The client has set up its own client-event handler using `notify_set_event_func()`.

- The application tells the Notifier that it wants to interpose its function in front of the client's event handler by calling `notify_interpose_event_func()` (which uses the same calling sequence as `notify_set_event_func()`).

- When the application's interposed function is called it tells the Notifier to call the next function, i.e., the client's function, via a call to `notify_next_event_func()` (which uses the same calling sequence as that passed to the interposer function, not described here).

19.9.3 An Interposition Example

You can notice when a frame opens or closes by interposing in front of the frame's *client-event handler*. The client-event handler is an XView-specific event handler which is built on top of the Notifier's general client-event mechanism.* To register an interposer, the following routine is used:

```
Notify_error
notify_interpose_event_func(client, event_func, type)
    Notify_client     client;
    Notify_func       event_func;
    Notify_event_type type;
```

The client must be the handle of the Notifier client in front of which you are interposing. In XView, this is the handle returned from `xv_create()`. The type is always `NOTIFY_SAFE` for XView clients.

Let's say that the application is displaying some animation and wants to do the necessary computation only when the frame is open. It can use interposition to notice when the frame opens or closes.

---

*The stream of events sent to a client-event handler is described in in Chapter 6, *Handling Input*.

Notifier

In Example 19-5, note the call to notify_next_event_func(), which transfers control to the frame's client-event handler through the Notifier. notify_next_event_func() takes the same arguments as the interposer.

Example 19-5. Transferring control through the Notifier

```
#include <xview/xview.h>

main()
{
    Frame frame;
    Notify_value my_frame_interposer();

    /* Create the frame */
    frame = window_create(NULL, FRAME, NULL);

    /* Interpose in front of the frame's event handler */
    (void) notify_interpose_event_func(frame,
            my_frame_interposer, NOTIFY_SAFE);
    ...

    /* Show frame and start dispatching events */
    xv_main_loop(frame);
}

Notify_value
my_frame_interposer(frame, event, arg, type)
Frame               frame;
Event               *event;
Notify_arg          arg;
Notify_event_type   type;
{
    int closed_initial, closed_current;
    Notify_value value;

    /* Determine initial state of frame */
    closed_initial = (int) window_get(frame, FRAME_CLOSED);

    /* Let frame operate on the event */
    value = notify_next_event_func(frame, event, arg, type);

    /* Determine current state of frame */
    closed_current = (int) window_get(frame, FRAME_CLOSED);

    /* Change animation if states differ */
    if (closed_initial != closed_current) {
        if (closed_current) {
            /* Turn off animation because closed */
            (void) notify_set_itimer_func(me, my_animation,
                ITIMER_REAL, ITIMER_NULL, ITIMER_NULL);
        } else {
            /* Turn on animation because opened */
            (void) notify_set_itimer_func(me, my_animation,
                ITIMER_REAL, &NOTIFY_POLLING_ITIMER, ITIMER_NULL);
        }
    }
    return (value);
}
```

In Example 19-5, the base event handler is intended to handle the event (so that the frame gets closed/opened). If the interposed function replaces the base event handler and you do

not want the base event handler to be called at all, your interposed procedure should not call
`notify_next_event_func()`.

19.9.4 Interposing on Resize Events

Another use of interposition is to give your application more control over the layout of its subwindows. To do this, you set up an interpose event handler which checks if the event type is `WIN_RESIZE`. If so, rather than calling `notify_next_event_func()` to dispatch the event to the normal handler for resizing, you call your own resize routine.

```
Notify_value
my_frame_interposer(frame, event, arg, type)
Frame              frame;
Event              *event;
Notify_arg         arg;
Notify_event_type  type;
{
    Notify_value value;

    if (event_action(event) == WIN_RESIZE)
        value = resize(frame);
    else
        value = notify_next_event_func(frame, event, arg, type);

    return(value);
}
```

NOTE

A `WIN_RESIZE` event is *not* generated until the frame is resized. If you want your resize procedure to be called when the window first appears, you must do so yourself. This is different from a canvas with the `CANVAS_RESIZE` attribute set, whose resize procedure is called the first time the canvas is displayed.

19.9.5 Modifying a Frame's Destruction

Suppose an application must detect when the user selects the "Quit" menu item in the frame menu in order to perform some application-specific confirmation. To accomplish this, the application should interpose a new function in front of the frame's *client-destroy event* handler using the following routine.

```
Notify_error
notify_interpose_destroy_func(client, destroy_func)
    Notify_client client;
    Notify_func   destroy_func;
```

Frame destruction may originate from several sources.

• The user may select the "Quit" menu item from the window manager's pulldown menu attached to the base frame.

Notifier

- The application may be terminated by a software interrupt from the calling process.

- The connection to the server has been lost and the Notifier is informing the application that it is dying.

- `xv_destroy(frame)` was called from within the application.

Each of these scenarios results in a different method for the frame's destruction. When the frame is going to be destroyed, the process happens in two phases. First, the frame's destroy-interposer is called informing it of the impending destruction. At this point, the interposer can *veto* the destruction or it can allow it to take place—at which time the Notifier proceeds to phase two, the actual frame destruction.

Destroy-event handlers use a status parameter to determine which phase of destruction the Notifier is in—whether the Notifier is requesting if it is feasible for the client to be terminated at present (phase one, `DESTROY_CHECKING`) or if it is making a request to terminate (phase two, `DESTROY_CLEANUP` or `DESTROY_PROCESS_DEATH`).

The destroy-interpose function takes the following form:

```
Notify_value
destroy_func(client, status)
    Notify_client client;
    Destroy_status status;

typedef enum destroy_status {
    DESTROY_PROCESS_DEATH,
    DESTROY_CHECKING,
    DESTROY_CLEANUP,
    DESTROY_SAVE_YOURSELF,
} Destroy_status;
```

If the `status` argument is `DESTROY_CHECKING` and the client cannot terminate at present, the destroy-event handler should call `notify_veto_destroy()`, indicating that termination would not be advisable at this time, and return normally. If the client can terminate at present, then the destroy handler should do nothing; a subsequent call will tell the client to actually destroy itself. This veto option is used, for example, to give a text subwindow the chance to ask the user to confirm the saving of any editing changes when quitting a tool.

If `status` is `DESTROY_PROCESS_DEATH`, then the client can count on the entire process dying and should do whatever it needs to do to cleanup its outside entanglements, such as updating a file used by a text subwindow. Since the process is about to die, it need not free allocated memory since it is implicitly freed by the process' termination.

Since the entire process is dying, you can*not* display a notice or do any sort of prompting with the user to try to veto this request.

However, if `status` is `DESTROY_CLEANUP` then the client is asked to destroy itself and to be very tidy about cleaning up all the process internal resources that it is using, as well as its outside entanglements. This may be called on frame's which are not the sole frames used by the application. If a frame is dismissed but the application is still running (e.g., dismissing a pinned up menu), then the frame should clean up—including freeing allocated memory.

The status is set to DESTROY_SAVE_YOURSELF when the window manager has sent a WM_SAVE_YOURSELF message to all the clients on the desktop. This means the user may have selected the "Save Workspace" option from an OPEN LOOK window manager's property sheet. Basically, this means that the application should save its current state in such a way that it could be resumed in the same state at a later time. For example, a text editing program would update the file being edited, a graphics program would output its image display to a file, or whatever.

Interposing a Client Destroy Handler

We present an example of interposing in front of the frame's client-destroy event handler. The following program displays a frame, a panel and a panel button labeled "Quit". When the user chooses the panel button or the frame's "Quit" menu selection, the interposer is called and indicates the fact that the frame is about to go away.

Example 19-6. The interpose.c program

```
/*
 * interpose.c -- shows how to use an interpose destroy function
 */
#include <xview/xview.h>
#include <xview/frame.h>
#include <xview/panel.h>
#include <xview/notice.h>

Frame frame;

Notify_value
destroy_func(client, status)
Notify_client client;
Destroy_status status;
{
    if (status == DESTROY_CHECKING) {
        int answer = notice_prompt(client, NULL,
            NOTICE_MESSAGE_STRINGS, "Really Quit?", NULL,
            NOTICE_BUTTON_YES,  "No",
            NOTICE_BUTTON_NO,   "Yes",
            NULL);
        if (answer == NOTICE_YES)
            notify_veto_destroy(client);
    } else if (status == DESTROY_CLEANUP) {
        puts("cleaning up");
        /* allow frame to be destroyed */
        return notify_next_destroy_func(client, status);
    } else if (status == DESTROY_SAVE_YOURSELF)
        puts("save yourself?");
    else
        puts("process death");
    return NOTIFY_DONE;
}

main (argc, argv)
int argc;
char *argv[];
{
    Panel panel;
```

Example 19-6. The interpose.c program (continued)

```
    int    quit();

    xv_init (XV_INIT_ARGC_PTR_ARGV, &argc, argv, NULL);

    frame = (Frame)xv_create (NULL, FRAME,
        FRAME_LABEL,      argv[0],
        XV_WIDTH,         200,
        XV_HEIGHT,        100,
        NULL);
    notify_interpose_destroy_func(frame, destroy_func);

    panel = (Panel)xv_create (frame, PANEL, NULL);
    (void) xv_create (panel, PANEL_BUTTON,
            PANEL_LABEL_STRING,        "Quit",
            PANEL_NOTIFY_PROC,         quit,
            NULL);
    xv_main_loop(frame);
}

int
quit()
{
    xv_destroy_safe(frame);
    return XV_OK;
}
```

The first time the interposer is called, the status is DESTROY_CHECKING. Here, we display a notice prompting the user to confirm the quit. We want the *default* action to be **No**, so we make the NOTICE_YES button have the label "No" and the NOTICE_NO button have the label "Yes." This is because the notice's *default* button is the NOTICE_YES button.

If the user selects the default "No" choice, then notify_veto_client() is called, vetoing the destruction request. Otherwise, the routine returns and the destruction sequence continues on as usual. The routine is then called again notifying that it is being destroyed this time. It calls notify_next_destroy_func() to allow the process to continue. This is where any process cleaning up should take place.

19.10 Notifier Control

The Notifier is started automatically by calling xv_main_loop(). It takes a window object (typically the base frame of the application) and sets XV_SHOW to TRUE. Then it calls notify_start() and the Notifier is running. notify_start() continuously loops through the Notifier's processing loop waiting for events in which its clients have expressed interest. This continues until the application calls notify_stop() or if there are no more clients registered. At this time, notify_start() returns and the application may continue.

When notify_start() is called, the Notifier takes over and none of the application code is executed unless it is directly or indirectly called by a *notify* or *callback* procedure. If the callback routine calls notify_stop(), when that callback function returns, notify_start() returns and, thus, xv_main_loop() returns. The Notifier can be stopped using this method despite the fact that there are still clients registered with the Notifier. At this point, the application may call `notify_start()` again or it may attempt to do either *implicit* or *explicit* dispatching of events.

Explicit dispatching is done by calling `notify_dispatch()`. Here, the Notifier steps through one iteration of its normal control loop. This allows you to monitor events during the execution of a time-consuming or computationally complex portion of the program. Say your application generates a complex fractal image. The process is initiated from the selection of a panel button. Because the generation of fractals is very time consuming, you may wish to check every once in a while to see if the user has generated any events that need to be processed—like selecting a panel button labeled `Stop`. In this case, the callback procedure for the panel button should call `notify_stop()` and return. The Notifier returns to the top-level, `notify_start()` returns (and thus, `xv_main_loop()` returns) and your application begins to generate the fractal image. During each iteration of the loop (or more often, if necessary), `notify_dispatch()` is called to be sure to process any pending events that the user might have generated.

Implicit dispatching indicates that you are going to make calls to `read()` or `select()`—system calls which *block*. If `notify_do_dispatch()` is called, then events that the user generates (such as moving the mouse or selecting a panel button) will continue to be processed even though the `read()` has not yet returned.

Implicit and explicit dispatching may be used before or after the call to `xv_main_loop()` or `notify_start()`, but it is not permitted to call these functions while the Notifier is looping on its own (from within a call to `notify_start()`). Therefore, you should never attempt to do direct dispatching from within a callback routine or any function that has been called indirectly by the Notifier.

These two methods of dispatching make porting programs that do not use the Notifier much easier. Thus, building an XView interface on top of a typical mainline-based input-driven program is also much easier. Programs written from scratch should try to follow the event-driven input style of program design and try to avoid using implicit or explicit dispatching whenever possible.

19.10.1 Implicit Dispatching

Implicit dispatching is used whenever you wish to loop on a call that might block, such as `read(2)`. Before calling `read()`, you should first call the function:

```
notify_do_dispatch();
```

This tells the Notifier that you are going to do implicit dispatching and that it should use its own version of `read()` rather than using the standard system call as the function. The two are equivalent with one exception—`read()` will return 0 on EOF rather than -1, as you might expect.

After `notify_do_dispatch()` has been called, you can either call `notify_dispatch()` directly (to process events you know to have been delivered already) or call `read()` (or both).

The following example program demonstrates how this can be done. The program creates our usual frame, panel and "Quit" panel button, but instead of calling xv_main_loop(), we create a small loop which reads stdin waiting for typed input.

Example 19-7. The ntfy_do_dis.c program

```
/*
 * ntfy_do_dis.c -- show an example of implicit notifier dispatching
 * by calling notify_do_dispatch().  Create a frame, panel and "Quit"
 * button, and then loop on calls to read() from stdin.  Event
 * processing is still maintained because the Notifier uses it's own
 * non-blocking read().
 */
#include <stdio.h>
#include <xview/xview.h>
#include <xview/frame.h>
#include <xview/panel.h>

Frame frame;

main (argc, argv)
int argc;
char *argv[];
{
    Panel panel;
    char  buf[BUFSIZ];
    int   n, quit();

    xv_init (XV_INIT_ARGC_PTR_ARGV, &argc, argv, NULL);

    frame = (Frame)xv_create (NULL, FRAME,
        FRAME_LABEL,    argv[0],
        XV_WIDTH,       200,
        XV_HEIGHT,      100,
        XV_SHOW,        TRUE,
        NULL);

    panel = (Panel)xv_create (frame, PANEL, NULL);

    (void) xv_create (panel, PANEL_BUTTON,
            PANEL_LABEL_STRING,        "Quit",
            PANEL_NOTIFY_PROC,         quit,
            NULL);

    /* Force the frame to be displayed by flushing the server */
    XFlush(xv_get(frame, XV_DISPLAY));

    /* tell the Notifier that it should use its own read() so that it
     * can also detect and dispatch events.  This allows us to loop
     * in this code segment and still process events.
     */
    notify_do_dispatch();

    puts("Frame being displayed -- type away.");
    while ((n = read(0, buf, sizeof buf)) >= 0)
        printf("read %d bytes\n", n);

    printf("read() returned %d\n", n);
}

int
quit()
```

Example 19-7. The ntfy_do_dis.c program (continued)

```
{
    xv_destroy_safe(frame);
    return XV_OK;
}
```

There are several things to note here. First, because `xv_main_loop()` is not called, we need to explicitly set the attribute `XV_SHOW` to `TRUE` for the base frame. Otherwise, it will never be displayed. Also, because of the nature of event dispatching, we must *flush* the connection between the X server and the application to make sure that the frame is displayed by the time the first `read()` call returns. If this is not done, the frame is not displayed until after the first `read()` returns.

19.10.2 Explicit Dispatching

Frequently, the programmer is plagued with the following problem: A great deal of processing has to be done to process something that the user has initiated. As mentioned before, the programmer might want to generate a fractal image or compute the value of *pi* when the user selects a panel button. Any time-consuming process that requires this type of functionality should utilize explicit dispatching. It seems like an easy solution to `fork()` and let the background process perform the operation, but this is frequently an *expensive* operation and should be avoided if explicit dispatching is sufficient. If forking is required, then Section 19.5.5, "Handling SIGCHLD," and Section 19.8.2, "Reading and Writing on Pipes," should be referenced.

The call `notify_dispatch()` does explicit event dispatching to service immediately an event that you know is waiting to be read and dispatched. Typically, this is called at particular locations within a control loop that is processing time-consuming tasks. It is assumed that this control loop does *not* call `read()` or `select()`. Rather, explicit dispatching is used within loops that might do heavy computation such as graphics processing or number crunching. This is necessary because while the computations are busy computing, the user might be attempting to interact with the application by selecting a panel button.

If `notify_dispatch()` is called frequently enough, then performance of the user interface may still be perceived as acceptable even though the program is very busy with its computations. Architecturally, such a program is designed in a similar way with *ntfy_do_dis.c* in Section 19.10.1, "Implicit Dispatching." That is, there is a central processing loop which is doing the main work of the program. In this case, `notify_do_dispatch()` is not called.

```
#include <xview/xview.h>
...
int finished;

main(argc, argv)
char *argv[];
{
    Display *dpy;
    Frame frame;

    ...
```

```
xv_create(NULL, FRAME, NULL);

...

dpy = (Display *)xv_get(frame, XV_DISPLAY);

/* flush everything before starting loop */
XFlush(dpy);
while (!finished) {
    notify_dispatch();
    XFlush(dpy);
    /* compute PI to the next place */
    process_pi();
}
}
```

Notice that after `notify_dispatch()`, `XFlush()` is called. It is imperative that this happen; otherwise, any Xlib calls (which result from many `xv_create()` or `xv_set()` calls) may not be displayed. You only need to call `XFlush()` once after one or more calls to a sequence of calls to `notify_dispatch()`. The rule of thumb is to flush the server whenever you want to see the latest display.

19.11 Error Codes

This section describes the basic error handling scheme used by the Notifier and lists the meaning of each of the possible error codes. Every call to the Notifier returns a value that indicates success or failure. On an error condition, `notify_errno` describes the failure. `notify_errno` is set by the Notifier much like `errno` is set by UNIX system calls, i.e., `notify_errno` is set only when an error is detected during a call to the Notifier and is not reset to `NOTIFY_OK` on a successful call to the Notifier.

```
enum notify_error {
    ... /* Listed below */
};
typedef enum notify_error Notify_error;

extern Notify_error notify_errno;
```

Table 19-1 contains a complete list of error codes.

Table 19-1. Notifier Error Codes

Error Code	Description
NOTIFY_OK	The call was completed successfully.
NOTIFY_UNKNOWN_CLIENT	The `client` argument is not known by the Notifier. A `notify_set_*_func` type call needs to be done in order for the Notifier to recognize a client.

Table 19-1. Notifier Error Codes (continued)

Error Code	Description
NOTIFY_NO_CONDITION	A call was made to access the state of a condition but the condition is not set with the Notifier for the given client. This can arise when a notify_get_*_func() type call was done before the equivalent notify_set_*_func() call was done. Also, the Notifier automatically clears some conditions after they have occurred; e.g., when an interval timer expires.
NOTIFY_BAD_ITIMER	The which argument to an interval timer routine was not valid.
NOTIFY_BAD_SIGNAL	The signal argument to an signal routine was out of range.
NOTIFY_NOT_STARTED	A call to notify_stop() was made but the Notifier was never started.
NOTIFY_DESTROY_VETOED	A client refused to be destroyed during a call to notify_die() or notify_post_destroy() when status was DESTROY_CHECKING.
NOTIFY_INTERNAL_ERROR	This error code indicates some internal inconsistency in the Notifier itself has been detected.
NOTIFY_SRCH	The pid argument to a child process control routine was not valid.
NOTIFY_BADF	The fd argument to an input or output routine was not valid.
NOTIFY_NOMEM	The Notifier dynamically allocates memory from the heap. This error code is generated if the allocator could not get any more memory.
NOTIFY_INVAL	Some argument to a call to the Notifier contained an invalid argument.
NOTIFY_FUNC_LIMIT	An attempt to set an interposer function has encountered the limit of the number of interposers allowed for a single condition.

The routine notify_perror() acts just as the library call perror(3).

```
notify_perror(str)
    char *str;
```

notify_perror() prints the string str, followed by a colon and followed by a string that describes notify_errno to stderr.

19.12 Issues

Here are some additional issues surrounding the Notifier:

- The layer over the UNIX signal mechanism is not complete. Signal blocking (sigblock(2)) can still be done safely in the flow of control of a client to protect critical portions of code as long as the previous signal mask is restored before returning to the Notifier. Signal pausing (sigpause(2)) is essentially done by the Notifier. Signal masking (sigmask(2)) can be accomplished via multiple notify_set_signal_func() calls. Setting up a process signal stack (sigstack(2)) can still be done. Setting the signal catcher mask and on-signal-stack flag (sigvec(2)) could be done by reaching around the Notifier but is not supported.

- Not all process resources are multiplexed (e.g., rlimit(2), setjmp(2), umask(2), setquota(2), and setpriority(2)); only ones that have to do with flow of control multiplexing. Thus, some level of cooperation and understanding needs to exist between packages in the single process.

- One might intercept close(2) and dup(2) calls so that the Notifier is not waiting on invalid or incorrect file descriptors if a client forgets to remove its conditions from the Notifier before making these calls.

- One might intercept signal(3) and sigvec(2) calls so that the Notifier does not get confused by programs that fail to use the Notifier to manage its signals.

- One might intercept setitimer(2) calls so that the Notifier does not get confused by programs that fail to use the Notifier to manage interval timers.

- One might intercept ioctl(2) calls so that the Notifier does not get fouled up by programs that use FIONBIO and FIOASYNC instead of the equivalent fcntl(2) calls.

- One might intercept readv(2) and write(2) just like read(2) and select(2) so that a program does not tie up the process.

- The Notifier is not a lightweight process mechanism that maintains a stack per thread of control. However, if such a mechanism becomes available, then the Notifier will still be valuable for its support of notification-based clients.

- Client events are disjoint from UNIX events. This is done to give complete freedom to clients as to how events are defined. One could imagine certain clients wanting to unify client and UNIX events. This could be done with a layer of software on top of the Notifier. A client could define events as pointers to structures that contain event codes and event specific arguments. The event codes would include the equivalents of UNIX event notifications. The event specific arguments would contain, for example, the file descriptor of an input-pending notification. When an input-pending notification from the Notifier was sent to a client, the client would turn around and post the equivalent client-event notification.

- One could imagine extending the Notifier to provide a record and replay mechanism that would drive an application. However, this is not supported by the current interface.

20
Color

In This Chapter:

XView Color Model 396
   Color and Pixel Values 396
Creating Colormap Segments 397
Changing Colormap Entries 402
Foreground and Background Colors 402
Coloring XView Objects 403
Coloring Panel Items 408

20
Color

The X Window System has various ways of allocating, specifying and using colors. While all of these methods are available to applications without XView intervening, XView provides its own model for color specification that may be used as an alternative. This model does not provide anything more than what is already available, but it may provide a simpler interface to request and specify colors. This model is especially useful when specifying colors for XView objects such as panel buttons and scrollbars.

There is no overlap between XView's color usage and Xlib's color usage. If you choose to use Xlib calls to create colormaps, to allocate color cells, and so on, you can only attach these colormaps to actual X windows, not XView objects. Thus, you would have to use `XChangeWindowAttributes` on the `XV_XID` of a canvas paint window, for example.

This chapter does not directly discuss how to use colors using *colormaps* and related Xlib color-specific functions. It discusses only the XView color model. See Chapter 7, *Color*, in Volume 1, *Xlib Programming Manual*.

Obviously, you cannot use color in your application unless you have a color display. But you cannot tell at the time your application is written whether the user's display is going to be able to support color. To do this, you can use the `DisplayPlanes()` macro to determine whether the display can handle color:

```
Display *dpy = (Display *)xv_get(frame, XV_DISPLAY);
extern use_colors = True;

if (DisplayPlanes(dpy, DefaultScreen(dpy)) == 1)
    use_color = False;
```

20.1 XView Color Model

The XView color model is based on *colormap segments*. A colormap segment is a subset of the available cells in a colormap on the X server. Applications define and refer to a colormap segment by assigning the segment a name. Colormap segments can be allocated as either *static* and *dynamic* colormap segments. These are XView entities (i.e., not Xlib) that provide a veneer over the Xlib color mechanism.

When you ask for a set of colors in a static colormap segment, XView attempts to allocate these colors read-only from the default colormap (using XAllocColor()). The closest match to the requested color is returned.

When you ask for dynamic colors in a colormap segment, XView sends a request to the server to allocate read-write colors. If the default visual is StaticColor or if the required number of cells cannot be allocated from a PseudoColor visual, a new PseudoColor colormap will be created and the color cells allocated from it.

Applications should always use static colormap segments unless they require exact color matches. Static colormap segments, by sharing color cells across applications, use the shared hardware colormap resources more efficiently. A newly created read-write colormap is installed and uninstalled by the window manager (in accordance with the ICCCM) based on some colormap focus policy (usually where the keyboard focus is). This installation procedure of the colormap may create a "flashing" affect when the user moves the pointer in and out of a window that has different colors in its colormap from other windows (despite the fact that you might have allocated only a small number of read-write cells in a colormap). Given the constraints of the X Protocol, there is no workaround for this problem.

Any object subclassed from the window object can allocate and use colormap segments. For example, setting colors on a text subwindow or canvas will propagate the colors to all the views of the object. However, the colors can also be set on a particular view.

20.1.1 Color and Pixel Values

A *color* is defined to be a set of red, green and blue (RGB) intensity values. For example, red is represented by a full intensity for the red value and no intensity for the green and blue values. More complicated colors, or color "shades," are achieved by raising or lowering the intensities of one or more of the RGB values.

A *colormap segment* represents an array of colors. A *pixel* represents the different colors from the array. The pixel values from a colormap can be obtained using the attribute WIN_X_COLOR_INDICES. Example 20-1 demonstrates the use of this attribute. For example let's assume a colormap segment associated with a canvas contains four colors.

```
unsigned long *colors;

colors = (unsigned long *)xv_get(canvas, WIN_X_COLOR_INDICES);
```

colors[0], colors[1], colors[2] and colors[3] contain the actual pixel values corresponding to these colors. These pixel values can be used in calls to XSet-Foreground().

More than one colormap segment may be in use at a time, and more than one XView object may reference the same colormap segment. To keep track of which segment is associated with which object, segments have names (char *) associated with them. When you change the *data* (actual colormap entries) for a colormap segment, all objects that share the same colormap are affected.

20.2 Creating Colormap Segments

The X11 protocol specifies that the Visual type of a window must be declared at the time it is created. Therefore, XView objects that allocated colormap segments are required, at create time, to specify the type of the colormap segment they propose to use. By default, windows are created using a static visual. However, you can set the Visual to be dynamic by setting the attribute WIN_DYNAMIC_VISUAL to TRUE.

The colormap segment (*cms*) data structure is declared in *<xview/cms.h>* as:

```
typedef struct xv_cmsdata {
    enum Xv_cmstype      type;
    short                size;
    short                index;
    short                rgb_count;
    unsigned char        *red;
    unsigned char        *green;
    unsigned char        *blue;
} Xv_cmsdata;
```

The break down of the cms data is as follows:

type	Indicates whether the cms is static or dynamic. It may have either of two values: XV_STATIC_CMS or XV_DYNAMIC_CMS.
size	Indicates the number of colors in this segment. Once set, this cannot be changed.
index	Specifies the starting origin to load rgb_count entries from the RGB arrays into the colormap segment.
rgb_count	Specifies the number of red, green, and blue values to load into the colormap segment starting at index.
red, green, blue	Specifies the actual RGB values associated with paricular index entries into the colormap.

The colormap segment data is assigned to colormap segements using the attribute WIN_CMS_DATA. The cms is typically one that has been named using WIN_CMS_NAME. A window's default colormap segment is derived from the default colormap obtained from the server (e.g., DefaultColormap()). When you use WIN_CMS_NAME to assign a new name to a colormap segment, the colormap is copied and subsequent assignments of WIN_CMS_DATA are assigned to the new colormap. Windows can change colormaps by setting its WIN_CMS_NAME to other allocated colormap segments.

For example, the following code segment shows how to assign certain RGB values representing specific colors to a colormap segment named "palette."

```
#define WHITE    0
#define RED      1
#define GREEN    2
#define BLUE     3
#define YELLOW   4

unsigned char   red[5], green[5], blue[5];

red[WHITE]  = 255;   green[WHITE]  = 255;   blue[WHITE]  = 255;
red[RED]    = 255;   green[RED]    = 0;     blue[RED]    = 0;
red[GREEN]  = 0;     green[GREEN]  = 255;   blue[GREEN]  = 0;
red[BLUE]   = 0;     green[BLUE]   = 0;     blue[BLUE]   = 255;
red[YELLOW] = 250;   green[YELLOW] = 230;   blue[YELLOW] = 30;

cms_data->type = XV_STATIC_CMS;
cms_data->size = 5;
cms_data->rgb_count = 5;
cms_data->index = 0;
cms_data->red = red;
cms_data->green = green;
cms_data->blue = blue;

canvas = (Canvas)xv_create(frame, CANVAS,
    WIN_CMS_NAME,             "palette",
    WIN_CMS_DATA,             &cms_data,
    NULL);
```

The #defines for colors are indices into the resulting colormap. The RGB values are assigned according to each color type; the RED color index has full red intensity, while the blue and green intensities are completely off. The cms type is set to XV_STATIC_CMS because we are deriving the colors from the static colormap. Thus, XView queries the server looking for colors in its color table that are the closest match to those specified. Had the type been XV_DYNAMIC_CMS, then the exact colors specified would be created in the new colormap segment. The cms data is set *after* the cms name is set to "palette."

The colors in the cms may be extracted and set as the GC's foreground and/or background pixel values. Example 20-1 shows how code similar to the fragment above can be used to set colors in a colormap segment and then use the GC and Xlib graphics calls to render various items in different colors.

Example 20-1. The x_draw.c program

```
/*
 * x_draw.c --
 *      Demonstrates the use of Xlib drawing functions inside an
 *      XView canvas.  Color is also used, but not required.
 */
#include <xview/xview.h>
#include <xview/canvas.h>
#include <xview/cms.h>
#include <xview/xv_xrect.h>

/* indices into color table renders specified colors. */
#define WHITE    0
#define RED      1
```

Example 20-1. The x_draw.c program (continued)

```
#define GREEN    2
#define BLUE     3
#define ORANGE   4
#define AQUA     5
#define PINK     6
#define BLACK    7

GC gc;    /* GC used for Xlib drawing */
unsigned long *colors; /* the color table */

/*
 * initialize cms data to support colors specified above.  Assign
 * data to new cms -- use either static or dynamic cms depending
 * on -dynamic command line switch.
 */
main(argc, argv)
int      argc;
char     *argv[];
{
    unsigned char red[8], green[8], blue[8];
    static char stipple_bits[] = {0xAA, 0xAA, 0x55, 0x55};
    Frame        frame;
    Canvas       canvas;
    XFontStruct *font;
    Display     *display;
    XGCValues    gc_val;
    XID          xid;
    void         canvas_repaint();
    Xv_cmsdata   cms_data;
    int          use_dynamic = FALSE;

    /* Create windows */
    xv_init(XV_INIT_ARGC_PTR_ARGV, &argc, argv, NULL);
    if (*++argv && !strcmp(*argv, "-dynamic"))
        use_dynamic = TRUE;

    frame = xv_create(NULL,FRAME,
        FRAME_LABEL,      "xv_canvas_x_draw",
        XV_WIDTH,         400,
        XV_HEIGHT,        300,
        NULL);

    /* initialize RGB values for specified colors */
    red[WHITE] = 255;    green[WHITE] = 255;    blue[WHITE] = 255;
    red[RED] = 255;      green[RED] = 0;        blue[RED] = 0;
    red[GREEN] = 0;      green[GREEN] = 255;    blue[GREEN] = 0;
    red[BLUE] = 0;       green[BLUE] = 0;       blue[BLUE] = 255;
    red[ORANGE] = 250;   green[ORANGE] = 130;   blue[ORANGE] = 80;
    red[AQUA] = 30;      green[AQUA] = 230;     blue[AQUA] = 250;
    red[PINK] = 230;     green[PINK] = 30;      blue[PINK] = 250;

    cms_data.type = use_dynamic? XV_DYNAMIC_CMS : XV_STATIC_CMS;
    cms_data.size = 8;
    cms_data.rgb_count = 8;
    cms_data.index = 0;
    cms_data.red = red;
    cms_data.green = green;
    cms_data.blue = blue;
```

Example 20-1. The x_draw.c program (continued)

```
    canvas = xv_create(frame, CANVAS,
        CANVAS_REPAINT_PROC,      canvas_repaint,
        CANVAS_X_PAINT_WINDOW,    TRUE,
        WIN_DYNAMIC_VISUAL,       use_dynamic,
        WIN_CMS_NAME,             "palette",
        WIN_CMS_DATA,             &cms_data,
        NULL);

    /* Get display and xid */
    display = (Display *)xv_get(frame, XV_DISPLAY);
    xid = (XID)xv_get(canvas_paint_window(canvas), XV_XID);

    if (!(font = XLoadQueryFont(display, "fixed"))) {
        puts("cannot load fixed font");
        exit(1);
    }

    /* Create and initialize GC */
    gc_val.font = font->fid;
    gc_val.stipple =
     XCreateBitmapFromData(display, xid, stipple_bits, 16, 2);
    gc = XCreateGC(display, xid, GCFont | GCStipple, &gc_val);

    /* get the colormap from the canvas now that
     * the cms has been installed
     */
    colors = (unsigned long *)xv_get(canvas, WIN_X_COLOR_INDICES);

    /* Start event loop */
    xv_main_loop(frame);
}

/*
 * Draws onto the canvas using Xlib drawing functions.
 */
void
canvas_repaint(canvas, pw, display, xid, xrects)
Canvas          canvas;
Xv_Window       pw;
Display         *display;
Window          xid;
Xv_xrectlist    *xrects;
{
    static XPoint box[] = {
        {0,0}, {100,100}, {0,-100}, {-100,100}, {0,-100}
    };
    static XPoint points[] = {
        {0,0}, /* this point to be overwritten below */
        {25,0}, {25,0}, {25,0}, {25,0}, {-100,25},
        {25,0}, {25,0}, {25,0}, {25,0}, {-100,25},
        {25,0}, {25,0}, {25,0}, {25,0}, {-100,25},
        {25,0}, {25,0}, {25,0}, {25,0}, {-100,25},
        {25,0}, {25,0}, {25,0}, {25,0}, {-100,25},
    };

    XSetForeground(display, gc, colors[RED]);
    XDrawString(display, xid, gc, 30, 20, "XFillRectangle", 14);
    XFillRectangle(display, xid, gc, 25, 25, 100, 100);
```

Example 20-1. The x_draw.c program (continued)

```
    XSetFunction(display, gc, GXinvert);
    XFillRectangle(display, xid, gc, 50, 50, 50, 50);
    XSetFunction(display, gc, GXcopy);

    XSetForeground(display, gc, colors[BLACK]);
    XDrawString(display, xid, gc, 155, 20, "XFillRect - stipple", 19);
    XSetFillStyle(display, gc, FillStippled);
    XFillRectangle(display, xid, gc, 150, 25, 100, 100);
    XSetFillStyle(display, gc, FillSolid);

    XSetForeground(display, gc, colors[BLUE]);
    XDrawString(display, xid, gc, 280, 20, "XDrawPoints", 11);
    points[0].x = 275; points[0].y = 25;
    XDrawPoints(display, xid, gc, points,
        sizeof(points)/sizeof(XPoint), CoordModePrevious);

    XSetForeground(display, gc, colors[ORANGE]);
    XDrawString(display, xid, gc, 30, 145, "XDrawLine - solid", 17);
    XDrawLine(display, xid, gc, 25, 150, 125, 250);
    XDrawLine(display, xid, gc, 25, 250, 125, 150);

    XSetForeground(display, gc, colors[AQUA]);
    XDrawString(display, xid, gc, 155, 145, "XDrawLine - dashed", 18);
    XSetLineAttributes(display, gc, 5,
        LineDoubleDash, CapButt, JoinMiter);
    XDrawLine(display, xid, gc, 150, 150, 250, 250);
    XDrawLine(display, xid, gc, 150, 250, 250, 150);
    XSetLineAttributes(display, gc, 0, LineSolid, CapButt, JoinMiter);

    XSetForeground(display, gc, colors[PINK]);
    XDrawString(display, xid, gc, 280, 145, "XDrawLines", 10);
    box[0].x = 275; box[0].y = 150;
    XDrawLines(display, xid, gc, box, 5, CoordModePrevious);

    XSetForeground(display, gc, colors[GREEN]);
    XDrawRectangle(display, xid, gc,
        5, 5, xv_get(pw, XV_WIDTH)-10, xv_get(pw, XV_HEIGHT)-10);
    XDrawRectangle(display, xid, gc,
        7, 7, xv_get(pw, XV_WIDTH)-14, xv_get(pw, XV_HEIGHT)-14);
}
```

x_draw.c uses Xlib routines to draw into the canvas's paint window. Therefore, the GC's foreground color is set to an index into the colormap used by the window being drawn into. In order to get the correct color from the colormap, we need to get the color table for the window using the attribute WIN_X_COLOR_INDICES. The repaint routine draws objects (points, lines, and rectangles) in the specified colors as indexed by the color-macros into the color table.

20.3 Changing Colormap Entries

When you change entries in a static colormap segment, the canvas's repaint procedure is called because you are changing actual pixel values. Therefore, windows using this colormap segment will have to repaint the portions of itself that have been painted with the changed pixel values. The repaint procedure is not called as a result of an event being generated; XView locates all windows with that particular colormap segment and calls its repaint routine directly.

If the application decides to track changes in the colormap segment itself and repaint the portions of the canvas that need to be repaired, a mechanism is required to prevent the canvas from generating repaints on color changes. This is accomplished by setting the Boolean attribute CANVAS_CMS_REPAINT. The default value for this attribute is TRUE if static colors are to be used in the window. It is FALSE if dynamic colors are to be used. That is, it is dependent on the value of WIN_DYNAMIC_COLOR.

When you change a color in the dynamic colormap segment, the pixel value remains the same but the *color* represented by the index into the colormap segment changes. Therefore, the repaint routine is not called and the window's appearance changes automatically. This method of colormap manipulation is used to implement color animation.

20.4 Foreground and Background Colors

The foreground and background colors of an XView object can be set either by using FRAME_FOREGROUND_COLOR and FRAME_BACKGROUND_COLOR or by using WIN_FOREGROUND_COLOR and WIN_BACKGROUND_COLOR. FRAME_FOREGROUND_COLOR and FRAME_BACKGROUND_COLOR require a single RGB value as an argument. A variable of type Xv_singlecolor is used to specify the color explicitly. The type is declared as:

```
typdef struct xv_singlecolor {
    unsigned char red, green, blue;
} Xv_singlecolor;
```

For example, the following code segment sets the foreground and background colors for a frame and provides for all child objects (canvases, panels, etc.) inherit the same foreground and background colors:

```
Frame              frame;
Xv_singlecolor     fg, bg;

bg.red = 250, bg.green = 230, bg.blue = 30;
fg.red = 180, fg.green = 100, fg.blue = 20;

xv_init(XV_INIT_ARGC_PTR_ARGV, &argc, argv, NULL);

frame = xv_create(XV_NULL, FRAME,
    FRAME_BACKGROUND_COLOR, &bg,
    FRAME_FOREGROUND_COLOR, &fg,
    FRAME_INHERIT_COLORS,   TRUE,
    NULL);
```

20.5 Coloring XView Objects

Once a colormap segment has been associated with an XView object, the foreground and the background color of the object can be set to any index value in the colormap segment using WIN_FOREGROUND_COLOR and WIN_BACKGROUND_COLOR. Note that these attributes take an index value (into the currently associated colormap segment) as the value.

Example 20-2 demonstrates how to set colors on specific XView objects. The user selects objects (from the "Objects" item) to be colored by selecting one of the color tiles from the "Colors" choice item. The callback function for this panel item calls color_notify(), which sets the currently selected colors on the foreground or background of the selected objects. Whether to use foreground or background colors is dependent on the value of the "Fg/Bg" panel item and the items whose colors are affected are retrieved by getting the value of the "Objects" panel item. Since more than one object can be selected from this item, the value is a mask of the selected items. We loop through each bit in the mask identifying which objects should have their colors set.

Example 20-2. The color_objs.c program

```
/*
 * color_objs.c --
 *      This program demonstrates the use of color in XView. It allows
 *      the user to choose the foreground and background colors of the
 *      various objects in an interactive manner.
 */
#include <X11/Xlib.h>
#include <xview/xview.h>
#include <xview/svrimage.h>
#include <xview/textsw.h>
#include <xview/panel.h>
#include <xview/icon.h>
#include <xview/cms.h>

#define SELECT_TEXTSW           0
#define SELECT_TEXTSW_VIEW      1
#define SELECT_SCROLLBAR        2
#define SELECT_PANEL            3
#define SELECT_ICON             4

#define NUM_COLORS              8

/* Icon data */
static short icon_bits[256]={
#include "cardback.icon"
};

Panel_item      objects;
Textsw          textsw;
Panel           panel;
Icon            icon;

/*
 * main()
 *      Create a panel and panel items. The application uses panel items
 *      to choose a particular object and change its foreground and
 *      background colors in an interactive manner. Create a textsw.
```

Example 20-2. The color_objs.c program (continued)

```
 *      Create an icon. All the objects share the same colormap segment.
 */
main(argc,argv)
int     argc;
char    *argv[];
{
    Frame           frame;
    Panel_item      panel_palette, panel_fg_bg;
    Xv_cmsdata      cms_data;
    unsigned char red[NUM_COLORS], green[NUM_COLORS], blue[NUM_COLORS];
    Server_image  chips[NUM_COLORS], icon_image;
    void            color_notify();
    extern void     exit();

    xv_init(XV_INIT_ARGC_PTR_ARGV, &argc, argv, NULL);

    /* Set up the RGB values and initialize the cms */
    initialize_cms_data(&cms_data, red, green, blue);

    frame = (Frame)xv_create(NULL, FRAME,
        FRAME_LABEL,    argv[0],
        NULL);

    /* Create panel and set the colormap segment on the panel */
    panel = (Panel)xv_create(frame, PANEL,
        PANEL_LAYOUT,   PANEL_VERTICAL,
        WIN_CMS_NAME,   "palette",
        WIN_CMS_DATA,   &cms_data,
        NULL);

    /* Create panel items */
    objects = (Panel_item)xv_create(panel, PANEL_TOGGLE,
        PANEL_LABEL_STRING,     "Objects",
        PANEL_LAYOUT,           PANEL_HORIZONTAL,
        PANEL_CHOICE_STRINGS,   "Textsw", "Textsw View",
                                "Scrollbar", "Panel", "Icon", NULL,
        NULL);

    panel_fg_bg = (Panel_item)xv_create(panel, PANEL_CHECK_BOX,
        PANEL_LABEL_STRING,     "Fg/Bg",
        PANEL_CHOOSE_ONE,       TRUE,
        PANEL_LAYOUT,           PANEL_HORIZONTAL,
        PANEL_CHOICE_STRINGS,   "Background", "Foreground", NULL,
        NULL);

    /* Initialize colored chips to be used as panel choice images */
    initialize_chips(panel, chips);
    panel_palette = (Panel_item)xv_create(panel, PANEL_CHOICE,
        PANEL_LAYOUT,           PANEL_HORIZONTAL,
        PANEL_LABEL_STRING,     "Colors",
        PANEL_CLIENT_DATA,      panel_fg_bg,
        XV_X,                   (int)xv_get(panel_fg_bg, XV_X),
        PANEL_NEXT_ROW,         15,
        PANEL_CHOICE_IMAGES,
            chips[0], chips[1], chips[2], chips[3], chips[4],
            chips[5], chips[6], chips[7], NULL,
        PANEL_NOTIFY_PROC,      color_notify,
        NULL);
```

Example 20-2. The color_objs.c program (continued)

```
    (void) xv_create(panel, PANEL_BUTTON,
        PANEL_LABEL_STRING,     "Quit",
        PANEL_NOTIFY_PROC,      exit,
        NULL);
    (void)window_fit_height(panel);

    /* create textsw and set the colormap segment for it */
    textsw = (Textsw)xv_create(frame, TEXTSW,
        WIN_CMS_NAME,     "palette",
        WIN_BELOW,        panel,
        WIN_ROWS,         15,
        WIN_COLUMNS,      80,
        NULL);

    /* adjust panel dimensions */
    (void)xv_set(panel, WIN_WIDTH, xv_get(textsw, WIN_WIDTH), NULL);

    icon_image = (Server_image)xv_create(NULL, SERVER_IMAGE,
        XV_WIDTH,             64,
        XV_HEIGHT,            64,
        SERVER_IMAGE_DEPTH,   1,
        SERVER_IMAGE_BITS,    icon_bits,
        NULL);
    /* associate icon with the base frame */
    icon = (Icon)xv_create(XV_NULL, ICON,
        ICON_IMAGE,       icon_image,
        WIN_CMS_NAME,     "palette",
        NULL);
    xv_set(frame, FRAME_ICON, icon, NULL);

    window_fit(frame);

    xv_main_loop(frame);
}

/*
 * initialize_cms_data()
 *    Initialize the colormap segment data and setup the RGB values.
 */
initialize_cms_data(cms_data, red, green, blue)
Xv_cmsdata      *cms_data;
unsigned char   *red, *green, *blue;
{
    /* white  */ (red)[0] = 255;  (green)[0] = 255;  (blue)[0] = 255;
    /* red    */ (red)[1] = 255;  (green)[1] = 0;    (blue)[1] = 0;
    /* green  */ (red)[2] = 0;    (green)[2] = 255;  (blue)[2] = 0;
    /* blue   */ (red)[3] = 0;    (green)[3] = 0;    (blue)[3] = 255;
    /* yellow */ (red)[4] = 255;  (green)[4] = 255;  (blue)[4] = 0;
    /* brown  */ (red)[5] = 188;  (green)[5] = 143;  (blue)[5] = 143;
    /* gray   */ (red)[6] = 220;  (green)[6] = 220;  (blue)[6] = 220;
    /* black  */ (red)[7] = 0;    (green)[7] = 0;    (blue)[7] = 0;

    cms_data->type = XV_STATIC_CMS;
    cms_data->size = NUM_COLORS;
    cms_data->rgb_count = NUM_COLORS;
    cms_data->index = 0;
    cms_data->red = red;
    cms_data->green = green;
    cms_data->blue = blue;
```

Example 20-2. The color_objs.c program (continued)

```
}
/*
 * initialize_chips()
 *      Create colored server images (pixmaps) to be used as
 * panel choice images.
 */
initialize_chips(panel, chips)
Panel           panel;
Server_image    chips[];
{
    register int    i;
    Display         *dpy = (Display *)xv_get(panel, XV_DISPLAY);
    unsigned long   mask, *pixels;
    XGCValues       values;
    Pixmap          pixmap;
    GC              gc;

    if (DefaultDepth(dpy, DefaultScreen(dpy)) == 1) {
        puts("You need a color display to run this program");
        exit(1);
    }
    /* setup gc for drawing colord squares (chips) */
    values.graphics_exposures = False;
    values.foreground = 1;
    mask = GCGraphicsExposures | GCForeground;
    gc = XCreateGC(dpy,
        RootWindow(dpy, DefaultScreen(dpy)), mask, &values);

    /* Get the actual X pixel values from the colormap.  The colormap
     * has been installed on the panel, so use that.  Any window with
     * a cms colormap will do.
     */
    pixels = (unsigned long *)xv_get(panel, WIN_X_COLOR_INDICES);
    for(i = 0; i < NUM_COLORS; i++) {
        chips[i] = (Server_image)xv_create(XV_NULL, SERVER_IMAGE,
            SERVER_IMAGE_COLORMAP, "palette",
            XV_WIDTH,           16,
            XV_HEIGHT,          16,
            SERVER_IMAGE_DEPTH, 8,
            NULL);
        XSetForeground(dpy, gc, pixels[i]);
        pixmap = (Pixmap)xv_get(chips[i], XV_XID);
        XFillRectangle(dpy, pixmap, gc, 0, 0, 16, 16);
    }
}

/*
 * This routine gets called when a color selection is made.
 * Set the foreground or background on the currently selected object.
 * WIN_FOREGROUND_COLOR & WIN_BACKGROUND_COLOR allow the application
 * to specify indices into the colormap segment as the foreground
 * and background values.
 */
void
color_notify(panel_item, choice, event)
Panel_item      panel_item;
```

Example 20-2. The color_objs.c program (continued)

```
int                choice;
Event              *event;
{
    int cnt;
    Xv_opaque get_object();
    unsigned objs = (unsigned)xv_get(objects, PANEL_VALUE);
    int fg = (int)xv_get(xv_get(panel_item, PANEL_CLIENT_DATA),
                    PANEL_VALUE);

    /* the value of the objects panel item is a bit mask ... "on" bits
     * mean that the choice is selected.  Get the object associated
     * with the choice and set it's color.  "&" tests bits in a mask.
     */
    for (cnt = 0; objs; cnt++, objs >>= 1)
        if (objs & 1)
            xv_set(get_object(cnt),
                fg? WIN_FOREGROUND_COLOR : WIN_BACKGROUND_COLOR,
                choice, NULL);

}

/*
 *      Return the XView handle to nth object.
 */
Xv_opaque
get_object(n)
int n;
{
    switch (n) {
        case SELECT_TEXTSW:
            return textsw;
        case SELECT_TEXTSW_VIEW:
            return xv_get(textsw, OPENWIN_NTH_VIEW, 0);
        case SELECT_SCROLLBAR:
            return xv_get(textsw, OPENWIN_VERTICAL_SCROLLBAR,
                                    xv_get(textsw, OPENWIN_NTH_VIEW, 0));
        case SELECT_PANEL:
            return panel;
        case SELECT_ICON:
            return icon;
        default:
            return textsw;
```

The panel item "Colors" has a choice of eight colors to choose from. The choice item uses
PANEL_CHOICE_IMAGES to display the color choices. The images are created in the function initialize_chips(). Here is where server images (pixmaps) are created. We color
them by setting the GC's foreground color using XSetForeground() to the appropriate
pixel value and using XFillRectangle() on the entire size of the image.

20.6 Coloring Panel Items

Panels are subclassed from the canvas object, so you can specify foreground and background colors for both objects in the same way. As you may have noticed by running *color_objs.c*, setting the *foreground* color in the panel also sets the colors for the panel items. However, you can specify the colors for panel items using the attribute PANEL_ITEM_COLOR. This attribute takes as a value an index into a colormap segment as discussed earlier. This attribute overrides the foreground color of the panel for the panel item.

A

Attribute Summary

A
Attribute Summary

This appendix lists all XView attributes in alphabetical order. Each attribute is described briefly. Following its description is a list of the attribute's type, default value and associated procedures. For brevity, the procedures `xv_create`, `xv_find`, `xv_get` and `xv_set` exclude the `xv_` prefix.

ATTR_LIST

Specifies a NULL-terminated attribute-value list. It has no value type or default, but when used, it must be the first attribute in an attribute-value list. Usage is:

```
xv_create(object, pkg,
        ATTR_LIST, avlist,
        other_attrs, ..., 0);
```

CANVAS_AUTO_EXPAND

If TRUE, canvas width and height are never allowed to be less than the edges of the canvas window.

Type:	Boolean
Default:	TRUE
Procs:	create, get, set

CANVAS_AUTO_SHRINK

If TRUE, canvas width and height are never allowed to be greater than the edges of the canvas window.

Type:	Boolean
Default:	TRUE
Procs:	create, get, set

CANVAS_CMS_REPAINT

Specifies whether the canvas package generates a repaint (i.e., invokes the repaint procedure) if the colors in its *static* cms are changed or if the colors in its foreground and/or background indices are changed.

Type:	Boolean
Default:	TRUE if static colors are to be used in the canvas; FALSE if dynamic colors are to be used (i.e., WIN_DYNAMIC_COLOR has been set to TRUE)
Procs:	create, get, set

CANVAS_FIXED_IMAGE

Sets the BitGravity for the canvas paint window to be NorthWestGravity when TRUE or ForgetGravity when FALSE.

Type:	Boolean
Default:	TRUE
Procs:	create, get, set

CANVAS_HEIGHT

Specifies the height of the canvas paint window in pixels.

Type:	int
Default:	0
Procs:	create, get, set

CANVAS_MIN_PAINT_HEIGHT

If CANVAS_AUTO_SHRINK is TRUE, limits shrinking of canvas paint window height to specified value.

Type:	int
Default:	0
Procs:	create, get, set

CANVAS_MIN_PAINT_WIDTH

If CANVAS_AUTO_SHRINK is TRUE, limits shrinking of canvas paint window width to specified value.

Type: int
Default: 0
Procs: create, get, set

CANVAS_NO_CLIPPING

Ignores clip rects in pixwin (pw_*) calls during repaints in all the paint windows of the canvas. (Sunview compatibility only)

Type: Boolean
Default: FALSE
Procs: create, get, set

CANVAS_NTH_PAINT_WINDOW

Returns the paint window associated with the *n*th view, and takes an argument of the value of *n*. 0 is the index of the first view.

Type: Xv_opaque
Procs: get

CANVAS_PAINT_CANVAS_WINDOW

Gets the canvas from a canvas paint window.

Type: Xv_window
Procs: get

CANVAS_PAINTWINDOW_ATTRS

Distributes modifications across all paint windows in a given canvas. It takes an in-line attribute-value list of window attributes.

Type: A-V list
Procs: create, set

CANVAS_REPAINT_PROC

Names a procedure called when canvas paint window has been damaged and must be repaired. See canvas_repaint_proc() in Appendix B, *Summary of Procedures and Macros*.

Default: NULL
Procs: create, get, set

CANVAS_RESIZE_PROC

Names a procedure called when canvas width or height changes. See canvas_resize_proc() in Appendix B, *Summary of Procedures and Macros*.

Default: NULL
Procs: create, get, set

CANVAS_RETAINED

Specified whether the X server should attempt to retain backing store for the canvas (and paint windows). Note, this does not guarantee that window are retained; the server may not be able to comply.

Type: Boolean
Default: TRUE
Procs: create, get, set

CANVAS_VIEW_CANVAS_WINDOW

Gets the canvas from a canvas view window.

Type: Xv_opaque
Procs: get

CANVAS_VIEW_PAINT_WINDOW

Gets the paint window for the specified canvas view window.

Type: Xv_window
Procs: get

CANVAS_VIEWABLE_RECT

Gets the visible part of the specified paint window in the paint window's coordinates.

Type: Rect *
Procs: get

CANVAS_WIDTH

Specifies the width of the canvas paint window in pixels.

Type: int
Default: 0
Procs: create, get, set

CANVAS_X_PAINT_WINDOW

When TRUE, adds additional parameters to the canvas_repaint_proc(). See Appendix B, *Summary of Procedures and Macros*.

Type: Boolean
Default: FALSE
Procs: create, get, set

CURSOR_BACKGROUND_COLOR

Specifies the background color of a cursor as an RGB triplet.

Type: Xv_singlecolor *
Default: white (255, 255, 255)
Procs: create, get, set

CURSOR_FOREGROUND_COLOR
Specifies the foreground color of a cursor as an RGB triplet.

Type: Xv_singlecolor *
Default: black (0, 0, 0)
Procs: create, get, set

CURSOR_IMAGE
Specifies the cursor's image.

Type: Server_image
Default: 16 x 16 x 1
Procs: create, get, set

CURSOR_X_HOT
Specifies the x coordinate of the hotspot. Its value cannot be negative.

Type: int
Default: 0
Procs: create, get, set

CURSOR_Y_HOT
Specifies the y coordinate of the hotspot. Its value cannot be negative.

Type: int
Default: 0
Procs: create, get, set

FONT_CHAR_HEIGHT
Gets the font's character height in pixels including ascenders and descenders.

Type: int
Procs: get

FONT_CHAR_WIDTH
Returns the width (int) of a specified character (char).

Type: int
Procs: get

FONT_DEFAULT_CHAR_HEIGHT
Gets the character height for the default font. Does not take a valve.

Type: char
Procs: get

FONT_DEFAULT_CHAR_WIDTH
Gets the character width for the default font. Does not take a valve.

Type: int
Procs: get

FONT_FAMILY
Specifies the name of a font family.

Type: char *
Default: none
Procs: create, find, get

FONT_RESCALE_OF
Given an existing font and a rescale factor, the returned font will be a similar font in the specified scale.

Type: Xv_Font, Window_rescale_
          state
Procs: create, find

FONT_SCALE
Specifies the relative scale of font with respect to other fonts within the same family and style.

Type: Window_rescale_state
Default: WIN_SCALE_MEDIUM
Procs: create, find, get

FONT_SIZE
Specifies the size of a font in pixels.

Type: int
Default: 12
Procs: create, find, get

FONT_SIZES_FOR_SCALE
Specifies a set of four integral sizes (measured in *points*) to which a font can be scaled.

Type: int, int, int, int
Default: 10, 12, 14, 19
Procs: create, find

FONT_STRING_DIMS
Given a string, returns the struct Font_string_dims giving the dimensions of that string.

Value type: char *
Return type: Font_string_dims
Procs: get

FONT_STYLE
Specifies a font style.

Type: char *
Default: NULL (Roman)
Procs: create, find, get

FRAME_BACKGROUND_COLOR

Specifies the frame's background color. This does not affect the title bar of the frame, which is controlled by the window manager. Use with FRAME_INHERIT_COLORS to propagate the specified colors to subwindows of the frame.

Type: Xv_singlecolor *
Default: 255, 255, 255
Procs: create, get

FRAME_BUSY

Sets label to gray and changes cursor to hour-glass.

Type: Boolean
Default: FALSE
Procs: create, get, set

FRAME_CLOSED

Sets or gets the frame's closed/iconified state.

Type: Boolean
Default: FALSE
Procs: create, get, set

FRAME_CLOSED_RECT

Sets the *size* of a closed frame base. Ignores x, y positioning.

Type: Rect *
Default: 64 x 64
Procs: create, get, set

FRAME_CMD_PANEL

Gets the default panel in the command frame.

Type: Panel
Procs: get

FRAME_CMD_PUSHPIN_IN

Indicates whether the pushpin is in or out.

Type: Boolean
Default: FALSE
Procs: create, get, set

FRAME_DEFAULT_DONE_PROC

The default procedure is to set the subframe to WIN_SHOW, FALSE.

Default: FRAME_DEFAULT_DONE_PROC
Procs: create, get, set

FRAME_DONE_PROC

Names a client's procedure to be called when user chooses Done from subframe's menu. See frame_done_proc() in Appendix B, *Summary of Procedures and Macros*.

Default: FRAME_DEFAULT_DONE_PROC
Procs: create, get, set

FRAME_FOREGROUND_COLOR

Specifies the frame's foreground color. This does not affect the title bar which is controlled by the window manager. Use with FRAME_INHERIT_COLORS to propagate the specified colors to subwindows of the frame.

Type: Xv_singlecolor *
Default: 0, 0, 0
Procs: create, get

FRAME_ICON

Identifies the base frame's icon.

Type: Xv_opaque
Default: NULL
Procs: create, get, set

FRAME_INHERIT_COLORS

Makes child windows inherit the foreground and background colors of the frame. Windows do not inherit colors in the title bar set by the window manager.

Type: Boolean
Default: FALSE
Procs: create, get

FRAME_LEFT_FOOTER

Specifies the left-justified footer.

Type: char *
Default: NULL
Procs: create, get, set

FRAME_NO_CONFIRM

If TRUE, allows destruction of base frame without confirmation.

Type: Boolean
Default: TRUE
Procs: create, get, set

FRAME_NTH_SUBFRAME
Gets the frame's *n*th (from 0) subframe.

Type: int
Default: NULL
Procs: get

FRAME_NTH_SUBWINDOW
Gets the frame's *n*th (from 0) subwindow.

Type: int
Default: NULL
Procs: get

FRAME_RIGHT_FOOTER
Specifies the right-justified footer.

Type: char *
Default: NULL
Procs: create, get, set

FRAME_SHOW_FOOTER
Indicates whether the footer is visible.

Type: Boolean
Default: FALSE
Procs: create, get, set

FRAME_SHOW_HEADER
Indicates whether the header is visible.

Type: Boolean
Default: TRUE
Procs: create, get, set

FRAME_SHOW_LABEL
Indicates whether the frame's label is displayed. This is equivalent to FRAME_SHOW_HEADER.

Type: Boolean
Default: TRUE
Procs: create, get, set

FRAME_SHOW_RESIZE_CORNER
Determines whether a frame has a resize corner. This applies only to command frames and property windows; not base frames.

Type: Boolean
Default: FALSE
Procs: create, get, set

FULLSCREEN_ALLOW_EVENTS
When in a fullscreen grab and the server has "frozen," sets the FULLSCREEN_ALLOW_EVENTS mode to thaw the grab according to the Xlib grab conventions. The values listed below are defined in *X.h*.

Type: Xv_opaque, where the value is any of the AllowEvents modes in *<X11/X.h>*.
Procs: create, set

FULLSCREEN_ALLOW_SYNC_EVENT
When in a synchronous grab mode, specifies that event processing should continue until the next mouse button or keyboard event.

Type: none
Procs: create, set

FULLSCREEN_COLORMAP_WINDOW
Uses colormap of specified window; xv_get identifies that window.

Type: Xv_window
Default: root window
Procs: create, get

FULLSCREEN_CURSOR_WINDOW
Restricts cursor to specified window; xv_get identifies that window.

Type: Xv_window
Default: none
Procs: create, get

FULLSCREEN_GRAB_KEYBOARD
Controls the keyboard portion of a grab.

Type: Boolean
Default: TRUE
Procs: create, get, set

FULLSCREEN_GRAB_POINTER
Controls the pointer portion of a grab.

Type: Boolean
Default: TRUE
Procs: create, get, set

FULLSCREEN_GRAB_SERVER
Controls the server portion of a grab.

Type: Boolean
Default: TRUE
Procs: create, get, set

FULLSCREEN_INPUT_WINDOW
Specifies the window from which input is read; xv_get identifies that window.

Type: Xv_window
Default: root window
Procs: create, get

FULLSCREEN_KEYBOARD_GRAB_KBD_MODE
Determines the grab mode for the keyboard when grabbing the keyboard.

Type: Fullscreen_grab_mode
Default: FULLSCREEN_ASYNCHRONOUS
Procs: create, get, set

FULLSCREEN_KEYBOARD_GRAB_PTR_MODE
Determines the grab mode for the pointer when grabbing the keyboard.

Type: Fullscreen_grab_mode
Default: FULLSCREEN_ASYNCHRONOUS
Procs: create, get, set

FULLSCREEN_OWNER_EVENTS
Determines whether events are reported normally (TRUE) or only with respect to the grab window (FALSE) if selected by the event mask.

Type: Boolean
Default: FALSE
Procs: create, get, set

FULLSCREEN_PAINT_WINDOW
Specifies or gets the canvas paint window.

Type: Xv_opaque
Default: root window
Procs: create, get

FULLSCREEN_POINTER_GRAB_KBD_MODE
Determines the grab mode for the keyboard when grabbing the pointer.

Type: Fullscreen_grab_mode
Default: FULLSCREEN_ASYNCHRONOUS
Procs: create, get, set

FULLSCREEN_POINTER_GRAB_PTR_MODE
Determines the grab mode for the pointer when grabbing the pointer.

Type: Fullscreen_grab_mode
Default: FULLSCREEN_ASYNCHRONOUS
Procs: create, get, set

FULLSCREEN_RECT
Returns a pointer to the rectangle containing the canvas paint window that is currently fullscreen.

Type: Rect *
Default: root window's bounding box
Procs: create, get

FULLSCREEN_SYNC
Specifies whether to grab in synchronous (TRUE) or asynchronous (FALSE) mode.

Type: Boolean
Default: FALSE
Procs: create, get, set

ICON_IMAGE
Sets or gets the remote image for icon's image.

Type: Server_image
Default: NULL
Procs: create, get, set

ICON_IMAGE_RECT
Sets or gets the bounding box (rect) for the icon's image.

Type: Rect *
Default: origin (0,0), width 64, height 64
Procs: create, get, set

ICON_LABEL_RECT
Sets or gets the bounding box for the icon's label. Relative to the icon, 0, 0 is upper-left corner of icon.

Type: Rect *
Default: bottom left-hand corner of icon
Procs: create, get, set

MENU_ACTION_IMAGE
Provides a shortcut for creating or modifying an *image* menu item (i.e., a Server_image) and associating it with a notify procedure. It takes two values: a server-image and a notify procedure.

Type: Server_image *,
          (void *) ()
Default: N/A
Procs: create, set

MENU_ACTION_ITEM
Provides a shortcut for creating or modifying a menu *item* and associating it with a notify procedure. It takes two values: a string and a notify procedure.

Type: char *, (void *) ()
Default: N/A
Procs: create, set

MENU_APPEND_ITEM
Appends an item to end of menu.

Type: Menu_item
Default: N/A
Procs: set

MENU_CLASS

Gets an enumerated type that identifies the menu class, as set by the package. One of MENU_CHOICE, MENU_COMMAND, or MENU_TOGGLE.

Type: Menu_class
Default: defined by package
Procs: get

MENU_COL_MAJOR

If TRUE, string items in the menu will be sorted in column-major order (like 1s (1)) instead of row-major order. This attribute does not apply unless the menu uses multiple columns.

Type: Boolean
Default: FALSE
Procs: create, get, set

MENU_DEFAULT

Default menu item as a position.

Type: int
Default: 1
Procs: create, get, set

MENU_DEFAULT_ITEM

Default menu item as opaque handle.

Type: Menu_handle
Default: handle of first item
Procs: get, set, create

MENU_DESCEND_FIRST

If this attribute is specified in xv_find, then the search will be done "depth first." If it is not specified, the search will be "deferred"; that is, it will be done horizontally through the menu structure.

Type: no value
Default: deferred
Procs: find

MENU_DONE_PROC*

Specifies a callback procedure that is called when the menu group is dismissed. See menu_done_proc() in Appendix B, *Summary of Procedures and Macros*.

Default: NULL
Procs: create, get, set

MENU_FEEDBACK

If FALSE, item is never inverted and is not selectable.

Type: Boolean
Default: TRUE
Procs: create, get, set

MENU_FIRST_EVENT

Gets the event which was initially passed into menu_show. (The event's contents *can* be modified.)

Type: Event *
Procs: get

MENU_GEN_PIN_WINDOW

Creates a command window as the pin window based on the static (not dynamic) menu's contents. The frame is the parent frame; the name is the pin window's name. All menu items *must* have notify procedures; MENU_NOTIFY_PROC for the menu itself is ignored.

Type: Frame, char *
Default: no pin window
Procs: create, set

MENU_GEN_PROC

Names a client-provided procedure that is called to generate a menu or menu item. See menu_gen_proc() in Appendix B, *Summary of Procedures and Macros*. This attribute takes two values: a string and a generate procedure.

Default: none
Procs: create, get, set

MENU_GEN_PROC_IMAGE

Defines the generate procedure and server image for a menu item.

Type: Server_image *,
           (* Menu) ()
Default: NULL
Procs: create, set

MENU_GEN_PROC_ITEM

Defines the generate procedure and text string for a menu item.

Type: char *,(* Menu)()
Default: NULL
Procs: create,set

MENU_GEN_PULLRIGHT

Defines the generate procedure for the menu
item's submenu.

Type: generate proc
Default: NULL
Procs: create,get,set

MENU_GEN_PULLRIGHT_IMAGE

Provides a shortcut for creating an image for
a menu item (or a menu item's submenu) and
associating it with a pullright-menu generate
procedure.

Type: Server_image *,
             (* Menu)()
Default: none
Procs: create,set

MENU_GEN_PULLRIGHT_ITEM

Provides a shortcut for creating a menu item
(or a menu item's submenu) and associating
it with a pullright menu generate procedure.
See menu_gen_proc() in Appendix B,
Summary of Procedures and Macros.

Type: char *,(* Menu) ()
Default: none
Procs: create,set

MENU_IMAGE

Specifies the menu item's server image.

Type: Server_image
Default: NULL
Procs: create,get,set

MENU_IMAGE_ITEM

Creates an image menu item with value
specified.

Type: Server_image
Default: none
Procs: create,get,set

MENU_IMAGES

Creates a menu item with multiple images.

Type: list of Server_image
Default: none
Procs: create,get,set

MENU_INACTIVE

If TRUE, item is grayed out and not selectable.

Type: Boolean
Default: FALSE
Procs: create,get,set

MENU_INSERT

Inserts new item after *n*th item in the menu.

Type: int,Menu_item
Default: N/A
Procs: create,get,set

MENU_INSERT_ITEM

Inserts the item given as the second value
after the one given as the first value.

Type: Menu_item,Menu_item
Procs: create,set

MENU_INVERT

If TRUE, item's display is inverted.

Type: Boolean
Default: FALSE
Procs: create,get,set

MENU_ITEM

Allows you to create menu items *in-line* with
the call to xv_create() used to create
your menu. Takes a *menu item*-specific attribute-value list that would otherwise be used
in a separate call to xv_create() to create
menu items with the MENUITEM package.

Type: A-V list
Procs: create,set

MENU_LAST_EVENT

Gets the last event read by the menu. (The
event's contents can be modified.)

Type: Event *
Procs: get

MENU_NCOLS

Sets or gets the number of columns in a
menu.

Type: int
Default: 1
Procs: create,get,set

MENU_NITEMS

Returns the number of items in a menu.

Type: int
Procs: get

MENU_NOTIFY_PROC

Names a procedure called when the user selects a menu item. See menu_notify_proc() in Appendix B, *Summary of Procedures and Macros*.

Default: NULL
Procs: create, get, set

MENU_NOTIFY_STATUS

If the menu is attached to a menu button that is part of an unpinned pop-up window, then the window is dismissed if MENU_NOTIFY_STATUS is XV_OK. If MENU_NOTIFY_STATUS is set to XV_ERROR, then the window is not dismissed.

Type: int
Default: XV_OK
Procs: create, get, set

MENU_NROWS

Sets or gets the number of rows in a menu.

Type: int
Procs: create, get, set

MENU_NTH_ITEM

Gets the *n*th menu item. *n* is counted from 1.

Type: int
Procs: get

MENU_PIN

Determines whether the menu will have pushpin.

Type: Boolean
Default: FALSE
Procs: create, get, set

MENU_PIN_PROC

Names a procedure called if user chooses the pin menu item. The default procedure displays a window whose layout is similar to the menu it replaces. See menu_pin_proc() in Appendix B, *Summary of Procedures and Macros*.

Default: menu_default_pin_proc()
Procs: create, get, set

MENU_PIN_WINDOW

Sets the handle of the command frame representing the pin window for the menu. Use MENU_PIN_WINDOW to attach a pin to a

dynamic (changing) menu.

Type: Frame_cmd
Default: none
Procs: create, get, set

MENU_PULLRIGHT

Item's pullright menu.

Type: Menu
Default: NULL
Procs: create, get, set

MENU_PULLRIGHT_IMAGE

Creates an image menu item with pullright submenu.

Type: Server_image, Menu
Default: N/A
Procs: create, set

MENU_PULLRIGHT_ITEM

Creates a string menu item with pullright submenu.

Type: char *, Menu
Default: N/A
Procs: create, set

MENU_RELEASE

Specifies that the item gets destroyed when its parent menu is destroyed (default for items created in-line).

Type: no value
Default: if in-line, destroy item; if Append/Replace, do *not* destroy item
Procs: create, set

MENU_RELEASE_IMAGE

Specifies that the string or Server_image associated with the item is freed when the item is destroyed.

Type: no value
Default: do not release text string or server image
Procs: create, set

MENU_REMOVE

Removes the *n*th item from the menu.

Type: int
Procs: set

MENU_REMOVE_ITEM

Removes the specified menu item.

Type: `Menu_item`
Procs: `set`

MENU_REPLACE
Replaces the *n*th item with specified item.

Type: `int, Menu_item`
Procs: `create, set`

MENU_REPLACE_ITEM
Replaces the item given as first value with the one given as the second value in the menu (the old item is not replaced in àny other menus in which it may appear).

Type: `Menu_item, Menu_item`
Procs: `create, set`

MENU_SELECTED
If TRUE, the item is currently selected.

Type: `Boolean`
Default: `FALSE`
Procs: `create, get, set`

MENU_STRING
Sets or gets the menu item's string.

Type: `char *`
Default: `NULL`
Procs: `create, get, set`

MENU_STRING_ITEM
Defines the text string and value for a menu item.

Type: `char *, Xv_opaque`
Default: `NULL`
Procs: `create, set`

MENU_STRINGS
Sets the string for multiple menu items.

Type: list of `char *`
Procs: `create, set`

MENU_TITLE
Specifies that the item is the menu's title. Returns TRUE or FALSE on `get`.

Type: no value on `set`, `Boolean` on `get`
Default: menu item is *not* the menu title
Procs: `create, get, set`

MENU_TITLE_ITEM
Creates a string title item. Must be used with menus that do not originate from pullright items or pulldown menu buttons.

Type: `char *`
Default: no title
Procs: `create, set`

MENU_TYPE
Returns `MENU_MENU` or `MENU_ITEM`. Informs you whether you have a menu or a menu item.

Type: `Menu_attribute` (an enum)
Default: `MENU_MENU`
Procs: `get`

MENU_VALID_RESULT
If TRUE, then a zero return value represents a legitimate value.

Type: `Boolean`
Default: `FALSE`
Procs: `create, get, set`

MENU_VALUE
Sets or gets the item's value.

Type: `Xv_opaque`
Default: `NULL`
Procs: `create, get, set`

NOTICE_BUTTON
Specifies a string to be displayed in a button and a value to use if the button is selected. Value is returned by `notice_prompt()`.

Type: `char *, int`
Default: none
Procs: `notice_prompt`

NOTICE_BUTTON_NO
Specifies a string associated with the NO (cancel) button, which can also be triggered via a keyboard accelerator. The value returned if this button is selected is `NOTICE_NO`.

Type: `char *`
Default: none
Procs: `notice_prompt`

NOTICE_BUTTON_YES
Specifies a string to associate with the YES (confirm) button, which is also triggered via a keyboard accelerator. The value returned when this button is selected is `NOTICE·YES`.

Type: `char *`
Default: none
Procs: `notice_prompt`

NOTICE_FOCUS_XY

Describes the x, y position, relative to the specified client window, from which the notice shadow emanates. (This is necessary because the pointer may move.)

Type: int, int
Default: mouse position
Procs: notice_prompt

NOTICE_FONT

Specifies the font to be used in the notice message(s).

Type: Xv_Font
Default: one size larger than that used by client frame
Procs: notice_prompt

NOTICE_MESSAGE_STRINGS

Specifies the strings to be displayed in the message area of the notice panel.

Type: list of char *
Default: NULL
Procs: notice_prompt

NOTICE_MESSAGE_STRINGS_ARRAY_PTR

Same as NOTICE_MESSAGE_STRINGS except the client need not know the actual strings being passed, just that the value is a pointer to the first of a null-terminated array of strings. The notice package will cast the value into a type char **.

Type: char**
Default: NULL
Procs: notice_prompt

NOTICE_NO_BEEPING

Allows a client to specify that no beeping should take place, regardless of defaults database setting. The default for this option is FALSE; that is, beep however many times specified in the database.

Type: int
Default: TRUE
Procs: notice_prompt

NOTICE_TRIGGER

Specifies an XView event that causes the notice to return. When this event occurs, the value returned is NOTICE_TRIGGERED. The event parameter to notice_prompt contains specifics about the event that triggered it.

Type: int
Default: N/A
Procs: notice_prompt

OPENWIN_ADJUST_FOR_HORIZONTAL_SCROLLBAR

Reserves space in openwin-class objects (e.g., canvas) for a horizontal scrollbar. On xv_set, adjusts (extends) the height of a subwindow that does *not* have a horizontal scrollbar to align properly with one that does.

Type: Boolean
Default: TRUE
Procs: create, get, set

OPENWIN_ADJUST_FOR_VERTICAL_SCROLLBAR

Reserves space in openwin-class objects (e.g., canvas) for a vertical scrollbar. On xv_set, adjusts (extends) the width of a subwindow that does *not* have a vertical scrollbar to align properly with one that does.

Type: Boolean
Default: TRUE
Procs: create, get, set

OPENWIN_AUTO_CLEAR

If TRUE, exposed areas of windows are cleared (i.e., painted the background color) before the repaint proc is called.

Type: Boolean
Default: TRUE unless subwindow's canvas is retained
Procs: create, get, set

OPENWIN_HORIZONTAL_SCROLLBAR

Returns the handle of the horizontal scrollbar associated with the specified view.

Type: Xv_scrollbar
Default: none
Procs: get

OPENWIN_NO_MARGIN

If TRUE, the view window's two pixel bottom and right margins are turned off.

Type: Boolean
Default: FALSE
Procs: create, get, set

OPENWIN_NTH_VIEW

Gets the handle of a specified openwin view window. Openwin view windows are numbered from 0.

Type: int, Xv_window
Procs: get

OPENWIN_NVIEWS

Gets the number of views contained in the open window.

Type: int
Default: 1
Procs: get

OPENWIN_SELECTED_VIEW

Specifies the currently selected openwin view.

Type: Xv_window
Default: none
Procs: create, get, set

OPENWIN_SHOW_BORDERS

Displays openwin borders. OPENWIN_ SHOW_BORDERS is set only on creation. This must remain on for openwin objects to have scrollbars attached to them.

Type: Boolean
Default: TRUE (FALSE for panels)
Procs: create, get

OPENWIN_SPLIT

Takes as its value a list of attribute-value pairs beginning with OPENWIN_SPLIT_.

Type: A-V list
Procs: create, set

OPENWIN_SPLIT_DESTROY_PROC

Names a procedure to call when a split openwin is destroyed. See openwin_ split_destroy_proc() in Appendix B, *Summary of Procedures and Macros.*

Default: NULL
Procs: create, get, set

OPENWIN_SPLIT_DIRECTION

Sets the direction of the split either horizontally or vertically.

Type: Openwin_split_direction
Default: OPENWIN_SPLIT_HORIZONTAL
Procs: create, set

OPENWIN_SPLIT_INIT_PROC

Names a procedure to call when a split window is created. See openwin_ init_split() in Appendix B, *Summary of Procedures and Macros.*

Default: NULL
Procs: create, get, set

OPENWIN_SPLIT_POSITION

Sets the position (in pixels) of the view.

Type: int
Default: none
Procs: set, create

OPENWIN_SPLIT_VIEW

Specifies which view to split. Its value is the handle of the view you want to split.

Type: Xv_window
Procs: set

OPENWIN_SPLIT_VIEW_START

Specifies which part of the data (measured in scrollbar-units) is displayed at the start of the view (*top* for vertical; *left* for horizontal).

Type: int
Default: continue from previous view
Procs: set, create, get

OPENWIN_VERTICAL_SCROLLBAR

Returns the handle of the vertical scrollbar associated with the specified view.

Type: Scrollbar
Default: none
Procs: get

OPENWIN_VIEW_ATTRS

Distributes modifications across all *views* in a given open window. It does not affect paintwindows.

Type: A-V list
Procs: create, set

PANEL_BACKGROUND_PROC

Names an event handling procedure called when an event falls on the background of the panel. See panel_background_proc() in Appendix B, *Summary of Procedures and Macros.*

Default: panel_default_handle_event
Procs: create, get, set

PANEL_CARET_ITEM

Specifies the text item that currently has the caret.

Type: `Panel_item`
Default: first text item
Procs: `create, get, set`

PANEL_CHOICE_IMAGE
Specifies the image for choice item indicated by the first argument.

Type: `int, server_image`
Default: none
Procs: `create, get, set`

PANEL_CHOICE_IMAGES
Specifies the image for each of several choices.

Type: list of `Server_image`
Default: `NULL`
Procs: `create, get, set`

PANEL_CHOICE_STRING
Sets the string for choice item specified by first argument.

Type: `int, char *`
Default: `NULL`
Procs: `create, get, set`

PANEL_CHOICE_STRINGS
Sets the string for each choice. You must specify at least one choice. The least you can specify is a single null string.

Type: list of `char *`
Default: `NULL`
Procs: `create, set`

PANEL_CHOICE_X
Second argument is left edge of choice specified by first argument.

Type: `int, int`
Default: determined by `PANEL_LAYOUT`
Procs: `create, get, set`

PANEL_CHOICE_XS
Left edge of each choice.

Type: list of `int`
Default: determined by `PANEL_LAYOUT`
Procs: `create, set`

PANEL_CHOICE_Y
Second argument is top edge of choice specified by first argument.

Type: `int, int`
Default: determined by `PANEL_LAYOUT`
Procs: `create, get, set`

PANEL_CHOICE_YS
Top edge of each set.

Type: list of `int`
Default: determined by `PANEL_LAYOUT`
Procs: `create, set`

PANEL_CHOOSE_NONE
Allows the scrolling list to have no currently selected item. This attribute is not applicable if `PANEL_CHOOSE_ONE` is `FALSE`.

Type: `Boolean`
Default: `TRUE`
Procs: `create, get, set`

PANEL_CHOOSE_ONE
If `TRUE`, creates an exclusive scrolling list. If `FALSE`, creates a non-exclusive scrolling list.

Type: `Boolean`
Default: `TRUE`
Procs: `create, get, set`

PANEL_DEFAULT_ITEM
Sets the default item on a panel or gets the handle to the current default item. The system default is the first item created.

Type: `Panel_item`
Default: first item
Procs: `create, get, set`

PANEL_DEFAULT_VALUE
Identifies the default choice item. Used only in `PANEL_CHOICE_STACK`.

Type: `int` or `unsigned`
Default: first choice
Procs: `create, get, set`

PANEL_DISPLAY_LEVEL
Specifies the number of choices to display. One of `PANEL_ALL`, `PANEL_CURRENT`, or `PANEL_NONE`.

Type: `char*`
Default: `PANEL_ALL`
Procs: `create, set`

PANEL_EXTRA_PAINT_HEIGHT
Defines the increment by which the panel grows in the y direction. It is used when `window_fit_height()` is called.

Type: int
Default: 1 pixel
Procs: create,get,set

PANEL_EXTRA_PAINT_WIDTH

Defines the increment by which the panel grows in the x direction. It is used when window_fit_width() is called.

Type: int
Default: 1 pixel
Procs: create,get,set

PANEL_FEEDBACK

Specifies feedback to give when an item is selected. If PANEL_DISPLAY_LEVEL is PANEL_CURRENT, the default is PANEL_NONE; otherwise, it is PANEL_MARKED.

Type: Panel_setting
Default: see description
Procs: create,get,set

PANEL_FIRST_ITEM

Gets the handle of the first item on a panel. The PANEL_EACH_ITEM macro (see Appendix B) can be used to iterate over each item in a panel, starting with this first item.

Type: Panel_item
Procs: get

PANEL_INACTIVE

If TRUE, panel button item cannot be selected. Inactive items are displayed with gray-out pattern.

Type: Boolean
Default: FALSE
Procs: create,get,set

PANEL_ITEM_CLASS

Gets the panel item *type* of the panel item specified.

Type: Panel_item_type
Procs: get

PANEL_ITEM_COLOR

Specifies the colormap index to use for the item. A value of –1 implies the foreground color for the panel window.

Type: int
Default: 0
Procs: create,get,set

PANEL_ITEM_MENU

Specifies the menu associated with the panel button item.

Type: Menu
Default: NULL
Procs: create,get,set

PANEL_ITEM_RECT

Gets the rectangle surrounding the panel item.

Type: Rect   *
Procs: get

PANEL_ITEM_X

Specifies the x position (in pixels) where the last panel item was created. If no item was created, then it specifies the x position where the first item will be created.

Type: int
Procs: create,get,set

PANEL_ITEM_X_GAP

Specifies the number of x-coordinate pixels between items. Provides space between items appearing in the same row.

Type: int
Default: 10 pixels
Procs: create,get,set

PANEL_ITEM_Y

Specifies the y position (in pixels) where the last panel item was created. If no item was created, then it specifies the y position where the first item will be created.

Type: int
Default: none
Procs: create,get,set

PANEL_ITEM_Y_GAP

Specifies the number of y-coordinate pixels between items. Provides space between items appearing in the same column.

Type: int
Default: 13 pixels
Procs: create,get,set

PANEL_LABEL_BOLD

If TRUE, item's label is rendered in bold. Only applies to PANEL_MESSAGE items.

Type: Boolean
Default: FALSE
Procs: create, get, set

PANEL_LABEL_IMAGE

Specifies the image for an item's label.

Type: Server_image
Default: NULL
Procs: create, get, set

PANEL_LABEL_STRING

Specifies the string for the item's label.

Type: char *
Default: NULL
Procs: create, get, set

PANEL_LABEL_WIDTH

Specifies the width of the panel label in pixels.

Type: int
Default: width of text string or server image
Procs: create, get, set

PANEL_LABEL_X

Specifies the x coordinate of the *label* portion of panel items that have *values* associated with them (e.g., text items). Intended to be used when PANEL_VALUE_X is specified.

Type: int (in pixels)
Default: PANEL_ITEM_X from parent panel.
Procs: create, get, set

PANEL_LABEL_Y

Specifies the y coordinate of the *label* portion of panel items that have *values* associated with them (e.g., text items). Intended to be used only if PANEL_VALUE_Y is specified.

Type: int (in pixels)
Default: PANEL_ITEM_Y from parent panel.
Procs: create, get, set

PANEL_LAYOUT

In a PANEL create call, this attribute controls the layout of panel items. When used in a create panel *item* call, this attribute controls the direction in which the item's *components* are laid out.

Type: Panel_setting
Default: PANEL_HORIZONTAL
Procs: create, get, set

PANEL_LIST_CLIENT_DATA

Sets or gets up to 32 bits of user-entered data from a row number on the list. This attribute takes two values: a row number, and a 32-bit data value.

Type: int, caddr_t
Default: NULL
Procs: create, get, set

PANEL_LIST_CLIENT_DATAS

Works much like its companion attribute, PANEL_LIST_ CLIENT_DATA, except that it takes a null-terminated value list of client data as its value. Position in the value list determines the row to which the data will be associated.

Type: list
Default: NULL
Procs: create, get, set

PANEL_LIST_DELETE

Deletes a row from the scrolling list. The list is adjusted automatically after the deletion.

Type: int
Default: none
Procs: create, set

PANEL_LIST_DISPLAY_ROWS

Sets the number of rows in a list that will be displayed.

Type: int
Default: 5
Procs: create, get, set

PANEL_LIST_GLYPH

Takes a row and Server_image to let you assign a glyph or icon to a row. The height of the glyph may not exceed the height of scrolling list row. Also see PANEL_ LIST_ROW_HEIGHT.

Value type: int, Server_image
Return type: Server_image
Default: NULL
Procs: create, get, set

PANEL_LIST_GLYPHS

Works the same as its companion attribute, PANEL_LIST_GLYPH, except that it takes a NULL-terminated value list as its value. The

height of the glyph may not exceed the
height of scrolling list row. Also see
`PANEL_LIST_ROW_HEIGHT`.

Type: list of `Server_image`
Default: `NULL`
Procs: `create, set`

PANEL_LIST_INSERT

Inserts a list item at a specified row number.
This attribute allocates space, attaches a row
number to the list, and inserts an empty
string. Clients must set `PANEL_LIST_`
`GLYPH` and/or `PANEL_LIST_STRING` at this
row number to set the glyph item and/or
string.

Type: `int`
Procs: `create, set`

PANEL_LIST_NROWS

Sets or gets the total number of rows in the
scrolling list.

Type: `int`
Default: `NULL`
Procs: `create, get, set`

PANEL_LIST_ROW_HEIGHT

Specifies the height of each row in the scrolling list.

Type: `int`
Default: height of panel's font
Procs: `create, get, set`

PANEL_LIST_SELECT

Takes two values: a row number and a
Boolean that lets you select (`TRUE`) or
deselect (`FALSE`) the specified row.

Type: `int, Boolean`
Default: `FALSE`
Procs: `set, create`

PANEL_LIST_SELECTED

Returns whether the specified row number is
selected (`TRUE`) or not (`FALSE`).

Value type: `int`
Return type: `Boolean`
Procs: `get`

PANEL_LIST_STRING

Sets (specifies) string to a specified row.
`xv_get` returns the pointer to the character
string assigned to the row.

Value type: `int, char *`
Return type: `char *`
Default: empty string
Procs: `create, get, set`

PANEL_LIST_STRINGS

Works the same as its companion attribute,
`PANEL_LIST_STRING`, except that it takes a
`NULL`-terminated list of strings as its value.

Type: `list, char *`
Default: empty string
Procs: `create, get, set`

PANEL_LIST_WIDTH

Sets or gets the width in pixels of the scrolling list. By default, the list will be just wide
enough to accommodate the largest item on
the list.

Type: `int`
Default: slightly larger than largest item
           on list
Procs: `create, get, set`

PANEL_MASK_CHAR

Specifies the character used to mask type-in
characters. Use the space character for no
character echo (caret does not advance). Use
the `NULL` character to disable masking.

Type: `char`
Default: `NULL`
Procs: `create, set, get`

PANEL_MAX_VALUE

Specifies the maximum value of the slider or
numeric text item.

Type: `int`
Default: `100`
Procs: `create, get, set`

PANEL_MIN_VALUE

Specifies the minimum value of the slider or
numeric text item.

Type: `int`
Default: `0`
Procs: `create, get, set`

PANEL_NEXT_COL

Specifies the amount of white space (in pixels) between the last column and the next
(new) column. If you specify −1, the default
gap (`PANEL_ITEM_X_GAP`) is used.

Type: Panel_item
Default: none
Procs: create

PANEL_NEXT_ITEM

Gets the handle of the next item on a panel.
Usage is:

```
next_item = xv_get(this_item,
              PANEL_NEXT_ITEM);
```

Type: Panel_item
Procs: get

PANEL_NEXT_ROW

Specifies the amount of white space (in pixels) between the last row and the next (new) row. If you specify −1, the default gap (PANEL_ITEM_Y_GAP) will be used.

Type: Panel_item
Default: none
Procs: create

PANEL_NOTIFY_LEVEL

Specifies when to call the notify function. Either PANEL_ALL, or PANEL_NONE.

Type: Panel_setting
Default: PANEL_SPECIFIED
Procs: create, get, set

PANEL_NOTIFY_PROC

Procedure to call when a panel item is selected. See panel_notify_proc() in Appendix B, *Summary of Procedures and Macros.*

Default: NULL
Procs: create, get, set

PANEL_NOTIFY_STATUS

If the panel item is part of an unpinned pop-up window, then the window is dismissed if PANEL_NOTIFY_STATUS is XV_OK. If PANEL_NOTIFY_STATUS is set to XV_ERROR, then the window is not dismissed.

Type: int
Default: XV_OK
Procs: create, get, set

PANEL_NOTIFY_STRING

String of characters that triggers notification when typed in a text item. Applies only when PANEL_NOTIFY_LEVEL is PANEL_SPECIFIED.

Type: char *
Default: \n \r \t (i.e., newline, carriage return, and tab)
Procs: create, get, set

PANEL_PAINT

Controls the panel item's painting behavior in xv_set calls. Possible values are PANEL_ITEM_CLEAR, PANEL_ITEM_NO_CLEAR, or PANEL_ITEM_NONE.

Type: Panel_setting
Default: PANEL_CLEAR
Procs: create, set

PANEL_PARENT_PANEL

Returns the panel that contains the item. Same as XV_OWNER.

Type: Panel
Procs: get

PANEL_READ_ONLY

For text and panel list items, if TRUE, editing is disabled; if FALSE, editing is enabled. xv_set applies to text items only.

Type: Boolean
Default: FALSE
Procs: create, get, set

PANEL_REPAINT_PROC

Specifies the name of the client-supplied panel repaint procedure. It takes the same arguments as canvas_repaint_proc (see Appendix B, *Summary of Procedures and Macros*).

Default: NULL
Procs: create, get, set

PANEL_SHOW_RANGE

If TRUE, shows the minimum and maximum slider values.

Type: Boolean
Default: TRUE
Procs: create, get, set

PANEL_SHOW_VALUE

If TRUE, shows the "value" part of item that have values.

Type: Boolean
Default: TRUE
Procs: create, get, set

PANEL_SLIDER_WIDTH
Specifies the width of the slider bar in pixels.

Type: int
Default: 100
Procs: create, get, set

PANEL_TOGGLE_VALUE
Specifies the value of a particular toggle choice. Second argument is value of choice specified by first argument.

Type: int, int
Default: NULL
Procs: create, get, set

PANEL_VALUE
If the item is of type PANEL_CHOICE_ITEM, the value is an ordinal position (from 0) of current choice. If the item is of type PANEL_TOGGLE_ITEM, the value is a bit-mask indicating currently selected choices (e.g., bit 5 is 1 of fifth choice selected). If text item, sets string value (char*). If list item, sets value in range PANEL_MIN_VALUE to PANEL_MAX_VALUE. Default is PANEL_MIN_VALUE.

Type: int or unsigned
Default: NULL
Procs: create, get, set

PANEL_VALUE_DISPLAY_LENGTH
Maximum number of characters to display in a text string. Note that the length of the value display may not be less than the combined width of the left and right "more text" buttons. In 12-point font, this is four characters.

Type: int
Default: 80
Procs: create, get, set

PANEL_VALUE_STORED_LENGTH
Maximum number of characters to store in the value string for text items.

Type: int
Default: 80
Procs: create, get, set

PANEL_VALUE_X
Specifies the x coordinate of the *value* portion of panel items that have separate *label* and *value* entities (e.g., text items). For use in conjunction with PANEL_LABEL_X.

Type: int
Default: (See Chapter 7, *Panels.*)
Procs: create, get, set

PANEL_VALUE_Y
Specifies the top edge of value. This is the companion attribute to PANEL_VALUE_X.

Type: int
Default: (See Chapter 7, *Panels.*)
Procs: create, get, set

SCREEN_NUMBER
Specifies the number of the screen associated with object.

Type: int
Default: 0
Procs: get

SCREEN_SERVER
Specifies the server associated with this screen.

Type: Display *
Default: value of DISPLAY environment
          variable
Procs: get

SCROLLBAR_COMPUTE_SCROLL_PROC
Specifies a procedure to compute the elevator and proportional indicator values.

Default: scrollbar_default_
          compute_scroll_proc
Procs: create, get, set

SCROLLBAR_DIRECTION
The orientation of the scrollbar as either SCROLLBAR_VERTICAL or SCROLLBAR_HORIZONTAL.

Type: Scrollbar_setting
Default: none
Procs: create, get

SCROLLBAR_LAST_VIEW_START
Specifies the offset of view into object prior to scroll.

Type: int
Default: 0
Procs: get

SCROLLBAR_MENU
Specifies a pointer to the scrollbar's menu. Clients can add items to the *default* menu but cannot remove items from it.

Type: Menu
Default: scrollbar creates a default menu
Procs: get

SCROLLBAR_NORMALIZE_PROC

Specifies a procedure that does normaliza-
tion (set the viewable area of the object that
the scrollbar scrolls).

Default: NULL
Procs: create, get, set

SCROLLBAR_NOTIFY_CLIENT

Used by the Notifier. Indicates client that is
notified when scrollbar is scrolled. See
Chapter 10, *Scrollbars*.

Type: Xv_opaque
Default: subwindow scrollbar is attached
           to contents
Procs: create, get, set

SCROLLBAR_OBJECT_LENGTH

Specifies the length of scrollable object in
scrollbar units. Value must be greater than or
equal to zero.

Type: int
Default: 0
Procs: create, get, set

SCROLLBAR_PAGE_LENGTH

Specifies the length of a page in scrollbar
units for page-scrolling purposes.

Type: int
Default: 0
Procs: create, get, set

SCROLLBAR_PIXELS_PER_UNIT

Specifies the number of pixels constituting a
scrollbar unit. For example, when scrolling a
list of icons, each unit might be 64 pixels.

Type: int
Default: 1
Procs: create, get, set

SCROLLBAR_SPLITTABLE

Indicates whether the object that contains the
scrollbar is splittable.

Type: Boolean
Default: FALSE
Procs: create, get, set

SCROLLBAR_VIEW_LENGTH

Specifies the length of viewing window in
scrollbar units.

Type: int
Default: 0
Procs: create, get, set

SCROLLBAR_VIEW_START

Specifies the current offset into scrollbar
object in scrollbar units. The value must be
greater than or equal to zero.

Type: int
Default: 0
Procs: create, get, set

SELN_REQ_BYTESIZE

Specifies the number of bytes in the selection.

Type: int
Default: none
Procs: selection_ask,
           selection_init_request,
           selection_query

SELN_REQ_COMMIT_PENDING_DELETE

Instructs the replier to delete any secondary
selection made in pending delete mode.

Type: none
Default: none
Procs: selection_ask,
           selection_init_request,
           selection_query

SELN_REQ_CONTENTS_ASCII

Specifies a null-terminated list of 4-byte
words containing the selection's ASCII contents. If the last word of the contents is not
full (including NULL terminator for the
string), it is NULL-padded.

Type: char *
Default: none
Procs: selection_ask,
           selection_init_request,
           selection_query

SELN_REQ_CONTENTS_PIECES

Specifies that the value is a NULL-terminated
list of 4-byte words containing the selection's contents described in the textsw's
piece-table format.

Type: char *
Default: none
Procs: selection_ask,
           selection_init_request,
           selection_query

SELN_REQ_DELETE

Instructs the holder of the selection to delete
the contents of the selection from its window
(used only by text subwindows).

Type: void
Default: none
Procs: selection_ask,
           selection_init_request,
           selection_query

SELN_REQ_END_REQUEST

Returns an error for failed or unrecognized
requests.

Type: void
Default: none
Procs: selection_ask,
           selection_init_request,
           selection_query

SELN_REQ_FAKE_LEVEL

Gives a level to which the selection should
be expanded before processing the remainder of this request. The original level should
be maintained on the display, however, and
restored as the true level on completion of
the request.

Type: int
Default: none
Procs: selection_ask,
           selection_init_request,
           selection_query

SELN_REQ_FILE_NAME

Specifies a null-terminated list of 4-byte
words. Contains the name of the file which
holds the *shelf* selection.

Type: char *
Default: none
Procs: selection_ask,
           selection_init_request,
           selection_query

SELN_REQ_FIRST

Gives the number of bytes that precede the
first byte of the selection.

Type: int
Default: none
Procs: selection_ask,
           selection_init_request,
           selection_query

SELN_REQ_FIRST_UNIT

Gives the number of units of the selection's
current level (line, paragraph, etc.) which
precede the first unit of the selection.

Type: int
Default: none
Procs: selection_ask,
           selection_init_request,
           selection_query

SELN_REQ_LAST

Gives the byte index of the last byte of the
selection.

Type: int
Default: none
Procs: selection_ask,
           selection_init_request,
           selection_query

SELN_REQ_LAST_UNIT

Gives the unit index of the last unit of the
selection at its current level.

Type: int
Default: none
Procs: selection_ask,
           selection_init_request,
           selection_query

SELN_REQ_LEVEL

Gives the current level of the selection.

Type: int
Default: none
Procs: selection_ask,
           selection_init_request,
           selection_query

SELN_REQ_RESTORE

Instructs the replier to restore the selection
referred to in this request, if it has maintained
sufficient information to do so.

Type: none
Default: none
Procs: selection_ask,
           selection_init_request,
           selection_query

SELN_REQ_SET_LEVEL

Gives a level to which the selection should be set. This request should affect the true level.

Type: int
Default: none
Procs: selection_ask,
           selection_init_request,
           selection_query

SELN_REQ_YIELD

Requests the holder of the selection to yield it. SELN_SUCCESS, SELN_DIDNT_HAVE, and SELN_WRONG_RANK are legitimate responses. The latter comes from a holder asked to yield the primary selection when it knows a function key is down.

Type: Seln_result
Default: none
Procs: selection_ask,
           selection_init_request,
           selection_query

SERVER_IMAGE_BITMAP_FILE

Specifies a file containing the X11 bitmap to be created. Refer to the Xlib documentation on XReadBitmapFile() for the file format.

Type: char *
Default: none
Procs: create

SERVER_IMAGE_BITS

Specifies the image bits for the server image. SunView pixrect data can be used.

Type: short *.
Default: uninitialized
Procs: create, set

SERVER_IMAGE_DEPTH

Specifies the bit plane depth of the server image. An xv_set of the SERVER_IMAGE_DEPTH on an existing server image will free it and allocate another server image with the requested depth.

Type: int
Default: 1
Procs: create, get, set

SERVER_IMAGE_PIXMAP

Allows an existing pixmap to be associated with a server image. An xv_get using this attribute is equivalent to an xv_get of the XV_XID of the server image.

Type: Pixmap
Default: none
Procs: create, get, set

SERVER_IMAGE_SAVE_PIXMAP

Allows the application to specify that the old pixmap must not be destroyed if a new pixmap is created as the result of changing the server image depth, width, height, image data (bits) or a new pixmap using SERVER_IMAGE_PIXMAP. You should retain a handle to old pixmap first.

Type: Boolean
Default: FALSE
Procs: get, set, create

SERVER_NTH_SCREEN

Specifies the screen with given number.

Type: int, Screen
Default: N/A
Procs: create, get, set

SERVER_SYNC

Synchronizes with the server once. Does not set synchronous mode.

Type: Boolean
Default: N/A
Procs: set

SERVER_SYNC_AND_PROCESS_EVENTS

Synchronizes with the server and processes any already delivered events.

Type: no value
Default: none
Procs: create, set

TEXTSW_AGAIN_RECORDING

If FALSE, changes to the textsw are not repeated when the user invokes AGAIN. Disabling reduces memory overhead.

Type: Boolean
Default: TRUE
Procs: create, get, set

TEXTSW_AUTO_INDENT

If TRUE, automatically indents a new line to match the previous line.

Type: Boolean
Default: FALSE
Procs: create, get, set

TEXTSW_AUTO_SCROLL_BY

Specifies the number of lines to scroll when type-in moves insert point below the view.

Type: int
Default: 1
Procs: create, get, set

TEXTSW_BLINK_CARET*

Determines whether the caret blinks (don't blink for better performance).

Type: Boolean
Default: FALSE
Procs: create, get, set

TEXTSW_BROWSING

If TRUE, prevents editing of displayed text. If another file is loaded in, browsing stays on.

Type: Boolean
Default: FALSE
Procs: create, get, set

TEXTSW_CHECKPOINT_FREQUENCY

Specifies the number of edits between checkpoints. Set to 0 to disable checkpointing.

Type: int
Default: 0
Procs: create, get, set

TEXTSW_CLIENT_DATA

Specifies the pointer to arbitrary client data.

Type: Xv_opaque
Default: NULL
Procs: create, get, set

TEXTSW_CONFIRM_OVERWRITE

Specifies confirmation of any request to write to an existing file.

Type: Boolean
Default: TRUE
Procs: create, get, set

TEXTSW_CONTENTS

Specifies the text for a subwindow. xv_get needs additional parameters (see Chapter 8, *Text Subwindows*).

Type: char *
Default: NULL
Procs: create, get, set

TEXTSW_CONTROL_CHARS_USE_FONT

If FALSE, control characters always display as an up arrow followed by a character instead of whatever glyph is in the current font.

Type: Boolean
Default: FALSE
Procs: create, get, set

TEXTSW_DISABLE_CD

Stops textsw from changing current working directory and grays out associated items in the menu.

Type: Boolean
Default: FALSE
Procs: create, get, set

TEXTSW_DISABLE_LOAD

Prevents files from being loaded into the textsw and grays out the associated items in the menu.

Type: Boolean
Default: FALSE
Procs: create, get, set

TEXTSW_EDIT_COUNT

Monotonically increments count of the number of edits made to the textsw.

Type: int
Procs: get

TEXTSW_FILE

For xv_create and xv_set, specifies the name of the file to load; for xv_get, returns the name of the file loaded or NULL if no file was loaded.

Type: char *
Default: NULL
Procs: create, get, set

TEXTSW_FILE_CONTENTS

Initializes the text subwindow contents from a file, yet still edits the contents in memory as if specified using TEXT_FILE_CONTENTS.

Type: char *
Default: NULL
Procs: create, set

TEXTSW_FIRST
Specifies the zero-based index of first displayed character.

Type: int
Procs: get

TEXTSW_FIRST_LINE
Specifies the zero-based index of first displayed line.

Type: int
Procs: get

TEXTSW_HISTORY_LIMIT
Specifies the number of user action sequences that can be undone.

Type: int
Default: 50
Procs: create, get, set

TEXTSW_IGNORE_LIMIT
Specifies the number of edits textsw allows before vetoing destroy. Valid values are 0, which means the destroy will be vetoed if there have been any edits, and TEXTSW_INFINITY, which means the destroy will never be vetoed.

Type: int
Default: 0
Procs: create, get, set

TEXTSW_INSERT_FROM_FILE
Inserts the contents of a file into a text subwindow at the current insertion point.

Type: char *
Default: none
Procs: set, create

TEXTSW_INSERT_MAKES_VISIBLE
Controls whether insertion causes repositioning to make inserted text visible. Possible values are TEXTSW_ALWAYS or TEXTSW_IF_AUTO_SCROLL.

Type: Textsw_enum
Default: TEXTSW_ALWAYS
Procs: create, get, set

TEXTSW_INSERTION_POINT
Specifies the index of the current insertion point.

Type: Textsw_index
Default: none
Procs: create, get, set

TEXTSW_LENGTH
Specifies the length of the textsw's contents.

Type: int
Procs: get

TEXTSW_LINE_BREAK_ACTION
Determines how the textsw treats file lines too big to fit on one display line. Possible values are TEXTSW_CLIP, TEXTSW_WRAP_AT_CHAR, or TEXTSW_WRAP_AT_WORD.

Type: Textsw_enum
Default: TEXTSW_WRAP_AT_CHAR
Procs: create, get, set

TEXTSW_LOWER_CONTEXT
Specifies the minimum number of lines to maintain between insertion point and bottom of view. A value of −1 turns auto scrolling off.

Type: int
Default: 0
Procs: create, get, set

TEXTSW_MEMORY_MAXIMUM
Specifies how much memory to use when not editing files (e.g., editing in memory). This attribute only takes effect at create time or after the window is reset with textsw_reset. The lower bound is 1K bytes, which is silently enforced.

Type: int
Default: 20000
Procs: create, get, set

TEXTSW_MODIFIED
Specifies whether the textsw has been modified.

Type: Boolean
Procs: get

TEXTSW_MULTI_CLICK_SPACE
Specifies the maximum number of pixels between successive mouse clicks to still have the clicks considered a multi-click.

Type: int
Default: 4
Procs: create, get, set

TEXTSW_MULTI_CLICK_TIMEOUT
Specifies the maximum number of milliseconds between successive mouse clicks to still have the clicks considered a multi-click.

Type: int
Default: 390
Procs: create, get, set

TEXTSW_NOTIFY_PROC
Names a notify procedure. See textsw_notify_proc in Appendix B, *Summary of Procedures and Macros*.

Default: NULL
Procs: create, set

TEXTSW_READ_ONLY
If TRUE, prevents editing of the displayed text. If another file is loaded in, read-only status is turned off again.

Type: Boolean
Default: FALSE
Procs: create, get, set

TEXTSW_STATUS
If set, specifies the address of a variable of type Textsw_status. A value that reflects what happened during the call to xv_create is then written into it.

Type: Textsw_status *
Default: none
Procs: create

TEXTSW_STORE_CHANGES_FILE
Controls whether the *target* filename given to textsw_store() to save the current contents to a file changes the name of the file being edited (TEXTSW_FILE).

Type: Boolean
Default: TRUE
Procs: create, set

TEXTSW_SUBMENU_EDIT
Returns the submenu associated with the Edit panel button.

Type: Menu
Procs: get

TEXTSW_SUBMENU_FILE
Returns the submenu associated with the File panel button.

Type: Menu
Procs: get

TEXTSW_SUBMENU_FIND
Returns the submenu associated with the Find panel button.

Type: Menu
Procs: get

TEXTSW_SUBMENU_VIEW
Returns the submenu associated with the View panel button.

Type: Menu
Procs: get

TEXTSW_UPPER_CONTEXT
Specifies the minimum number of lines to maintain between the start of the selection and top of view. A value of –1 means defeat the normal actions.

Type: int
Default: 2
Procs: create, get, set

TTY_ARGV
The command, specified as an argument vector, that the tty subwindow executes.

Type: char**
Default: none
Procs: create, set

TTY_ARGV_DO_NOT_FORK
Lets a user start a tty subwindow without forking off a shell.

Type: char**
Default: none
Procs: create

TTY_CONSOLE
If TRUE, tty subwindow grabs console output.

Type: Boolean
Default: FALSE
Procs: set, create

TTY_PAGE_MODE

If TRUE, output will stop after each page.

Type:	Boolean
Default:	FALSE
Procs:	create, get, set

TTY_PID

The process ID of the program being run in the tty subwindow.

Type:	int
Default:	none
Procs:	create, get, set

TTY_QUIT_ON_CHILD_DEATH

If TRUE, window_done is called on the parent frame of the tty window when its child terminates.

Type:	Boolean
Default:	FALSE
Procs:	set, create

TTY_TTY_FD

Gets the file descriptor of the pseudo-tty associated with the tty subwindow.

Type:	int
Procs:	get

WIN_ALARM

Rings the bell for that window.

Type:	no value
Default:	off
Procs:	set, create

WIN_ALARM_DATA

Sets the number of flashes and number of beeps used as alarm.

Type:	Xv_opaque
Default:	1 beep, 1 flash
Procs:	get

WIN_BACKGROUND_COLOR

Specifies the background color of a window as an index into the colormap segment associated with the window.

Type:	int
Default:	0
Procs:	create, get, set

WIN_BELOW

Causes the window to be positioned below the sibling window given as the value. Restricted to windows with the same imme-diate parent (i.e., subwindows). Does not affect the xv_x of the window.

Type:	Xv_Window
Default:	varies
Procs:	set, create

WIN_BIT_GRAVITY

Sets the Xlib-specific "bit gravity" property on the underlying X window associated with the object. See *<X11/X.h>* for list of legal values.

Type:	int
Default:	NorthWestGravity
Procs:	set, create

WIN_CMD_LINE*

Lets an individual application save its *specify command line* flag. When a user invokes *Save Workspace* from an OPEN LOOK window manager, the string is written to *~/.openwin-init*. The handle for xv_set should be the base frame.

Type:	string
Default:	none
Procs:	create, get, set

WIN_CMS_DATA

Specifies the data for the colormap segment associated with the window. The data is written into the currently allocated colormap segment. If a new segment is desired, set it using WIN_CMS_NAME first.

Type:	Xv_cmsdata *
Default:	none
Procs:	create, get, set

WIN_CMS_NAME

Specifies the colormap segment to be associated with the window.

Type:	char *
Default:	none
Procs:	create, get, set

WIN_COLLAPSE_EXPOSURES

Collapses multiple Exposure (and GraphicsExpose) events destined for the same window.

Type:	Boolean
Default:	TRUE
Procs:	create, get, set

WIN_COLUMNS
Specifies the window's width (including left and right margins) in columns relative to the width of the window's font.

Type: `int`
Default: varies
Procs: `create, get, set`

WIN_CONSUME_EVENT
Specifies that the window will accept an event of type specified.

Type: event code
Default: none
Procs: `create, get, set`

WIN_CONSUME_EVENTS
Specifies a null-terminated list of event types that this window accepts.

Type: list XView Events.
Default: Varies from package to package.
Procs: `create, set`

WIN_CONSUME_X_EVENT_MASK
The input mask is specified using X event masks found in *<X11/X.h>*.

Type: `unsigned long`
Default: Varies from package to package.
Procs: `create, get, set`

WIN_CURSOR
Specifies the window's cursor.

Type: `Xv_Cursor`
Default: default cursor
Procs: `create, get, set`

WIN_DEPTH
Specifies the pixel depth of the window.

Type: `int`
Default: function of the screen
Procs: `create, get`

WIN_DESIRED_HEIGHT
Specifies the desired height of the window in pixels. This is subtly different from using XV_HEIGHT.

Type: `int`
Default: none
Procs: `create, get, set`

WIN_DESIRED_WIDTH
Specifies the desired width of the window in pixels. This is subtly different from using XV_WIDTH.

Type: `int`
Default: none
Procs: `create, get, set`

WIN_DYNAMIC_VISUAL
Specifies the type of colormap segment to be used with the window. This attribute needs to be set on the actual drawing window of an object that uses dynamic colors. (SunView-compatible `pw_putcolormap` and `pw_setcmsname` routines must set this attribute to TRUE during creation.)

Type: `Boolean`
Default: `FALSE`
Procs: `create`

WIN_EVENT_PROC
Used by canvas and panel. Be sure to set `WIN_EVENT_PROC` and `WIN_CONSUME_EVENTS` on the *canvas paint window*, not on the canvas or the canvas view window.

Type: `int`
Default: none
Procs: `create, get, set`

WIN_FIT_HEIGHT
Causes the window to shrink or expand its height according to the window's contents leaving a margin specified by the value given. Typically used with panels to fit panel items.

Type: `int`
Default: depends on window size
Procs: `get`

WIN_FIT_WIDTH
Causes the window to shrink or expand its width according to the window's contents leaving a margin specified by the value given.

Type: `int`
Default: depends on window size
Procs: `get`

WIN_FOREGROUND_COLOR
Specifies the foreground color of a window as an index into the colormap segment associated with the window.

Type: `int`
Default: `size -1` (where `size` is the number of colors in the colormap segment associated with the window)
Procs: `create, get, set`

WIN_FRAME
Specifies the window's frame.

Type: `Frame`
Default: `NULL`
Procs: `get`

WIN_GRAB_ALL_INPUT
Specifies that the window will get all events regardless of location of the pointer.

Type: `Boolean`
Default: `FALSE`
Procs: `set, create`

WIN_HORIZONTAL_SCROLLBAR
A handle to the horizontal scrollbar for that window.

Type: `Scrollbar`
Default: `NULL`
Procs: `create, get, set`

WIN_IGNORE_EVENT
Specifies that the window will not receive this event. (Certain events cannot be ignored.)

Type: XView event code
Default: none
Procs: `set, create`

WIN_IGNORE_EVENTS
Specifies a `NULL`-terminated list of events that this window will not receive. (Certain events cannot be ignored.)

Type: list of event codes
Default: none
Procs: `set, create`

WIN_INPUT_MASK
Specifies the window's input mask.

Type: `Inputmask *`
Default: Varies from package to package.
Procs: `create, get, set`

WIN_INPUT_ONLY
Specifies that a window can receive input only; although it has other window properties, it cannot be drawn into.

Type: none
Default: not transparent
Procs: `create`

WIN_IS_CLIENT_PANE
If `TRUE`, the window is considered to be an OPEN LOOK GUI application-specific pane which can override OPEN LOOK GUI defaults, such as fonts. Currently, the only packages that support this are `text` and `tty/term`.

Type: `Boolean`
Default: `FALSE`
Procs: `create, get, set`

WIN_KBD_FOCUS
Indicates whether the window has the keyboard focus.

Type: `Boolean`
Default: `FALSE`
Procs: `create, get, set`

WIN_MAP
Indicates whether to map or unmap the window. This does not imply *raised* (to the top of the window tree).

Type: `Boolean`
Default: `FALSE`
Procs: `create, get, set`

WIN_MENU
Specifies the window's menu, if applicable. (Scrollbars and text subwindows, but not canvases or panels.)

Type: `Menu`
Default: none
Procs: `create, get, set`

WIN_MOUSE_XY
Specifies the mouse's position within the window. Returns a static `Rect *` on `get`.

Type: `int, int`
Default: current mouse position
Procs: `create, get, set`

WIN_NOTIFY_IMMEDIATE_EVENT_PROC
Used to specify a notify interpose function, as in:

```
notify_interpose_event_func
(window, func,
 NOTIFY_IMMEDIATE)
```

See `window_interpose_func()` in Appendix B, *Summary of Procedures and Macros*.

Default: `NULL`
Procs: `create, get, set`

WIN_NOTIFY_SAFE_EVENT_PROC

Used to specify a notify interpose function, as in:

```
notify_interpose_event_func
(window, func,
 NOTIFY_SAFE)
```

See `window_interpose_func()` in Appendix B, *Summary of Procedures and Macros*.

WIN_NO_CLIPPING

Ignores clip rects in pixwin (`pw_*`) calls during repaints in all paint windows of the window. SunView compatibility only.

Type: `Boolean`
Default: `FALSE`
Procs: `create, get, set`

WIN_NO_DECORATIONS

Establishes that this window is not controlled by the window manager. (`Override-Redirect` is set to `TRUE`.)

Type: `Boolean`
Default: `FALSE`
Procs: `set, create`

WIN_PARENT

Specifies the window's parent in the window tree. Same as `XV_OWNER`.

Type: `Xv_Window`
Default: `none`
Procs: `create, get, set`

WIN_PERCENT_HEIGHT

Sets a subwindow's height as a percentage of the frame's height.

Type: `int`
Default: `0`
Procs: `create, get, set`

WIN_PERCENT_WIDTH

Sets a subwindow's width as a percentage of the frame's width.

Type: `int`
Default: `0`
Procs: `create, get, set`

WIN_RECT

Specifies the bounding box of a window.

Type: `Rect *`
Default: `NULL`
Procs: `create, get, set`

WIN_RETAINED

Sets hint that server should keep a backing store for this window. The server may ignore this request.

Type: `Boolean`
Default: `FALSE`
Procs: `create, get, set`

WIN_RIGHT_OF

Causes a sibling window to be laid out just to the right of the window given as the value. Restricted to windows that share the same immediate parent. Does not set `XV_Y`.

Type: `Xv_Window`
Default: `arbitrary`
Procs: `set, create`

WIN_ROW_GAP

Specifies the gap between rows in the window.

Type: `int`
Default: `0`
Procs: `create, get, set`

WIN_ROW_HEIGHT

Specifies the height of a row in the window.

Type: `int`
Default: `font's default height`
Procs: `create, get, set`

WIN_ROWS

Specifies the window's height (including top and bottom margins) in rows.

Type: `int`
Default: `34`
Procs: `create, get, set`

WIN_SAVE_UNDER

Provides hints about whether or not the screen area beneath a window should be saved while a window, such as a pop-up menu, is in place. This saves obscured windows from having to redraw themselves

when the pop-up is removed. This is not the
same as WIN_ RETAINED.

Type: Boolean
Default: FALSE
Procs: set

WIN_SCREEN_RECT
Returns the bounding box of the screen containing the window. Data points to per-pro-
cess static storage.

Type: Rect *
Default: screen dependent
Procs: get

WIN_SET_FOCUS
Gets the input from the window, if possible.

Type: no value
Default: none
Procs: set, create

WIN_TOP_LEVEL
Establishes whether the window is the child
of another window or is a frame.

Type: Boolean
Default: varies
Procs: get

WIN_TRANSPARENT
Specifies that the window's background
pixmap should be transparent.

Type: none
Default: not transparent
Procs: create

WIN_VERTICAL_SCROLLBAR
Specifies that scrollbar orientation is vertical.

Type: Scrollbar
Default: none
Procs: create, get, set

WIN_WINDOW_GRAVITY
Window gravity lets you define how the window should be repositioned if its parent is
resized.

Type: int
Default: NorthWestGravity
Procs: set, create

WIN_X_COLOR_INDICES
Translates the logical indices of the window's colormap segment (from 0 to
size-1) into the actual indices into the

colormap used by the window.

Type: unsigned long *
Procs: get

WIN_X_EVENT_MASK
Expects an X event mask. Acts in the same
manner as WIN_CONSUME_X_EVENT_MASK,
but instead of appending to the current input
mask, replaces it with a new mask.

Type: unsigned long
Default: none
Procs: create, get, set

XV_AUTO_CREATE
Specifies whether to create an object not
found by xv_find().

Type: Boolean
Default: TRUE
Procs: find

XV_BOTTOM_MARGIN
Specifies the margin at the bottom of an
object.

Type: int
Default: varies with object
Procs: create, get, set

XV_FONT
Specifies an object's font.

Type: Xv_Font
Default: lucida medium
Procs: create, get, set

XV_HEIGHT
Specifies the height of an object in pixels.

Type: int
Default: N/A
Procs: create, get, set

XV_HELP_DATA
Specifies the help string used by the help
package to display on-line help. The text
string has the form file:keyword. The
help package looks for the key keyword in
the file $HELPDIR/file.info.

Type: char *
Default: no help available
Procs: create, get, set

XV_INIT_ARGC_PTR_ARGV
Interprets command line `args`. Strips `-W` command-line frame arguments out of `argv`, and decrements `argc` accordingly.

Type: `int *, char **`
Default: none
Procs: `create`

XV_INIT_ARGS
Interprets command line arguments. Does not strip `-W` command-line frame arguments out of `argv`.

Type: `int, char **`
Default: none
Procs: `create`

XV_KEY_DATA
Stores a 32-bit data value on an object. You may set multiple `XV_KEY_DATA` values on objects by using different keys.

Type: `int, XV_opaque`
Default: none
Procs: `create, get, set`

XV_LABEL
Specifies a frame's header or an icon's label.

Type: `char *`
Default: `NULL`
Procs: `create, get, set`

XV_LEFT_MARGIN
Specifies the margin at the left of the object.

Type: `int`
Default: Varies with object
Procs: `create, get, set`

XV_MARGIN
Specifies the offset from the border of this object.

Type: `int`
Default: varies with object
Procs: `create, get, set`

XV_NAME
Specifies an optional name for an object. In some cases, this attribute is used internally by packages (e.g., the `SERVER` package sets the display connection name using this attribute).

Type: `char *`
Default: varies with object
Procs: `create, get, set`

XV_OWNER
Specifies the object's owner. For example, if a panel is created on a frame, an `xv_get(panel, XV_OWNER)` would yield the frame handle.

Type: `Xv_opaque`
Procs: `get`

XV_RECT
Specifies the object's bounding box; that is, the smallest rectangle that contains the object.

Type: `Rect *`
Default: none
Procs: `create, get, set`

XV_RIGHT_MARGIN
Specifies the margin at the right of the object.

Type: `int`
Default: varies with object
Procs: `create, get, set`

XV_ROOT
Specifies the root window for an object. (Object must contain a window.)

Type: `Xv_object`
Default: root window for default screen
Procs: `get`

XV_SHOW
Causes the object to be displayed or undisplayed. If object is a window, bring object to the top.

Type: `Boolean`
Default: varies
Procs: `create, get, set`

XV_TOP_MARGIN
Specifies the margin at the top of the object.

Type: `int`
Default: varies with object
Procs: `create, get, set`

XV_TYPE

Returns the package that belongs to an object.

Type: Xv_pkg *
Default: varies with object
Procs: get

XV_WIDTH

Specifies the width of the object in pixels.

Type: int
Default: none
Procs: create, get, set

XV_X

Specifies the x position of the object relative to its parent.

Type: int
Default: varies with object
Procs: create, get, set

XV_XID

Gets the XID of the specified object such as the pixmap associated with a Server_ image or the X Window associated with a canvas paint window.

Type: int
Default: varies with object
Procs: get

XV_Y

Specifies the y position of the object relative to its parent.

Type: int
Default: varies with object
Procs: create, get, set

B

Summary of Procedures and Macros

Procedures
and Macros

B
Summary of Procedures and Macros

This appendix lists the XView procedures and macros in alphabetical order and describes each of them briefly. The description includes the call that uses the procedure or macro.

CANVAS_EACH_PAINT_WINDOW()

Macro providing built-in support for iteration across all the paint windows contained in a given canvas. Allows you to perform operations on multiple paint windows for which there are no canvas attributes.

CANVAS_END_EACH

Closes the loop started by CANVAS_EACH_PAINT_WINDOW(). These two macros are meant to be used together.

canvas_paint_window()

Returns the paint window associated with the first view in the canvas. If the canvas is not split, first view is the only view.

```
Xv_window
canvas_paint_window(canvas)
        Canvas          canvas;
```

This is defined to be

```
xv_get(canvas, CANVAS_NTH_PAINT_WINDOW, 0);
```

canvas_repaint_proc()

Client-supplied callback procedure called when getting a WIN_REPAINT event. Function is attached to a canvas by setting WIN_EVENT_PROC on the canvas' *paint window*.

```
void
canvas_repaint_proc(canvas, paint_window, repaint_area)
        Canvas          canvas;
        Xv_Window       paint_window;
        Rectlist        *repaint_area;
```

If CANVAS_X_PAINT_WINDOW is TRUE, the repaint callback is called:

```
void
canvas_repaint_proc(canvas, paint_window, display, xid,
                    xrectlist)
        Canvas          canvas;
        Xv_Window       paint_window;
        Display         *display;
        Window          xid;
        Xv_xrectlist    *xrects;
```

display is the display handle to the X11 server connection. xid is the X11 window identifier for the canvas paint window. The Xv_xrectlist structure contains an array of XRectangles and a count that specifies the repaint area for the canvas paint window.

canvas_resize_proc()

Procedure called when canvas width or height changes. This function is installed using the attribute CANVAS_RESIZE_PROC.

```
void
canvas_resize_proc(canvas, width, height)
        Canvas          canvas;
        int             width;
        int             height;
```

cursor_copy()

Creates and returns a copy of src_cursor.

```
Xv_Cursor
cursor_copy(src_cursor)
        Xv_Cursor       src_cursor;
```

frame_get_rect()

Gets the rect of the frame. x, y is the upper-left corner of the window coordinate space. Width and height include the window manager decoration.

```
void
frame_get_rect(frame, rect)
        Frame           frame;
        Rect            *rect;
```

frame_set_rect()

Sets the rect of the frame. `x, y` is the upper-left corner of the window coordinate space. Width and height include the window manager decoration.

```
void
frame_set_rect(frame, rect)
        Frame           frame;
        Rect            *rect;
```

menu_action_proc()

See `menu_notify_proc()` below.

menu_done_proc()

The procedure called whenever a menu group is dismissed by the user. Installed by `MENU_DONE_PROC`.

```
void
menu_done_proc(menu, result)
        menu            menu;
        Xv_opaque       result;
```

`menu` is the base (top) level menu, as specified in `menu_show()`. `result` is the value of the item selected, unless the user specifies `menu_return_item`. You can get notification that any menu in a menu group is done by attaching `MENU_DONE_PROC` to each menu. However, you will get better results with `menu_item` notify procedures.

menu_gen_proc()

This menu generating procedure is called whenever a menu item that has the `MENU_GEN_PROC` attribute set and the menu needs to be displayed or traversed. It should return a handle to a menu that has either been dynamically created or statically stored.

```
Menu
menu_gen_proc(m, op)
        Menu               m;
        Menu_generate      op;
```

MENUITEM_SPACE

Used to create a blank menu item.

menu_notify_proc()

The notify procedure is attached to menus and menu items using `MENU_NO-TIFY_PROC`. This function is called whenever the user selects a menu item.

```
Xv_opaque
menu_notify_proc(menu, menu_item)
        Menu            menu;
        Menu_item       menu_item;
```

The `menu` identifies which menu the `menu_item` belongs to.

menu_pin_proc()

This client supplied procedure is called whenever the user attempts to pin up a menu. Attached to menus using the attribute, MENU_PIN_PROC.

```
void
menu_pin_proc(menu, x, y)
        Menu           menu;
        int            x, y;
```

x, y are the fullscreen coordinates of the upper-left corner of the pin window.

menu_return_item()

Predefined notify procedure which, if given as the value for MENU_NOTIFY_PROC, causes the menu_done_proc() (if any) to return the selected item rather than its value.

```
Menu_item
menu_return_item(menu, menu_item)
        Menu           menu;
        Menu_item      menu_item;
```

menu_return_value()

Predefined notify procedure which, if given as the value for MENU_NOTIFY_PROC, causes the menu_done_proc() (if any) to return the value of the selected item rather than the item itself.

```
void
menu_return_value(menu, menu_item)
        Menu           menu;
        Menu_item      menu_item;
```

menu_show()

Displays menu and gets a selection from the user.

```
void
menu_show(menu, window, event, NULL)
        Menu           menu;
        Xv_Window      window;
        Event          *event;
```

window is the handle of the window over which the menu is displayed. event is the event which causes the menu to come up. The final NULL is required for public (non-XView internal) usage.

notice_prompt()

Displays notice and does not return until the user pushes a button or until its trigger or the default has been seen. It returns a value of NOTICE_FAILED if notice_prompt() fails for any reason; otherwise, it is equivalent to the ordinal value of the button which caused the return (i.e., button actually selected or default button if default action triggered return). The client_window should be the window for which the notice has been generated. (This is important for fonts and positioning information. If a window object is not available, NULL may be passed and defaults used. For the correct positioning of the notice, clients should specify NOTICE_FOCUS_XY.) The event will be completely filled in at the time the `notice_prompt()` returns. The possible status values that may be returned from this function are:

- The `int()` value passed with every `NOTICE_BUTTON` attribute.

- `NOTICE_YES` if a confirm button or trigger was pushed.

- `NOTICE_NO` if a cancel button or trigger was pushed.

- `NOTICE_FAILED` if the notice failed to pop up.

```
int
notice_prompt(window, event, attributes)
        XV_Window            window;
        Event                *event;
        attribute-list       attributes;
```

OPENWIN_EACH_VIEW()

Macro providing built-in support for iteration across all the views contained in a given openwin. Allows you to perform operations on multiple views for which there are no openwin attributes.

OPENWIN_END_EACH

Closes the loop started by `OPENWIN_EACH_VIEW()`. These macros are meant to be used together, as in the following example:

```
OPENWIN_EACH_VIEW(openwin, view)
        Openwin              openwin;
        Openwin_item         item;
        xv_set(openwin, attributes, 0);
OPENWIN_END_EACH;
```

openwin_init_split()

Procedure installed by applications using `OPENWIN_SPLIT_INIT_PROC`. This function is called when the user *splits* two views. The attributes passed are handles to the openwin and the new view.

```
openwin_init_split(openwin, view)
        Openwin              openwin;
        Xv_Window            view;
```

openwin_split_destroy_proc()

Procedure installed by applications using `OPENWIN_SPLIT_DESTROY_PROC`. This function is called when the user *joins* two views.

```
openwin_split_destroy_proc(openwin)
        Openwin              openwin;
```

panel_advance_caret()

Advances the caret to the next text item. If on the last text item, rotate back to the first. Returns the new caret item or NULL if there are no text items.

```
Panel_item
panel_advance_caret(panel)
        Panel           panel;
```

panel_background_proc()

Event handling procedure called when an event falls on the background of the panel (e.g., not on any panel items). This is installed by the client using PANEL_BACKGROUND_PROC.

```
void
panel_background_proc(panel, event)
        Panel           panel
        Event           *event
```

panel_backup_caret()

Backs the caret up to the previous text item. If already on the first text item, rotate back to the last. Returns the new caret item, or NULL if there are no text items.

```
Panel_item
panel_backup_caret(panel)
        Panel           panel;
```

PANEL_CHECK_BOX

Macro for "PANEL_TOGGLE, PANEL_FEEDBACK, PANEL_MARK." Creates non-exclusive choice item(s) with check_boxes instead of boxes.

```
xv_create(panel, PANEL_CHECK_BOX, NULL);
```

PANEL_CHOICE_STACK

Macro for "PANEL_CHOICE, PANEL_DISPLAY_LEVEL, PANEL_CURRENT." Creates an OPEN LOOK abbreviated menu button.

```
xv_create(panel, PANEL_CHOICE_STACK, NULL);
```

panel_default_handle_event()

Default event procedure for panel items PANEL_EVENT_PROC and for the panel's background (PANEL_BACKGROUND_PROC). Implements the standard event-to-action mapping for the item types.

```
panel_default_handle_event(panel_object, event)
        Xv_object       panel_object;
        Event           *event;
```

Note that panel_object may be a PANEL or PANEL_ITEM.

PANEL_EACH_ITEM()

Macro to iterate over each item in a panel. The corresponding macro `panel_end_each` closes the loop opened by `PANEL_EACH_ITEM()`.

```
PANEL_EACH_ITEM(panel, item)
        Panel           panel;
        Panel_item      item;
```

PANEL_END_EACH

Closes the loop started by `PANEL_EACH_ITEM()`. Same usage as `OPENWIN_EACH_VIEW()`.

panel_event_proc()

Client specified event handling procedure for handling events on panel items. This procedure is installed using `PANEL_EVENT_PROC`.

```
void
panel_event_proc(item, event)
        Panel_item      item
        Event           *event
```

panel_notify_proc()

Client specified callback routine invoked when the user *activates* panel items (accepts preview). The form for button, text, and numeric text items is:

```
notify_proc(item, event)
        Panel_item      item;
        Event           *event;
```

For buttons, the return value of `notify_proc` is of type `int` and is either `XV_OK` or `XV_ERROR`. For text and numeric text items, the return value type is `Panel_setting` and is one of `PANEL_INSERT`, `PANEL_NEXT`, `PANEL_NONE`, or `PANEL_PREVIOUS`.

Choice and slider items have an additional parameter that specifies the current value:

```
notify_proc(item, value, event)
        Panel_item      item;
        int             value;
        Event           *event;
```

For nonexclusive items, the value parameter is of type `unsigned int` because it represents a *mask* of choices that are selected (e.g., if the first and third items are selected, then the first and third bits in the `value` parameter are on—this value happens to be five). For slider, choice, and toggle (nonexclusive settings) items, `panel_notify_proc` is of type `void`; that is, it does not return a value.

The form for panel list items is:

```
int
notify_proc(item, op, event)
        Panel_item              item;
        Panel_list_op           op;
        Event                   *event;
```

For panel list items, op indicates a select, validate, or delete operation. Of these, only PANEL_LIST_OP_VALIDATE requires a return value: XV_OK to validate a change or XV_ERROR to invalidate a change.

panel_paint()

Paints an item or an entire panel. paint_behavior can be either PANEL_CLEAR, which causes the area occupied by the panel or item to be cleared prior to painting, or PANEL_NO_CLEAR.

```
int
panel_paint(panel_object, paint_behavior)
        Xv_object           panel_object;
        Panel_setting       paint_behavior;
```

Note that panel_object may be a PANEL or PANEL_ITEM.

panel_text_notify()

Default notify procedure for panel text items. Causes caret to advance on Return or Tab, caret to back up on Shift-Return or Shift-Tab, printable characters to be inserted into item's value, and all other characters to be discarded.

```
Panel_setting
panel_text_notify(item, event)
        Panel_item          item
        Event               *event
```

PANEL_TOGGLE

Macro for "PANEL_CHOICE, PANEL_CHOOSE_ONE, FALSE." Used to create non-exclusive choice item(s).

```
xv_create(panel, PANEL_TOGGLE, NULL);
```

SCROLLABLE_PANEL

Used to create a scrollbar panel. To add a scrollbar after creating the panel, create a scrollbar with the panel as its parent. Example:

```
panel = xv_create(frame, SCROLLABLE_PANEL, NULL);
xv_create(panel, SCROLLBAR, NULL);
```

Note: scrollable panels are not OPEN LOOK-compliant.

scrollbar_default_compute_scroll_proc()

Computes default scrolling based on scroll position. pos is the position from the start of the cable event. length is the length of the cable. offset and object_length are output parameters. The offset is given in client units to scroll by. The object length is in client units.

```
void
scrollbar_default_compute_scroll_proc(
        scroll_public, pos, available_cable, motion,
        offset, object_length)
                Scrollbar             scroll_public
                Scrollbar             scroll_public
                int                   pos;
                int                   available_cable;
                Scroll_motion         motion;
                unsigned long         *offset;
                unsigned long         *object_length;
```

scrollbar_paint()

Repaints all portions of the scrollbar.

```
void
scrollbar_paint(scrollbar)
        Scrollbar             scrollbar;
```

selection_acquire()

Acquires the selection of a specified rank. This is typically used internally by XView packages. It is not used to *inquire* about the current selection.

```
Seln_rank
selection_acquire(server, client, asked)
        Xv_Server     server;
        Seln_client   client;
        Seln_rank     asked;
```

client is the opaque handle returned from selection_create(). The client uses this call to become the new holder of the selection of rank asked. asked should be one of SELN_CARET, SELN_PRIMARY, SELN_SECONDARY, SELN_SHELF, or SELN_UNSPECIFIED. If successful, the rank actually acquired is returned.

If asked is SELN_UNSPECIFIED, the client indicates it wants whichever of the primary or secondary selections is appropriate given the current state of the function keys; the one acquired can be determined from the return value.

selection_ask()

selection_ask() is a simplified form of selection_request() that looks and acts very much like seln_query(). The only difference is that it does not use a callback proc and so cannot handle replies that require more than a single buffer (e.g., long text selections). If it receives a reply consisting of more than one buffer, it returns the first buffer and discards the rest. The return value is a pointer to a static buffer; in case of error, this will be a valid pointer to a NULL buffer:

```
buffer->status = SELN_FAILED
```

The call looks like this:

```
Seln_request *
selection_ask(server, holder, attributes, ..., NULL)
    Xv_Server     server;
    Seln_holder   *holder;
    Attr_union    attributes;
```

selection_clear_functions()

The server is told to forget about any function keys it thinks are down, resetting its state to all-up. If it knows of a current secondary selection, the server will tell its holder to yield.

```
void
selection_clear_functions()
```

selection_create()

The server is initialized for this client. `Client_data` is a 32-bit opaque client value which the server will pass back in callback procedures, as described above. The first two arguments are addresses of client procedures which will be called from the selection functions when client processing is required. These occasions occur when the server sees a function-key transition which may interest this client and when another process wishes to make a request concerning the selection this client holds.

```
Seln_client
selection_create(
    server, function_proc, request_proc, client_data)
        Xv_Server,      server;
        void            (*function_proc) ();
        Seln_result     (*request_proc) ();
        Xv_opaque       client_data;
```

selection_destroy()

A client created by `selection_create` is destroyed—any selection it may hold is released, and various pieces of data associated with the selection mechanism are freed. If this is the last client in this process using the Selection Service, the RPC socket is closed and its notification removed.

```
void
selection_destroy(server, client)
    Xv_Server     server;
    Seln_client   client;
```

selection_done()

Client indicates it is no longer the holder of the selection of the indicated rank. The only cause of failure is absence of the server. It is not necessary for a client to call this procedure when it has been asked by the server to yield a selection.

```
Seln_result
selection_done(server, client, rank)
    Xv_Server     server;
    Seln_client   client;
    Seln_rank     rank;
```

selection_figure_response()

Procedure to determine the correct response according to the standard user interface when `seln_inform()` returns `*buffer` or the client's `function_procs` called with it. The `addressee_rank` field in `Seln_function_buffer` will be modified to indicate the selection which should be affected by this client; `holder` will be set to point to the element of `*buffer` which should be contacted in the ensuing action, and the return value indicates what that action should be. Possible return values are `SELN_DELETE`, `SELN_FIND`, `SELN_IGNORE`, `SELN_REQUEST`, and `SELN_SHELVE`.

```
Seln_response
selection_figure_response(server, buffer, holder)
        Xv_Server                       server;
        Seln_function_buffer    *buffer;
        Seln_holder             *holder;
```

selection_hold_file()

The server is requested to act as the holder of the specified rank, whose ASCII contents have been written to the file indicated by path. This allows a selection to persist longer than the application which made it can maintain it. Most commonly, this will be done by a process which holds the shelf when it is about to terminate.

```
Seln_result
selection_hold_file(server, rank, path)
        Xv_Server       server;
        Seln_rank       rank;
        char            *path;
```

selection_inform()

Low-level, policy-independent procedure for informing the server that a function key has changed state. Most clients will prefer to use the higher-level procedure `seln_report_event`, which handles much of the standard interpretation required.

```
Seln_function_buffer
selection_inform(server, client, which, down)
        Xv_Server               server;
        Seln_client             client;
        Seln_function           which;
        int                     down;
```

selection_init_request()

Procedure used to initialize a buffer before calling `selection_request`. (It is also called internally by `selection_ask` and `seln_query`.) It takes a pointer to a request buffer, a pointer to a `struct` referring to the selection holder to which the request is to be addressed, and a list of attributes which constitute the request to be sent. The attributes are copied into `buffer->data`, and the corresponding size is stored into `buffer->buf_size`. Both elements of `reques-ter_data` are zeroed; if the caller wants to handle long requests, consumer-proc and context pointers must be entered in these elements after `selec-tion_init_request` returns.

```
void
selection_init_request(
        server, buffer, holder, attributes, ..., NULL)
        Xv_Server              server;
        Selection_request      *buffer;
        Seln_holder            *holder;
        char                   *attributes;
```

selection_inquire()

Returns a `Seln_holder` structure containing information which enables the holder of the indicated selection to be contacted. If the `rank` argument is `SELN_UNSPECIFIED`, the server will return access information for either the primary or the secondary selection holder, as warranted by the state of the function keys it knows about. The `rank` element in the returned struct will indicate which is being returned.

This procedure may be called without `selection_create()` having been called first.

```
Seln_holder
selection_inquire(server, rank)
        Xv_Server      server;
        Seln_rank      rank;
```

selection_inquire_all()

Returns a `Seln_holders_all` struct from the Selection Service; it consists of a `Seln_holder` struct for each of the four ranks.

```
Seln_holders_all
selection_inquire_all()
```

selection_query()

Transmits a request to the selection holder indicated by the `holder` argument. `consume` and `context` are used to interpret the response and are described below. The remainder of the arguments to `selection_query` constitute an attribute-value list which is the request. (The last argument should be a 0 to terminate the list.) The procedure pointed to by `reader` will be called repeatedly with a pointer to each buffer of the reply. The value of the `context` argument will be available in `buffer->requester_data.context` for each buffer. This item is not used by the selection library; it is provided for the convenience of the client. When the reply has been completely processed (or when the `con-sume` proc returns something other than `SELN_SUCCESS`), `selection_query` returns.

```
Selection_result
selection_query(
        server, holder, reader, context, attributes, ...,
    NULL)
                Xv_Server        server;
                Seln_holder     *holder;
                Seln_result     (*reader)();
                char *          *context;
                A-V list         attributes;
```

selection_report_event()

High-level procedure for informing the server of a function key transition which may affect the selection. It incorporates some of the policy of the standard user interface and provides a more convenient interface to `selection_inform`.

`Seln_client_node` is the client handle returned from `selection_create`; it may be 0 if the client guarantees it will not need to respond to the function transition.

`Event` is a pointer to the struct `inputevent` which reports the transition `seln_report_event`. `selection_report_event` generates a corresponding call to `seln_inform` and, if the returned struct is not null, passes it to the client's `function_proc` callback procedure.

```
void
selection_report_event(server, client, event)
        Xv_Server               server;
        Seln_client_node       *client;
        Event                   *event;
```

selection_request()

Low-level, policy-independent mechanism for retrieving information about a selection from the server. Most clients will access it only indirectly, through `selection_ask` or `selection_query`.

`selection_request` takes a pointer to a holder (as returned by `seln_inquire`) and a request constructed in `*buffer`. The request is transmitted to the indicated selection holder, and the buffer rewritten with its response. Failures in the RPC mechanism will cause a `SELN_FAILED` return; if the process of the addressed holder is no longer active, the return value will be `SELN_NON_EXIST`. Clients which call `selection_request` directly will find it most convenient to initialize the buffer by a call to `selection_init_request`.

Request attributes which are not recognized by the selection holder will be returned as the value of the attribute `SELN_UNRECOGNIZED`. Responses should be provided in the order requests were encountered.

```
Seln_result
selection_request(server, holder, buffer)
        Xv_Server        server
        Seln_holder    *holder;
        Seln_request  *buffer;
```

selection_yield_all()

Procedure that queries the holders of all selections and, for each which is held by a client in the calling process, sends a yield request to that client and a Done to the server. It should be called by applications which are about to exit or to undertake lengthy computations during which they will be unable to respond to requests concerning selections they hold.

```
void
selection_yield_all()
```

textsw_add_mark()

Adds a new mark at position. flags can be either TEXTSW_MARK_ DEFAULTS or TEXTSW_MARK_MOVE_AT_INSERT.

```
Textsw_mark
textsw_add_mark(textsw, position, flags)
        Textsw               textsw;
        Textsw_index         position;
        unsigned             flags;
```

textsw_append_file_name()

Returns 0 if textsw is editing a file and, if so, appends the name of the file at the end of name.

```
int
textsw_append_file_name(textsw, name)
        Textsw          textsw;
        char           *name;
```

textsw_delete()

Returns 0 if the operation fails. Removes the span of characters beginning with first and ending one before last_plus_one.

```
Textsw_index
textsw_delete(textsw, first, last_plus_one)
        Textsw                textsw;
        Textsw_index          first, last_plus_one;
```

textsw_edit()

Returns 0 if the operation fails. Erases a character, word or line, depending on whether unit is SELN_LEVEL_FIRST or SELN_LEVEL_LINE. If direction is 0, characters after the insertion point are affected; otherwise, characters before the insertion point are affected. The operation will be done count times.

```
                    Textsw_index
                    textsw_edit(textsw, unit, count, direction)
                            Textsw          textsw;
                            unsigned        unit, count, direction;
```

textsw_erase()

Returns 0 if the operation fails. Equivalent to `textsw_delete()` but does not affect the global shelf.

```
                    Textsw_index
                    textsw_erase(textsw, first, last_plus_one)
                            Textsw                  textsw;
                            Textsw_index            first, last_plus_one;
```

textsw_file_lines_visible()

Fills in `top` and `bottom` with the file line indices of the first and last file lines being displayed in `textsw`.

```
                    void
                    textsw_file_lines_visible(textsw, top, bottom)
                            Textsw          textsw;
                            int             *top, *bottom;
```

textsw_find_bytes()

Beginning at the position addressed by `first`, searches for the pattern specified by `buf` of length `buf_len`. Searches forward if flags is 0, else searches backward. Returns −1 if no match, else matching span placed in indices addressed by `first` and `last_plus_one`.

```
                    int
                    textsw_find_bytes(
                            textsw, first, last_plus_one, buf, buf_len, flags)
                            Textsw                  textsw;
                            Textsw_index *first, *last_plus_one;
                            char            *buf;
                            unsigned        buf_len, flags;
```

textsw_find_mark()

Returns the current position of `mark`. If this operation fails, it will return `TEXTSW_INFINITY`.

```
                    Textsw_index
                    textsw_find_mark(textsw, mark)
                            Textsw                  textsw;
                            Textsw_mark             mark;
```

textsw_first()

Returns the first `textsw` view.

```
                    Textsw
                    textsw_first(textsw)
                            Textsw          textsw;
```

textsw_index_for_file_line()

Returns the character index for the first character in the line given by `line`. If this operation fails, it will return `TEXTSW_CANNOT_SET`.

```
Textsw_index
textsw_index_for_file_line(textsw, line)
        Textsw          textsw;
        int             line;
```

textsw_insert()

Inserts characters in `buf` into `textsw` at the current insertion point. The number of characters actually inserted is returned. This will equal `buf_len` unless there was a memory allocation failure. If there was a failure, it will return 0.

```
Textsw_index
textsw_insert(textsw, buf, buf_len)
        Textsw          textsw;
        char            *buf;
        int             buf_len;
```

textsw_match_bytes()

Searches for a block of text in the `textsw`'s contents; ends with characters matching `end_sym`. This function places the starting index of the matching block in `first` and its ending index in `last`.

```
int
textsw_match_bytes(
        textsw, first, last_plus_one, start_sym,
        start_sym_len, end_sym, end_sym_len, field_flag)
                Textsw          textsw;
                Textsw_index *first, *last_plus_one;
                char            *start_sym, *end_sym;
                int             start_sym_len, end_sym_len;
                unsigned        field_flag;
```

textsw_next()

Returns the next view in the set of `textsw` views.

```
Textsw
textsw_next(textsw)
        Textsw          textsw;
```

textsw_normalize_view()

Repositions the text so that the character at `position` is visible and at the top of the subwindow.

```
void
textsw_normalize_view(textsw, position)
        Textsw          textsw;
        Textsw_index    position;
```

textsw_notify_proc()

Notify procedure installed by application using TEXTSW_NOTIFY_PROC.

```
void
notify_proc(textsw, avlist)
      Textsw          textsw
      Attr_avlist     avlist
```

textsw_possibly_normalize()

If the character at position is already visible, this function does nothing. If it is not visible, it repositions the text so that it is visible and at the top of the subwindow.

```
void
textsw_possibly_normalize(textsw, position)
      Textsw               textsw;
      Textsw_index         position;
```

textsw_remove_mark()

Removes an existing mark from textsw.

```
void
textsw_remove_mark(textsw, mark)
      Textsw               textsw;
      Textsw_mark          mark;
```

textsw_replace_bytes()

Replaces the character span from first to last_plus_one with the characters in buf. The return value is the number of bytes inserted or deleted. The number is positive if bytes are inserted, negative if bytes are deleted. (The number is also negative if the original string is longer than the one that replaces it.) If this operation fails, it will return a value of 0.

```
Textsw_index
textsw_replace_bytes(
      textsw, first, last_plus_onebuf, buf_len)
            Textsw          textsw;
            Textsw_index    first;
            Textsw_index    last_plus_one;
            char            *buf;
            unsigned        buf_len;
```

textsw_reset()

Discards edits performed on the contents of textsw. If needed, a message box will be displayed at x, y.

```
void
textsw_reset(textsw, x, y)
      Textsw          textsw;
      int             x, y;
```

Procedures
and Macros

textsw_save()

Saves any edits made to the file currently loaded into textsw. If needed, a message box will be displayed at x, y.

```
unsigned
textsw_save(textsw, x, y)
        Textsw          textsw;
        int             x, y;
```

textsw_screen_line_count()

Returns the number of screen lines in textsw.

```
int
textsw_screen_line_count(textsw)
        Textsw          textsw;
```

textsw_scroll_lines()

Moves the text up or down by count lines. If count is positive, then the text is scrolled up on the screen. If negative, the text is scrolled down (backward in the file).

```
void
textsw_scroll_lines(textsw, count)
        Textsw          textsw;
        int             count;
```

textsw_set_selection()

Sets the selection to begin at first and includes all characters up to last_plus_one. A type value of 1 indicates primary selection, 2 indicates secondary selection.

```
void
textsw_set_selection(textsw, first, last_plus_one, type)
        Textsw                  textsw;
        Textsw_index            first, last_plus_one;
        unsigned                type;
```

textsw_store_file()

Stores the contents of textsw to the file named by filename. If needed, a message box will be displayed at x, y.

```
unsigned
textsw_store_file(textsw, filename, x, y)
        Textsw          textsw;
        char            *filename;
        int             x, y;
```

ttysw_input()

Appends `len` number of characters from `buf` onto `tty`'s input queue. It returns the number of characters accepted.

```
int
ttysw_input(tty, buf, len)
        Tty     tty;
        char    *buf;
        int     len;
```

ttysw_output()

Appends `len` number of characters from `buf` onto `tty`'s output queue; it sends them through the terminal emulator to the TTY. It returns the number of characters accepted.

```
int
ttysw_output(tty, buf, len)
        Tty     tty;
        char    *buf;
        int     len;
```

window_done()

Destroys the entire hierarchy to which `win` belongs.

```
int
window_done(win)
        Xv_Window       win;
```

window_fit()

Causes `win` to fit its contents in the dimensions specified with `WIN_FIT_HEIGHT` and `WIN_FIT_WIDTH`. A macro, defined as:

```
int
xv_set(win, WIN_FIT_HEIGHT, WIN_FIT_WIDTH, 0, 0)
window_fit(win)
        Xv_Window       win;
```

window_main_loop()

Displays `base_frame` on the screen and begins the processing of events by passing control to the Notifier.

```
void
window_main_loop(base_frame)
        Frame           base_frame;
```

window_read_event()

Reads the next input event for `window`. In case of error, sets the global variable `errno` and returns −1.

```
int
window_read_event(window, event)
        Xv_window       window;
        Event           *event;
```

WIN_NOTIFY_EVENT_PROC

> #defined to be WIN_NOTIFY_SAFE_EVENT_PROC.

window_interpose_func()

> Client function specified by using:
>
> ```
> xv_set(window,
>     WIN_NOTIFY_EVENT_PROC, window_interpose_function,
>     NULL);
> ```
>
> or by using:
>
> ```
> notify_interpose_event_func(window,
>     window_interpose_func, how);
> ```
>
> how is either NOTIFY_SAFE or NOTIFY_IMMEDIATE. The window_inter-
> pose_func() takes the following parameters when called:
>
> ```
> Notify_value
> window_interpose_func(window, event, arg)
>     Xv_Window   window;
>     Event       *event;
>     Xv_opaque   arg;
> ```

wmgr_bottom()

> Sets stackmode to Below in XConfigureWindow.
>
> ```
> void
> wmgr_bottom(frame)
>     Frame       frame;
> ```

wmgr_changelevel()

> Sets stackmode in XConfigureWindow.
>
> ```
> void
> wmgr_changelevel(window,parent,top)
>     Xv_Window   window;
>     int         parent;
>     int         top;
> ```

wmgr_close()

> Sets wmhints.initial_state to ICONICSTATE.
>
> ```
> void
> wmgr_close(frame)
>     Frame       frame;
> ```

wmgr_completechangerect()

Calls XConfigureWindow with a new rect.

```
void
wmgr_completechangerect(window, rectnew, rectoriginal,
    parentprleft, parentprtop)
        Xv_window       window;
        Rect            *rectnew, *rectoriginal;
        int             parentprleft, parentprtop;
```

wmgr_open()

Sets wmhints.initial_state to NORMALSTATE.

```
void
wmgr_open(frame)
        Frame           frame;
```

wmgr_refreshwindow()

Calls XConfigureWindow repeatedly.

```
void
wmgr_refreshwindow(window)
        Xv_window       window;
```

wmgr_top()

Sets stackmode to Above in XConfigureWindow.

```
void
wmgr_top(frame)
        Frame           frame;
```

xv_col()

Returns an integer representing the number of pixels, excluding the left margin of the window.

```
int
xv_col(window, column)
        Xv_Window       window
        int             column;
```

xv_cols()

Returns an integer representing the number of pixels, including the left margin of the window.

```
int
xv_cols(window, columns)
        Xv_Window       window
        int             columns;
```

xv_create()

To create *any* XView object, call the generic procedure xv_create. This procedure will return a handle to some XView object. It takes as parameters the owner of the object being created, the type of object to create, and a list of attributes. The attribute list must terminate with a NULL. In specifying the type, you must use the name of some XView package. That name must be in all capital letters to distinguish it from the corresponding data type. The package is the name of the package to which the object you wish to create belongs.

The procedure `xv_create()` returns either the handle for the new object or XV_NULL if the attempt at object creation fails.

```
Xv_opaque
xv_create(owner, package, attributes)
        Xv_object          owner;
        Xv_pkg             *package;
        attribute-list     attributes;
```

xv_destroy()

To destroy an XView object and any subframes owned by that object, use the procedure `xv_destroy()`. It will return either XV_ERROR or XV_OK.

```
int
xv_destroy(object)
        Xv_object      object;
```

XV_DISPLAY_FROM_WINDOW()

Macro to get at the handle to the display object from a window object.

```
Xv_opaque
XV_DISPLAY_FROM_WINDOW(window)
        Xv_Window      window;
```

xv_find()

To find any XView object, use the procedure `xv_find()`. If the object is not found, `xv_find` will automatically attempt to create it.

```
Xv_opaque
xv_find(owner, package, attributes)
        Xv_object          owner;
        Xv_pkg             *package;
        attribute-list     attributes;
```

xv_get()

To get the value of any single attribute of *any* XView object, use the procedure `xv_get()`.

```
Xv_opaque
xv_get(object, attribute)
        Xv_object          object;
        attribute-list     attributes;
```

The procedure returns 0 for failure. As a result, you cannot detect errors when retrieving the values of attributes which might return 0 as a valid value. Note that, although you can supply XV_NULL as the owner when you create a new object with `xv_create`, you *must* give the object when asking for the value of an attribute.

For example, you cannot just ask for:

```
xv_get(XV_NULL, XV_FONT)
```

to determine the default font, but you can ask for the font associated with a particular screen, as in:

```
xv_get(Screen1, XV_FONT)
```

Some attributes require a screen or server to be supplied to `xv_get()`. For such attributes, you should ask any window you think should be on the same screen what to identify as its screen or server, using the attributes XV_SCREEN and XV_SERVER.

If you know your application only runs on a single screen, you can use the global values xv_default_server and xv_default_screen or you can ask the defaults database what the server is.

xv_init()   To initialize the Notifier, use the procedure xv_init(). It reads any passed attributes and the '/.Xdefaults Database as well as initializing the Defaults/Resource-Manager Database and loading the Server Resource-Manager Database.

```
int
main(argc, argv)
        int     argc;
        char    **argv:
{
/* initialization/declarations */
        .
        .
        .
    (void)xv_init(XV_INIT_ARGC_PTR_ARGV, &argc, argv, 0);
    frame = xv_create(NULL, FRAME, FRAME_LABEL, "foo", 0);
}
```

xv_row()   Returns an integer representing the number of pixels, excluding the top margin of the window.

```
int
xv_row(window, row)
        Xv_Window       window
        int             row;
```

xv_rows()   Returns an integer representing the number of pixels, including the top margin of the window.

```
int
xv_rows(window, rows)
        Xv_Window       window
        int             rows;
```

XV_SCREEN_FROM_WINDOW()

Macro to return the handle to the screen object from the window object.

```
XV_SCREEN_FROM_WINDOW(window)
        Xv_Window       window;
```

xv_send_message()

Lets two separate processes communicate with each other. You can specify the addressee field either with one of the constants XV_POINTER_WINDOW or XV_FOCUS_WINDOW or with the window's XID, if known. If the addressee is XV_POINTER, then the message is sent to the window that the pointer is in. If the addressee is XV_FOCUS_WINDOW, then the message is sent to the window that currently has the focus, regardless of the pointer position. If the addressee is a windows XID, then the message is sent to the window with the corresponding ID.

```
void
xv_send_message(
        window, addressee, msg_type, format, data, len)
            Xv_object       window;
            Xv_opaque       addressee;
            char            *msg_type;
            int             format;
            Xv_opaque       *data;
            int             len;
```

XV_SERVER_FROM_WINDOW()

Macro to get at the handle to the server object from a window object.

```
Xv_opaque
XV_SERVER_FROM_WINDOW(window)
    Xv_Window      window;
```

xv_set()   To set the value of one or more attributes of *any* XView object, call the procedure xv_set with the handle to the object whose attributes you wish to set and a list of attribute-value pairs terminating in a zero.

```
Xv_object
Xv_set(owner, type, attributes)
    Xv_object          owner;
    vu type            *type;
    attribute-list     attributes;
```

The procedure xv_set() returns XV_OK if it succeeds; otherwise, it returns an error code indicating that the attribute on which it ran encountered problems.

C
Data Types

C
Data Types

The following is a list of XView data types and their descriptions.

Canvas	Handle to an opaque structure that describes a canvas.
Canvas_attribute	One of the canvas attributes (CANVAS_*).
Xv_Cursor	Handle to an opaque structure that describes a cursor.
Xv_Cursor_attribute	One of the cursor attributes (CURSOR_*).
Destroy_status	Enumeration: DESTROY_PROCESS_DEATH DESTROY_CHECKING DESTROY_CLEANUP DESTROY_SAVE_YOURSELF
Event	The structure that describes an input event. Use macros for access.
Xv_Font	Pointer to an opaque structure that describes a font.
Xv_Font_attribute	One of the font attributes (FONT_*).
Frame	Pointer to an opaque structure that describes a frame.
Frame_att	One of the frame attributes (FRAME_*).
Window_scale_state	Enumeration: WIN_SCALE_SMALL WIN_SCALE_MEDIUM WIN_SCALE_LARGE WIN_RESCALE_EXTRALARGE
Fullscreen	Handle to an opaque structure that describes a fullscreen.
Fullscreen_attribute	One of the fullscreen attributes (FULLSCREEN_*).
Icon	Handle to an opaque structure that describes a icon.
Icon_attribute	One of the icon attributes (ICON_*).
Inputmask	Mask specifying which input events a window will receive.

Menu	Pointer to an opaque structure that describes a menu.
Menu_attribute	One of the menu attributes (MENU_*).
Menu_generate	Enumerated type for the operation parameter passed to generate procs.
Menu_item	Pointer to an opaque structure that describes a menu item.
Notice_attribute	One of the notice attributes (NOTICE_*).
Notify_arg	Opaque client optional argument.

Notify_destroy	Enumeration:
	    NOTIFY_SAFE
	    NOTIFY_IMMEDIATE

Notify_event	Opaque client event.

Notify_event_type	Enumeration of errors for notifier functions:
	    NOTIFY_SAFE
	    NOTIFY_IMMEDIATE

Notify_func	Notifier function.

Notify_signal_mode	Enumeration:
	    NOTIFY_SYNC
	    NOTIFY_ASYNC

Notify_value	Enumeration of possible return values for client notify procs:
	    NOTIFY_DONE
	    NOTIFY_IGNORED
	    NOTIFY_UNEXPECTED

Openwin_split_direction	Enumeration:
	    OPENWIN_SPLIT_HORIZONTAL
	    OPENWIN_SPLIT_VERTICAL

Panel	Pointer to an opaque structure that describes a panel.
Panel_attr	One of the panel attributes (PANEL_*).
Panel_item	Pointer to an opaque structure that describes a panel item.

Panel_item_type	Enumerated type:
	    PANEL_BUTTON_ITEM
	    PANEL_ITEM
	    PANEL_LIST_ITEM
	    PANEL_MESSAGE_ITEM
	    PANEL_NUMERIC_TEXT
	    PANEL_SLIDER_ITEM
	    PANEL_TEXT_ITEM
	    PANEL_TOGGLE_ITEM

Panel_list_op

Enumerated type:
```
PANEL_LIST_OP_DELETE
PANEL_LIST_OP_DESELECT
PANEL_LIST_OP_SELECT
PANEL_LIST_OP_VALIDATE
```

Panel_setting

Enumerated type:
```
PANEL_CLEAR
PANEL_NO_CLEAR
PANEL_NONE
PANEL_ALL
PANEL_NON_PRINTABLE
PANEL_SPECIFIED
PANEL_CURRENT
PANEL_DONE
PANEL_MARKED
PANEL_VERTICAL
PANEL_HORIZONTAL
PANEL_INVERTED
PANEL_INSERT
PANEL_NEXT
PANEL_PREVIOUS
PANEL_NONE_DOWN
PANEL_LEFT_DOWN
PANEL_MIDDLE_DOWN
PANEL_RIGHT_DOWN
PANEL_CHORD_DOWN
```

Rect

The structure describing a rectangle:
```
typedef struct rect {
        short  r_left;
        short  r_top;
        short  r_width;
        short  r_height;
} Rect;
```

Rectlist

A list of rectangles:
```
typedef struct rectlist {
        short rl_x, rl_y;
        Rectnode *rl_head;
        Rectnode *rl_tail;
        Rect rl_bound;
} Rectlist;
```

Rectnode

One of the individual rectangles in a `rectlist`:
```
typedef struct rectnode {
        Rectnode *rn_next;
        Rect        rn_rect;
} Rectnode;
```

Data Types

Xv_Screen	Pointer to an opaque structure that describes a screen.
Xv_Screen_attr	One of the screen attributes (SCREEN_*).
Scrollbar	The opaque handle for a scrollbar.
Scrollbar_attr	One of the scrollbar attributes (SCROLL_*).
Scrollbar_motion	Enumeration: SCROLL_ABSOLUTE SCROLL_POINT_TO_MIN SCROLL_PAGE_FORWARD SCROLL_LINE_FORWARD SCROLL_MIN_TO_POINT SCROLL_PAGE_BACKWARD SCROLL_LINE_BACKWARD SCROLL_TO_END SCROLL_TO_START SCROLL_NONE
Scrollbar_setting	Enumeration: SCROLL_VERTICAL SCROLL_HORIZONTAL
Seln_attribute	One of the seln attributes.
Xv_Server	Pointer to an opaque structure that describes a server.
Server_attr	One of the server attributes.
Server_image	Pointer to an opaque structure that describes a server image.
Server_image_attribute	One of the Server_image attributes: SERVER_IMAGE_DEPTH SERVER_IMAGE_BITS
Textsw	Pointer to an opaque structure that describes a text subwindow.
Textsw_action	Enumeration of actions defined for client provided notify_proc: TEXTSW_ACTION_CAPS_LOCK TEXTSW_ACTION_CAPS_LOCK TEXTSW_ACTION_EDITED_FILE TEXTSW_ACTION_EDITED_MEMORY TEXTSW_ACTION_FILE_IS_READONLY TEXTSW_ACTION_LOADED_FILE TEXTSW_ACTION_SAVING_FILE TEXTSW_ACTION_STORING_FILE TEXTSW_ACTION_USING_MEMORY TEXTSW_ACTION_WRITE_FAILED TEXTSW_ACTION_REPLACED TEXTSW_ACTION_PAINTED TEXTSW_ACTION_SCROLLED

```
                                  TEXTSW_ACTION_DESTROY_VIEW
                                  TEXTSW_ACTION_SPLIT_VIEW
```

Textsw_attribute   One of the textsw attributes.

Textsw_enum   Enumeration:
```
                                  TEXTSW_NEVER
                                  TEXTSW_ALWAYS
                                  TEXTSW_ONLY
                                  TEXTSW_IF_AUTO_SCROLL
                                  TEXTSW_CLIP
                                  TEXTSW_WRAP_AT_CHAR
                                  TEXTSW_WRAP_AT_WORD
                                  TEXTSW_WRAP_AT_LINE
```

Textsw_index   An index for a character within a text subwindow's text stream.

Textsw_view   Pointer to an opaque structure that describes a text subwindow view.

Textsw_expand_status   Enumeration describe expand status of text subwindow operations:
```
                                  TEXTSW_FULL_BUF
                                  TEXTSW_EXPAND_OK
                                  TEXTSW_EXPAND_OTHER_ERROR
```

Textsw_status   Enumeration describing the status of text subwindow operations:

Tty   Pointer to an opaque structure that describes a TTY subwindow.

Xv_Window   Pointer to an opaque structure that describes a window.

Window_attr   One of the window attributes (WIN_*).

Window_scale_state   Enumeration:
```
                                  WIN_SCALE_SMALL
                                  WIN_SCALE_MEDIUM
                                  WIN_SCALE_LARGE
                                  WIN_SCALE_EXTRALARGE
```

Xv_error_action   Enumeration:
```
                                  XV_ERROR_CONTINUE
                                  XV_ERROR_RETRY
                                  XV_ERROR_ABORT
```

Xv_error_attr   Enumeration:
```
                                  XV_ERROR_SYSTEM
                                  XV_ERROR_BAD_VALUE
                                  XV_ERROR_CREATE_ONLY
                                  XV_ERROR_CANNOT_SET
                                  XV_BERROR_CANNOT_GET
                                  XV_ERROR_SERVER
                                  XV_ERROR_STRING
```

Data Types

	XV_ERROR_INVALID_OBJ XV_ERROR_INTERNAL
Xv_error_severity	**Enumeration:** XV_ERROR_RECOVERABLE XV_ERROR_NON_RECOVERABLE
Xv_object	Pointer to an opaque structure that describes an XView object.
Xv_opaque	Pointer to an opaque structure.
Xv_Xrectlist	A list of rectangles returned by XView in X/11 rectangle list format.

D
Event Codes

D
Event Codes

Table D-1 lists the predefined event codes and their values:

Table D-1. Event Codes

Value	Event Code	Description
0	ASCII_FIRST	Marks beginning of ASCII range
127	ASCII_LAST	Marks end of ASCII range
128	META_FIRST	Marks beginning of META range
255	META_LAST	Marks end of META range
31744	ACTION_NULL_EVENT	Event is *not* translated into an action
31745	ACTION_ERASE_CHAR_BACKWARD	Erase char to the left of caret
31746	ACTION_ERASE_CHAR_FORWARD	Erase char to the right of caret
31747	ACTION_ERASE_WORD_BACKWARD	Erase word to the left of caret
31748	ACTION_ERASE_WORD_FORWARD	Erase word to the right of caret
31749	ACTION_ERASE_LINE_BACKWARD	Erase to the beginning of the line
31750	ACTION_ERASE_LINE_END	Erase to the end of the line
31752	ACTION_GO_CHAR_BACKWARD	Move the caret one character to the left
31753	ACTION_GO_CHAR_FORWARD	Move the caret one character to the right
31754	ACTION_GO_WORD_BACKWARD	Move the caret one word to the left
31755	ACTION_GO_WORD_FORWARD	Move the caret one word to the right
31756	ACTION_GO_WORD_END	Move the caret to the end of the word
31757	ACTION_GO_LINE_BACKWARD	Move the caret to the start of the line
31758	ACTION_GO_LINE_FORWARD	Move the caret to the start of the next line
31759	ACTION_GO_LINE_END	Move the caret to the end of the line
31760	ACTION_GO_LINE_START	Move the caret to the beginning of the line
31761	ACTION_GO_COLUMN_BACKWARD	Move the caret up one line, maintaining column position
31762	ACTION_GO_COLUMN_FORWARD	Move the caret down one line, maintaining column position
31763	ACTION_GO_DOCUMENT_START	Move the caret to the beginning of the text
31764	ACTION_GO_DOCUMENT_END	Move the caret to the end of the text
31765	ACTION_GO_PAGE_FORWARD	Move the caret to the next page
31766	ACTION_GO_PAGE_BACKWARD	Move the caret to the previous page

Value	Event Code	Description
31767	ACTION_STOP	Stop the operation
31768	ACTION_AGAIN	Repeat previous operation
31769	ACTION_PROPS	Show property sheet window
31770	ACTION_UNDO	Undo previous operation
31771	ACTION_REDO	Repeat previous operation
31772	ACTION_FRONT	Bring window to the front of the desktop
31773	ACTION_BACK	Put the window at the back of the desktop
31774	ACTION_COPY	Copy the selection to the clipboard
31775	ACTION_OPEN	Open a window from its icon form (or close if already open)
31776	ACTION_CLOSE	Close a window to an icon
31777	ACTION_PASTE	Copy clipboard contents to the insertion point
31778	ACTION_FIND_BACKWARD	Find the text selection to the left of the caret
31779	ACTION_FIND_FORWARD	Find the text selection to the right of the caret
31780	ACTION_REPLACE	Show find and replace window
31781	ACTION_CUT	Delete the selection and put on clipboard
31782	ACTION_SELECT_FIELD_BACKWARD	Select the previous delimited field
31783	ACTION_SELECT_FIELD_FORWARD	Select the next delimited field
31784	ACTION_COPY_THEN_PASTE	Copy, then paste, text
31785	ACTION_STORE	Store the specified selection as a new file
31786	ACTION_LOAD	Load the specified selection as a new file
31787	ACTION_INCLUDE_FILE	Includes the file
31788	ACTION_GET_FILENAME	Get the selected filename
31789	ACTION_SET_DIRECTORY	Set the directory to the selection
31790	ACTION_DO_IT	Do the appropriate default action
31791	ACTION_HELP	Set the directory to the selection
31792	ACTION_INSERT	"INSERT" key*
31796	ACTION_CAPS_LOCK	Toggle caps-lock state
31799	ACTION_SELECT	Left mouse button down or up
31800	ACTION_ADJUST	Middle mouse button down or up
31801	ACTION_MENU	Right mouse button down or up
31802	ACTION_DRAG_MOVE	For moving text
31803	ACTION_DRAG_COPY	Attempting to drag copy
31803	ACTION_SPLIT_HORIZONTAL	Split pane horizontally
31804	ACTION_DRAG_LOAD	Attempting to drag load
31806	ACTION_SPLIT_VERTICAL	Split pane vertically
31807	ACTION_SPLIT_INIT	Initialize a split pane
31808	ACTION_SPLIT_DESTROY	Destroy a split of a pane
31809	ACTION_RESCALE	Rescale a pane
31810	ACTION_PININ	Pop up's OPEN LOOK pushpin in window header is in
31811	ACTION_PINOUT	Pop up's OPEN LOOK pushpin in window header is out
31812	ACTION_DISMISS	OPEN LOOK "dismiss" of pop-up window

Value	Event Code	Description
31815	ACTION_TAKE_FOCUS	Take the input focus
31818	KBD_MAP	KeymapNotify
31819	WIN_GRAPHICS_EXPOSE	GraphicsExpose
31820	WIN_NO_EXPOSE	NoExpose
31821	WIN_VISIBILITY_NOTIFY	VisibilityNotify
31822	WIN_CREATE_NOTIFY	CreateNotify
31823	WIN_DESTROY_NOTIFY	DestroyNotify
31824	WIN_MAP_REQUEST	MapRequest
31825	WIN_REPARENT_NOTIFY	ReparentNotify
31826	WIN_GRAVITY_NOTIFY	GravityNotify
31827	WIN_RESIZE_REQUEST	ResizeRequest
31828	WIN_CONFIGURE_REQUEST	ConfigureRequest
31829	WIN_CIRCULATE_REQUEST	CirculateRequest
31830	WIN_CIRCULATE_NOTIFY	CirculateNotify
31831	WIN_PROPERTY_NOTIFY	PropertyNotify
31835	WIN_COLORMAP_NOTIFY	ColormapNotify
31836	MAPPING_NOTIFY	MappingNotify
31895	ACTION_MATCH_DELIMITER	Select text up to a matching delimiter
31897	ACTION_QUOTE	Cause next event in the input stream to pass untranslated by the keymapping system
31898	ACTION_EMPTY	Empty out the object or window.
32000	PANEL_EVENT_CANCEL	The panel or panel item is no longer "current"
32001	PANEL_EVENT_MOVE_IN	The pointer enters panel or panel item with no mouse buttons down
32002	PANEL_EVENT_DRAG_IN	The pointer enters panel or panel item with one or more mouse buttons down
32256	SCROLLBAR_REQUEST	Request the scrollbar client to scroll paint window to a new view start
32512	LOC_MOVE	Pointer moves
32513	LOC_WINENTER	Pointer enters window
32514	LOC_WINEXIT	Pointer exits window
32515	LOC_DRAG	Pointer moves while a button was down
32516	WIN_REPAINT	Some portion of window requires repainting
32517	WIN_RESIZE	Window has been resized
32518	WIN_MAP_NOTIFY	Notification of window being mapped
32519	WIN_UNMAP_NOTIFY	Notification of window being unmapped
32520	KBD_USE	Window is now the focus of keyboard input
32521	KBD_DONE	Window is no longer the focus of keyboard input
32522	WIN_CLIENT_MESSAGE	A message from another client
32563+i-1	BUT(i)	Press pointer buttons 1–10
32563	MS_LEFT	Press left mouse button
32564	MS_MIDDLE	Press middle mouse button
32565	MS_RIGHT	Press right mouse button
32573+i-1	KEY_LEFT(i)	Press left function keys 1–15

Value	Event Code	Description
32589+i-1	`KEY_RIGHT(i)`	Press right function keys 1–15
32605+i-1	`KEY_TOP(i)`	Press top function keys 1–15
32621+i-1	`KEY_BOTTOM(i)`	"BOTTOM" keys*
32621	`KEY_BOTTOMLEFT`	
32621	`KEY_BOTTOMFIRST`	
32622	`KEY_BOTTOMRIGHT`	
32636	`KEY_BOTTOMLAST`	

* May not be available on all keyboards.

E

Command Line Arguments

E
Command Line Arguments

In XView, each property can be set in one of three ways:

1. By specifying the short flag name plus its value (if any) on the command line.

2. By specifying the long flag name plus its value (if any) on the command line.

3. By editing the corresponding default or defaults in your ⁷/.Xdefaults file.

In the absence of any of these actions, the default action is taken. Methods 1 and 2 each take precedence over method 3.

Naturally, an application can override defaults through the use of XView attributes, but a well-behaved application will always override application defaults with the command line arguments.

Arguments are all set in *italics*. Those arguments in parentheses describe the value or values. Arguments not in parentheses indicate a list from which you must choose.

Table E-1. XView Command Line Arguments

Short Flag	Long Flag	Default Argument(s)	Value	Example
-Wx	-scale	*medium*	small medium large extra_large	-Wx large
-Wt	-font	*(fontname-size)*	lucidasans-12	-Wt screen-14
-Ww	-width	*(columns)*	80	-Ww 120
-Wh	-height	*(rows)*	34	-Wh 24
-Ws	-size	*(pixels pixels)*	80 columns by 34 rows	-Ws 500 400
-Wp	-position	*(x y)*	from top left to bottom right of screen	-Wp 237 625

Short Flag	Long Flag	Default Argument(s)	Value	Example
-WP	-icon_position	*(x y)*	along edge of screen	-WP 500 0
-Wl	-label	*(header_string)*	none	-Wl "My tool"
-Wi	-iconic		open	-Wi
-Wf	-foreground_color	*(red green blue)*	black	-Wf 0 0 0
-Wb	-background_color	*(red green blue)*	white	-Wb 255 255 255
-Wg	-set_default_color		no	-Wg
-WI	-icon_image	*(pixmap_pathname)*	blank	-WI mytool.icon
-WL	-icon_label	*(footer_string)*	none	-WL "Idle"
-WT	-icon_font	*(fontname-size)*	lucidasans-12	-WT screen-10
-Wr	-display	*(hostname:display)*	DISPLAY environment variable	-Wr myhost:0
-Wdr	-disable_retained		enable retained windows on monochrome displays	-Wdr
	-disable_screen_saver	*0*	XSetScreenSaver not called	-disable_ screen_ saver 1
		1	XSetScreenSaver called	--disable_ screen_ saver 0
	-sync	*0*	run asynchronously	-sync 0
		1	run synchronously	-sync 1
-WH	-help			
-Wdxio	-disable_xio_error_handler			-Wdxio

Table E-2. Resource Names of Command Line Arguments

Short Flag	Resource Name(s)
−Wx	window.scale
−Wt	font.name
−Ww	window.columns
−Wh	window.rows
−Ws	window.width
..	window.height
−Wp	window.x
	window.y
−WP	icon.x
	icon.y
−Wl	window.header
−Wi	window.iconic
−Wf	window.color.foreground
−Wb	window.color.background
−Wg	window.inheritcolor
−WI	icon.pixmap
−WL	icon.footer
−WT	icon.font.name
−Wr	server.name
−Wdr	window.mono.disableRetained 0
−WH	(Prints out a list of generic command line arguments.)
−Wdxio	(Disables the I/O error handler installed by xv_init().)

F

OPEN LOOK
User Interface Compliance

In This Chapter:

Level 1 Features Not Supported in XView 491
   Keyboard and Mouse Customization 491
   Input Focus Feedback 492
   Menu Default Setting 492
   Default Buttons in Pop Ups 493
   Help 493
   Window Background 493
   Notices 493
   Text Functions 493
   Control Items 494
   Scrolling Lists 494
   Property Windows 495
   Inactive Controls 495
Level 2 Features Supported in XView 496
Level 2 Features Not Supported in XView 496

OPEN LOOK User Interface Compliance

This appendix lists the ways that the XView toolkit is not compliant with the *OPEN LOOK Graphical User Interface Functional Specification*. It is not a complete list of the ways that OpenWindows 1.0 is not an OPEN LOOK UI-compliant environment. OPEN LOOK UI compliance has two components: toolkit compliance and environment compliance.

An OPEN LOOK UI-compliant toolkit allows a developer to write an application that will be OPEN LOOK UI-compliant if run with an OPEN LOOK UI window manager. The toolkit might also support the application running successfully with, for example, a MOTIF™ window manager, but in such a configuration, the application would not be OPEN LOOK UI-compliant. An OPEN LOOK UI-compliant environment consists of an OPEN LOOK UI window manager, file manager, workspace properties window, and other such utility programs. To guarantee an OPEN LOOK UI application, the developer must write the application with an OPEN LOOK UI-compliant toolkit *and* run the application in an OPEN LOOK UI-compliant environment.

This list is in three parts. The first part consists of those features missing from XView 1.0 that are specified as Level 1 OPEN LOOK UI features. The second part lists some of the Level 2 OPEN LOOK UI features supported by XView 1.0. The third part lists the rest of the Level 2 OPEN LOOK UI features, which are not supported by XView 1.0.

Level 1 Features Not Supported in XView 1.0

The Level 1 features listed on the following pages are not supported in XView 1.0.

Keyboard and Mouse Customization

XView 1.0 hard-codes the bindings for function keys, mouse buttons, and mouse modifiers that OPEN LOOK UI says the user should be able to customize.

An OPEN LOOK UI toolkit should allow the user to specify the keys used for CUT, COPY, PASTE, PROPERTIES, UNDO, CANCEL, DEFAULTACTION, NEXTFIELD, and PREVFIELD.

- In XView 1.0, these key bindings are hard-coded to L10, L6, L8, L3, L4, L1, Return, Tab, and Shift-Tab.

An OPEN LOOK UI toolkit should allow the user to change the mouse buttons used for SELECT, ADJUST, and MENU; the specified default mouse button bindings are LEFT, MIDDLE, and RIGHT.

- In XView 1.0, the specified default mouse button bindings are hard-coded.

An OPEN LOOK UI toolkit should allow the user to change the mouse modifiers used for SETMENUDEFAULT, DUPLICATE, PAN, and CONSTRAIN. The specified default modified mouse actions are Control-RIGHT for SETMENUDEFAULT, Control-LEFT for DUPLICATE, Meta-LEFT for PAN, and LEFT-and-MIDDLE-chorded for CONSTRAIN.

- In XView 1.0, the specified defaults for SETMENUDEFAULT and DUPLICATE are hard-coded, and PAN and CONSTRAIN are not supported.

In an OPEN LOOK UI toolkit, clicking ADJUST when there is no selection will set an initial insert point (the same as clicking SELECT).

- In XView 1.0, this selects a single character.

In an OPEN LOOK UI toolkit, the user can bind a modified mouse action to selecting a single character, but the default binding is NONE.

- In XView 1.0, selecting a single character is hard-coded to clicking ADJUST when there is no selection.

Input Focus Feedback

In an OPEN LOOK UI toolkit, only one text area (that is, text field or text pane) within a window may have a caret, whether active or inactive.

- XView 1.0 allows multiple inactive carets to be displayed in a single window (but only one active caret). As a result, if you use the *follow-mouse* input focus model instead of the *click-to-type* model, you may believe that an inactive caret is not being properly activated. In fact, that inactive caret should not have been displayed.

Menu Default Setting

In an OPEN LOOK UI toolkit, the user can press or release the SETMENUDEFAULT mouse modifier either before or after pressing MENU to change the menu default setting, thus allowing the user to change the menu default and invoke the new default in a single menu action.

- In XView 1.0, the user must press SETMENUDEFAULT before pressing MENU to change the menu default.

Default Buttons in Pop Ups

In an OPEN LOOK UI toolkit, notices, command windows, and property windows must always have a "default button," even when there is only one button, and that the DEFAULTACTION keyboard accelerator always invokes the default button.

* XView 1.0 does not provide this automatically, but applications can implement this feature using XView primitives.

Help

In an OPEN LOOK UI toolkit, help text can have bold text, italic text, and glyphs (small pictures).

* XView 1.0 does not support this.

In an OPEN LOOK UI toolkit, applications can add a More button to the help window.

* XView 1.0 does not allow this.

Window Background

In an OPEN LOOK UI toolkit, window backgrounds are used to access the Window menu, to select a window, and to move it by dragging.

* XView 1.0 does not support this.

Notices

In an OPEN LOOK UI toolkit, notices do not freeze the screen; input to other applications is always possible.

* In XView 1.0, notices block input to all applications.

In an OPEN LOOK UI toolkit, each window of an application displays the standard busy pattern in the header when a notice is displayed.

* XView 1.0 does not give the window manager enough information for this to work.

Text Functions

In an OPEN LOOK UI toolkit, an UNDO after an UNDO reverses the effect of the UNDO, restoring the original state.

* In XView 1.0, the second UNDO undoes the next-previous edit. There is no way in XView 1.0 to reverse the effect of an UNDO.

Control Items

In an OPEN LOOK UI toolkit, an abbreviated menu button can have a text field to the right of the menu button. The text field is used to add items to the menu.

- XView 1.0 does not have this feature.

In an OPEN LOOK UI toolkit, menu buttons (and abbreviated menu buttons) highlight on MENU down, and change to the standard busy pattern on MENU-up in stay-up mode.

- XView 1.0 does not provide this.

In an OPEN LOOK UI toolkit, a default setting for exclusive and non-exclusive settings is only displayed when the controls are used on a menu.

- XView 1.0 indicates a default setting for exclusive and non-exclusive settings even when the controls are used in command and property windows.

In an OPEN LOOK UI toolkit, a slider can be shown with a read-only current value.

- XView 1.0 does not support this.

In an OPEN LOOK UI toolkit, the user can click SELECT to the left or right of a slider drag box on the slider bar to decrement or increment respectively, the setting by one unit. The pointer jumps as needed to allow repeated clicks.

- XView 1.0 does not support this.

In an OPEN LOOK UI toolkit, some exclusive settings can have no choice selected; the user clicks SELECT on the current choice to cause it to be deselected, yielding a value of "none."

- XView 1.0 requires exclusive settings to have one choice selected.

In an OPEN LOOK UI toolkit, an indeterminate state is defined on exclusive and non-exclusive settings.

- XView 1.0 does not support this.

In an OPEN LOOK UI toolkit, the bold border width on exclusive and non-exclusive settings is adjusted (to either 2 or 3 pixels) depending on the display resolution.

- XView 1.0 does not provide this.

Scrolling Lists

In an OPEN LOOK UI toolkit, scrolling lists can be put into an editable mode, and in that mode, the item selected for editing is inverted.

- XView 1.0 does not allow scrolling lists to be edited; they can only be changed by the application.

In an OPEN LOOK UI toolkit, scrolling lists can support no current choice (display or edit only), one current choice (exclusive list), or zero or more current choices (non-exclusive list).

- XView 1.0 only provides non-exclusive lists.

In an OPEN LOOK UI toolkit, a current choice in a non-exclusive list can be "deselected" by clicking on it.

- XView 1.0 does not support this.

Property Windows

In an OPEN LOOK UI toolkit, there is a required Settings pop-up menu for a property window.

- XView 1.0 does not provide this automatically, but applications can implement this menu themselves.

In an OPEN LOOK UI toolkit, property windows have two required buttons, `Apply` and `Reset`, and an optional button, `Set Default`.

- Again, XView 1.0 does not provide this automatically, but applications can implement this feature using XView primitives.

In an OPEN LOOK UI toolkit, there is a way to have two active selections when using property windows.

- XView 1.0 does not support this.

In an OPEN LOOK UI toolkit, when there are two active selections, the `Apply` button becomes a menu button with `Original Selection` and `New Selection` items.

- XView 1.0 does not support this.

Inactive Controls

In an OPEN LOOK UI toolkit, the scrollbar up or down arrow is dimmed when the scroll elevator is at the beginning or end of the document, respectively. When there is no data in the document, both arrows are dimmed.

- XView 1.0 does not support this.

In an OPEN LOOK UI toolkit, a menu's pushpin is dimmed if the menu has already been pinned.

- XView 1.0 does not support this.

Level 2 Features Supported in XView 1.0

The following Level 2 features are supported in XView 1.0.

- Abbreviated buttons

- Nonstandard basic windows

- Numeric text fields with increment/decrement buttons

- Some keyboard accelerators

- Splittable panes

    - *Missing*: Dimming the pane's border or its contents to indicate that the pane is about to disappear when removing a split pane using cable anchors.

- Split View and Join Views items on Scrollbar menu

- Dragging text to move/copy

    - *Missing*: Text duplicate and text move pointers should use a more-arrow instead of an ellipsis ...

- Quick Move and Quick Duplicate on (most) text

- Some Level 2 Workspace Properties

Level 2 Features Not Supported in XView 1.0

The following Level 2 features are not supported in XView 1.0.

- Blocking pop-up windows

- Change bars in property windows

- Color

    - Window manager provides color in headers and footers

    - Color backgrounds are supported in notices (only)

    - *Missing*: Color backgrounds in control areas and menus

    - *Missing*: Grayscale/color glyphs for "3-D" appearance

- Multi-line text areas

- Edit menu for text fields

- Read-only gauges

- Menus containing more than one type of control

- Resizable panes

- Selectable panes

- Minimum scrollbar
- View must be updated while scrollbar elevator is dragged
- Page-oriented scrollbar
- Automatic scrolling
- Panning
- Glyphs in scrolling lists
- Hierarchical scrolling lists
- Sliders with end-boxes and tickmarks
- Vertical sliders
- Soft function keys
- Window scaling

G

Example Programs

In This Chapter:

item_move.c 502
xv_termsw.c 508
scroll_cells2.c 510
menu_dir2.c 514
type_font.c 519
fonts.c 521
seln.c 526
seln_line.c 529
x_draw.c 531

G
Example Programs

This appendix contains nine example programs that supplement the programs in the chapters:

- *item_move.c*
- *xv_termsw.c*
- *scroll_cells2.c*
- *menu_dir2.c*
- *type_font.c*
- *fonts.c*
- *seln.c*
- *seln_line.c*
- *x_draw.c*

Some of these programs are extensions to programs presented earlier in this book; they are listed here to demonstrate extended usage. Other programs in this appendix attempt to integrate features from unrelated XView packages that exceeded the scope of a particular chapter.

item_move.c

The first program demonstrates how you can use an event handler within a panel to allow the user to create panel items, move them around within the panel, and delete them. Chapter 7, *Panels*, discusses specifics about how panels work. Chapter 5, *Canvases and Openwin*, discusses the canvas and openwin issues, since the panel is subclassed from those packages.

Example G-1. The item_move.c program

```
/*
 * item_move.c
 *     Move items around in a panel using an event handler specific
 * to the panel.  Two panels are created -- the left panel contains
 * panel buttons that allow you to create certain types of items that
 * are put in the second panel.  Use the ADJUST mouse button to move
 * items around in the second panel.
 */
#include <stdio.h>
#include <xview/xview.h>
#include <xview/panel.h>

/* we need handles to the base frame and a panel -- instead of using
 * global variables, we're going to attach the objects to the objects
 * which need to reference them.  Attach using XV_KEY_DATA --
 * here are the keys.
 */
#define PACKAGE_KEY     100
#define FRAME_KEY       101
#define PANEL_KEY       102

main(argc, argv)
int argc;
char *argv[];
{
    Frame          frame;
    Panel          panel;
    Panel_item     create_text, item;
    void           quit(), my_event_proc();
    int            selected(), create_item();

    xv_init(XV_INIT_ARGC_PTR_ARGV, &argc, argv, NULL);

    frame = (Frame)xv_create(XV_NULL, FRAME,
        FRAME_LABEL,            "Use Middle Button To Move Items",
        FRAME_SHOW_FOOTER,      TRUE,
        NULL);
    /*
     * Create panel for known panel items.  Layout panel vertically.
     */
    panel = (Panel)xv_create(frame, PANEL,
        PANEL_LAYOUT,           PANEL_VERTICAL,
        NULL);

    /*
     * Create the standard "Quit" button to exit program.
     */
    (void) xv_create(panel, PANEL_BUTTON,
        PANEL_LABEL_STRING,     "Quit",
```

```
        PANEL_NOTIFY_PROC,        quit,
        XV_KEY_DATA,              FRAME_KEY,        frame,
        NULL);

    /*
     * create text panel item, attach the frame as client data for
     * use by the notify procedure create_item().  Text items inherit
     * the layout of "label" and "value" from its parent panel.
     * override for the text item by setting PANEL_LAYOUT explicitly.
     */
    create_text = (Panel_item)xv_create(panel, PANEL_TEXT,
        PANEL_LABEL_STRING,       "Create Button:",
        PANEL_NOTIFY_PROC,        create_item,
        PANEL_LAYOUT,             PANEL_HORIZONTAL,
        PANEL_VALUE_DISPLAY_LENGTH,   10,
        NULL);

    /*
     * panel button determines which type of button to create -- a
     * button or a message item.  See create_item().
     */
    item = (Panel_item)xv_create(panel, PANEL_CHOICE,
        PANEL_DISPLAY_LEVEL,      PANEL_CURRENT,
        PANEL_LAYOUT,             PANEL_HORIZONTAL,
        PANEL_LABEL_STRING,       "Item type",
        PANEL_CHOICE_STRINGS,     "Button", "Message", "Text", NULL,
        NULL);
    window_fit(panel);

    /* Create a new panel to be used for panel creation.  The panel
     * from above is no longer referenced.  The panel created here
     * is the panel used throughout the rest of this program.  The
     * panel referenced in WIN_RIGHT_OF and XV_HEIGHT is the old one
     * since the new one isn't created yet.
     */
    panel = (Panel)xv_create(frame, PANEL,
        WIN_RIGHT_OF,             canvas_paint_window(panel),
        XV_WIDTH,                 300,
        XV_HEIGHT,                xv_get(panel, XV_HEIGHT),
        OPENWIN_SHOW_BORDERS,     TRUE,
        NULL);

    /* Install event handling routine for the panel */
    xv_set(canvas_paint_window(panel),
        WIN_EVENT_PROC,           my_event_proc,
        XV_KEY_DATA,              PANEL_KEY,        panel,
        NULL);
    /* attach various items to the text item for text_select() */
    xv_set(create_text,
        XV_KEY_DATA,              FRAME_KEY,        frame,
        XV_KEY_DATA,              PACKAGE_KEY,      item,
        XV_KEY_DATA,              PANEL_KEY,        panel,
        NULL);
    window_fit(frame);
    xv_main_loop(frame);
}

/*
```

```
 * Process events for the panel's subwindow.  This routine gets -all-
 * events that occur in the panel subwindow and does not interfere
 * with the normal processing of events dispatched to panels items.
 * my_event_proc is only interested in ADJUST button events that
 * happen on top of panel items.  When the user clicks and _drags_ the
 * ADJUST button on a panel item, the item is moved to where the mouse
 * moves to.
 */
void
my_event_proc(window, event)
Xv_Window window;
Event *event;
{
    static Panel_item   item;
    static int  x_offset, y_offset;
    Panel       panel = (Panel)xv_get(window, XV_KEY_DATA, PANEL_KEY);
    Frame       frame = (Frame)xv_get(panel, XV_OWNER);
    Rect        *rect, *item_rect;
    char        buf[64];

    /*
     * If the mouse is dragging an item, reset its new location.
     */
    if (event_action(event) == LOC_DRAG && item) {
        Panel_item pi;
        Rect r;
        /*
         * Get the rect of item, then *copy* it -- never change data
         * returned by xv_get().  Modify the copied rect reflecting
         * new X,Y position of panel item and check to see if it
         * intersects with any existing panel items.
         */
        rect = (Rect *)xv_get(item, XV_RECT);
        rect_construct(&r, /* see <xview/rect.h> for macros */
            rect->r_left, rect->r_top, rect->r_width, rect->r_height);
        r.r_left = event->ie_locx - x_offset;
        r.r_top = event->ie_locy - y_offset;
        PANEL_EACH_ITEM(panel, pi)
            if (pi == item)
                continue;
            /* don't let panel items overlap */
            item_rect = (Rect *)xv_get(pi, XV_RECT);
            if (rect_intersectsrect(item_rect, &r))
                return;
        PANEL_END_EACH
        /* no overlap -- move panel item. */
        xv_set(item,
            PANEL_ITEM_X, r.r_left,
            PANEL_ITEM_Y, r.r_top,
            NULL);
    }
    /* If it's not the ADJUST button, we're not interested */
    if (event_action(event) != ACTION_ADJUST)
        return;
    /*
     * next two cases is ADJUST button just-down or just-released
```

```
        */
    if (event_is_down(event)) {
        /* Middle button down on an item -- determine panel item */
        PANEL_EACH_ITEM(panel, item)
            rect = (Rect *)xv_get(item, XV_RECT);
            if (rect_includespoint(rect,
                event->ie_locx, event->ie_locy)) {
                x_offset = event->ie_locx - rect->r_left;
                y_offset = event->ie_locy - rect->r_top;
                break;
            }
        PANEL_END_EACH
        if (item)
            sprintf(buf, "Moving item: '%s'",
                (char *)xv_get(item, PANEL_LABEL_STRING));
        else
            buf[0] = 0;
    } else if (item) {
        char *name = (char *)xv_get(item, PANEL_LABEL_STRING);

        /* test if item is inside panel by comparing XV_RECTs */
        rect = (Rect *)xv_get(panel, XV_RECT);
        if (!rect_includespoint(rect,
            event->ie_locx + rect->r_left,
            event->ie_locy + rect->r_top)) {
            /* item is outside the panel -- remove item */
            xv_destroy(item);
            sprintf(buf, "Removed '%s' from panel", name);
        } else
            sprintf(buf, "'%s' moved to %d %d", name,
                (int)xv_get(item, XV_X), (int)xv_get(item, XV_Y));
        /* set "item" to null so that new drag
         * events don't attempt to move old item.
         */
        item = NULL;
    }
    xv_set(frame, FRAME_LEFT_FOOTER, buf, NULL);
}

/*
 * Callback routine for all panel buttons except "Quit".
 * If the panel item is the text item, determine the name of the new
 * panel button the user wishes to create.  Loop through all the
 * existing panel items looking for one with the same label.  If so,
 * return PANEL_NONE and set the frame's footer with an error message.
 * Otherwise, create a new panel item with the label, reset the text
 * item value and return PANEL_NEXT.
 */
int
create_item(item, event)
Panel_item item;
Event *event;
{
    Xv_pkg      *pkg;
    Panel       panel = (Panel)xv_get(item, XV_KEY_DATA, PANEL_KEY);
    Frame       frame = (Frame)xv_get(item, XV_KEY_DATA, FRAME_KEY);
    Panel_item  pi, pkg_item;
```

```
    char        buf[64];

pkg_item = (Panel_item)xv_get(item, XV_KEY_DATA, PACKAGE_KEY);
(void) strncpy(buf, xv_get(item, PANEL_VALUE), sizeof buf);
if (!buf[0])
    return PANEL_NONE;
switch((int)xv_get(pkg_item, PANEL_VALUE)) {
    case 1: pkg = PANEL_MESSAGE; break;
    case 2: pkg = PANEL_TEXT; break;
    default: pkg = PANEL_BUTTON;
}
/* loop thru all panel items and check for item with same name */
PANEL_EACH_ITEM(panel, pi)
    if (!strcmp(buf, xv_get(pi, PANEL_LABEL_STRING))) {
        xv_set(frame, FRAME_LEFT_FOOTER, "Label Taken", NULL);
        return PANEL_NONE;
    }
PANEL_END_EACH
(void) xv_create(panel, pkg,
    PANEL_LABEL_STRING,     buf,
    PANEL_NOTIFY_PROC,      selected,
    XV_KEY_DATA,            FRAME_KEY,      frame,
    /* only for text items, but doesn't affect other items */
    PANEL_VALUE_DISPLAY_LENGTH, 10,
    PANEL_LAYOUT,           PANEL_HORIZONTAL,
    NULL);
xv_set(item, PANEL_VALUE, "", NULL);
return PANEL_NEXT;
}

/*
 * For panel buttons. return XV_OK or XV_ERROR if the item was
 * selected using the left mouse button or not.
 */
int
selected(item, event)
Panel_item item;
Event *event;
{
    Frame       frame = (Frame)xv_get(item, XV_KEY_DATA, FRAME_KEY);
    char        buf[64];

    if (event_action(event) == ACTION_SELECT) {
        sprintf(buf, "'%s' selected", xv_get(item, PANEL_LABEL_STRING));
        xv_set(frame, FRAME_RIGHT_FOOTER, buf, NULL);
        return XV_OK;
    }
    return XV_ERROR;
}

/*
 * callback for the "Quit" item.  Destroy the frame, which
 * causes xv_main_loop() to return.
 */
void
quit(item, event)
Panel_item item;
```

```
Event *event;
{
    Frame frame = (Frame)xv_get(item, XV_KEY_DATA, FRAME_KEY);
    if (event_action(event) == ACTION_SELECT)
        xv_destroy_safe(frame);
}
```

xv_termsw.c

This book has never discussed the *term* subwindow. Basically, it is a tty subwindow that can be edited like a text subwindow. It may also contain a scrollbar. *xv_termsw.c* shows you how to create a *term* subwindow.

Example G-2. The xv_termsw.c program

```
/*
 * xv_termsw.c
 * Demonstrate incorporation of a Term subwindow in an application;
 * keyboard input to the termsw can come either directly to the
 * termsw or from an adjoining panel text item.
 */
#include <stdio.h>
#include <xview/xview.h>
#include <xview/panel.h>
/* #include <xview/tty.h> */
#include <xview/termsw.h>

Termsw          term;
Panel_item      text_item;

main(argc,argv)
int     argc;
char    *argv[];
{
    Frame       frame;
    Panel       panel;
    int         notify_proc();

    xv_init(XV_INIT_ARGS, argc, argv, NULL);

    frame = (Frame)xv_create(NULL, FRAME, NULL);
    panel = (Panel)xv_create(frame, PANEL, NULL);
    text_item = (Panel_item)xv_create(panel, PANEL_TEXT,
        PANEL_LABEL_STRING,         "Command:",
        PANEL_NOTIFY_PROC,          notify_proc,
        PANEL_VALUE_DISPLAY_LENGTH, 20,
        NULL);
    (void) xv_create(panel, PANEL_BUTTON,
        PANEL_LABEL_STRING,     "Apply",
        PANEL_NOTIFY_PROC,      notify_proc,
        NULL);
    window_fit_height(panel);

    term = (Termsw)xv_create(frame, TERMSW, NULL);

    window_fit(frame);
    xv_main_loop(frame);
}
/*
 * This procedure is called when the user this return on the
 * panel text item or clicking on the <apply> button.
 * Use ttysw_input() to feed the string to the termal window.
 */
int
notify_proc(item,event)
```

```
Panel_item      item;
Event   *event;
{
    char        str[81];

    sprintf(str, "%.81s\n", (char *)xv_get(text_item, PANEL_VALUE));
    ttysw_input(term, str, strlen(str));
    xv_set(text_item, PANEL_VALUE, "", NULL);
    return XV_OK;
}
```

Example
Programs

scroll_cells2.c

This program is based heavily on *scroll_cells.c*, which is found in Chapter 10, *Scrollbars*. This version of the program deals with resize events. When a resize occurs, the `object`, `view`, and `page` length attributes are set to correctly reflect the size of the scrollbar with respect to the object it scrolls.

Example G-3. The scroll_cells2.c program

```
/*
 * scroll_cells2.c -- scroll a bitmap of cells around in a canvas.
 * This is a simplified version of scroll_cells.c graphically. That
 * is, it does not display icons, just rows and columns of cells.
 * The difference with this version is that it attempts to accommodate
 * resize events not addressed in the scroll_cells.c.
 * This new function is at the end of the file.
 */
#include <stdio.h>
#include <X11/X.h>
#include <X11/Xlib.h>     /* Using Xlib graphics */
#include <xview/xview.h>
#include <xview/canvas.h>
#include <xview/scrollbar.h>
#include <xview/xv_xrect.h>

#define CELL_WIDTH          64
#define CELL_HEIGHT         64
#define CELLS_PER_HOR_PAGE  5 /* when paging w/scrollbar */
#define CELLS_PER_VER_PAGE  5 /* when paging w/scrollbar */
#define CELLS_PER_ROW       16
#define CELLS_PER_COL       16

Pixmap          cell_map;          /* pixmap copied onto canvas window */
Scrollbar       horiz_scrollbar;
Scrollbar       vert_scrollbar;
GC              gc;                 /* General usage GC */

main(argc, argv)
int argc;
char *argv[];
{
    Frame       frame;
    Canvas      canvas;
    void        repaint_proc(), resize_proc();

    /* Initialize, create frame and canvas... */
    xv_init(XV_INIT_ARGC_PTR_ARGV, &argc, argv, NULL);

    frame = xv_create(XV_NULL, FRAME,
        FRAME_LABEL,            argv[0],
        FRAME_SHOW_FOOTER,      TRUE,
        NULL);

    canvas = xv_create(frame, CANVAS,
        /* make subwindow the size of a "page" */
        XV_WIDTH,               CELL_WIDTH * CELLS_PER_HOR_PAGE,
        XV_HEIGHT,              CELL_HEIGHT * CELLS_PER_VER_PAGE,
        /* canvas is much larger than the window */
```

```
            CANVAS_WIDTH,               CELL_WIDTH * CELLS_PER_HOR_PAGE,
            CANVAS_HEIGHT,              CELL_HEIGHT * CELLS_PER_VER_PAGE,
            /* CANVAS_AUTO_EXPAND,   FALSE, */
            /* CANVAS_AUTO_SHRINK,   FALSE, */
            /* don't retain window -- we'll repaint it all the time */
            CANVAS_RETAINED,           FALSE,
            /* We're using Xlib graphics calls in repaint_proc() */
            CANVAS_X_PAINT_WINDOW,     TRUE,
            CANVAS_REPAINT_PROC,       repaint_proc,
            CANVAS_RESIZE_PROC,        resize_proc,
            OPENWIN_AUTO_CLEAR,        FALSE,
            NULL);

    /*
     * Create scrollbars attached to the canvas. When user clicks
     * on cable, page by the page size (PAGE_LENGTH). Scrolling
     * should move cell by cell, not by one pixel (PIXELS_PER_UNIT).
     */
    vert_scrollbar = xv_create(canvas, SCROLLBAR,
        SCROLLBAR_DIRECTION,           SCROLLBAR_VERTICAL,
        SCROLLBAR_PIXELS_PER_UNIT,     CELL_HEIGHT,
        NULL);
    horiz_scrollbar = xv_create(canvas, SCROLLBAR,
        SCROLLBAR_DIRECTION,           SCROLLBAR_HORIZONTAL,
        SCROLLBAR_PIXELS_PER_UNIT,     CELL_WIDTH,
        NULL);

    /*
     * create pixmap and draw cells into it.  This portion of the
     * program could use XCopyArea to render real icons whose sizes
     * do not exceed whatever CELL_WIDTH and CELL_HEIGHT are defined
     * to be.  The cell_map will be copied into the window via
     * XCopyPlane in the repaint procedure.
     */
    {
        short           x, y, pt = 0;
        XPoint          points[256];
        XGCValues       gcvalues;
        Display *dpy = (Display *)xv_get(canvas, XV_DISPLAY);

        cell_map = XCreatePixmap(dpy, DefaultRootWindow(dpy),
            CELLS_PER_ROW * CELL_WIDTH + 1,
            CELLS_PER_COL * CELL_HEIGHT + 1,
            1); /* We only need a 1-bit deep pixmap */

        /* Create the gc for the cell_map -- since it is 1-bit deep,
         * use 0 and 1 for fg/bg values.  Also, limit number of
         * events generated by setting geraphics exposures to False.
         */
        gcvalues.graphics_exposures = False;
        gcvalues.background = 0;
        gcvalues.foreground = 1;
        gc = XCreateGC(dpy, cell_map,
            GCForeground|GCBackground|GCGraphicsExposures, &gcvalues);

        /* dot every other pixel */
        for (x = 0; x <= CELL_WIDTH * CELLS_PER_ROW; x += 2)
            for (y = 0; y <= CELL_HEIGHT * CELLS_PER_COL; y += 2) {
```

```
                    if (x % CELL_WIDTH != 0 && y % CELL_HEIGHT != 0)
                        continue;
                    points[pt].x = x, points[pt].y = y;
                    if (++pt == sizeof points / sizeof points[0]) {
                        XDrawPoints(dpy, cell_map, gc,
                            points, pt, CoordModeOrigin);
                        pt = 0;
                    }
                }
            }
        if (pt != sizeof points) /* flush out the remaining points */
            XDrawPoints(dpy, cell_map, gc,
                        points, pt, CoordModeOrigin);
        /* label each cell indicating the its coordinates */
        for (x = 0; x < CELLS_PER_ROW; x++)
            for (y = 0; y < CELLS_PER_COL; y++) {
                char buf[8];
                sprintf(buf, "%d,%d", x+1, y+1);
                XDrawString(dpy, cell_map, gc,
                    x * CELL_WIDTH + 5, y * CELL_HEIGHT + 25,
                    buf, strlen(buf));
            }
        /* we're now done with the cell_map, so free gc and
         * create a new one based on the window that will use it.
         */
        XFreeGC(dpy, gc);
        gcvalues.background = WhitePixel(dpy, DefaultScreen(dpy));
        gcvalues.foreground = BlackPixel(dpy, DefaultScreen(dpy));
        gcvalues.plane_mask = 1L;
        gc = XCreateGC(dpy, DefaultRootWindow(dpy),
            GCForeground|GCBackground|GCGraphicsExposures, &gcvalues);
    }

    /* shrink frame to minimal size and start notifier */
    window_fit(frame);
    xv_main_loop(frame);
}

/*
 * The repaint procedure is called whenever repainting is needed in
 * a paint window.  Since the canvas is not retained, this routine
 * is going to be called anytime the user scrolls the canvas.  The
 * canvas will handle repainting the portion of the canvas that
 * was in view and has scrolled onto another viewable portion of
 * the window.  The xrects parameter will cover the new areas that
 * were not in view before and have just scrolled into view.  If
 * the window resizes or if the window is exposed by other windows
 * disappearing or cycling thru the window tree, then the number
 * of xrects will be more than one and we'll have to copy the new
 * areas one by one.  Clipping isn't necessary since the areas to
 * be rendered are set by the xrects value.
 */
void
repaint_proc(canvas, paint_window, dpy, win, xrects)
Canvas          canvas;
Xv_Window       paint_window;
Display         *dpy;
Window          win;
```

```
Xv_xrectlist      *xrects;
{
    int x, y;

    x = (int)xv_get(horiz_scrollbar, SCROLLBAR_VIEW_START);
    y = (int)xv_get(vert_scrollbar, SCROLLBAR_VIEW_START);

    for (xrects->count--; xrects->count >= 0; xrects->count--) {
        printf("top-left cell = %d, %d -- %d,%d %d,%d\n", x+1, y+1,
            xrects->rect_array[xrects->count].x,
            xrects->rect_array[xrects->count].y,
            xrects->rect_array[xrects->count].width,
            xrects->rect_array[xrects->count].height);

        XCopyPlane(dpy, cell_map, win, gc,
            x * CELL_WIDTH,
            y * CELL_HEIGHT,
            xv_get(paint_window, XV_WIDTH),
            xv_get(paint_window, XV_HEIGHT),
            0, 0, 1L);
    }
}

/*
 * If the application is resized, then we may wish to reset the
 * paging and viewing parameters for the scrollbars.
 */
void
resize_proc(canvas, new_width, new_height)
Canvas canvas;
int new_width, new_height;
{
    int page_w = (int)(new_width/CELL_WIDTH);
    int page_h = (int)(new_height/CELL_HEIGHT);

    if (!vert_scrollbar || !horiz_scrollbar)
        return;

    printf("new width/height in cells: w = %d, h = %d\n",
        page_w, page_h);

    xv_set(horiz_scrollbar,
        SCROLLBAR_OBJECT_LENGTH,        CELLS_PER_ROW,
        SCROLLBAR_PAGE_LENGTH,          page_w,
        SCROLLBAR_VIEW_LENGTH,          page_w,
        NULL);
    xv_set(vert_scrollbar,
        SCROLLBAR_OBJECT_LENGTH,        CELLS_PER_COL,
        SCROLLBAR_PAGE_LENGTH,          page_h,
        SCROLLBAR_VIEW_LENGTH,          page_h,
        NULL);
}
```

Example
Programs

menu_dir2.c

In Chapter 11, *Menus*, the program *menu_dir.c* demonstrates the use of an XView menu in a canvas subwindow. A menu is brought up with the MENU mouse button and displays menu choices representing the files in the directory. The problem with *menu_dir.c* is that the entire menu cascade is created for all the subdirectories at the very beginning of the program. If the directory stack is very deep, it could take a very long time to build. You could also run out of memory in the process. Further, if the contents of the directory tree is dynamic, the menu entries could become invalid over time.

These problems are solved in *menu_dir2.c* because it creates only the top-level menu. For each directory entry under the top-level, rather than creating an associated pullright menu, a MENU_GEN_PULLRIGHT procedure is specified. This routine creates that menu only at the time it is needed. So, when the user invokes the menu and tries to descend into a submenu representing a subdirectory in the directory tree, only then is the directory entry searched and a new submenu created. When the user backs out of the menu, the menu is destroyed—attempting to re-enter the submenu causes the process to be repeated.

An exercise for the ambitious programmer would be to modify this program so that the submenus are not destroyed until the entire menu cascade has been dismissed. This enhancement would optimize the perceived performance of the program for the user because, once a directory subpath has been searched and a menu created, the menu is cached so that re-entry into the same submenu would be instantaneous.

Example G-4. The menu_dir2.c program

```
/*
 * menu_dir2.c -
 * Demonstrate the use of an XView menu in a canvas subwindow.
 * A menu is brought up with the MENU mouse button and displays
 * menu choices representing the files in the directory.  If a
 * directory entry is found, a new pullright item is created with
 * that subdir as the pullright menu's contents.  This implementation
 * creates directories on an as-needed basis.  Thus, we provide a
 * MENU_GEN_PULLRIGHT procedure.
 *
 * argv[1] indicates which directory to start from.
 */
#include <xview/xview.h>
#include <xview/canvas.h>
#include <sys/stat.h>
#include <sys/dir.h>
#include <X11/Xos.h>
#ifndef MAXPATHLEN
#include <sys/param.h>
#endif /* MAXPATHLEN */

Frame       frame;

main(argc,argv)
int         argc;
char        *argv[];
{
    Canvas          canvas;
```

```
    extern void exit();
    void        my_event_proc();
    Menu        menu;
    Menu_item   mi, add_path_to_menu();

    xv_init(XV_INIT_ARGC_PTR_ARGV, &argc, argv, NULL);

    frame = (Frame)xv_create(NULL, FRAME,
        FRAME_LABEL,                argv[1]? argv[1] : "cwd",
        FRAME_SHOW_FOOTER,          TRUE,
        NULL);
    canvas = (Canvas)xv_create(frame, CANVAS,
        FRAME_LABEL,    argv[0],
        XV_WIDTH,       400,
        XV_HEIGHT,      100,
        NULL);

    mi = add_path_to_menu(argc > 1? argv[1] : ".");
    menu = (Menu)xv_get(mi, MENU_PULLRIGHT);
    /* We no longer need the item since we have the menu from it */
    xv_destroy(mi);

    /* associate the menu to the canvas win for easy etreival */
    xv_set(canvas_paint_window(canvas),
        WIN_CONSUME_EVENTS,     WIN_MOUSE_BUTTONS, NULL,
        WIN_EVENT_PROC,         my_event_proc,
        WIN_CLIENT_DATA,        menu,
        NULL);

    window_fit(frame);
    window_main_loop(frame);
}
/*
 * my_action_proc - display the selected item in the frame footer.
 */
void
my_action_proc(menu, menu_item)
Menu    menu;
Menu_item       menu_item;
{
    xv_set(frame,
        FRAME_LEFT_FOOTER,      xv_get(menu_item, MENU_STRING),
        NULL);
}

/*
 * Call menu_show() to display menu on right mouse button push.
 */
void
my_event_proc(canvas, event)
Canvas  canvas;
Event *event;
{
    if ((event_id(event) == MS_RIGHT) && event_is_down(event)) {
        Menu menu = (Menu)xv_get(canvas, WIN_CLIENT_DATA);
        menu_show(menu, canvas, event, NULL);
    }
}
```

```
/*
 * return an allocated char * that points to the last item in a path.
 */
char *
getfilename(path)
char *path;
{
    char *p;

    if (p = rindex(path, '/'))
        p++;
    else
        p = path;
    return strcpy(malloc(strlen(p)+1), p);
}

Menu
gen_pullright(mi, op)
Menu_item mi;
Menu_generate op;
{
    Menu menu;
    Menu_item new, old = mi;
    char buf[MAXPATHLEN];

    if (op == MENU_DISPLAY) {
        menu = (Menu)xv_get(mi, MENU_PARENT);
        sprintf(buf, "%s/%s",
            xv_get(menu, MENU_CLIENT_DATA), xv_get(mi, MENU_STRING));
        new = add_path_to_menu(buf);
        /* if item has a pullright menu, free it (its data first) */
        if (menu = (Menu)xv_get(mi, MENU_PULLRIGHT)) {
            free(xv_get(menu, MENU_CLIENT_DATA));
            xv_destroy(menu);
        }
        if (new) {
            menu = (Menu)xv_get(new, MENU_PULLRIGHT);
            xv_destroy(new);
            return menu;
        }
    }
    if (!(menu = (Menu)xv_get(mi, MENU_PULLRIGHT)))
            menu = (Menu)xv_create(NULL, MENU,
                MENU_STRINGS, "Couldn't build a menu.", NULL,
                NULL);
    return menu;
}

/*
 * The path passed in is scanned via readdir().  For each file in the
 * path, a menu item is created and inserted into a new menu.  That
 * new menu is made the PULLRIGHT_MENU of a newly created panel item
 * for the path item originally passed it.  Since this routine is
 * recursive, a new menu is created for each subdirectory under the
 * original path.
 */
Menu_item
```

```
add_path_to_menu(path)
char *path;
{
    DIR                 *dirp;
    struct direct       *dp;
    struct stat         s_buf;
    Menu_item           mi;
    Menu                next_menu;
    char                buf[MAXPATHLEN];
    static int          recursion;

    /* don't add a folder to the list if user can't read it */
    if (stat(path, &s_buf) == -1 || !(s_buf.st_mode & S_IREAD))
        return NULL;
    if (s_buf.st_mode & S_IFDIR) {
        int cnt = 0;
        if (!(dirp = opendir(path)))
            /* don't bother adding to list if we can't scan it */
            return NULL;
        if (recursion)
            return (Menu_item)-1;
        recursion++;
        next_menu = (Menu)xv_create(XV_NULL, MENU, NULL);
        while (dp = readdir(dirp))
            if (strcmp(dp->d_name, ".") && strcmp(dp->d_name, "..")) {
                (void) sprintf(buf, "%s/%s", path, dp->d_name);
                mi = add_path_to_menu(buf);
                if (!mi || mi == (Menu_item)-1) {
                    int do_gen_pullright = (mi == (Menu_item)-1);
                    /* unreadable file or dir - deactivate item */
                    mi = (Menu_item)xv_create(XV_NULL, MENUITEM,
                        MENU_STRING,  getfilename(dp->d_name),
                        MENU_RELEASE,
                        MENU_RELEASE_IMAGE,
                        NULL);
                    if (do_gen_pullright)
                        xv_set(mi,
                            MENU_GEN_PULLRIGHT, gen_pullright,
                            NULL);
                    else
                        xv_set(mi, MENU_INACTIVE, TRUE, NULL);
                }
                xv_set(next_menu, MENU_APPEND_ITEM, mi, NULL);
                cnt++;
            }
        closedir(dirp);
        mi = (Menu_item)xv_create(XV_NULL, MENUITEM,
            MENU_STRING,          getfilename(path),
            MENU_RELEASE,
            MENU_RELEASE_IMAGE,
            MENU_NOTIFY_PROC,     my_action_proc,
            NULL);
        if (!cnt) {
            xv_destroy(next_menu);
            /* An empty or unsearchable directory - deactivate item */
            xv_set(mi, MENU_INACTIVE, TRUE, NULL);
```

```
        } else {
            xv_set(next_menu,
                MENU_TITLE_ITEM, strcpy(malloc(strlen(path)+1), path),
                MENU_CLIENT_DATA, strcpy(malloc(strlen(path)+1), path),
                NULL);
            xv_set(mi, MENU_PULLRIGHT, next_menu, NULL);
        }
        recursion--;
        return mi;
    }
    return (Menu_item)xv_create(NULL, MENUITEM,
        MENU_STRING,            getfilename(path),
        MENU_RELEASE,
        MENU_RELEASE_IMAGE,
        MENU_NOTIFY_PROC,       my_action_proc,
        NULL);
}
```

type_font.c

This very simple program captures keyboard events in a canvas and uses XDrawString() to render what the user types. It also looks for backspacing. This is not intended to replace the text subwindow in any way, but rather to demonstrate how some text rendering functions can be implemented. See Chapter 16, *Fonts*, for more information about fonts.

Example G-5. The type_font.c program

```
/*
 * simple_font.c -- very simple program showing how to render text
 * using fonts loaded by XView.
 */
#include <ctype.h>
#include <X11/X.h>
#include <X11/Xlib.h>
#include <xview/xview.h>
#include <xview/panel.h>
#include <xview/font.h>

Display *dpy;
GC      gc;
XFontStruct *font_info;

main(argc, argv)
int     argc;
char    *argv[];
{
    Frame       frame;
    Panel       panel;
    Canvas      canvas;
    XGCValues   gcvalues;
    Xv_Font     font;
    void        my_event_proc();
    extern void exit();

    xv_init(XV_INIT_ARGC_PTR_ARGV, &argc, argv, NULL);

    frame = (Frame)xv_create(XV_NULL, FRAME,
        FRAME_LABEL,            argv[0],
        NULL);

    panel = (Panel)xv_create(frame, PANEL,
        PANEL_LAYOUT,           PANEL_VERTICAL,
        NULL);
    xv_create(panel, PANEL_BUTTON,
        PANEL_LABEL_STRING,     "Quit",
        PANEL_NOTIFY_PROC,      exit,
        NULL);
    window_fit(panel);

    canvas = (Canvas)xv_create(frame, CANVAS,
        XV_WIDTH,               400,
        XV_HEIGHT,              200,
        CANVAS_X_PAINT_WINDOW,  TRUE,
        NULL);
    xv_set(canvas_paint_window(canvas),
        WIN_EVENT_PROC,         my_event_proc,
```

```
        NULL);

    window_fit(frame);

    dpy = (Display *)xv_get(frame, XV_DISPLAY);
    font = (Xv_Font)xv_get(frame, XV_FONT);
    font_info = (XFontStruct *)xv_get(font, FONT_INFO);

    gcvalues.font = (Font)xv_get(font, XV_XID);
    gcvalues.foreground = BlackPixel(dpy, DefaultScreen(dpy));
    gcvalues.background = WhitePixel(dpy, DefaultScreen(dpy));
    gcvalues.graphics_exposures = False;
    gc = XCreateGC(dpy, RootWindow(dpy, DefaultScreen(dpy)),
        GCForeground | GCBackground | GCFont | GCGraphicsExposures, &gcvalues);

    xv_main_loop(frame);
}

void
my_event_proc(win, event)
Xv_Window win;
Event *event;
{
    static int x = 10, y = 10;
    Window xwin = (Window)xv_get(win, XV_XID);
    char c;

    if (event_is_up(event))
        return;

    if (event_is_ascii(event)) {
        c = (char)event_id(event);
        if (c == '\n' || c == '
            y += font_info->max_bounds.ascent +
                        font_info->max_bounds.descent;
            x = 10;
        } else if (c == 7 || c == 127) { /* backspace or delete */
            if (x > 10)
                x -= XTextWidth(font_info, "m", 1);
            /* use XDrawImageString to overwrite previous text */
            XDrawImageString(dpy, xwin, gc, x, y, "  ", 2);
        } else {
            XDrawString(dpy, xwin, gc, x, y, &c, 1);
            x += XTextWidth(font_info, &c, 1);
        }
    } else if (event_action(event) == ACTION_SELECT) {
        x = event_x(event);
        y = event_y(event);
    }
}
```

fonts.c

This program is similar to *type_font.c* above. However, *fonts.c* provides an interface for the user to pick and choose from a subset of the font families and styles available on the X server. If a font "name" is specified, then the family, style and size choices are ignored. Using the SELECT button on the canvas window positions the current typing location at the x,y coordinates of the button-down event. The characters typed are printed in the current font.

Example G-6. The fonts.c program

```
/*
 * fonts.c -- provide an interface for the user to pick and choose
 * between font families and styles known to XView.  The program
 * provides several panel buttons to choose between font types, and
 * a canvas window in which the user can type.  The characters typed
 * are printed in the current font.  If a font "name" is specified,
 * then the family, style and size are ignored.  Using the SELECT
 * button on the canvas window positions the current typing location
 * at the x,y coordinates of the button-down event.
 */
#include <ctype.h>
#include <X11/X.h>
#include <X11/Xlib.h>
#include <xview/xview.h>
#include <xview/panel.h>
#include <xview/font.h>

Display *dpy;
GC      gc;
XFontStruct *cur_font;
Panel_item family_item, style_item, scale_item, name_item;
int canvas_width;

main(argc, argv)
int     argc;
char    *argv[];
{
    Frame       frame;
    Panel       panel;
    Canvas      canvas;
    XGCValues   gcvalues;
    Xv_Font     font;
    void        change_font();
    void        my_event_proc(), my_resize_proc();
    int         change_font_by_name();
    extern void exit();

    xv_init(XV_INIT_ARGC_PTR_ARGV, &argc, argv, NULL);

    frame = (Frame)xv_create(XV_NULL, FRAME,
        FRAME_LABEL,            argv[0],
        FRAME_SHOW_FOOTER,      TRUE,
        NULL);

    panel = (Panel)xv_create(frame, PANEL,
        PANEL_LAYOUT,           PANEL_VERTICAL,
```

```
            NULL);
    (void) xv_create(panel, PANEL_BUTTON,
        PANEL_LABEL_STRING,     "Quit",
        PANEL_NOTIFY_PROC,      exit,
        NULL);
    family_item = (Panel_item)xv_create(panel, PANEL_CHOICE,
        PANEL_LABEL_STRING,     "Family",
        PANEL_LAYOUT,           PANEL_HORIZONTAL,
        PANEL_DISPLAY_LEVEL,    PANEL_CURRENT,
        PANEL_CHOICE_STRINGS,
            FONT_FAMILY_DEFAULT, FONT_FAMILY_DEFAULT_FIXEDWIDTH,
            FONT_FAMILY_LUCIDA, FONT_FAMILY_LUCIDA_FIXEDWIDTH,
            FONT_FAMILY_ROMAN, FONT_FAMILY_SERIF, FONT_FAMILY_COUR,
            FONT_FAMILY_CMR, FONT_FAMILY_GALLENT,
            FONT_FAMILY_OLGLYPH, FONT_FAMILY_OLCURSOR, NULL,
        PANEL_NOTIFY_PROC,      change_font,
        NULL);
    style_item = (Panel_item)xv_create(panel, PANEL_CHOICE,
        PANEL_LABEL_STRING,     "Style",
        PANEL_LAYOUT,           PANEL_HORIZONTAL,
        PANEL_DISPLAY_LEVEL,    PANEL_CURRENT,
        PANEL_CHOICE_STRINGS,
            FONT_STYLE_DEFAULT, FONT_STYLE_NORMAL, FONT_STYLE_BOLD,
            FONT_STYLE_ITALIC, FONT_STYLE_BOLD_ITALIC, NULL,
        PANEL_NOTIFY_PROC,      change_font,
        NULL);
    scale_item = (Panel_item)xv_create(panel, PANEL_CHOICE,
        PANEL_LABEL_STRING,     "Scale",
        PANEL_LAYOUT,           PANEL_HORIZONTAL,
        PANEL_DISPLAY_LEVEL,    PANEL_CURRENT,
        PANEL_CHOICE_STRINGS,
            "Small", "Medium", "Large", "X-Large", NULL,
        PANEL_NOTIFY_PROC,      change_font,
        NULL);
    name_item = (Panel_item)xv_create(panel, PANEL_TEXT,
        PANEL_LABEL_STRING,     "Font Name:",
        PANEL_LAYOUT,           PANEL_HORIZONTAL,
        PANEL_VALUE_DISPLAY_LENGTH, 20,
        PANEL_NOTIFY_PROC,      change_font_by_name,
        NULL);
    window_fit(panel);

    canvas = (Canvas)xv_create(frame, CANVAS,
        XV_WIDTH,               400,
        XV_HEIGHT,              200,
        CANVAS_X_PAINT_WINDOW,  TRUE,
        CANVAS_RESIZE_PROC,     my_resize_proc,
        NULL);
    xv_set(canvas_paint_window(canvas),
        WIN_EVENT_PROC,         my_event_proc,
        WIN_CONSUME_EVENT,      LOC_WINENTER,
        NULL);

    window_fit(frame);

    dpy = (Display *)xv_get(frame, XV_DISPLAY);
    font = (Xv_Font)xv_get(frame, XV_FONT);
```

```
    cur_font = (XFontStruct *)xv_get(font, FONT_INFO);
    xv_set(frame, FRAME_LEFT_FOOTER, xv_get(font, FONT_NAME), NULL);

    gcvalues.font = cur_font->fid;
    gcvalues.foreground = BlackPixel(dpy, DefaultScreen(dpy));
    gcvalues.background = WhitePixel(dpy, DefaultScreen(dpy));
    gcvalues.graphics_exposures = False;
    gc = XCreateGC(dpy, RootWindow(dpy, DefaultScreen(dpy)),
        GCForeground | GCBackground | GCFont | GCGraphicsExposures,
        &gcvalues);

    xv_main_loop(frame);
}

void
my_event_proc(win, event)
Xv_Window win;
Event *event;
{
    static int x = 10, y = 10;
    Window xwin = (Window)xv_get(win, XV_XID);
    char c;

    if (event_is_up(event))
        return;

    if (event_is_ascii(event)) {
        c = (char)event_action(event);
        XDrawString(dpy, xwin, gc, x, y, &c, 1);
        /* advance x to next position.  If over edge, linewrap */
        if ((x += XTextWidth(cur_font, &c, 1)) >= canvas_width) {
            y += cur_font->max_bounds.ascent +
                    cur_font->max_bounds.descent;
            x = 10;
        }
    } else if (event_action(event) == ACTION_SELECT) {
        x = event_x(event);
        y = event_y(event);
    } else if (event_action(event) == LOC_WINENTER)
        win_set_kbd_focus(win, xwin);
}

/*
 * check resizing so we know how wide to allow the user to type.
 */
void
my_resize_proc(canvas, width, height)
Canvas canvas;
int width, height;
{
    canvas_width = width;
}

void
change_font(item, value, event)
Panel_item    item;
Event        *event;
{
    static int  family, style, scale;
```

```
        char        buf[128];
        Frame       frame;
        char        *family_name;
        char        *style_name;
        int         scale_value;
        Xv_Font     font;

        frame = (Frame)xv_get(xv_get(item, PANEL_PARENT_PANEL), XV_OWNER);
        family_name = (char *)xv_get(family_item, PANEL_CHOICE_STRING, value);
        style_name = (char *)xv_get(style_item, PANEL_CHOICE_STRING, value);
        scale_value = (int) xv_get(scale_item, PANEL_VALUE);
        xv_set(frame, FRAME_BUSY, TRUE, NULL);
        font = (Xv_Font)xv_find(frame, FONT,
            FONT_FAMILY,     family_name,
            FONT_STYLE,      style_name,
            /* scale_value happens to coincide with Window_rescale_state */
            FONT_SCALE,      scale_value,
            FONT_SIZES_FOR_SCALE, 12, 14, 16, 22,
            NULL);
        xv_set(frame, FRAME_BUSY, FALSE, NULL);

        if (!font) {
            if (item == family_item) {
                sprintf(buf, "cannot load '%s'", family_name);
                xv_set(family_item, PANEL_VALUE, family, NULL);
            } else if (item == style_item) {
                sprintf(buf, "cannot load '%s'", style_name);
                xv_set(style_item, PANEL_VALUE, style, NULL);
            } else {
                sprintf(buf, "Not available in %s scale.",
                    xv_get(scale_item, PANEL_CHOICE_STRING, scale));
                xv_set(scale_item, PANEL_VALUE, scale, NULL);
            }
            xv_set(frame, FRAME_RIGHT_FOOTER, buf, NULL);
            return;
        }
        if (item == family_item)
            family = value;
        else if (item == style_item)
            style = value;
        else
            scale = value;
        cur_font = (XFontStruct *)xv_get(font, FONT_INFO);
        XSetFont(dpy, gc, cur_font->fid);
        sprintf(buf, "Current font: %s", xv_get(font, FONT_NAME));
        xv_set(frame, FRAME_LEFT_FOOTER, buf, NULL);
}

change_font_by_name(item, event)
Panel_item item;
Event *event;
{
    char buf[128];
    char *name = panel_get_value(item);
    Frame frame = (Frame)xv_get(xv_get(item, XV_OWNER), XV_OWNER);
    Xv_Font font;
```

```
    xv_set(frame, FRAME_BUSY, TRUE, NULL);
    font = (Xv_Font)font = (Xv_Font)xv_find(frame, FONT,
        FONT_NAME,        name,
        NULL);
    xv_set(frame, FRAME_BUSY, FALSE, NULL);

    if (!font) {
        sprintf(buf, "cannot load '%s'", name);
        xv_set(frame, FRAME_RIGHT_FOOTER, buf, NULL);
        return PANEL_NONE;
    }
    cur_font = (XFontStruct *)xv_get(font, FONT_INFO);
    XSetFont(dpy, gc, cur_font->fid);
    sprintf(buf, "Current font: %s", xv_get(font, FONT_NAME));
    xv_set(frame, FRAME_LEFT_FOOTER, buf, NULL);
    return PANEL_NONE;
}
```

seln.c

seln.c is a simple program demonstrating some uses of the selection service. See Chapter 18, *The Selection Service*, for more information.

Example G-7. The seln.c program

```c
/*
 * seln.c -- print the primary selection from the server.  If the
 * selection is in a text subwindow, then print information about
 * the line number(s) the selection spans and the indexes of the
 * bytes within the textsw's text stream.  This simple program
 * may not be sufficient for general usage -- see comments in
 * get_selection() comments below.
 */
#include <stdio.h>
#include <xview/xview.h>
#include <xview/textsw.h>
#include <xview/panel.h>
#include <xview/server.h>
#include <xview/seln.h>

Xv_Server       server;
Textsw          textsw;

char *get_selection();

main(argc, argv)
char *argv[];
{
    Frame           frame;
    Panel           panel;
    void            print_seln(), exit();

    xv_init(XV_INIT_ARGC_PTR_ARGV, &argc, argv, NULL);

    frame = (Frame) xv_create(NULL, FRAME,
        FRAME_LABEL,            argv[0],
        NULL);
    panel = (Panel) xv_create(frame, PANEL,
        WIN_WIDTH,              WIN_EXTEND_TO_EDGE,
        NULL);
    (void) xv_create(panel, PANEL_BUTTON,
        PANEL_LABEL_STRING,     "Quit",
        PANEL_NOTIFY_PROC,      exit,
        NULL);
    (void) xv_create(panel, PANEL_BUTTON,
        PANEL_LABEL_STRING,     "Get Selection",
        PANEL_NOTIFY_PROC,      print_seln,
        NULL);
    window_fit(panel);

    textsw = (Textsw)xv_create(frame, TEXTSW,
        WIN_X,                  0,
        WIN_BELOW,              panel,
        WIN_ROWS,               10,
        WIN_COLUMNS,            80,
        TEXTSW_FILE_CONTENTS,   "/etc/passwd",
        NULL);
```

```
    window_fit(frame);

    server = (Xv_Server)xv_get(xv_get(frame, XV_SCREEN), SCREEN_SERVER);

    xv_main_loop(frame);
}

void
print_seln()
{
    char *text = get_selection();

    if (text)
        printf("---selection---\n%s0-end seln---0, text);
}

/*
 * Get the selection using selection_ask().  Note that if the
 * selection is bigger than about 2K, the whole selection will
 * not be gotten with one call, thus this method of getting the
 * selection may not be sufficient.
 */
char *
get_selection()
{
    long            sel_lin_num, lines_selected;
    Textsw_index    first, last;
    Seln_holder     holder;
    Seln_result     result;
    int             len;
    Seln_request    *request;
    static char     selection_buf[BUFSIZ];
    register char   *ptr;

    /* get the holder of the primary selection */
    holder = selection_inquire(server, SELN_PRIMARY);

    /* If the selection occurs in the text subwindow, print lots
     * of info about the selection.
     */
    if (seln_holder_same_client(&holder, textsw)) {
        /* ask for information from the selection service */
        request = selection_ask(server, &holder,
            /* get the index of the first and last chars in seln */
            SELN_REQ_FIRST,             NULL,
            SELN_REQ_LAST,              NULL,
            /* get the actual selection bytes */
            SELN_REQ_CONTENTS_ASCII,    NULL,
            /* fool the textsw to think entire lines are selected */
            SELN_REQ_FAKE_LEVEL,        SELN_LEVEL_LINE,
            /* line numbers of beginning and ending of the seln */
            SELN_REQ_FIRST_UNIT,        NULL,
            SELN_REQ_LAST_UNIT,         NULL,
            NULL);
        /* set the ptr to beginning of data -- SELN_REQ_FIRST */
        ptr = request->data;
        /* "first" is data succeeding SELN_REQ_FIRST -- skip attr */
        first = *(Textsw_index *)(ptr += sizeof(SELN_REQ_FIRST));
        ptr += sizeof(Textsw_index); /* skip over value of "first" */
```

```
        /* "last" is data succeeding SELN_REQ_LAST -- skip attr */
        last  = *(Textsw_index *)(ptr += sizeof(SELN_REQ_LAST));
        ptr += sizeof(Textsw_index); /* skip over value of "last" */

        /* advance pointer past SELN_REQ_CONTENTS_ASCII */
        ptr += sizeof(SELN_REQ_CONTENTS_ASCII);
        len = strlen(ptr); /* length of string in request */
        (void) strcpy(selection_buf, ptr);
        /*
         * advance pointer past length of string.  If the string
         * length isn't aligned to a 4-byte boundary, add the
         * difference in bytes -- then advance pointer passed "value".
         */
        if (len % 4)
            len = len + (4 - (len % 4));
        ptr += len + sizeof(Seln_attribute); /* skip over "value" */

        /* advance past SELN_REQ_FAKE_LEVEL, SELN_LEVEL_LINE */
        ptr += sizeof(SELN_REQ_FAKE_LEVEL) + sizeof(SELN_LEVEL_LINE);

        sel_lin_num = *(long *)(ptr += sizeof(SELN_REQ_FIRST_UNIT));
        ptr += sizeof(long);
        lines_selected = *(long *)(ptr += sizeof(SELN_REQ_LAST_UNIT));
        ptr += sizeof(long);

        /* hack to workaround bug with SELN_REQ_LAST_UNIT always
         * returning -1.  We have to count the line numbers ourselves.
         */
        if (lines_selected < 0) {
            register char *p;
            lines_selected++;
            for (p = selection_buf; *p; p++)
                if (*p == '\n')
                    lines_selected++;
        }
        printf("index in textsw: %d-%d, line number(s) = %d-%d\n",
            first+1, last+1, sel_lin_num+1,
            sel_lin_num+lines_selected+1);
    } else {
        /* the selection is not in the text subwindow */
        request = selection_ask(server, &holder,
            SELN_REQ_CONTENTS_ASCII, NULL,
            NULL);
        if (request->status != SELN_SUCCESS) {
            printf("selection_ask() returns %d\n", request->status);
            return "";
        }
        (void) strcpy(selection_buf,
            request->data + sizeof(SELN_REQ_CONTENTS_ASCII));
    }
    return selection_buf;
}
```

seln_line.c

seln_line.c demonstrates another use of the selection service. See Chapter 18, *The Selection Service*, for more information.

Example G-8. The seln_line.c program

```
/*
 * seln_line.c -- demonstrate how to use the selection service to get
 * the line number of the primary selection in a textsw.
 */
#include <stdio.h>
#include <xview/xview.h>
#include <xview/textsw.h>
#include <xview/panel.h>
#include <xview/seln.h>

Textsw   textsw;

main(argc, argv)
char *argv[];
{
    Frame          frame;
    Panel          panel;
    void           exit();
    int            seln_proc();

    xv_init(XV_INIT_ARGC_PTR_ARGV, &argc, argv, NULL);

    frame = (Frame)xv_create(NULL, FRAME,
        FRAME_SHOW_FOOTER,        TRUE,
        NULL);

    panel = (Panel)xv_create(frame, PANEL,
        WIN_WIDTH,                WIN_EXTEND_TO_EDGE,
        NULL);

    (void) xv_create(panel, PANEL_BUTTON,
        PANEL_LABEL_STRING,       "Quit",
        PANEL_NOTIFY_PROC,        exit,
        NULL);
    (void) xv_create(panel, PANEL_BUTTON,
        PANEL_LABEL_STRING,       "Get Selection",
        PANEL_NOTIFY_PROC,        seln_proc,
        PANEL_CLIENT_DATA,        frame,
        NULL);
    (void) xv_create(panel, PANEL_TEXT,
        PANEL_LABEL_STRING,               "No-op:",
        PANEL_VALUE_DISPLAY_LENGTH,       30,
        NULL);

    window_fit(panel);

    textsw = (Textsw)xv_create(frame, TEXTSW,
        WIN_X,                    0,
        WIN_BELOW,                panel,
        WIN_ROWS,                 10,
        WIN_COLUMNS,              80,
        TEXTSW_FILE_CONTENTS,     "/etc/passwd",
```

```
        NULL);
    window_fit(frame);
    xv_main_loop(frame);
}

int
seln_proc(item, event)
Panel_item item;
Event *event; /* unused */
{
    Frame           frame = (Frame)xv_get(item, PANEL_CLIENT_DATA);
    Seln_holder     holder;
    Seln_request    *buffer;
    int             line_number;
    char            *msg[32];

    /*
     * get primary selection
     */
    holder = seln_inquire(SELN_PRIMARY);
    /*
     * ask for the data containing line number of the first
     * character of the selection
     */
    buffer = seln_ask(&holder,
        SELN_REQ_FAKE_LEVEL, SELN_LEVEL_LINE,
        SELN_REQ_FIRST_UNIT, 0,
        NULL);
    /*
     * determine the window that contains the selection
     */
    if (seln_holder_same_client(&holder, textsw)) {
        xv_set(frame,
            FRAME_LEFT_FOOTER, "selection in textsw",
            NULL);
        /*
         * convert data into the line number
         */
        sprintf(msg, "Selection: line %ld",
            *(long *)(buffer->data + 3 * sizeof(Seln_attribute)));
        xv_set(frame,
            FRAME_RIGHT_FOOTER, msg,
            NULL);
    } else
        xv_set(frame,
            FRAME_LEFT_FOOTER, "selection elsewhere",
            NULL);

    return XV_OK;
}
```

x_draw.c

This program uses several Xlib drawing functions to draw various types of geometric objects
We integrate the XView color model (see Chapter 20, *Color*) to render each object in a different color.

Example G-9. The x_draw.c program

```
/*
 * x_draw.c -- demonstrates the use of Xlib drawing functions
 * inside an XView canvas.  Color is also used, but not required.
 */
#include <xview/xview.h>
#include <xview/canvas.h>
#include <xview/cms.h>
#include <xview/xv_xrect.h>

/* indices into color table renders specified colors. */
#define WHITE    0
#define RED      1
#define GREEN    2
#define BLUE     3
#define ORANGE   4
#define AQUA     5
#define PINK     6
#define BLACK    7

GC gc;                     /* GC used for Xlib drawing */
unsigned long *colors; /* the color table */

/*
 * initialize cms data to support colors specified above.  Assign
 * data to new cms -- use either static or dynamic cms depending
 * on -dynamic command line switch.
 */
main(argc, argv)
int      argc;
char     *argv[];
{
    unsigned char red[8], green[8], blue[8];
    static char stipple_bits[] = {0xAA, 0xAA, 0x55, 0x55};
    Frame        frame;
    Canvas       canvas;
    XFontStruct *font;
    Display     *display;
    XGCValues    gc_val;
    XID          xid;
    void         canvas_repaint();
    Xv_cmsdata   cms_data;
    int          use_dynamic = FALSE;

    /* Create windows */
    xv_init(XV_INIT_ARGC_PTR_ARGV, &argc, argv, NULL);
    if (*++argv && !strcmp(*argv, "-dynamic"))
        use_dynamic = TRUE;

    frame = xv_create(NULL,FRAME,
        FRAME_LABEL,    "xv_canvas_x_draw",
```

```
        XV_WIDTH,           400,
        XV_HEIGHT,          300,
        NULL);

    /* initialize RGB values for specified colors */
    red[WHITE] = 255;    green[WHITE] = 255;    blue[WHITE] = 255;
    red[RED] = 255;      green[RED] = 0;        blue[RED] = 0;
    red[GREEN] = 0;      green[GREEN] = 255;    blue[GREEN] = 0;
    red[BLUE] = 0;       green[BLUE] = 0;       blue[BLUE] = 255;
    red[ORANGE] = 250;   green[ORANGE] = 130;   blue[ORANGE] = 80;
    red[AQUA] = 30;      green[AQUA] = 230;     blue[AQUA] = 250;
    red[PINK] = 230;     green[PINK] = 30;      blue[PINK] = 250;

    cms_data.type = use_dynamic? XV_DYNAMIC_CMS : XV_STATIC_CMS;
    cms_data.size = 8;
    cms_data.rgb_count = 8;
    cms_data.index = 0;
    cms_data.red = red;
    cms_data.green = green;
    cms_data.blue = blue;

    canvas = xv_create(frame, CANVAS,
        CANVAS_REPAINT_PROC,     canvas_repaint,
        CANVAS_X_PAINT_WINDOW,   TRUE,
        WIN_DYNAMIC_VISUAL,      use_dynamic,
        WIN_CMS_NAME,            "palette",
        WIN_CMS_DATA,            &cms_data,
        NULL);

    /* Get display and xid */
    display = (Display *)xv_get(frame, XV_DISPLAY);
    xid = (XID)xv_get(canvas_paint_window(canvas), XV_XID);

    if (!(font = XLoadQueryFont(display, "fixed"))) {
        puts("cannot load fixed font");
        exit(1);
    }

    /* Create and initialize GC */
    gc_val.font = font->fid;
    gc_val.stipple =
     XCreateBitmapFromData(display, xid, stipple_bits, 16, 2);
    gc = XCreateGC(display, xid, GCFont | GCStipple, &gc_val);

    /* get the colormap from the canvas now that
     * the cms has been installed
     */
    colors = (unsigned long *)xv_get(canvas, WIN_X_COLOR_INDICES);

    /* Start event loop */
    xv_main_loop(frame);
}
/*
 * Draws onto the canvas using Xlib drawing functions.
 */
void
canvas_repaint(canvas, pw, display, xid, xrects)
Canvas          canvas;
Xv_Window       pw;
```

```
Display          *display;
Window           xid;
Xv_xrectlist     *xrects;
{
    static XPoint box[] = {
        {0,0}, {100,100}, {0,-100}, {-100,100}, {0,-100}
    };
    static XPoint points[] = {
        {0,0}, /* this point to be overwritten below */
        {25,0}, {25,0}, {25,0}, {25,0}, {-100,25},
        {25,0}, {25,0}, {25,0}, {25,0}, {-100,25},
        {25,0}, {25,0}, {25,0}, {25,0}, {-100,25},
        {25,0}, {25,0}, {25,0}, {25,0}, {-100,25},
        {25,0}, {25,0}, {25,0}, {25,0}, {-100,25},
    };

    XSetForeground(display, gc, colors[RED]);
    XDrawString(display, xid, gc, 30, 20, "XFillRectangle", 14);
    XFillRectangle(display, xid, gc, 25, 25, 100, 100);
    XSetFunction(display, gc, GXinvert);
    XFillRectangle(display, xid, gc, 50, 50, 50, 50);
    XSetFunction(display, gc, GXcopy);

    XSetForeground(display, gc, colors[BLACK]);
    XDrawString(display, xid, gc, 155, 20, "XFillRect - stipple", 19);
    XSetFillStyle(display, gc, FillStippled);
    XFillRectangle(display, xid, gc, 150, 25, 100, 100);
    XSetFillStyle(display, gc, FillSolid);

    XSetForeground(display, gc, colors[BLUE]);
    XDrawString(display, xid, gc, 280, 20, "XDrawPoints", 11);
    points[0].x = 275; points[0].y = 25;
    XDrawPoints(display, xid, gc, points,
        sizeof(points)/sizeof(XPoint), CoordModePrevious);

    XSetForeground(display, gc, colors[ORANGE]);
    XDrawString(display, xid, gc, 30, 145, "XDrawLine - solid", 17);
    XDrawLine(display, xid, gc, 25, 150, 125, 250);
    XDrawLine(display, xid, gc, 25, 250, 125, 150);

    XSetForeground(display, gc, colors[AQUA]);
    XDrawString(display, xid, gc, 155, 145, "XDrawLine - dashed", 18);
    XSetLineAttributes(display, gc, 5,
        LineDoubleDash, CapButt, JoinMiter);
    XDrawLine(display, xid, gc, 150, 150, 250, 250);
    XDrawLine(display, xid, gc, 150, 250, 250, 150);
    XSetLineAttributes(display, gc, 0, LineSolid, CapButt, JoinMiter);

    XSetForeground(display, gc, colors[PINK]);
    XDrawString(display, xid, gc, 280, 145, "XDrawLines", 10);
    box[0].x = 275; box[0].y = 150;
    XDrawLines(display, xid, gc, box, 5, CoordModePrevious);

    XSetForeground(display, gc, colors[GREEN]);
    XDrawRectangle(display, xid, gc,
        5, 5, xv_get(pw, XV_WIDTH)-10, xv_get(pw, XV_HEIGHT)-10);
    XDrawRectangle(display, xid, gc,
        7, 7, xv_get(pw, XV_WIDTH)-14, xv_get(pw, XV_HEIGHT)-14);
}
```

Example
Programs

Index

A

abbreviated choice item 147, 151
accelerator keys, used in notices 267
ACTION_DRAG_COPY event 121
ACTION_DRAG_MOVE event 121
ACTION_MENU event 236
ACTION_SELECT event 116
alarm() system call 356
applications, structure of 41
attribute, ATTR_LIST 411
  CANVAS_AUTO_CLEAR 87
  CANVAS_AUTO_EXPAND 92, 411
  CANVAS_AUTO_SHRINK 92, 411
  CANVAS_CMS_REPAINT 402, 411
  CANVAS_FIXED_IMAGE 82, 87, 411
  CANVAS_HEIGHT 92, 411
  CANVAS_MIN_PAINT_HEIGHT 92, 411
  CANVAS_MIN_PAINT_WIDTH 92, 412
  CANVAS_NO_CLIPPING 412
  CANVAS_NTH_PAINT_WINDOW 97, 412
  CANVAS_NTH_PAINT_WONDOW 445
  CANVAS_PAINTWINDOW_ATTRS 354, 412
  CANVAS_REPAINT_PROC 85, 412
  CANVAS_RESIZE 381
  CANVAS_RESIZE_PROC 94, 412, 446
  CANVAS_RETAINED 82, 412
  CANVAS_VIEWABLE_RECT 412
  CANVAS_VIEW_CANVAS_WINDOW 412
  CANVAS_VIEW_PAINT_WINDOW 97, 98, 412
  CANVAS_WIDTH 92, 412
  CANVAS_X_PAINT_WINDOW 88, 412
  CURSOR_BACKGROUND_COLOR 412
  CURSOR_FOREGROUND_COLOR 413
  CURSOR_IMAGE 275, 413
  CURSOR_MASK_CHAR 277
  CURSOR_SRC_CHAR 277
  CURSOR_X_HOT 413
  CURSOR_Y_HOT 413

FONT_CHAR_HEIGHT 315, 413
FONT_CHAR_WIDTH 315, 413
FONT_DEFAULT_CHAR_HEIGHT 315, 413
FONT_DEFAULT_CHAR_WIDTH 315, 413
FONT_FAMILY 311, 413
FONT_FAMILY_DEFAULT 311
FONT_FAMILY_DEFAULT_FIXEDWIDTH 311
FONT_INFO 315
FONT_NAME 315
FONT_RESCALE_OF 314, 413
FONT_SCALE 413
FONT_SIZE 311, 312, 413
FONT_SIZES_FOR_SCALE 413
FONT_STRING_DIMS 315, 413
FONT_STYLE 311, 413
FONT_STYLE_DEFAULT 312
FRAME_BACKGROUND_COLOR 73, 402, 414
FRAME_BUSY 72, 414
FRAME_CLOSED 287, 414
FRAME_CLOSED_RECT 65, 414
FRAME_CMD_PANEL 414
FRAME_CMD_PUSHPIN_IN 68, 414
FRAME_DEFAULT_DONE_PROC 414
FRAME_DONE_PROC 414
FRAME_FOREGROUND_COLOR 73, 402, 414
FRAME_ICON 65, 414
FRAME_INHERIT_COLORS 73, 82, 402, 414
FRAME_LABEL 63
FRAME_LEFT_FOOTER 414
FRAME_NO_CONFIRM 66, 414
FRAME_NTH_SUBFRAME 74, 415
FRAME_NTH_SUBWINDOW 74, 415
FRAME_RIGHT_FOOTER 415
FRAME_SHOW_FOOTER 63, 415
FRAME_SHOW_HEADER 63, 415
FRAME_SHOW_LABEL 415
FRAME_SHOW_RESIZE_CORNER 71, 415
FULLSCREEN_ALLOW_EVENTS 415
FULLSCREEN_ALLOW_SYNC_EVENT 415

FULLSCREEN_COLORMAP_WINDOW 415
FULLSCREEN_CURSOR_WINDOW 415
FULLSCREEN_GRAB_KEYBOARD 415
FULLSCREEN_GRAB_POINTER 415
FULLSCREEN_GRAB_SERVER 415
FULLSCREEN_INPUT_WINDOW 415
FULLSCREEN_KEYBOARD_GRAB_KBD_MODE 416
FULLSCREEN_KEYBOARD_GRAB_PTR_MODE 416
FULLSCREEN_OWNER_EVENTS 416
FULLSCREEN_PAINT_WINDOW 416
FULLSCREEN_POINTER_GRAB_KBD_MODE 416
FULLSCREEN_POINTER_GRAB_PTR_MODE 416
FULLSCREEN_RECT 416
FULLSCREEN_SYNC 416
ICON_IMAGE 288, 416
ICON_IMAGE_RECT 288, 416
ICON_LABEL_RECT 288, 416
MENU_ACTION_IMAGE 241, 416
MENU_ACTION_ITEM 240, 241, 416
MENU_APPEND_ITEM 242, 416
MENU_CLASS 417
MENU_CLIENT_DATA 255
MENU_COL_MAJOR 417
MENU_DEFAULT 417
MENU_DEFAULT_ITEM 253, 417
MENU_DESCEND_FIRST 252, 417
MENU_DONE_PROC 249, 447
MENU_FEEDBACK 417
MENU_FIRST_EVENT 237, 417
MENU_GEN_PIN_WINDOW 248, 417
MENU_GEN_PROC 242, 417, 447
MENU_GEN_PROC_IMAGE 417
MENU_GEN_PROC_ITEM 417
MENU_GEN_PULLRIGHT 245, 418
MENU_GEN_PULLRIGHT_IMAGE 418
MENU_GEN_PULLRIGHT_ITEM 245, 418
MENU_IMAGE 241, 418
MENU_IMAGE_ITEM 418
MENU_IMAGES 243, 418
MENU_INACTIVE 249, 418
MENU_INSERT 418
MENU_INSERT_ITEM 418
MENU_INVERT 418
MENU_ITEM 240, 254
MENU_LAST_EVENT 237, 418
MENU_NCOLS 247, 418
MENU_NITEMS 418
MENU_NOTIFY_PROC 239, 249, 419, 447, 448
MENU_NOTIFY_STATUS 419
MENU_NROWS 247, 419
MENU_NTH_ITEM 419
MENU_PIN 249, 419
MENU_PIN_PROC 249, 419, 447

MENU_PIN_WINDOW 249, 419
MENU_PULLRIGHT 243, 419
MENU_PULLRIGHT_IMAGE 243, 419
MENU_PULLRIGHT_ITEM 243, 419
MENU_RELEASE 243, 253, 419
MENU_RELEASE_IMAGE 244, 419
MENU_REMOVE 419
MENU_REMOVE_ITEM 419
MENU_REPLACE 420
MENU_REPLACE_ITEM 420
MENU_SELECTED 420
MENU_SELECTED_ITEM 253
MENU_STRING 240, 241, 420
MENU_STRING_ITEM 420
MENU_STRINGS 239, 420
MENU_TITLE 420
MENU_TITLE_ITEM 239, 420
MENU_TYPE 420
MENU_VALID_RESULT 420
MENU_VALUE 420
NOTICE_BUTTON 267, 420
NOTICE_BUTTON_NO 266, 420
NOTICE_BUTTON_YES 266, 420
NOTICE_FOCUS_XY 266, 421
NOTICE_FONT 421
NOTICE_MESSAGE_STRINGS 267, 421
NOTICE_MESSAGE_STRINGS_ARRAY_PTR 421
NOTICE_NO 384
NOTICE_NO_BEEPING 269, 421
NOTICE_TRIGGER 421
NOTICE_YES 384
OPENWIN_ADJUST_FOR_HORIZONTAL_SCROLLBAR 421
OPENWIN_ADJUST_FOR_VERTICAL_SCROLLBAR 421
OPENWIN_AUTO_CLEAR 87, 421
OPENWIN_HORIZONTAL_SCROLLBAR 421
OPENWIN_NO_MARGIN 421
OPENWIN_NTH_VIEW 97, 421
OPENWIN_NVIEWS 422
OPENWIN_SELECTED_VIEW 422
OPENWIN_SPLIT 96, 422
OPENWIN_SPLIT_DESTROY_PROC 97, 422
OPENWIN_SPLIT_DIRECTION 422
OPENWIN_SPLIT_INIT_PROC 97, 422
OPENWIN_SPLIT_POSITION 422
OPENWIN_SPLIT_VIEW 422
OPENWIN_SPLIT_VIEW_START 422
OPENWIN_VERTICAL_SCROLLBAR 422
OPENWIN_VIEW_ATTRS 422
PANEL_BACKGROUND_PROC 173, 174, 422, 450
PANEL_CARET_ITEM 162, 173, 422
PANEL_CHOICE_IMAGE 143, 423

PANEL_CHOICE_IMAGES 148, 407, 423
PANEL_CHOICE_STRING 423
PANEL_CHOICE_STRINGS 148, 423
PANEL_CHOICE_X 149, 423
PANEL_CHOICE_XS 149, 423
PANEL_CHOICE_Y 149, 423
PANEL_CHOICE_YS 149, 423
PANEL_CHOOSE_NONE 423
PANEL_CHOOSE_ONE 157, 423
PANEL_CLIENT_DATA 166
PANEL_DEFAULT_ITEM 423
PANEL_DEFAULT_VALUE 423
PANEL_DISPLAY_LEVEL 148, 423
PANEL_EVENT_PROC 173, 174, 451
PANEL_EXTRA_PAINT_HEIGHT 142, 423
PANEL_EXTRA_PAINT_WIDTH 142, 424
PANEL_FEEDBACK 424
PANEL_FIRST_ITEM 144, 424
PANEL_INACTIVE 424
PANEL_ITEM_COLOR 408, 424
PANEL_ITEM_RECT 424
PANEL_ITEM_X 140, 424
PANEL_ITEM_X_GAP 139, 424
PANEL_ITEM_X_START 140
PANEL_ITEM_Y 140, 424
PANEL_ITEM_Y_GAP 139, 424
PANEL_ITEM_Y_START 140
PANEL_LABEL_BOLD 157, 424
PANEL_LABEL_IMAGE 299, 425
PANEL_LABEL_STRING 145
PANEL_LABEL_WIDTH 425
PANEL_LABEL_X 142, 425
PANEL_LABEL_Y 142, 425
PANEL_LAYOUT 139, 149, 161, 425
PANEL_LIST_CLIENT_DATA 425
PANEL_LIST_CLIENT_DATAS 425
PANEL_LIST_DELETE 156, 425
PANEL_LIST_DISPLAY_ROWS 425
PANEL_LIST_GLYPH 153, 425
PANEL_LIST_GLYPHS 425
PANEL_LIST_INSERT 156, 426
PANEL_LIST_NROWS 426
PANEL_LIST_ROW_HEIGHT 154, 426
PANEL_LIST_SELECT 156, 426
PANEL_LIST_SELECTED 426
PANEL_LIST_STRING 153, 426
PANEL_LIST_STRINGS 153, 426
PANEL_LIST_WIDTH 153, 426
PANEL_MASK_CHAR 161, 426
PANEL_MAX_VALUE 159, 426
PANEL_MIN_VALUE 159, 426
PANEL_NEXT_COL 139, 426
PANEL_NEXT_ITEM 144, 427

PANEL_NEXT_ROW 139, 427
PANEL_NOTIFY_LEVEL 160, 163, 427
PANEL_NOTIFY_PROC 427
PANEL_NOTIFY_STRING 163, 427
PANEL_PAINT 427
PANEL_PARENT_PANEL 427
PANEL_READ_ONLY 427
PANEL_REPAINT_PROC 169, 427
PANEL_SHOW_RANGE 427
PANEL_SHOW_VALUE 159, 427
PANEL_SLIDER_WIDTH 428
PANEL_TOGGLE_VALUE 428
PANEL_VALUE 143 - 144, 428
PANEL_VALUE_DISPLAY_LENGTH 161, 428
PANEL_VALUE_STORED_LENGTH 161, 162, 428
PANEL_VALUE_X 142, 428
PANEL_VALUE_Y 142, 428
SCREEN_NUMBER 294, 428
SCREEN_SERVER 296, 428
SCROLLBAR_COMPUTE_SCROLL_PROC 227, 428
SCROLLBAR_DIRECTION 428
SCROLLBAR_LAST_VIEW_START 428
SCROLLBAR_MENU 428
SCROLLBAR_NORMALIZE_PROC 227, 429
SCROLLBAR_NOTIFY_CLIENT 429
SCROLLBAR_OBJECT_LENGTH 220, 429
SCROLLBAR_PAGE_LENGTH 220, 222, 429
SCROLLBAR_PIXELS_PER_UNIT 220, 221, 429
SCROLLBAR_SPLITTABLE 429
SCROLLBAR_VIEW_LENGTH 220, 222, 429
SCROLLBAR_VIEW_START 220, 429
SELN_LEVEL_LINE 343
SELN_REQ_BYTESIZE 429
SELN_REQ_COMMIT_PENDING_DELETE 429
SELN_REQ_CONTENTS_ASCII 337, 342, 429
SELN_REQ_CONTENTS_PIECES 429
SELN_REQ_DELETE 430
SELN_REQ_END_REQUEST 430
SELN_REQ_FAKE_LEVEL 342, 343, 430
SELN_REQ_FILE_NAME 430
SELN_REQ_FIRST 338, 430
SELN_REQ_FIRST_UNIT 343, 430
SELN_REQ_LAST 338, 430
SELN_REQ_LAST_UNIT 343, 430
SELN_REQ_LEVEL 430
SELN_REQ_RESTORE 430
SELN_REQ_SET_LEVEL 343, 431
SELN_REQ_YIELD 431
SERVER_IMAGE_BITMAP_FILE 298, 431
SERVER_IMAGE_BITS 297, 431
SERVER_IMAGE_COLORMAP 298
SERVER_IMAGE_DEPTH 298, 431
SERVER_IMAGE_PIXMAP 298, 431

Index

SERVER_IMAGE_X_BITS 297
SERVER_NTH_SCREEN 431
SERVER_SYNC 431
SERVER_SYNC_AND_PROCESS_EVENTS 296, 431
TEXTSW_ACTION_CAPS_LOCK 200
TEXTSW_ACTION_CHANGED_DIRECTORY 200
TEXTSW_ACTION_EDITED_FILE 200, 201
TEXTSW_ACTION_EDITED_MEMORY 200
TEXTSW_ACTION_FILE_IS_READONLY 200
TEXTSW_ACTION_LOADED_FILE 200, 201
TEXTSW_ACTION_TOOL_CLOSE 200
TEXTSW_ACTION_TOOL_DESTROY 200
TEXTSW_ACTION_TOOL_MGR 201
TEXTSW_ACTION_TOOL_QUIT 201
TEXTSW_ACTION_USING_MEMORY 201
TEXTSW_AGAIN_RECORDING 431
TEXTSW_AUTO_INDENT 431
TEXTSW_AUTO_SCROLL_BY 432
TEXTSW_BLINK_CARET 432
TEXTSW_BROWSING 432
TEXTSW_CHECKPOINT_FREQUENCY 432
TEXTSW_CLIENT_DATA 432
TEXTSW_CONFIRM_OVERWRITE 432
TEXTSW_CONTENTS 186, 191, 432
TEXTSW_CONTROL_CHARS_USE_FONT 432
TEXTSW_DISABLE_CD 432
TEXTSW_DISABLE_LOAD 432
TEXTSW_EDIT_COUNT 432
TEXTSW_FILE 183, 432
TEXTSW_FILE_CONTENTS 190, 432
TEXTSW_FIRST 183, 433
TEXTSW_FIRST_LINE 193, 433
TEXTSW_FOR_ALL_VIEWS 192
TEXTSW_HISTORY_LIMIT 433
TEXTSW_IGNORE_LIMIT 433
TEXTSW_INSERT_FROM_FILE 191, 433
TEXTSW_INSERTION_POINT 185, 433
TEXTSW_INSERT_MAKES_VISIBLE 185, 194, 433
TEXTSW_LENGTH 182, 433
TEXTSW_LINE_BREAK_ACTION 192, 433
TEXTSW_LOWER_CONTEXT 433
TEXTSW_MEMORY_MAXIMUM 188, 433
TEXTSW_MODIFIED 183, 433
TEXTSW_MULTI_CLICK_SPACE 433
TEXTSW_MULTI_CLICK_TIMEOUT 434
TEXTSW_NOTIFY_PROC 199, 434
TEXTSW_READ_ONLY 434
TEXTSW_STATUS 182, 183, 191, 434
TEXTSW_STORE_CHANGES_FILE 190, 434
TEXTSW_SUBMENU_EDIT 434
TEXTSW_SUBMENU_FILE 434
TEXTSW_SUBMENU_FIND 434
TEXTSW_SUBMENU_VIEW 434

TEXTSW_UPPER_CONTEXT 434
TEXTSW_WRAPAROUND_SIZE 188
TTY_ARGV 205, 210, 434
TTY_ARGV_DO_NOT_FORK 211, 434
TTY_CONSOLE 434
TTY_PAGE_MODE 435
TTY_PID 210, 435
TTY_QUIT_ON_CHILD_DEATH 210, 435
TTY_TTY_FD 211, 435
WIN_ALARM 435
WIN_ALARM_DATA 435
WIN_BACKGROUND_COLOR 403, 435
WIN_BELOW 435
WIN_BIT_GRAVITY 88, 435
WIN_CLIENT_MESSAGE_DATA 124
WIN_CLIENT_MESSAGE_FORMAT 124
WIN_CLIENT_MESSAGE_TYPE 124
WIN_CMS_DATA 397, 435
WIN_CMS_NAME 397, 435
WIN_COL_GAP 139
WIN_COLLAPSE_EXPOSURES 86, 435
WIN_COLUMNS 436
WIN_CONSUME_EVENT 99, 111, 436
WIN_CONSUME_EVENTS 111, 436
WIN_CONSUME_KBD_EVENTS 53
WIN_CONSUME_PICK_EVENTS 53
WIN_CONSUME_X_EVENT_MASK 110, 436
WIN_CURSOR 436
WIN_DEPTH 436
WIN_DESIRED_HEIGHT 436
WIN_DESIRED_WIDTH 436
WIN_DYNAMIC_VISUAL 397, 436
WIN_EVENT_PROC 99, 173, 436
WIN_FIT_HEIGHT 436
WIN_FIT_WIDTH 436
WIN_FOREGROUND_COLOR 403, 436
WIN_FRAME 437
WIN_GRAB_ALL 120
WIN_GRAB_ALL_INPUT 437
WIN_GRAPHICS_EXPOSE 114
WIN_HORIZONTAL_SCROLLBAR 437
WIN_IGNORE_EVENTS 437
WIN_IGNORE_X_EVENT_MASK 110
WIN_INPUT_MASK 126, 437
WIN_INPUT_ONLY 437
WIN_IS_CLIENT_PANE 437
WIN_KBD_FOCUS 437
WIN_LEFT_MARGIN 140
WIN_MAP 437
WIN_MENU 437
WIN_MOUSE_XY 278, 437
WIN_NO_CLIPPING 89, 438
WIN_NO_DECORATIONS 438

WIN_NOTIFY_EVENT_PROC 53, 463
WIN_NOTIFY_IMMEDIATE_EVENT_PROC 437
WIN_NOTIFY_SAFE_EVENT_PROC 438
WIN_PARENT 438
WIN_PERCENT_HEIGHT 438
WIN_PERCENT_WIDTH 438
WIN_RECT 438
WIN_RESIZE 381
WIN_RETAINED 82, 95, 171, 438
WIN_RIGHT_OF 438
WIN_ROW_GAP 139, 438
WIN_ROW_HEIGHT 438
WIN_SAVE_UNDER 438
WIN_SCALE_EXTRALARGE 313
WIN_SCALE_LARGE 313
WIN_SCALE_MEDIUM 313
WIN_SCALE_SMALL 313
WIN_SCREEN_RECT 439
WIN_SET_FOCUS 439
WIN_TOP_MARGIN 140
WIN_TRANSPARENT 439
WIN_WINDOW_GRAVITY 439
WIN_X_COLOR_INDICES 396, 401, 439
WIN_X_EVENT_MASK 439
XV_AUTO_CREATE 253, 439
XV_BOTTOM_MARGIN 439
XV_DISPLAY 293, 395
XV_ERROR_PROC 54
XV_FONT 439
XV_HEIGHT 297, 439
XV_HELP_DATA 439
XV_INIT_ARGC_PTR_ARGV 45, 46, 63, 440
XV_INIT_ARGS 46, 63, 440
XV_KEY_DATA 166, 239, 440
XV_LABEL 288, 440
XV_LEFT_MARGIN 440
XV_MARGIN 440
XV_NAME 295, 440
XV_OWNER 440
XV_RIGHT_MARGIN 440
XV_ROOT 440
XV_SCREEN 294
XV_SHOW 67, 384
XV_TOP_MARGIN 440
XV_TYPE 441
XV_USAGE_PROC 46
XV_WIDTH 297, 441
XV_X 140
XV_XID 88, 308, 441
XV_Y 140, 441
attributes, attribute-value pair 22, 23
  changing 22
  generic and common; described 22

naming conventions 22
Textsw_action 200
ATTR_LIST attribute 411
auto-expand 92
auto-shrink 92

B

base frame, closed 64
  creating 61
  defined 60
  FRAME_CLOSED_RECT attribute 65
BitGravity, set for canvases 82
  windows 87
blocking 370
busy frames 72
BUT macro 119
button item 145
  label 145
  selection 145

C

callback procedure 35, 107
callback style of programming 35
canvas, about 29, 79, 80
  automatic sizing 92
  callback procedures 99
  controlling size of 91
  creating 82
  default input mask 99
  drawing in 83
  getting view windows 97
  handling input 99
  height of subwindow 92
  model of 80
  paint window 79, 80
  repaint procedure 85 - 91
  repainting 83, 88
  resize procedure 94
  scrolling 94
  splitting views 95
  subclassed from openwin 79
  subwindow 79, 80
  tracking changes in size 94
  tracking events 114
  view window 79, 80
  width of subwindow 92
CANVAS_AUTO_CLEAR attribute 87

CANVAS_AUTO_EXPAND attribute 92, 411
CANVAS_AUTO_SHRINK attribute 92, 411
CANVAS_CMS_REPAINT attribute 402, 411
CANVAS_EACH_PAINT_WINDOW() macro 98, 445
CANVAS_END_EACH macro 98, 445
CANVAS_FIXED_IMAGE attribute 82, 87, 411
canvas.h header file 82
CANVAS_HEIGHT attribute 92, 411
CANVAS_MIN_PAINT_HEIGHT attribute 92, 411
CANVAS_MIN_PAINT_WIDTH attribute 92, 412
CANVAS_NO_CLIPPING attribute 412
CANVAS_NTH_PAINT_WINDOW attribute 97, 412
CANVAS_NTH_PAINT_WONDOW attribute 445
canvas_paint_window() procedure 445
CANVAS_PAINTWINDOW_ATTRS attribute 354, 412
CANVAS_REPAINT_PROC attribute 85, 412
  event handling 114
canvas_repaint_proc() procedure 445
CANVAS_RESIZE attribute 381
CANVAS_RESIZE_PROC attribute 94, 412, 446
  event handling 114
canvas_resize_proc() procedure 446
CANVAS_RETAINED attribute 82, 412
CANVAS_VIEWABLE_RECT attribute 412
CANVAS_VIEW_CANVAS_WINDOW attribute 412
CANVAS_VIEW_PAINT_WINDOW attribute 97, 98, 412
CANVAS_WIDTH attribute 92, 412
CANVAS_X_PAINT_WINDOW attribute 88, 412
cascading menu (See pullright menu).
chained inheritance 18
checkbox item 147, 151
choice item 147
  abbreviated 147, 151
  checkbox 147
  checkboxes 151
  display 148
  exclusive and nonexclusive 147, 150
  getting image 143
  layout 148
  notification 152
  parallel lists 149
  selection 152
class hierarchy 18
client, about 5
  events 366, 390
  messages 108, 114, 120; interpreting 120;
    sending and reading 124
clipboard 186, 333
closing frames (See iconification).
cms.h header file 280

collapsing expose events 86
color, background 402
  colormap segment 396; creating 397; default
    397; definition of 396; dynamic 396;
    static 396
  colormap table; definition of 396
  cursor, setting for 280
  definition of RGB 396
  differences between XView and Xlib 395
  foreground 402
  inheriting from parent frame 82
  panel items; example of 408
  pixel values 396
  setting for frame 73
  XFillRectangle procedure 407
  XSetForeground procedure 407
command frame 27, 67
  defined 60
common attributes 22
compiling XView programs 41
confirmation of quit, FRAME_NO_CONFIRM attri-
    bute 66
connection, between server and client 6
control area, implemented as panel 135
copy_func() procedure 368
create_cursor() procedure 280
curses(3X) 205, 211
cursor, about 275
  as font character 277
  color 277
  color, setting 280
  hotspot 278
  predefined 277
  Xv_Cursor 275
CURSOR package 275 - 281
CURSOR_BACKGROUND_COLOR attribute 412
cursor_copy() procedure 446
CURSOR_FOREGROUND_COLOR attribute 413
CURSOR_IMAGE attribute 275, 413
CURSOR_MASK_CHAR attribute 277
cursors.h header file 275
CURSOR_SRC_CHAR attribute 277
CURSOR_X_HOT attribute 413
CURSOR_Y_HOT attribute 413

D

DefaultColormap() macro 397
defaults, package 319 - 327
  (See also resources)

defaults_get_boolean() procedure 323
defaults_get_character() procedure 324
defaults_get_enum() procedure 325
defaults_get_integer() procedure 324
defaults_get_string() procedure 325
defaults.h header file 322
defaults_init() procedure 322
defaults_load_db() procedure 322
defaults_set_boolean() procedure 323
defaults_set_character() procedure 324
defaults_set_integer() procedure 324
defaults_set_string() procedure 325
defaults_store_db() procedure 322
delayed binding 235, 286
    scrollbars 218
DESTROY_CHECKING 369, 382
DESTROY_CLEANUP 382
destroying frames 75
DESTROY_PROCESS_DEATH 369, 382
DESTROY_SAVE_YOURSELF Destroy_status 383
Destroy_status 382
    DESTROY_SAVE_YOURSELF 383
destruction of objects 382
    safe 369
dispatching, explicit 387
dispatching by Notifier, explicit 385
    implicit 385
display, distinguished from screen 6
Display structure 293
displaying frames 67
distributed processing, about 6
drag-and-drop operation 120
draw programs 83
drawing in a canvas
dup2() system call 373

E

edit log 188
editing (see text subwindow)
enum, ITIMER_REAL 360
    ITIMER_VIRTUAL 360
    NOTIFY_ASYNC 358
    NOTIFY_SYNC 358
enumerated resources 325
error_proc() procedure 54
errors, at run-time 54
    recovery 54
    types 54
escape sequences, sending to TTY subwindows

207
event, ACTION_DRAG_COPY 121
    ACTION_DRAG_MOVE 121
    ACTION_MENU 236
    ACTION_SELECT 116
    Expose 86
    GraphicsExpose 86
    KBD_DONE 113
    KBD_USE 113, 119
    LOC_DRAG 99, 112
    LOC_MOVE 99, 112
    LOC_WINENTER 99, 112, 119
    LOC_WINEXIT 99, 112
    MapNotify 53
    MS_LEFT 116
    realize 53
    WIN_ASCII_EVENTS 99, 113
    WIN_COLORMAP_NOTIFY 112
    WIN_EVENT_PROC 445
    WIN_LEFT_KEYS 113
    WIN_META_EVENTS 113
    WIN_REPAINT 86, 114, 445
    WIN_RESIZE 114
    WIN_RIGHT_KEYS 113
    WIN_TOP_KEYS 113
    WIN_UP_ASCII_EVENTS 113
    WIN_UP_EVENTS 113
    WIN_UP_META_EVENTS 113
    WM_SAVE_YOURSELF 383
    XClientMessage 108
    XClientMessageEvent 124
event handling, in CANVAS package 99
event_action macro 116
event_action() procedure 164
event_button_is_down macro 119
event-driven input handling 354
event_id macro 116
event_is_button macro 119
event_is_down macro 117
event_is_key_bottom macro 118
event_is_key_left macro 118
event_is_key_right macro 118
event_is_key_top macro 118
event_is_up macro 117
event_left_is_down macro 119
event_middle_is_down macro 119
event_right_is_down macro 119
events 10
    about 10, 107
    classes of 108
    client 390
    communicating with client 366
    determing state of event 117

differences between X and XView 53, 116
event ID 109, 116
Event structure 20, 115 - 116
event-to-action mapping 109, 116; default for
    panel items 172
keyboard 113
keyboard focus 113
masks 53, 107, 131
modifier keys 117
mouse 112
posting 370
posting destroy 369
registering 109
relationship to Notifier 35
repaint 114
resize 114
semantic 109
XEvent structure 116
event_string() macro 117
event_xevent() macro 86
exclusive and nonexclusive choices 147, 150
exec() system call 373
expanding size of canvas 92
Expose event 86

F

file descriptors, use in Notifier 370
files, reading 371
FIOASYNC 356
FIONBIO 356
flow of control in Notifier-based programs 35
font conventions (in this book), boldface xxvi
  italics xxvi
  typewriter font xxvi
font family (See fonts).
font ID 307
FONT package 307 - 317
FONT_CHAR_HEIGHT attribute 315, 413
FONT_CHAR_WIDTH attribute 315, 413
FONT_DEFAULT_CHAR_HEIGHT attribute 315, 413
FONT_DEFAULT_CHAR_WIDTH attribute 315, 413
FONT_FAMILY attribute 311, 413
FONT_FAMILY_DEFAULT attribute 311
FONT_FAMILY_DEFAULT_FIXEDWIDTH attribute
   311
FONT_INFO attribute 315
FONT_NAME attribute 315
FONT_RESCALE_OF attribute 314, 413
fonts 25, 49, 307
  creating 308
  dimensions 315

family 307, 311
  rescaling 314
  scale 307
  scaling 313
  size 307, 312
  specifying font by name 314
  style 307, 311
  using xv_find() 308
  WINDOW attributes 313
FONT_SCALE attribute 413
fonts.h header file 308
FONT_SIZE attribute 311, 312, 413
FONT_SIZES_FOR_SCALE attribute 413
FONT_STRING_DIMS attribute 315, 413
Font_string_dims structure 316
FONT_STYLE attribute 311, 413
FONT_STYLE_DEFAULT attribute 312
footer, FRAME_SHOW_FOOTER attribute 63
  of a frame 63
fork() system call 373
frame, about 26 - 27
  base frame 26, 60, 61
  closed base frame 64
  command frame 60, 67
  headers and footers 63
  in class hierarchy 18
  inheriting colors 73, 82
  initialization 62
  modifying destruction using the Notifier 381
  modifying open/close using the Notifier 379
  pop-up 26
  providing visual feedback 72
  role of window manager 61
  setting colors 73
  setting display of 67
  setting the size of 72
  subframe 60
FRAME package 59 - 75
  capabilities 59
  (See also FRAME_CMD package)
FRAME_BACKGROUND_COLOR attribute 73, 402,
   414
FRAME_BUSY attribute 72, 414
FRAME_CLOSED attribute 287, 414
FRAME_CLOSED_RECT attribute 65, 414
FRAME_CMD package 67
  (See also FRAME package)
FRAME_CMD_PANEL attribute 414
FRAME_CMD_PUSHPIN_IN attribute 68, 414
FRAME_DEFAULT_DONE_PROC attribute 414
FRAME_DONE_PROC attribute 414

FRAME_DONE_PROC() procedure 70
frame_fit_all macro 74
FRAME_FOREGROUND_COLOR attribute 51, 73, 402, 414
frame_get_rect() procedure 72, 446
FRAME_ICON attribute 65, 414
FRAME_INHERIT_COLORS attribute 73, 82, 402, 414
FRAME_LABEL attribute 63
FRAME_LEFT_FOOTER attribute 414
FRAME_NO_CONFIRM attribute 66, 414
FRAME_NTH_SUBFRAME attribute 74, 415
FRAME_NTH_SUBWINDOW attribute 74, 415
FRAME_RIGHT_FOOTER attribute 415
frame_set_rect() procedure 72, 446
FRAME_SHOW_FOOTER attribute 63, 415
FRAME_SHOW_HEADER attribute 63, 415
FRAME_SHOW_LABEL attribute 415
FRAME_SHOW_RESIZE_CORNER attribute 71, 415
freeing the server 300
FULLSCREEN package 300
FULLSCREEN_ALLOW_EVENTS attribute 415
FULLSCREEN_ALLOW_SYNC_EVENT attribute 415
FULLSCREEN_COLORMAP_WINDOW attribute 415
FULLSCREEN_CURSOR_WINDOW attribute 415
FULLSCREEN_GRAB_KEYBOARD attribute 415
FULLSCREEN_GRAB_POINTER attribute 415
FULLSCREEN_GRAB_SERVER attribute 415
FULLSCREEN_INPUT_WINDOW attribute 415
FULLSCREEN_KEYBOARD_GRAB_KBD_MODE attribute 416
FULLSCREEN_KEYBOARD_GRAB_PTR_MODE attribute 416
FULLSCREEN_OWNER_EVENTS attribute 416
FULLSCREEN_PAINT_WINDOW attribute 416
FULLSCREEN_POINTER_GRAB_KBD_MODE attribute 416
FULLSCREEN_POINTER_GRAB_PTR_MODE attribute 416
FULLSCREEN_RECT attribute 416
FULLSCREEN_SYNC attribute 416
function (See procedure).

G

gap between panel items 139
GC, about 90 - 91
    font ID 307
    fonts 310
    repainting objects; example of 91
    setting foreground and background colors 398, 407

generic, attributes 22
    functions; table of 21
Generic Object 18, 24 - 25
getitimer() system call 356
global variables 166
glyphs 154, 277, 307
grabbing the server 300
graphics, CANVAS_X_PAINT_WINDOW 88
    cursor images 275
    draw programs 83
    exposure events 86, 114
    paint programs 84
    rendering in color 398
    rendering methods 85
    rendering text; example of 310
    SunView 85
    text-based programs 84
    visualization programs 84
    Xlib drawing; example of 280
    XView model 85
    (See also server image)
GraphicsExpose event 86

H

handle, for object 19
header, FRAME_SHOW_HEADER attribute 63
    of a frame 63
header file, canvas.h 82
    cms.h 280
    cursors.h 275
    defaults.h 322
    fonts.h 308
    icon.h 286
    notice.h 264
    notify.h 356
    openmenu.h 235
    panel.h 137
    rect.h 65
    screen.h 294
    server.h 295
    signal.h 358
    svrimage.h 297
    textsw.h 182
    tty.h 205
    win_event.h 111, 116
    win_input.h 111, 115, 116
    X.h 110
    Xlib.h 90, 294
    xv_error.h 55
    xview.h 42

Index

header files, about 42
help frame 27
hidden class 79
hints, to window manager 61

I

ICCCM (See Inter-Client Communications Conventions Manual).
icon 64, 65
  about 33, 285
  creating 286
  positioning image 288
  server image 286
  size 288
  text label 288
ICON package 285 - 289
icon.h header file 286
iconification 64, 286
ICON_IMAGE attribute 288, 416
ICON_IMAGE_RECT attribute 288, 416
ICON_LABEL_RECT attribute 288, 416
include files (See header files).
inheritance 18, 79, 82
initialization 45, 62
  (See also xv_init() procedure)
input, about 10
  handling; event-driven 354; mainline 353
  handling of 107 - 131
  in CANVAS package 99
input masks 107
Inputmask structure 111, 125
interclient communication 9, 331 - 349
Inter-Client Communications Conventions Manual, about 9
interposition 38, 378 - 384
Intrinsics (See Xt Intrinsics).
ioctl() system call 356
ITIMER_REAL enum 360
ITIMER_VIRTUAL enum 360

K

KBD_DONE event 113
KBD_USE event 113, 119
keyboard, event states 117
keyboard events 113
keyboard focus, about 4
  defined by window manager 9
  directing under program control 119
  events 113

grabbing 120, 300
KEY_BOTTOM macro 118
KEY_LEFT macro 118
KEY_RIGHT macro 118
KeySym 109
KEY_TOP macro 118

L

libraries, for XView 42
line, editing in text subwindow 192
list item, adding and deleting 156
  displaying 153
  notification 157
  selection 157
LOC_DRAG event 99, 112
LOC_MOVE event 99, 112
LOC_WINENTER event 99, 112, 119
LOC_WINEXIT event 99, 112

M

macro, BUT 119
  CANVAS_EACH_PAINT_WINDOW() 98, 445
  CANVAS_END_EACH 98, 445
  DefaultColormap() 397
  event_action 116
  event_button_is_down 119
  event_id 116
  event_is_button 119
  event_is_down 117
  event_is_key_bottom 118
  event_is_key_left 118
  event_is_key_right 118
  event_is_key_top 118
  event_is_up 117
  event_left_is_down 119
  event_middle_is_down 119
  event_right_is_down 119
  event_string() 117
  event_xevent() 86
  frame_fit_all 74
  KEY_BOTTOM 118
  KEY_LEFT 118
  KEY_RIGHT 118
  KEY_TOP 118
  OPENWIN_EACH_VIEW 98
  OPENWIN_END_EACH 449
  PANEL_CHECK_BOX 151
  PANEL_CHOICE_STACK 151
  PANEL_EACH_ITEM 144

PANEL_END_EACH 144, 451
panel_set_value() 165
PANEL_TOGGLE 150
window_fit() 142
window_fit_height() 142
window_fit_width() 142
XV_INIT_ARGS 46
mainline input handling 353
MapNotify event 53
masks (see events)
menu, about 31, 231
  adding menu items 242
  appending new item 240
  creating 235
  default item 253
  destroying 253
  display stage of menu processing 246
  displaying image 241, 243
  finding items 252
  freeing allocated strings 254
  freeing pullright menus 254
  generation procedures 245
  notification procedures 249
  owner of 235
  pin-up 248
  pullright menus 233
  selected item 253
  setting inactive items 249
  string handling 239
  toggle (nonexclusive) settings 246
  XView implementation 233
menu buttons, on panels 146
MENU package 231 - 259
MENU_ACTION_IMAGE attribute 241, 416
MENU_ACTION_ITEM attribute 240, 241, 416
menu_action_proc() procedure 447
MENU_APPEND_ITEM attribute 242, 416
MENU_CHOICE_MENU package 236
MENU_CLASS attribute 417
MENU_CLIENT_DATA attribute 255
MENU_COL_MAJOR attribute 417
MENU_DEFAULT attribute 417
MENU_DEFAULT_ITEM attribute 253, 417
MENU_DESCEND_FIRST attribute 252, 417
MENU_DONE_PROC attribute 249, 447
menu_done_proc() procedure 447
MENU_FEEDBACK attribute 417
MENU_FIRST_EVENT attribute 237, 417
MENU_GEN_PIN_WINDOW attribute 248, 417
MENU_GEN_PROC attribute 242, 417, 447
menu_gen_proc() procedure 245, 447

MENU_GEN_PROC_IMAGE attribute 417
MENU_GEN_PROC_ITEM attribute 417
MENU_GEN_PULLRIGHT attribute 245, 418
MENU_GEN_PULLRIGHT_IMAGE attribute 418
MENU_GEN_PULLRIGHT_ITEM attribute 245, 418
MENU_IMAGE attribute 241, 418
MENU_IMAGE_ITEM attribute 418
MENU_IMAGES attribute 243, 418
MENU_INACTIVE attribute 249, 418
MENU_INSERT attribute 418
MENU_INSERT_ITEM attribute 418
MENU_INVERT attribute 418
MENU_ITEM attribute 240, 254
  (See also MENUITEM package)
MENUITEM package 240, 241
MENU_LAST_EVENT attribute 237, 418
MENU_NCOLS attribute 247, 418
MENU_NITEMS attribute 418
MENU_NOTIFY_PROC attribute 239, 249, 419, 447,
  448
menu_notify_proc() procedure 239, 249, 447
MENU_NOTIFY_STATUS attribute 419
MENU_NROWS attribute 247, 419
MENU_NTH_ITEM attribute 419
MENU_PIN attribute 249, 419
MENU_PIN_PROC attribute 249, 419, 447
menu_pin_proc() procedure 447
MENU_PIN_WINDOW attribute 249, 419
MENU_PULLRIGHT attribute 243, 419
MENU_PULLRIGHT_IMAGE attribute 243, 419
MENU_PULLRIGHT_ITEM attribute 243, 419
MENU_RELEASE attribute 243, 253, 419
MENU_RELEASE_IMAGE attribute 244, 419
MENU_REMOVE attribute 419
MENU_REMOVE_ITEM attribute 419
MENU_REPLACE attribute 420
MENU_REPLACE_ITEM attribute 420
menu_return_item() procedure 448
menu_return_value() procedure 448
menus, pullright 243
MENU_SELECTED attribute 420
MENU_SELECTED_ITEM attribute 253
menu_show() procedure 236, 448
MENU_STRING attribute 240, 241, 420
MENU_STRING_ITEM attribute 420
MENU_STRINGS attribute 239, 420
MENU_TITLE attribute 420
MENU_TITLE_ITEM attribute 239, 420
MENU_TOGGLE_MENU package 236
MENU_TYPE attribute 420
MENU_VALID_RESULT attribute 420

MENU_VALUE attribute 420
message item 157
  selection 157
messages, client 114
modifier keys 117
motion events 112
mouse, button events 112
  button; re-mapping 109
  event states 117
  getting coordinate position 278
  motion events 112
  position 115
mouse; button events; registering interest in 111
MS_LEFT event 116

N

nonexclusive choice 150
nonvisual objects 293 - 303
  about 33
notice, about 27, 263
  creating 264
  displaying 264
  implementation 263
  origin 266
  responses 266
  suppressing beep 269
  triggers 267
NOTICE package 263 - 272
  use of FULLSCREEN package 300
NOTICE_BUTTON attribute 267, 420
NOTICE_BUTTON_NO attribute 266, 420
NOTICE_BUTTON_YES attribute 266, 420
NOTICE_FOCUS_XY attribute 266, 421
NOTICE_FONT attribute 421
notice.h header file 264
NOTICE_MESSAGE_STRINGS attribute 267, 421
NOTICE_MESSAGE_STRINGS_ARRAY_PTR attribute
  421
NOTICE_NO attribute 384
NOTICE_NO_BEEPING attribute 269, 421
notice_prompt() procedure 264, 448
NOTICE_TRIGGER attribute 421
NOTICE_YES attribute 384
notification, menus 249
notification procedures, in a text subwindow
  199
Notifier 353 - 390
  about 10, 353
  base event handler 378
  client 356
  client events 366

control 384
definition 355
destroy event delivery time 369
error codes 388
explicit dispatching 385, 387
file descriptors 370
flow of control in Notifier-based programs 35
handling X events 52
implicit dispatching 385
interposing on frame open/close 379
interposing on resize events 381
interposition 378
miscellaneous issues 390
operation 354
overview 35
pipes 373
posting client events 367
posting destroy events 369
posting events 370
posting events with an argument 368
procedures of 354
prohibited signals 357
reading 371
role of xv_main_loop procedure 52
safe destruction 369
signal handling 357
SIGTERM handling 364
timers 360
Notifier procedures, copy_func() 368
  notify_default_wait3() 365
  notify_do_dispatch() 385
  notify_interpose_destroy_func() 381
  notify_interpose_event_func() 379
  notify_next_event_func() 380
  notify_post_destroy() 369
  notify_post_event() 370
  notify_post_event_and_arg() 368
  notify_set_destroy_func() 357
  notify_set_exception_func() 358
  notify_set_input_func() 358, 371
  notify_set_itimer_func() 355, 360
  notify_set_output_func() 358, 371
  notify_set_signal_func 358
  notify_set_signal_func() 359
  notify_set_wait3_func() 357, 365
  notify_veto_destroy() 382
notify procedure 35
Notify_arg 368, 370
NOTIFY_ASYNC enum 358
NOTIFY_BADF 388

NOTIFY_BAD_ITIMER 388
NOTIFY_BAD_SIGNAL 388
Notify_client 370
Notify_copy 368
NOTIFY_COPY_NULL 368
notify_default_wait3() procedure 365
NOTIFY_DESTROY_VETOED 369, 388
notify_dispatch() procedure 385
notify_do_dispatch() procedure 385
NOTIFY_DONE 365, 370
notify_errno 388
Notify_error 388
Notify_event 367, 370
Notify_event_type 370
NOTIFY_FUNC_LIMIT 388
notify.h header file 356
NOTIFY_IGNORED 365, 367, 370
NOTIFY_IMMEDIATE 367, 370
NOTIFY_INTERNAL_ERROR 388
notify_interpose_destroy_func() procedure 356, 381
notify_interpose_event_func() procedure 379
notify_interpose_wait3_func() procedure 210
NOTIFY_INVAL 369, 388
notify_next_event_func() procedure 380
NOTIFY_NO_CONDITION 367, 388
NOTIFY_NOMEM 388
NOTIFY_NOT_STARTED 388
NOTIFY_OK 388
notify_perror() procedure 389
notify_post_destroy() procedure 369
notify_post_event() procedure 367, 370
notify_post_event_and_arg() procedure 368
notify_proc() procedure 199
Notify_release 368
NOTIFY_RELEASE_NULL 368
NOTIFY_SAFE 367, 370
notify_set_destroy_func() procedure 364
notify_set_event_func() procedure 370
notify_set_exception_func() procedure 358
notify_set_input_func() procedure 358, 371
notify_set_itimer_func() procedure 355, 360
notify_set_output_func() procedure 358, 371
notify_set_signal_func() procedure 358, 359
notify_set_wait3_func() procedure 357, 365, 373
NOTIFY_SRCH 388
notify_start() procedure 384
notify_stop() procedure 384
NOTIFY_SYNC enum 358
NOTIFY_UNKNOWN_CLIENT 367, 388

NULL 22
numeric text item 161, 165

O

object, destruction of 382
object-oriented programming 17
objects, canvas subwindows 29
    class hierarchy 18
    destroying 50
    frames 26
    Generic Object 18, 24
    icons 33
    menus 31
    nonvisual 18, 33
    panels 30
    relationship to Notifier 36
    scrollbars 32
    text subwindows 30
    use of object handle 19
    windows 25
opaque data types 20
OPEN LOOK, about 13
    as standard 13
    control area; about 135
    documentation 14
    menus; about 231
    scrollbars; about 217
openmenu.h header file 235
OPENWIN package 79
    split views 218
OPENWIN_ADJUST_FOR_HORIZONTAL_SCROLLBAR
        attribute 421
OPENWIN_ADJUST_FOR_VERTICAL_SCROLLBAR
        attribute 421
OPENWIN_AUTO_CLEAR attribute 87, 421
OPENWIN_EACH_VIEW macro 98
OPENWIN_EACH_VIEW() procedure 449
OPENWIN_END_EACH macro 449
OPENWIN_HORIZONTAL_SCROLLBAR attribute 421
openwin_init_split() procedure 449
OPENWIN_NO_MARGIN attribute 421
OPENWIN_NTH_VIEW attribute 97, 421
OPENWIN_NVIEWS attribute 422
OPENWIN_SELECTED_VIEW attribute 422
OPENWIN_SPLIT attribute 96, 422
OPENWIN_SPLIT_DESTROY_PROC attribute 97, 422
openwin_split_destroy_proc() procedure 449
OPENWIN_SPLIT_DIRECTION attribute 422
OPENWIN_SPLIT_INIT_PROC attribute 97, 422

Index

Index

OPENWIN_SPLIT_POSITION attribute 422
OPENWIN_SPLIT_VIEW attribute 422
OPENWIN_SPLIT_VIEW_START attribute 422
OPENWIN_VERTICAL_SCROLLBAR attribute 422
OPENWIN_VIEW_ATTRS attribute 422
override_redirect 263
ownership of objects 48

P

package, CURSOR 275 - 281
  FONT 307 - 317
  FRAME 59 - 75
  FRAME_CMD 67
  FULLSCREEN 300
  ICON 285 - 289
  MENU 231 - 259
  MENU_CHOICE_MENU 236
  MENUITEM 240, 241
  MENU_TOGGLE_MENU 236
  NOTICE 263 - 272
  PANEL 135 - 177
  SCREEN 294
  SCROLLBAR 217 - 228
  SELN 331
  SERVER 295
  SERVER_IMAGE 297
  TEXTSW 181 - 203
  TTYSW 205
packages 43
  about 18
paint programs 84
paint window 80
  controlling size 92
  definition of 79
  handling events 99
panel, about 30, 135
  creating 137
  event codes 175
  event handling 135, 172
  iterating over items 144
  layout 139
  minimum size 142
  ordering of item 138
  repainting 169
  sizing 142
  subclassed from canvas 135
  item (See panel item).
panel item, about 135
  attaching data 166
  button 145
  choice 147

  classes 144
  creating 138
  destroying 144
  gap 139
  iteration 144
  layout 139
  menu buttons 146
  messages 157
  numeric text 161
  ordering 138
  repainting 172
  scrolling lists 153
  setting values 143
  setting x and y coordinates 140
  slider 159
  text 161
  types 138
  values 143
panel items, color 408
PANEL package 135 - 177
  summary 176
panel_advance_caret() procedure 449
PANEL_BACKGROUND_PROC attribute 173, 174, 422, 450
panel_background_proc() procedure 450
panel_backup_caret() procedure 450
PANEL_CARET_ITEM attribute 162, 173, 422
PANEL_CHECK_BOX macro 151
PANEL_CHECK_BOX procedure 450
PANEL_CHOICE_IMAGE attribute 143, 423
PANEL_CHOICE_IMAGES attribute 148, 407, 423
PANEL_CHOICE_STACK macro 151
PANEL_CHOICE_STACK procedure 450
PANEL_CHOICE_STRING attribute 423
PANEL_CHOICE_STRINGS attribute 148, 423
PANEL_CHOICE_X attribute 149, 423
PANEL_CHOICE_XS attribute 149, 423
PANEL_CHOICE_Y attribute 149, 423
PANEL_CHOICE_YS attribute 149, 423
PANEL_CHOOSE_NONE attribute 423
PANEL_CHOOSE_ONE attribute 157, 423
PANEL_CLIENT_DATA attribute 166
panel_default_handle_event() procedure 450
PANEL_DEFAULT_ITEM attribute 423
PANEL_DEFAULT_VALUE attribute 423
PANEL_DISPLAY_LEVEL attribute 148, 423
PANEL_EACH_ITEM macro 144
PANEL_EACH_ITEM() procedure 450
PANEL_END_EACH macro 144, 451
PANEL_EVENT_PROC attribute 173, 174, 451
panel_event_proc() procedure 451

PANEL_EXTRA_PAINT_HEIGHT attribute 142, 423
PANEL_EXTRA_PAINT_WIDTH attribute 142, 424
PANEL_FEEDBACK attribute 424
PANEL_FIRST_ITEM attribute 144, 424
panel.h header file 137
PANEL_HORIZONTAL, value of PANEL_LAYOUT 139
PANEL_INACTIVE attribute 424
PANEL_ITEM_COLOR attribute 408, 424
PANEL_ITEM_MENU procedure 424
PANEL_ITEM_RECT attribute 424
PANEL_ITEM_X attribute 140, 424
PANEL_ITEM_X_GAP attribute 139, 424
PANEL_ITEM_X_START attribute 140
PANEL_ITEM_Y attribute 140, 424
PANEL_ITEM_Y_GAP attribute 139, 424
PANEL_ITEM_Y_START attribute 140
PANEL_LABEL_BOLD attribute 157, 424
PANEL_LABEL_IMAGE attribute 299, 425
PANEL_LABEL_STRING attribute 145
PANEL_LABEL_WIDTH attribute 425
PANEL_LABEL_X attribute 142, 425
PANEL_LABEL_Y attribute 142, 425
PANEL_LAYOUT attribute 139, 149, 161, 425
PANEL_LIST_CLIENT_DATA attribute 425
PANEL_LIST_CLIENT_DATAS attribute 425
PANEL_LIST_DELETE attribute 156, 425
PANEL_LIST_DISPLAY_ROWS attribute 425
PANEL_LIST_GLYPH attribute 153, 425
PANEL_LIST_GLYPHS attribute 425
PANEL_LIST_INSERT attribute 156, 426
PANEL_LIST_NROWS attribute 426
PANEL_LIST_ROW_HEIGHT attribute 154, 426
PANEL_LIST_SELECT attribute 156, 426
PANEL_LIST_SELECTED attribute 426
PANEL_LIST_STRING attribute 153, 426
PANEL_LIST_STRINGS attribute 153, 426
PANEL_LIST_WIDTH attribute 153, 426
PANEL_MASK_CHAR attribute 161, 426
PANEL_MAX_VALUE attribute 159, 426
PANEL_MIN_VALUE attribute 159, 426
PANEL_NEXT_COL attribute 139, 426
PANEL_NEXT_ITEM attribute 144, 427
PANEL_NEXT_ROW attribute 139, 427
PANEL_NOTIFY_LEVEL attribute 160, 163, 427
PANEL_NOTIFY_PROC attribute 427
PANEL_NOTIFY_STRING attribute 163, 427
PANEL_PAINT attribute 427
panel_paint() procedure 172, 452
PANEL_PARENT_PANEL attribute 427
PANEL_READ_ONLY attribute 427

PANEL_REPAINT_PROC attribute 169, 427
panel_set_value() macro 165
PANEL_SHOW_RANGE attribute 427
PANEL_SHOW_VALUE attribute 159, 427
PANEL_SLIDER_WIDTH attribute 428
panel_text_notify() procedure 452
PANEL_TOGGLE macro 150
PANEL_TOGGLE procedure 452
PANEL_TOGGLE_VALUE attribute 428
PANEL_VALUE attribute 143 - 144, 428
PANEL_VALUE_DISPLAY_LENGTH attribute 161, 428
PANEL_VALUE_STORED_LENGTH attribute 161, 162, 428
PANEL_VALUE_X attribute 142, 428
PANEL_VALUE_Y attribute 142, 428
PANEL_VERTICAL, value of PANEL_LAYOUT 139
parallel lists for choice item 149
pattern matching (see text subwindow)
pipe() system call 373
pipes 373
pixel, definition of 396
    value of 396
pixmap 84
primary selection, in a text subwindow 198
procedure, canvas_paint_window() 445
    canvas_repaint_proc() 445
    canvas_resize_proc() 446
    copy_func() 368
    create_cursor() 280
    cursor_copy() 446
    defaults_get_boolean() 323
    defaults_get_character() 324
    defaults_get_enum() 325
    defaults_get_integer() 324
    defaults_get_string() 325
    defaults_init() 322
    defaults_load_db() 322
    defaults_set_boolean() 323
    defaults_set_character() 324
    defaults_set_integer() 324
    defaults_set_string() 325
    defaults_store_db() 322
    error_proc() 54
    event_action() 164
    FRAME_DONE_PROC() 70
    frame_get_rect() 72, 446
    frame_set_rect() 72, 446
    menu_action_proc() 447
    menu_done_proc() 447
    menu_gen_proc() 245, 447
    menu_notify_proc() 239, 249, 447
    menu_pin_proc() 447

Index

menu_return_item() 448
menu_return_value() 448
menu_show() 236, 448
notice_prompt() 264, 448
notify_default_wait3() 365
notify_dispatch() 385
notify_do_dispatch() 385
notify_interpose_destroy_func() 356, 381
notify_interpose_event_func() 379
notify_interpose_wait3_func() 210
notify_next_event_func() 380
notify_perror() 389
notify_post_destroy() 369
notify_post_event() 367, 370
notify_post_event_and_arg() 368
notify_proc() 199
notify_set_destroy_func() 364
notify_set_event_func() 370
notify_set_exception_func() 358
notify_set_input_func() 358, 371
notify_set_itimer_func() 355, 360
notify_set_output_func() 358, 371
notify_set_signal_func() 358, 359
notify_set_wait3_func() 357, 365, 373
notify_start() 384
notify_stop() 384
OPENWIN_EACH_VIEW() 449
openwin_init_split() 449
openwin_split_destroy_proc() 449
panel_advance_caret() 449
panel_background_proc() 450
panel_backup_caret() 450
PANEL_CHECK_BOX 450
PANEL_CHOICE_STACK 450
panel_default_handle_event() 450
PANEL_EACH_ITEM() 450
panel_event_proc() 451
PANEL_ITEM_MENU 424
panel_paint() 172, 452
panel_text_notify() 452
PANEL_TOGGLE 452
release_func() 368
SCROLLABLE_PANEL 452
scrollbar_default_compute_scroll_proc() 452
scrollbar_paint() 453
selection_acquire() 453
selection_ask() 335, 336, 343, 453
selection_clear_functions() 454
selection_create() 454
selection_destroy() 454
selection_done() 454
selection_figure_response() 455
selection_hold_file() 455

selection_inform() 455
selection_init_request() 455
selection_inquire() 335, 456
selection_inquire_all() 456
selection_query() 456
selection_report_event() 457
selection_request() 457
selection_yield_all() 458
textsw_add_mark() 196, 458
textsw_append_file_name() 188, 458
textsw_delete() 186, 458
textsw_edit() 187, 458
textsw_erase() 186, 187, 459
textsw_file_lines_visible() 193, 459
textsw_find_bytes() 194, 459
textsw_find_mark() 197, 459
textsw_first() 198, 459
textsw_index_for_file_line() 193, 459
textsw_insert() 185, 460
textsw_match_bytes() 195, 460
textsw_next() 198, 460
textsw_normalize_view() 194, 460
textsw_notify_proc() 460
textsw_possibly_normalize() 194, 461
textsw_remove_mark() 197, 461
textsw_replace_bytes() 188, 461
textsw_reset() 190, 461
textsw_save() 185, 189, 461
textsw_screen_line_count() 193, 462
textsw_scroll_lines() 193, 462
textsw_set_selection() 198, 462
textsw_store_file() 185, 189, 462
toggle_notify() 247
ttysw_input() 207, 462
ttysw_output() 207, 463
window_done() 463
window_fit() 463
window_interpose_func() 464
window_main_loop() 463
window_read_event() 463
win_set_kbd_focus() 119
WIN_VERTICAL_SCROLLBAR 439
wmgr_bottom() 464
wmgr_changelevel() 464
wmgr_close() 464
wmgr_completechangerect() 464
wmgr_open() 465
wmgr_refreshwindow() 465
wmgr_top() 465
XAllocColor() 396
XChangeWindowAttributes() 395
XCopyPlane() 223
XGrabPointer() 236

XLookupString() 117
XNextEvent() 125
XRebindKeysym() 116, 117
XSendEvent() 108, 120
XSetForeground() 396
XSetForeground 407
XTranslateCoordinates() 266
xv_col() 140, 465
xv_cols() 465
xv_create() 47, 465
xv_destroy() 50, 137, 466
xv_destroy_safe() 50, 166
XV_DISPLAY_FROM_WINDOW() 466
xv_error() 54
xv_find() 49, 466
xv_get() 50, 466
xv_init() 45, 62, 295, 467
xv_input_readevent() 111, 125, 302
xv_main_loop() 52, 384
xv_row() 140, 467
xv_rows() 467
XV_SCREEN_FROM_WINDOW() 467
xv_send_message() 108, 120, 124, 467
XV_SERVER_FROM_WINDOW() 468
xv_set() 50, 468
property sheets 135
pullright menus 243
pushpin, about 27, 68
    close procedure 70
    command frame 68
    use in menus 248

Q

quit action 66
quit confirmation, FRAME_NO_CONFIRM attribute
    66
quit.c program 44

R

read() 370
readv() system call 390
realize event 53
reaping child process 364, 365
Rect structure 20, 65
rect.h header file 65
Rectlist structure 20, 88
release_func() procedure 368

rendering graphics 85
repaint, canvas; about 83; form of procedure
    85; procedures used to draw 83 - 85;
    when procedure is called 85
    event 54, 114
    panel item 172
    panels 169
reserved names, table of 43
resize corners, displaying 71
resize event 114
resources 319 - 327
    boolean 323
    boolean resources 323
    character resources 324
    enumerated resources 325
    integer resources 323
    lookup 325
    pairs 325
    predefined default values; table of 319
    string resources 324
rlimit() system call 390
run-time errors 54

S

SCREEN package 294
Screen structure 294
Screen type 294
screen.h header file 294
SCREEN_NUMBER attribute 294, 428
screens, multiple 294
SCREEN_SERVER attribute 296, 428
SCROLLABLE_PANEL procedure 452
scrollbar, about 32, 217
    creating 218
    managing 227
    OPEN LOOK description 217
    owner 218
    relationship to objects 220
    split views 218
    use with canvases 94
SCROLLBAR package 217 - 228
SCROLLBAR_COMPUTE_SCROLL_PROC attribute
    227, 428
scrollbar_default_compute_scroll_proc() proce-
    dure 452
SCROLLBAR_DIRECTION attribute 428
SCROLLBAR_LAST_VIEW_START attribute 428
SCROLLBAR_MENU attribute 428
SCROLLBAR_NORMALIZE_PROC attribute 227, 429

SCROLLBAR_NOTIFY_CLIENT attribute 429
SCROLLBAR_OBJECT_LENGTH attribute 220, 429
SCROLLBAR_PAGE_LENGTH attribute 220, 222,
    429
scrollbar_paint() procedure 453
SCROLLBAR_PIXELS_PER_UNIT attribute 220, 221,
    429
SCROLLBAR_SPLITTABLE 95
SCROLLBAR_SPLITTABLE attribute 429
SCROLLBAR_VIEW_LENGTH attribute 220, 222,
    429
SCROLLBAR_VIEW_START attribute 220, 429
scrolling lists 153
secondary selection, in a text subwindow 198
selection, about 331
    copying to clipboard 333
    getting from holder 335
    in a text panel item 162
    in a text subwindow 197
    rank 333, 334
    service 331
selection package (See SELN package).
selection_acquire() procedure 453
selection_ask() procedure 335, 336, 343, 453
selection_clear_functions() procedure 454
selection_create() procedure 454
selection_destroy() procedure 454
selection_done() procedure 454
selection_figure_response() procedure 455
selection_hold_file() procedure 455
selection_inform() procedure 455
selection_init_request() procedure 455
selection_inquire() procedure 335, 456
selection_inquire_all() procedure 456
selection_query() procedure 456
selection_report_event() procedure 457
selection_request() procedure 457
selection_yield_all() procedure 458
SELN package 331
SELN_CARET enum 335
SELN_LEVEL_LINE attribute 343
SELN_PRIMARY enum 335
SELN_REQ_BYTESIZE attribute 429
SELN_REQ_COMMIT_PENDING_DELETE attribute
    429
SELN_REQ_CONTENTS_ASCII attribute 337, 342,
    429
SELN_REQ_CONTENTS_PIECES attribute 429
SELN_REQ_DELETE attribute 430
SELN_REQ_END_REQUEST attribute 430
SELN_REQ_FAKE_LEVEL attribute 342, 343, 430

SELN_REQ_FILE_NAME attribute 430
SELN_REQ_FIRST attribute 338, 430
SELN_REQ_FIRST_UNIT attribute 343, 430
SELN_REQ_LAST attribute 338, 430
SELN_REQ_LAST_UNIT attribute 343, 430
SELN_REQ_LEVEL attribute 430
SELN_REQ_RESTORE attribute 430
SELN_REQ_SET_LEVEL attribute 343, 431
Seln_request structure 336, 337
SELN_REQ_YIELD attribute 431
SELN_SECONDARY enum 335
SELN_SHELF enum 335
SELN_UNKNOWN enum 335
SELN_UNSPECIFIED enum 336
sending client messages 124
server, about 5, 295
    freeing 300
    grabbing 300
    identifying 296
    object 295
    opening a connnection 295
    synchronizing 296
    windows retained 82
server image 297
    as panel image 299
    attached to other objects 298
    creating 297
    destroying pixmap 298
    pixmaps 297
    Server_image object 297
    used for cursor 275, 277
SERVER package 295
server-client model 5
server.h header file 295
SERVER_IMAGE package 297
SERVER_IMAGE_BITMAP_FILE attribute 298, 431
SERVER_IMAGE_BITS attribute 297, 431
SERVER_IMAGE_COLORMAP attribute 298
SERVER_IMAGE_DEPTH attribute 298, 431
SERVER_IMAGE_PIXMAP attribute 298, 431
SERVER_IMAGE_X_BITS attribute 297
SERVER_NTH_SCREEN attribute 431
SERVER_SYNC attribute 431
SERVER_SYNC_AND_PROCESS_EVENTS attribute
    296, 431
setjmp() system call 390
setpriority() system call 390
setquota() system call 390
settimer() system call 355
shelf 333
SIGALRM 357

sigblock() system call 390
SIGCHLD 357, 364
SIGIO 358
sigmask() system call 390
signal handling 357
signal() system call 355, 358, 377
signal.h header file 358
sigpause() system call 390
sigstack() system call 390
SIGTERM 357, 364, 369
SIGURG 358
sigvec() system call 390
sigvec(2) 355
SIGVTALRM system call 357
slider item 159
   displaying 159
   selection 159
split views, about 29
   function of scrollbar 218
   in a text subwindow 198
   in canvas 95
static subclassing 18
structure, Display 293
   Event 20, 115
   Font_string_dims 316
   Inputmask 111, 125
   Rect 20, 65
   Rectlist 20, 88
   Screen 294
   Seln_request 336, 337
   XEvent 116
   XFontStruct 315
   XTextExtents 316
   Xv_cmsdata 397
   Xv_Screen 294
subframe 60
subframes 67
subwindows, about 28
   laying out in frames 74
SunView 12
   graphics 85
svrimage.h header file 297
system call, alarm() 356
   calls to avoid 355
   dup2() 373
   exec() 373
   fork() 373
   getitimer() 356
   ioctl() 356
   pipe() 373
   readv() 390
   rlimit() 390
   setjmp() 390

setpriority() 390
setquota() 390
settimer() 355
sigblock() 390
sigmask() 390
signal() 355, 377
sigpause() 390
sigstack() 390
sigvec() 390
SIGVTALRM 357
system() 356, 373
umask() 390
wait() 356
wait3() 356, 365
write() 390
system() system call 356, 373

T

terminal emulator (See TTY subwindow).
text item 143, 161
   ASCII events 173
   notification 162, 164
   numeric 161, 165
   selection 162
text item, setting a value
text subwindow, about 30, 181
   checking status 184
   contents of 182
   creating 182
   deleting text 186
   determining what lines are visible 193
   discarding edits 190
   edit log 188
   editing 183
   emulating an editing character 187
   getting a text selection 197
   getting filename 188
   index 182
   interaction with file system 189
   lines on screen and in file 192
   loading a file 183
   marking positions 196
   notification 199
   pattern matching 194
   positioning text 192
   positioning views 192
   reading from 185
   replacing characters 187
   saving edits 189
   scrolling 193
   setting initial contents 190

Index

setting insertion point 185
split views 198
storing edits 189
subclassed from OPENWIN 182
undo 188
use of clipboard 186
writing to 185
text subwindow package (see TEXTSW package)
text-based programs 84
TEXTSW package 181 - 203
Textsw_action attributes 200
TEXTSW_ACTION_CAPS_LOCK attribute 200
TEXTSW_ACTION_CHANGED_DIRECTORY attribute 200
TEXTSW_ACTION_EDITED_FILE attribute 200, 201
TEXTSW_ACTION_EDITED_MEMORY attribute 200
TEXTSW_ACTION_FILE_IS_READONLY attribute 200
TEXTSW_ACTION_LOADED_FILE attribute 200, 201
TEXTSW_ACTION_TOOL_CLOSE attribute 200
TEXTSW_ACTION_TOOL_DESTROY attribute 200
TEXTSW_ACTION_TOOL_MGR attribute 201
TEXTSW_ACTION_TOOL_QUIT attribute 201
TEXTSW_ACTION_USING_MEMORY attribute 201
textsw_add_mark() procedure 196, 458
TEXTSW_AGAIN_RECORDING attribute 431
textsw_append_file_name() procedure 188, 458
TEXTSW_AUTO_INDENT attribute 431
TEXTSW_AUTO_SCROLL_BY attribute 432
TEXTSW_BLINK_CARET attribute 432
TEXTSW_BROWSING attribute 432
TEXTSW_CHECKPOINT_FREQUENCY attribute 432
TEXTSW_CLIENT_DATA attribute 432
TEXTSW_CONFIRM_OVERWRITE attribute 432
TEXTSW_CONTENTS attribute 186, 191, 432
TEXTSW_CONTROL_CHARS_USE_FONT attribute 432
textsw_delete() procedure 186, 458
TEXTSW_DISABLE_CD attribute 432
TEXTSW_DISABLE_LOAD attribute 432
textsw_edit() procedure 187, 458
TEXTSW_EDIT_COUNT attribute 432
textsw_erase() procedure 186, 187, 459
TEXTSW_FILE attribute 183, 432
TEXTSW_FILE_CONTENTS attribute 190, 432
textsw_file_lines_visible() procedure 193, 459
textsw_find_bytes() procedure 194, 459
textsw_find_mark() procedure 197, 459
TEXTSW_FIRST attribute 183, 433
textsw_first() procedure 198, 459
TEXTSW_FIRST_LINE attribute 193, 433

TEXTSW_FOR_ALL_VIEWS attribute 192
textsw.h header file 182
TEXTSW_HISTORY_LIMIT attribute 433
TEXTSW_IGNORE_LIMIT attribute 433
Textsw_index type 182
textsw_index_for_file_line() procedure 193, 459
TEXTSW_INFINITY value
textsw_insert() procedure 185, 460
TEXTSW_INSERT_FROM_FILE attribute 191, 433
TEXTSW_INSERTION_POINT attribute 185, 433
TEXTSW_INSERT_MAKES_VISIBLE attribute 185, 194, 433
TEXTSW_LENGTH attribute 182, 433
TEXTSW_LINE_BREAK_ACTION attribute 192, 433
TEXTSW_LOWER_CONTEXT attribute 433
textsw_match_bytes() procedure 195, 460
TEXTSW_MEMORY_MAXIMUM attribute 188, 433
TEXTSW_MODIFIED attribute 183, 433
TEXTSW_MULTI_CLICK_SPACE attribute 433
TEXTSW_MULTI_CLICK_TIMEOUT attribute 434
textsw_next() procedure 198, 460
textsw_normalize_view() procedure 194, 460
TEXTSW_NOTIFY_PROC attribute 199, 434
textsw_notify_proc() procedure 460
textsw_possibly_normalize() procedure 194, 461
TEXTSW_READ_ONLY attribute 434
textsw_remove_mark() procedure 197, 461
textsw_replace_bytes() procedure 188, 461
textsw_reset() procedure 190, 461
textsw_save() procedure 185, 189, 461
textsw_screen_line_count() procedure 193, 462
textsw_scroll_lines() procedure 193, 462
textsw_set_selection() procedure 198, 462
TEXTSW_STATUS attribute 182, 183, 191, 434
TEXTSW_STORE_CHANGES_FILE attribute 190, 434
textsw_store_file() procedure 185, 189, 462
TEXTSW_SUBMENU_EDIT attribute 434
TEXTSW_SUBMENU_FILE attribute 434
TEXTSW_SUBMENU_FIND attribute 434
TEXTSW_SUBMENU_VIEW attribute 434
TEXTSW_UPPER_CONTEXT attribute 434
TEXTSW_WRAPAROUND_SIZE attribute 188
tiled windows, definition of 28
timers 360
toggle_notify() procedure 247
toolkit, XView 12
toolkit (See X Window System).
triggers 267
TTY subwindow, about 205
    creating 205
    escape sequences 207
    input and output routines 207

monitoring 210
  under program control 207
TTY_ARGV attribute 205, 210, 434
TTY_ARGV_DO_NOT_FORK attribute 211, 434
TTY_CONSOLE attribute 434
tty.h header file 205
TTY_PAGE_MODE attribute 435
TTY_PID attribute 210, 435
TTY_QUIT_ON_CHILD_DEATH attribute 210, 435
TTYSW package 205
ttysw_input() procedure 207, 462
ttysw_output() procedure 207, 463
TTY_TTY_FD attribute 211, 435
type, about 19
  Screen 294
  Textsw_index 182
  Visual 397
  Window_rescale_state 313
  Xv_Cursor 275
  Xv_Font 308
  Xv_object 20, 48
  Xv_opaque 20
  Xv_singlecolor 82, 280, 402
typecasting 51
types, defined in XView 43

U

umask() system call 390
UNIX facilities used by applications 355
UNIX system calls and XView 355
user interface components 7
user interface standards 13

V

view window 80
  definition of 79
views (See split views).
Visual type 397
visualization programs 84

W

wait() system call 356
wait3() function 210
wait3() system call 356, 365
widget sets 7

WIN_ALARM attribute 435
WIN_ALARM_DATA attribute 435
WIN_ASCII_EVENTS event 99, 113
WIN_BACKGROUND_COLOR attribute 403, 435
WIN_BELOW attribute 435
WIN_BIT_GRAVITY attribute 88, 435
WIN_CLIENT_MESSAGE_DATA attribute 124
WIN_CLIENT_MESSAGE_FORMAT attribute 124
WIN_CLIENT_MESSAGE_TYPE attribute 124
WIN_CMS_DATA attribute 397, 435
WIN_CMS_NAME attribute 397, 435
WIN_COL_GAP attribute 139
WIN_COLLAPSE_EXPOSURES 114
WIN_COLLAPSE_EXPOSURES attribute 86, 435
WIN_COLORMAP_NOTIFY event 112
WIN_COLUMNS attribute 436
WIN_CONSUME_EVENT attribute 99, 111, 436
WIN_CONSUME_EVENTS attribute 111, 436
WIN_CONSUME_KBD_EVENTS attribute 53
WIN_CONSUME_PICK_EVENTS attribute 53
WIN_CONSUME_X_EVENT_MASK attribute 110,
  436
WIN_CURSOR attribute 436
WIN_DEPTH attribute 436
WIN_DESIRED_HEIGHT attribute 436
WIN_DESIRED_WIDTH attribute 436
window manager, authority of 9
  definition 9
  hints 61
  role of 61
window_done() procedure 463
window_fit() macro 142
window_fit() procedure 463
window_fit_height() macro 142
window_fit_width() macro 142
window_interpose_func() procedure 464
window_main_loop() procedure 463
window_read_event() procedure 463
Window_rescale_state type 313
windows, as objects 25
  creation 53
WIN_DYNAMIC_VISUAL attribute 397, 436
win_event.h header file 111, 116
WIN_EVENT_PROC attribute 99, 173, 436
WIN_EVENT_PROC event 445
WIN_FIT_HEIGHT attribute 436
WIN_FIT_WIDTH attribute 436
WIN_FOREGROUND_COLOR attribute 403, 436
WIN_FRAME attribute 437
WIN_GRAB_ALL attribute 120
WIN_GRAB_ALL_INPUT attribute 437

Index

WIN_GRAPHICS_EXPOSE attribute 114
WIN_HORIZONTAL_SCROLLBAR attribute 437
WIN_IGNORE_EVENTS attribute 437
WIN_IGNORE_X_EVENT_MASK attribute 110
win_input.h header file 111, 115, 116
WIN_INPUT_MASK attribute 126, 437
WIN_INPUT_ONLY attribute 437
WIN_IS_CLIENT_PANE attribute 437
WIN_KBD_FOCUS attribute 437
WIN_LEFT_KEYS event 113
WIN_LEFT_MARGIN attribute 140
WIN_MAP attribute 437
WIN_MENU attribute 437
WIN_META_EVENTS event 113
WIN_MOUSE_XY attribute 278, 437
WIN_NO_CLIPPING attribute 89, 438
WIN_NO_DECORATIONS attribute 438
WIN_NO_EVENTS 112
WIN_NOTIFY_EVENT_PROC attribute 53, 463
WIN_NOTIFY_IMMEDIATE_EVENT_PROC attribute 437
WIN_NOTIFY_SAFE_EVENT_PROC attribute 438
WIN_PARENT attribute 438
WIN_PERCENT_HEIGHT attribute 438
WIN_PERCENT_WIDTH attribute 438
WIN_RECT attribute 438
WIN_REPAINT event 86, 114, 445
WIN_RESIZE attribute 381
WIN_RESIZE event 114
WIN_RETAINED attribute 82, 95, 171, 438
WIN_RIGHT_KEYS event 113
WIN_RIGHT_OF attribute 438
WIN_ROW_GAP attribute 139, 438
WIN_ROW_HEIGHT attribute 438
WIN_SAVE_UNDER attribute 438
WIN_SCALE_EXTRALARGE attribute 313
WIN_SCALE_LARGE attribute 313
WIN_SCALE_MEDIUM attribute 313
WIN_SCALE_SMALL attribute 313
WIN_SCREEN_RECT attribute 439
WIN_SET_FOCUS attribute 439
win_set_kbd_focus() procedure 119
WIN_TOP_KEYS event 113
WIN_TOP_MARGIN attribute 140
WIN_TRANSPARENT attribute 439
WIN_UP_ASCII_EVENTS event 113
WIN_UP_EVENTS event 113
WIN_UP_META_EVENTS event 113
WIN_VERTICAL_SCROLLBAR procedure 439
WIN_WINDOW_GRAVITY attribute 439
WIN_X_COLOR_INDICES attribute 396, 401, 439

WIN_X_EVENT_MASK attribute 439
wmgr_bottom() procedure 464
wmgr_changelevel() procedure 464
wmgr_close() procedure 464
wmgr_completechangerect() procedure 464
wmgr_open() procedure 465
wmgr_refreshwindow() procedure 465
wmgr_top() procedure 465
WM_SAVE_YOURSELF event 383
write() 370
write() system call 390

X

X Protocol 6
X Window ID (See XV_XID attribute).
X Window System, events 86; differences
    between X and XView 116
  extensibility 9
  interclient communications 9, 331
  overview 3
  protocol 6
  role of window manager 9
  server and client relationship 5
  software hierarchy 6
  specifying event masks 110
  toolkits 7
  X Window ID for paint window 88
  Xlib 6
XAllocColor() procedure 396
XChangeWindowAttributes() procedure 395
XClientMessage event 108
XClientMessageEvent event 124
XCopyPlane() procedure 223
XEvent structure 116
XFontStruct structure 315
XGrabPointer issued by pop-up menu 236
XGrabPointer() procedure 236
X.h header file 110
Xlib 6
  repainting canvas 89
  using to draw; example 280
Xlib.h header file 90, 294
XLookupString() procedure 117
XNextEvent() procedure 125
XRebindKeysym() procedure 116, 117
XSendEvent() procedure 108, 120
XSetForeground() procedure 396
XSetForeground procedure 407
XTextExtents structure 316

XTranslateCoordinates() procedure 266
XV_AUTO_CREATE attribute 253, 439
XV_BOTTOM_MARGIN attribute 439
Xv_cmsdata structure 397
xv_col() procedure 140, 465
xv_cols() procedure 465
xv_create() procedure 47, 465
xv_create() procedure; compared to xv_find()
   49
Xv_Cursor type 275
xv_destroy() procedure 50, 137, 466
  used for frames 75
xv_destroy_safe() procedure 50, 166
XV_DISPLAY attribute 293, 395
XV_DISPLAY_FROM_WINDOW() procedure 466
XV_ERROR 51
xv_error() procedure 54
Xv_error_action 54
xv_error.h header file 55
XV_ERROR_PROC attribute 54
xv_find() procedure 49, 466
XV_FONT attribute 439
Xv_Font type 308
xv_get() procedure 50, 466
XV_HEIGHT attribute 297, 439
XV_HELP_DATA attribute 439
XView, about 3, 7, 10
  as object-oriented system 17
  compiling programs 41
  concept of windows differs from X 25
  data types; table of 20
  example of programming interface 43
  frames and subframes 26
  generic functions 21
  Generic Object 24
  libraries 42
  notification 10, 35
  objects 23
  objects and owners; table of 20
  objects; list of 43
  packages 18, 43
  programmer's model 17 - 23
  programming interface 41
  programs; initialization 45, 62
  reserved names 43
  reserved prefixes 43
  structure of applications 41
  subwindows 28
  toolkit 12
  types 43
  window objects 25

xview.h header file 42
xv_init() procedure 45, 62, 295, 467
XV_INIT_ARGC_PTR_ARGV attribute 45, 46, 63,
   440
XV_INIT_ARGS attribute 46, 63, 440
XV_INIT_ARGS macro 46
xv_input_readevent() procedure 111, 125, 302
XV_KEY_DATA attribute 166, 239, 440
XV_LABEL attribute 288, 440
XV_LEFT_MARGIN attribute 440
xv_main_loop() procedure 52, 384
XV_MARGIN attribute 440
XV_NAME attribute 295, 440
XV_OBJECT 18
Xv_object type 20, 48
Xv_opaque type 20
XV_OWNER attribute 440
XV_RIGHT_MARGIN attribute 440
XV_ROOT attribute 440
xv_row() procedure 140, 467
xv_rows() procedure 467
XV_SCREEN attribute 294
Xv_Screen structure 294
XV_SCREEN_FROM_WINDOW() procedure 467
xv_send_message() procedure 108, 120, 124,
   467
XV_SERVER_FROM_WINDOW() procedure 468
xv_set() procedure 50, 468
XV_SHOW attribute 67, 384
Xv_singlecolor type 82, 280, 402
XV_TOP_MARGIN attribute 440
XV_TYPE attribute 441
XV_USAGE_PROC attribute 46
XV_WIDTH attribute 297, 441
XV_X attribute 140
XV_XID attribute 88, 308, 441
XV_Y attribute 140, 441 •

Z

Z-ordering 138, 176

Overseas Distributors

Effective January 1, 1990, customers outside the U.S. and Canada will be able to order Nutshell Handbooks and the X Window System Series through distributors near them. These overseas locations offer international customers faster order processing, more local bookstores and local distributors, and increased representation at trade shows worldwide, as well as the high level, quality service our customers have always received.

AUSTRALIA & NEW ZEALAND
(orders and inquiries)
Addison-Wesley Publishers, Pty. Ltd.
6 Byfield Street
North Ryde, N.S.W. 2113
AUSTRALIA
Telephone: 61-2-888-2733
FAX: 61-2-888-9404

UNITED KINGDOM & AFRICA
(orders and inquiries)
Addison-Wesley Publishers, Ltd.
Finchampstead Road
Wokingham, Berkshire RG11 2NZ
ENGLAND
Telephone: 44-734-794-000
FAX: 44-734-794-035

EUROPE & THE MIDDLE EAST
(orders and inquiries)
Addison-Wesley Publishers B.V.
De Lairessestraat 90
1071 PJ Amsterdam
THE NETHERLANDS
Telephone: 31-20-764-044
FAX: 31-20-664-5334

ASIA inquiries (excluding Japan)
Addison-Wesley Singapore Pte. Ltd.
15 Beach Road #05-09/10
Beach Centre
Singapore 0718
SINGAPORE
Telephone: 65-339-7503
FAX: 65-339-9709

ASIA orders (excluding Japan)
Addison-Wesley Publishing Co., Inc.
International Order Department
Route 128
Reading, Massachusetts 01867 U.S.A.
Telephone: 1-617-944-3700
FAX: 1-617-942-2829

JAPAN
(orders and inquiries)
Toppan Company, Ltd.
Ochanomizu Square B, 1-6
Kanda Surugadai
Chiyoda-ku, Tokyo 101
JAPAN
Telephone: 81-3-295-3461
FAX: 81-3-293-5963

O'Reilly & Associates, Inc.
Creators and Publishers of Nutshell Handbooks

Nutshell Handbooks

Learning the UNIX Operating System
DOS Meets UNIX
Learning the vi Editor
UNIX in a Nutshell, System V
UNIX in a Nutshell, Berkeley

Handbooks on Communications:

!%@:: A Directory of Electronic
Mail Addressing and Networks
Using UUCP and Usenet
Managing UUCP and Usenet

Handbooks on Programming:

Using C on the UNIX System
Checking C Programs with lint
Understanding and Using COFF
Programming with curses
termcap and terminfo
Managing Projects with make

The X Window System series

Vol. 0 *X Protocol Reference Manual*
Vol. 1 *Xlib Programming Manual*
Vol. 2 *Xlib Reference Manual*
Vol. 3 *X Window System User's Guide*
Vol. 4 *X Toolkit Intrinsics*
        Programming Manual
Vol. 5 *X Toolkit Intrinsics Reference*
        Manual
Vol. 7 *XView Programming Manual*

For HyperCard on Macintosh:

UNIX in a Nutshell for HyperCard
(includes 1.8MB of HyperCard
stackware, *User's Guide*, and a copy of
Learning the UNIX Operating System)

Other UNIX books:

UNIX Text Processing

Send me more information on:

☐ Retail sales

☐ Licensing

☐ Review copies for instructors

☐ Magazine press kits for new books

☐ Education policy

☐ Bookstore locations

☐ Overseas distributors

☐ Additional copy of Nutshell News

☐ Upcoming books on the subject:

_____
_____

☐ Writing a Nutshell Handbook

O'Reilly & Associates, Inc.
Creators and Publishers of Nutshell Handbooks

Nutshell Handbooks

Learning the UNIX Operating System
DOS Meets UNIX
Learning the vi Editor
UNIX in a Nutshell, System V
UNIX in a Nutshell, Berkeley

Handbooks on Communications:

!%@:: A Directory of Electronic
Mail Addressing and Networks
Using UUCP and Usenet
Managing UUCP and Usenet

Handbooks on Programming:

Using C on the UNIX System
Checking C Programs with lint
Understanding and Using COFF
Programming with curses
termcap and terminfo
Managing Projects with make

The X Window System series

Vol. 0 *X Protocol Reference Manual*
Vol. 1 *Xlib Programming Manual*
Vol. 2 *Xlib Reference Manual*
Vol. 3 *X Window System User's Guide*
Vol. 4 *X Toolkit Intrinsics*
        Programming Manual
Vol. 5 *X Toolkit Intrinsics Reference*
        Manual
Vol. 7 *XView Programming Manual*

For HyperCard on Macintosh:

UNIX in a Nutshell for HyperCard
(includes 1.8MB of HyperCard
stackware, *User's Guide*, and a copy of
Learning the UNIX Operating System)

Other UNIX books:

UNIX Text Processing

Send me more information on:

☐ Retail sales

☐ Licensing

☐ Review copies for instructors

☐ Magazine press kits for new books

☐ Education policy

☐ Bookstore locations

☐ Overseas distributors

☐ Additional copy of Nutshell News

☐ Upcoming books on the subject:

_____
_____

☐ Writing a Nutshell Handbook

☐ Please send me the information
I have asked for on the reverse
side of this card.

Name _____

Company _____

Address _____

City _____

State, ZIP _____

(Fill out or tape
business card here)

Nutshell Handbooks

NUTSHELL
HANDBOOKS
O'Reilly & Associates, Inc.
632 Petaluma Avenue
Sebastopol CA 95472

☐ Please send me the information
I have asked for on the reverse
side of this card.

Name _____

Company _____

Address _____

City _____

State, ZIP _____

(Fill out or tape
business card here)

Nutshell Handbooks

NUTSHELL
HANDBOOKS
O'Reilly & Associates, Inc.
632 Petaluma Avenue
Sebastopol CA 95472